Dreams and
Beyond

Finding Your Way in the Dark

Dreams and Beyond

Finding Your Way in the Dark

Madhu Tandan

HAY HOUSE
Australia • Canada • Hong Kong • India
South Africa • United Kingdom • United States

First published and distributed in the United Kingdom by:
Hay House UK Ltd, 292B Kensal Rd, London W10 5BE. Tel.: (44) 20 8962 1230;
Fax: (44) 20 8962 1239. www.hayhouse.co.uk

Published and distributed in the United States of America by:
Hay House, Inc., PO Box 5100, Carlsbad, CA 92018-5100. Tel.: (1) 760 431 7695 or
(800) 654 5126; Fax: (1) 760 431 6948 or (800) 650 5115. www.hayhouse.com

Published and distributed in Australia by:
Hay House Australia Ltd, 18/36 Ralph St, Alexandria NSW 2015. Tel.: (61) 2 9669 4299;
Fax: (61) 2 9669 4144. www.hayhouse.com.au

Published and distributed in the Republic of South Africa by:
Hay House SA (Pty), Ltd, PO Box 990, Witkoppen 2068. Tel./Fax: (27) 11 467 8904.
www.hayhouse.co.za

Published and distributed in India by:
Hay House Publishers India, Muskaan Complex, Plot No.3, B-2, Vasant Kunj,
New Delhi – 110 070. Tel.: (91) 11 4176 1620; Fax: (91) 11 4176 1630.
www.hayhouse.co.in

Distributed in Canada by:
Raincoast, 9050 Shaughnessy St, Vancouver, BC V6P 6E5. Tel.: (1) 604 323 7100;
Fax: (1) 604 323 2600

A catalogue record for this book is available from the British Library.

ISBN 978-1-4019-2014-2

Printed and bound at
Thomson Press (India) Ltd.

To

Sri Madhava Ashish,
the best of teachers.

Rajeev,
for weaving and being woven into the fabric of this book.

Purnima,
who serendipitously stood back from her dreams.

Had I the heavens' embroidered cloths,
Enwrought with golden and silver light,
The blue and the dim and the dark cloths
Of night and light and the half-light,
I would spread the cloths under your feet:
But I, being poor, have only my dreams;
I have spread my dreams under your feet;
Tread softly because you tread on my dreams.

— W. B. YEATS

CONTENTS

PART 4
The Dream: A Window to Reality

PART 5
The Dream: A Gateway to Transcendence

Acknowledgements

In all ways this book has been a joint effort with my husband Rajeev. From researching to structuring, his indefatigable energy and unusual ideas helped mould it. He is the primary author of part 2 and the last chapter. Without him it would have been only half a book.

Purnima Mehta whose interest remained steadfast over the years as she edited the manuscript through its endless permutations, nurturing it with her belief. Her giving and involvement ultimately go far beyond the book.

Malashri Lal and Katharina Poggendorf-Kakar for their discerning suggestions. Their enthusiasm and friendship were beacons when my inspiration wavered. And to V.K. Karthika – without her insightful comments this book may not have found its present direction.

Pervin Mahoney, Hartosh Singh Bal, Pushkar Johari, Monisha Mukundan, Robey Lal, Serinity Young, Usha Kumar, Sudhir Kakar, Namita Unnikrishnan, Padmini Mongia, Satish Pandey, Kersy Katrak, and Trinath Mishra for their involvement at one stage or the other.

To Komal Narayan, Avani Mehta Sood, and Shalini Kahlon who made sure that I got any book I needed from overseas. My thanks also to Sangeeta Kaul and the Delnet service, and to Sushma and the staff of the IIC library for ensuring that I had access to articles and journals whenever I needed them. My parents, specially my mother, for reading chapters from various drafts and being patient when the only conversation in the house was on dreams. To my father-in-law, Ramesh Tandan, who was keenly interested in what I wrote. Aruna Mehta for reinforcing the title of the book. Nirmal Masurekar and Amy Rose Grigoriou for the cover of the book.

To the International Retreat for Writers at Hawthornden Castle, Edinburgh, where a fellowship allowed me to re-vision the book.

Ashok Nagpal, Honey Oberoi, Anurag Mishra, Vineeta Kshetrapal, and Mallika Akbar, my teachers at the Centre for Psychoanalytic Studies at Delhi University, who helped deepen my understanding and appreciation of Freud; together with the students with whom many lively exchanges created bonds I value.

To Ashok Chopra, my publisher, whose belief in the book has taken it to distant lands. Often the last phase of a book proves to be the most intense. I am truly thankful that Ratika Kapur, my editor, was there to help me negotiate it. She managed to chisel and sharpen its original mass with her gentle nudges and valuable questionings all the while remaining attuned to the essence of the book. Her thoroughness and interest managed to bring out the best in the manuscript. The book is as much hers.

Lastly, to the many people whom I cannot name, who shared a part of their lives with me. I can only hope that I have done justice to their dreams.

PART 1

THE MANY STRANDS OF THE DREAMING MIND

It can be estimated that in the course of our lives, we enter our dream worlds half a million times. This state of affairs presents us all with a challenge: as we neglect or cultivate the world of our dreams, so will this realm become a wasteland or a garden. As we sow, so shall we reap our dreams. With the universe of experience thus open to you, if you must sleep through a third of your life, as it seems you must, are you willing to sleep through your dreams too?

Stephen La Berge, Lucid Dreaming

Chapter 1

THE MULTIPLICITY
OF DREAMS

Will it not be enough to say that in dreams *anything* is
possible – from the deepest degradation of mental life to an
exaltation of it which is rare in waking hours?

Sigmund Freud

*F*or many people, dreams are meaningless hallucinations that arise
when the rational intellect has been disarmed by the delirium of the
night. Some even deny that we regularly dream; to the occasional dream
they accord only a somatic reality as a result of, say, indigestion. Still
others believe that dreams merely replay the happenings of the previous
day and that's about all they have to offer. Their opponents – those who
ascribe meaning to dreams – while conceding that dreams are founded
on the day's residue, argue that many things happen during the day,
but that a dream does not portray them all, choosing only certain
events over others. So why does this happen? Is this choice important
in some way to the dreamer? Does the dream contain a clue to this
significance, a hidden meaning? They also point to another facet of the
dream: it does not replay the chosen event as it had actually occurred,
but something is added to or subtracted from it. This alteration, they
believe, indicates that the dream is a symbolic allusion; that dreams
mean something other than what they appear to depict.

Human beings have puzzled over dreams ever since they
first recorded them on clay tablets some five thousand years ago.

Interestingly, all known cultures have delved into dreams and their meanings. Intrigued by the strange evanescent images of dreams and their cargo of symbolism, people have sought to crack the armour of their unintelligibility and fathom their significance. This has spawned a host of theories on how to decode a dream. Some see it as a somatic communication alerting the dreamer to a malfunctioning organ of the body, while others view it as a prognostication that warns or heralds an impending event. Modern-day belief considers the dream to be a comment on the psychological reality of the dreamer, his or her feelings, anxieties, and internal conflicts; most religions, on the other hand, approach the dream as a meeting with the sacred.

At the outset it must be clarified that neither the rationalist (who denies meaning to a dream) nor the hermeneutist (who ascribes meaning to it) can boast of concrete proof either way. The scientifically oriented person who denounces dreams is making as much of an assumption based on subjective belief as the person who swears to their meaningfulness. I like to believe that the evidence tilts towards the latter point of view, and my bias is evident in this book.

The debate on dreams, however, is not that easily polarized between the two coordinates of the rational and the hermeneutic. The hermeneutists do not speak in a unified voice; often the conceptions of one dream theorist will conflict with another. To do justice to what is a complex and rather wide-ranging debate, this book deals with two major aspects of dreams. Both are concerned with multiplicity: the multiplicity of dream types and the multiplicity of meaning in dreams.

We often adopt a one-dimensional approach to the dreaming mind. The rationalist believes that dreams amount to nothing at all; Freudians treat every dream as a wish-fulfilment; Jungians decipher most dreams as though they are mainly compensatory of our waking attitudes; and others scan dreams for their precognitive content. Most theorists are seeking the essence of dreaming, reducing it to a nothing-but phenomenon as though it is just one thing. But this approach excludes the natural varieties of the dreaming mind. To this end, my book aims to show that dreams range over a wide variety of types.

The main bulk of dreaming consists of 'ordinary' or 'little' dreams. These dreams are relatively short and mundane episodes beset by strange elements, and appear to be based on the manipulation and recombination of memories, recent or of the past. There are also full-length theatrical productions with complex, meandering themes. Apart from these is the nightmare, with its frightening images of bizarre creatures and threatening forms. But dreams are not limited to psychological commentaries. There is the medical or somatic dream that apprises the dreamer about the state of the body. Then there are problem-solving dreams where unexpected answers and creative solutions to problems are revealed. For such dreams we can only ascribe a creative imagination to them. On the ascending scale of creativity, there are the prophetic-telepathic dreams. These are intuitive dreams that have occurred to all people at all times. Perhaps exhibiting even more intuitiveness (or creative imagination) than these kinds of dreams are the 'extraordinary' or 'big' dreams that linger in consciousness, demanding to be understood. They are a point of contact with the sacred and may have a transcendent, cosmic quality to them. Standing apart from all these types is the lucid dream, where the dreamer is actually aware that he or she is dreaming.

Importantly, a dream may not be limited to one type. It may be a combination of two or more types of dreams. For example, during a nightmare the dreamer may become lucid, realizing that it is only a dream. Or a prophetic dream may be set against a background in which there is an obvious recombination of current and childhood memories. Or a mythic being may provide the solution to a problem about a computer program that the dreamer is grappling with while awake.

Besides the variety of dream types, the other aspect this book engages in is how the same dream can be understood in different ways. At first glance this appears to be the same as the previous point – since there are numerous types of dreams, naturally there would be different meanings of dreams. Though there may be some overlap in these two aspects, there is a distinction between them. A multiplicity of dream types has to do with the different categories of dreams. However, the second aspect of the issue alludes to the plurality of interpretations of a single dream. Or, one can say, there are many keys that can unlock the meaning of the dream. This means that even when we identify a dream to be a particular type, say, a psychological comment, it may still yield different interpretations, alerting the dreamer to diverse facets of the personality. Part of the fascination of dreams resides in their ability to reveal different aspects of our lives – our mind, body, feelings – and, at times, offer intimations of something even beyond them. For example, my neighbour had a dream from which several meanings could be gleaned. She is in her mid-forties, and lives with her husband and in-laws. Her marriage, for the most part, is an indifferent one. Now that her daughter is married and well settled, she divides her time between walks and yoga in the mornings, and visits in the evenings to her ageing parents who live in an adjacent neighbourhood. At the time when she had this dream, her father was suffering from a malfunctioning prostrate and was hospitalized. She dreamt:

> *My husband is bringing my father out of the hospital. My dad has just been discharged and they are both standing outside the hospital building. An old black Fiat drives up and my father's deceased brother emerges from it. My uncle is looking much younger; in fact, he is looking in his prime. He asks my father to sit in the front seat and they drive off. I find myself sitting in the back seat and I soon realize that my uncle has come to take my father away. I feel a sense of finality to this act. In desperation I try and phone my husband to tell him that Dad will not be coming back. I watch them as they drive into an underpass.*

At first glance this dream certainly substantiates the belief that dreams replay the events of the past day – her father had been hospitalized and subsequently discharged, and the dream had depicted this with some embellishment. But it is also a reflection of my neighbour's anxiety about her father's health, a continuation of the remains of her day where, unsupported, she feels trapped between the desire to help her parents and the need to fulfil her obligations towards her marital home. The dream portrays her loneliness, vulnerability, and her impotence. Her husband, even though he is present after the father's discharge, just stands there and makes no effort to escort him home. This is left to her and a dead uncle. Since dead people may not be of much use in assisting someone home, the responsibility, in effect, is only hers. The dream bluntly voices her apprehension – will she be able to cope with looking after her parents in their fading years?

Another view would not treat this as an anxiety dream, but would hold that it presents an inversion of her actual relationship with her father and thereby supports her self-image of a mature individual. Perhaps she had never emerged from the awe in which she held her father as a child. The dream, after all, is about dependence and assistance, portraying an ailing parent and a daughter's desire to help him. It has displaced her sense of dependence on her father and projected it onto his weak health, consequently portraying him as the dependent figure. This neatly reverses the roles and now she is the caretaker – the stronger, superior one. The only way she can maintain this superiority in the face of an unequal relationship with her father is to portray him in her dream as passive and helpless.

Or is the dream about a malaise in her marriage – the larger than life image she has of her father that is affecting her relationship with her husband? The husband, escorting the father out of the hospital, signifies that he is instrumental in bringing to the surface this fixation on her father. This issue has remained dormant (dead) in their marriage as portrayed by the dead uncle who has come to take him away. She finds herself in the family car with the husband conveniently forgotten. Also, it seems that she drives her marriage from the back seat as seen by her position in the car. She attempts to assure the husband by telling him over the phone that the father will not come back (between them). The father and uncle go underground – the underpass – indicating that the 'sick' father fixation is being buried once again. Viewed thus, the dream appears to be commenting on the 'sickness' within her marriage, her father fixation being the root cause.

These are just three of the many psychological interpretations one could give to the dream. Those inclined towards such a psychological reading will, no doubt, be able to detect the different theories supporting these interpretations. Each of them explores a somewhat different aspect of the dreamer's personality, which is usually inaccessible to the normal waking gaze. However, there can be a totally different rendering of this dream. It could be anticipating the imminent death of the father. He will come out of the hospital, but may succumb to unforeseen complications soon afterwards. A messenger from the world of death – her deceased uncle – has come to assist him in the crossing, which is depicted in the dream by his departing with the brother. But her attachment propels her into the back seat of the car. This, however, can only be for a very short distance, after which she can only be a mere spectator from her world as they cross over into the 'other' world (a vehicular underpass takes you to the other side). Her desperate bid to phone her husband is perhaps reflective of the shock surrounding the death of the father – *'Dad will not be coming back.'* This interpretation, of course, nudges us into a dimension altogether different from the psychological paradigm of dreams. The dream becomes a premonition.

The distinction between the multiplicity of dream types and the many meanings of a dream becomes evident through this dream. The first three interpretations reflect the different meanings of a psychological dream, while the last one considers the dream to be a different type. This last interpretation reveals another expression of the dreaming mind – its paranormal voice. Perhaps it needs to be stressed that one meaning does not exclude the other. Every one of the interpretations of my neighbour's dream may be applicable to her – relevant to her life situation. Her dream could be a comment on her current anxiety, her seeming impotence in front of the father, and her estrangement from her marriage, and it could also be anticipating an actual event. In other words, the appropriateness of the psychological interpretations need not preclude the paranormal meaning of the dream. In fact, the dream had other paranormal elements as well, as I was soon to learn.

Curiously, three weeks after my neighbour had recounted her dream to me, we found ourselves walking abreast one morning. For a while we walked in silence. She broke it by reminding me of her dream. 'Little did I realize that the dream was foretelling my father's death. There had been nothing in his condition that was alarming. Neither had the doctors any inkling that he would go away so suddenly.'

Maybe it was her way of telling me that my psychological rendering of her dream was not a correct assessment. Her father had been perfectly well when he was discharged, but then he developed one complication after another, and had died a week later.

'I am so sorry to learn about your father ...' I commiserated.

She began telling me about the funeral, describing the calm expression on her father's face just prior to the cremation. Then she paused and said, 'My husband said that when they were dressing the body it smelt of cigars ... like the residual smell after a cigar smoker has left the room.'

'That's odd,' I replied. 'Did your father like cigars?'

'Not at all! He never smoked.'

My mind struggled for an explanation. Was it a combination of association and imagination that had triggered her husband's olfactory senses to believe he had smelt cigar smoke in the room? Of course, in the Hindu tradition, it would have been sacrilegious for anyone to smoke while the body was being dressed and anointed for the cremation.

She addressed my thoughts without my voicing them: 'No one in the room was a cigar smoker. My husband is a down-to-earth, nuts-and-bolt sort who isn't given to flights of fancy.'

We walked on in silence, unable to solve the mystery.

She then suddenly said, 'My husband does not even know about my dream.' She paused before continuing: 'My uncle, he was the cigar smoker!'

At that moment my rational beliefs wavered. Was she implying that the cigar aroma was a signature of her dead uncle who had come to ensure a safe passage for his brother into the 'other' world, just as her dream had foretold?

More than one person has recounted vivid dreams in which they have been 'visited' by a loved one who has passed away. I could have treated these dreams as merely psychological projections, where a powerful wish to contact the departed soul metamorphosed into a potent dream of an actual visitation. Such a view, however, would not preserve the potency of the dreamer's experience – perhaps it could even do violence to it. If, however, we allow for a broader understanding of dreams, my neighbour's dream could be read as a visitation from her deceased uncle, who had come to warn her of her father's death. He (from the land of the dead) had come to take him. There was a *finality to this act … Dad will not come back.*' Her dead uncle drove him into the earth (the underpass) to reach the other side – the 'other' world.

Given our rational difficulties with the visitation dream, we may easily dismiss it by denying its validity. But a similar problem would then be encountered with telepathic, prophetic, healing, and problem-solving dreams. How are we to understand these dreams? Can they be accorded any reality outside the rational (psychological) paradigm? If we limit ourselves to this paradigm alone, then would it not amount to an imposition of the analyst's belief on the dreamer's experience? Also, is such a belief justified? Perhaps it is the limits of our belief that circumscribe our understanding of psychic realities that defy explanation. If we have a surer grasp of the dream phenomenon we may then have clearer answers to questions that challenge our rationality. I have therefore allowed the debate on dreams to spill over into these and other related areas.

Confronted with this multiplicity we may ask: How are we to make sense of these diverse interpretations? In fact, can dreams really be understood? Are their multiple meanings a testimony to their essential meaninglessness? Dream theorists counter that this is akin to the arts, where the beauty of a painting is dependent on the multiple meanings it can evoke. The same is true of literary texts, for which multiple interpretations, even contradictory interpretations, of the same text do not render them meaningless, but enrich them further. If we can accept multiple meanings in literature and art, then why not in dreams? Dreams may not have verifiable meanings like that of scientific postulates, which can be tested, but that does not empty them of significance.[1]

Initially it is difficult to accept that a simple artefact of our daily life is actually a complex web of psychic tissue and open to myriad ways of understanding. When I was barely through the first draft of the book I asked a psychoanalyst friend who wrote extensively, 'How come you haven't written a book on dreams?'

My enthusiasm had perhaps eclipsed the presumptuosness of the question. He smiled and said, 'It's too vast a subject.'

Next time we met he and his wife loaned me two books – one on anthropological dreaming, which explored the comparative history of dreaming in different cultures, and the other on religious dreaming. Much later, after my enthusiasm had been tempered with reading and pondering, I understood the truth of his remark.

Slowly it became evident that currently we are poised at a time where there is an increased interest in dreams – much of it backed by scientific research – and clusters of theorists and researchers have formed, focusing on various approaches to understand dreams: physiological, psychoanalytical, phenomenological, metaphorical, and content analysis. Added to these are the cognitivists and the post-modernists, who view the dream as a memory and/or a linguistic process. This increasingly heterogeneous mix of dream theories and research findings over the last century has considerably increased our understanding of the variations within the dream experience itself. In turn, these approaches have paved the way for a new level of questioning in which some researchers have attempted to relate dreams to altered states of consciousness, apart from both waking and dreaming consciousness. This work on dreams and dreaming affords an unparalleled opportunity to take a fresh look at the full range of the dreaming mind.[2]

Dreams and Beyond explores the different avenues of dreaming and debates their relevance, and much like the peeling of an onion, each layer informs the reader about the developments, discoveries, new facets, and controversies regarding the various approaches.

Beginning with what appeared to be a trivial aspect of our daily inventory of experience, I soon realized that dreams have fanned out to embrace a plethora of issues. Besides exploring the cultural dream patterns evidenced by different societies separated by time and distance, dreaming forces one to ask some pretty basic questions. For instance, about evolution (Do all creatures dream?), brain structures (What triggers a dream?), the states of waking and sleeping (Are daydreams the same as nocturnal dreams?), reality and illusion (Do dreams allude to a real or imaginary realm?). The issues are endless. Indeed, as my friend had said, dreaming is a vast subject. Perhaps the simplest question that can be posed is about how we interpret them! The more I explored, the more there was to explore. Yet all the while I felt like a person walking the shores of the ocean of dreaming and all that I had managed to collect were a few pebbles lying on its beaches – pebbles that shone with enough affirmation to continue searching for others.

There was a time when I felt disadvantaged due to my lack of specialization, even though I majored in psychology and have faithfully kept a record of my dreams for more than thirty years. But as I actively engaged with the world of dreaming I realized that what I had considered my handicap was also an advantage. The expert adopts but one specialized approach towards dreams and their meanings. The distinct advantage I had was that while giving cognizance to various dream theories, I was not wedded to any particular one. That gave me the freedom to explore the myriad avenues that dreaming takes, all the while being aware that these diverse theories had underlying assumptions that needed to be appreciated without exclusively subscribing to any one of them. Perhaps a pluralistic approach may afford a wider perspective to dreaming. For it is just this multiplicity – the ability of the dream content to evoke more than one significance – that weaves richness into a dream tapestry.

In this book I explore this multiple evocation, in range and in meaning, through the lives of people I met and interviewed. Their dreams are not representative of a specialized group, but are the dreams of ordinary people. It is a known fact that a specialized setting, say, of psychoanalysis, evokes dreams congruent to the beliefs of the analyst. The dreams narrated to me were spontaneous remembrances and were recounted without any obligation save the desire to share them. And perhaps by analysing them we may learn a little more about our waking behaviour and aspirations, and also further understand the world we live in.

The next chapter narrates my own dreams. They have been culled from my dream journal and span various stages of my life. My attempt in recounting them is not mere self-indulgence, but a way to present in personal terms the different facets of the dreaming mind.

Chapter 2

MY DIALOGUE WITH DREAMS: A PERSONAL INTRODUCTION

What is there which the dream cannot, on occasion, embody? Dreams may give expression to ineluctable truths, to philosophical pronouncement, illusions, wild fantasies, memories, plans, anticipations, irrational experiences, even telepathic visions and heavens knows what besides.

C. G. Jung, *Modern Man in Search of a Soul*

*A*t the age of eighteen I was fairly confused about what I wanted to do with my life. The world opened up many possibilities, yet I was not sure which path was mine to follow. It was then that I met my Teacher. After a thirty-six-hour journey, the bus dropped me at a sleepy village in the Himalayan foothills, where the last stretch to his hermitage was a forty-five-minute walk up a steep mountain track rustling with burnished pine needles.

In the evening by the light of an oil lamp, the dark stillness of the mountains enclosing us, my Teacher asked me, 'What brings you here?'

Instead of answering him, all that I could do was ask more questions: What should I do with my life? What direction should I take, and how will I know?

The tall English engineer-turned-Hindu monk, sitting cross-legged opposite me, startled me by saying, 'If you like, record your dreams. They will tell you what to tackle first.'

'But I don't remember my dreams,' I said.

'You will if you pay attention to them. They'll respond to your interest in them. Keep a notebook next to your bed and jot down whatever you remember in the morning – even if it is the tail-end of a dream. Then see how you feel about them.'

At the time, his suggestion to record my dreams did not mean much to me. It seemed like a far-fetched idea that anything of significance could be known through dreams. How could those jumbled, disjointed, often weird, nightly visuals hold a key to knowing about myself? Yet his words were like an unnoticed stimulant injected into my sleep, for I found myself waking in the morning with vague but persistent memories of dreams that made me mildly curious about them. A few months later I recalled a dream with absolute clarity because it was so frightening.

We are travelling in a caravan. A car stops in front of us. Two people get out of it. One of them is Annie Besant. She lifts a small girl of about nine or ten, who appears to be dead, out of the car. Suddenly Annie Besant's face changes and begins to look frightening as it enlarges and sags, making her look ninety-years-old.

I wrote about it to him and he responded promptly: 'The dream probably alludes to an emotional trauma you experienced. I wonder if you know that Annie Besant "adopted" Krishnamurti as her son, to finally groom him to become her successor at the Theosophical Society. The dream is probably centred on the theme of adoption, since it has picked up symbols connected with that topic. When dreams refer to particular numbers, try and look for what their association is for you. Did something happen at the age of nine or ten that felt like a kind of emotional death? Can you try and remember what it was, at that time, which suddenly made everything seem very frightening?'[1]

I read his letter twice before I could even begin to make sense of it. How could he have known from my dream about a conflict I had not even admitted to myself? Then he had asked me to think back on what happened at the age of nine or ten, as though the age of the dead girl in the dream had something to do with me.

Looking back, I know it was neither his suggestion to note my dreams, nor his book-lined study with all the high priests of dream analysis like Freud and Jung rubbing shoulders with each other that had impressed me about him. It was his interpretation of my dream that stunned me. He accurately pinpointed something long-buried within me that needed to be confronted. Only I had to agree to do so.

I am grateful to him for many things that he taught me, but I owe him a special debt of gratitude for providing me this dream compass to navigate the unmapped terrain of my inner and outer life. And, ever since, dreams have been my gateway to the inner courtyard. Throughout my twenty years of association with him I took as many dreams as I could remember to discuss with him.

As time went by I was repeatedly struck by my dreams' remarkably accurate portrayal of my concerns, my psychic state, the truth of my life. The waking mind may fool itself and blur the distinction between the desirable and the real. The dreaming mind never does so. It never equivocates. It tells the truth as plainly as a mirror. But what is this 'truth' we are talking about? I believe the truth that dreams reflect allows us to go backward in time to revisit and heal dumb wounds marooned within our growing years; dreams allow us to explore current concerns, trivial or pivotal, inner or material; they also permit us to transcend the dreary limits of space and time to glimpse the metaphysical context of our life. This, for me, is the truth that dreams uphold: the vision of our evolution from being creatures buffeted by chance and necessity, driven by animal instincts, fed on a diet of self-indulgent emotions, to becoming beings who sense a greater purpose to life and try to honour that call.

Straight out of college I wondered more than once about what kind of work I could get. I was very keen to get a job, but felt underqualified in a world peopled by specialists. I then had a dream:

> It is the 26th of January and I find myself at the Republic Day parade in New Delhi at India Gate. I am standing in one corner as I see thousands and thousands of people, as far as the eye can see, filling the roads. The line of humanity awaiting entry seems to snake in 'S' bends and I feel I'll never get a place for myself among these teeming millions. Suddenly a jeep pulls up next to me and an official at the parade invites me to sit in the jeep. He drives me past two or three pavilions to an area where he points out a small spot and says, 'That's your place.'
>
> I am inordinately happy as I open my small bundle of clothes, take out a mat, and settle myself in the place shown to me.

I had already begun to appreciate how dreams tell stories in a symbolic language. I was anxious to find my place in the world. The dream, by depicting thousands and thousands of people who were attempting to do the same thing as I was, conveyed my uncertainty. Furthermore, it not only depicted what I was feeling, but also brought the story to a culmination. For, within the dream – amidst my self-doubt – a figure appeared and took me to a place that was reserved for me. Though the place was small and modest, it satisfied me, as it felt just right.

And I did find a place for myself in the world. My first job was modest but appropriate for me. The dream had reassured me that there was a spot that was only mine to fill, and so it happened.

Over the years, I found that my dreams had an uncanny ability of not only representing a current concern, but also indicating a life trend. Five years after being married, Rajeev and I decided to uproot ourselves from work, family, and friends to live in our Teacher's hermitage, in what was to become for us the continuous unfolding of a great challenge. Before the decision was taken, we were unaware of being on the verge of such a momentous step. But, somehow, my dreams knew. In fact, they nudged me not to refuse the call. It was only that at the time I did not know what they were alluding to.

> *We are in a plane with no seats. A friend and a few other people are there. At a predetermined moment we are all expected to jump out without parachutes. My friend says that it's impossible to take such a high-risk jump without appropriate training. While she is speaking, I look out of the plane and see far away in the distance the outlines of people who have already jumped. I realize that they are not falling, but seem to have touched invisible ground in mid-air. Each of them has a look of great happiness.*
>
> *I point them out to my friend and say, 'Look at them. They made the jump although they were untrained. We've got to do it, otherwise this plane will be our home forever.'*
>
> *The hatch at the bottom of the plane opens and we prepare to jump.*

I had this dream maybe six months before our decision to relocate. Yet it related the entire story of how I would doubt my capabilities to make the jump from city life to rural living, where twelve hours of manual work would entail learning how to plant, weed, and harvest crops, besides leading a life shorn of most urban conveniences – even the nearest market was an hour away by jeep. No wonder my friend in the dream expressed all my doubts: It's impossible to take such a high-risk jump without appropriate training. I felt the odds were against me, being unfamiliar with such a life. Would I ever be able to cope?

While we were living in the ashram, I had quite casually related a dream to a friend, in which I had found myself in Oxford, walking along a covered area that looked into a library. I had vividly described the books and the tables at which people were reading, and ended by saying that, perhaps, the dream was mirroring my desire to study in Oxford. My friend, who had graduated from Oxford, found the dream interesting for a very different reason. She felt my dream had quite accurately described the Bodleian Library, as though I had actually seen it. Since I had never travelled overseas at the time, nor did I have any memory of ever seeing a photograph of the library, what exactly had happened? Had I travelled there 'astrally' to be able to describe it? Was it sheer coincidence? Or had my description triggered an association in my friend's mind, conflating memory with image?

Many years later I did go to Oxford, and, needless to say, one of the first places I wanted to visit was the Bodleian Library. I was stunned – my dream had captured the essence of what my eyes beheld now. No doubt it was not identical – the dream had confused many of the details – but it was not enough to convince me that the dreamt image was illusory. The dream had enough visual images of the library, but they were superimposed with elements that I can only call projective content: a half-and-half situation, which neither dismisses the dream as 'illusion', nor confirms it as 'astral travel'.

I was very puzzled by this dimension to dreams that seemed to suggest a non-ordinary vista of perception. The fact was that, coincidence or not, I had been able to describe something that existed in real time without my ever having visited it and, more importantly, someone familiar with it was able to identify it as such.

There was another dream that I found puzzling. Unlike the previous one, whose impact dawned on me only after my friend had reacted to it, this dream needed no one else's substantiation – the ensuing events provided confirmation. Our Teacher had left the ashram for a two-week-long trip, and as the days passed we found ourselves looking forward to his return eagerly, even though he had categorically told us that he would be back on the sixteenth of that month. I had a short dream:

Our Teacher has returned to the ashram on the fourteenth, two days before he was expected, and I am very surprised to see him.

I say to him, 'But you were supposed to return on the sixteenth.'

He does not answer, but his lips betray a smile, possibly amused by my confusion. His eyes look straight at me as though searching for an explanation.

My surprise knew no bounds when he actually did return on the fourteenth, exactly as my dream had foretold! When asked about his early return, he replied matter-of-factly: 'The work finished earlier, so I came.' Then, as if in response to my surprise, he asked, 'Should I have stayed on?'

I was left bewildered. Had I been privy to a clue by which my subconscious mind had calculated that he would return earlier and expressed its deduction through the dream? If the past is one such clue, then it went against my dream-dictated thesis because whenever our Teacher had left the ashram he would more often than not have to extend his trip due to delays in his work. Never had he come back earlier. I asked the other residents of the ashram whether they had entertained the possibility of his early return, but they had all been surprised by his premature homecoming. If no subliminal hint had existed, then what was my dream? Precognition? Or do we once again invoke 'coincidence'? Precognition presents its own difficulties by relying on a source of information beyond 'normal' parameters. It defies the thesis that dreams retrieve information already embedded in memory. If my dream had not relied on any memory mechanism for its knowledge, from where had the dream sourced its information? Did it exist elsewhere, outside the realm of my experience? If so, then whose province is it?

Some people believe that dreams, at least a majority of them, are premonitory. They would eagerly read the few dreams I have mentioned above in this manner. The symbols in the 26 January dream foretold that I would find a job, even if it was a modest one. The hatch-opening dream disclosed the choice that would be exercised six months later, and the dream about the Bodleian Library merely alerted me sixteen years earlier that I would, one day, visit Oxford. All these dreams were casting a glance towards the future. If dreams can anticipate events, then it would not be long before predestination becomes a handmaiden to my beliefs: events are already written, like a script, and all we do is read the lines, at the appropriate time. And yet the precognition in the last dream is essentially different from the earlier dreams.

Others would argue that although in this case the event matched the dream, there will be hundreds of instances when there is no outcome to attest the dream episode. Then why are we ready to link this dream precognitively to the event? I do not pretend to have the answers, but we will explore this relationship in greater depth later in the book.

The challenges of my new life in the hermitage seemed, at times, so overwhelming that often I did not know where I was going. Then a dream would come, encouraging, warning, or cautioning me, like a beam of light on a dark road. In those moments they seemed to possess a breadth of vision I could never honestly claim as my own.

At one phase during our years at the ashram, I had sunk into such an abyss of despair that I had abandoned all hope. My expectations were at their lowest. All roads seemed like dead ends. Then, totally unexpectedly, I was touched by something profoundly mysterious. It taught me, it guided me, and sometimes it gave me glimpses of a state of being against which the limitations of my everyday reality stood out.

I do not pretend to understand the full import of this mystery, yet it commanded my attention as it increasingly directed the theatre of my dream life, helping me transform many of my perceptions. For instance, it questioned my limited view on the nature of life's sufferings and pointed its finger in a direction that transcended them:

A practice session of judo is in progress. Students in traditional judo attire are performing various exercises. I am part of a group that is running up and down staircases and tackling minor obstacles, in an effort to increase our stamina. Unexpectedly, the judo master appears. He is Japanese and a venerated figure. He looks at me and says, 'Come here.'

I go and stand in front of him. Before I know it, he raises his hand and brings it down in a swift, painful crack at the base of my neck. The impact is so strong that I faint. When I come around I see him standing near me, watching. I'm very angry and say, 'You knew I couldn't handle that, yet you hit me.'

'I did it so that you are never caught unawares again. Be always in a state of readiness. Now I will teach.' He paused and looked at me gently. 'The first rule is that when a blow is coming, go soft, go plastic ... Let the blow strike through you like air. The impact of the blow must not be such that your own resistance rips you apart.' He comes near me and demonstrates. The motion is so fluid, yielding, and graceful that I feel awed. I bow my head.

This appeared to be a totally different type of dream; I felt no need to pass it through the sieve of analysis. I chose to understand the message in the dream literally. A judo master was teaching me an important lesson: Don't stiffen up with fear and anxiety. Go fluid, become pliant, yield. The dream challenged the common conception that suffering can be best avoided by resisting it.

A seventy-five-year-old friend, who had had a few drinks, slipped while descending a rather steep staircase and went tumbling down the full flight of fifteen steps. Miraculously, he did not suffer a bruise. His inebriated condition probably did not allow him to tense up, so that his body had not resisted the fall but had *yielded* to it! As Confucius said: a man comes safely down a roaring waterfall, who abandons himself to the nature of falling water.

I believed in my dream because through it I learnt a simple but profound truth: The assaults of life are best taken by yielding, not resisting. Yielding does not imply fatalistic passivity; in fact, it pushes one to grapple with and understand suffering. Perhaps we gloss over the distinction between pain and suffering. 'Pain is physical; suffering is mental. Beyond the mind there is no suffering. Pain is merely a signal that the body is in danger and requires attention.' We suffer when our self-conception is threatened by loss or change.[2]

When Rajeev and I decided after seven years to return to the city, what I dreaded most was the absence of the unique atmosphere of the Himalayas, where our Teacher's presence and the environment he had created had afforded us the best opportunity for our inner search. Once distant from that, would we lose touch with what we believed to be most essential in life? Above all, I wondered whether the few glimpses I held precious in my dream life would ever be repeated or whether they would simply get submerged in the swamp and mire of city life.

Yet in the transition from the quiet, concentrated mountain life to the noisy jostle of the city, my dreams ran a dialogue with me. Initially there were many typical anxiety dreams: I am searching for something I have lost; or I find guests in the house and there is no food; or my school results are being announced and I cannot find my name on the list of those who have passed. These were dreams reflecting my feeling of being lost, ill-prepared, unsure. They pointed at my fears about whether I had failed in the challenge I had left behind, and how I would cope with the life that lay ahead. I dreamt so often of our life in the mountains, of our tiny cottage – it was evident that although I had physically moved away from the ashram, emotionally I was still there. Then, many months later, I dreamt:

*I'm closing the gate right outside our mountain cottage and I walk
down the road without a backward glance.*

Maybe it was from this point onwards that I did manage to *'close the
gate'* on our life in the mountains, and without a *'backward glance'* I made
an important emotional shift to my new life. But I knew that a great
deal more had to be tackled before I could say that the transition was
complete. The power of our years in the ashram lay in the complexity
of our experience. I was finding it very difficult to resolve the utter
polarity of those years – on one hand there had been struggle and
suffering, while on the other hand the experience had been magical
and transforming. I oscillated between the inspiration of those years
and the abyss of despair to which I had also plummeted. I could not
find a bridge between the two. In order to understand my experiences
better, I began to write.

I wrote for about six months, trying to maintain some chronological
order of what our Teacher had taught us. I kept myself distant from
what I was writing. My pen seemed afraid to flow. I did not quite
realize what I was going through at the time, but once again my
dreams did:

*There is a house under construction, which has a basic wall, a
rudimentary roof, and no floor. Construction material – sand, cement,
rubble – is lying all around as I enter this structure. The only furniture
inside is an old table on which my typewriter rests. I begin typing
from the notes I had made the previous day.*

*A woman wearing stiletto heels enters. She has long painted
fingernails, perfectly groomed hair, and rather fancy clothes. As she
moves towards me her high heels wobble on the uneven floor. Her
carefully modulated voice, her fancy clothes, her made-up face do
not sit comfortably in this rough environment. I get up and after a
few polite words usher her out. I then take the typewriter from the
table and set it down on the ground.*

It seemed a strange dream, initially difficult to interpret. In my
confused state I had forgotten the simple rule of dreams – they respond
to whichever area your energies are focused upon. The typewriter gave
me the initial clue that the dream was centred on my writing, since I
used it to record my thoughts. Other images became clearer. I began
to see that the house under construction was a symbol alluding to my
manuscript. I felt I had a story to tell, but the problem lay in the telling.
It was, as described by the dream, at a very rudimentary stage – the

'structure' of the story was still very basic. There was construction material lying around, indicating that the material for the book was available, but I still had to give it form. In the dream a well-groomed woman entered, whose presence I found incongruous in that setting. I asked myself what was manicured or superficial in my current draft. Once more, the clue lay within the dream itself – again in the typewriter: I picked it up from the table and placed it on the floor. The dream was urging me to 'ground' my writings, to base them on my own experiences. The ground was a symbol of being earthed; being in touch with what is authentic.

So far my draft was only a record of incidents and teachings, as though I was not a participant, but merely a scribe noting events without daring personal involvement. As a result, it was a superficial work, out of touch with my own feelings. What I had not perceived, my dream had dredged from the unconscious and placed before me.

I heeded my dream advice and began rewriting.

What kind of dream was this one? We cannot think of it as precognitive, nor is it an ordinary dream rummaging through the residues of the day spent in writing. Was it a problem-solving dream? It certainly offered me advice, and quite creatively at that.

I am not suggesting at all that every time I had a problem a dream would miraculously give me the solution. There were a number of long stretches when I could not remember any dream, and there were times when they seemed to say nothing about what I thought was important. It was as though my dream life had simply gone to sleep. But I do not think that was really the case. My dream life was just marking time till the intensity of the problem had built up sufficiently for its insights to be ingested. Then, a dream would come to appease the hunger of my waiting.

Over the years I realized there were different dream types. There were dreams that unearthed old wounds, as in the Annie Besant dream; dreams of reassurance where I found my 'spot', like in the Republic Day dream; anticipatory dreams, such as the one in which the hatch opened and we jumped into the unknown – a new way of life. Travelling to the Bodleian Library or the unexpected return of my Teacher seemed yet another class of dreams where information otherwise inaccessible became known to me. Then there was the all-important teaching dream in which a judo master instructed me on how to handle suffering. This dream spoke of suffering, while the next one dealt with healing – a process marked by my closing the gate outside our cottage in the ashram.

At quite another level was the dream of the chic woman entering the half-built house and striking a discordant note vis-à-vis my writing. It was truly a problem-solving dream, suggesting impediments and offering ideas on how to rework my manuscript. From psychological to paranormal, problem-solving to existential, to my amazement the range continued to expand over the years. The mystery of dreams grew for me. And maybe in a need to understand the range of the dreaming mind, this book was born. I became an apprentice to its mystery.

Perhaps the dreaming mind's most powerful yet inscrutable face is its metaphysical one, where it asks questions whose answers seem to go far beyond merely the inner and outer life of the individual. It directs the dreamer's gaze to the root and source of human consciousness. At one level dreams explore the entire field of human consciousness and, at another level, they ask you to go beyond it.

The last of my dreams that I will recount belongs to that potent category of transpersonal dreams, where answers lie neither at an emotional nor intellectual level, but demand a transformation of consciousness.

By the time I was forty I had come full circle. Twenty-two years earlier, I had ventured out to discover my path. I had since met a charismatic teacher, under whose vigilant tutelage I had lived for seven years. Another seven years had elapsed since our return to the city – time enough to assimilate the intense experience of discipleship. But now I was confronted with an even more fundamental question – how deep was my commitment to my inner search? It was no longer being shouldered by my Teacher, for he had passed on. I was confronted with assuming the responsibility of sustaining my search without any inputs, save my own commitment to it. What had been taken for granted when he was alive had to be revivified entirely by my own effort. It raised uncomfortable questions about my dedication. How much did I really want it? How much was I prepared to give to it?

I oscillated between the travails of holding onto it and the painful awareness when I let my grip loosen. That I often fell short was apparent to me. The following dream came against the backdrop of this unarticulated conflict:

> I'm sitting for an examination and the invigilator hands me the question paper. I realize this is no ordinary examination – it is a life exam. The first question is: What is your gravest doubt in life?

I answer: My doubt is that nothing is permanent. Everything changes. Today's pleasure is tomorrow's sorrow; despair turns to hope, health to illness, love to indifference. In this constant flux what is permanent?

I continue to write in this vein for some time and then feel that I need to get on to the next question, since time is running out. Even though I have not completed my answer, curiosity compels me to turn the page over and look at what the next question is. In rather bold letters it asks: Who are you?

I awoke from this dream with the sense of deep reassurance that comes when a conflict is directly addressed. I realized it would take me time to understand the full import of the dream. However, at an instinctive level it affirmed that if I needed direction, it would be given. If I lost my way I would be guided. By asking me who I was, the dream highlighted what was essential. It was very similar to the central teaching of the great south Indian sage Ramana Maharshi. He believed that the best way to realize the true nature of the Self is through an assiduous enquiry centred on the question: Who am I? Though the question came out of the blue and startled me, it was nonetheless comforting, for it clearly defined my next step.

The dream surprised me at various levels. If someone had asked me while I was awake what my gravest doubt was, I would have fumbled for an answer. Yet in the dream I suffered from no such ambiguity. As though by making me aware of my gravest doubt, the next question – Who are you? – could be asked. If everything changes, if all is transitory, then my quest for permanence could only be answered by knowing who I am.

On the face of it, not knowing who one is seems ludicrous. Yet I knew it was not a trivial question, but a serious one: it was an enquiry into my essential identity. And if I persisted along this line of questioning, I might get a clue to 'the unchanging and the permanent'.

In the days that followed I remained perplexed. I began to realize how difficult the exercise was. No matter how much I thought about it, I was confronted with inadequate answers. If I addressed the question by my gender (woman), or my roles (wife, daughter, writer), or by abstract personal qualities (empathetic, extroverted, impractical), it did not provide any satisfactory answers.

It seems that I am something more than my body, more than its desires and fears, more than the mind with all its thoughts and creativity. I may think that the sum of my personality traits, my thoughts, and my emotions define the person I am, but in essence that is still not 'me', for when asleep they are not in evidence, yet I still am. Furthermore, my thoughts and emotions constantly change, my body undergoes changes, my personality traits change, so how can I search for an answer based on ever-changing attributes? There has to be a permanent 'someone' to whom these changes occur. Who is that 'someone', the unchanging 'I'?

Till today, I continue to seek the answer to that question.

While dreams often allude to our inner world, revealing an earlier trauma, or point to a disguised desire, or present a metaphorical assessment of our current dilemmas, at other times they cannot be denied a phenomenological[3] reality and may be regarded as a prophetic intimation, an intuitive insight addressing concrete outer events. At certain junctures of our lives, dreams may also address our spiritual concerns; they become a ladder of awareness that takes us to a realm beyond the everyday self. Then there may be some dreams that are prosaic and trivial, and others that are totally unintelligible. Though each of us has a predominant style of dream experience – our dream idiom – most of us will experience the full spectrum of the dreaming mind.

Both my own experiences and those of others repeatedly affirmed to me that there is a mystery at the heart of every dream. And it is this mystery – which can never be proved and yet is ever-present in a dream – that enthrals and captures our imagination. The book emerged out of reverence for such a mystery: the sheer desire to remain in its presence long enough in the hope that it will occasionally lift its veil to one of its seekers.

Chapter 3

THE INTERPLAY BETWEEN
BELIEF AND BIZARRENESS

'Explain all that,' said the Mock Turtle.
'No, no! The adventures first,' said the Gryphon in an
impatient tone: 'explanations take such a dreadful time.'

Lewis Carroll, *Alice's Adventures in Wonderland*

The psychologically-minded may not concur with my understanding
of the dreams in the last chapter. They may feel the interpretations
are simple and linear, lacking any theoretical grounding to inform their
analysis; that my Teacher's and my interpretations had a common
orientation – the inner life. However, would psychologists of different
persuasions attribute identical meanings to my dreams? We have already
seen with my neighbour's dream that various theorists, based on their
conception of what a dream is, would attribute different meanings to
it. This leads us to conjecture that, perhaps, something else besides
the dream is required to arrive at the significance of the dream. Most
psychologists believe that the personal associations of the dreamer to the
dream images are fundamental in the understanding of the dream. Some
also use mythology and folklore to amplify these images and symbols.
Others hold that more than the associations, the interpretation should
focus on the dreamer's experience itself. It seems the interpretation of
a dream may not be such a simple matter, as attendant factors become

as important as the dream content itself.[1] These factors include the beliefs and conceptions permeating the interpretation of a dream, and often invading it.

Dreams are primarily expressed in the language of the night, which largely comprises visual imagery in contrast to the usually imageless thoughts of waking life. Our attempt at interpretation is a process of transposing the language of the night into the thoughts of the waking world. During this process, our beliefs make their invisible entry and dictate our interpretation of the dream.

To elaborate, if dreaming is considered a metaphor that provides insights into the dreamer's neglected thoughts and emotions, then my neighbour's dream is a comment on her marriage. If dreaming is considered a communication where subtle influences, which remain unheeded due to daytime preoccupations, may be heard, then the dream warns her about her father's imminent death. These divergent beliefs about dreaming give rise to radically different interpretations of the dream. Thus before decoding dreams we have to clarify the underlying beliefs that lend substance to their interpretation.

The fundamental issues

The different approaches to dreaming may perhaps be quickly grasped by asking a few basic questions about dreams.[2] Possibly the most fundamental question we can ask is about the function of dreams. Is there a reason or purpose for why we dream? Does the dream have any role in the conduct of our lives, helping the dreamer to adapt to external circumstances or to one's internal network of emotions? Interlinked with the role of dreams is the question about their source. How are they formed? Are they a product of our reasoning faculty, or do they arise from our emotional nature? We certainly do not feel responsible for what we dream. If dreams are not willed by us – rationally or imaginatively – then what gives rise to them? Are they born outside us and visit us at night? The way we answer these questions is bound to affect our method of interpreting a dream.

Maybe this can be illustrated with Calpurnia's oft-repeated dream in Shakespeare's *Julius Caesar*: She saw Caesar's statue 'which like a fountain with an hundred spouts / Did run blood'. Calpurnia was convinced she had dreamt of Caesar's assassination: 'Thrice hath Calpurnia in her sleep cried out, / "Help, ho! They murder Caesar!"'[3] It must be appreciated that more than the 'truth' of her dream images, it was her historical context that made her believe that the dream was an obvious prognostication intended to safeguard the life of her husband. She was being 'told' to restrain Caesar from attending the Senate.

The ancient world considered dreams to be a message from an external source, and restricted the function of dreams to pronouncements about an unforeseeable future. Hence it was important to dream about victory before the war, of game before the hunt. In fact, Decius duplicitously tells Caesar that Calpurnia's dream indicates victories for Rome promising that 'from you great Rome shall suck / Reviving blood'.[4] Here again we witness multiple meanings of the same dream, even though both interpretations assume dreams to be prognostications.

On the other hand, the modern belief is that they are psychological messages from within us. Had Calpurnia lived in modern times, her analyst would have led her through a psychological labyrinth of infantile urges to comprehend her dream: she was expecting to find a replica of her father in her spouse, and finding him lacking actually wished his death. Analysts today, governed by their particular beliefs about dreaming, would treat her dream only as a therapeutic device that promises psychological health to Calpurnia's marriage.

In other words, the significance of a dream is subsumed by our cultural perceptions about the role of dreams. If we deem them to be internal messages, we are given to believing that their role is to help the dreamer understand emotional relationships or personal feelings. If we are of the view that dreams come from an external source, we look upon them as messages of deep import about forthcoming events.

Differences surface not only when we ascribe a particular role to the dream as a whole, but also if we were to read a single element within the dream. Our ability to attribute symbolic significance to any image within the dream is also guided by our conceptions of dreaming. The Hellenic Greeks treated the penis in a dream as representative of speech and education, among other things, because the penis, like speech, is very fertile.[5] The South American Jivaro Indians, who hunt with blowguns and poisoned darts, interpret an erect penis in a dream as a symbol of a snake.[6] (For them the ultimate significance of a dream rests in its ability to aid the hunt – and snake venom is prized ammunition.) A modern analyst, on the other hand, would treat the erect penis in a dream as a symbol for the power of Eros. Interestingly, a therapist of a different persuasion would reverse the symbolism treating a snake in a dream as a penile symbol. Once again, belief is the net by which dreams and their symbols are caught and understood.

This is all very well, we tell ourselves, but which one would be the right meaning of the dream? This poses yet another basic question about dreaming: Do dreams have but one fundamental meaning? Or does a network of meanings reside in them, which collectively reflects the mental, emotional, and physical state of the dreamer, even commenting on the dreamer's environment at times? We somehow expect that a dream should have only one 'true' interpretation, that the others only carry the burden of our errors in decoding them. This belief persists notwithstanding the fact that history has not only substantiated Calpurnia's interpretation, but it has also justified Decius's rendering of the dream. The Roman legions under Augustus – Julius Caesar's successor – did subsequently fan out and revive Roman hegemony over the Mediterranean and much of Europe, ushering in the Golden Age of Rome. Further, we cannot really limit the dream to being a mere personal and social prophecy, foretelling the fate of Caesar and Rome. It would not be too far-fetched to see the psychological truth of the dream as well. After all, Caesar had not exactly walked the straight and narrow path of matrimony; he had reputedly sired a son by Cleopatra. Besides, his ambition laced with his megalomania must have translated into pretty selfish behaviour at home, robbing Calpurnia of any form of companionship. Her dream may very well have been an expression of her deep marital dissatisfaction and their bleeding, dying relationship. Whichever way we look, our perceptions of dreaming inform how we interpret the dream and it seems they can all yield relevant interpretations. The Jewish scholar 'Rabbi Binza reported that he once consulted twenty-four dream interpreters who were in Jerusalem at one time and received different interpretations of his dream from each, all of which were subsequently realized.'[7]

This only raises further questions: Can we entrust our dreams only to a trained analyst for interpretation, or can any person, with a little familiarization, learn to interpret his or her own dreams? Some hold that the dreamer is the best person to fully comprehend the dream as it actually belongs to that person and no one else. Only the dreamer can know whether the dream is masking a personal truth or not – the rest are only reading confirmations of their theories in the dream. This, in turn, raises another issue: Is the dream private to the dreamer and can it then really be shared with others? All these questions will be addressed in the course of the book.

The strangeness of the dream

By now one fact is evident: humankind's divergent perceptions about dreaming have spawned widely differing theories about dreams. Paradoxically, these disparate theories rely on a single feature of dreams to posit their views: the strangeness of the dream. The situation is comparable to the six blind men and the proverbial elephant they hope to describe. Each touches a different part of the elephant and comes up with dissimilar versions. It would have been truly amazing if, instead, all of them had felt the trunk and still described the elephant differently. This is precisely what has happened to dream theories. Each grapples with the strangeness of the dream – its incongruity with the waking world – and describes a very different elephant.

My neighbour's dream amply demonstrates that differing perceptions about the strange or bizarre images in a dream lead to varied interpretations. The strange part of her dream was her dead uncle coming to escort her father from the hospital. The sheer implausibility of such an occurrence would lead some to treat the dream as nothing more than a hallucination. They would find it absurd to search for meaning in such imagery. Others would say that this incongruity indicates that the dream is a disguise of a deeper wish and of something repressed, which cannot be accepted by the waking mind. They would probe this camouflage by evoking associations to the dead uncle in an effort to cull meaning from her dream. Still others feel dreams never express themselves in a logical way, but always in the language of metaphor. Thus their strangeness is but a device that only serves to attract attention. If we interpret the dead uncle as a metaphor of her marital estrangement, then the dream is only projecting her lack of reliance on her husband as an obviously absurd proposition – a dead uncle helps her escort the father home! If we believe the dream focuses on feelings of superiority/inferiority, then we will analyze the dead uncle as an imaginary support that enables her to defend her sense of self-worth in the face of an overwhelming father. And if the dream is perceived as a literal comment on reality, then the uncle becomes a messenger of death, alerting the dreamer that her father may die in the near future. So many different interpretations emanate from one strange element – the dead uncle.

Alongside we must admit that it is the strange qualities of dreams – their discontinuities and incongruities, *dream bizarreness* – that initially attract our attention to recall and relate them. It is these strange elements – kings turning into cabbages or horses that sing – that lift dreams above the monotony of everyday life. We remember and retell them because of their sheer unusualness and lack of conformity to what is 'normal' to waking life. There are many different ways in which to familiarize the reader with the range of dream theories. However, I have not resorted to a linear historical sequence. Instead I have attempted to trace the evolution of dream theories from this single feature of dreaming – the strangeness of the dream.

We have seen how belief determines the meaning of dreams. Now we see that belief is also locked in a tight embrace with bizarreness. I am not suggesting a linear relationship between them – bizarreness shapes belief, which in turn colours the meaning of a dream. On the contrary, each affects the other. To illustrate, if a dream is strange we believe it contains a hidden meaning. Here bizarreness has triggered a particular belief. However, it is equally true that beliefs have a characteristic way of viewing bizarreness. For example, if we believe dreams are thoughts that are converted into visual imagery, then dream bizarreness would be viewed as a translation error that creeps into this process of conversion. Much like a book that when converted into a film script is invariably 'impaired' by jumps and distortions.

Expressed differently, beliefs and bizarreness are the two strands on which any dream theory is built. Belief imbues a function to dreaming, and with its help the theory comments on the purpose of dreams. While bizarreness alerts us to the method of understanding dreams, it also helps to affirm the beliefs of the theory. Based on these two components, each theory hopes to comprehend different types of dreams by constructing a full metaphysic about them.

Each theory may be viewed as a matrix that attempts to answer four basic questions about dreams: Where do they come from? Why are they so strange? What function(s) do they serve? How are they interpreted?[8] The questions sound simple enough, but the diversity of answers given by theorists through the millennia affects the way we comprehend any dream.

The earliest conception of dreams in antiquity was that the source of dreams was from the gods or from the supernatural world. Their function was to guide, warn, and inspire man to realize his destiny. Dreams were strange because god spoke in parables. Dream bizarreness was attributed to the imperfect understanding of man, who was unable to comprehend god's language. Interpretation would enable the dreamer to fulfil god's bidding.

In direct contrast are the modern scientific theories, which rely on brain chemistry to answer these very questions. They trace the source of dreams to the neural activity in the brainstem, and their strangeness to a medley of imperfectly assimilated images, randomly generated as a by-product of periodic neuronal firing within the sleeping brain. Their function is the daily clean up of the brain's neural circuitry. The bizarre nature of dreams is proof enough that they are inherently meaningless. Whatever we read into them is only a secondary effect of waking thought, superimposed upon an episode recalled after awakening.

Away from the gods and brain neurology stands Freud, straddling twentieth-century dream discourse with his remarkable insights. He treated dreams as an internal psychic event that arises from the unconscious. The unconscious is equated neither with an external god nor with brain activity, but is situated within man, being the submerged part of the human psyche that controls all conscious behaviour. For him, and subsequently for psychology, it remains the source of all dreams. Freud attributed the strangeness of dreams to a disguise wrought by the psyche to mask an unacceptable and therefore repressed wish, which is usually sexual. Its function is to preserve sleep, and the method used to interpret dreams is to reverse the disguise with the help of a chain of free associations. We do not remember dreams because they are intimations of a painful happening in the past.

It is evident from this how the twin strands of belief and bizarreness allow a theory to ascribe significance to dreaming. These are only three theories; other theorists have understood dreams still differently. It is perhaps for this reason that we have many meanings of a single dream.

Interesting though these views are, unfortunately the Gryphon within me complained and shrank from the Mock Turtle's demand to 'explain, all that' about dreaming. The adventure of specific dreams and their interpretation are more interesting and 'explanations take such a dreadful time.' But could we have ignored the Mock Turtle's request?

Chapter 4

DREAM PARADIGMS

'Why,' said the Dodo, 'the best way to explain it is to do it.'

Lewis Carroll, *Alice's Adventures in Wonderland*

One of the challenges I faced when writing this book was in finding a basis for grouping together the dreams that were narrated to me. For example, when I attempted to organize them according to the dreamer, often one set of dreams would challenge the fundamental tenets of another. Like in my dreams related earlier, the underlying beliefs of the Bodleian Library dream challenged the beliefs that supported the interpretation of the Annie Besant dream. After considerable thought, I realized that the system of grouping together dreams that are paradigmatically similar lends itself best to my pursuit.

But how is a paradigm different from a theory? Though each theory of dreaming, founded on the twin notions of beliefs and bizarreness, is different from all other theories, some of them do draw upon common beliefs and assumptions. When these theories that share a common foundation are viewed together they may be called a paradigm of dreaming. However, a paradigm that works very well for some dreams, may fail to grasp the significance of others. Consequently we need different paradigms if we are to understand the full range of the dreaming mind. Though Calpurnia and Decius shared the same cultural beliefs, they attributed different meanings to the same dream. Calpurnia had interpreted her dream as a personal omen, while Decius had viewed it as a comment on the social destiny of Rome. This apparent contradiction is easier to understand if we say that they had used different paradigms to decode her dream. My attempt here is not to define a neat taxonomy, but to offer some sort of classification that would adequately explain the multiplicity of dream types.

However, before we proceed any further, there are a few issues that need to be negotiated. Firstly, if we consider the way I have interpreted my dreams in chapter 2, it is fairly clear that most of the dream images have been interpreted as though they were analogous to the circumstances of my life. For example, the chic lady in the building under construction has been treated as a symbol of my manuscript, and her actions in the dream have been transposed as comments on my writing. In short, the dreams have been comprehended symbolically. On the other hand, in some dreams the messages have been construed literally from the dream images, as though their meanings were no different from what was conveyed by the imagery. Like the dream about the early arrival of my Teacher – no interpretation was used to decode its content. It was understood to presage his actual date of arrival.

This categorization of dreams into literal and symbolic reflects dichotomies at a number of levels. Most of my dreams appeared to be expressions of my internal psychological reality, where concealed motives, unexpressed wishes, and unresolved conflicts surfaced to address the concerns of the moment. The dream becomes a metaphor for an unfinished emotional situation. In contrast to these symbolic dreams, the literal dreams deal with the world of actions, commenting directly on events in the everyday life of the dreamer. Each category becomes an expression of an underlying system of belief, a paradigm. In other words, a way of classifying paradigms slowly suggested itself: literal as opposed to symbolic; psychological as opposed to paranormal; rational as opposed to romantic.

I soon realized that this classification was real and not arbitrary. My neighbour's dream when viewed from the psychological paradigm would be a comment on the state of her mind / emotions, while the paranormal paradigm would treat it as a premonition about an imminent event and even as a paranormal visitation.

Another example may prove illustrative in a different way. This dream is from the files of the Jungian psychotherapist Marie Louise von Franz.[1] A domineering woman with a very strong power complex dreamt of three tigers seated threateningly in front of her. Her analyst counselled her that the dream was indicative of her devouring attitude towards other people, as symbolized by the three tigers. It seemed a very apt interpretation, given the personality of the dreamer. Except that when the dreamer and her friend were strolling along Lake Zurich later that very afternoon, they noticed a crowd gathered near a barn and their curiosity led them to enquire about what was occupying these people's attention. The lady was shocked to see three tigers sitting in a row, exactly as in her dream! Now can we be sure that the psychological interpretation of the dream encompasses the full intent of the dreaming mind? Could not the dream also have been informing our domineering woman of sighting something unusual the next day? After all, it's perhaps rare even in an Indian jungle to witness three tigers sitting together in a row – and this was Switzerland! (The tigers were part of a circus spending the night in town.)

Even if this dream did not foretell anything of serious significance, its unusual gaze into the future would certainly provoke the question: Where did the dream source its information from? Certainly not from memory. It highlights that the distinction between a psychological and phenomenological dream is not always clear-cut. Further, more than one paradigm is necessary to understand the multiplicity of dream types.

Before we explore the paradigms that ascribe meaning to dreams, we may need to consider the scientific one, which views dreams to be meaningless. In its view, the debate on whether the dream is a message about our outward circumstances or our internal condition is akin to worrying over the choice of a vocation for the son of a barren woman. This doubt about whether dreams are, in fact, meaningful or not is probably something that has dogged each of us at one point or another in our lives. We can never know whether Calpurnia actually did dream of Caesar's death, or whether it was simply a literary device employed by the creative genius of Shakespeare, or Plutarch for that matter.[2]

The scientific view of dreams

Dreams are no longer a speculative subject, but have been taken into the temples of Science – the research laboratory. Modern researchers have established that each of us dreams a minimum of four dreams every night. Physiological processes, they assert, author dreams and not external factors or psychological compulsions. Their formation has been traced to the neural activity in a particular part of the brain, the brainstem. The proof resides in the fact that if the brainstem is stimulated while a person is asleep, immediately a dream is experienced. When the brainstem is bombarded by electro-chemical signals, the sleeping brain generates random visual images as a by-product, and this imagery is what we experience as a dream. It explains the sudden scene changes that occur while we dream, as also the strange and disconnected content (dream bizarreness). Dreams are, therefore, nothing more than the meaningless by-products of the central nervous system stimulated during sleep.

This mounting experimental evidence should have silenced psychologists and parapsychologists once and for all. But this did not happen because scientific theories stalled at this juncture. The dream is strange – at variance with reality – but only at some points; otherwise it maintains a pretty cohesive story. My neighbour's dream had only one strange element – a dead uncle driving a car; other than that, the narrative had a plausible and definite storyline. If all the images are randomly generated, then how can we account for the successive images in her dream that followed a cohesive thread? This scientific lapse permits entry to other theories that attribute meaning to the dream. It also opens the proverbial Pandora's box by allowing for a host of other questions to be raised.

If most of the dream unfolds sequentially, who infuses this order into the otherwise randomly generated imagery? Does this ordering agency follow a plan? Then, is the meaning of the dream inherent in it, or is it implanted by the dreamer/interpreter? Is the dream a device that manipulates our stored memories, or is it a product of our creative imagination? Does the dream represent a reality in itself, or is its vocabulary limited to the alphabets of our everyday concerns? The issues are endless. My intention is not to dwell on the philosophical subtleties of these issues, but to give an introductory flavour in the hope that the reader's dialogue with his or her own dreams becomes more significant. Perhaps the impact of one of these issues on the meaning of the dream can be briefly illustrated.

Is the dream a thought expressed as visual imagery, or is it merely the product of a sensation? In other words, is the dream a somatic signal as some believe, which alerts the dreamer to the internal needs of the body (hunger, cold, illness) or at times even to an external stimulus? While dreaming, Alfred Maury, a nineteenth-century Frenchman, found himself being tried during the French Revolution and sentenced to the guillotine. So real was the dream that he felt the blade fall, but just as it was about to sever his neck from his body he awoke. He found that the bed rail had fallen on his neck. This only leads one to conclude that the bed rail falling on his neck had triggered the dream, which had imaginatively located the sensation in his neck into a historically charged context, and thereby created the potency of the dream.[3]

Maury, it seems, experimented further: when someone held a burning match under his nose while he slept he dreamt that the gunpowder store on the ship he was sailing in had caught fire. Replacing the lit match with cologne produced a dream of a perfume factory in Cairo. And, when a pair of tweezers was reverberated close to his ear, he dreamt of bells ringing during the French Revolution.[4]

Maury's theory that dreams are caused by external stimulation has been modified by current research to show that dreams can be *influenced* by such stimulation. This is an important difference, for what Maury was suggesting was that the dream is essentially a sensation and consequently devoid of any inherent meaning. The modern modification implies that the dream is visual imagery that can, at times, incorporate external as well as bodily sensation. It, therefore, does not preclude meaning from it. Thus one's conception of a dream as meaningless or meaningful may dramatically alter based on whether we view it as a reflex sensation or a succession of images that may be reflective of an ordering agency.

In the beginning of the book, before discussing the paradigms that attribute meaning to dreams, I consider the standpoint of science and its resistance to grant any real significance to dreams. I have also cast a backward glance to outline how dreams have been viewed historically. Though humanity's earliest perception of dreaming was only reverential, somewhere in history dreams were discredited in the Western world. It is important that we understand why and how this happened in order to appreciate the resurgence of interest in dreams in modern times.

Thereafter, I delve into the various dream theories, which I have arranged under three broad paradigms. In doing so, I am aware that I have neither been comprehensive in detailing the theories discussed, nor have I been exhaustive in delineating all the formulations. Nor can I claim that I have limited myself to the most important schools. Yet, what I hope to convey through these three paradigms are three important facets of the dreaming mind.

The dream as a mirror of the personality

The first of these paradigms views the dream as a purveyor of our psychological reality. This is currently the dominant Western model, and it sees the dream as a reflection of our wishes, desires, concerns, and aspirations. It considers the dream to be a mirror of the personality.

I discuss how some of its exponents – Freud, Jung, Perls, Ullman, Hall – perceive the dream, attempting through each theory to highlight an unfoldment within the psychological paradigm itself.

Freud, who had founded this approach, understood dreams to be a disguise for ungratified wishes. Jung, while agreeing that some dreams are clearly wish-fulfilments, added another dimension to dream discourse by stating that dreams are compensatory of the imbalances in the dreamer's conscious waking attitudes. Freud and Jung had posited an 'unconscious' to understand dreams and they both believed that only a trained analyst can uncover the meaning of a dream. Later theorists like Perls and Ullman questioned this belief, arguing that the dream really belongs to the dreamer and no one else. In making this claim, they freed the dream from the clinic or the couch and brought it into everyone's bedroom. Calvin Hall went a step further to enquire whether the Freudian or Jungian superstructure (the unconscious) is required in understanding dreams. His approach envisioned the dream to be a continued expression during the night of our waking conceptions and the world that surrounds us. My interviews with people about their dreams are interwoven with these theories and this both explicates and helps classify them.

This model, though adequate for normative dreaming, finds it difficult to acknowledge phenomenological or literal dreams, which convey information that would otherwise be inaccessible to the dreamer. Freud, for example, viewed the precognitive dream only as a wish aching to be fulfilled. Jung, perhaps, came closest to acknowledging it, but retreated into a rationally safe position by calling it an 'anticipatory' dream.[5] Admittedly, if a Mrs Smith dreams of her husband being stabbed at work, no one will entertain the possibility that it is prophetic, preferring to explore its meaning along psychological coordinates. Yet this does not preclude the prophetic dream from being a part of our conceptual vocabulary. It can happen, however remote the possibility, as Calpurnia would testify. Perhaps a modern example would be more compelling.

A member of the New York Stock Exchange dreamt: 'we should sell all our stocks including box stock (one considered very good). I saw a bull following my wife, who was dressed in red.' He consulted the American psychic Edgar Cayce on 5 March 1929 for an interpretation of his dream. Cayce advised him that his dream is 'an impression of a condition which is to come about, a downward movement of long duration ... Dispose off all held, even box.'[6] Cayce may have understood the red dress in the dream to signify danger and the bull to mean a bull market that was about to exit. The stock market crash of 1929 substantiated the interpretation. It seems the dream was prophetic in more ways than one. The stockbroker's wife asked him for a divorce a few months later![7] Could this be seen in the bull chasing the wife out? Like Calpurnia's, this dream, it seems, was prophetic of both his personal and social destiny. The rationalist would only enquire: Was it? Could not the dreamer (and Cayce) have somehow anticipated the trend of Wall Street, the dream merely stating its natural corollary? Just like Calpurnia, subliminally sensing Brutus's disappointment and her own astute awareness of Caesar's unchecked megalomania, may have anticipated his assassination through a dream. The believer in the prophetic ability of the dream will answer one way, the psychologist another way.

The dream as a window to reality
The psychological model, however, does not exhaustively define the dream. It allows no philosophical space for the varieties of dream types – problem-solving, precognition of events and illness, telepathic and shared dreams – even though many people experience them. This necessitates the second paradigm, which views the dream as a window to outward reality.

These two paradigms of dreaming – the psychological and paranormal – exemplify the eternal debate between the rational and the romantic views. Despite laboratory confirmation of telepathy and precognition, the scientific and psychological schools are suspicious of anything that borders on the unknown – anything that is removed from the 'truth' of their conceptions. The romanticists, in a typically humanist vein, insist that any phenomenon experienced by people warrants attention and should be explored rather than disregarded just because it is alien to our beliefs. They argue that sometimes a dream can provide 'insights so novel and personally revealing that it feels ungracious to regard the dream as anything but an intentional communication of some sort'.[8] I work this debate through this section of the book, detailing the experimental evidence accumulated in the last fifty years and how it has impacted on paranormal dreaming.

In both these paradigms the dream penetrates to something hidden, to some mystery: the psychological dimension seeks to discover the hidden fount of the personality, while the paranormal explores phenomena hidden from our everyday consciousness. But what about the greatest mystery that is veiled from us – what lies at the root of human consciousness: the mystery of being?

We may thus need yet another paradigm of dreaming that is beyond the psychological and the paranormal, the rational and the romantic, and that gives credence to this mystery. The last of my dreams that I related earlier, which dealt with the question: Who are you? refuses to be slotted into any of these categories. It certainly does not display any paranormal ability, nor have I decoded it by using the psychological key. Had I availed of this key it would have yielded an answer only about my psychophysical identity, which, given the nature of the question, would have been banal. It, perhaps, is reflective of another order of dreaming that did not really expect a rational answer, but intended to introduce me to a much deeper enigma: my essential identity.

Earlier it had been asserted that people dream and interpret dreams within a pattern established by their culture. This additional paradigm gives the dream an opportunity to break free from our cultural norms and beliefs. For any one of us, this dimension of dreaming 'can interrupt the mundane reality of the waking world by positing an alternative reality that needs, somehow, to be incorporated into waking life'.[9] It must have been through dreams that the ancient world got its first inkling of another reality. Just like my dream was introducing me to a deeper reality within me. It is towards this essential identity that this 'higher' dimension of dreaming addresses itself.

Dreams as a gateway to transcendence

This is perhaps the subtlest of all the dimensions, in which dreams are a gateway to transcendence. It addresses ultimate questions of who we are, where we come from, and to what purpose we exist.

I know some would question whether there is a transpersonal aspect to our existence, and if so how our lives reflect this transcendental function. I prefer not to be engaged by that debate. Instead, like the Hindus and Buddhists, I questioned myself: Why are we confusing dreaming, which is actually a state of consciousness, with the condition – waking or sleeping – of the body? Normally we bind the dream irretrievably to sleep, when we enter a private imaginary world where the intrusion of an external reality is reduced to a bare minimum and the voluntary direction of attention is relinquished.[10] If this defines the dream, then don't all these characteristics also apply to our daydreams? Can the daydream be distinguished in any essential manner from the nocturnal dream? Then, there is the reverie, trance, hypnotic state, and the Jungian technique of active imagination[11] – all close cousins of the dream. The nearest in lineage is, possibly, the hypnagogic state experienced at sleep onset, when consciousness is neither awake nor asleep yet it is both 'aware' and in a dreamlike condition. What this strongly indicates is that the dreaming mode of consciousness is not always bound to a supine body; it can manifest independently. If we can 'dream' when the body is awake, couldn't there be a possibility that we can be 'awake' while the body sleeps and also be able to direct our attention? This is a totally different dimension of dreaming – lucidity – wherein the dreamer is aware during the currency of a dream that he or she is dreaming and can exercise volitional control over the dream. The reality of lucid dreaming has been attested in research laboratories, hence its inclusion.

Traditionally, this kind of dreaming has been the prerogative of the religious/mystical schools, where after gaining lucidity, the disciple attempts to control the dream in an effort to harness his or her consciousness towards transcendence. The aim is to identify an awareness that stands apart from the action in the dream in a silent state of contentless awareness.

In essence, it seems the full spectrum of the dreaming mind is concerned only with the dreamer. The dreaming mind looks at you, inside you, through you, and finally beyond you. When it looks at you it defines your somatic reality; when inside you it describes your psychological reality; when it looks through you it portrays outward events, concerning people and happenings in your life; when it looks beyond you it catches glimpses of the great mystery that animates consciousness.

At another level the whole of dreaming is an enquiry into how we define our identity, who we are. Dreams confirm for the neurologist that cells and neurons define who we are – mere materiality. For Freud, dreams demonstrate that our actual identity lies fragmented in the hidden caverns of the unconscious. The mystical schools, with the help of dreaming, aim to transcend personal identity and penetrate into the mystery: Who dreams the dream?

PART 2

DREAMS AND THE FUNDAMENTAL QUESTION OF MEANING

The issue of meaning is fundamental to dream studies ... [and] will continue to interest human society as long as people dream.

Harry Hunt

Legend has it that when the gods made the human race, they fell to arguing as to where to put the answers to the great questions of life so that human beings would have to search for them.

One of them said, 'Let's put the answers on top of a mountain. They will never look for them there.'

'No,' said the others. 'They'll find them right away.'

Another said, 'Let's put them in the centre of the earth. They will never look for them there.'

'No,' said the others. 'They'll find them right away.'

Then another spoke, 'Let's put them at the bottom of the sea. They will never even think of looking there.'

'No,' said the others. 'They will find that too obvious.'

Silence fell …

After a while another god spoke. 'We can put the answers to the great questions of life within them. They will never look for them there.'

And that is what they did.

Quoted from Fraser Boa's book The Way of the Dream

Chapter 5

AN INSIGNIFICANT DREAM
AND THE BIOLOGY OF DREAMING

It has long been an axiom of mine that the little things are
infinitely the most important.

Sherlock Holmes

Artemidorus, a second-century Greek scholar, discloses in his
Oneirocritica the secret of understanding dreams: In order to
interpret dreams one needs to know all about the dreamer, his or her
moods, character, situation. It is also essential to know the story of
the circumstances in which the dream appeared because it may have
occurred when an issue had assumed great importance.

Dr 'Gilani's'[1] is one such story. He has headed the neurosurgery
department of more than one of Delhi's leading hospitals. This is also
the story of a woman who had a tumour in her brain and of Dr Gilani's
commitment to finding out the exact nature of that tumour. For days
he pondered over it, went to the library to read, but was still not certain
if he was near the correct diagnosis. Then one night, still debating the
problem in his mind, he went to sleep. He had a dream that night, a
seemingly insignificant dream. Yet some instinct prompted Dr Gilani
to follow the lead that the dream gave him, and to this day his voice
is tinged with surprise and wonder at the outcome, even though the
dream occurred many years ago.

It all began when Dr Gilani got an invitation from the Clinico-Pathological Conference (CPC), which the All India Institute of Medical Sciences (AIIMS) in Delhi hosts. At the CPC a difficult and controversial case, often a fatal one, is chosen, and an eminent doctor is given the case material in advance – the patient's history, symptoms and signs, and the investigative findings – but the post-mortem report is withheld. The doctor presents the diagnosis to a panel of doctors who had handled the actual case, doing so in the full glare of an audience comprising the medical fraternity, hospital consultants, students, and anyone else who wishes to attend. The doctor explicates his or her diagnosis, provoking a debate in which experts quiz the line of argument chosen. No one knows the final diagnosis, except the histopathologist who had performed the biopsy. After the debate is over he or she is called to read out what had actually transpired.

Dr Gilani looked at the history sheet; it spoke of a forty-five-year-old woman who had come to AIIMS to show her eyes. Over the last six months there had been a gradual reduction in vision, along with an inability to focus her eyes or to concentrate, and this was accompanied with headaches. The eye specialist had found the eyes normal, except that their field of vision was reduced and the disc was pale. He had thus referred her to the neurology department, where further symptoms were noted – weight gain and a frequent urge to pass urine.

Dr Gilani resisted the urge to see the radiological findings. He wanted to mull over these symptoms, understand what they were indicating. As always, he wanted the case to come alive. He visualized the woman sitting in front of him. What could she be feeling? Bewilderment, he supposed, tinged with fear. She must have presumed that hers was a simple, open-and-shut case of eyestrain. Given her age she had no unusual symptoms – weight gain is a common malaise, as is frequent urination. Yet the woman who had simply come to have her eyes checked had died. It was now up to Dr Gilani to ascertain what had caused her death.

Later that night, after his family had gone to bed, he opened the case notes once more. As he read, his mind started to come to terms with the case. It wasn't a simple case of eyestrain because the eye specialist had found the optic system all right, yet both the eyes showed some kind of malfunction. This could only mean that the problem lay at the junction of the optic nerves. Possibly there was something pressing this area from beneath, causing the patient's frequent headaches and inability to focus her eyes. What could be causing this pressure, this stretching?

Dr Gilani opened the CT scan. A tumour was visible at the pituitary gland. He studied the plates carefully to see if he could glean any additional information that may have escaped the radiologist's attention. It was in vain. Not only the plates, but the whole file afforded no further clues. The cause of the problem and its position had been easy to diagnose; the difficulty now lay in determining the exact nature of the tumour, its differential diagnosis.

The next afternoon he went to the library to read about pituitary tumours. They were of several kinds – chordoma, which is congenital; a growth hormone tumour, which causes the enlargement of all organs; prolactinoma, affecting lactation in women and impotency in males; Cushing's disease, associated with fat deposits, hair growth, and blood pressure; or, it could be a tissue epidermoid tumour.

The case details fitted each of these, but not completely. The patient had gained weight but there wasn't any sign of hair growth. So was it Cushing's or not? And a chordoma would have shown up as calcification within the tumour in the CT scan. Days passed with Dr Gilani spending longer and longer hours in the library poring over a stack of medical tomes.

The conference was only ten days away, and he still had five types of tumours between him and the differential diagnosis. The auditorium would be full of doctors – his peers, as well as his seniors from whom he had learnt much, many of whom he regarded as experts in the field. They would question his diagnosis, probe into its every aspect, examine the relevance of his conclusions; the best minds would test him with the most intelligent questions. He must have the differential diagnosis. On the wings of such a desire, he wafted into sleep, and he dreamt:

I open the bottom-most drawer of my card index, and in the third section from the front is a card in Dr 'Kapur's' writing. I take out the card.

Before he can read the card, the dream is over.

At first glance this seems an insignificant dream. There is no evident medical revelation, no symbolic references to the problem vexing him, but only what might be a dream about an anxious doctor rummaging through his drawers in search of elusive information.

Dr Gilani lay in bed wondering about the dream. Surely there must be some significance in the fact that the dream pointed to a particular card in the third section of the filing cabinet. Could it be nudging him towards something? Was there a message in the dream, a small clue ...?

Dr Gilani got out of bed with a strange sense of excitement brewing within him. He tried to check his unholy hurry, convincing himself that after all, *it's only a dream*. To little avail. On reaching the hospital he rushed straight to his chambers. The cleaning staff was puzzled: doctor *sahib* comes early, but this early? The bottom drawer slid open cleanly, his fingers ran through the cards like a banker counting currency notes. They paused and then stopped dead in their tracks. The third section had a card with Dr Kapur's handwriting. He slowly pulled it out. His mind reeled with disbelief. The card contained notes about a particular type of pituitary tumour.

What were these cards that Dr Gilani maintained? It was his habit to make notes of medical details. After an operation he would record his observations, his errors, and his conclusions. Slowly, over the years, he had amassed a data bank based not only on his personal experiences, but anything new or unusual he came across in medical journals. On occasion, when he was too busy, he would ask his colleague, Dr Kapur, to make the card. This was the only card in the third section that bore her writing – just as the dream had indicated.

He had come across a reference to a pituitary null cell tumour in a medical journal, which Dr Kapur had scanned and filed. It is a recherché tumour, not commonly found. The tumour cell does not obey the sacrosanct cellular law of contact inhibition. It continues to enlarge but does not otherwise perform functions inherent to a cell of the pituitary gland. This results in headaches, and in some cases blindness. Behavioural changes may also occur, depending on which part of the brain is impinged upon by the tumours. The null cell doesn't secrete hormones like other pituitary tumours, but only continues to grow; its homeostasis is affected and this manifests in the malfunction of the concerned part or function of the body. Little is known about it because it is a rare kind of tumour that fortunately afflicts very few.

So the dream was not irrelevant, nor was it being irreverent. On the contrary, it was steering him towards a particular type of pituitary tumour, albeit a very rare one. Dr Gilani was amazed with the turn of events – his dream and then finding the predicted card in exactly the same location. The timing of the dream – barely a week before the CPC, and after Dr Gilani had exhausted himself in weighing all the possibilities – was also intriguing. Dr Gilani felt convinced that his dream had urged him in the right direction, since the symptoms indicated a null cell tumour more than any other type of tumour. He now believed that this is what the woman had died of. But what would he say in the CPC? 'I had a dream ...' like Martin Luther King had said? A dream I dared to believe in?

The day of the conference arrived. The hall was full. The panel was on the stage. At a solitary desk sat Dr Gilani facing the panel. The details of the case were read out and Dr Gilani was asked to present his diagnosis.

Dr Gilani went through the case, outlining the various possible types of tumours, and then, very quietly, he said that according to him it was a null cell tumour.

There was a long silence before the questions and objections hit him like a volley of cannon fire. 'All the symptoms seem to point to a growth hormone tumour,' one doctor argued. 'Doesn't this show, and my experience confirms, that it is a tissue tumour?' another said.

Throughout the vigorous debate Dr Gilani held his ground. He acknowledged the validity of the arguments given, countering them to show that they were not conclusive and by the same token could very well indicate a null cell tumour. The debate was long and animated. Dr Kapur, sitting in the audience, wondered why her colleague was taking such a definitive position. She wondered how he could be so sure. Little did she know that she was instrumental in crystallizing his opinion.

Finally the histopathological findings were tabled before the full conference. The patient had died and the biopsy report would give a conclusive answer to what had been hotly debated. Opinion was divided in favour of the commonly known tumours, except for Dr Gilani's lone voice for the null cell tumour.

The histopathologist gave the details of his findings and ended by stating that it was a null cell tumour.

Dr Gilani felt a surge of relief. He suddenly found himself surrounded by people congratulating him. Among them was his mentor, Dr Tandon: 'You were very convincing in your arguments, which finally have been proven right! But tell me what made you decide that it was a null cell?'

Inwardly Dr Gilani answered, 'A dream. An insignificant dream.'

Driving back to his house, Dr Gilani couldn't help but be vexed by another question: If the dream had come to the surgeon who had treated the woman, would it have saved her life? And who would be responsible if the surgeon had dismissed it as just a dream?

What is intriguing about Dr Gilani's story is the connection between his dilemma and his dream. It is not being suggested that the dream had actually provided the answer; it only alerted his attention to null cell tumours. The question is how did the dreaming mind allude to something so relevant, and in such a specific manner? Had his dreaming mind known of his concerns? Or was the allusion merely coincidental? Dr Gilani, or anyone who has had such a dream, will never view it as coincidental, but attribute a mysterious guiding intentionality to the dream. This, rather than resolving the issue, raises many more questions: Is this intelligence, distinct from our waking one, the architect of our dreams? Does it possess superior or greater knowledge than the waking mind? If its intention was to help then why did it take so long to give the struggling doctor a clue? Many of these questions seem relevant only to specific dreams, like Dr Gilani's, and may not be pertinent to other dreams. However, some questions are fundamental to all dreams: What are dreams? What is their essential nature? Do ordinary people dream? From where do these evanescent phenomena materialize? And why do they vanish from memory when we wake, even when we attempt to recall them? Do they, or can they, have any purpose or significance?

I wished to explore these issues with Dr Gilani by asking him what he, a medical professional, felt about dreaming. There is also another aspect – a human one – to Dr Gilani's story, which is truly courageous: confronted with such a dream, how many of us would follow its suggestion? If we have eagerly planned a holiday and then dreamt of a plane crash, how many of us would cancel or postpone the trip?

'What made you believe in your dream?' I asked Dr Gilani.

Somewhat hesitantly he said, 'I really don't know.'

'You are a doctor, a man of science, yet you had the courage to trust a dream, which most people would relegate to the non-rational side of life.'

'That may not be entirely true. Dreams have now been researched in scientific laboratories for the last fifty years,' he said, and paused before continuing with a wry smile on his face, 'and as a brain surgeon I should be curious about anything that goes on within the brain.'

'But most people swear they never dream,' I replied.

'That is because they do not remember their dreams, which is not the same as not dreaming. The sleeping brain is operating under the influence of a special neurotransmitter that tends to inhibit memory. However, when we are awake the brain is dominated by a different set of neurons, which are memory-preserving. If you wake up in the middle of the night and attempt to recall the dream before falling asleep again, then you shift the brain into a better mode for remembering the dream than if you tried to remember it when you awoke in the morning. By then much of it may be forgotten as the sleeping brain has not processed it into its memory.'

'Then how come some dreams are remembered when we wake in the morning?'

'Think of it like this – while dreaming the dream content stays in temporary memory, and we forget it because no command is given by the brain to embed it permanently into memory. However, sometimes it may leave an impress on it and then those traces may be remembered as snatches of dream episodes that are partially remembered and mostly forgotten. The resolve to remember your dream before going to bed may perhaps act like a command which instructs the sleeping cortex to embed the dream into memory.'

All this talk of cells and circuits would make anyone wonder if it is possible that research in a laboratory can provide us with a causal theory that explains every aspect of a dream – how and why they are formed (source), what determines their imagery (content), and what their purpose is (meaning). Is a subjective experience such as a dream actually amenable to this kind of objective verification?

The discovery of a physiological basis of dreaming

Modern research into the physical patterns of dreaming began serendipitously in the sleep laboratories of the University of Chicago in 1953, when American physiologist Nathaniel Kleitman was studying the sleeping behaviour of infants in their cribs. He was interested in observing the slow rolling of the eyes that accompanies sleep onset to determine whether they are related to the quality of sleep. He assigned the responsibility of monitoring eye movements through the night to Eugene Aserinsky, a graduate student. Aserinsky noticed that at certain times, for short periods, the eyes of the sleeping subject began to dart about furiously beneath the closed eyelids. These were startlingly different movements from the familiar, slow pendular movements that were the original object of the study. Further studies revealed that similar movements were also present in sleeping adults. Sleep comprises, they concluded, of two distinct phases: *REM (rapid eye movement) sleep* and another phase, which is characterized by the absence of rapid movements of the eyeballs – *NREM (non-rapid eye movement) sleep*. These rapidly moving eyeballs gave the impression that the sleeping person was scanning an internal landscape, the eyes sometimes moving from left to right and vice versa, akin to watching a game of tennis; at other times the eyes moved up and down as though watching someone walking up and down a flight of stairs. Aserinsky and Kleitman decided to wake up their subjects during this phase of eye movement to enquire whether they were dreaming. A large number of the subjects were able to describe their dreams in detail. However, when awoken during the phase in which there were no movements of the eyeballs (the NREM phase), they usually failed to remember a dream. This established that REM sleep is directly associated with dreaming. This was the breakthrough: the discovery of a link between eye movement and dreaming, which would revolutionize dream research.

Kleitman expanded his team to include another medical sophomore, William Dement, and they decided to measure these bursts of rapid eye movements (REM) more precisely on the polygraph that was monitoring the subjects. Gradually it emerged that during the course of sleep there was a cyclic pattern to these movements – after every ninety minutes the slow rolling of the eyes was interrupted by bursts of rapid eye movements. Electroencephalogram (EEG) readings, which record the electrical activity of the brain, revealed that these periods of eye movements correspond with particular brain rhythms that are different from either the waking or the sleeping ones. This REM phase was also accompanied by a change in breathing and other physiological departures from the normal pattern of sleep. Sleep research was no longer the preserve of insomnia, but had opened exciting possibilities that could forever change our conceptions about dreams and dreaming.

What happens when we go to sleep

Not only has the occurrence of dreams been objectively verified, in fact, researchers have extensively studied and mapped the entire sleeping state. Our nocturnal rest fosters two entirely different phenomena, REM and NREM, each characterized by recognizably different physiological indicators. Besides these two phases of sleep, scientists also distinguish a short period of transition between waking and sleeping, which is called *sleep onset* or the *hypnagogic* state. It is very difficult to pinpoint the exact instant of sleep onset, but it is said to occur when a stimulus, like a flashing light, fails to elicit its customary response from the person. Perhaps we can say that the difference between wakefulness and sleep is the loss of awareness. One second we are awake, seeing, hearing, responding, and in the next second we are blind to that flashing light, deaf to noise, and are asleep. Frequently associated with sleep onset is a feeling of floating or falling, which can often terminate abruptly in a jerk, and return us to wakefulness. Such starts generally occur only during the first five minutes of sleep, and sometimes represent an arousal response to a very weak, insignificant external stimulus.

Visual perception ceases with the onset of sleep and the eyes begin to drift slowly from side to side. This rolling is a reliable indicator that sleep has commenced. There is a gradual transition in brain activity from the characteristic rhythms of wakefulness to that of NREM sleep. Researchers further characterize the NREM phase into four distinct stages, which are simply termed as Stage 1, Stage 2, Stage 3, and Stage 4. Dreaming or REM sleep, of course, is different from any of these four stages of NREM sleep.

When we move from wakefulness to sleep, after the period of sleep onset, we progressively descend deeper into sleep; within the first fifteen minutes we enter the NREM phase of sleep, beginning with Stage 1. Each new stage is announced by its own typical pattern in the EEG, the brain waves becoming slower in each successive stage. After only a few minutes of Stage 1, Stage 2 is established. Several minutes later the much slower brain waves of Stage 3 become apparent. Another ten minutes and the EEG signals that the sleeper has entered Stage 4, or the deepest part of sleep. In this stage the body is at its most relaxed and brain rhythms are at their slowest. It is therefore not surprising that it is extremely difficult to awaken the sleeper at this point. When awoken, if your child takes a few minutes to reach full awareness, it is likely that he or she has been aroused from Stage 4 NREM sleep. It is also during this stage of sleep that sleep talking, sleepwalking, night terrors, and bed-wetting are initiated in young children.[2]

All this has happened in the thirty or forty minutes following sleep onset. Soon a series of body movements, like turning on one's side, indicates that the sleeper has now started the re-ascent through the stages of NREM sleep. Gradually the familiar pattern of Stage 1 resurfaces on the EEG. After approximately ninety minutes of sleep, the sleeper will now display strikingly different physiological characteristics, and markedly different brain rhythms are recorded on the EEG. Cerebral blood flow and brain temperature soar to new heights, but despite this the body remains totally immobile, and only small convulsive muscular twitches manifest on the face and fingertips. Snoring (if any) ceases, and the breathing becomes irregular – very fast, then slow. Under the eyelids the eyeballs start to move in frenzied bursts. If the eyelids are gently pulled back the sleeper appears to be actually witnessing something. The first REM period of the night has begun. In other words, the first dream of the night has begun. Typically the dream will last for ten minutes. Unfortunately the dream experience associated with this first REM period is more difficult to recall in the morning. As suddenly as it had begun, the burst of eye activity subsides into the placid rolling of the eyes from side to side – NREM sleep has been re-established. The REM state mostly occurs when we are emerging from Stage 1 of NREM sleep, and not when we enter it.

Thereafter, the process of descent and ascent through the stages of NREM sleep is repeated four to seven times during the night, though we rarely again reach the state of deep sleep of Stage 4. Each successive REM episode becomes progressively longer, as does the frequency and rapidity of eye movement, so that the final REM phase can last as long as thirty or forty minutes. The average adult has a minimum of four dreams every night, spending about one-and-a-half hours in dreaming sleep.[3] The last dream is generally the one we tend to remember in the morning and is liable to be more elaborate than the earlier dreams of the night.

This research, perhaps, rescues the dream from the hazy realm of speculation surrounding it in the minds of most people. Everyone dreams whether they remember their dreams or not. There are no non-dreamers. Incidentally, blind people also have REM periods, that is, if their eye muscles have not atrophied. These REM states are accompanied by dreams, which are visual if they had sight at some period of their lives. Studies have indicated that people who become blind before the age of five do not have visual imagery, while if the impairment set in later than five years then their dreams are visual. Helen Keller (1880–1968), who became blind and deaf after scarlet fever at the age of nineteen months, was perhaps an exception as evidenced by her graphic description of a pearl 'seen' in her dream:

> Once in a dream I held in my hand a pearl. I have no memory-vision of a real pearl. The one I saw in my dream must, therefore, have been a creation of my imagination. It was a smooth, exquisitely molded crystal. As I gazed into its shimmering deeps, my soul was flooded with an ecstasy of tenderness, I was filled with wonder, as one who should for the first time look into the cool, sweet heart of a rose. My pearl was dew and fire, the velvety green of moss, the soft whiteness of lilies, and the distilled hues and sweetness of a thousand roses. It seemed to me the soul of beauty was dissolved in its crystal bosom.[4]

It is remarkable how Helen Keller's description of colour was so vivid and real, in spite of her very early blindness. In fact, modern researchers have found that people dream in colour far more than they are aware of. Most people think they dream in black and white, but actually colour is intrinsic; when asked what colour the sky was in their dream they would immediately say, 'Blue, of course!' Some people always dream in colour, while others have elements of colour in their dreams, which may be forgotten on awakening.

Is sleep meant to rest the body?

For centuries it was assumed – and perhaps a lot of us still do – that the sole purpose of sleep is to rest the body. This belief had to be relinquished when it was found that resting while awake tends to rejuvenate the muscles in much the same manner as in sleep. But rest without sleep still leaves us tired.

Experiments have shown that rats chronically deprived of sleep died after about two to three weeks; rats deprived only of REM sleep survived about twice as long.[5] Sleep-deprivation experiments have shown that the cognitive functions of the brain have been affected when human subjects are denied sleep and thereby REM dreaming. Peter Tripp, an American disc jockey, agreed to be kept awake for 72 hours as a publicity stunt. He did this in full public glare by continuing to broadcast without a break for this period. His hyped radio chatter was gradually replaced by fixed paranoid delusions.[6] It seems there is a fine balance that sustains our being rational, and perhaps sleep and dream hold one key to upholding it. Little wonder that Shakespeare so poetically describes:

Sleep, that knits up the ravell'd sleave of care,
The death of each day's life, sore labour's bath,
Balm of hurt minds, great Nature's second course,
Chief nourisher in life's feast ...[7]

It is not only sleep deprivation that we find difficult to cope with; even a change in the pattern of sleep is disorienting, irrespective of the body having been rested. For example, the disorientation experienced after a long flight – jet lag. Some researchers argued that it is not the body but the brain that needs to rest while we sleep. The waking state is full of sensory input stimulating activity within the brain, while sleep, it was felt, results from a gradual extinguishing of brain activity. Induced by fatigue, the brain 'switches off' and can thereby recuperate in the darkness of mental inactivity. The dream, then, was, perceived as an aberration; not every part of the brain comes to rest equally, that 'some areas of it, under the influence of unknown stimuli, endeavoured to go on working but were only able to do so in a very incomplete fashion'.[8] Contrary to this perception, laboratory studies indicate that sleep is an actively induced, highly organized brain state. Cells that are crucial for the normal waking state decrease their activity during sleep, while the activity of other cells intensify. So the brain, rather than reducing its activity while dreaming, was found to be equally active as in its waking mode. This implied that the function of dreaming is not so much to rest the brain as to reorganize its information, thus representing a shift in research focus from energy to information.

The reliable indicator of a dream

Michel Jouvet, a young neurosurgeon in Lyon, France, was studying the learning abilities of the brain. Interestingly, his experimental subjects, cats, who naturally spend two-thirds of their life in sleep, behaved like human beings: when exposed to learning stimuli they became bored, their attention wandered, and they entered a state similar to sleep. Since the EEG of the sleeping cats registered brain activity akin to when they were awake, 'the journals of the Lyon lab in the late 1950s contain words to the effect that the animal appears to be asleep but the EEG shows it to be awake'.[9] It was only after Jouvet learnt about the discovery of REM sleep that he was able to appreciate that his cats were dreaming. The EEG indication of a state had been misunderstood to signify the waking state itself. We will continue to witness this time and again – belief beclouding perception – when we dig deeper into the mysteries of dreaming. It is to Jouvet's credit that, once rid of this initial belief, his subsequent research significantly helped efforts to understand dreaming.

It was not only Jouvet who needed research evidence to clarify his innate perceptions of dreaming – we all do. I, personally, found these laboratory studies very illuminating as they helped me confront notions about dreaming that I had unwittingly imbibed and never challenged. Perhaps a brief digression may prove interesting.

One of the nuns in my school had communicated to many of us her beliefs about dreaming through an intriguing anecdote. A man, so the story goes, had fallen asleep in church. Like Alfred Maury, he was transported in his dream to the days of the French Revolution.

> *He was brought before the revolutionary council, tried, and sentenced to death by the guillotine. He was led to the place of execution where a large crowd had gathered. As he climbed on to the scaffold and*

*was being bound to the plank by the executioner, he could hear the
mob baying for blood. The blade of the guillotine was released. Terror
took hold of him as he realized that in a matter of a few breaths his
head would be severed from his body.*

Meanwhile his wife, a devout Christian, was embarrassed that her
husband had dozed off in the middle of the Sunday service. At first,
she had confused his closed eyelids for inward contemplation, but by
now his head had limply drooped to one side and his breathing was
short and fast. Afraid that he would start snoring she gently tapped his
neck with her Bible, hoping to wake him up without being noticed.
This coincided exactly with the descent of the guillotine in his dream.
She had tapped him at the very spot that the blade of the guillotine
would actually have struck. So real was his dream that he suffered a
heart attack and died immediately.

We stared at the nun, enthralled by the power of the dream. She
seemed to enjoy our sense of wonderment, but then wrenched us from
our speculations by informing us that dreams are merely imaginary
things, a kind of poetic licence to spin an interesting yarn. We looked
at her, puzzled by her insinuation. If the man had died in his sleep,
she explained, how could we know that he had been dreaming? Her
argument was reasonable and persuasive. Without realizing it most of
us had absorbed her conclusions about dreams.

Jouvet, however, would not have shared the nun's scepticism and,
in fact, he would have asserted that she was mistaken! It was amply
evident from the wife's description that the sleeping man had been
dreaming. His neck muscles had gone loose and his breathing had
become erratic – sure bodily indicators that he had entered the REM
state. Also, he would not have started to snore,[10] since the physical
indicators of dreaming had been initiated. Of course, this does not tell
us about the actual content of his dream.

Jouvet would be certain in his belief because he and his colleagues
had observed something significant about cats when they were exposed
to learning stimuli. The heads of the cats would begin to droop after
they had lost interest in the learning exercise and they would enter REM
sleep. Not only did their neck muscles lose their tightness, their whole
body would lose all its muscular tonicity.[11] It has now been confirmed
that this always occurs when we are dreaming: the muscles become
loose, perhaps to prevent us from enacting the contents of the dream.
In fact, this loss of tonicity is one of the most reliable physiological
indicators of dream sleep.

The necessity of dreams

Research has uncovered a strange paradox about REM dreaming: there
is brain activity, akin to wakefulness, yet it is coupled with muscular
slackness as expected in deep sleep. Jouvet therefore named this strange
state *paradoxical sleep*.[12] It is also called fast-wave or active sleep, rapid-
eye-movement (REM) sleep, and dreaming sleep, whereas the sleep
that precedes it is often called slow-wave or quiet sleep, NREM sleep,
and dreamless sleep. To recapitulate, we live in three distinct states
of consciousness that can be described in purely physiological terms:
Wakefulness is accompanied by fast, low-voltage electrical activity in
the brain, a significant amount of tonus in the muscular system, and
eye motility. Sleep, or NREM sleep, is characterized by a slackening of
electrical activity in the brain, retention of muscular tension (contrary to
the belief of resting the body), and the absence of rapid eye movements.
Dreaming, or paradoxical sleep, presents a more complex picture – the
brain activity registers as fast waves accompanied by phasic high-voltage
bursts, and though there is muscular atonia (slackness) the oculomotor
system generates rapid movements of the eyeballs. The limpness in the
neck muscles of the man in the nun's anecdote is indicative of muscular
atonia, which grips the body once dreaming commences.

What this research into the varied patterns of sleep indicates is that
there may be another purpose for why we sleep, besides physiological
or psychological fatigue. Mystifying matters further, laboratory findings
confirm that not only do we need to sleep for reasons other than resting,
but we also need to dream! Research has established that REM sleep
may be essential for our psychological well-being.

In the 1960s scientists discovered that REM sleep deprivation
appears to lead to daytime irritability, fatigue, memory loss, and
poor concentration. Research also showed that when volunteers were
systematically deprived of REM sleep by being roused whenever they
entered this phase, they made up for this on subsequent nights by
engaging in more REM sleep than usual. This is called *REM rebound*.
'If a subject is faced with total sleep deprivation, because of illness or
other factors, the REM state has even been known to force its way into
waking consciousness.'[13] This finding has been proven again and again.
In the summer of 2004, twenty-nine-year-old Mike Trevino slept nine
hours in nine days because he was participating in a 3,000 mile cross-
country bicycle race. For the first 38 hours he did not sleep at all, and
later he restricted sleep to just ninety-minute naps each night. Soon
he began to imagine that his support crew was part of a bomb plot. 'It

was almost like riding in a movie. I thought it was a complex dream, even though I was conscious,' said Trevino, after finishing second in the race.[14]

These research findings, as enumerated above, may not fully answer the question about the function of dreams. But at least we are sure about two aspects of dreaming – firstly, that dreams actually happen and secondly, that an overfed stomach does not cause them! It appears that dreaming is not only important physiologically, but it may also be critical for our psychological health. In fact, a number of American dream researchers have even suggested that REM sleep warrants recognition as a third basic state of human awareness, thereby confirming the ancient Hindu tradition that consciousness is modified in three distinct ways: *jagrat* (waking), *swapna* (dreaming), and *sushupti* (dreamless sleep). However, a niggling question still remains: Is it possible to comprehend a state of consciousness – dreaming – by an empirical exploration of its physiological mechanisms and their corresponding manifestations?

What is a dream?
Although there can never be a rigid definition, an empirical investigation into the state of dreaming allows us to identify certain characteristic features of a dream. Essentially, during a dream external sensory information is blocked and the muscles lose their tension so that we cannot enact any dream command or execute any other movement, with the exception of eye movements. Paradoxically, this does not inhibit the sleeping brain from experiencing motor sensations like walking, running, swimming, even flying. Other cognitive features also continue to function normally. Internal information is generated and dreams have a preponderance of visual imagery, as also of auditory and tactile sensations. Taste and smell are not very commonly experienced, nor is pain, even though the dreamer may be involved in frightening dream situations. Everything appears real, though typically there are some elements in the narrative structure of the dream that are bizarre – incongruities (features that do not fit together), discontinuities (changes in time and scene), and identity transformations. The dreamer, however, does not perceive these elements as bizarre during the currency of the dream, never doubting it to be different from everyday reality. There is an absence of self-reference, wherein one can reflect on oneself, and the dreamer has no volitional control over the dream sequence. Instead the dreamer is single-mindedly absorbed in the content of the dream. Any

theory that endeavours to understand dreams must be able to address these elements. It should also be able to explain where dreams come from, before attempting to answer the most difficult question of them all: What is their purpose? Dr Gilani has already provided a biochemical explanation of why we forget them.

Modern theory of dreams – the computational model

The scientific study of dreams has given rise to a host of theories about the role of dreams. Based on the emerging computational models of the mind, it became fashionable to explain dreaming in terms of computer functioning. This resulted in dreams being perceived merely as information in the form of visual images stored in our memory tapes, much like the computer stores a poem in binary code. A poem, stored in our computer, if read in machine language would appear as a curious string of zeroes and ones and would not make much sense. Similarly, dreams are our thoughts read in binary code during the night, which also explains why they contain bizarre elements.

A British psychologist, Christopher Evans, proposed a theory comparing the dreaming brain to a computer that is 'off-line'. While processing information a computer does not accept any new data input and is thus considered to be 'off-line'. Similarly, the brain absorbs experiences during the day, and while asleep it does not accept any fresh sensory input but sorts and updates its memory files. This process of sorting is what we experience as dreams.[15] It is a necessary and meaningful activity rather like that of the old-fashioned bank clerk who spends the morning depositing and withdrawing money, but then needs the afternoon to him or herself to update the ledgers.

'We dream in order to forget'

In 1983, Francis Crick and Graeme Mitchison carried the computational analogy one step further when they proposed their 'reverse learning' theory of dreams, which claims that due to the brain's – specifically the neocortex's – limited size, each night it needs to discard information that is occupying space in its memory areas in order to accommodate fresh inputs. This was founded on their understanding of networks, which suggested that when there is an information overload the system fosters unwanted or 'parasitical' modes of behaviour. They argued that the brain being a network of interconnected cells, if it were not regularly purged of excess information, then it would similarly develop false or 'parasitical' thoughts when overburdened by fresh informational inputs. This would jeopardize the true and orderly storage of memory. REM sleep then is the mechanism that serves to erase these spurious associations as also to replace redundant information with the more important newer inputs. Hence their catch phrase, 'We dream in order to forget.'[16] According to them, dreams, therefore can be thought to be garbage (redundant information) that is being excreted by the brain at night – a process of 'reverse learning'. This process of dumping obsolete information is experienced as jumbled dream images: an unimportant snippet from one episode, the tail-end of another, half an opening sequence of a different situation – all compounded to form the bizarre dream content. According to this theory, a remembered dream reflects a fundamental error in the dreaming process, and it then becomes totally nonsensical to attempt to understand the dream. However radical the theory may seem, it very easily accounts for the bizarreness found in dreams.

It may be interesting to see how this theory works in an actual dream. A man related 'how when he was a child he used often to go from Meaux, which was his birthplace, to the neighbouring village of Trilport, where his father was superintending the building of a bridge'. Many years later he dreamt:

> He found himself in Trilport and was once more playing in the village street. A man came up to him who was wearing a sort of uniform. [He] asked him his name and he replied that he was called C. and was a watchman at the bridge.

The man awoke feeling sceptical about the accuracy of his memory. He asked an old maidservant, who had been with him since his childhood, whether there was a man by that name. 'Why, yes,' was the reply, 'he was the watchman at the bridge when your father was building it.'[17]

This is an intriguing dream. It forcefully registers that something not available to waking memory was dredged up by the dreaming mind. The question is why? There was no suggestion that this trivial detail was of any consequence to the dreamer. Crick and Mitchison believed that the brain, via the dream, was throwing out this irrelevant detail of the watchman's name. It was needlessly occupying space in memory, and it had to be dumped to make room for other, more important, information.

The theory provides a plausible explanation for the latter part of the dream, but it does not account for the neat narrative structure and coherent plot outlined in the dream. After all, the dream was not merely a collection of motley images, all of them ready to be expunged from memory. Even Dr Gilani's dream was certainly not a jumble of images. Instead, it described a progression of events – opening drawers, searching for a particular card, and finding it in the third section. A minimal story sequence, but nevertheless a logical storyline. Also, Dr Gilani had not stepped near that filing cabinet the previous day, so why was the dream sorting information about the filing cabinet? If it was processing information from a past event, then why so on this particular night? And if a past event had been chosen, then what had dictated that choice? Why had it not decided to sort information from his childhood, or his marriage, or the dinner he had attended three nights ago? If the dream was 'excreting' from memory the information on that card because it was redundant, surely that was a gross error of judgement. And was there an 'intelligent supervisor' (to use Crick and Mitchison's term) who decreed what to discard and what to retain?

These two theories do not have any experimental evidence to substantiate their claims; they are only speculative, relying by analogy on a technology – computers – that has strongly impacted our lives. The physiological arousal or the source of the dream remains unstated in them. It was the activation-synthesis model that incorporated the gathering laboratory evidence to identify the stimulus of a dream and detail its genesis, and perhaps Crick and Mitchison also rely on this to explain the genesis of the dream.

The activation-synthesis model of dreaming

J. Allan Hobson and Robert McCarley, from the Harvard Medical School, proposed an entirely neurophysiological theory of dreaming – the *activation-synthesis* model – to explicate the source of the dream. Their goal was to trace the neurological spur of a dream and thereby isolate its biochemical origins. They deduced that dreams are a consequence of 'turning on' a neuronal switch within the brainstem – a neuron is a special type of cell capable of transmitting nerve impulses and so carries information from one part of the body to another. This 'turning on' bombards the forebrain with neural signals, *activating* its visual areas and thereby generating random images within it. Confronted with these triggered images, the forebrain, which deals with higher functions like thinking, as distinct from the involuntary reflex action of stimulus and response, attempts to *synthesize* them by evoking connected images from its memory banks. This synthesis helps provide the link between the disparate images activated by the neuronal firing in the brainstem, and this synthesized episode is experienced as a dream. This, very briefly, is the Hobson-McCarley model.

The biochemical secret of dreams

Though the Hobson-McCarley explanation may seem complex, its foundation rests on elementary facts: that we periodically alternate between waking and sleeping, and that while we are asleep dreams occur regularly every ninety minutes. Rather than gloss over such trivial facts, researchers felt that any dream theory must be able to explain the periodic alternation of waking, sleeping, and dreaming. As noted earlier, this recurring pattern cannot be merely ascribed to fatigue and rest. The regularity and cyclical nature of waking and sleeping implies that sleep results from involuntary processes rooted in our physiology. Studies further suggested that the primary motivating force for dreaming is not psychological but, perhaps, metabolic. In other words, it was suspected that our ability to wake, sleep, and dream is dependent on processes within the brainstem, the primitive part of the brain responsible for involuntary functions. Confirmation came when the brainstem of a cat was cut at the level of the pons. The upper brain was now rendered inactive, and the cat became an insomniac. It exhibited a cycle of waking and dreaming only – without ever falling asleep! This demonstrated that our ability to sleep is controlled by a region within the brainstem. If the cut is applied a little lower down the brainstem, ahead of the medulla oblangata, the cat does not even dream, but stays awake all the time. This was striking proof that the trigger for initiating dreams lies not in any other part of the brain, but in the middle section of the primitive brainstem. The secret trigger that initiates sleeping and dreaming, which had eluded man for millennia, had finally been found. This trigger resides in the brainstem, acting like a selector switch; in one position it puts the brain into its waking mode, in another it triggers sleep, and in a third position it initiates dreaming.

The activation-synthesis hypothesis believes that this 'switching' is achieved by the constant competition between groups of neurons in the brain. The inhibition and activation of different neurons lead to cycles of waking, sleeping, and dreaming. Expressed differently, dreams are triggered when certain neurons in the brainstem are victorious, and the other neurons fall silent. The firing of the victorious neurons gives rise to spontaneous excitations that travel mainly to the forebrain's visual tracts, and it seems that these excitations are related to the formation of the images that one 'sees' in dreams.

Regardless of how strongly the brain is stimulated by these spontaneous impulses during sleep, the body's motor system remains inactive since it is also controlled by the brainstem. There was striking experimental confirmation of this when the area in the brainstem that controls muscular movement was destroyed in a cat. The cat could now both dream and enact its dreams. While asleep, it periodically exhibited a spasm of active physical behaviour and performed bodily movements of rage or fear as though it was under threat. On other occasions it indulged in pursuit-like activity for a minute or two. The sleeping animal's behaviour at times was so fierce that even the experimenter recoiled.[18] It follows from this that not only are we sure that cats dream, but we also have a very good idea of what they dream about!

How does the brain construct a dream?
According to the activation-synthesis model, not only does the firing of brainstem neurons trigger rapid eye movements (REM), but it was also found that the direction of eye movements faithfully replicates the pattern of existing neuronal activity. During this activity strong pulses of excitation, in precise association with these eye movements, are conducted from the brainstem, via independent pathways, to the image-making areas of the forebrain.[19] This stimulates visual receptors, giving dreams their largely visual character. Other areas of the brain are also similarly activated. Meanwhile, sensory data from the outside world fed into the brain is blocked by the same neurons that initiate eye movement. Brainstem neurons also prevent any signals being sent to the muscular system resulting in muscular atonia. This denial, however, does not eliminate the arousal of internal messages generated by the brainstem activity, and the forebrain is kept busy processing them. But since we are unable to respond to these messages as we would when we are awake, the results of this processing are 'seen' by the sleeping brain in dreams. For example, the signals that prevent physical movement would be experienced in terrifying dreams as the inability to move. Similarly, the arousal of the part of the brain (the vestibular areas) responsible for balance could lead to the sensations of flying and falling in dreams.[20] The predominantly visual character of dreams is attributed to the stimulation of the visual cortex, the sense of movement is fostered by the activation of the motor cortex, while the intensity of signals gives vividness to the dream elements, and the pattern of signalling dictates shifts in scenery and plots. The Hobson-McCarley model, therefore, concludes that the dream gets activated as a by-product of neuronal firing in the brainstem.

According to Hobson and McCarley, the genesis of the dream does not end with the activation phase; they invoke the synthesis aspect of their theory to transform the neuronal activation into a consistent narrative. They feel that once activated, the brain then tries its best to lend coherence to the random images being continuously triggered in the image-making area of the brain. The aim is to synthesize this bizarre data by invoking other data from its memory banks, which will connect the already activated but disparate images and thereby impart continuity to them. This attempt at synthesis produces in dreams 'such features as scene shifts, time compression, personal condensations, splitting, and symbol formation'.[21]

The bizarre elements that colour a dream are attributed to the inadequate attempt of the forebrain to create a coherent narrative out of the unconnected images generated by the neuronal chatter of the brainstem. In short, 'the forebrain may be making the best of a bad job in producing even partially coherent dream imagery from the relatively noisy signals sent up to it from the brain stem.'[22]

This process may be best described by considering separately the activation and synthesis attempts of the brain during dream generation. Let us say a man goes to sleep and the chance images generated are of himself, of a child of maybe six to eight years, of buildings, and of mud. Besides activating random images of people and objects, the neuronal firing also triggers sensations, say, of movement, and feelings of friendliness and unfamiliarity. This is the activation phase of a dream; it has triggered disparate images, sensations, and feelings as an extraneous by-product of neuronal firing, like foam on beer. When confronted with these disjointed images, the forebrain attempts to inject meaning by ordering their haphazardness into a story. It can do this in a variety of ways, for example, by combining two images into one: the man and the child can be fused into a single image of his childhood when he was six-years-old. Of course, there are other ways of bringing order to these images: he and a child of eight are walking on a street past a building. The *walking on a street* has been taken from memory to create a cohesive whole. This latter method of ordering by the forebrain has the added advantage of including the sensation of movement into the story. The secondary process of synthesis in the Hobson-McCarley theory will weave all the evoked imagery into a consistent narrative, and it is the brain's cortex that is responsible for this function. The random imagery activated in the above example, including the man, the child, mud, buildings, movement, and the feelings of warmth and alienation, can be synthesized into a cohesive plot as in the following dream:

> *Walking South on 14th St., just south of Pennsylvania Ave. Street was very muddy. A few blocks (about 3) south of the avenue (Pa. Ave.) I turned east, passing behind various buildings none of which seemed large. No one in sight except my companion, a child of perhaps 6 to 8 years, who later turned into Jason but who, at first, seemed like a stranger.*[23]

The disparate images have been knit into a narrative concerning a walk in downtown Washington DC. The bizarre part of the dream is that the unfamiliar child (a stranger), who is the companion, has been replaced by the dreamer's nephew Jason, of whom he is very fond. The cortex has retrieved from memory the image of Jason in its attempt to synthesize the imagery. Can a companion be a stranger? It is an obvious contradiction, which the cortex needs to rectify. This stranger-turning-into-a-nephew also effectively incorporates into the dream the otherwise unrelated feelings of unfamiliarity and friendliness.

Hobson believes that the brain does this because the cognitive cortex is so bent upon the quest for meaning that it ascribes and even creates meaning where little or none is to be found in the data it is asked to process.[24] Perhaps a glimmer of a similar process is apparent in our attempt to discern patterns in the stars shining in the night sky – the animal representations are not inherent in the zodiacal constellations, but have been imposed on to the stars to help classify the night sky. Meaning, therefore, does not reside within the stars, or dreams themselves, but is granted to them by the beholder. Hobson emphasizes that this does not imply that dreams do not have any purpose. They help the brain maintain its basic neural circuits because waking activities do not draw on all the potential abilities of the brain. Hobson likens the brain to a car parked in the garage – we need to 'rev our cerebral motor' at least once a day to keep it in working order.[25]

What brain neurology cannot explain about dreams

The activation-synthesis theory not only gives a very detailed neurological description of what activates the dream, but also attempts at length to account for its unusual properties. However, on applying this hypothesis to a reading of Dr Gilani's dream, several problems arise. Dr Gilani's dream was suspiciously linked to his waking concerns; it was not a collection of random images triggered by inchoate neuronal chatter.

In fact, his dream image was neither random nor bizarre. In hindsight it is more than evident that it was a very significant dream. Another example may substantiate this difficulty even more forcefully:

> *I once dreamt of a young woman with golden hair, whom I saw talking to my sister while showing her some embroidery. She seemed very familiar to me in the dream and I thought I had seen her very often before.*

After the dreamer woke up, he still had her face very clearly before him. He tried to recollect who she was or where he had met her, but he simply could not remember or recognize her. He went to sleep again, and the woman appeared again. But in this second dream a strange development took place:

> *I spoke to the fair-haired lady and asked her if I had not had the pleasure of meeting her before somewhere. 'Of course,' she replied, 'don't you remember the plage* [beach] *at Pornic?'*

He immediately woke up again and was then able to recollect clearly all the details associated with the attractive woman in his dream.[26]

The first dream had presented the dreamer with an unidentified memory and, peculiarly, the second dream had completed the recognition. In a manner of speaking, the initial dream had presented him a problem, which the subsequent one had solved.

Presumably, the initial neural firing in the brainstem, triggering the first dream, had randomly thrown up two images – his sister and a pretty girl. His sleeping cortex, in its search for meaning, had synthesized these unrelated images by linking them through a common interest in embroidery. This is a perfectly plausible image as women can bond by means of a shared interest. This connection between the sister and the stranger was, nevertheless, not completely satisfactory, and this inadequacy expressed itself as a vague feeling of familiarity about the stranger. In neurological language, the cortex had not been able to fully synthesize the disparate imagery into a cohesive narrative and this was reflected in the incomplete identification of the blonde woman in the dream. So far, the first dream faithfully echoes the Hobson-McCarley theory. However, difficulty looms large with every image in the second dream. It turns on its head the Hobson-McCarley theory. Rather than the neocortex providing a connecting link to bridge disparate images, the second dream cogently (and correctly) answers a doubt posed by the waking mind – the identity of the woman.

The activated imagery is not randomly generated; instead it repeats the images of the previous dream. Not only the image of the woman, but the puzzlement of the earlier dream persists in this one, and has crescendoed into a direct enquiry to end the confusion over the identity of the blonde stranger. Hobson and McCarley's theory would have expected the sleeping cortex to revert to the store of waking memories to provide the identification; instead we find that the waking brain (in between the dreams) was unable to locate the missing information in its memory store. It was the sleeping brain that provided the key, and this was confirmed later when the dreamer awoke. Whatever be the exact mechanics of memory retrieval, surely we cannot believe that these were random images coincidentally evoked in successive dreams, that they coincidentally addressed the same dilemma. The second dream clearly demonstrated that memory recall was more intensified in the dream state than while awake. Perhaps it may not be too outrageous to posit a dreaming intelligence that comprehends, and sometimes answers, our waking concerns, whether they are about the identity of a woman or a recherché tumour!

This only leads one to question: Could not the neuronal firing in the brainstem itself have been triggered by a persistent thought?

How else would you explain to yourself that, after having experienced a dream of feasting on food, on awakening you realize that you are famished? Presumably, you would surmise that hunger triggered the dream about food, not the other way round; that by chance the brainstem activation evoked images of food and on awakening you realized it coincided with your visceral status. If an internal somatic need can excite a dream, then may we not presume that Dr Gilani's brain, immersed in thoughts about pituitary tumours, precipitated a dream about a rare kind of it?

Are dreams meaningful?

Hobson, however, forecloses the possibility of dream stimulation being a two-way street of this kind. If a thought, he argued, had triggered the dream then, perhaps, the first stimulus would have been observed within the cortex – the part of the brain that deals with thoughts – and this would signal the brainstem neurons to 'switch on' the mechanism of dreaming. Unfortunately, this sequence has never been observed in the laboratory. Invariably the stimulus for the dream image is initiated by the brainstem, which controls involuntary functions like breathing. Dreams are thus a consequence of metabolic processes as evidenced by their regular periodicity – every ninety minutes of our sleep.

Is it then being suggested that if dreams are the result of a biological process, they are essentially meaningless? Like the digestive process, which, once triggered, calls upon different enzymes to break down different foods, the cortex calls upon its memory banks to digest (synthesize) the triggered images. Can we call our digestive process meaningful? Purposive – yes. But meaningful?

Strangely, Hobson stresses again and again that dreams are not meaningless. He likens the dream to a Rorschach inkblot into whose irregular and random shape we read a story, which certainly does not exist in the inkblot itself, but is a measure of our creative imagination. Rather than clarifying the issue, all this further mystifies our quest to comprehend dreaming. At one level Hobson states that blind forces within the primitive brainstem stir dreams, at another level he says the cognitive cortex infuses the dream with meaning. A blind force never discerns, it only acts whenever triggered by circumstances; on the other hand a meaningful activity presumes assessment, discrimination, and choice. In this sense meaningfulness is antithetical to the blind or random forces of stimulus and response.

What, then, are we to understand from the Hobson theory? Are dreams as meaningful as our digestive system, since both depend upon random metabolic processes? Or are they meaningful in the same way as meaning is granted to the zodiac? Perhaps Hobson's conception is that dreams start with the intention of a metabolic process, but their generation is completed by implanting meaning into the products of biology. 'Dumb' biology gives way to 'smart' psychology. However, Hobson further confounds the issue by suggesting: 'During REM sleep, the brain and its mind seem to be engaging in a process of fantastic creation.'[27] And further that 'certain phases of the learning process – such as the consolidation of memory traces and comparison of old and new information – may take place during sleep … Carrying this notion a step further, it is possible to suggest that the brain is actually creative during sleep. New ideas arise and new solutions to old problems may be consciously or unconsciously derived during sleep.'[28]

If the dreaming brain can provide novel solutions, then surely it can alert a perplexed brain surgeon about a recherché pituitary tumour with the intention of providing him a solution to the problem that was vexing him. If we concur with this, then we return full circle to the question that arose from Dr Gilani's dream: Was the dreaming intelligence assiduously following his waking concerns? And if, as Hobson says, the dream was indulging in problem-solving, then all the more credit to the sleeping brain for 'remembering' that its waking counterpart had read about null cell tumours and had filed a card about it; a fact that had eluded its cognitively superior waking cousin. Furthermore, are we to infer that the waking and dreaming intelligences have separate domains within our minds and lives, like the sun and the moon have in the sky? Or is it that like the moon remains hidden during the day, so the dreaming mind stays in the background during the day silently watching over its cousin's shoulder and offers its advice when disinhibited in the darkness of the night?

The 'random' images of the night appear to be trivial, yet they can startle us with meaningful insights into our lives. The dreaming world, it appears, will not fully lift its veil and divulge its mysteries even to the exacting gaze of neurological research. In fact, none of the prevalent empirical theories, while vastly enlarging the dream perspective, can boast of having grasped or assimilated the entire dialogue of the dreaming mind. None of the sciences – physiology, neurobiology, and now neurophilosophy – by themselves, or in combination with each other, are able to provide a comprehensive understanding of dreaming. When viewed against this background the activation-synthesis theory is but the latest offering at the altar of dreams.

Modern theory has only put into scientific terminology what has engaged human beings for millennia. Perhaps in our attempt to unravel the dream, we should cast a backward glance to other times, when other people and other cultures debated the secrets of dreaming.

Chapter 6

THE LEGACY OF DREAMS:
A BACKWARD GLANCE

'Dreams, sir,' said the cautious Penelope, 'are awkward and
confusing things ...'

Homer, *The Odyssey*

The source of dreams

When confronted with the mysterious world of dreams one of the
first questions that arise relate to their origin. Who scripts this
nocturnal drama and to what purpose? Dreams seem to point to the
concerns of our waking life, yet follow none of its sequential orderliness.
They appear to be the spontaneous products of our imagination, yet
their content is beyond our conscious control. Like us, people in ancient
times felt as if they were passive recipients of this nocturnal experience,
since the twin notions of personal responsibility and the ability to
direct and control the dream were absent. Because a dream occurred
whether the dreamer willed it or not, the dreamer could not consider
him or herself to be its causative agent. But if the dreamer was not the
cause of the dream then who was? The ancient world concluded that
dreams were messages from a transpersonal realm – the world of the
gods and the supernatural world.

Another reason why the ancients attributed dreams to an external
agency was the strangeness of the dream. They believed that the
dream's tantalizing ambivalence, though unintelligible, was still open

to understanding. Compelled to dwell on the secret behind this enigma they sensed a warning, a promise awaiting fruition, a call of destiny. Since information conveyed in dreams appeared to be outside the waking experience of the dreamer, they concluded that the origin of dreams lay in a realm beyond human consciousness, and only a power greater than them could author them. That power was god. Once the source of the dream was determined, all other pieces of the dream jigsaw now fell into place. The dream did not conform to the waking world, they said, as the gods spoke in parable and allegory, and the language of dream was a more natural language for the gods to send messages to humankind. The bizarreness in the dream was ascribed to the parts of the message that were outside the ken of human understanding and hence appeared garbled.

Our knowledge of dream beliefs of ancient times comes mainly from inscriptions and the corpus of extant religious texts and literary compositions. The further back we go in history the scarcer these become, and the paucity of available material limits our scope of research. The accounts that have survived pertain to rulers and their high priests. Maybe special attention was accorded to the dreams of royalty because the gods were more likely to appear to the highest amongst humans.

What these accounts show is that modern dream theorists were not the first to inquire about the source, strangeness, and significance of dreams. Throughout history the same lines of enquiry have been pursued and reflected upon, and models were developed to understand the mystery of dreams. The ancients, too, devised interpretational techniques to decode meaning from the alluring and cryptic dream text.

The earliest surviving records detailing dream lore are from Mesopotamia (present-day Iraq). Archaeologists date the cuneiform clay tablets of the Sumerians – the first cultural group to reside there – from the early fourth millennium to the late third millennium BC. Among other events, these tablets chronicle the epic of their hero-king Gilgamesh – a tale in which dreams play a very significant role. Two of the tablets inform us that nearly a thousand years later – in 2200 BC – the Sumerian king Gudea wished to honour his god with a temple. The god sent him a symbolic dream with a cast of divine characters, a goddess explained the meaning of the dream, and the god appeared himself in another dream promising to give a sign to indicate when the work should commence.[1]

This is a dream type most commonly encountered in accounts from the ancient Near East – the *message* dream.[2] Simply put, in these kinds of dreams a deity appears and delivers a message about an impending event of significance. They unfold in a typical style – by stating who the dreamer is, and describing the setting and the time of the dream, and the dreamer's circumstances. Strangely, it is customary in these dream narratives to stress that the dreamer has gone to bed and is fast asleep, as though to highlight the supernatural origin of the dream and the person's receptive between god and the dreamer. The god, usually, stands over the head of the dreamer, who is overcome by the god's towering stature and superhuman attributes. In some dream accounts the deity repeatedly calls the name of the dreamer, as though preparing the dreamer for the approaching revelation. In these message dreams the deity is invariably the central, if not the only, figure in the dream. The encounter also ends typically: the dreamer awakes either with a start, or is refreshed by the dream.[3]

For the ancients the dream was a means to knowledge, which was otherwise inaccessible to normal waking consciousness. The passivity of the dreamer in the message dream could be understood to signify that ordinary consciousness becomes passive or dormant in sleep, while something unknown (therefore external and higher) is communicating with him or her – a fact modern psychology still subscribes to: the dream is the nocturnal discourse of the unknown layers of the psyche. In the ancient world the psyche alluded to the spirit, the soul, or the breath of life.

The deity could also appear 'unsolicited' to the dreamer to demand an act of piety towards itself. Plutarch, the Greek biographer, records the dream of Ptolemy Soter: The king of Egypt dreamt of a colossal statue, which ordered him to take it back to Alexandria where it was formerly situated. On awakening the king made enquiries and realized that indeed a similar statue did exist. It was located and brought back to Alexandria where it was recognized as the statue of the god Serapis.[4]

The gods also came to grant boons and favours that would benefit the community, and such accounts abound in every culture.[5] The Siva Sutra was reportedly discovered through a dream. Shiva, one of the principle Hindu deities, appeared to Vasugupta (860–925), a sage, in a dream and revealed to him the secret location of the seventy-seven aphorisms that are the Siva Sutra. Upon awakening, Vasugupta promptly went to the indicated spot and found the promised text inscribed on a rock.[6] These unsolicited message dreams could also include warnings, which, if heeded, would guarantee the safety or prosperity of the nation.

The divine source of dreams was further strengthened with the *sought* dream – in which gods were beseeched for help and guidance. Divine communication and intervention in human life now occurred much more frequently and reversed the earlier position wherein god came to human beings; now people went to god soliciting a favour. In exceptional circumstances such intervention also occurred in the waking world – for example, the request for the safe exodus of the Jews to the Promised Land. Generally, the gods were supplicated through a formal ritual especially designed for the purpose. From the moment the supplicant entered the sanctuary the priests guided him or her. The supplicant performed special actions involving fasting, abstinence, and other purifications of the body before invoking the deity to answer the request. At night, lying on stone slabs, amidst burning torches and the low chants of temple priests, the dreamer was in a state of preparedness to receive an answer to his or her request. This ritualized sought dream crystallized into the process known as *incubation*, and was widely practised in Chaldea, Egypt, the Hellenic world, India, and China.

The Greeks borrowed extensively from their Egyptian and Mesopotamian brethren as regards the sought dream, and built more than three hundred shrines to participate in this special form of direct communication between the dreamer and god. However, soon the dialogue came to be limited exclusively to ailments, and cults specializing in healing took root fast. The most famous was the oracle of Aesculapius at Epidaurus (Greece), where the god of healing himself diagnosed and cured the supplicant, or advised treatment through dreams. These dreams were used as a basis for a medical diagnostic system in which certain dream elements represented certain body parts and their possible malfunctioning and cures. In Indian texts, the earliest example of the incubated dream is from the Chandogya Upanishad (ninth to seventh century BC).[7]

The sought dream raises some awkward questions that even the dream biologist will find difficult to answer. This dream type is clearly not an involuntary experience sparked by random processes, but an explicit request that the dream initiate a specific dialogue with the sleeper. This is part of a design and cannot be attributed to chance. The ancient mind understood this interaction without much trouble since, unlike in modern-day thought, no rigid distinction existed between reality and dream, and a porous boundary allowed experience to permeate sleeping and waking. A question (or a request) had been put to god and god had answered back through the dream. The answer received was seen as both relevant and meaningful. It was not perceived as a mere chaotic jumble of irrelevant images; instead, the dream was a directed conversation about the issue at hand. No doubt Dr Gilani did not believe that his dream came from the gods, but it does exemplify the point that dreams can often appear highly directed in answering a specific concern – quite contrary to the point of view that considers them as random neuronal excretions. With the sought dream, another element of dream generation had been formulated by the ancient world.

The Homeric epics, *The Iliad* and *The Odyssey* (eighth century BC), contain numerous instances of gods intervening in the affairs of humankind.[8] These reveal an important modification effected by the Greeks in the message dream. In some of them god dispenses with a personal visit. Divine messages are delivered through a hero, or even the spirit of a dead person. Possibly, this was a mid-way position designed to show that the gods may not be the source of all dreams. The Mesopotamian message dream owed its validity to the presence of the deity; now, the Greeks were satisfied with a surrogate presence. Aware of this difficulty the later Vedic texts also introduced a caveat stipulating that those dreams that are conditioned by the dreamer's temperament are not sent from the gods.[9] Perhaps the divine source of dreams was only the initial conception in early antiquity. Gradually more than one factor was being introduced to identify the origin of the dream. This dilution of divinity suggests that the ancient world realized that most dreams did not have a god in them, nor a cast of divine characters. So what could be the source of these dreams, and who sends them?

The Hellenic world came up with a very interesting formulation to explain the birth of a dream and the regions it traversed to reach the sleeper. This Greek conception of dream formation was no doubt different from Hobson and McCarley or Crick and Mitchison, but it was grappling with the same problem – the source of a dream.

The spatio-temporal view of the Hellenic world answers these questions. In general, it was believed that dreams were objective and external to the dreamer. They originated from the world of sleep. This was not an allegory as the Grecian *kosmos* was organized in space and time not as abstract constructs, but as experiential categories. They believed that along the dimension of time, there were eras when humanity was ignorant of civilized forms of existence – Prometheus had not yet gifted them fire and they did not know how wheat was

grown. Further back was the time of the Giants and the Titans. Prior to
that, there was a time when even the gods did not exist, when Uranus
and Gaea by their embrace blocked the birth of life, and still beyond
that there existed only Chaos and its children, Night and Erebus (god
of darkness). Similar formulations existed in the dimension of space,
sequentially leading back to non-order – to spatial chaos. Beyond the
Greek Isles were the barbarous countries, then the imaginary countries,
and even beyond the Isles of the Blessed lay the outermost edge of the
kosmos, the Okeanos itself. Somewhere past that lay the land of dreams,
close to the world of the dead.[10] And from this land, dreams came as
nocturnal visitants to humankind.[11]

Thus when Hesiod (Homer's contemporary) says in *Theogony,* a rich
collection of religious lore, that the 'people of dreams' were brought
forth by Night, it was not an allegorical statement: we experience dreams
when we sleep at night; hence dreams are the children of the night. In
the Hellenic imagination, Nyx (night), the daughter of Chaos, when
impregnated by Erebus, gave birth to Thanatos (death), to Hypnos
(sleep), and to the people of dreams.[12] Homer, in *The Odyssey*, also
regards dreams as actual beings – there is a 'people of dreams' living
in the 'village of dreams' (*oneiros demiros*) on the dim path to the land
of the dead.[13]

According to an alternative view documented by Euripides (480–
406 BC), dreams are 'truth's shadows upfloating from Earth's dark womb'.
The goddess Chthon, the primordial and darker aspect of Earth, had
held sway over the oracle at Delphi till Apollo had usurped it, killing
her sacred serpent. In retaliation she 'bred a band of dreams':

> But Earth had wished to save the oracle
> For Themis, Her own daughter,
> And so in anger bred a band of dreams
> Which in the night should be oracular
> To men, foretelling truth.[14]

Thus a different explanation of dreams emerges: it is Earth who
produces prophetic visions of the future, suggesting that dreams received
at certain sacred spots, such as Delphi, would be oracular in character
due to the inherent virtues of the location itself. Later, this was refined
to the theory that dreams occurring in these places were directly inspired
by the god to whom the seat of prophecy was consecrated. Thus the
oracle of Delphi came into the possession of Apollo, and the god, besides
revealing the future through his 'inspired' priestess (the Pythia), sent

veridical visions and dreams.[15]

As Greek thought evolved, a new dimension was introduced to the mystery of dreams when Aristotle refuted the notion that dreams were sent by the gods. He argued that the gods would send them only to people who could make use of them. But dreams came to everybody. Since people did not always make use of them, they could not have originated from the gods. By this reasoning Aristotle reduced dreams merely to an activity of the senses, for they incorporate sensations experienced when asleep and change them into intense dream images. He wrote, 'One imagines [dreams] that one is walking through fire and feels hot, if this or that part of the body becomes only slightly warm.' Thus dream sensations are indicators of a malfunctioning in the body. Hippocrates, the father of modern medicine, also came to a similar conclusion, and used dreams to diagnose ailments in his patients. These views signalled a major turning away from the predominant beliefs about dreaming in the Hellenic era, and pointed towards a new dimension to the dreaming process known as *prodromal* dreams. That dreams give indications of the onset of an ailment has been observed and confirmed by modern research. This aspect of dreaming is discussed later in the book. However, it appears that the time was not right for this theory to fire popular imagination, and the course of dream theory in the these regions did not alter. The notion that attributed the source of dreams to agencies external to the dreamer continued to hold.

Classification of dream content

In addition to determining their source, another fundamental point in our attempt to understand dreams concerns whether they have any significance or not, and if they do, what the nature of this significance is. We have already seen that to the neurologist the dream is essentially an empty structure, a random episode of the brain. Any meaning attributed to it is what is imputed to it. To the ancient world, dreaming was full of import, particularly the message dream and the encounter with a god therein (directly or vicariously). But such dreams were fairly rare, and only experienced by royalty and priests. Are we then not attributing a misplaced significance to dreaming on the strength of a few highborn dreams? What about other dreams, devoid of divine content? And what about the common dreams of the laity? How was their content to be treated?

It raises the natural question: can the content of common dreams be studied, considering their bafflingly immense variety? One way of understanding a phenomenon, and bringing order and shape to it is by categorizing it. Just as the night sky was a jumble of myriad twinkling objects, once classified into stars and planets (and thereafter into solar systems and galaxies), the heavens began to assume intelligibility. Perhaps we can similarly penetrate the mystery of dreams by classifying them.

The simplest categorization of dream content would be based on an assessment of whether a dream is a literal or a symbolic one. We can introduce a slight sophistication into this elementary taxonomy by another polarization that distinguishes between meaningful and insignificant dreams. This simple scheme creates a tripartite classification of dreams: *literal* dreams, *symbolic* dreams, and *insignificant* dreams. The first two are subcategories of the meaningful dream. (Of course, no ostensible purpose would be served if we distinguished between a literal and symbolically insignificant dream!) This basic classification would also provide a yardstick for comparison with a modern theorist's view of dreams.

The power of the literal dream resides in its clarity, and its directness has always evoked a tremendous sense of awe and wonderment. Shorn of obscure symbols, its apprehension of reality has often foretold events and wrought transformations in the world. The message dreams – both the unsolicited and the sought – do not require interpretation, and hence they are examples of literal dreams. Similarly, all the dreams related in Homeric texts are literal dreams conveying direct and simple messages: a divine figure appears and commands or forbids the dreamer to adopt a particular course of action. All dreams, however, do not conform to waking reality. Just like in our waking speech we use metaphors, the ancient world believed that the dream similarly employs allegories and indirect allusions to convey its message. Whether this was intended to dramatize the communication or it represented human fallibility in comprehending the message is difficult to assess. One thing was certain: a different category of dream had been identified and had become an acceptable mode of dreaming.

Julius Caesar, after his victories in Gaul, reported a dream in which he was having sexual intercourse with his mother.[16] Comprehended as a literal dream this imagery would be considered a depraved and bizarre dream. Obviously the dream's message lay elsewhere. The image of his mother would have to be understood symbolically, and according to Caesar's dream interpreter it represented his taking possession of the Earth (Mother Earth). A well-known oracle had decreed that the conquest of Rome would fall to him who should first kiss his mother! The message in the dream was not literal, pertaining to an Oedipal conflict in Caesar, but that he would soon possess Rome, his mother city. Bolstered by this augury Caesar crossed the Rubicon, led his army southward, and entered Rome without a struggle. Interestingly, two thousand years later Freud felt this dream revealed a true psychological insight: those who are favoured by the mother conquer the world.[17]

This dream is an example of the second category of our threefold classification, the symbolic dream. Even if a god or his messenger were not present, these message dreams were accorded great importance and significance because they contained a divine message albeit communicated symbolically. As noted earlier, the Greeks had replaced the appearance of the deity in the message dream with another figure without sacrificing the veracity of the communication. When this is taken one step further, and the words of the message are replaced by analogous content, it then becomes the symbolic dream.

Sometimes the symbolism is not as easily apparent as in Caesar's dream of sleeping with his mother. In the story of the Indian princess Damayanti, separated for twelve years from her husband Nala, the ruler of Kosala, the symbolism is more complex. She saw the following dream, as reported in the Jaina text Trisastisalakapurusacarita (Vol. V: 144):

I saw the goddess Nirvrti today at dawn, while I was comfortably asleep. She showed me in the sky a garden of Kosala where she had flowers and fruits. She put a blooming lotus in my hand. When I had climbed the tree, a bird, which had gone up before, fell to the ground at once.

King Bhima, her father, said: 'Daughter, this is a very fine dream. Surely, the goddess Nirvrti is your heap of merit which has matured. The garden of Kosala seen in the air confers lordship over Kosala on you. According to the climbing of the mango [tree], you will soon meet your husband. The bird that had climbed there first and fell – King Kubara will doubtless fall from the throne. From seeing the dream at dawn Nala will meet you today. For a dream at this time bears fruit quickly.'[18]

Notably the Indian text also adheres to the narrative style mentioned earlier, stating that she was asleep when she had the dream, and giving the exact time of its occurrence. This information is factored into the interpretation. The dream equated the climbing of the tree to a reunion with her husband. Previously a bird had climbed it but had now fallen, showing that the earlier domination of her husband by his enemies would be reversed. Her ascending the mango tree with a blooming lotus given by the goddess augured well for a reunion with her estranged husband.

Lastly is the category of the insignificant dream. The insignificance implied in this category is not to be confused with the 'meaninglessness' attributed to the dream by modern theorists. To the ancient world, since the insignificant dream did not predict future events, it was of no interest, but it could present a few difficulties. Here it needs to be emphasized that the symbolic dream is inextricably linked to its interpretation, both forming one unit. A symbolic dream that does not have any interpretation automatically becomes the insignificant dream. The ancient world thought of the insignificant dream as either pleasant or unpleasant. Pleasant dreams were no cause for worry, and the unpleasant ones deserved some consideration (not interpretation) if they were particularly disturbing. They were then considered 'evil' dreams and were conceived of as a disease, or at least as an expression of a poor state of health. They allegedly occurred because protective spirits had abandoned their ward and therefore evil dreams, ill health, and other misfortunes plagued such a person. The unprotected were also prey to magical manipulation by their enemies who could send them tormenting dreams. In both instances, evil dreams were conceived of as demonic phenomena. Their influence could be so ominous that no allusion was made of them; they were only referred to in the anonymity of the plural – one of those evil dreams visited me last night! In fact, according to the Mesopotamians, the very narration of this type of dream increased their potency for harm, and the dreamer had to undergo cathartic rites to be rid of its influence.[19] The *Susruta Samhita*, an ancient Sanskrit text on surgery, similarly cautioned against relating a bad dream to anyone. Perhaps it is for this reason that it is difficult to find an example of an evil dream. The Vedas, a vast collection of Sanskrit texts that are believed to be the oldest sacred literature of the Hindus, tend to treat evil dreams as calamities comparable to sin or disease, as pollutants the soul encounters during its journeys outside the body. The Rig Veda contains several hymns to dispel the consequences of evil dreams.[20] The Atharva Veda advises utmost care with evil dreams and prescribes chants to ward them away.[21] Elsewhere it is blandly stated that even Indra, king of the gods, is not exempt from sufferings consequent to evil dreams.[22]

It is more than apparent that the foundation of this tripartite classification rested on whether the dream was foretelling the future or not. The literal dream did so plainly and the symbolic one couched it in allegory, and the insignificant dream was dismissed simply on its inability to prognosticate coming events.

Although the dream was primarily a medium of discourse about the future, it also had other roles. In Mesopotamian and other earlier cultures it became the medium that signalled god's acceptance of the actions of the royalty or the clergy. Sometimes this acceptance had to do with a change in royal circumstances, like the ascension of a new ruler to the throne. The dream was used to sanction the conduct of the ruler, as it conferred authority on the dreamer. Besides investing authority in the dreamer, the Greeks also ascribed to dreams the alternate role of problem-solving. This is abundantly evident in Homer, and other classical writers. Characteristically they would bring dreams to their protagonists at times of crisis. *The Iliad* describes a 'baneful dream' sent by Zeus to Agamemnon in the climactic year of the Trojan War urging him to attack and 'take the wide-wayed city of the Trojans'.[23] This underscores the fact that Agamemnon did not attack Troy just to claim his brother Menelaus's wife, Helen, back. It was not merely personal revenge, but his act had divine sanction – Zeus himself had sent a dream – authorizing the war.

Another fact needs to be stressed at this point. Initially it was believed that the gods sent dreams; soon this divine origination was replaced by the belief that dreams arise from a supernatural world (messengers of god, spirits, ancestors). Around the same time another shift became evident: dreams were not limited to royalty or clergy, but included ordinary people, providing auguries to the common people about their personal destiny.

Though the method of classification based on dream content – literal versus symbolic – is elementary, it is not always that simple to slot a specific dream into any one of these categories. At times the demarcating lines between literal and symbolic dreams get blurred. This dilemma is best exemplified by the self-explanatory message dreams of Joseph in the Old Testament. The dreams of the sheaves making obeisance (Gen. 37:5), and the luminaries and eleven stars showing their submission to Joseph (Gen. 37:9) foretell his supremacy over his family. These dreams are not a straightforward message; they require decoding. Joseph's dreams are considered message dreams as the inherent meaning is easily unravelled by replacing the images with their hidden counterparts. This substitution between image and message is not as easily accomplished in the Indian princess Damayanti's dream. Even Calpurnia's portent of Caesar's assassination, for that matter, did not show blood pouring from Caesar himself, but out of his statue. Perhaps a dream where the symbolic allusion is easily transposed to unveil its meaning could also be classified as a literal dream. The subtle variations of dream types necessitated further refinements in the basic taxonomy, which Greek dream theorists developed without changing the foundation of the classification.

A panorama of the evolution of these theories over the millennia, of the nuances introduced by them to unravel the mystery of dreams, culminating in the discrediting of dreams in Christian times, would provide a broad historical sweep of dreaming in the ancient world. Since there is much more literature extant detailing the Mediterranean dream, the discussion of ancient theories is largely embedded in the evolution of the Hellenic conception of the dream. Other cultures that framed their understanding of dreams along similar lines are the Judaic, early Christian, Islamic, Chinese, Buddhist, and Hindu.

As we have seen, the Homeric dream was a literal one, always alluding to waking reality directly, presaging the events about to transpire. There was little need for interpretation as there was hardly any evident symbolism. Experience, presumably, taught them that all dreams do not fulfil their promise. Some dreams do not come true. This necessitated a distinction between true and false dreams. The Homeric Greek theorized that there are two gates through which dreams pass before reaching us – one is fashioned of horn and the other of sawn ivory. 'Those that come through the ivory gate cheat us with empty promises that never see fulfilment; while those that issue from the gate of burnished horn inform the dreamer what will really happen.'[24] Thus an elementary classification between true and false dreams emerged. True dreams bear fruit – what they foretell will come to pass. These could be literal or symbolic dreams, while the false dream is the insignificant dream of our taxonomy. Further refinements in these categories were enumerated first by Artemidorus of Daldus and then Macrobius.

The most complete book on dreams that we have inherited from the Hellenic world is the *Oneirocritica* (interpretation of dreams), compiled by Artemidorus. He lived in the second century (AD), and was a contemporary of the physician Galen (one of the few who looked upon dreams as messengers of bodily ailments) and the astronomer Ptolemy. He refers to many other manuals that he had read, including those written by quacks! By this we conjecture that a lively practice of dream interpretation existed in the region. The *Oneirocritica* preserves the Homeric distinction between true and false dreams, but calls them *oneiros* and *enupnion*, or dreams that are significant and those that are not. The latter (*enupnion*) was considered meaningless because it predicted nothing; in sleep it simply reproduced the daytime preoccupations of the dreamer. The former (*oneiros*) was the significant or prophetic dream, which functioned by 'calling to the dreamer's attention a prediction of future events'. Artemidorus believed the *oneiros* to be 'a movement or fiction of the soul that takes many shapes and signifies good or bad things that will be'.[25] He maintained that the soul is naturally insightful, and bridges the distance between the present and the future. He further distinguished between two types of *oneiros* (the true or significant dream). The first, *theorematic* dreams, predict the future clearly and unambiguously, and 'come true just as they are seen' – as exemplified by a man at sea who dreamt of a shipwreck and barely escaped drowning when his ship actually sank the next day. Such dreams do not need interpretation because image and event correspond identically. They are literal dreams. The second category consists of the *allegorical* dream, which is the symbolic dream of our classification. Artemidorus would have classified the Indian princess Damayanti's dream into this category. The images are allusive; they are predictive of an outcome, which they signify through riddles and thus need interpretation. The content of an allegorical dream is always enigmatic – signifying one thing by means of another.

This basis of categorization was to hold sway for a long time, till Macrobius, writing in the fourth century AD, elaborated on Artemidorus's elementary classification to detail a five-fold taxonomy of dreams. This affected the perception of dreams in Europe till the Middle Ages, and perhaps much later too. According to Macrobius, all dreams were interesting and most of them were true. However, only three out of his five categories were appropriate for divination. He believed it was not enough to only specify the literal dream. Communication in dreams may be of different orders and these needed to be distinguished. Firstly, there is the prophetic vision (*visio*), where something has been 'seen' by the dreamer and this provides the prognostic content of the dream. Then there is the dream that is like an oracle (*oraculum*), where a parent, or a pious or honourable person, or even a god reveals what will transpire, and what action is to be taken or avoided. The third type of dream fit for divination was the symbolic dream, which Macrobius called *somnium*, where the profundity of the dream is concealed by cryptic images whose import can only be revealed through interpretation.[26]

Artemidorus had called the insignificant dream the *enupnion*. Macrobius had further refined this by distinguishing two types of insignificant dreams, even though they held no mantic significance and thus were unfit for interpretation. *Insomnium,* the first of the two types, only mirrors the travails of the body (gluttony, hunger), emotional states (love, threat), or professional issues (to win or lose office). The other category, *visum*, causes anxiety and nightmares.[27] Surprisingly, these dreams, which would catapult the modern therapist into an interpretational frenzy, were summarily dismissed by Macrobius seventeen hundred years ago!

Oneirology – the science of interpreting dreams

Whether it was Artemidorus in the second century or scientists today, what has been the central focus to the understanding of dreaming is the strangeness of the dream, its bizarreness. For the ancient world this strangeness was a riddle, which if solved would lead to rich, meaningful content.

The basis of our classification rests on a scale of increasingly bizarre content in the dream. The literal dream was the least bizarre, the symbolic one introduced strangeness into its imagery, and the insignificant dream had so much bizarre content that it was considered untranslatable and thus discarded.

It is reported that Alexander the Great was accompanied on most of his campaigns by Aristander, his dream interpreter. Plutarch, the biographer, reports that after Alexander had laid siege to the city of Tyre for seven months, resulting in an exhausting stalemate, he had a dream:

> *A satyr appeared to him at a distance, and sported with him, but when he endeavoured to catch him, ran away, and that, at length, after much trouble, he caught him.*[28]

Is this dream meaningless nonsense randomly generated by the sleeping brain of a fatigued world conqueror, or is it possible to scrutinize this dream for its mantic meaning? Does it contain an augury that could aid the Macedonian conqueror to plan the future of his campaign? His dream interpreters certainly felt it did! They seized on the strange part of the dream and unpacked the riddle contained within it. A satyr in Greek mythology is a woodland deity in human form with a bizarre anatomy – pointed ears, pug nose, short tail, and budding horns. Aristander decoded the dream by breaking the Greek word for satyr – *satyros* – into 'sa' and 'tyros': Tyre is thine. Alexander had contemplated lifting the siege and returning home, but now, encouraged by his dream, he intensified his efforts and captured the city.

Another popular method to decipher the dream riddle was to employ the logic of contrariness. An example from a Hindu text reads, 'The one who enjoys the pleasure of the company of an unchaste woman, he achieves a good wife.'[29] An impure liaison in the dream signifies its opposite. Often there was no obvious connection between the dream content and the prediction based on it, save only a paronomastic – puns and plays on words – relationship between image and outcome. For example, for the Egyptians, dreaming of buttocks signified that the dreamer's parents would die – the word for buttocks closely resembling the word for orphan in their language.[30]

It was the job of the interpreter to understand the secret code. The first problem encountered was to establish whether the dream is devoid of meaning (and consequently to be discarded), or is endowed with mantic import. The next step was to ascertain whether the meaning of the dream symbol is ominous or portended good. King Bhima began the interpretation of his daughter's dream by declaring it to be a fine dream. Most cultures had worked this polarization into their dream manuals. The *T'ung Shu*, an ancient Chinese text, contains a section called 'Chou Kung's Book of Auspicious and Inauspicious Dreams'.[31] The ancient Hindu text Brahmavaivarta Purana[32] alludes to the Sama Veda, another sacred text that discusses the nature of dreams, which describes the distinction between them, and proceeds to highlight good and bad dreams.

The unravelling of dream symbols was initially the purview of the priests, but soon specialist dream interpreters also undertook the task. In Egypt they were known as 'Masters of the Secret Things'.[33] It is easy to see why they were held in such high esteem. On them lay the responsibility of recognizing the import of a dream. At times, their decoding of the dream was not sufficient, and the interpretation would then have to be confirmed by other signs (*omina*). One of the most powerful confirmatory signs was when the dream repeated itself, immediately underlining its import and inducing a sense of reverence to its contents. Repetition meant not only a replay of the contents of the dream, but the recurrence of its message, irrespective of whether a symbol may have been exchanged for another. In Joseph's dreams the message remained the same despite the sheaves being replaced by the stars. Another confirmatory sign could be the *parallel* or *shared* dream – the same message being relayed to different people on the same night. Thus the importance of the Buddha's departure from his home is signalled by his father, aunt, and wife 'sharing' prophetic dreams.[34] Three different people had dreams predicting his departure; this was enough to attest and bring significance to the message heralding the first step of his journey to become a world saviour. The Mesopotamian king Assurbanipal reports that, on the eve of making a difficult river-crossing, the goddess Ishtar appeared in a dream to his dejected army with words of encouragement.[35] A dream simultaneously dreamt by an entire army is bound to lift their morale. The shared dream is not the preserve of ancient cultures or Buddhism alone, it pervades every culture down to present times.

In an effort to translate enigmatic dreams into understandable terms each culture compiled their own dream dictionaries. These volumes, with their exhortations and warnings, bespeak of the prevalent traditions and beliefs of their times – something we, today, casually dismiss as irrational and superstitious elements. The Chinese believed that to dream of an orchard bowed down with ripe fruit portends many children, while to see a parrot calling in a dream means a major quarrel is brewing. If in a dream you see the flight of a swallow, a friend will come to visit you from far away.[36] The Indian text *Prasastapada Bhashya* states that it is lucky to dream of riding an elephant, while to ride a donkey is an inauspicious augury.[37] In Nepal, a tooth falling could symbolize the death of someone in the family. A lower tooth could mean it would be someone younger than you, and an upper tooth signifies someone older. Later, while discussing typical dreams, we will consider how dreams of falling teeth are understood by the modern therapist.

The ancient world relied on two essentially different methods to interpret dreams. In the first method the contents of the dream were taken as a whole – *en masse* – and sought to be replaced by another more intelligible situation.[38] For example, Joseph's interpretation of the Pharaoh's dream in the Old Testament, of seven fat kine followed by seven lean ones that ate up the fat kine, was taken to symbolically prophesy seven years of famine in Egypt, which would devour all the benefits of the seven plentiful years preceding them. This method, bordering on the artistic, relies on the interpreter using his or her intuitive perception to arrive at a symbolic interpretation. No wonder it was assumed that the interpreter possessed an exalted gift, which could stem only from the numinous. However, the gifts of the interpreter were severely tested when confronted with unwieldy and disjointed dreams. The second method of interpretation – *en detail* – guarded against this problem by treating the dream as a cryptogram in which each image would be decoded into something else with the help of a fixed key.[39] For example, if you had a dream in which a butterfly came and sat on your ring finger, then it might presage the death of your fiancée. This is assuming that the dream dictionary decoded the butterfly image as the spirit of a relative or friend and the ring finger signified the betrothed; combining both these symbols would provide the interpretation. It was always a dream dictionary and not the inspirational faculties of the analyst that provided the 'key'. The Egyptians, as early as 2,000 BC, were using both these methods – en masse and en detail – and documented guidelines for their application, thereby systematizing much of their oneiromancy. These texts could typically read: If a man dreams of spattering urine on himself, then he will forget what he has said, for incontinence is associated with senility.

The Greeks made an important contribution in the understanding of dreams by taking into account not only the content of the dream, but also the character and circumstances of the dreamer. Thus the same dream dreamt by two people having dissimilar life situations would have entirely different interpretations. This point never took root in Mesopotamia, where a person's social standing did not interfere with the meaning of his dream. Though Artemidorus made copious lists, including a detailed account of explicit sexual dreams with the mother, he still emphasized that personal experience is the only reliable guide to dream interpretation. The Hindus also believed that the state of the dreamer and not merely the oneiric content dictates the meaning of the dream. The Matsya Purana, oldest of the Indian Puranas, qualifies its list of auspicious dreams, which in ordinary circumstances promise wealth to the dreamer; however, if these are the dreams of a sick person then they foretell not wealth but a quick cure.[40] Some Hindu texts organize dreams according to the physical temperament of the dreamer (fiery, watery, windy), and according to the time of the night the dream occurs.[41] They also inform us that the temperament of the dreamer can be ascertained by the dream! The Brahmavaivarta Purana[42] goes one step further by not only considering the dreamer, but including the state of the person to whom the dream is narrated. Thus the outcome of a dream is affected by a fusion of three factors: dream, dreamer, and interpreter. Modern therapists are not unaware of this relationship when they state that people dream in the dialect of their analyst.[43] In other words, if you are going to a Freudian analyst your dreams will be replete with Freudian symbolism, and a Jungian therapist will be able to identify many archetypes in the dreams, underscoring that oneiric content is often influenced by the beliefs of the interpreter. This influence is not restricted to beliefs alone, but can spill over into the language used by the dream. Sudhir Kakar, a well-known Indian psychoanalyst, recounts his experience while training to become a therapist: 'This intense need to be understood, paradoxically by removing parts of the self from the analytic arena of understanding, was brought home to me by the fact that during my own training analysis I started dreaming in the language of my analyst, German, something I have not done before or after that period.'[44]

The Christian discrediting of dreams

In the early fourth century AD, the Roman persecution of Christians stopped with the conversion of Emperor Constantine to Christianity. It is said that he was converted because of a dream. No surprise then that the initial Christian approach to dreams had its roots in the Hellenic conception – that the dream is a dialogue with the gods. Tertullian (early third century AD), one of the first Christians to write on dreams, states that 'the majority of mankind learn to know God through dreams'.[45] The ordinary dream is scarcely mentioned in the early Christian accounts. They, however, focused on visions.[46] Throughout antiquity an ascetic approach had been employed to encourage visions, similar to the sought dream with its attendant practice of incubation, which still continued, however, no longer in god's temple, but at the martyr's tomb.[47] The Christians retained the fasting and prayer of the pagan approach, but officially banned dream interpreters. This despite the injunction in the Bible that 'I speak to him in dreams,' (Num. 12:6) and 'your young men will see visions, your old men will dream dreams.' (Acts 2:17). Tertullian suggests that Christians must interpret dreams in a new way.[48] This way, affirmed by the texts but curbed by their ideology, encouraged Christians to seek visions yet simultaneously discouraged the world of ordinary dreams. This approach helped replace the plethora of pagan gods by a monotheistic God, and consequently the demonic plural found a strong focus in the antithesis to God, Satan, to whom were attributed most dreams, thus justifying the injunction to avoid dreams.

Christian authors desirous of departing from the Hellenic classification of the oneiric experience emphasized other methods suited to the new ideology's perception of relations between humans and divinity. However, Tertullian attributed the origin of dreams to the same three agencies as the Greeks (Stoics) – gods, soul, demons – except that now they were dressed in Christian robes. In the Christian methodology (as explicated by Tertullian) it was necessary to first ascertain the source of dreams, whether they came from God (if all ideological considerations were fulfilled), the Devil (the most frequent source), or from the dreamer him/herself.[49] This last source was sometimes referred to as the soul, and it was influenced by the person's mind, daytime activities, and body. 'It was usually considered a bad sign when dreams were stimulated by overeating and drinking, or by the urges of the flesh' (the standard explanation of the wet dream).[50]

St Augustine (AD 354–430) considered dreams to be an important tool for grasping the inner workings of the mind, and not a form of privileged access to divine truth. However, difficulty arises in the Christian view when we focus on St Paul's vision of his ascension to the third heaven (2 Cor. 12:1–4). Are the scriptures alluding to a physical vision involving the senses, or to a spiritual one? And was the apostle asleep or awake when taken there? Are the texts referring to a dream or an ecstatic vision? To sort out this confusion St Augustine was forced to distinguish between different kinds of visions, and to define *ekstasis*, which involves having visions while remaining awake.[51] Thus, many centuries later, Hildegard of Bingen (AD 1098–1178), the Christian mystic, could not describe her visions as dreams (to avoid suspicion of being diabolically motivated), nor as a result of sensory experience, but as wakeful visions.[52] A vision is 'seeing' in an altered state of consciousness and it seems incongruous to imprison that state to a particular condition of the body – waking or sleeping. If chained to the waking condition it becomes difficult to distinguish between vision and hallucination, as Hildegard herself concedes in *Liber Scivias*.[53] And if visions are bound to dreaming then they are apt to be confused with the imaginary. Possibly the state in which one experiences a vision subsumes both waking and dreaming, and is not in the least affected by the condition of the body prior to attaining the vision. In other words, it is inappropriate to assess the quality of a vision – divine or diabolical, inspired or delusional – solely from the condition of the body.

Dreams had come full circle. They had begun as divine messages, but gradually the divine content was diluted. Also the dream was no longer restricted to royalty and clergy, but it visited people regardless of distinction or status. Aristotle and Hippocrates had enlarged the scope of dreaming to include somatic sensations. Artemidorus and Macrobius, of course, considered dreams born from emotional subjective distortions as insignificant – the *enupnion*. Gradually the belief that dreams were of divine origin underwent changes, to the extent that Artemidorus declines to engage in the debate about whether dreams come from the gods:

> I do not, like Aristotle, inquire as to whether the cause of our dreaming is outside of us and comes from the gods or whether it is motivated by something within, which disposes the soul in a certain way and causes a natural event to happen to it. Rather, I use the word in the same way that we customarily call all unforeseen things god-sent.[54]

The Christians reversed this position back to earlier times – dreams were messages from God for his elect. The laity was excluded from this communication; their dreams were inspired by the Devil. Over the centuries, the Church gained both political and moral ascendancy in Europe. It dictated the norms on thought and behaviour for the proletariat. The belief that God communicated directly with humans was perceived as inimical to the power and the interests of the Church. The word of God had been given to the Church through the Pope. The people had no need to speak directly with God through dreams. Any further communication outside the ambit of the Church was not needed.[55] Anything that vitiated this doctrine was to be discouraged and condemned. The belief that dreams were sent by God was gradually exorcized from the minds of the masses, and the dream gradually sank to the level of superstition, and was left to gypsies and fortune-tellers.

The Christian discrediting of dreams successfully managed to diminish the value of dreaming in the European world. Whatever residual meaningfulness of dreams that may have survived was robbed by the emergence of the Cartesian mechanistic dualism in the seventeenth century, which finally consigned dreaming into the realm of fantasy, hallucination, and irrational experience.[56]

From the Pacific coastline of China to the Atlantic shores of Europe, from the equatorial reaches of the Indian subcontinent to the Arctic limits of Scandinavia, the theories abounding around the world at the time were similar in their treatment of dreams. No fresh input had stimulated their understanding; the old notions had run their course, and now the subject had fallen into disrepute, discredited by a growing belief in Science. And maybe, we, today, have in some way inherited the vestiges of that bias against dreams. We have to wait till the twentieth century and Sigmund Freud (1856–1939) to provide the next clue to the enigma of dreams and their bizarreness.

Chapter 7

FREUD FASHIONS A NEW PATHWAY:
THE UNCONSCIOUS

[The unconscious] contains, even according to my present-day
judgement, the most valuable of all the discoveries which it
has been my good fortune to make. Insight such as this falls
to one's lot but once in a lifetime.

Sigmund Freud, preface to *The Interpretation of Dreams*

*T*he human race, in its infancy, had projected onto the heavens
– as gods or demons – powers and forces that it found difficult to
comprehend or conceptualize. The mysterious world of dreams was one
such realm of their daily experience. Dreams could only be explained as
a gift from the heavens. Although this view gradually gave way to the
belief that dreams emanated from a supernatural world, their source
always remained external to human beings. Freud, at the turn of the
twentieth century, withdrew much of what was projected outwards and
internalized it within us. Our drives are the demons that chase us, and
our aspirations are the gods that motivate us. He thus attributed dreams
to our inner gods and demons. Though Freud's view was revolutionary,
perhaps it only echoed anew the direction in which humankind had
begun to perceive reality.

The early picture of the universe was one of an ordered and
harmonious whole, governed by a system of hierarchy in which

everything in Creation, from the luminous heavens to a quivering blade of grass, had its appointed place. Humankind, it was always assumed, was at the centre of this system. By extension, the earth they inhabited was the centre of the universe; the heavens revolved around it. This Ptolemaic view of the cosmos held sway for a long time until Copernicus replaced this geocentric definition of the universe with a heliocentric conception. The earth from being the centre of the cosmos became just a planet; one among others, orbiting the all-important sun. Galileo, Newton, and Kepler circumscribed the universe within the laws of mechanics and mathematical equations. First the earth and now the sun, too, lost its centrality, when it was realized that it was not at the centre of the heavens, but merely a humdrum star consigned to a far-flung corner of a nondescript galaxy. With the rise of the mechanistic view, celestial entities lost their numinosity. The cosmos was no longer run by the whims of gods who till then were believed to have been the causative agents for all phenomena and events. Forces and gravitational fields replaced them. Literally and metaphorically humankind was displaced from the centre of the universe, resulting in a dramatic shift in perception about their role in the cosmos. Plato and the ancient world could not grasp human beings outside of their relationship with the cosmos; St Augustine and the Christians could not imagine human beings outside their relationship with God. Beginning with the dualism of Descartes, philosophers introduced a radical division between the soul (mind) and soma (body), and sought to comprehend their relationship with each other in mechanistic terms. The human soul no longer remained the pawn of God, nor was it obligated to the cosmos. Human beings were now considered to be self-enclosed entities endowed with the capacity to think and use reason to explore and order their own life. The human body was perceived as a mechanism, much like the mechanistic cosmos surrounding it, and was something that could and ought to be controlled.[1] As if this was not enough, Darwin and his theory of natural selection erased any illusions that human beings were set apart from the rest of the animal kingdom. Bluntly the evolutionary doctrine stated: human beings were primates and their descent was from the apes, further eroding the belief in their divine origins. This radical view meant that human beings had to be studied along naturalistic lines. Freud drove the last nail in the coffin when he informed us that it is not our consciousness that is central to our life but the *unconscious*.[2]

We assume that we know what transpires in our mental world, that we are aware of the origins of our emotional attitudes and understand the motives behind our actions. It had been assumed since antiquity that consciousness is an island, and that reason and feelings are its only inhabitants. Now it was being suggested that the island is actually a peninsula, with the mainland shrouded by a permanent mist. Thus human beings contain an unknown part within themselves, the existence of which had never been suspected. The obscured continent is the unconscious.[3]

Freud was to bring to light that the conscious mind is not the sole architect of our life, but that the human psyche has depths beyond our realization, and somewhere within these depths lurk primitive tendencies, which play a very large part in shaping our conduct and feelings. Our psychic activity for the most part proceeds unconsciously, and only fragments of this activity emerge temporarily into consciousness. Thus, far from controlling our inner life, we are actually subject to its domination. In fact, Freud believed that psychologically we are 'not master in our own house'. His uniqueness lies in attributing such a decisive role to the unconscious. Based on his division of the human mind into conscious and unconscious terrains, Freud postulated his dream theory, which has been the foundation of psychoanalysis.

Dreams, according to Freud, are instigated when the memory of recent experiences (*day residue*) stirs up unconscious wishes from their shackles. These seek fulfilment and threaten to invade consciousness, but are denied expression by the *censor* as they may disrupt sleep. The only way these wishes can get past the censor is by disguising their urges. This transformed content is what we experience as dream images. This, very briefly, is Freud's disguise-censorship theory. Contrary to the common belief that dreams disturb sleep, Freud perceived them as the guardians of sleep. Dreams, he asserted, perform the useful function of preserving sleep from disturbances, defending the sleeper from awakening.

A five-year-old boy, sleeping in a laboratory, had got the wormlike soft-plastic chain of the monitoring equipment wrapped around his neck. The researchers only noticed this when he screamed aloud; meanwhile the instruments had registered that he had already experienced a dream for a full four minutes. He still had not awakened. They decided to wake him and record the dream. He reported that he was in the family car and that his brother put crawly 'caterpillar worms' on his sister's leg. Clearly, the electrode chain wrapped around his neck had stimulated the dream. His screams were indicative of his feeling choked, yet it had not awakened him. Had the boy not been aroused by the researchers he would have continued to sleep. The dream had successfully disguised the threatening stimulus – by displacing it from his neck to his sister's leg – to ensure prolonged sleep.[4]

This totally new perspective on dreams given by a medical doctor, trained in Vienna, drew on the speculative curiosity of earlier dream interpreters, connecting dream interpretation with the now prevalent explanatory model of the natural sciences. Thus stepping beyond divination, Christian morals, and eschatology, he replaced them with the determinism of the human psyche. It is Freud's pioneering contribution to the evolution of dream theory that the unconscious is not conceived as an exterior power, like the pagan gods or fate, but is located within the human being.[5] Dreams were now an internal experience, a state of mind, with the unconscious expressing itself through them.

This is best understood if we consider a dream related to Freud by a lady, who, though she was still young, had been married for ten years:

> She was at the theatre with her husband. One side of the stalls was completely empty. Her husband told her that Elise L. and her fiancé had wanted to go too, but had only been able to get bad seats – three for 1 florin 50 kreuzers – and of course they could not take those. She thought it would not really have done any harm if they had.[6]

In fact, her husband had informed her the previous day that Elise L., her friend who was three months her junior, had just become engaged to a very nice man, and strangely she had felt angry. It seems the dream was precipitated by this recent event, the day residue, or as a reaction to it. Besides Elise and her fiancé there are other elements in the dream also excavated from events that had recently occurred. The dreamer had gone to see a play the previous week. Her keenness had made her buy the tickets too early – so early that she actually had to pay a booking fee. When they got to the theatre it turned out that her anxiety had been unfounded, as one side of the stalls was completely empty. Her husband had teased her for having been in such a hurry. Apparently the dream had borrowed its image of empty stalls from this incident.

Even the strange element of three seats for 1 florin and 50 kreuzers had been prompted by an event the previous day. Her sister-in-law had been given a present of 150 florins by her husband and in a great hurry she had rushed to the jewellers and bought a piece of jewellery. Perhaps the dream had split the amount and represented it as 1 florin and 50. But what had prompted the number three? Possibly it alluded to her newly engaged friend being three months younger than her. The different elements of the dream appeared to have been plucked from unrelated recent events.

The common belief that dreams merely replay the happenings of the recent past is certainly attested by this dream. Hobson, however, would remind us that the dream constituted only unconnected memories of recent events – information imparted by her husband, the visit to the theatre, and her sister-in-law's gift. The firing in the brainstem had randomly triggered these disparate memories and out of them the cortex had constructed a plausible scenario. Its attempt had failed to convincingly synthesize the number three and the sum of 150 florins, and this had remained the bizarre part of the narrative. Need we, then, ascribe any meaning into this dream?

Surprisingly, Freud told the lady that the dream revealed her regret at having married so early: that underlying the dream were her feelings of dissatisfaction with her husband and regret that she might have got a better husband if only she had waited. He suggested to her that she believed she could have got a man a hundred times better than her husband, considering the quantum of dowry that had been paid.

The interpretation is certainly a revelation, and one wonders how Freud 'divined' it. There was nothing in the imagery that suggested what Freud insinuated. It was therefore startling when Freud stated that he had deciphered the dream using the principles of analysis. Needless to say, the lady agreed with the interpretation, but at the same time she was completely astonished by it. The analysis accurately portrayed her deepest reservations though they were not her conscious thoughts and had never been articulated, even to herself.

Freud asserted that the dream is never derived from conscious thoughts, but from unconscious wishes and feelings. The correlations between what the dream says and its underlying thoughts are neither simple nor straightforward. They admittedly stretch the imagination. If we wish to understand the Freudian conception of the dream it is necessary to become familiar with certain distinctions he introduced in the structure and dynamics of dream formulation. Fundamental to Freud are two dichotomies, the first being the divide between the conscious and the unconscious, and the second, the distinction between a dream's manifest and latent content. Though the concept of the unconscious had antecedents and parallels in philosophy and literature, such as in the Romantic Movement, it was Freud who seized on this concept and mapped its contents, which had hitherto not been done. And this unconscious became the framework for deciphering dreams in psychoanalysis.

The unconscious

Our waking faculties can never fully explain all the facts of experience. Often a name or date may not be recalled at one moment, only to appear in the mind at a later time – indicating that such information is retained in the mind but isn't always accessible to consciousness. While hidden from awareness, where does it reside? Then there are ideas and thoughts that are denied expression. Do we presume that the arrest or the expulsion of a thought is its annihilation? Or can we say that the excluded idea does continue to exist although in an unconscious form, since it is able to return to consciousness? The latter idea was bound to meet with resistance going as it did against the grain of the established and prevalent view of the supremacy of the mind. Unwilling to accept the hypothesis of the unconscious, Freud's critics contended that within conscious activity many gradations in intensity or clarity can be distinguished. Some of these activities are vividly discernible while others are faintly noticeable, yet all are parts of consciousness. Then why must we postulate that the forgotten name or date has estranged itself from consciousness to reside outside it, within a newly posited unconscious? They are difficult to discern merely because they have lost their brightness and become very dim. Furthermore, they will be visible in consciousness once again when they regain their clarity. Arguing in a similar vein, Freud countered their objection. He said that using the argument of 'gradations' to deny the existence of the unconscious would amount to a denial of darkness and death. 'There are so very many gradations in illumination – from the most glaring and dazzling light to the dimmest glimmer – therefore there is no such thing as darkness at all'; or, 'there are varying degrees of vitality, therefore there is no such thing as death'.[7] Thus, the unconscious refers to those phenomena within an individual that proceed without his or her awareness. This may include processes like the digestion of food, which also occur below the level of awareness, but we are not interested in this type of unconscious activity. We are concerned with those unconscious processes that may affect our behaviour even though we cannot account for them.

For Freud, these ideas were just the first step towards exploring and understanding the new pathway that he would eventually blaze. The unconscious, he believed, is the repository of unresolved conflicts, traumatic past events, forgotten experiences of childhood, as also innate, instinctual urges that have never become conscious. He held that unadmitted desires that are considered threatening, and consequently restrained from expression, also reside in the unconscious after being expelled from consciousness.

The lady's unexplained anger, when she learnt of Elise's betrothal, had no conscious basis and therefore she was not aware of what had sparked it. The deeply buried regret about her marriage was never allowed entry into her conscious thoughts, but banished before it could find expression. Our dreamer thus never appeared dissatisfied with her early marriage. It is her anger that betrayed her unconscious regret. The news of the friend's betrothal (or the anger) by itself was not capable of creating the dream, unless an old wish lying in the unconscious had been resurrected. Her anger harked back to a time when early marriage fulfilled the wishful impulses of simple-minded girls to dwell on the sexual truths of adult life. Marriage also lifted restraints from their going to the theatre to see all the plays – a hitherto prohibited activity. The emotional charge of this old wishful impulse had perhaps stimulated her dream. The unconscious wish gave the dream its structure by replacing 'marriage' with 'going to the theatre'. Freud was struck by the repetitive theme provided by the events associated with the dream imagery. She bought the theatre tickets *too early,* so *hurriedly* that she had to pay more than was necessary. Similarly her sister-in-law had been *in a hurry* to go to the jewellers and buy some jewellery with the recently gifted money, as though she would otherwise *miss it*. In addition to these allusions to *hurry,* Freud took into account the precipitating cause of the dream – the news that her friend, only *three* months her junior, had nevertheless got an excellent husband. This confirmed the central element underlying the dream: regret at having married early and the low value she assigned to her husband. In effect, the news about Elise had inflamed a buried (unconscious) desire and created a conflict within her that provoked her anger. So that she may continue sleeping, the dream had to substitute this conflict and resultant feelings for the pleasant experience of 'going to the theatre'. Thus the experience of the dream had given expression to her wishful impulse and yet preserved her sleep.

The unconscious, which was used in a purely descriptive sense before, now implied something more – a separate space in the human psyche: 'a particular realm of the mind with its own wishful impulses, its own mode of expression and its peculiar mental mechanisms which are not in force elsewhere'.[8] Only fragments of its activity emerge temporarily into consciousness, and this is not because the unconscious idea is necessarily a weak impulse, but because it operates under its own dictates. Unconscious processes are closer to hallucination than they are to thinking in words, for in them logic and the consequential cause-effect connections are missing. The unconscious only contains content that is *cathected* (emotionally invested) or charged with greater or lesser strength. Emotional charge is easily transferred from the actual content to something else; opposites may merge and become one and the same thing; several single figures are amalgamated to mixed figures. Chronology and the effects of time do not exist in the unconscious. Memories and traumas from early childhood may remain imbued with the same charge for years. For example, when very young I might have felt terrified of a growling black dog, but years later, even though I have now grown much bigger than the dog, my fear of black dogs persists unchanged. The unconscious also contains instinctual desires, which are often in conflict with the demands of the external world. Thus, there is little regard for external reality, time, or causality in the unconscious; everything is comprehended only by emotional dictates. The functioning appears to be extraordinarily primitive, perhaps no different from what presumably prevails in an infant before the acquisition of language. Freud termed this as a *primary process* – 'primary' in contrast to the more evolved conscious thinking, the *secondary process*.[9] 'Primary process thought is instinctual, wishful, irrational; its sole concern is to seek pleasure. In contrast, secondary process thought is sober, controlled, rational; it works to regulate the fulfillment of instinctual wishes in accordance with the demands of reality.'[10] Primary processes rule the unconscious, while secondary processes dominate the conscious and the preconscious.

The preconscious

Complicating matters further Freud introduces another level in the unconscious: the *preconscious*. In his view, thought processes that temporarily leave the realm of consciousness and can reclaim their hold on it without any difficulty are located in the preconscious; they lie in wait in the forecourt of consciousness. Our conscious mind is constantly bombarded with sense stimuli from the external world. We simply cannot focus attention on all of them and must necessarily put some of them aside, otherwise we will fail to perform our daily business. The repository for these recent memories is the preconscious. This is the day residue lodged in the preconscious, some of which may initiate a dream, especially those with greater emotional resonance. The contents of the preconscious differ from the unconscious because they share a permeable boundary with consciousness and can cross over into it with ease. On the other hand, unconscious processes are cut off and can only pierce into consciousness when a certain amount of energy is available for this task. Don't we often notice that in trying to retrieve an unconscious memory a distinct feeling of *repulsion* has to be overcome? Correspondingly, when attempting to evoke another's unconscious memory we will encounter his or her *resistance* to it. These forces of resistance and repulsion keep the conscious and the unconscious asunder.

This mapping of the mind – its contents and functioning – enables us to understand how a dream is born. In the above example, Elise's news had been relegated to the preconscious of the dreamer. As the day residue, it had succeeded in finding a connection with an unconscious wish present in her ever since childhood. Normally, the unconscious wish is prevented from entering consciousness during the day. But at night, the lowered state of defence and the strength of the instinctual material pressing for satisfaction had combined with the facts of recent experience – Elise's engagement – to construct the dream. Alternatively, the emotional charge borrowed from the unconscious impulse helped activate the day residue that expressed itself in the dream. The dream thus becomes the means for the unconscious, with the help of the preconscious, to make evident its wishful impulses to the sleeping consciousness.

Freud thus very neatly explained why a dream arises. Unlike Hobson, he did not invoke metabolic processes to author the dream; instead we are told that psychological compulsions beget this child of the night. This, however, does not explain the senseless and contradictory character of dreams – their bizarreness – which had intrigued and captivated the imagination of humankind.

In the lady's dream there is a distinctly absurd element – three tickets required for two people, as also their absurd cost: three for 1 florin 50! Freud believed this bizarreness was not dream nonsense, but a deliberate disguise, a concerted attempt not to expose the real wishful impulse behind the dream. The dream content, he implied, is only a false façade camouflaging something else – the real intent of the dream.

The underlying emotion in the lady's dream was the absurdity of her marrying so early. This was replaced by the absurd action of buying tickets so early. In fact, the main theme of early marriage has been completely masked by the dream imagery. It then becomes the job of the analyst to rescue the actual content powering the dream from the camouflage of the manifest dream imagery. With this basis in place we are now in a position to describe fully Freud's understanding of the lady's dream.

The news about Elise acquiring a good husband had created a ripple in her unconscious, stimulating regret that her dowry amount could have got her a much better husband, if only she had waited. She felt defeated by Elise's triumph. The creation of the dream story had helped deflect the charge of the awakened impulse. The dream had replaced her recent feelings of defeat by an old triumph where her early marriage had permitted her to view and indulge in activities forbidden to Elise and other unmarried girls. If the power of the emotional disturbance (regret) created within her was expressed directly and blatantly, without any disguise, its force would prevent continued sleep.

At its core the Freudian dream is given its form by two conflicting psychical forces operating while we are asleep – one that seeks expression and the other that strives to prevent its expression. When this constant conflict ends in a compromise a dream is born. The communicating force manages to express itself, but not in the way it desired; the restraining force meanwhile succeeds only in softening the impact by distorting the infantile wish seeking expression into an unrecognizable dream form.[11] The situation is analogous to that of a political journalist who when writing about those in power cannot present the undisguised truth due to the threat of censorship. The journalist has to learn to couch and soften (and thereby distort) the expression of his or her opinion. The extent of censorship will ascertain whether certain thoughts are eliminated, or spoken in allusions, or concealed beneath an innocent metaphorical disguise. The stricter the censorship, the more ingenious the disguise and consequently the greater the distortion will be.

Similarly at night an unconscious force stimulated by the day residue in the preconscious attempts to express the instigated and ungratified wish through a dream. It is restrained by another force that exercises censorship upon this dream wish and forcibly brings about a distortion in its expression. Freud likened the restraining force to a censor, which polices the boundary between the conscious and the unconscious, preventing any banished or instinctual material from forcing itself into consciousness. The same censor thwarts any threatening thoughts from invading our waking consciousness by forcing them down into the unconscious. The censor does its policing work by using the force of *repression*, and the banished idea is thus called a *repressed thought*. Later in his writings Freud referred to the censor as the *superego*.[12]

Manifest and latent content

At this juncture, the other dichotomy – the cornerstone of Freudian dream theory – needs to be introduced. Freud distinguished between two levels of the dream. The dream content with its visual experience, which is recalled in the morning, is referred to as the *manifest content* of the dream. Freud did not accord any significance or meaning to the imagery in the dream, its manifest content, since he considered it the disguised representation of another, more significant, underlying content, which is the unconscious material hidden behind it. This concealed material, the undisguised thoughts seeking expression, is the *latent content* of the dream. He also called them *dream thoughts*. These comprise the repressed wishes and primal instincts from the unconscious. The latent content cannot express itself as it is denied entry into consciousness by the censor. Only by disguising itself can it gain access to it. Thus the 'true' thought of the dream – its latent content – by changing its form to evade the censor, becomes the meaningless manifest content, or what we experience as the dream. The following dream of a middle-aged man may be illustrative:

> We are going for a picnic on our bicycles, with our neighbours Vikram and Anjali. Anjali's cycle doesn't have enough air. I quickly pump air into the tyre before we set off.

The dreamt images narrate a mundane enough episode that seems trivial. But the latent content of this dream may turn out to be rather potent, disclosing the dreamer's secret desire for sexual union with Anjali. Since she was married, this forbidden wish, if expressed in its raw, elemental form during sleep, without the control of the censoring ego, would violate the dreamer's sense of morality and shock him into wakefulness. The censor prevents this by disguising his urge, and replacing it with an acceptable and harmless image of pumping air into her bicycle tyre. The manifest content of this dream, unlike most other dream imagery, does not need much elaboration to arrive at its underlying thought. It expresses his desire, yet disguises its potency. This kind of transformation of content is not the province of dreams only, but we occasionally employ such disguises in our waking lives also. When one excuses oneself to go to the 'powder room' or 'rest room', the manifest speech is being used to express the latent desire: I wish to go and urinate.[13] The 'powdering' or the 'resting' are actually totally meaningless in the context of the communication.

Another example. A man dreamt:

An angry tiger was chasing a poor little dog. I try to fight the tiger and protect the little animal, but the tiger gets stronger and stronger.[14]

On the previous day the dreamer, out of envy, had been very unkind to a friend and wished to forget the whole episode. During the night this day residue had instigated the dream; his preconscious memory had possibly stimulated other unkind and envious actions from his distant past. Actually, a painful memory, forgotten and buried deep in his unconscious, had been rekindled: Once, out of sibling jealousy, he had pushed his little brother off his tricycle, wounding him badly. The meaning of the dream, though camouflaged, now becomes evident. It alluded to his guilt surrounding that incident and was a reminder of the anger at his parent for neglecting him. Both these cathected feelings – jealousy and anger – had been stored in his unconscious. It is also clear that the dream itself – the manifest content – is only a disguise and devoid of any meaning except that it leads to the all-important underlying truth – the latent content – which is something far removed from the manifest content.

Dreams: the royal road to the unconscious

As mentioned earlier, the unconscious was known prior to Freud. But the importance Freud ascribed to it was entirely revolutionary. The powers of the unconscious became apparent to Freud while he was working with hysterical patients. He realized that their hysteria was the product of an emotional trauma that had been forgotten by the patients themselves. Painful memories and unacceptable desires had been repressed and forced underground into the unconscious. This defensive repression of forbidden wishes was responsible for the patient's distortion of reality. The mind had turned against its own desires to evade the harsh demands of the outer world. Rather than dismiss the hysteria of his patients as delusional, Freud used their obsessional outpourings to explore their unconscious and discover the underlying repressed wishes. Inevitably this discovery led to a cure. Freud further argued that the unconscious does not intrude only into the conscious life of neurotic patients, but also expresses itself in the lives of normal people. Repressed material in the unconscious finds an outlet through phenomena that pepper our lives every single day. It manifests in trivial but faulty acts like forgetting names, misplacing things, misreading, mishearing, and making slips of the tongue and the pen – commonly referred to as the Freudian slip. The underlying assumption is that a fear, a memory, or a desire that has been repressed from the conscious mind, rather than disappearing, seeks a way back into consciousness. Take for example how after a sumptuous meal, the president of a club prefaced his concluding speech with these remarks: 'Since we are all fed up, I will not take much of your time …' Unwittingly his boredom with the earlier part of the meeting had expressed itself behind his intent to compliment the lunch. These slips, Freud maintained, are neither as accidental nor as innocent as they appear. The 'accidental slip' can reveal much repressed material. Our everyday life is filled with these unconscious expressions. They are observed in every healthy person and have nothing to do with any form of illness. Freud called them *parapraxes*.[15] Even jokes people relate are the product of such unconscious mechanisms. Dreams are another prominent area in everyday life where the unconscious manifests itself. In fact, dreams are for Freud the royal road into the unconscious of any person, affording a view of his or her unconscious thoughts and memories. Freud believed that at the heart of every dream lies a wish seeking fulfilment. This conclusion is not immediately apparent from the lady's dream about Elise or from our own dreams, but when we consider the dreams of small children they, perhaps, best illustrate this articulation of unfulfilled wishes. The dreams of children below four years require no great interpretative skills – all one need do is enquire into the child's experiences the previous day. Freud's nineteen-month-old daughter Anna had had an attack of vomiting one morning and had consequently been kept without food all day. During the night she was heard calling out excitedly in her sleep: 'Anna Fweud, stwawbewwies, wild stwawbewwies, omblet, pudden!'[16] Clearly, the feast in her dream was expressive of her uppermost desire that had remained unfulfilled the previous day.

An eight-year-old boy dreamt that he was driving in a chariot with Achilles and that Diomede was the charioteer.[17] On being informed that a book on Greek legends had excited the boy the previous day, it immediately becomes apparent that the boy wished to be with the Trojan heroes. Similarly, a young girl dreamt often that God wore a paper cocked-hat on his head. The meaning of the dream becomes evident when it is disclosed that during meals she was required to wear a similar hat to ensure that she did not see the size of her sibling's helpings. The dream was stating that despite the hat she could see everything, just like God can see everything.[18]

These simple transparent childhood dreams become more and more disguised as the child grows and learns to camouflage wishes and desires. This need for disguise is most evident when they are toilet-trained; they soon learn that their fascination with their excreta must not be indulged in. Contrarily it is to be considered as 'dirty'. It is equally confusing when their genital urges are also restrained. A mother, while bathing her five-year-old son, was horrified to see that the boy had experienced an erection. She could only express her shock by sternly reprimanding him with the rhetorical question: What is it you are doing? The boy was both bewildered and ashamed – he had merely responded to the warm water and the gentle caressing of his mother soaping him. Young children are amoral and possess no internal inhibitions against the expression of their impulses. His mother's disapproval was a reminder that he had to control his instinctual responses. As the child grows up such parental controls continually reinforce this, with offerings of love and with threats of punishment. Gradually the child internalizes this external restraint. Parental authority is replaced by a self-censoring agency – the conscience. The urge to engage in a particular activity is abandoned if the child's conscience does not concur, and if the urge overcomes this restraint and persuades the child into indulgence, then the conscience punishes the child with feelings of remorse or guilt. Without the child realizing it, a mechanism is being instilled that is not only judgemental, but helps censor the arousal of unacceptable desires. Slowly the child learns which desires can never be fulfilled and therefore should never even be articulated, and which desires have to be garbed in their expression. Gradually the stage has been prepared for a lifelong conflict between desire and guilt. Perhaps an analogous mechanism operates within the arena of dreams, and children learn to create a comparable camouflage. So that when they are mature their dreams do not directly express the desires underlying them, but, like the hysterical symptom, they distort the unfulfilled wish. This disguised substitute is unintelligible when it appears in the dream, as it seems the farthest away from any wish demanding fulfilment. The distortion is the work of the same defensive forces of resistance within the dreamer, which in waking life disguises impulses and at times altogether prevents their expression, so that 'the dreamer can no more understand the meaning of his dreams than the hysteric can understand the connection and significance of his symptoms'.[19]

A lady questioned Freud about his claim that dreams fulfil wishes. She had had a dream whose subject was the opposite – her wish was not satisfied.

> *I wanted to give a supper-party, but I had nothing in the house but a little smoked salmon. I thought I would go out and buy something, but I remembered then that it was Sunday afternoon and all the shops would be shut. Next I tried to ring up some caterers, but the telephone was out of order. So I had to abandon my wish to give a supper-party.*

The associations she produced were not sufficient to interpret the dream. Freud pressed her for some more. After a short pause (indicative that she was overcoming a resistance) she related that the day before she had visited a woman friend. She confessed she felt jealous of the friend as her husband constantly praised her. Fortunately the threatened feelings had remained contained because her friend was skinny and thin, while her husband admired a plumper figure. During the visit her friend had asked her, 'When are you going to ask us to another meal? You always feed one so well.'

The meaning of the dream was now clear to Freud. The dream was actually fulfilling her wish: She would rather not give another supper-party, so that her friend does not become plump and attractive to her husband![20]

Freud's division of the dream into two distinct levels was radically different from all other attempts till then to decode the dream. Every analyst, since antiquity, had viewed only the manifest dream image and never looked elsewhere to explain the dream. All interpretations comprised permutations of the manifest content. Freud introduced a new class of material between the dream image and its interpretation – the latent content, or the dream thoughts. 'It is from these dream-thoughts and not from a dream's manifest content that we disentangle its meaning.'[21] As soon as we know the latent content the dream becomes immediately comprehensible. The dreamer usually attempts to understand the dream solely on the merits of the manifest content and is thus led into error about the meaning of the dream. Freud compared the dream content to a rebus, a picture puzzle. Then, rather than view the disparate images as incongruous or bizarre and therefore meaningless, it is advisable to lay aside criticisms on their composition and, instead, try to replace each dream element by something else that is representative of it in another manner. When done this way the apparent worthlessness of the dream may give way to meaning.

Dreams, Freud felt, could be categorized into three broad groups depending upon the extent of disguise enforced on the latent dream thoughts. 'In the first place, we may distinguish those dreams which make sense and are at the same time intelligible.'[22] It is easy to understand their import in the context of our waking life; they are usually short and do not contain anything astonishing or strange within them. 'A second group is formed by those dreams which, though they are connected in themselves and have a clear sense, nevertheless have a bewildering effect, because we cannot see how to fit that sense into our mental life ... The third group, finally, contains those dreams which are without either sense or intelligibility, which seem *disconnected*, *confused* and *meaningless*.'[23] Freud's categorization is akin to the taxonomy outlined earlier. The first group is the literal dream of our classification, while the second and third groups correspond to the categories of the symbolic and insignificant dreams. In ancient times an interpreter would first ascertain whether the dream is fit for interpretation or if it is empty of any meaning and therefore to be discarded as an *enupnion*. Freud reversed this priority by focusing on the discovery of meaning in the 'disconnected' and 'confused' *enupnion*.

Obviously it is only in Freud's second and third groups that we can distinguish between the latent and manifest content of a dream. Dreams in the first category are easily intelligible as their manifest and latent contents coincide. Children's dreams, as we said earlier, exhibit this tendency clearly with no pretence or disguise in them. Usually it is the third group that is most bewildering because the disguise wrought by the dream is most effective, completely hiding the latent dream thoughts behind the dreamt images.

Freud believed that an intimate relationship exists between the confused nature of dreams and the underlying intelligible latent content. We have already seen how the dream censorship disguises the unconscious wish to enable it to evade the censor. This attempt at disguise is reminiscent of the children's game of speaking in P-language, which allows them to freely communicate without adults being able to figure out what they are talking about. Simply, it allows kids to disguise what may be considered objectionable. The method of disguise is simple – a 'p' is inserted after every vowel sound in a word, and the vowel sound is then replicated. Thus, for example, our horrified mother's question (What is it you are doing?) would be pronounced – Whapat ipis ipit youpou apare dopoiping? (The underlined alphabets are the inserted 'p' in each word.) A simple question has become a bizarre communication.

But could the strangeness of a dream be attributed to a disguise employing a fixed and systematic method of scrambling dream thoughts like, say, in P-language or in software encry`ption? The method of disguise in dreams is not just convoluted, but also wide-ranging and variable. Dream bizarreness, according to Freud, is the product of a far more complex process, and dream censorship and the scrambling of dream thoughts cannot be the only mechanism that distorts dreams; there has to be something else that gives the dream its bizarre quality.

Freud calls the process of transforming latent content into manifest content *dream work*. Interpretation would then become the process of reversing the disguise wrought by the dream work and dream censorship.

Dream work achieves its aim of masking the unfulfilled wish underlying the dream in four ways. The first of these processes is *condensation*, whereby the dream work combines a number of elements in the unconscious wish and represents them by a single image in the dream. Condensation performs its work by either omitting some elements of the dream thoughts, or by including only a fragment of them, or by combining two or more elements into a single unity. Thus we can dream of a composite person who looks like A, but is dressed like B, and performs actions that are typical of C. This composite image is possible only if these three people have something in common with the underlying wish of the dream. All we recall on awaking is that we dreamt of a strange person! Like the familiar though strange mythical centaur, a composite image of man and beast, fused to represent the dual aspect – human and animal – of our nature. Condensation also applies to places, objects, and concepts; the more unfamiliar these are the more bizarre is the image in the dream. Thus, every image in a dream may correspond to many dream thoughts. Consider another example: a Roman soldier in a dream may allude to an authoritarian father associated with strictures imposed in childhood, and at the same time the image may represent a sexual relationship in late adolescence, which the father had disapproved of and opposed. One image in the dream alludes to two separate underlying thoughts. Thus both the feared father and the desired lover are condensed into the single dream figure of the Roman soldier.[24] Condensation can also act in another manner: a single element in the underlying content may be reflected by many dream images. Like the lady's regret at marrying too early finds expression in two of the dream images – empty stalls and 1 florin 50.

Although condensation makes dreams obscure, it does not appear to achieve its end in the same manner as censorship does. This clearly reflects that they are different processes.[25] Dream censorship uniformly objects to all disagreeable material, like the man's desire for Anjali in the bicycle dream. However, the translation effected by dream work through its processes is not the result of a fixed method or rule as in the case of P-language; it isn't a letter-for-letter or sign-for-letter conversion found, for instance, in World War II ciphers.

To exemplify further how the dream work disguises and constructs the dream let us return to the five-year-old boy (aroused while being bathed), who has in the meanwhile grown up. Suppose much later in his life, he had, on the pretext of work, slipped out of office to buy a present for his wife – a silk scarf. Later that very day his boss had yelled at him for not finishing his work on time. Presumably the day's residue had awakened the memory of his mother's reprimand, and his consequent feelings of smallness and guilt. The resurrected unconscious wish of his arousal while being bathed by his mother will transfer its desires onto the recent material. This wish seeks to force itself upon his sleeping consciousness, but it comes up against the censor. The mother's horrified question in response to his erection would have to be camouflaged as it pointed towards his repressed desire to sexually posses his mother (Oedipal urge). This latent wish was seeking expression through a dream, but the censor will not allow it entry into consciousness unless it disguises itself.

To illustrate the specific steps involved in the construction of a dream, I will attempt an imaginative recreation by presuming that P-language was the initial disguise employed to evade the censor. This scrambled reprimand of his Oedipal desire, however, by itself does not have sufficient force to construct a dream. Its further advance towards consciousness will be foiled at the boundary of the preconscious because an unconscious primary process is attempting expression in a domain ruled by secondary processes. It is at this juncture that the dream work would cast its magical spell, reformulating (distorting) the mother's question (stated in P-language) to enable it to be experienced as a dream and thereby drawing attention to the instigating desire. Condensation would obfuscate the response of the shocked mother by altering it to 'hat pipit pure dope', condensing the thirty-four alphabets contained in the original six words to sixteen letters in the four modified words, and thereby transforming the mother's question into something unintelligible. The disguise has been effected by combining some elements of the sentence and partly omitting some of them: 'Pipit' (as in pipette) is an amalgamation of 'ipis' and 'ipit', which in turn were disguises of 'is' and 'it'; similarly 'pure' is an amalgamation of 'youpou' and 'apare', themselves disguises of 'you' and 'are' in her question; while 'hat' and 'dope' have omitted an alphabet or two.

Transformation of the latent wish cannot be effected by condensation alone. It goes hand in hand with another process, *displacement*, or the shifting of emotional emphasis. Different ideas in the dream thoughts are not all of equal value; they are imbued with varying magnitudes of emotion or affect. It is this affect that determines their importance or insignificance. If the dream thoughts have to be transformed, then not only will they be compressed, but the emotional emphasis would also have to be disguised. The dream work, so to speak, separates the idea from the emotion attached to it. Ideas that are important in the dream thought are stripped of their importance. Instead, importance is conferred to those dreamt images that have been disguised from insignificant ideas or trivial details within the dream thoughts. In the dream about the theatre tickets, the underlying judgement that it was absurd to marry so early has been replaced by going to the theatre and buying the tickets in a hurry. This central element has been displaced from the dream, and as a result the manifest content has become so unlike the latent content. Perhaps no other mechanism renders the dream as strange and incomprehensible as this shift in importance – displacement. It is principally responsible for the distortion of the underlying ideas, which produce the manifest images of the dream.[26] We see this mechanism operative in many jokes.

If I am permitted to persist with my example of the question stated in P-language, then the work of displacement would alter its emotional affect by converting the question into a command: 'Put hat, pure pope!' The stupid person – dope (what the little boy felt after being reprimanded) – has been transformed into the important personage of the pope, and the measuring object – pipette (a disguise for the penis whose length has increased beyond measure) – has become the definitive command 'put' (an involuntary activity, his erection, has become purposive). A change in the sequence of the words has achieved the remaining effect of altering the original rhetorical question. The mother's horror, alluding to the 'impure' response of the boy, has been displaced by the purity of the pope and his vestments.

There are still two more processes, says Freud, that work on the distorted dream thoughts before the dream images can be experienced by the dreamer. They would best be described by continuing with our example, which has already been distorted by the twin processes of condensation and displacement. 'Put hat, pure pope!' is easily comprehended if it remains as a spoken command, but there may be difficulty in depicting this in images. Dreams do not *say* things, they *show* things. To achieve this, the dream work takes recourse to another mechanism at its disposal, *visual representation*, which converts the text of the dream thoughts into images, involving a still further alteration. Don't we witness such a change when a book is converted into its film script, however faithful the script? Visual representation would modify our above example by portraying the pope donning his hat. The command has become a ritual adornment.

Finally, the mechanism of *secondary revision* gives the finishing touches to the dream; it improves the narrative coherence of the dream content. If, in our example, that evening the dreamer had seen a film on the holy Indian city of Benares, then this day residue might have found expression in his dream. Undergoing a secondary revision, the manifest content of the dream becomes:

The Pope is visiting Benares. He is presented a silk hat, which has been brought on a trishul [three-pointed spear].

The silk of the Pope's hat has also been taken from the day residue of buying a silk scarf for his wife. The dreamer would wonder at the strangeness of this dream, little realizing that through it a long buried conflict was surfacing. We have seen how beginning with a latent thought – his instinctual indiscretion eliciting his mother's reprimand – the dream work distorts the underlying desire into the manifest images of dream.

How the dream work and the censor help form a dream:

What is it you are doing?	mother's reprimand (Oedipal urge)
Whapat ipis ipit youpou apare dopoiping?	P-language disguise evades censor
Hat pipit pure dope	condensation
Put hat, pure pope!	displacement
The pope dons his hat.	visual representation
The pope is visiting Benares. He is presented a silk hat, which has been brought on a trishul.	secondary revision uses day's residue (film and scarf for wife)

It is interesting to note the difference between Freud's explanation of the bizarreness in dreams and Hobson's, who had posited the neurological mechanism of synthesis to explicate the strangeness of the dream. Freud employs a psychological mechanism to accomplish the same objective. The two mechanisms, however, are intrinsically poles apart. The Hobson mechanism initiates order into a chaotic situation – the forebrain attempts to lend cohesion and meaning to the random images generated by neuronal activity. On the other hand, Freudian dream work, through censorship, condensation, displacement, visual representation, and secondary revision, injects disorder into intelligible but unfulfilled wishes.

The reverse process, the interpretation of the dream, beginning with the dream images, would unravel them to expose the underlying unconscious desire. The dream, when retraced by the work of interpretation, would lead to the memory of the question asked by his shocked mother. If asked to give his associations, the dreamer would immediately identify the day residue in the dream. The silk had its origin in the scarf, while the image of Benares had been stimulated by the memory of the film he had seen the previous evening. His associations to the other elements of the dream had elicited the contrast between the holy (pure) pope and the unholy (impure) thoughts that sometimes coursed through his mind, especially when he was an adolescent in school. In particular he remembered a chemistry class in which while measuring the volume of a fluid through a pipette his body suddenly and inexplicably shook with sexual desire. In another science class the instructor had called him a dope and made him stand in a corner. Rebelliously, his mind had thought of imaginative uses for the instructor's silk tie, visualizing it as a hat. Somehow this led him to remember that his mother insisted on washing all the silk clothes herself rather than have them washed by the washer-woman, and from thereon his associations sped to his mother bathing him once a week when he was young. It is only a small step in the flow of his associations to recall her horror, which, in turn, betokens the genital urges aroused within the child during his bath. Though this may be considered an imaginative recreation of the individual steps involved in the construction of the dream, they will be borne out by the dreamer's associations to the dream imagery. It seems the manifest dream makes 'an abbreviated selection from the associations'.[27] The only image that cannot be traced back is the three-pointed spear, which is dwelt on a little later.

Perhaps it may be appropriate to pause a little here and clarify the larger perspective against which Freud was labouring the mechanisms involved in dreaming. We all know that there is a strangeness to the language of dreams; it contains bizarre elements, which have mystified the imagination of the sage, soothsayer, and scientist alike. Their explanations have spawned widely differing theories of dreaming. However, all of them have ascribed the authorship of the dream to a source alien to our waking consciousness. Freud, also arguing that dreams do not originate in consciousness, believed that they stem from the unconscious, and the disparate images of a dream are evidence of an underlying text, latent dream thoughts – a medley of instinctual impulses and forbidden wishes – which have to be camouflaged to escape censure. His dream work is the mechanism by which this disguise is accomplished. The consequent distortion is experienced as the bizarre element in dreams, immediately suggesting an explanation for the strangeness of the dream world. The peculiar imagery of the dream, for Freud, is not simply the use of another language, but the product of a deliberate effort to conceal the meaningfulness of the underlying wishes. Dreaming thus becomes a kind of pathological mental activity, analogous to neurotic symptom formation.[28]

The significance of these theoretical considerations will become evident when we consider the practical part of dream interpretation. Since dreams conceal the true motive of the dreamer, Freud advocated the method of *free association* to arrive at their interpretation. However seductive the manifest content of a dream, attention has to be diverted away from it as a whole. Instead, in free associating, each portion of the dream must be considered independently, as though it requires separate assessment.[29] While engaged thus the dreamer must renounce all criticism and painstakingly report in succession every association that comes to mind in relation to each of the individual elements of the dream. A chain of associations will now seem to emerge 'of its own free will', each association linked to the next one. To exemplify, let us return to the man who dreamt of a tiger chasing a small dog. After recounting the dream the dreamer suddenly said, 'I don't know why, but that reminds me that yesterday I had a very angry discussion with one of my colleagues. I felt bad afterwards.' This was the day residue that had prompted the dream. The dreamer allowed his flow of associations to range freely from thereon. 'He is a young colleague and looks up to me – but he sometimes says such stupid things! I shouldn't have been so unkind ... I'm thinking right now about my little brother who was eighteen months younger than me. I really loved him and we used to have such fun. Oh dear! I suddenly remember one holiday ... he was riding down the path on his tricycle and I pushed him over – he scratched both his knees and his chin had a huge bleeding gash and he started to cry. How horrible! Why did I do that to Bobby? Well ... I guess I was angry with my mother. She was always busy, and then she got pregnant with my sister ... I don't know why she had to have three children!'[30]

Following these connections we quickly arrive from the remote dream world – a fight between animals – to the real life of the dreamer and his frustration over having to share his mother's attention. The associations may invoke memories from the previous day or from times long past, or they may involve reflections, discussions, confessions, or enquiries. In short, we must allow thoughts to wander where they will without dismissing them.

Confronted with a dream element the dreamer is asked to indulge in a chain of verbal associations. Once the train of associations is triggered off it becomes evident that they reverse the process initiated by the dream work. A specific image may fan out into many diverse memories, all of them sharing something in common, so that the initial image appears to be condensed from them. At times they may involve feelings that have a contrasting emotional affect from the original image, or these associations may take us into memories that may be very distant from the initiating image – displacement. The disparate associations evoked will certainly not be cohesive; what the chain of associations has undone is the process of secondary revision, which had fused diverse memories into the tight narrative content of the dream. The predominantly visual imagery lacks overt connections with the dreamer's life, but on exposure to free association it metamorphoses into verbal expressions that are largely centred on narcissistic infantile impulses. This reveals the dream work mechanism of visual representation. Freud hypothesized that if free association can reverse everything that happens in dream formation, then it could be used as a valuable clue to the unconscious impulses supporting the dream.[31]

These free associations should not be equated with latent dream thoughts. They are merely a means of providing explanations, transitions, and connections required for unravelling the dream imagery. Soon the flow of associations will come to an abrupt end and this occurs precisely at the point of revelation of the underlying dream thought. At this point the analyst intervenes, fills in the gap, draws the undeniable but unstated conclusion, and explicitly details what the associations are hinting at.[32] In short, free association unravels the process of dream work to reach the latent content.

An example of how a dream is interpreted may illuminate this approach more clearly. The examples cited by Freud himself are rather long, but a dream interpreted by his colleague Frink may provide a simpler but equally vivid example.

A young American woman dreamed that she was walking on Fifth Avenue with a friend, looking for a new hat. Finally she went in [to a shop] *and bought one.*[33]

This seems like a trivial dream and it certainly isn't spilling over with repressed infantile wishes. At best it expresses a desire to buy a hat from a fashionable store, which surely is not something that women repress from their waking minds! However, after Frink had elicited the dreamer's associations they revealed a dramatically different content underlying the harmless images of the dream. The young woman had actually gone for a walk the previous day, on Fifth Avenue. But she had not purchased a new hat. Her husband had been ill the whole day and she had found herself worrying over whether he would die, even though he was suffering from a minor ailment. Noticing her quietness and gloom, he had suggested that she go out with a friend who had called her. During the walk their discussion had wandered to a man whom she had known before marriage. Here her associations ceased. When the analyst asked her to proceed, she eventually revealed that long ago she had been in love with this man. When asked whether she had considered marrying him, she said that he had never asked her, their disparate social and financial status had not let them think of it. She was unable to describe this association any further; instead she began to associate about buying hats. She wanted to buy many hats but, in fact, she and her husband could not afford this kind of expenditure. She then suddenly remembered that the hat she had bought in her dream was a black one. 'It was a mourning hat ...' she had added.

In the course of interpreting a dream, frequently a previously omitted fragment emerges, which until that instant had been totally forgotten. This fragment, wrested from forgetfulness, Freud believed, is always the most important part in interpretation.[34]

The wrested detail about the hat made the dream clear to the analyst. The dreamer had feared that her husband might die and her dream had shown this by her purchasing a mourning hat, suggesting a forbidden wish for her husband's death. Though she could not afford the hat she had bought it without hesitation in the dream, indicating that she would have been better off had she married the other man. Not only did she wish this, but had believed that despite the social difference he too had wanted to marry her. It emerged that the dream had condensed and disguised three different repressed wishes, all of them forbidden by her real circumstances, to which she was consciously reconciled: her husband's death, to marry the man she first loved, and to have plenty of money. The woman acknowledged to her analyst that every aspect of this was true and that in the past few weeks she had often thought about this first man whom she might have married.

Even though it is a short dream the analyst had not attempted to interpret it en masse, as one collective image, as Joseph had done with the Pharaoh's dream. The interpretation became evident only after the dreamer had provided her personal associations to the individual images in the dream. These free associations forged the link between her unconscious desire and the dream. Whereas earlier cultures had relied on a dream dictionary to decode dreams, the new Freudian theory, in one stroke, rendered all dictionaries obsolete. The only dictionary we need to interpret our dreams, Freud said, does not lie on our bookshelves, but exists in our minds.[35]

Besides the day residue and the images freely bringing forth associations, there is another class of material in the dream imagery that evokes no associative response whatsoever from the dreamer. We are not talking about those elements that after some persuasion will yield related ideas, but to certain images that leave the dreamer mute.

This does not represent a failure of the technique, but is the work of a fresh general principle. Freud found that this failure in associations regularly occurred in connection with particular dream elements. Whenever he imputed a fixed meaning to these elements they fitted into the general scheme of the dream and made satisfactory sense of it. An accumulation of many such cases where the meaning fitted the element convinced him that these portions of the dream could be understood without the dreamer's associations. This stable relationship between a dream element and its translated meaning was described by Freud as a 'symbolic' one, and the dream element a 'symbol' of unconscious dream thought.[36] This fixed symbolic relationship does not replace the associative technique, but supplements it. In fact, symbols and associations become the two bridges that link the manifest dream to its underlying and all important latent content.

The interpretation of the bicycle dream, without any helpful associations from the dreamer, relied on reading 'pumping' as a symbol of the sexual act. Thus a simple replacement of it in the dream imagery makes its meaning apparent. In the dream about the pope and the hat, the spear (*trishul*) did not have any associations and therefore would be interpreted as a phallic symbol, its three points further emphasizing the sexual symbolism – the number three alluding to the three male genitals.

Freud believed that not every object appears as a symbol in a dream, but only certain definite elements of the dream thought are symbolized. The range of things symbolically represented in a dream is limited to the human body, parents, siblings, birth, death, and nakedness. A survey conducted by Calvin Hall and his students to determine the referents commonly symbolized in psychoanalytic literature yielded 102 symbols for the penis, 95 for the vagina, 55 for coitus, 25 for masturbation, 13 for breasts, and 12 for castration, out of a total of 709 symbols identified.[37] Symbols are employed in dreams to give expression and gratification to our sexual conflicts (wish-fulfilment), and also to depotentize them by concealing them so that sleep is uninterrupted. Symbols thus become both an expression and a concealment of our sexual urge. Say you dream of a gun. According to Freud, it would be a symbol of the phallus. In his view, 'All elongated objects, such as sticks, tree-trunks and umbrellas ... may stand for the male organ – as well as all long, sharp weapons, such as knives, daggers and pikes ... Boxes, cases, chests, cupboards and ovens represent the uterus, and also hollow objects, ships, and vessels of all kinds ... Steps, ladders or staircases, or, as the case may be, walking up or down them, are representations of the sexual act.'[38]

The path led from dreams to the unconscious, to the life of the instincts, and then to sexuality. This last step – the insistence that symbols are pre-eminently sexual and that the sexual life of human beings does not begin at puberty – with physical maturing – but much earlier, in infancy, through the infant's relationship with the mother, perhaps earned Freud the greatest resistance to his ideas. He, however, stuck to his position, even claiming experimental confirmation in support of his thesis. An experiment was conducted on deeply hypnotized subjects who were instructed to dream of sexual themes. Their dreams employed the same symbols as found in Freudian theory. In other experiments, psychotic patients were told stories of a grossly sexual kind and when asked to repeat them, they reproduced the sexual organs as symbols that Freud had earlier described. Interestingly, some of them represented sexual intercourse as a staircase, which is difficult to reach even by conscious intent.[39]

That sexual imagery is often a predominant theme is confirmed not only from such experiments, but also in folklore and rituals. To give but one example: the symbol of a cloak. In a woman's dream it stands for a man. 'During the extremely ancient bridal ceremonial of the Bedouins, the bridegroom covers the bride with a special cloak known as "Aba" and speaks the following ritual words: "Henceforth none save I shall cover thee!"'[40] In the Punjabi marriage ritual in India, which is performed even today, the bride is adorned with a cloak (*chunni*) given by the bridegroom in a special ceremony devoted solely to consecrate it.

'Thus symbolism is a second and independent factor in the distortion of dreams, alongside of the dream-censorship. It is plausible to suppose, however, that the dream-censorship finds it convenient to make use of symbolism, since it leads towards the same end – the strangeness and incomprehensibility of dreams.'[41]

Freud broke with tradition by attributing the unusual form of the dream, not to its 'messaging' content from a suprapersonal world, but to defensive forces. The emphasis of interpretation shifted from the deciphering of a communication from an outer agency to the unmasking of internal impulses disguised by the censor. The dream from being abandoned as an outcast in the Christian world was included in the rational precinct of analysis and therapy.

The function of the dream, according to Freud, is to preserve sleep.

The role of the dream is to defensively protect the sleeper from two forces – external and internal. An external stimulation, for example, the ringing of an alarm clock, would be incorporated into the dream, say, as the peeling of a distant church bell, thus ensuring continued sleep. Protection from external stimulation is assigned a relatively minor role in Freudian theory in comparison to the more important protection against internal stimulation, both somatic (bladder pressure, hunger pangs) and psychological (aroused memories).[42] As noted, Freud assigned the greatest significance to the protection against threatening internal impulses (memory) pressing for discharge from the unconscious.

Freud's conception of dreams and psychology is known as psychoanalysis, as distinct from other psychological schools of personality development. Psychoanalysis is not only a theory of personality or the mind, but also a method of therapy that aims at comprehending dreams by investigating the interaction of conscious and unconscious elements. Classically, its methodology relies on the patient free associating in such a way that repressed wishes, which are buried in the unconscious, are made to surface and subsequently be dealt with.

Psychoanalysis is an outgrowth of Western civilization, and its impact is not limited to the precincts of mental health professionals, but has spread far and wide. Freud always strove to understand the link between the mind and the body. He made us aware that every bodily state has an effect on the mind and that nothing happens in the mind that does not also affect the body. Only after Freud did we begin to think of bodily illness as connected with the mind.

Freud's division of the mind into the conscious and the unconscious has influenced every aspect of life. Freudian terms such as 'subconscious', 'repressed urges', 'inhibition', 'fixation', and 'identification' have passed into popular parlance. The substance of psychoanalytic disclosures, as understood by the artist's imagination, has often dominated the content of literary works. Novelists familiar with the processes of dream work and the behaviour of the unconscious have exploited these ideas for their craft. Visual artists have also borrowed the mode of psychoanalytic discourse and begun to freely express unconscious elements in their paintings and sculptures. Freud's *Interpretation of Dreams* is now considered to be more than a book about dreams. It expounds Freud's theory of the mind and maps its dynamics. Despite the initial resistance to his ideas, so foundational have his theories proved to be that they have shaped many areas of contemporary thought: gender, memory, literary criticism, construction of the self, etc. The advent of psychoanalysis also released people from the restraints imposed by traditional mores, sparking social change and sexual permissiveness. Further, it provided a language for the discussion of sexual matters within and across generations.

Who then was Freud? Dream artisan, psychologist, medical practitioner, philosopher, or social activist? Early in his life he had learnt the lesson that conformity meant stultification. He questioned everything: Why do we dream? Why do people become ill and how can they be cured? Why do we have wars? Why are some groups persecuted?[43] His attempt was to elucidate and comprehend some of the riddles of nature and society. Possessed of a rare acuity, he tirelessly sought to contribute something towards their solutions. Freud cannot be judged by ordinary standards. As W. H. Auden said of him, Freud 'is no more a person now but a whole climate of opinion'.[44]

Chapter 8

ARE DREAMS 'DUMB' BIOLOGY OR 'SMART' PSYCHOLOGY?

If sleep does not serve an absolutely vital function, then it is the biggest mistake the evolutionary process ever made. Sleep precludes hunting for and consuming food. It is incompatible with procreation. It produces vulnerability to attack from enemies. Sleep interferes with every voluntary adaptive motor act in the repertoire of coping mechanisms. How could natural selection with its irrevocable logic have 'permitted' the animal kingdom to pay the price of sleep for no good reason?

Allan Rechtschaffen

The discovery that there is an inexorable regular periodicity to dreaming – they punctuate our sleep every ninety minutes – led researchers to believe that dreams are a product of physiological processes and nothing else. This fact, coupled with their random and bizarre imagery, made neurologists declare that dreaming is essentially meaningless. Our ability to detect a pattern in them is reflective more of our ingenuity than any intentionality of the dream. Contrarily, the ancient world and the romantics treated this same strangeness of the dream as an encoded message and read a meaningful intentionality into its symbolic or metaphorical content. They ascribed the sudden scene shifts in the dream to its remarkable facility in skipping the 'dull' stretches, or the insignificant parts of the story. Freud also found intentionality in dreams but believed it emanates from the unconscious. He attributed the apparent unintelligibility of the dream to a drive-discharge transformational algorithm, whereby the ego, because of its constant conflict with the unconscious, defends itself by distorting the drives seeking discharge. Who is right? In essence, the debate is whether dreams should be understood as instances of 'smart' psychology or 'dumb' biology.[1] Or can they, apart from biology and psychology, have any reality at all? Is there any meaning (censored or metaphoric) in them, or are they like the digestive system – a necessary biological process?

Do REM findings confirm Freud?

Freud did not live to see the laboratory research on dreaming. What if Freud had been awakened night after night in a dream laboratory and asked to record his dreams? Or, if he had pored over the REM bursts generated by the dreaming brain, would he have altered his theory? Some believe that the discovery of REM sleep disproved Freud's theory. Conversely, his daughter Anna, who went on to make important psychoanalytic contributions, felt that the physiological research demonstrated significant affinities with Freud's work. Consider, for example, the discovery that while dreaming the body experiences muscular atonia, which forecloses any movement during the currency of the dream. Perhaps this is Nature's method of providing a somatic mechanism so that the dreamer does not awaken and thus sleep is preserved, regardless of the provocation within the dream – a striking confirmation of Freud's basic postulate that dreams are the guardians of sleep. Further, physiologists inform us that the sensorimotor system of the body blocks all input while we are asleep. And if any external stimulus squeezes past this inhibition, it partially arouses the sleeper; sleep becomes lighter and brain activity increases. Freud believed that it is at this juncture that a dream story is generated within the mind, which incorporates the disturbing stimulus, as was well illustrated in the instance of the ringing of an alarm clock stimulating the dream of church bells pealing in the distance. In this way Freud's dream work prevents the sleeper from being fully aroused by inconsequential disturbances that might otherwise keep him or her awake half the night. His theory neatly dovetails with laboratory observations of the blocking of sensory input during sleep – the effort of both being to preserve sleep. Another confirmation of Freud's theory is the role played by day residues in dream content. Experiments have demonstrated that pre-sleep influences do insinuate their way into the narrative content of the dream.

Freud and Hobson compared

However, the psychoanalytical account of the dream is radically different from the neurophysiological description, and it may prove useful to juxtapose the two. Initially it may appear incompatible to assess a psychological theory with a biological model, but Freud's work not only dealt with the interpretation of dreams, but also with the process of dreaming.

Freud constructed a framework of dreaming using only psychological determinants. He had striven to create a scientific psychology in a manner similar to the more established natural sciences of his day. An explanation was considered scientific if it could mould its content to the dictates of a mechanical system and if it adopted concepts synonymous with those prevalent in the physical sciences. Therefore it is not surprising that Freud formulated his psychodynamic theory of dreams in terms of forces (of repression and censure) and energy (unconscious, libidinal), which like any pressurized hydraulic system 'builds up' and 'presses for discharge'. In fact, the early neurological assumptions persist in Freud's model; he equated the build-up of stimulation as painful and its discharge as pleasurable.[2] In this sense the underlying attempt of both the theories – neurological and psychological – was very similar, even though their content apparently differed widely. Just as in neurological research, psychoanalysis also addressed basic questions about dreaming that had been raised earlier.

What is the source of the dream? The laboratory theory asserts that the occurrence and character of dreaming are both determined and shaped by physiological processes; that dreams are an epiphenomenon of the brain's periodical self-activation, a by-product of its biochemical compulsions. The psychoanalyst affirms that it is the day residue that stirs up unconscious wishes, which are constantly seeking discharge, and this gives birth to the dream.

Why are dreams so strange? The activation-synthesis model attributes the strangeness of the dream to the imperfect integration of disparate and chaotic internal data generated in the absence of external sensory inputs or internal chemical controls, both of which are necessary for logical thought or insight.[3] The Freudian theory, on the other hand, ascribes the strangeness of the dream to the active disguising of unacceptable wishes by the dream work to evade the censor. Conflict is fundamental and is at the root of this defensive encoding, while in the Hobson theory conflict is only incidental in the constant competition of neuronal populations that excite or inhibit the dream.

Why are dreams hard to recall in the morning? The laboratory theory assigns this amnesia to the neuronal firing that determines the metabolic mode of the brain, and consequently fails to instruct the forebrain to 'remember' the dream experience.[4] Freud believed that our failure to recall dreams is part of the ego's resistance to the dream. The censor opposed its expression and it is but natural that it would not be embedded into memory and available for recall.

Hobson and the neurological school asserted that Freud had got the mechanism of dreaming wrong. The stimulus for the Freudian dream lies in the unconscious, a special kind of memory, and if this could be neurologically located it would have to reside in the cognitive region of the brain – the cortex. But we do know that dreams are triggered from the primitive section of the brain, the brainstem. Freudians concede that Freud may have got the biology of dreaming wrong, but he had not erred in its psychology, and perhaps this was what actually interested him about the dream. To Freud the dream is not as important as the dreamer's response to it.

Freudian theory, however, scores over Hobson's hypothesis because it takes into cognizance the emotive affect in dreams. A simple activity like crossing the road, which is effortlessly performed every day, may generate extreme emotions in a dream – the magnitude of which may never have been experienced in reality. We will witness Kavita's inability to execute this elementary task in her dream related in a later chapter. Hobson's thesis relies on the cortex synthesizing the disparate elements by invoking its memory banks. Since we may never have been paralysed by fear when crossing the neighbourhood street there may not be such an emotion-laden incident stored in memory. To produce a dream with such an affect, Hobson would need to invoke the emotion-producing centres of the brain. Unfortunately, specific physiological evidence of this is absent and his neurological theory is silent about it.[5] In fact, the original article states that it 'cannot yet account for the emotional aspects of the dream experience'.[6] We have already seen how Freud easily explains this shift in affect – from a mundane activity to one replete with terror – by the mechanism of displacement.

The Freudian hypothesis received a major confirmation with the advent of newer imaging technologies like the positron emission tomography (PET), which made it possible to simultaneously look at the activity of many different regions of the brain. The data thus collected was compatible with the formal features of dreaming. The findings revealed that vast areas of the limbic forebrain, responsible for mediating emotions and motivational behaviour, are activated when dreaming is initiated, including areas that control fear and provide associations. Clearly this neatly accommodates the more emotional nature of dreams, which are motivated by instinct. The lack of cognitive elements in dreams – diminished self-awareness, a reduced sense of reality, and impaired logic – is attributed to the inactivation of the regions of the brain that control these features during waking. Even Hobson, a bitter critic of Freud in his earlier writings, is forced to concede that 'all the features of dreaming that Freud wanted to explain with his wish-fulfilment, disguise-censorship theory are explained in just the way he hoped might ultimately be possible – by the physiology and chemistry of the brain'.[7] This has dictated a shift of emphasis in laboratory research, possibly best described by the modified terminology: from neurophysiology to neuropsychology.

An evolutionary perspective on dreaming

Not all researchers, however, subscribe to the activation-synthesis model; it is the hypothesis of two neurologists. Others read an entirely different story from the gathering laboratory evidence about sleep and dreams. We have seen that research had concentrated on cats for REM data and its inferences. The natural question that arose from these findings was: do other animals also exhibit REM in their pattern of sleep?

Research was then extended to many animals[8] and it was consistently observed that most if not all mammals sleep and dream, though it varies greatly across species. The duration of sleep ranges from about four to five hours in giraffes and elephants, to eighteen hours or more in bats, opossums, and giant armadillos. Smaller mammals need to sleep more than their larger phylogenetic cousins. The length of REM episodes also differ; mammals born immature tend to have more REM sleep, both in infancy and adulthood, than mammals who are born mature. Presumably, some of these specific characteristics of sleep and dream may have evolved as adaptations to their habitat. For example, marine mammals are sometimes asleep only in one side of their brain, apparently to be able to maintain respiration. If a dolphin is awakened when only one hemisphere is asleep, later that hemisphere shows a sleep rebound (greater need to sleep) while the other one does not. In other words, though there may be some differences, a recognizable pattern of sleep – cyclically interspersed by dreaming – is evident in all mammals.

This discovery is important because if every living creature indulges in REM sleep then we will attribute a biological function to dreaming, like we do to breathing – creatures breathe to live. However, if only some species dream then the purpose of dreaming will be sought using parameters specific to those species. REM sleep is not exhibited in all creatures. In fact, as we go down the evolutionary ladder to the amphibians, even sleep and waking states cannot be clearly demarcated. What is observed is that they merely experience quiescent periods that resemble sleep behaviourally, but it is not clear whether these periods are actual sleep or whether they are simply a form of rest. Reptiles, higher on the evolutionary scale than amphibians, become a point of interest as they are perhaps the earliest species to display mammalian sleep. Some researchers, however, assert that they do not sleep, while others believe they indulge only in non-REM sleep, and consequently do not dream. It is thus doubtful whether the reptilian kingdom knows of the circadian rhythm of sleep, a luxury afforded to their more evolved brethren. For the larger population, their metabolic imperatives, like those of their amphibian predecessors, allow them only a cycle that alternates between activity and rest. Higher up the scale, birds exhibit very well developed sleep (NREM) and show occasional, very brief (about a few seconds) episodes of what appears to be an evolutionary precursor of REM sleep. Rarely do they experience muscular atonia during the REM phase, and they also frequently register sleep in only one hemisphere of the brain. [9]

Fully developed sleep and dream patterns exist only within the mammalian world. An interesting hypothesis advanced by researchers is that mammals, as distinct from amphibians, have eyes on the same side of the head and that rapid eye movement during sleep serves to train mammalian eyes to work together. Amphibian eyes do not have to work together and thus show little or no rapid eye movement during sleep. [10] Intriguing though this thesis is, it surely cannot be the only reason why we dream.

This brief survey shows that dreaming possibly evolved with the advent of mammals from their cold-blooded reptilian ancestors; perhaps the same may be conjectured for sleep also. The point in outlining this research is that it leads to the all-important question: Why did these two events – the advent of mammals and sleep / dream – coincide evolutionally? Do dreams (and sleep) have a biological role in mammalian evolution? If they are functionally insignificant, 'then they must represent Nature's most stupid blunder and most colossal waste of time. When an animal is asleep it cannot

protect itself from predators, cannot forage for its food, cannot pro-
create, or defend its territory or its young. Yet for over 130 million
years, despite enormous evolutionary changes, sleeping and dreaming
have persisted in large numbers of species.'[11] It is likely that sleeping
and dreaming are functionally important because despite phylogenetic
differences they have been ubiquitous in the mammalian world and
persistent over time.

REM sleep helps to mature the brain

Coinciding with the apparent introduction of REM sleep in mammals
was a remarkable neuroanatomical change. Initially, brain size
had continually increased to accommodate the increased needs
of evolutionary advancement. A larger brain could handle more.
Strangely we do not find this when we reach the mammals. The brain
(prefrontal cortex), rather than enlarge to serve the needs of the more
intelligent mammals, reduced in size when compared to the brain of
their evolutionary ancestors.[12] Size was perhaps offset by complexity of
functioning. Mammalian brains have more complex networks and thus
are able to service their enhanced needs. An analogous demonstration
is the 'brain' of the computer, the chip, which gets smaller every year,
but is able to 'do' more because of its increased complexity.

The conjecture is that REM sleep may have aided the maturational
process of the brain. This hypothesis fits in neatly with the research
findings in the sleep patterns of the immature young, whether a human
baby, a kitten, or a puppy. All of them experience a lot more REM
sleep when born in comparison to their adult years. For example, the
human foetus, when thirty weeks old, spends all its uterine time in REM
sleep – complete with eye motility and facial expressions. This complete
preoccupation with dreams is sharply reduced to a mere eight hours in
a day, or 50 percent of its sleep, by the time its umbilical connections
are cut.[13] This further decreases to three hours of REM sleep by the age
of two years and soon afterwards the adult pattern of a little less than
two hours (or 25 percent of sleep) is established. It is also a fact that the
newborn baby's brain is not fully developed, but reaches full maturity
around the same time as REM dreaming starts to decrease. This has led
to the hypothesis that REM sleep is connected in some way with the
maturation of the brain.

The predominance of REM sleep in early life is not specific to the
human baby alone, but is also observed in the newborn puppy, rat,
and hamster. These young ones, like the human child, after birth

take a period of time to reach maturity. One of the exceptions in the mammalian world is the newborn guinea pig who is born mature and its brain does not develop after birth. It exhibits very little REM sleep after birth, thus corroborating our hypothesis.[14] Another confirmation comes from the fact that a premature human baby spends an increased time (75 percent) in REM sleep as compared to the normal baby, since the brain is less developed. The occurrence of so much REM sleep raises some difficult questions about the relationship of REM sleep and dreaming. For example, if in the early intrauterine life of the human foetus REM sleep is the all-encompassing mode of existence, then what could it be dreaming of, without any life experience to dream from? Traditional Hindus would, of course, affirm that it is recapitulating its past-life experiences! They, of course, viewed life, death, and the afterlife as a continuum, a theme we will reflect on in the last part of the book.

The other functions of REM sleep

Some researchers link the scanning activity of the eyes during REM, which we share with other mammals, as part of our instinctual apparatus for self-preservation. We perform a similar activity in the waking state when we walk into a strange room and our eyes dart back and forth to take in as much as possible. Perhaps this vigilance mechanism persists periodically even when we are asleep and defenceless.[15]

Other research data has highlighted a correlation between survival and dreams. When an animal is coping in a manner that involves its survival, like the predatory behaviour in a hungry cat, or the flight syndrome in apprehensive rabbits, or the defensive exploration in a starving rat, their brains emit the same signal – theta rhythms. Conversely, it is argued that when theta rhythms are detected then it indicates that the animal is behaving in a manner crucial for its survival, in other words coping with a situation. It was discovered that all animals emit theta rhythms during REM sleep. This led Jonathan Winson of Rockefeller University to conclude that REM episodes are the nightly record of a basic mammalian memory process: information gathered during waking is being reprocessed during REM sleep into memory for the purpose of survival, or for the organism to cope with the demands of living.[16]

Could these be the reasons why we need to sleep and dream? Unfortunately there are no definitive answers; these are only speculations. Though each of these hypotheses enjoys some experimental support, the mechanism of sleep and hence dreaming is still not wholly understood. Many questions remain unanswered. For all we know there may not be a single common function. Perhaps sleep and dream serve as a still unknown cellular function that supports maturational processes in the young, temperature regulation in small animals,[17] and/or higher mental processes in adult humans, among other functions. We thus cannot ascribe only an evolutionary or biological imperative to dreaming; it just may be that dreams cater to developmental needs and may still be imbued with inherent meaning. No scientific discovery or research artefact has been able to convincingly demonstrate that dreams do not have any meaning.

REM research has reached a hiatus

Laboratory dream research had, by the late eighties, reached a point of diminishing returns. The discovery of a relationship between dreaming and objectively verifiable states of sleep in the fifties had heralded the hope that, after millennia spent in speculation, we had finally penetrated the essence of dreaming, its fundamental building blocks. It was believed that dream episodes would be faithfully and exclusively mapped by the neurological events of REM sleep, as both of them represent different aspects of the same activity. It was now a matter of painstakingly detailing the features of REM sleep, secure in the assumption that the dreaming process was also being documented. Once completed it would enable neurophysiologists to confidently expound on the dreaming process, its function, and meaning. Unfortunately the aim of a one-to-one linkage of the events in dreams with the physiology of the brain during REM has proven too ambitious. Another reason that shook the neurophysiological theory from its roots, and also contributed to this hiatus, involved asking some very basic questions, which were thought to have been settled much earlier but were not.

The implication of Aserinsky and Kleitman's momentous discovery of the cyclical recurrence of REM sleep was that it is identical with dreaming. All along it has been argued that we dream when we are in REM sleep, and we do not dream when we are in NREM sleep. Conversely, whenever we dream we have to be exhibiting REM sleep characteristics. Researchers began to allude to REM sleep as a necessary and sufficient condition for dream sleep. Thus when an animal exhibited REM sleep it was concluded that it was dreaming.

David Foulkes, a cognitive psychologist, and other researchers felt this REM sleep-dreaming equation may be hasty and far too general a conclusion. They questioned the common-sense definition of a dream. Foulkes asked whether any report of mental content, including thoughts, recalled from sleep could be classified as a dream. Kleitman and Dement had accepted as dreams only coherent, fairly detailed descriptions; vague or fragmentary impressions were not recorded as dream recall.[18] Foulkes, to circumvent this definitional issue, did not ask his subjects when awakened, 'Were you dreaming?' but asked, 'Was anything going through your mind?' This approach elicited a lot more material that hitherto had not been labelled as dreaming. We give below two dreams reported by the same person on the same night. The first report was when this person was experiencing NREM sleep, while the second report is from a REM awakening later that night:

> NREM report: *I had been dreaming about getting ready to take some kind of an exam. It had been a very short dream. That's just about all that it contained. I don't think I was worried about it.*

> REM report: *I was dreaming about exams. In the early part of the dream, I was dreaming that I had just finished taking an exam and it was a very sunny day outside. I was walking with a boy who was in some of my classes with me. There was a sort of a ... a break, and someone mentioned a grade they had gotten in a social science exam, and I asked them if the social science marks had come in. They said yes. I didn't get mine because I had been away for a day.*[19]

Both reports appear to be about the same subject. Clearly Foulkes was justified in his redefinition; the first report is as much a dream as the second one. There are, of course, differences between the two. The former is more thoughtlike, while the latter is more dreamlike with the perceptual vividness and imagery that is associated with dreaming. NREM reports of dreams tend to be shorter, with less intense visual imagery, and lower levels of physical activity and emotional involvement than dream reports from the REM stage of sleep. Foulkes's study reported a dramatic number of mental occurrences that happened outside REM sleep.

Subjects awakened during the brief sleep-onset transitional period – the hypnagogic state – produced dream reports in 90–100 percent of experimental trials. This frequency is the same as that of dream reports elicited from awakenings from the REM state. Even non-REM awakenings produced dream reports in 20–60 percent of experimental trials.[20] This shows that every time a person dreams, he or she does not necessarily have to be experiencing REM, which goes against the earlier assumption that if we are not exhibiting a REM episode we could not be dreaming. Clearly, dreams can and do occur outside the narrow confines of the REM state. A number of studies were conducted with this renewed criterion of dreaming. The evidence trickling out of sleep laboratories confirmed that REM sleep is not the only condition for dreaming. Currently almost all researchers believe that REM is not synonymous with dreaming, NREM sleep is not a dreamless void, and that mental activity, in one form or the other, occurs through all stages of the sleep cycle.

What has emerged is that different stages of sleep and sleep onset are associated with discernibly different dream characteristics. In the early period of sleep onset there may only be incomplete images (like a number hanging in mid-air), or even one image superimposed on another. Since hypnagogic dreams occur in a transitional period – from wakefulness to sleep – they are mostly concerned with everyday experience, as though events are not as yet distant from the sleeping mind but are being mulled over. There is not much emotional affect in them. In contrast, REM-state dreams display a maximal organization of images from which coherent narrative reports emerge. These are the dreams we are familiar with. NREM reports, on the other hand, are usually purely verbal. They may easily be mistaken for thinking, being more akin to thoughts and generally lacking in expressive imagery like motion, vivid colour, or emotional involvement.[21] Perhaps in the early phase of sleep-laboratory research, subjects when awakened from NREM sleep and asked to relate a dream would have drawn a blank. They would have thought that they had been thinking and not dreaming!

Foulkes, in addition to this, discovered through laboratory studies that there are lower levels of dreaming in children until the age of about nine to eleven. In young children, REM awakenings did not reliably translate into dream retrieval. Foulkes denies that this represents a failure to recall or articulate dreams on the part of children, but is reflective of a lack in dream generation. Other studies did confirm his thesis but were unable to silence its critics. Support, however, came from an unexpected source. It was found that patients with brain lesions registered REM activity but failed to have dreams. Based on this, and the studies conducted on children, can we speculate that REM sleep is neither sufficient nor necessary for dreaming? Other stages of sleep also foster dreams. In short, REM sleep cannot be equated to dreaming, nor is NREM a state from which dreams are totally absent. Furthermore, dreamlike experiences can occur at all times of the night, and sometimes can even be elicited during quiet wakefulness. This would imply that REM physiologists may not be better equipped to identify and comment on the function of dreams, nor can we claim that their theories are the ultimate explanation of all dream phenomena. Nevertheless, the above does not imply that there is no connection between REM sleep and dreams; it only implies that the relationship is not exclusive. REM sleep remains the state from which long vivid dreams can be most reliably retrieved. The task that lies ahead of us is to identify a mechanism or a model of the mind that encompasses dreaming. 'Decades of psychophysiological research has made it clear that this is not a job that dream biology can and will do for us.'[22]

The need to go beyond Hobson and Freud

Perhaps, as Dr Harry Hunt from Brock University points out, there is a common approach between the psychoanalysts and the neuro-physiologists,[23] and we may have to go beyond both of them. Both analyse the dream as the interaction between two agencies – for the former, they are the ego and the unconscious, and for the latter, the brainstem and the cortex. Furthermore, both acknowledge that dreams result from a competition between a coherent organizing system (order) and a more primitive and ultimately disruptive tendency (chaos). Freud believed the dream is a delirium, a compromise between the ego and infantile impulses; Hobson attributes the genesis of the dream to competing neuronal populations within the primitive brainstem, the cognitive cortex synthetically making cohesive the dream's inherent randomness. Again both conceive a 'higher' agency imposing order on the input from the 'lower'. They then attribute a varying level of meaning to the resulting compromise: Freud denies any meaning to the dream itself, attributing it solely to the underlying cause; Hobson grudgingly concedes implied meaning to an otherwise empty structure. Disagreeing with them are other dream theorists who maintain that not all of dreaming is from a 'primitive' or 'disruptive' source. They view dreams as the spontaneous expressions of a symbolic intelligence that is different but not inferior to wakeful cognition, and which often can be self-referential, as it can be sensitive to current emotional concerns. Rather than view the unconscious as a constantly threatened collection of repressed desires, these other thinkers have broadened the Freudian conception to make it friendlier, more accessible. No longer is it swamped only with dreaded urges. Instead, they have redefined the role of the unconscious as an ally, eager to rehearse strategies that are important to our waking reality, like solving problems that periodically arise. This, in turn, would affect our understanding of consciousness, the model of dreaming, and, ultimately, how we view ourselves.

Possibly this represents a decisive step away from dreams being considered utterly insignificant. The two modern models – 'one controlling sleep, the other controlling mood' – have not given completely satisfactory answers, but they have shepherded us away from the belief that dreams are insignificant. If I am allowed to borrow Hobson's analogy,[24] our cup of conviction about the significance of dreams is now at least half-full, whereas previously it was completely empty.

Freud, like many before and possibly after him, believed he had understood the essence of dreaming. In a letter[25] alluding to the house where he had first analysed his own dream and, encouraged by his analysis, had consequently proceeded to formulate his theory, Freud had mused, 'Do you suppose that some day a marble tablet will be placed on the house, inscribed with these words? – "In This House, on July 24th, 1895 the Secret of Dreams was Revealed to Dr. Sigm. Freud."'

He continued to add, quite rightly, 'At the moment there seems little prospect of it.'

Perhaps it was also evident to one of dreaming's most evolved initiates that the children of the night had still not divulged all of their secrets! If humankind wanted to fully comprehend dreaming, then clearly more was required. It was towards this end that Jung made his own unique descent into the unconscious. Humankind's dialogue with dreams continued.

PART 3

THE DREAM:
A MIRROR OF THE PERSONALITY

The dream possesses two characteristics which should make it highly eligible for serious and systematic investigation. It is a personal document and it is a projection. As a personal document it is more frank and intimate than a diary and as a projection it requires no ink-blots or pictures to bring it into existence.

Calvin Hall

Chapter 9

JUNG LIBERATES
THE UNCONSCIOUS

Anyone who is conscious of his guiding principle knows with
what indisputable authority it rules his life. But generally
consciousness is too preoccupied with the attainment of
some beckoning goal to consider the nature of the spirit that
determines its course.

C. G. Jung

The burden of every dream theory that we have looked at so far
– ancient, psychoanalytical, and physiological – is the bizarre nature
of dreams. But are most dreams bizarre? There may be some dreams that
do not conform to the waking world, but there are many that simply
aren't that strange. In fact, recent studies involving a large number of
dreams have also revealed that relatively few dreams are very bizarre.[1]
Perhaps they have acquired a reputation for being so because mostly it
is the bizarre dream, or the bizarre part of a dream, that is remembered
and narrated.

Dreams have a story to tell
Scant notice has been given to another attribute that is possibly more
distinctive of dreaming than its strangeness. Dreams usually have
a coherent train of related images. Very rarely is a scene in a dream

impinged upon simultaneously by another scene or by different thoughts and images. Rather, they are episodic in nature; there is an unfoldment akin to the narration of a plot. A jumble of disparate images does not constellate most dreams. They are thematically single-minded, with a tendency to tell one story at a time. Possibly this kind of focus is not available even in wakefulness; one is listening to a speaker and one's mind is elsewhere. Could there be an organizing, ordering principle evident in dreams similar to the order and structure we impose on all narration? Perhaps this inherent order is best illustrated through a dream. A retired military general dreamt:

> I was on parade with a number of young officers, and our commander-in-chief was inspecting us. Eventually he came to me, but instead of asking a technical question he demanded a definition of the beautiful. I tried in vain to find a satisfactory answer, and felt most dreadfully ashamed when he passed on to the next man, a very young major, and asked him the same question. This fellow came out with a damned good answer, just the one I would have given if only I could have found it. This gave me such a shock that I woke up.[2]

The dream seems preposterous at first glance – an army chief quizzing a general on the definition of beauty at a parade! Notwithstanding this strange question, the dream does have a consistent theme unfolding through a dramatic plot. The dream opens with an exposition, revealing the characters and setting up the plot. It involves a parade, which is being inspected by the chief. The plot unfolds with the chief questioning the general. Instead of asking a question related to the military, the chief asks the general to define 'beautiful', which takes the latter by surprise. A definite tension emerges as this complication in the story is introduced. His inability to answer develops into a conflict within the protagonist of the dream. The young major's excellent answer represents the response to this conflict and signals the conclusion of the dream plot.

The dreamer had narrated this dream as an example of the inherent worthlessness of dreams to a co-passenger on a train who happened to be a dream analyst. When the analyst asked him if he had noted anything interesting about the major, the general felt that the young officer had looked just like he did when he was a young major. The analyst suggested that the dream was perhaps drawing the general's attention to something he had possessed when he was a major but had since forgotten or lost. After some reflection the general remembered that he had been deeply interested in art, but this interest had to be sacrificed due to the pressures of his profession. The dream was prompting him to pick up his old interest, which was related to beautiful things – art. Not only was the dream a coherent, structured episode, it also conveyed a message of significance to the general. The bizarreness of the dream rested in the general being portrayed as two separate people: the major, representing the person he was in his youth, and his present self, which was enacted by the general himself. The dream, like nature, may often be obscure, but it is not deceitful, nor does it distort or disguise; instead it portrays what it intends to convey. Dreams only appear misleading because the conscious mind is unable or unwilling to comprehend the point in question, like the general had not understood the actual intent of the dream – to highlight his inability to make space for his interest in art throughout his professional life.

If we view a dream as a structured episode – a tale being told with characters and settings, with a distinct beginning, middle, and end – will we have to set aside those theories that do not ascribe to dreams their intrinsic organization? Have these theories – focusing only on the aberrant part of the dream, its incongruence – ignored the central feature of dreaming: telling a story? The elements that appear strange in it may but be a lisp, a fumble, as we often make while conversing. A stumble over a part of a sentence does not mean that the entire thought is meaningless (Hobson), or that it has to be paraphrased by another thought (Freud).

If we are honest about it we would have to concede that dream images are so captivating that they lead us to believe that we are seeing real events till we awaken. Furthermore, we are often awestruck by the creativity of dreams. For most of us, our imaginative ability in waking life is not as impressive as the storytelling ability of our dreaming mind. As Dostoevsky said, dreams 'often have a singular actuality, vividness and extraordinary semblance of reality. ... the whole picture ... filled with details so delicate, so unexpected, but so artistically consistent, that the dreamer, were he an artist ... could never have invented them in the waking state'.[3]

Dreams are inherently imaginative creations and not merely sense perception

Another reason to question the hypothesis that dreams are meaningless sensory perceptions (because of their bizarreness) and support their being an imaginative or creative act is the inability of the modern dream theorists – for example, Hobson and Freud – to incorporate the creative potential of the sleeping mind. Freud had denied any significance to the actual dream, and then, to add insult to injury, devalued its underlying content to archaic/primitive perceptions capable of only primary-process expression. This effectively relegated dreaming to a reflexive drive-discharge mechanism that eventually represents unconscious impulses as visual perception. The neurobiologists similarly restrict dreaming by attributing dreams to a neuronal stimulus triggering a response in the visual areas of the brain, again dismissing it as mere sense perception rather than assigning any higher mental phenomenon in the dream's generation. Even if we concur with the biologists and psychoanalysts that dream images are akin to sense perceptions, they cannot still be divorced completely from some intrinsic creative or imaginative involvement. In fact, current cognitive psychology views all perception as a constructive mental act,[4] to the extent that even the sensory images we experience while awake are ascribed a creative cognitive component.

Let us elucidate this by considering an incontestable sensory perception: grass is green. To characterize this as a pure sense perception is but convenient shorthand for a larger creative function. For within the boundaries of this simple perception a creative intelligence, a cognitive ability, is at work. A detailed description of this simple act would state that light bouncing off the grass (the stimulus) strikes the retinal mechanism of the eye (receptor), and is converted into neural impulses. These, in turn, activate the visual areas of the brain. At this point a truly remarkable transformation occurs. Colourless light reflected by a colourless object (grass) and collected by a colourless receptor (retina) gives rise to the experience of colour in consciousness.[5] Though there is an invariable correlation between colour and the frequency of light, this transformational act cannot be exercised primarily by purely stimulus-receptor mechanisms. A higher-order phenomenon of recognition capable of distinguishing, sorting, and comparing has to be invoked. Thus, even if we accept dreams as sense phenomena, we will have to invoke an organizing tendency, an 'intelligent supervisor' that directs and guides the sensory images. Furthermore, if we cling to the simplistic notion that when awake we see images because actual objects stimulate them, then how do we explain the presence of imagery during a dream in the absence of any external stimulus? Would we then grant reality to these dream objects? And to what would we ascribe the origin of dream imagery involving surreal objects or alien images that have no material counterparts? Clearly it would be simpler to postulate that some cognitive mechanism (or supernatural agency) operates to activate and integrate stored memory into the images of dreams.[6] In other words, sense perceptions tell us something *is*. But they do not tell us *what* it is. This is not told to us by a physiological process of perception, but by the psychic process of *apperception*.[7]

In saying all this the intention is not to digress into philosophical subtleties of 'image' and 'perception', but rather to point out that the exclusive concentration on but one aspect of the dream has generated theories, which, though distinct from each other, have only conceived dreaming as an inferior activity. The Hobson dream arises from biological processes that are as creative as our digestive system, while to Freud the dream is a product of infantile drives seeking discharge, developmentally no different than a primitive mechanism of stimulus-and-response. A different view of the formal features of dream, like its narrative coherence and/or creative imagination, would necessitate it to be cast in a very different mould. The chaos that was foundational to the dream would then have to be replaced by order. This order would then become fundamental to dreaming and thereby affect its analysis. Another example of a dream and its interpretation may be illustrative:

> I was in a house I did not know, which had two storeys. It was 'my house'. I found myself in the upper storey, where there was a kind of salon furnished in fine old pieces in rococo style ... But then it occurred to me that I did not know what the lower floor looked like. Descending the stairs, I reached the ground floor. There everything was much older, and I realised this part of the house must date from about the fifteenth or sixteenth century ... I came upon a heavy door, and opened it. Beyond it, I discovered a stone stairway that led down into the cellar. Descending again, I found myself in a beautifully vaulted room which looked exceedingly ancient ... I knew the walls dated from Roman times ... I looked more closely at the floor ... and again I saw a stairway of narrow stone steps leading down into the depths. These, too, I descended, and entered a low cave cut into the rock. Thick dust lay on the floor, and in the dust were scattered bones and broken pottery, like remains of a primitive culture. I discovered two human skulls, obviously very old and half disintegrated.[8]

Is this dream characterized only by bizarreness? Or is it a lucid narrative about an imaginative exploration of the dreamer's house? There are, no doubt, some strange twists and turns as the story unfolds.

The explorer keeps discovering new staircases, which take him into ever-older parts of the house. Is this dream totally empty of meaning?

If, like Freud, we consider the dream to be a façade – a mere perception – behind which its meaning is hidden, then the most important image of this dream are the two skulls. In fact, the whole dream appears to be an exploration aimed specifically at uncovering these two objects. To decode the dream the psychoanalyst would strive to find a wish connected with these skulls. This can only be a secret death wish, which the dreamer feels towards someone he knows, and the identification of this would uncover the 'true' meaning of the dream. Thus, in effect, the significance of the dream does not rest in the story told by the images, but resides elsewhere. The imagery in itself is meaningless except that it provides an association to guide the analysis towards the real issue underlying the dream.

On the other hand, if a dream is considered to be a direct and honest portrayal of the dreamer's inner world, then the above dream would be understood very differently. The house then represents the dreamer's psyche, his waking mind represented by the salon. The dream also suggests that there are many levels of the mind/psyche, which have not been explored by the dreamer. If the exploration is undertaken it would take the dreamer to those caverns of the mind that are historically ancient, seemingly unrelated to and far removed from his present life and experience. Yet these deep, dark reaches of the psyche are somehow related to his current state of consciousness: they support the uppermost storey of the house. The chambers constructed in past times perhaps signify bygone stages of consciousness. The deeper the dreamer descended, the more alien and remote the chamber became. The last chamber – a cave – depicts the remains of a primitive culture, which perhaps suggests that a part of his mind borders on the life of an animal – indicative of the animal urges that reside within us but which, checked by the process of civilization, lie in abeyance. The dream is then a well-knit story about the structure of the dreamer's psyche. Indeed, it might be an accurate map of the entire territory of the human mind!

The analyst alluded to above was Sigmund Freud himself and the dream belonged to a disciple, who Freud was grooming as his successor. The dream marked a turning point in the relationship between the two men. This disciple was not prepared to view the dream merely as a hidden death wish about his wife and sister-in-law, as Freud was prone to suggest. He wished to probe much deeper into the dream imagery.

His probing would necessitate a major overhaul of our conception of the unconscious that supports our consciousness and behaviour. Our next clue to the puzzle of dreaming is provided by this very same disciple of Freud – Carl Gustav Jung.

Jung

Jung (1875–1961) broke away on ideological grounds, disagreeing with Freud's insistence that the dream is merely the distorted version of underlying latent thoughts that more truly represent the dreamer's subjective state. Jung says, 'To me dreams are a part of nature, which harbours no intention to deceive, but expresses something as best as it can.' He, therefore, did not accept Freud's distinction between the manifest and latent content of a dream. Jung also disagreed with the Freudian conception that the conscious and unconscious stand opposed to each other. Jung felt the psyche is a self-regulating system that maintains equilibrium as the body does. Every process that goes too far immediately calls for a compensatory activity. The dream, according to Jung, is the expression of an involuntary psychic process that tends to function in compensatory relation to one's conscious outlook. Dreams appear strange to us because we fail to see the dream's intent. They are not meaningless, but rather they are like a text we cannot read and whose language we may have to learn to understand. Jung saw the bizarreness in dreams as characteristic of dream language – exaggerations to attract attention. By this Jung had answered the fundamental questions of dreaming differently from Freud.

Needless to say, the implications of this disagreement for dream analysis were profound. Though Jung acknowledged Freud's contributions, he was unwilling to submit to Freudian dogma. Jung was not prepared to attribute exclusive importance to infantile sexual trauma nor grant psychological universality to sexuality. Difficulty arose primarily with the Freudian contention that most symbols are a disguise for the genitals or the sexual act. To Jung, the sexual component of dreams is often the means of expression and not always the meaning and the aim of the dream. Just like in waking life the use of sexual slang ('prick', 'motherfucker') is not intended to refer to genitals or sexual practices as such, but simply to attack someone who has offended us on quite different grounds.[9]

Jung looked for a meaning that accorded with the overall context of the dream. For example, a tree in a dream cannot be taken only as a phallic object, harking back to the strong libidinal conflicts experienced by the pubertal dreamer while resting under it. Its shelter and shade can also represent security and support. At a deeper level, trees may symbolize equilibrium because their profusion signifies the ecological balance between man and nature. And, at a transcendental level, a tree may represent the Tree of Life, as in the Kabbalah, expressing the cosmology of all creation and the myriad interrelationships existing within it.

Let us analyse a dream using both the Freudian and Jungian approaches to demonstrate their differences clearly. An unmarried woman patient of Jung dreamt that *'someone gave her a wonderful, richly ornamented, antique sword dug up out of a tumulus'*.[10]

The dreamer associated the sword with her father's dagger, which he had once flashed in the sun in front of her. It had made a great impression on her. Her father had died when she was young. He had been an energetic, strong-willed man with an impetuous temperament, and had been adventurous in his love affairs.

A Freudian analysis would immediately circumscribe the dream to a phallic fantasy, the antique sword representing the dreamer's infantile wish for the father's weapon, her 'penis envy'. Instead of restricting this weapon to elementary sexual urges, Jung's approach would associate the sword to the dreamer's Celtic ancestry – to an intractable, impulsive temperament similar to her father's. The dream had no latent content as it had clearly stated its intention – that her temperament, inherited from the father, had been buried too long. Till then she had been a spoilt child and completely given to sexual fantasies. The dream was not deceiving but was compensating. It was telling her that she needed to claim the strong weapon of her father's personality as her own. Thus the dream about the buried sword alluded to something beyond sexual compulsions, representing the neglected truth about her own personality, which Jung excavated through constructive analysis.

Perhaps the essential difference between the two approaches rests in the decoding of a symbol. The psychoanalytic inability to transcend the sexual nature of a symbol may be encapsulated in a question often asked of Freudians: If most elongated objects are symbols of the phallus, then what does the phallus, in a dream, represent?[11] Jung saw the sexual symbolism that emerged in dreams as indicative of a deeper, non-sexual level of meaning.

Jung had been introduced to this dimension of dreams when he was young. He had dreamt that in the meadow of a vicarage (his father was a pastor) he suddenly discovered a subterranean chamber with a massive tree trunk made of skin and naked flesh, with a rounded head and no hair. The image was an obvious phallus that was standing on a wonderfully rich golden throne.[12] It had paralysed him with terror, and for years he was haunted by this dream. Only much later did he realize that what he had seen in the dream was a phallus. It would still take many more years for him to understand that it was a ritual phallus, not to be confused with the penis; that it was not a sexual allusion but an iconoclastic image of an exalted pagan symbol challenging the conceptions of a Christian pastor's son.

Also, for Jung the notion of wish-fulfilment was altogether too confining a container to hold dreams. He felt that our psyche is much deeper, and consequently dreams have a much wider significance. Consider, for example, Jung's dream/vision of Zeus and Hera making love. To Freud, this dream would be representative of 'primal scene' material; it arises from the child's early experience of his or her parents as omnipotent and omniscient, and therefore they are personified in dreams as powerful mythological beings. For Jung, however, these mythological beings were the only suitable symbolic vehicle for something abstract and numinous that encompasses and transcends us, but cannot be contained in discursive formulation. He, thus, took his dream as a vision of the sacred *Hieros Gamos*, representing the marriage of psychic opposites.[13] The two interpretations are poles apart. Freud believed that the grandiose and mythological character of the imagery was expressive of a distortion of the parental image, making it disproportionately powerful, and thus highlighting a malaise. Jung saw the same images as the symbolic union of opposites. The dream for Jung has become a cohesive unifying metaphor for individuation (personal growth), while for Freud it remains a loose array of personal memories and mere current conflicts. And by this Jung had widened dream perception, lifting dreams from the shackles of repression, and restoring in them the dignity they deserve.

This completely different approach to dreaming was possible because for Jung a dream is a subjectively powerful and cohesive experience, not a clouded episode born of a compromise between contradictory primary personal forces. Jung believed that dreams emanate from the deeper depths of the psyche, which is inherently ordered and intrinsically creative, in contradistinction to the Freudian unconscious that is fractured by conflicting urges. The psyche is not merely seeking satisfaction through the dream, but aims to make the person whole by uniting and integrating the personality with its unconscious roots. Thus the dream is not an automatic response, but a purposive and flexible message from the psyche to the personality.

The dream is no longer hostage to desire and the remains of the day world; instead it now has the freedom to assemble images from a vast collective reservoir, which is not limited merely to personal memory. Freud had a monotony of interpretation that excavated only the sexual foundations, and resolved the dream into components of ungratified infantile memories. What the psyche had made of the instinctual impulse was omitted from the interpretation.

To Jung, dream formation is not an isolated event unrelated to other aspects of the dreamer's life, but it can become a part of an ongoing process of dialogue between the dreamer and his or her psyche, where the preceding dreams were amplifications of the imagery and content of the current dream. Dreams on subsequent nights become a verification to confirm or correct a previous interpretation. Hence the dream as a series of communications becomes more important than the individual episode. Jung asserted, 'I attach little importance to the interpretation of single dreams.'[14]

Thus, to Jung the dream is a coherent and creative message with the intent to reveal and not conceal the objectively autonomous nature of the underlying psyche. The aim of the dream is wholeness and its intention is to regulate the personality to serve its vision of order and balance.

A new conception of dreaming necessitates a reformulation of our understanding of dreaming – the source of dreams, their form, and function. This can only be done if we revamp our Freudian conceptions of the unconscious, its contents, and its interactions. It thus may be appropriate to digress a little and appreciate the key concepts of Jung's psychology around which the personality of an individual revolves. All of Jung's theories are attempts to illuminate the workings of the human psyche. Most are closely related to his work on dreams. Perhaps his conception would aid in grasping dreaming in a totally different manner.[15]

Psyche and consciousness

Jung called the personality as a whole the *psyche*. Its original Latin meaning is 'spirit' or the 'soul', but in Jungian psychology it embraces all thought, feeling, and behaviour, both conscious and unconscious.

It functions as a guide that regulates and adapts the individual to his or her social and physical environment. Jung said, 'Psychology, however, is neither biology nor physiology nor any other science than just this knowledge of the psyche.'[16]

The concept of the psyche affirms Jung's primary idea that a person is a whole to begin with. Freud had assumed that the personality is an assemblage of parts, acquired layer by layer in the process of growing up. Jung explicitly rejects this conception of personality. Human beings do not strive for wholeness; they already have it, they are born with it.

The role of experience, then, lies in the development of what already inheres as wholeness in the psyche, rather than being the fulcrum that organizes an unstructured personality. Jung distinguishes three levels of the psyche: *consciousness*, *personal unconscious*, and the *collective unconscious*.

Consciousness is the only part of the mind that is known directly by the individual. It appears early in life, probably prior to birth. Consciousness is gradually nourished as the child grows, through the application of the four mental functions that Jung identified as *thinking*, *feeling*, *sensing*, and *intuiting*. As it grows, the child's character will develop one or more of these functions at the cost of others, distinguishing itself, say, as a predominantly thinking or feeling type. The process by which the consciousness of a person becomes individualized or differentiated from other people is known as *individuation*.[17]

Individuation and ego

Individuation and consciousness go hand in hand in the development of personality. The greater the individuation, the more consciousness that is attained. The goal of individuation is to achieve wholeness. From the process of individuation of consciousness a new element is produced, which Jung called the *ego*.

The ego is composed of conscious perceptions, memories, thoughts, and feelings. It plays the critical role of gatekeeper to consciousness, and only it can sanction an idea, a feeling, a memory, or a perception to be brought into consciousness. Perhaps that explains why, sometimes, even though an object is lying in front of our eyes we fail to notice it; the ego does not allow it to be 'seen'. (As we have discussed earlier, seeing is not just a matter of light waves bouncing off an object and collected by the eye, something else is involved.) This selective perception serves the important role of protecting consciousness from being overwhelmed by the mass of impressions that bombard us at every moment. Possibly this enables us to remain sane and focused. But what governs this filtering process? Partly it is determined by the function dominant in the personality. For example, a thinking personality will allow entry to ideas more readily than feelings. Another filtering mechanism is one in which ideas and memories that evoke anxiety are refused entry. However, this may not always be successful. Sometimes the strength or intensity of an experience is powerful enough to batter its way through the gates of the ego. Weaker ones are usually repelled. Possibly the most important factor is the level of individuation – a progressive integration of unconscious contents; a more individuated person will allow more things to become conscious. Those experiences that are denied entry into consciousness by the ego are not lost to the psyche, but are stored, as Freud told us, within the unconscious.

Complexes

Jung asserted that the contents of the unconscious are grouped together in clumps to form what he called *complexes*. This word and its more popular synonym *hang-up* have become a part of our daily vocabulary, and we owe their origin to Jung. It is common to speak of a person having a complex, insinuating that the person is strongly preoccupied by something that swamps his or her thinking and actions. An oft-cited and easily perceived example described by Jung is the mother complex. A man with this complex is dominated by the mother and is extremely sensitive to what she says or feels; her image is always foremost in his mind. All evaluations in his life are made by comparing them with her standards, her ideals, her preferences, and her interests. He will gravitate towards her friends, preferring the company of older women to those of his own age. This tendency, when taken to its extreme, may make him see his mother in every woman. He may never, therefore, be able to perceive any woman as a lover, and this tendency, if not addressed, can only lead to psychological impotence.

But a complex, as Jung discovered, need not be a hindrance in the personality. It actually has quite a contrary side. It is perhaps because of their mother fixation that men control their libidinous desires, and show courtesy and respect to women. The complex can also often provide the drive, the energy, that is essential for outstanding achievement. Most achievers, when viewed intimately, will display a drive powered by a complex. This leads us to the natural question: How do complexes originate?

Two kinds of unconscious

Initially, under the influence of Freud, Jung was inclined to believe that complexes originated in the traumatic experiences of early childhood. This explanation did not contain Jung's curiosity for very long, and led to his discovery of the collective unconscious. He broke free from the belief that our mind (psyche) is determined only by its environmental conditioning, and showed that evolution and heredity provide the blueprints of the psyche, just as they provide the blueprints of the body. There is unquestionable evidence that we have acquired our anatomy as a result of an evolutionary process. Traces of gills appearing during embryonic development attest to our aquatic ancestry, and vestiges of a tailbone in the foetus reflect our mammalian heritage. Thus Jung believed that 'just as the human body represents a whole museum of organs, each with a long evolutionary history behind it, so we should expect to find that the mind is organised in a similar way. It can no more be a product without history than is the body in which it exists.'[18]

The mind, according to Jung, has a form of innate programming, which is imprinted in the psyche at birth. This predisposes the human being to meet life experiences in a particular manner. Freud had linked every person to his or her own past; Jung extended this link from the person's infancy to the past of the species and, even prior to that, to the long stretch of organic evolution. The traces of this past, in the form of racial memory, reside in the collective unconscious. Jung thus effectively placed the psyche within the evolutionary process, visualizing the unconscious as two distinct chambers.

The division of the unconscious into two parts was arguably Jung's greatest contribution to psychology. Some things are personal and peculiar to each of us and they reside in our personal unconscious. However, this personal unconscious rests upon a deeper layer that is not personal, but has contents that the human race shares irrespective of geographical divides. This grid or underpinning to the personal unconscious appears in different forms in different cultures, empowering their myths and religious legends; it also manifests itself in diverse forms in our deepest and most meaningful dreams. This deeper layer he termed the collective unconscious. In addition to many of his own dreams, some of his patients' dreams contained images that were unlikely to have been a part of the individual's personal experience. For example: 'A patient saw a penis coming out of the centre of the Sun, moving and producing the wind. This made no sense; until Jung came across a reference to the pre-Christian Mithraic religion which described how the wind originated from a tube hanging from the centre of the sun. The patient knew nothing of this Mithraic image, so where did it come from?'[19] These images could not have been authored by a personal unconscious, but only by humankind's unconscious. Jung hypothesized that these motifs – for example, the mandala or the cross – arise out of a common substratum: the collective unconscious.

The collective unconscious is a reservoir of latent images that are predispositions or potentialities for experiencing and responding to the world in age-old ways. Consider, for example, our fear of snakes or of the dark. Typically, the fear is not due to any individual experiences with snakes or the dark, but an inherited disposition. Our primitive ancestors may have experienced this fear for countless generations and they have been imprinted on the psyche. In other words, these fears are not dependent upon personal experience, but owe their origin to collective memory.

Jung posited that the collective unconscious is formed of two components, *instincts* and *archetypes*. They exercise a preformed pattern for personal behaviour to be followed from the day a person is born. 'The form of the world into which he is born is already in him as a virtual image.'[20] A baby does not need to be taught how to draw milk from his or her mother. All that the mother does is to offer her breast and the child responds (instinct).

'Instincts are impulses which carry out actions from necessity, and they have a biological quality, similar to the homing instinct in birds. Instincts determine our actions. Yet in the same manner, Jung suggests that there are innate, unconscious modes of understanding which regulate our perception itself.'[21] These are the archetypes.

Archetypes

Jung believed that human beings are born with numerous predispositions for perceiving and experiencing in specific ways; we are not born tabula rasa, a blank slate. This innate aptitude remains an unconscious potentiality till it comes into contact with the actual experience in life. Consider, for example, the mother: because a virtual image (archetype) of the mother exists in the collective unconscious, it will quickly manifest in a child's perception, and the child will thus respond to the actual mother. The archetypes are crucial in determining our mode of apprehension, just like the instincts determine our actions. 'How we apprehend a situation (archetype) determines our impulse to act. Unconscious apprehension through the archetype determines the form and direction of the instinct. On the other hand, our impulse to act (instinct) determines how we apprehend a situation (archetype).'[22]

Archetypes operate below the threshold of consciousness and therefore their functioning cannot be perceived. Yet they govern every area of our life – birth, forming attachments, puberty, adulthood, courtship, marriage, bringing up children, mid-life concerns, and dying – imbuing them with characteristic behavioural patterns and ideas. Despite obvious variability, the patterns of behaviour that result in mating, in the care of babies and young children, and in the strong attachment of the young to their parents are found in almost all members of the human race. This is archetypal behaviour, which, like instinctual behaviour, is common throughout the human species.

Symbols

Symbols are the outward manifestation of archetypes. Archetypes can only be expressed through symbols because they are deeply buried within the collective unconscious, unknown and unknowable in themselves. The two concepts of the archetype and the symbol are crucial to the Jungian dream and are intimately related. By analysing and interpreting the symbols, whether of dream or art, myth or fantasy, we can capture a glimpse of the collective unconscious and the operation of archetypes.

This is a powerful method because it can seize on any aspect of our life, analyse its involvements, and from it understand our deepest longings and aspirations. Symbols appear not only in nocturnal dreams but also in waking life. Sometimes even inanimate objects co-operate with the unconscious in expressing symbolic patterns. There are numerous well-authenticated accounts of clocks stopping at the moment of their owner's death; mirrors that break; or a picture falling when a death occurs or when someone is going through an emotional crisis. I have a personal example: I was very fond of an old lady who lived at my Teacher's hermitage. After I had returned to the city, she had presented me with two jasmine plants. They invariably reminded me of her. Strangely, within the space of three days both the plants, which were till then healthy, suddenly withered and died. I wondered what had happened. A few days later, news reached me that the dear old lady had passed away.

Jung broke away from Freud's conception that symbols have a fixed meaning. For Jung, symbols have layer upon layer of meaning that analysis would uncover the deeper it probed. A man may dream of inserting a key in a lock, of wielding a heavy stick, or of breaking down a door with a battering ram. Each of these can be treated as a sexual symbol. Jung questioned that if all images symbolize the same thing, then why is one symbol chosen over the other in a dream? The fact that the unconscious prefers one of these specific images is, perhaps, also significant. The task of interpretation is to understand why one symbol has been chosen over another – why the key has been chosen rather than the stick, or the stick rather than the ram. This may lead us to the discovery that the symbol is not sexual in nature but something altogether different.[23]

For Freud the symbol could only be a disguise for a wish seeking fulfilment. Jung took a more holistic view by treating a symbol in two ways. At one level, it is an attempt to satisfy an instinctual impulse that has been frustrated. Our wishes and desires that remain inhibited in waking life account for many of the symbols in dreams. Jung, however, believed that a symbol is more than a disguise. It is also a transformation of instinctual drives. For example, sexual energy is diverted into dance as an art form, or aggression is diverted into competitive games. However, Jung said that a symbol is not mere substitution or a displacement of instinctual energy from its original object to another one. Dance is not only a substitute for sexual activity, it is something much more.

The essential feature of Jung's theory of symbolism is that 'the symbol is not a sign that veils something everybody knows. Such is not its significance; on the contrary, it represents an attempt to elucidate, by means of an analogy, something that still belongs entirely to the domain of the unknown or something that is yet to be.'[24] 'What is it that is "as yet completely unknown and only in the process of formation"? It is an archetype buried in the collective unconscious. A symbol, above all, is an attempt to represent an archetype, but the result is always imperfect.'[25] In the final analysis, symbols are representations of the psyche; they are projections of all aspects of our nature. They not only contain the wisdom of the race, but also the wisdom individually acquired by the person. They can also represent that person's future levels of development. However, the knowledge stored in the symbol is not directly apprehensible and the symbol must be deciphered in order to discover its message.

A symbol thus has two aspects, one *retrospective* and guided by the instincts, the other *prospective* and guided by the ultimate goals of the transcendent personality. A dream can be analysed using either of these aspects. A retrospective analysis will expose the instinctual basis of the symbolism, and a prospective analysis reveals the yearnings of the individual for completion, rebirth, harmony, and purification.[26] The dream about the antique sword dug out of a tumulus exemplifies this distinction. A causal reductive type of analysis would view this image as the father's 'weapon'; while a teleological, finalistic type of analysis would understand it as an insight marking the process of individuation. Jung believed that the prospective character of a symbol has been disregarded in favour of its instinctual origins. For a complete understanding of the symbol or dream both its aspects should be considered because there is both a driving and an attracting force involved in the creation of a symbol. The push is provided by instinctual energy, the pull by transcendental goals. Neither of them alone suffices to create a symbol.

Dreams

Jung, as mentioned earlier, disagreed with the Freudian conception of the dream. To him the unconscious is not a chaotic cauldron seething with repressed infantile desires or an undifferentiated primeval soup, but contains the collective wisdom of the species. He insisted that the human psyche is structured around an inherently organizing principle, which is also evidenced in dreams.

Like Freud, Jung also believed that dreams are a product of psychical activity. Though some images may be influenced by external or internal stimuli, mainly the images are determined by the unconscious. Their point of departure arose due to their differing conceptions of the unconscious. Jung argued that if the unconscious were akin to the Freudian conception of it, then the lifting of repression by dream analysis (or any other means) would lower unconscious activity. Those who attend to their dreams would dream less, and the evolved elect, in the foreseeable future, might even dispense with dreaming altogether. However, studies indicate that as we grow older the time spent in dreaming does not vary, barring a very small decline in old age. Consequently, a decrease in dreaming may have more to do with age rather than with emotional maturity, or with the draining of the unconscious of its cathected content.

Based on this observation that dreaming persists, Jung deduced that an underlying process continuously generates dreams, only a small proportion of which surfaces into awareness. The dream for him is not the 'remnants left over from the day, as the crumbs that fall into the twilit world from the richly laden table of our consciousness'. In Freudian theory, the dark depths of the night are nothing but an empty sack, containing no more than what falls into it from above – the conscious day world. For Jung it was the other way round: the day world or consciousness contains whatever happens to fall into its lap from the unconscious.[27] This does not mean that the dream cannot have conscious determinants, but that all psychic contents must have their roots in the unconscious. It is from there that waking life derives its meaning. Jung said, 'A dream is nothing but a lucky idea that comes to us from the dark, all-unifying world of the psyche. What would be more natural, when we have lost ourselves amid the endless particulars and isolated details of the world's surface, than to knock at the door of dreams and inquire of them the bearings which would bring us closer to the basic facts of human existence?'[28] He ascribed to the unconscious an objective intelligence that can perceive, intuit, gauge, and judge as an autonomous psychic entity whose wisdom far exceeds that of the conscious personality. Through the dream it manifests its capacity to direct and guide consciousness. This objective feature of the unconscious is often unknown to our ego personality. Jung called this objective wisdom of the unconscious the *Self* – the inner guiding factor that is different from the conscious personality and can only be grasped through the investigation of our dreams. This Self is the regulating centre of the psyche and through dream symbols attempts to bring about a constant extension and maturing of the personality by compensating for its shortfalls. How far the personality can develop depends on how much the person is capable of heeding the messages of the Self.

The function of dreaming: compensation

We have arrived at the heart of Jung's dream theory. His keystone hypothesis of dream interpretation is that almost all dreams are *compensatory*. The dream material that emerges takes on the role of modifying, balancing, and adjusting consciousness, thereby restoring psychic equilibrium and ultimately leading to wholeness. It compensates for the neglected aspects of the personality and amends any attitude that has become one-sided. For example, a humble and self-effacing man frequently had dream encounters with great figures from history, such as Napoleon and Alexander the Great. Such illustrious dream acquaintances were compensating for his modest sense of importance, which always made him politely take a back seat.[29]

The compensatory function of dreams is the psyche's attempt at self-regulation. Just as the body attempts to maintain a steady temperature, perspiring when the temperature rises and shivering when the temperature drops, the psychic goal of achieving individuation can only be realized when all of the components of one's psyche are balanced in the quest for wholeness. Compensation then becomes the manifestation of the ordering, objective, purposeful function of the unconscious that is aware of the imbalance in the conscious attitude. It assesses and creates dream symbols that tell an appropriate regulating story to balance and direct consciousness to achieve greater fullness by incorporating the unconscious directives.

Jung questioned the belief that dreams merely reproduce the events of the previous day. Dreams rarely repeat events in an exact manner; they add or subtract something, or round off the experience.[30] Jung felt that this deviation – adding, subtracting, or rounding off (the bizarreness of the dream) – is compensatory in character. Compensation represents a broadening of Freud's wish-fulfilment. Both concepts rely on the dream to provide contents that are denied to consciousness. They differ, however, in that the Jungian dream aspires to wholeness by equalizing and balancing, while the Freudian one regresses to gratify infantile desires. The former represents an intelligent assessment out of a need for order, and is resourceful and flexible, while the latter is automatic and blind.

In Jung's view, the material supplied from the unconscious may be unpleasant or even painful because it shows the dreamer those aspects of his or her life that are going wrong, but which the dreamer has not admitted to him or herself. Dreams express what the ego does not know or understand.

When attempting to understand a dream, Jung always found it helpful to ask: What conscious attitude does it compensate for? Jung quotes the case of a lady known for her stupid prejudices and stubbornly superior arguments. She dreamt:

There is a great social affair to which she is invited. She is received by her hostess (a very bright woman) at the door with the words: 'Oh, how nice that you have come, all your friends are already here and are expecting you.' She leads her to a door, opens it, and the lady steps into – a cowshed.[31]

The dreamer's personality traits that were exaggerated and offensively one-sided were compensated for in the dream by showing them as bovine and mindless. Besides highlighting our blind spots as the above dream shows, compensatory dreams also bring to our awareness neglected areas of our personality.

Jung, as we said, was told a dream by a general in which the commander-in-chief asked him the definition of 'beautiful', which he was unable to answer but a young major in the parade could. That was a compensatory dream, for it pointed out a neglected area of interest that needed to be resurrected and developed. The one-sidedness of the general's rigid, military life was being compensated for by the reminder of his previously stimulating, now abandoned interest in art.

Although the preponderance of dreams is compensatory, some are not. Non-compensatory dreams may be *prospective*, *archetypal*, *extrasensory*, or *traumatic*.

The prospective or anticipatory nature of dreams

Probably the most numerous of the non-compensatory dreams are the anticipatory or prospective dreams. These, too, are dedicated to the realization of the development of the personality, for they come about when the conscious attitude is highly unsatisfactory and the unconscious is attempting to show the dreamer the consequences of continuing on a particular path. Anticipation is a form of warning, a looking forward by the psyche of what will happen if a particular course continues to be taken. According to Jung, 'Dreams prepare, announce, or warn about certain situations, often long before they actually happen. This is not necessarily a miracle or a precognition. Most crises or dangerous situations have a long incubation, only the conscious mind is not aware of it. Dreams can betray the secret.'[32] A prospective dream he said 'results from the fusion of subliminal elements and is thus a combination of all the perceptions, thoughts, and feelings which consciousness has not registered because of their feeble accentuation'.[33] They are not any more prophetic than 'a medical diagnosis or a weather forecast. They are merely an anticipatory combination of probabilities which may coincide with the actual behaviour of things but need not necessarily agree in every detail.'[34] For example, you may have dreamt that the wooden staircase in your house has collapsed, only to find that two days later it actually does collapse. To a Jungian this is not a prophetic dream; it is an example of an anticipatory dream. It is difficult to deny that while traversing up or down you had not heard a barely audible creak, or subliminally not sensed an additional deflection under your weight. The dream is then not precognitive, but merely a conclusion, anticipating information privy to the body, which had registered below the level of conscious awareness.

Anticipatory dreams can be likened to 'a preliminary exercise or a sketch, or a plan roughed out in advance'.[35] This is possible because the psyche takes in both the unconscious and conscious factors in a situation, and armed with foresight can surmise towards what conclusion these forces are headed. By doing so it may even outline the solution for an unusually difficult conflict or it may prepare the dreamer for a future attitude. The dream can be either positive or negative in its import; it may foreshadow specific good fortune or catastrophe.

Archetypal or 'big' dreams

Some dreams go beyond what is only of personal significance. Such dreams often make use of surprising and even incomprehensible symbols (dream bizarreness), and their relationship to the dreamer is difficult to trace. Such dreams are often accompanied with a vividness that compels attention, and they appear as memorable exceptions. These are the kind of dreams that people treasure for years after they have dreamt them; they are archetypal dreams. The major defining features are their uncanny, numinous quality; aesthetically rich structure; geometric and mandala-like patterns; mythological and metaphysical thinking; and the powerful sense of felt meaning conveyed directly in them. These archetypal dreams emerge from the collective unconscious and reappear in symbolic form again and again in myths, religious motifs, and dreams. Often, these dreams provide their own context of meaning, for they are a powerful, non-verbal and relatively ineffable experience. Even if the dream is not understood, it enriches the dreamer's experience because they are more like self-sufficient or cohesive visions, not the patchwork of ordinary dreams that involve the reorganization of memory. Archetypal dreams have about them what Jung called a 'cosmic quality'; a sense of temporal or spatial infinity; movement at tremendous speed over vast distances similar to a comet-like flight through space; an experience of hovering above the Earth; meeting with particular gods or goddesses; a sense of expansion of the self till it transcends its narrow individuality and embraces all of creation.

Archetypal dreams are most likely to occur at important transitional points in life. They also occur at times of upheaval and uncertainty, and mark the process of individuation towards greater cohesion in the personality.

To understand them Jung recommends historical and mythological analogies, or *amplification*, in which associations become more impersonal as they circle around the striking details of the dream imagery. Traditionally, some dreamers have felt the need to hide archetypal dreams as 'precious secrets'. Paradoxically, others, including poets and storytellers, have a strong impulse to relate such dreams. Is their impulse to share them because these dreams have a general meaning that reflects on common human problems? Or do they believe that the endlessly repeated eternal truths are brought to focus through these archetypal dreams?

However, it must be stressed that a purely archetypal dream is a somewhat misleading term. Dreams containing archetypal content nearly always have some personal element in them as well. Perhaps it might be more appropriate to allude to them not as archetypal dreams but as archetypal images or motifs that are the components of the dream. A dream containing one or more such allusions may thus require archetypal amplification.

The first step in analysing any dream: the conscious situation of the dreamer

Jung treated the dream as the psyche's response to the dreamer's conscious or waking situation – events, thoughts, emotions, hopes, fears, and conflicts crowding the person's waking life. The dream, he said, often contains the unconscious complement or compensatory aspect of the current waking situation of the dreamer. Further, the conscious situation that stimulates a dream usually rises from experience that impinges on a complex, or from a problem on which inadequate judgement has been made. This judgement may be a decision, an attitude towards another person, or a self-evaluation. The following example illustrates the need to consider the dreamer's conscious situation while interpreting a dream:

> *My father is driving away from the house in his new car. He drives very clumsily, and I get very annoyed over his apparent stupidity. He goes this way and that, forwards and backwards, and manoeuvres the car into a dangerous position. Finally he runs into a wall and damages the car badly. I shout at him in a perfect fury that he ought to behave himself. My father only laughs, and then I see that he is dead drunk.*[36]

The dream has no foundation in the waking life of the dreamer. His father would never behave as he does in the dream, even if he were drunk. The dreamer had a good relationship with his father. Without knowledge of this the analyst may be prone to finding fault in the father-son relationship because the dream is presenting such an unfavourable picture of the father. Should the analysis of the dream veer towards suggesting that his good relationship with his father is superficial, and therefore founded on deeply entrenched resistances? Once again, if the conscious situation of the dreamer does not betray any neurotic ambivalence in relation to his father, would it be justified to infer such a destructive pronouncement interpretatively? Rather, the meaning of the dream would have to incorporate their actual relationship in its interpretation. In fact, his relationship with his father was not only good but too good. His father was still too much the guarantor of his existence and on account of this the dreamer was unable to see his own reality. In order to bring this to light the unconscious resorts to a kind of artificial blasphemy so as to lower the father's image and elevate the son's. This is done to enable the son to contrast himself with his father, which is the only way he can become conscious of himself. And this would urge the young man to become aware of his own strengths as distinct and apart from his father's. Without knowledge of the conscious situation of the dreamer the real meaning of the dream would have remained in doubt. By understanding the dreamer's waking world, we can rightly view the dream as a compensation of his real-life situation. Here again the self-regulatory nature of the psyche is in evidence. An inadequate conscious attitude is being corrected by the objective eye of the unconscious.

The importance of the conscious situation in dream analysis can be further seen when similar imagery appears in dreams of different people. Would the imagery be interpreted in the same manner for all the dreams? Like Artemidorus nearly two thousand years earlier, Jung concurred that the circumstances of the dreamer would dictate the analysis. Jung illustrated this in the case of two men, one young and the other old, who had both brought him essentially the same dream:

> *A company of young men are riding on horseback across a wide field. The dreamer is in the lead and jumps a ditch of water, just clearing it. The others fall into the ditch.*[37]

The imagery speaks of the dreamer's ability to overcome an obstacle that others are unable to do. For the young man who was cautious and introverted, the dream indicates the possibilities in his life, which he was not exploring and fulfilling. For the old man, an invalid who stubbornly ignored medical instructions, the dream indicated that he had an illusion about his capacities, far above that which held true for his age and situation. In both cases, however, the compensatory mechanism of dreams was operative – for the younger fellow it was a correction of his lack of self-confidence, while for the older man it was redressing his overestimation of himself.

The second step: subjective or objective level of interpretation
Once the context of the dream has been established, it becomes necessary to decide the level at which the dream is to be understood. Jung believed that dreams could be interpreted at either a *subjective* or an *objective* level. Subjective interpretation in this context does not carry the customary connotation of something insubstantial, personal, or illusory. The question to be posed is: Are the figures in the dream to be taken as whoever they are in real life, or are they representative of facets of the dreamer's personality?

A figure is characterized as objective when it appears in the dream as an actual person in his or her actual relationship with the dreamer. Its characterization is subjective when its appearance in the dream portrays a part of the dreamer's personality. The objective approach is indicated if the dream figure is a person important to the dreamer, such as a spouse, members of the dreamer's immediate family, or a close friend. But if the dream figure is not highly significant to the dreamer, a subjective interpretation would be appropriate. Remote relatives, someone the dreamer has not seen for a long time, historical personages, even unknown figures will be subjectively characterized while interpreting the dream. These people then become the personification of something within the dreamer's personality.

Jung used the example of a dream in which a friend appears in the form of a black sheep. If the friend is someone whom the dreamer has not seen for a long time, the figure should be taken subjectively. The dreamer has something of this 'black sheep' in his or her psyche. But if the friend is someone currently important to the dreamer, the interpretation would be objective: The friend is a dishonourable person or there is something dark between him or her and the dreamer.

A woman who dreams of her father may need to face a problem connected with him as the external object of reference, or some aspect of her relationship to him. This would be an objective reading of the dream. Alternatively, subjective interpretation may be understood to mean that she needs to recognize the male principle (as personified by her father) in herself, as in the dream of an ancient dagger in a tumulus. Jung had characterized that dream subjectively, while Freud had given an objective interpretation.

Another criterion for choosing either the objective or the subjective interpretation is the manner in which the dream figure is depicted. If he or she is someone well known to the dreamer and appears photographically (as he or she is), the dream figure is interpreted objectively. But if the dream depicts the figure inaccurately, the misleading traits are likely to be the attributes of the dreamer or the effects of the dreamer's behaviour in a particular situation.

An example is a man's dream in which appeared a drunken, dishevelled, vulgar woman called his 'wife' (though in reality his wife was totally different). Since the dream was grossly inaccurate about the description of his wife, it represented an aspect of himself that was behaving like a degenerate female.

Besides this, the emotional charge associated with a figure in a dream is also significant. When a person with whom the dreamer has a strong emotional connection in waking life appears as an unimportant figure in the dream, a subjective interpretation should be favoured. Freud had called this displacement of emotional affect a disguise, but according to Jung it is a means of separating the emotion from the person in an effort to indicate an erroneous or inadequate attitude. 'For example, when a person important to the dreamer appears in a dream as a slave, the unconscious may be reminding the dreamer that the person is not so powerful as the dreamer consciously believes.'[38]

The subjective interpretation of dreams is no longer as controversial as when Jung first introduced it as an alternative to the almost exclusively objective approach prevalent then. Freudian analysis treats the dream content in terms of the elements of our waking experience, that is, objectively or as an impulse towards other people and external objects. Many of the current dream theorists, including some neo-Freudians, have increasingly started using the subjective interpretation.[39] Jung was the first analyst to propose specific criteria to ascertain whether the dream should be understood objectively or subjectively.

Amplification and direct association
Jung used the methods of *direct association* and amplification in understanding dream images, rather than the free-association technique

advocated by Freud. For the latter, when confronted with a bull as dream image, the dreamer's series of continuous sequential associations may run such: cow, milk, bottle, baby, crying, hungry. According to Jung, such a method allows the mind to wander and freewheel, leading the dreamer away from the original dream image. His method of direct association entails preventing the person's train of thought from wandering by bringing it back again and again to the original oneiric image. His method would lead the dreamer to associate with the same image of a bull – it is large, it is strong, it is dangerous, it is used for breeding – till a point is reached when the meaning of the image reveals itself. Jung conceded that free association does yield valuable psychological insights, but thought that these insights may often bear no connection with the message contained in the dream. One might as well take any word at random from a dictionary, and use that as an initial image.

Jung also favoured the amplification of dream symbols, a technique that draws out a richer and thereby deeper meaning of symbols by placing them in their wider mythological and transpersonal context. Initially, it involves the exploration of the personal associations attached to the dream image, say the bull. The next stage focuses on the cultural meaning attached to that image. The bull image for a Spaniard accustomed to bloody bull fights[40] would have a different meaning from that of an Indian, who sees them wandering unharmed on every street. A still deeper level of amplification involves attempting to find the archetypal connection to the image. During this third phase the analyst may help by referring to a particular fairy tale, myth, or religious practice. For the Hindus it could be the bull Nandi, which carried the god Shiva, thereby lending a sacred element to the dream image; similarly, for the ancient Egyptians, the sacred bull Apis, who was worshipped as the reincarnation of the god Ptah; or in Persia, the bull in the Mithraic cult. These mythic connections help the dreamer link with the transpersonal dimensions of life. Later in the book we will discuss specific archetypal images that appeared to Manish Chawla at puberty, and Kavita Nayar at the time of her marriage. These dreams, so striking in character, were of fundamental importance to the dreamers at turning points in their lives.

Freud and Jung compared
The question is whether the Jungian conception of the dream and its method of interpretation is somehow 'deeper' or more fundamental as

compared to the defensive conception of Freud. Jung felt our everyday dreams are based largely on the assimilation of memory and reflective of daily personal concerns, however the archetypal or 'big' dream became the focal point, which gave his dream theory deeper meaning. Freud saw archetypal dreaming as dominated by secondary revision – a superficial accommodation of primary personal forces. Also Freud reduced all numinous dreams to the Oedipal arena. Jung refused to let him explain the ineffable in this manner; it would be akin to using the stone in the masonry of a temple to explain its design and purpose.

Freud believed that dreams reflect past conflicts, from which the dreamer needs to be defended. Hence his message: Reveal your dreams and I will show you the origins of your disturbance. Jung, on the other hand, perceived them as communications purposive towards individuation. He therefore asserted: Reveal your dreams and I will show you what you are striving to achieve and what obstructs your path.[41] Freud gazed towards the earlier part of life – childhood; Jung glanced towards the latter part of life – maturation. Both stressed the existence and importance of the unconscious aspects of the mind, and both regarded dreams as conveyors of messages from within.

The day residue sparks the Freudian dream by stimulating an earlier conflict. For Jung it opens an area of experience not attended to while awake. He emphasized the present predicament of the dreamer rather than concentrating on past conflicts.

Freud had told us that the function of dreaming is to preserve sleep by modulating instinctual tensions within the dreamer. The dream helps discharge repressed instinctual impulses. Jung, on the other hand, felt that the function of dreams is compensatory – to help achieve psychic balance by orienting the dreamer to unacknowledged aspects of the self. Jung also believed that the dream 'prepares the dreamer for the events of the following day'[42]: it has a prospective function.

Freud had solved the problem of dreams by positing a fundamental dichotomy between the manifest and latent contents of the dream. To him the manifest dream is a mere façade, a false or disguised rendering of the underlying latent dream thoughts. Jung had disagreed, believing that the manifest façade is the dream, and that there is no other dream. He felt that the interpretation of the dream must be a reflection of the needs of the imagery.

To Freud the dream itself is worthless, save as an initial trigger to free associate to the all-important latent content. It is therefore not surprising that Freud regarded the dream as completely *asocial*: It has nothing to communicate to anyone else; it arises within the subject as a compromise between the mental forces struggling in the person; it remains unintelligible to the subject and is for that reason uninteresting to other people. To Jung dream formation can become a part of an ongoing dialogic process. He advised to view dreams as a series and not as isolated episodes, so that the meaning of a symbol must find confirmation by a subsequent dream. This dream dialogue would also anticipate future images as the whole process is an unfoldment and what comes subsequently depends on earlier imagery as proto-symbols. He thus believed that it is of the utmost importance to maintain a dream diary, while in stark contrast Freud discouraged his patients from writing down their dreams.[43]

Jung's and Freud's theories of dream function and the methods of dream interpretation seem to reflect and evolve from their own personal dream experiences. Jung's own dreams are narratively cohesive and are organized around unusually high levels of geometric-mandala symbols, other-worldly and/or mythological settings, and uncanny numinous emotions. Freud's dreams, on the other hand, are a loose array of personal memories and current concerns. Jung's interpretative attitude therefore revolved around viewing the dream as a coherent unifying metaphor where amplification further integrates the material. For Freud, the method of free association resolved the issue into personal memories that were fragmented and disconnected, clouded by a distant, dissolving past.[44]

Both Freud and Jung spent several years engaged in self-analysis and used dreams as important tools of discovery while making their inner journeys. They returned with divergent views on what is buried in the unconscious. Perhaps their method of interpreting dreams followed as a consequence of their forms of dreaming. This difference is borne out in recent studies with university students. Some students actually dreamt in cohesive metaphors, while others dreamt in more delirious aggregates. It also showed that some find one method of interpretation convenient and the other more difficult to apply. Perhaps some people are natural free associaters, while others are natural amplifiers.[45] As Jung is reported to have commented to a colleague, 'A man cannot transcend himself. So the fact is that Freud's, Adler's and my psychology are all generalizations and abstractions of our own psychology.'[46]

More recent methods of dream interpretation
We noted the importance of the oneirologist in antiquity. Freud and Jung had also outlined a method of understanding dream language

that needed a trained analyst to interpret the dream. Later positions appeared no different – only the analyst is equipped to understand the meaning of the dream. More recent theories, however, no longer require specialized analysts and feel the best judges are the dreamers themselves. The role of the analyst is only that of a facilitator who helps to enlarge the dreamer's understanding of any dream symbol. Perhaps a brief look at the techniques of two modern-day interpreters may further the picture of oneirology today.

Frederic Perls, trained in the Freudian school, moved away to start the Gestalt method. He felt that dreams are best interpreted in a group rather than in a psychotherapy session with an analyst. *Gestalt* is a German word that may be translated to mean 'whole' or 'pattern', and a Gestalt session aims at uncovering the 'pattern' of the dream taken as a 'whole'. There is no standardized way or theory involved. Perls believed that dreams represent unfinished emotional business, or 'emotional holes' in the dreamer's life history, and that the content of dreams alludes to these personal experiences rather than to instinctual or collective drives. He also believed that every character and object in our dreams is a projection of our own self, and the way we have been living our lives. He thus wanted the dreamer to experience the various elements of the dream. For example, if a woman dreamt of a quilt, then she may describe herself as a quilt: warm, colourful, soft, or heavy. The dreamer is then asked to differentiate between various aspects of the dream by enacting each part and setting up a dialogue with the different elements of the dream. This is called *role playing,* and is enacted with the help of two chairs. The dreamer is in the hot seat, and on the other empty chair the dreamer assigns any person with whom there is an unfinished situation. Not only is it possible to represent other people in this way, but the empty chair can be any dream element, such as emotions, abstractions, or even parts of oneself. The dreamer then expresses what she feels about the 'other' in the empty chair, after which she is asked: If you are the 'other', how will you answer yourself? She moves from chair to chair and engages with each of the elements in the dream. This technique will help the dreamer explore her polarities by understanding her desires, needs, and potentials, on the one hand, and, on the other hand, by identifying the excuses, pretexts, and obstacles she puts in her own way. The dreamer must experience these so that she can accept the responsibility for her actions and relationships. She may choose to drape herself around some group member, and thereby realize that the other person may experience her apparent warmth as 'clinging' and therefore inhibitive. Thus the dream content is not considered as something in the past, but by enactment it becomes a current experiential reality, through which insights are gained.

Montague Ullman developed an entirely different group approach. In the Gestalt tradition, dreamers explore their dreams largely on their own with an occasional grilling by the conductor to drive home a point; the group participates only vicariously. However, Ullman's method aims to provide a gentle, sharing environment for the dreamers to discuss their dreams. The setting is democratic and non-threatening for the dreamer as each member of the group shares their personal associations with the individual elements of the dream related. In a typical session the dreamer volunteers a dream, the group 'may ask questions to clarify the dream and to grasp it as clearly and completely as possible. Any real characters in the dream are briefly identified.'[47]

The group members then comment on the dream as if it were their own, taking care to preface their statements with 'If this was my dream ...', and they attempt to reflect upon the feelings they experience in response to the dream. This then leads them to identify the *metaphorical* content of the dream. Ullman describes the next stage as 'returning the dream to the dreamer'. The group has given their reactions and feelings to the various dream elements; they have tried to establish the metaphors in the dream. Now, if willing, the dreamer shares how far he or she has come in understanding the dream. At no point is the person grilled or pressured into responding, Gestalt style. Ullman emphasizes safety and discovery. Safety because the dreamer 'is exposing a most personal and vulnerable side of himself';[48] the dreamer must be secure in the knowledge that he or she is in control at all times so that privacy and authority over the dream is assured. The discovery aspect becomes operative when the group responds to the dream by giving their individual responses. This can help the dreamer in discerning the meaning of the dream.

Chapter 10

THE METAPHORICAL
LANGUAGE OF DREAMS

I believe it to be true that dreams are the true interpreters of our
inclinations, but there is art required to sort and understand
them.

Michel de Montaigne

It is time now to heed the Gryphon's lament. The explanations over,
we can indulge in the adventure of interpreting dreams. But what
else have we been doing until now? We have taken a detailed look at
how Freud and Jung would approach the interpretation of a dream.
Both of them, however, embed the dream in a theoretical framework
that requires a specialist to decode the dream. Does this mean that we
have to go to a psychotherapist to interpret our dreams? Can we not
understand them ourselves, or rely on a spouse or a close friend to help
unravel them?

Modern therapists like Montague Ullman argue that the dream
essentially belongs to the dreamer, and at no point should the analyst
wrest control of it. It is the dreamer who is the truly decisive factor in
uncovering the meaning of the dream. To reinforce this point we have
seen that even the specialist requires something more than the imagery
to plumb the dream. These are usually the dreamer's associations
about the images, and without this crucial input the dream remains

unfathomable. If the specialist needs some inputs from the dreamer to unlock the meaning of the imagery, then surely the dreamer with a little familiarization with dream language can understand his or her own dreams.

I intend to sketch out a simple method by which the reader can grasp the import of the dream message. This is not an attempt to outline a definitive method, or present a standard formula for handling each and every type of dream. This method has been fashioned by borrowing largely from Ullman, as also from other interpreters. The dialect of this method relies on current psychological terminology. However, we are not restricted by the psychologist's beliefs. Neither is a specialist's knowledge required, nor is any training necessary; all that is needed is a fascination with dreams peppered with a healthy dose of curiosity. It is also hoped that once readers become familiar with the language of dreams, they will adopt a technique that suits them best. This is but a scaffolding, which should be dismantled once the reader gets the 'feel' for interpreting dreams.

Most of us, when confronted with our own dreams, fail to make sense of them. We have seen that throughout history it is the symbolic dream that has posed a dilemma to dreamer and interpreter alike. The literal dream does not suffer from these difficulties. It is the language of the symbolic dream that needs to be understood. Our method will have to primarily address this.

The method I am suggesting views the dream as a metaphorical communication about a waking life experience. This form of communication does not usually reflect the real-life situation directly as it is. Though a metaphorical depiction has the ability to find a likeness between things that are apparently disparate, there are a few inherent difficulties. For one, it allows the dream to be interpreted in multiple and sometimes diverse ways, and this may leave us unsure about the meaning of the dream. Take the example of the colour blue. In a dream it can allude to pornography, aristocracy, grief, freedom, or infinity, thereby demonstrating the unrelated directions that the interpretation may take.[1]

Conceiving the dream as a metaphor may raise another difficulty: We have talked of symbols in the dream so far, but what is the difference between a symbol and a metaphor? Often the boundaries between them become blurred, as there is a definitional overlap. The distinction between symbols and metaphors has been intentionally created in the hope that it will help us identify two essentially different aspects of the dream. Most dreams have a storyline – its plot – which unfolds as the dream progresses, like in a play. Each play has a number of characters who enact its storyline, but the thematic content is itself distinct from them. Similarly, a dream may have many symbols (the characters in the play), but these symbols when put together allude to a particular theme – its *metaphorical* message – which is distinct from the symbols. So, a dream speaks in the language of symbols but conveys its meaning through metaphors.[2] The ability to use metaphors depends on the capacity to see a similarity between things that are otherwise dissimilar, as when a ferocious man is called a tiger or a sunset is used to denote old age. With the ingenious use of visual metaphors, dreams tend to elaborate upon the issues invoked in the course of our lives, the emotional dilemmas each of us inevitably must face. A person who dreams that his car is hurtling down a cliff will experience the sensation of being in an uncontrollably dangerous situation far more powerfully than ordinary language can convey. In waking life, when we need to express abstract notions we resort to art, music, or poetry to state inexpressible feelings. While dreaming, a metaphorical mode of communication may best reflect the range of emotions we experience. A woman's dream of a stillborn child, perhaps, expresses far more powerfully than words can, her feelings of disappointment and failed expectations. Thus we read in a little-known essay by Ernest Fenollosa, published by Ezra Pound, 'Metaphor is … the very substance of poetry; [without it] there would have been no bridge whereby to cross from the minor truth of the seen to the major truth of the unseen.'[3]

We use metaphors all the time when we converse, so why does their nocturnal use astound us and compel us to label the dream discourse as bizarre? When Balzac likened clumsy men making love to gorillas playing violins,[4] we call it a powerful metaphor. But if in a dream we see a gorilla playing a violin we will term the dream as bizarre and not a metaphor.

In a dream, 'a metaphor is an attention-getting, powerful device'.[5] Mostly it is this attention-grabbing element that we term the dream's bizarreness. Every dream will have one or more of such elements that will attract attention; this could be an obvious incongruity, a powerful emotion, or an element that is repeated again and again in the dream. It is as if that element is beckoning for attention.

That is easily said, but a welter of confusion confronts us when we come across contradictory images in a dream. To exemplify, a person

dreamt of a cactus growing on the North Pole.[6] The sheer oddity of
a plant, let alone a cactus, growing on the North Pole is bound to
be confusing, and defies identification of any plot or metaphor in
the dream. However, there is a powerful metaphor involved in this
dream – a cactus is found in hot deserts, while the North Pole is a cold
desert. By telescoping these two aspects into one image the dreamer is
being alerted to 'desert', and its many meanings – being jilted, feeling
alone or abandoned – to identify the underlying thematic content of
the dream.

It is very important to bring the personal association of the dreamer
to the dream images. We cannot hope to rely on a dictionary of set
meanings since metaphors are created according to the dreamer's ability
to see the connection between two dissimilar things. The best way to
approach a dream, when no associations are triggered, is to focus on
the feelings evoked by the dream imagery and connect them to waking
concerns. Gayle Delaney, in her book *Breakthrough Dreaming*[7], likens this
process to forming a *bridge* from the images in the dream to something
in the dreamer's life.

To illustrate, in a dream you might find yourself on a battlefield,
apparently oblivious to the shells and bullets flying around you. Unless
you are a soldier on furlough this may not represent your real-life
situation. In order to understand the message of the dream you may
have to form a bridge from the dream to your actual situation. This
can be done by asking yourself what feelings predominated in the
dream, or were conspicuously absent. In the above dream the dreamer
is unaffected in a dangerous situation – an inappropriate feeling within
the context of the dream. You may then need to find a connection
between the dream emotion and a life situation in the past or present
that others regarded as dangerous but you did not. Or perhaps the
question could be: What situation of danger were you in that you were
unaware of?[8]

The identification of the metaphor immediately makes the message
of the dream transparent. Dreams can have a single-metaphor theme
or may have more than one metaphor. In a multi-metaphor dream,
it would be advisable to determine the main or lead metaphor. The
others then become secondary to it. The secret to understanding a
dream, therefore, is to spot its lead metaphor and then interpret the
rest of the images around it. 'The most effective way to do this is to
begin by breaking the dream down into its various scenes, consider
each scene first as a unit, and then work with the individual elements

in that scene.'[9] Even if we find sequential scenes disparate, we will still have to find the thread that sews the scenes into a single metaphorical theme.

Perhaps a few examples, starting with a very simple single-metaphor dream, may elucidate the process. 'Mala Saxena' dreamt:

> *I get into my car, but much to my horror realize that the car has no steering wheel.*

The dream vividly conveys that Mala is unable to direct her car, or some aspect of her life. The main metaphor in the dream is the steering wheel; its absence has, possibly, caused her lack of direction.

I asked Mala if she was feeling unsure about the direction in which she was heading.

Her eyes grew sad. 'Yes, I am. I lost my father six months ago. He was not just a father to me. He was a friend, an advisor, in fact, my mentor. Now that he has gone I am feeling adrift.'

She had provided the bridge from the dream to her circumstances. The dream had rather eloquently and with cryptic economy portrayed her feeling rudderless.

Another example: 'Sanjay Dhir' dreamt:

> *I'm on a cricket field where I am expected to bowl. I make my way towards the bowling run-up but suddenly realize that the pitch looks much longer than the usual twenty-two yards. I begin to feel unsure about my ability to bowl effectively on such a long pitch. But when I approach the bowling crease I find that the pitch is a normal one, and suddenly feel capable of giving a good delivery.*

The dominant metaphor in this dream is the pitch, and the dreamer's reaction to it is expressed through two emotions, appearing sequentially. Initially there is a feeling of inadequacy that then changes to confidence. This was the dream of a father whose young child needed surgery, and this was possible only in a town that was unfamiliar to him. He worried about whom he could turn to if the need arose. In fact, he was uncertain on many counts. The dream describes his anxiety through a cricket pitch – *it is too long for an effective delivery*. However, it also reassures him by showing him that once he gets into the situation – when he nears the crease – it is a normal one, and he'll be able to cope.

Sanjay had this dream before he left for his son's surgery and I heard him relate it in a workshop on dreams after the operation. The operation was successful, his son improved steadily, and before long they were back home. Sanjay remarked, 'When I awoke from the dream I felt reassured that things were going to be manageable. I remember the dream clearly because it helped me feel better.'

What we have done in trying to understand these dreams is to identify its metaphorical statement, locate its central theme, and then relate it to something in the dreamer's life.

What happens if we have a long meandering dream? Would it be easy to identify its central metaphor? A long dream may also give us the opportunity to explore the Freudian and Jungian approaches to a dream. Particularly, with the aid of the Jungian method of amplification, we may be able to explore in depth the many facets of a dream. The following is the dream of a young boy, 'Manish Chawla', who is soon to enter his teens:

We are playing marbles during the lunch recess when a lion roars his way into the school compound. We all run into the school building and hide. He frightens us – he is on the rampage, destroying everything. My friend is confused: He cannot even see us, nor did we tease him, so why is he so angry? Suddenly my father arrives in the school with his twelve-bore gun. Though I am very relieved, I don't go up to him because I am afraid to let him see that I'm actually scared.

My father goes out into the courtyard, and I quietly follow him, without his knowing it. He fires twice at the lion, but I am surprised that nothing happens to it. Dad quickly reloads the gun and shoots. I can see the bullet as it speeds towards the lion's head. The lion just stands on his hind legs and eats the bullet. All that happens is that his mane of hair slips back so that instead of being at his neck it is now around the lower part of his stomach, and his two hind legs have become wheels. This enables him to come faster towards us. Before my father can reload his gun, the lion swallows us both.

I open my eyes to find my father massaging my neck where the lion had bit it. He is not annoyed with me for following him, but says that I must not make any noise as we are in the stomach of the lion and he must not know that we are alive. We start moving very quietly through the valleys and mountains, keeping a look-out for wild animals. After a long, long time we are able to cut our way out of the lion's stomach with the help of a hunting knife.

The scene changes, my father and I are watching a Bharat Natyam dance performance. I think the other people must think that our clothes, after the adventure we have been through, are so smelly

and full of blood. But they don't seem to notice. I look at my clothes
and see that we are actually nicely dressed. Even I am wearing a dark
suit and necktie and my shoes are perfectly polished. Had I imagined
the lion, or were we watching a dance that had a lion? No, I am sure,
we were not [imagining the lion]. *I look back on to the stage – all*
the performers are girls.
       Then I woke up.

At first glance this seems a long, rambling dream that promises to
be difficult to interpret. We wonder whether there is any structure or
storyline behind this apparently meaningless dream of an adolescent
boy. To help identify the main metaphor it may be useful to divide the
dream into its component scenes.[10] If we condense each of these scenes
to its main thrust, we might characterize the dream thus: an angry lion
enters the school compound; the father attempts to subdue it; instead,
the lion swallows the father-son duo but they manage to escape from
the lion's stomach; and finally, the boy finds himself attending a
classical Indian dance recital. With this break-up it is easy to identify
that there are two metaphors running through the dream. The first is
the lion and the second is the father. We have to ascertain which out
of the two is the primary metaphor. The lion dominates the dream, and
the thematic content of the plot hinges around it, while the father's
role is dependent on the lion and could, therefore, be considered the
secondary metaphor.

If we can make a bridge from the lead metaphor – the lion – to
something in Manish's life, we may then understand the significance
of each of these four scenes and thereby attempt to piece together the
meaning of the dream. What did the lion mean to Manish? It was
difficult to get any kind of association out of him.[11] However, I was
struck by the way he pronounced lion: '*a* loin *roars his way ... speeds*
towards loin*'s head ... the* loin *just stands on his hind legs ...*' He had,
unwittingly, provided the clue: the lion was actually the *loins*.[12] I used
this lead to make the bridge. However, it must be emphasized that in
no way did Manish make this connection, but his pronunciation of lion
as 'loin' had inadvertently provided the pathway by which a further
exploration became possible.[13] The main metaphor it seems is centred
on the theme of sexual awakening. Manish may have already been aware
of the stirrings of erotic energy coursing through his body, probably
finding it both stimulating and pleasurable, but those are really only
initial instinctual explorations, wherein boys discover and familiarize
themselves with their bodies. In all probability this, however, was his

very first real encounter with his libido. It is only now that the full force
of awakening may have burst upon him, like the dramatic entry of the
lion in the dream. Sexual awakening is often felt as an alien, powerful
force, erupting into a boy's consciousness as something fearful, awe-
inspiring and uncontrollable – similar to Manish's reaction to the lion
in the dream.

Once this has been established, it is easier to understand the
significance of each of the divisions of the dream in relation to this
metaphor for puberty. The first scene announces the boy's sexual
awakening. The lion on the rampage, uncontrolled within the school
compound, is indicative of instinctive urges running riot within the
enclosure of Manish's personal world – his thoughts. Puberty is not
merely a marker of the sexual maturing of the child; it involves every
aspect of him, and the next scene comments on his relationships – with
his parents and with others. When this hitherto alien force explodes
in him it metaphorically devours him, and this is bound to alter his
perception of the world – symbolized by his entry into the belly of the
lion and his experience within it. He then emerges transformed. The
secondary metaphor – the father – tries to help Manish handle this phase
of turbulence and 'rebirth'. The last scene depicts his transformation:
his clothes change, his demeanour alters. After the battle with the
power of the 'loins' he finds himself settled in a cultured, mature
environment.

The dream has many metaphors embedded in it, and we will
attempt to interpret them with the bridge already established by the
lead metaphor and the hindsight of psychoanalytical understanding.
The dream sequence opens with Manish and his friends playing marbles,
indicating his boyish inclinations before the advent of puberty. His
friend's puzzlement about the unreasonableness of the lion, points,
perhaps, to the bewilderment Manish faced with the build-up in his
instinctual life.

It may be necessary to point out here that psychoanalysts believe
that all of us undergo a sexual period early in our infancy, when
instinctual urges dominate the child's world. Is it not common for
every child to put everything in its mouth (oral urge), or exhibit a
great curiosity for its own excreta (anal urge)? This is soon followed by
a phallic urge. (One mother described the involuntary tendency in this
phase by asking her son: 'Darling, why can't you leave the family jewel
alone?') The child can only gratify these needs, as it does not have, as
yet, any means to combat them. Puberty is the first recapitulation of this

period.[14] After the early infantile sexual period the child starts to develop a sense of self (ego) as a result of the restraints put on its instinctual urges, and slowly over time the child feels equal to grappling with them. In other words, children gradually establish a modus vivendi between urges and their control, replacing parental disapproval with a sense of 'conscience' and 'guilt'. After some time the equilibrium circumscribing the world of boys is disturbed by the infusion of greater urgency in their instinctual nature as puberty approaches. The prepubescent boy is not entirely sure whether to attribute his earlier subjugation of instinctive desires to his self or to filial pressure, which wagging its parental finger had admonished him as 'naughty'. Possibly, it was this dilemma that Manish's friend had projected on to the lion's behaviour and found puzzling.

During this prepubescent phase the boy's feelings towards his parents are bound to be ambivalent as his reliance on them is waning in direct proportion to his growing sense of self and the consequent decrease of his fear of the outside world. However, he has still not acquired the confidence to relate with the world independently. The dream describes this eloquently: Manish is relieved at the father's arrival, but is hesitant to greet him in case his quailing legs betray his internal confusion. And again, his hesitation in confronting the father does not detract from his wilfulness in trailing behind him towards the lion. This may refer to Manish's feeling that he has a new ally – his developing conscience – to combat his rampaging urges; the dream symbol, however, informs us that this ally is not strong enough to meet the lion alone but needs the cover of parental protection. Boys are not apt to talk about this emerging experience of puberty with their fathers, feeling shy, awkward, and fearful about its import; yet he is the only one, the dream tells us, who wields a gun (we all know how Freudians would decode that symbol!). Also a boy's relationship with his father feeds his image of manhood, and without this role model he may even distrust his own emerging masculinity. Common sense hopes that it is the father who would instruct his son into the mysteries of puberty, helping him understand the difficulties he will inevitably encounter on the road to manhood. Unfortunately, this is not the case. The boy does not want the advice of adults as he is testing his own abilities and wants to form relationships independent of them; he prefers to consult his friends and peers.[15] The dream states that the father's bullets (parental guidance) bounce off; the lion (the pubescent boy) is impervious to them. If we had any residual doubt about the symbolic significance of the dream then the next depiction of the lion should dispel it – the mane slips back to present a hairless member raising itself: an erect 'loin'.

In its next scene, the dream is symbolically stating that the boy has to 'die' to his childhood ways, if he has to attain maturity. This change that is upon Manish cannot be averted or postponed; the lion has to swallow him. He has to sacrifice his childhood personality at the altar of puberty. In the process, his relationship with his environment has to change, as will his relationship with his parents – in the metaphorical language of the dream, the father also has to be swallowed by the lion. The lion swallowing the father-son duo would thus symbolize that the life-sustaining power of Eros has devoured Manish, meaning his assessment of himself has to change. Their journeying together in the lion's stomach is indicative that it will take a little time for this awakening, and its attendant changes, to be assimilated by Manish; the 'battle' lies ahead of him. It is not only reflective of biological changes and psychological re-evaluations, but every aspect of his life would undergo transformation. They would be able to cut their way out of the lion's belly only when he is ready to be 'reborn'.

This is a very interesting dream indeed, not only because it very neatly dovetails with the Freudian template of the developmental stages leading to puberty, but it also demonstrates the Jungian conception of the collective unconscious – that mankind shares an underlying psychic substratum common across time and cultural divides. Confronted with an important transitional phase in his life, Manish dreamt of being swallowed by a lion, eventually to cut his way out of its belly. This is a universally recurrent image found in the myths and legends of many cultures. The hero, instead of conquering or being able to placate the powers that oppose him, is swallowed by them. Hiawatha, the American Indian chief, and his canoe were swallowed by Mishe-Nahma – the King of Fishes. The Inuit of the Bering Strait tell the tale of their hero Raven being swallowed by a whale, and how he then stood inside its belly and looked around, while the Zulus have a story of a mother and her two children, in which an elephant swallowed the mother. When the woman reached the belly of the elephant 'she saw large forests and great rivers, and many high lands', a similar sight confronted by Manish in the lion's belly. In the German fairy tale, Red Riding Hood was swallowed by a wolf. And, the whole Greek pantheon, with the sole exception of Zeus, was swallowed by Kronos (Time).[16]

It seems that Manish's dream of being swallowed was neither all that bizarre nor personal to him. Myths all over the world have woven their stories around this theme. At any rate, there appears to be a close connection between dream and myth. Joseph Campbell believes a dream is a personalized myth; the myth a depersonalized dream. In dreams the forms are 'quirked' by the peculiar troubles of the dreamer, whereas in myth the problems and solutions shown are directly valid for all humankind.[17]

Possibly, Jung was fully justified in his conception of the collective unconscious, and it may prove illuminating to take another look at the dream using Jungian principles. It would cast the dream in another dimension altogether. Our interpretation has viewed everything in the dream from the prism of genital urges; now let us see whether Jungian archetypes can raise that urge to a different level of expression. However, it must be remembered that, at its core, it is still the dream of a pubescent Manish grappling with his confusion when confronted by a developmental dictate.

The archetypal motif emphasized in Manish's dream, and in these 'swallowing' myths, is the symbol of death and rebirth. Manish, or the hero in these myths, must be overwhelmed by that with which he is struggling. He must endure a process that in some way annihilates him. He has to disappear, 'die' to the life he once lived; only then can he be born again to a new life. 'No creature,' writes Ananda Coomaraswamy, 'can attain a higher grade of nature without ceasing to exist.'[18] The death of the hero does not imply that he exits from the world, but rather that he is expected to go inwards into himself to sever himself from the stage of life he needs to leave behind, and prepare for the imperatives of the new phase. Thus Manish had to leave his boyish games in pursuit of more adult interests.

Returning to the specifics in the dream we find that the main metaphor of the lion – the instinctual turbulence of puberty – intertwines itself with the secondary metaphor: the father, who helps Manish handle this phase of emotional volatility. The dream-father is a symbol of the guiding voice that the young boy so desperately needs now. Suddenly, Manish's relationship with the father changes after the lion has swallowed them. The latter is no longer the distant figure of the earlier phase, and is found massaging his neck rather than scolding him for following him. They are now shown journeying together. The boy becomes a junior apprentice to the father. Later in the dream we witness still another change in their relationship when they emerge from this ordeal and sit together, like two adults, at the dance performance. All these metaphorical allusions are not a comment on the change in his relationship with his father, but they refer to the archetypal symbol of the father – the image of father as guide. This archetypal father's influence extends far beyond Manish's sexual maturation process and his evolving psychodynamics. He acts as the bridge between the individual and the collective, between family and society, and even beyond that to the transpersonal. He plays the *instrumental* role, which should be distinguished from the mother's *expressive* role.[19] Typically, in India, the father plays no significant role in the early development of the child – Manish's awe of him in the dream speaks of their emotional distance. With mothers, on the other hand, there is both a physical and psychological closeness. 'Constantly held, cuddled, crooned and talked to, the Indian infant's experience of his mother is a heady one. His contact with her is of an intensity and duration that differentiates it markedly from the experience of infancy in western worlds.'[20] This expressive bond with the mother restricts the boy's gaze to home and family, while his developmental dictate at puberty leads him out of the house and into the world outside. It is the archetypal father whose role will be instrumental in facilitating the young adult's transition from home to the world. And this initiation is likely to be completed – the dream informs us – only after many trials, when Manish and the 'father' emerge from the lion's belly.

We had started this analysis with the express aim of learning to interpret a complicated dream, but a dream has many layers of meaning and our attempt must incorporate as much of its significance as we can.

Freud believed the dream to be like a house of which the manifest dream is only a façade, in the negative sense of being a false front that conceals the true meaning of the dream. For Jung, however, 'the "manifest" dream-picture is the dream itself and contains the whole meaning of the dream ... We say that the dream has a false front only because we fail to see into it.'[21] Perhaps the incomprehensibility of the dream is its false front. Jung therefore treated the dream as though it were a text that he could not fathom. If we come across Latin or Sanskrit words that we do not understand it isn't as if they are concealing something from us; we simply do not know the language. The philologist, when confronted with a very rare word, would try to seek parallels by studying text passages where that word also occurs, and then apply the understanding gained from the other texts into the new text. And that is the way Jung's method of amplification attempts to read dreams. It looks for parallels elsewhere to grasp the full import of the dream.

Initially there is an attempt to explore personal associations attached to the dream, then the attention focuses on the cultural significance of the dream. A still deeper level of amplification involves finding transpersonal connections to the images in the dream. We have seen Manish's personal significance with the dream, as also some parallels in myths. However, there are other parallels in rituals that ceremonially and silently address Manish's dilemma at a cultural and transcendental level.

The ancient world instinctively, perhaps, used rituals to help its members negotiate these transitional periods. It seems there is something within our psyche that responds to ritual in a meaningful manner. The ritual is almost like an organic enactment that communicates at many levels the many aspects of the transition to the participant. Or, put the other way, the culmination of a phase desires the pageantry of ritual to help assimilate its import and to celebrate the advent of the next phase. A modern illustration of this is the pageantry involved in the ritual enacted at university graduation ceremonies. It may not be articulated as such, but to the graduating student the regalia imparts a closure to a phase. Possibly, without it, the whole educational period would remain incomplete.

Many Australian tribes require every male member to be circumcised during the tribal initiation at puberty. The ritual surrounding it usually involves the boy being symbolically swallowed and disgorged by a monster; just like Manish's dream many thousands of miles – and cultures – away. Among the Kai, a New Guinea tribe, the ritual is more graphically expressed by making the boys 'pass under a scaffold on which stands a man, who makes a gesture of swallowing and takes in fact a gulp of water as each trembling novice passes beneath him'.[22] All this underscores the fact that deep within our psyches – whether tribal or 'civilized' – some phases are common, and they elicit similar responses in myth and in dream. Rather than view rituals as regurgitations from our primitive past, they can be seen as an ally, helping people across difficult transitions, like birth, puberty, marriage, or death. Not only do they ferry the person across these stages, but also aid other people involved. These are the 'rites of passage'. The amazing fact is that many of these ritual enactments appear automatically in dreams the moment the person is ready to negotiate these transitions. May we infer from this that one of the possible functions of ritual, myth, and dream is to supply the symbols that may aid the development of the individual, and not let him or her stay trapped in the eddies of fantasy or fear that deplete one of energy and intent?

Puberty is not only a biologically important transition, it also marks the boy's cutting away from the mother, and his induction into the society and lore of men. Henceforth, the boy will take his place in the conclave of men and not view the world through the gender-oblivious amorphousness of childhood. Manish belonged to a progressive Hindu family and had not undergone any of the religious ceremonies of *namakarana* (naming) or *mundan* (tonsuring). Had he been born in a traditional Indian family, the *upanayana* ceremony – performed for a boy anywhere between the ages of eight to twelve years – might have helped him through this difficult period at puberty.

In the traditional ceremony the boy is smeared all over with a yellow paste (turmeric) on the night prior to the initiation ceremony. He is then made to spend the whole night in a pitch-dark room in absolute silence – an obvious attempt to recreate the embryonic state. The imagery of the dark womblike room is rather similar to the belly-womb images of the myths we touched upon earlier, as also found in Manish's dream. The silence is intended to make the boy feel like a speechless child anew. These trials of darkness and silence are deemed prerequisites for his new incarnation.

The following day the boy emerges to participate in one of the most moving and poignant ceremonies, the sharing of a meal with his mother. This is the last time the mother and son will ever eat together, clearly marking the grand end of childhood;[23] it signals his 'second birth'. After the meal, he is shaved and bathed, symbolic of the purification required of the mind and body. The bath over, the boy is given a *kaupina* (loincloth) to wear – his sexual energy needs to be masked, or rather, harnessed and refined. A girdle is tied round his waist to support the *kaupina*, and then he is invested with the 'sacred thread' made of triple cotton cord, spun by a virgin Brahmin girl.[24] Sometimes the three strands make way for six – the extra three for his future wife! These indirect allusions leave an overarching impression that the ritual has a strong connection with the emerging sexuality at puberty, just as in Manish's dream.

Most societies believe that for the mental development of the individual it is absolutely essential to restrain and displace the young adolescent's sexual energy. The more complete this instinctual renunciation, the higher the cultural development. The individual has to learn to control the gratification of his or her sexual drives, redirecting them into socially acceptable and culturally creative channels for the greater common good. Consequently these cultures tend to delay marriage, or, at any rate, its consummation, rather than give the sexual urge unfettered expression at puberty, as evidenced in sex dormitories for adolescent boys and girls in some Eastern Indian tribes. Also, the sanctity of this restraint is enforced in the monogamous nature of their marriages. The raw power of the sexual urge at puberty, felt alike by tribal and 'civilized' man, is the same, but the difference is that the latter sublimates it by restraining its outflow and channelling it into the training of the mind.[25] Invariably these cultures will divert their energy towards education. In Indian antiquity, the *upanayana* was an educational *samskara* – a request from a pubescent boy to his guru to accept him as a disciple. The ceremony was a recognition of and commitment to the fact that if he transmuted his sexual energies, it would illuminate his whole being. In the dream Manish is shown that if he can conquer the sexual beast – release himself from the lion's belly – then he may be enriched, symbolized by his participation in a culturally evolved activity – the Bharat Natyam dance. All that Manish notices, after emerging from the encounter with the 'loin', is that the dance performance is filled with girls – perhaps an apt testimony to what pervades his pubescent mind. However, he is expected to sublimate his emerging sexuality, as seen in the dream by his distant participation as a member of the audience.

This power of the 'loins' can catapult Manish into realizing his highest potential, meaning that he has the potential of refining his energies to the highest level within his cultural paradigm. The dance is a very subtle and refined art form, an epitome of the cultural process. Manish emerges to find himself attending a Bharat Natyam dance recital. Gone are the symbolic bloodied clothes torn in his combat with the power of the 'loin', a metaphor for Manish's inner encounter with his sexuality. He has metamorphosed from someone playing the boyish games of marbles into an adult engaged in a considerably more sophisticated pursuit, and his emerging interest in girls is given precedence over his male friends. His attire also reflects the change in his maturing consciousness – from the indifference of preadolescent clothes to the formal suit, necktie, and polished shoes of adulthood. He is now a *dvija,* or twice born, transformed into a new life.

This is a 'new' life in many ways. Apart from the changes taking place within him, his mode of relating to others will also undergo a radical transformation. Initially as an infant he had only dimly perceived an instinctual sense of 'I' within his nebulous consciousness. This feeling was gradually stabilized thanks to the relentless nurturing by the mother.

Now he has begun to appreciate, in a very real sense, the fundamental polarity in life. Not only is he aware of gender distinctions, but also his pubertal strivings are now irresistibly drawn to form a relationship away from the mother. Besides this, he also begins to realize that, willy-nilly, he belongs not only to himself, but also to a larger collective whole – family, school, society. His sublimated urges have lost their urgency for instinctual satisfaction and have been transformed into a desire to lose himself in the experience of the 'other': individually, in his relationship with a woman, and functionally, in participating in the collective – be it his school or an ideology. Erik Erikson, the psychologist, believes that 'the young adult is eager and willing to fuse his identity with that of others. He is ready for intimacy.'[26]

I am not for a moment suggesting that Manish, or any other pubescent boy, is able to articulate all this to himself; his consciousness is crammed with great question marks looming in every direction. He simply tries to cope with what is arising out of his being, expressing his sporadic attempts within the assumptions of his family, his socio-economic environment. He will get hurt, stumble and learn and rise again, all the while groping to understand what he is supposed to do, and whether he will be able to do it well.

With Jung's method of amplification we have moved from Manish's personal association of the dream to a cultural one informed by myths and rituals, finding parallels in them that help vivify and universalize the theme of his dream. Through an anonymous boy somewhere in India, dealing privately with his pubescent stirrings, we discover that the dream belongs to a wider territory, which concerns human beings all over the world, at a similar stage in their life. This transition connects Manish at many levels – personal, cultural, and transpersonal.

In the dream, a lion swallows Manish and yet he remains alive, symbolically introducing him to another reality. The outer world of events has been eclipsed to introduce him to the worlds within him. There are a number of myths that do just this. When he opens his mouth the child Krishna (an incarnation of the Indian god Vishnu) reveals another universe to his mortal mother Yashoda, indicating that we do not live only in the world of events, but in another greater reality that is interior to and sustains this world.[27] In the ancient scripture Matsya Purana, Vishnu swallows the sage Markandeya, and only after emerging from the belly of the god does the sage question the nature of reality and illusion. The myth continues to ferry Markandeya back and forth between the two worlds, into the belly of the god and out again, till finally he is released from all delusion, discovering the true nature of reality (*Brahman*).[28] Manish being swallowed could symbolize that he has been introduced to the core of the lion (or to the heart of his sexuality), which may transform him when he is returned to his former world. In some sense the transformed Manish would then have assimilated the lion into himself. In the language of the myth, he would become half-man, half-lion. This image is very sacred to the Hindus – Narasimha, one of the ten avatars of Vishnu, was a man-lion. A wealth of meaning lies within the belly of the lion. Perhaps the dream is stating that hidden within the sexual urge of puberty is the opportunity to gain access to another realm. It is the power that brought him into this world, and it can also help him transcend it. The 'lion-loin' energy at one level is experienced as raw, sexual energy, and at another level it is felt as something awe-inspiring, powerful, and beyond the personal – in its association with the gods.

It is normally with the rise of sexual energies at puberty that the feeling of a power greater than one's own limited consciousness is experienced. This power demands submission at various levels. Biologically, the human species lays claims on the child – he is ready for procreation. The adolescent is also increasingly claimed by society as he proceeds to high school and college. Individually he has the personality-transcending function of propagating the species; collectively he will contribute to his society by propagating its primary structure – the family.

It is at puberty itself that the transpersonal also stakes its claim on the individual. This hitherto alien power, which engulfs the individual, reminds the adolescent about his numinous origins. Such is the overwhelming nature of this primal power that humankind, from time immemorial, has accorded it a stature beyond temporal reality. The Hindus recognized that it is this transpersonal ancestry of the child that will infuse purpose, and inform his personal and collective goals with meaning. Therefore, they planted the seed of his divine roots into his mind at the *upanayana* thread ceremony with the help of the Gayatri Mantra. No doubt the young man will remain unaware of his transcendental connections till the soil is ready to let the seed sprout and mature. This hidden dimension becomes visible in Manish's dream since his psyche utilized the symbol of a Bharat Natyam recital – a dance form that traces its origins to the ancient art of temple dances in South

India. As we noted earlier, Manish's attending this recital became an expression of the sublimation of his energies as expressed through a culturally refined art form. The Bharat Natyam dance form is this and much more; it is a form of divine worship and service, culminating as a self-offering to the deity. Its outstanding function is to give symbolic expression to abstract religious concepts. The close relationship between dance and religion, particularly as a philosophical metaphor, began very early in Hindu thought.[29] From its journey as an esoteric temple ritual to its current form as an artistic presentation in theatres, Bharat Natyam is still imbued with the power of a culture's continual striving to establish a connection with the divine. Thus, in Manish's dream, his experience of the Bharat Natyam recital becomes a multi-layered symbol.

Promptings, like this dream, are akin to archetypes pushing through our unconscious to make their power felt in the nitty-gritty of our lives. What defines these dreams is the powerful sense of felt meaning that seems to resist articulation. So it is not surprising that Jung chose not decoding, analysis, or free association to understand these dreams, but amplification as the natural pathway for their full understanding. Free associations to dreams usually branch out into personal memories, but archetypal dreams tend to become more impersonal, more universal, and it is thus preferable to circumambulate the dream, always reconnecting with its details. This often heightens the inherent sense of significance of the dream.

Perhaps that is the real power of the archetype – it has many levels of meaning. The deeper we dig, the larger is the metaphor's significance. If we restrict its operation to the outer arena of activity then it reveals only a genital striving. However, if we are prepared to probe deeper, a wealth of meaning emerges that lends dignity to our dreams. As Joseph Campbell says, 'Apparently, there is something in the initiatory images so necessary to the psyche that if they are not supplied from without, through myth and ritual, they will have to be announced again, through dream, from within – lest our energies should remain locked in a banal, long outmoded toy room, at the bottom of the sea.'[30]

The unravelling of young Manish's dream was simplified because we were able to identify its lead metaphor and the secondary ones. It seems that the skill, or the art, in grasping a dream lies in deciding which metaphor is most important. No hard and fast rules govern this, but generally a few important features would help to alert the attention to the main metaphor in your dream. The golden rule is not to hunt for them; let them attract your attention. Let them speak to you. There will always be some element or elements in the dream demanding to be heard, and they may do so in a variety ways.

Possibly, the easiest to spot is an obvious incongruity, as in Mala's dream, where the steering wheel of the car was missing. Take another dream example: a woman is walking her dog in the park. Nothing in the dream stands out. However, if the woman is, say, Indira Gandhi or Jackie Kennedy, then this metaphor attracts attention, and the dream interpretation will be built around it. Alternatively, if the dog bites a passer-by then this particular aspect would assume significance and the interpretation would lead in a different direction. The trouble begins if the woman is Mrs Gandhi and the dog also bites a passer-by. Then we would have to accord relative importance to the competing metaphors, like we did to the lion and the father in Manish's dream, and knit the two metaphors together in the interpretation.

Another way in which a dream element assumes prominence is by repetition. If the dog continues to bite every passer-by then it will certainly deserve special attention. Or if the woman stops every now and then and asks the passers-by, 'Do you get messages from the unconscious?', then the bizarre nature of the sentence and not the woman will merit attention. However, if the sentence is a standard pleasantry – 'Have a good day' – then it is not important and cannot be considered the lead metaphor.

Another form of repetition that attracts attention is the recurrence of a symbol. The woman may not be Mrs Gandhi and the dog may not bite, but if night after night you dreamt that a woman is walking her dog in the park – the same woman, the same dog in the neighbourhood park – the sequence, by its sheer recurrence, will cry out for attention. The dream may even assume a reality that compels you to contemplate verifying whether such a woman or a similar dog does actually frequent the nearby park. Similarly, a metaphor recurring in dream after dream alerts you to its significance.

What happens when there is no incongruity, repetition, or recurrence? Continuing with our example of the lady walking in the park, if none of the attention-grabbing devices are present in the dream, and the woman is the dreamer's neighbour and her dog is a placid creature, we could attempt to identify the metaphorical allusion by asking the dreamer if there's any overriding trait in the neighbour that comes to mind. Or, we could ask the dreamer to try and characterize the neighbour. This may then lead us towards the significance of the dream. If, for instance, the response is that the neighbour is very organized, then the dream is asking the dreamer to look at the decisive / scattered aspects in his or her life, perhaps in regard to routine activities (the dog has to be walked every day). It is perhaps obvious that it is the perception of the neighbour – the dreamer's particular response – and not the actual traits of the neighbour that is critical to the association.

If the neighbour is just a name in the phone book, with no personal involvement, then her name may provide the clue. If it is Asha it could allude to the Hindi word for hope, if David, then perhaps to the righteousness of the biblical figure. We do not have to restrict ourselves to the people in the dream. If the neighbour has not registered in any way in the dreamer's memory and his or her name does not ring any bells, we could explore the associations with the dog, or with dogs in general, and make a bridge from those attributes to something in the dreamer's life. As always, the association of the dreamer is most important and holds the key to the dream.

In chapter 2 I recounted my dream in which a woman wearing fancy clothes and stiletto heels enters a house under construction, only to be ushered out as she does not belong there. Three metaphors in this dream vie for attention: Firstly, we have the construction site with building material lying around, which provides the setting for the dream. The next thing that draws our attention is that the inside of the room is totally bare except for a typewriter on an old table – as though the dream deliberately kept the room empty, barring these two objects, to single them out. Lastly, the groomed woman in fancy clothes competes for attention, as she is utterly incongruous in these surroundings.

What is the lead metaphor of this dream, given the fact that all three images – the half-built structure, the typewriter on the table, and the decked-out lady – make a strong statement in the dream? The most striking element, however, is the woman who, due to her incongruity in that setting, does not belong there. One can say that the house under construction and the old typewriter somehow belong to the same genre, but the inappropriate attire of the woman is the most attention-grabbing device of the dream. Without her, the plot of the dream has no tension to unfold. Her presence suggests that there is something misplaced, something not right. She, thereby, becomes the lead metaphor of the dream. Had this lady appeared in a dream of a dinner party, she would not have been incongruous and thus would not qualify as the lead metaphor. Once I had identified the metaphorical message of the dream – that there was something incongruous in what I was attempting to do – I now had to discover what it was. My association with the old typewriter formed the bridge to the area of the incongruity in my waking life. The typewriter became the secondary metaphor because it described the nature of the problem, which could not have come into play had the primary focus – the woman – not first stated it and brought it to my notice. The typewriter was an obvious allusion to my writings. The half-built structure metaphorically confirmed that the allusion was to my writing. Something in the way I was writing was like the woman in the dream – superficial, ornamental, out of place. My ushering the woman out of the building became a symbolic injunction to rid the draft of these weaknesses.

Next, let us look at the dream that my Teacher had interpreted, involving Annie Besant and the dead child. Annie Besant – one of the early presidents of The Theosophical Society – draws our attention. But so does the apparently dead girl, and perhaps more strikingly. May we not immediately surmise that the dream is about a young girl, who is dead metaphorically? I am choosing the dead girl in the dream as the main metaphor because it is around her that the dream plot unfolds. Annie Besant, no doubt, claims attention due to her stature, but her bringing out a dead child from the car – an utterly unusual act – suggests that she was bringing out, exposing, the main issue of the dream. Mrs Besant would then become the supportive metaphor giving additional clues about the theme of the dream. Like Manish, I was unable to provide any association to Mrs Besant for my Teacher to make the bridge. But, because we have chosen the little girl as the pivotal message of the dream, we can pay attention to another attention-grabbing device: a repetition. Mrs Besant appeared to be ninety years old, while the almost dead girl was nine or ten years old. The dream idiom had used a mathematical repetition – ninety is equal to nine times ten. As my Teacher had suggested, numbers in dreams can also be understood as referring to an event that may have occurred that many years ago or, alternatively, when the dreamer was as old as the dream number. Once the dream had been unravelled thus far, my Teacher's question to me seems the only logical climax: What happened to you when you were nine or ten years old that felt like an emotional death?

Numbers need not only be representative of age; there are many ways of understanding their significance as the following dream shows. Immediately after getting his Senior Cambridge exam results,[31] my husband Rajeev dreamt:

A school friend is with me and we go to the market to buy cloth for a shirt. The cloth costs three rupees, but the stitching charges for the shirt are twenty-one rupees! We find this very puzzling.

He related the dream to an uncle who was interested in dreams, adding that dreams do get things mixed up; it might have been more realistic to dream that the cloth cost twenty-one rupees and the stitching charges were only three rupees.

The uncle replied, 'If that would be so, then the dream would be telling you nothing.'

'But, what is it saying?'

His uncle was silent for a while, then said, 'You are puzzled about your school results. There is something you don't agree with, or are surprised about.'

Rajeev was taken aback as the results had just been communicated by post from his school and he hadn't told his uncle any of its details.

His uncle continued, 'It seems you are puzzled about scoring a 3 in some subject.'

Rajeev had felt he had done better in the physics exam than in chemistry and was surprised when he got a 2 in chemistry and a 3 in physics. He was happy about the chemistry result, but he felt that he deserved at least a grade 2 in physics.

A few days later, a letter came from the school apologizing for an error in communicating Rajeev's results. The grades were corrected to a 2 in physics and a 3 in chemistry. Needless to say, Rajeev confronted the uncle with the letter, asking, 'How did you do it? Magic?'

'Your dream was screaming it loud and clear, but you thought it had no idea of prices in the real world. By presenting an anomaly it was drawing your attention to the number three. The cloth was for three rupees and the stitching charge of twenty-one can also be read as two plus one, which is again a three.'

There is something impressive when a dream is interpreted in this fashion, and it seems Rajeev's uncle had the knack for it. He was quick to spot the lead metaphor to be a number, and the repetition of the number three in the dream helped him identify the cause for concern in Rajeev's teenage mind. However, most dreams are difficult to interpret in this manner; Rajeev's uncle had provided the bridge intuitively, without asking him for his associations. This is possible only if the interpreter knows the dreamer well, and is well versed with his or her concerns.

If a number can alert one to the lead metaphor so can a significant date, as in my dream recounted earlier in the book of the parade on 26

January. There are other metaphorical images embedded in this dream: the teeming millions, the official-in-charge identifying a spot for me, and above all what he says to me. Yet what struck me immediately was that a nationally important date was being highlighted, possibly as a metaphor for the theme of the dream. The Constitution of India came into force on 26 January, Republic Day; the nation had defined its identity as a democracy. I, too, was in need of an identity after graduating – seeking to define myself in the world.

Before we can interpret our dreams, it is important to remember them. The best way to start remembering your dreams is to tell yourself before you drift into sleep: I will remember my dream tonight.

I recall my Teacher introducing someone to dreams.

Promptly came the reply, 'But I don't dream.'

My Teacher ignored the objection and continued to discuss late into the night the significance of dreams and how to record them.

Next morning the man reported with astonishment, 'I had six dreams last night! And, I was able to write them down.'

A little interest in the subject had stimulated the dreaming mind to respond. If you are interested in your dreams, maintain a notebook specifically to record your dreams. Keep it with a pen on your bedside table. Before going to sleep write down the date on a fresh page. If ever you awaken during the night, write down whatever comes to you – even if it is only a mood, or an image. If you do not write down the dream immediately it would probably have disappeared by the morning.

Upon awakening train yourself not to open your eyes immediately, but to dwell on any dream feelings or images that you can recall. In order to focus, lie quietly, do not move or change position, or switch on the light. Just stay with the dream, undistracted, however small the fragment that you remember. Try and relive the mood of the dream images.

If, even after a few days of trying, you are unable to remember a dream, then don't bother recalling them. Instead, aim to recollect what you had been thinking at the moment of awakening. Once that has been recalled, try to find out why you were thinking those thoughts. This process may lead you to the memory of a dream, after which, like an angler, you can reel in the other segments of the dream.

It is important to record a dream as close to the time it happened, otherwise one might lose the details, or forget large chunks of it. After writing down the dream, record your feelings. What was the most dominant emotion? Write down any associations you may have with the dream images – people, situations, or objects in the dream. With these associations ask yourself: What is the symbolic story that the dream is telling and what could it be referring to within my current life situation?

If you're having trouble interpreting your dreams, don't worry. Keep the dream diary going. After a month reread the dreams. You may find that most of them are centred on one particular theme. The thread in them may help you clarify a dream you were not able to understand earlier. It seems that the dreaming intelligence presents the same theme from many perspectives, in an attempt to help us see the situation from various angles. It tells us: Look at it this way. If we can't, then it says, Hey, what about this angle? Got it? Once we're able to grasp the issue then it may build on our understanding by giving us many more insights and further information. This dreaming intelligence is also very gentle with us, especially when we are struggling with something that is difficult to cope with. It may say, I suppose that's enough for the time being. We'll come back to it a little later. Let's talk of something else. And it will start on a new series of dreams.

Many of our dreams portray and comment on our everyday concerns. For this reason it is necessary to define the relevant waking experiences that could have triggered a dream. Try to remember what you were thinking of before going to sleep because that can often be an important clue to the context of the dream. If this does not give a lead to the dream imagery, then think back in detail to all you did on the day preceding the dream. Unless we are successful in building the bridge between the imagery and our present life context we may not completely fathom what our dreams are trying to tell us.

Chapter 11

TYPICAL DREAMS
AND THE NIGHTMARE

The most skilful interpreter of dreams is he who has the faculty
of observing resemblances.

Aristotle

As we have seen, dream worlds are built according to individual
peculiarities; a person's dreams can therefore be interpreted only
by his or her personal associations to the symbols in the dream. This
approach does away with the dream dictionaries that have proliferated
since antiquity. According to Freud, 'The only dictionary we need
to decode our dreams is not on our bookshelves but in our heads.'[1]
However, in his effort to identify the dream stimulus – libidinal impulses
seeking gratification – he followed a method in which every symbol
was unlocked only by this one 'key'. An unintended consequence
was the emergence of rather fixed symbols; whether it was walking
through a room or using a nail file, each one alluded to the sexual act. A
predetermined meaning was the case with many other symbols as well.
Ironically, it gave impetus to Freudian analysts to form a new dictionary!
Jung gave freedom to dreamers in their choice of symbol as long as the
dream was dredging material from the personal unconscious. When it
came to the collective unconscious and its archetypes we were back,
once again, to a predetermined understanding of them. If we dream of

a professor, doctor, or priest, Jungian analysts will often see in this the 'wise old man' archetype, personifying a source of growth and wisdom. This was in complete contrast to the attempt to view dream symbols in a purely personal context without fixed predetermined meanings. It is to Freud's credit that he acknowledged this aberration.[2] He argued that there were certain dreams that almost everyone dreamt alike, leading him to conclude that these presumably had the same meaning. Such dreams as a rule failed to produce any associations, which would ordinarily help in their decoding.[3] This led to the identification of the *typical* dream, and most analysts agree on the validity of using a common approach to their meaning.

Typical dreams include sitting for an examination, missing a train, being pursued by a hostile stranger or predatory animal, falling from a great height, flying, finding oneself naked in company, or having one's teeth fall out. These themes, with the same basic plot and events, express common human concerns.

Calvin Hall, an American psychologist and dream researcher (whose dream theory we will discuss in a later chapter), statistically compounded dream components and further added to the list of typical dreams by including the following: dreams of having sex; getting married; giving birth; watching fires; swimming; or being confined in an underground place. These themes are meant to be illustrative and are not a complete listing of them. He believed that 'typical dreams express the shared concerns, preoccupations, and interests of all dreamers. They may be said to constitute the universal constants of the human psyche.'[4]

Hall spent most of the 1950s and 1960s collecting and categorizing dreams and their contents from large numbers of subjects from various parts of the world. Together with Vernon Nordby he examined 50,000 dreams and concluded that a number of 'typical' themes are represented over and over again. 'This is true for individual dream series as well as for sets of dreams obtained from groups of people,' Hall and Nordby wrote. 'These typical dreams, as we shall call them, are experienced by virtually every dreamer, although there are differences in the frequency with which these dreams occur among individual dreamers.'[5]

The dream themes discussed below are not intended to be an exhaustive exploration of typical dreams. Also, some of the themes mentioned might not strictly fall under this category, but their constant occurrence and the interest that so many people have in them warrants their inclusion.

Being chased

I'm being chased by a band of robbers. I'm running fast in a dark alley, with my pursuers gaining ground. Their footsteps are as loud as galloping horses. My heart is pounding more with fear than exertion as I try and zigzag my way without looking back. I just keep running from the threat, which may overwhelm me any moment.

This is a typical dream of being pursued. Such dreams are accompanied by a great sense of dread. Normally the dreamer does not offer any kind of resistance by turning around to face the pursuer or by fighting back. Interestingly, the pursuer never actually overwhelms the dreamer, but the threat is unremitting. The dreamer's terror usually ends by awakening from the dream. Mostly, the pursuer is a threatening person, a wild animal, or even a ghost.

Hall's studies indicate that dreams of being pursued are one of the two most common kinds of dreams, the other being the 'falling' dream. His survey in the mid-fifties of 517 American college students found that 93 percent of the males and 98 percent of the females had had one or both of these dreams. In analysing the content of 106 such dreams he found that both men and women typically dreamed of an unprovoked physical attack by a male to which the dreamer responded by fleeing.[6]

Hall believed that when such dreams appear, they represent the dreamer's self-conception of being a weak, passive, inferior, or helpless person, typified by a display of poor resistance.[7] This low self-image could be attributed to threatening external circumstances. According to others, the pursuer is not necessarily an external threat, but representative of the dreamer's feelings threatening to get out of control.[8] Sometimes such dreams could also be projections of 'disowned parts of the dreamer's personality'.

It is commonly perceived that most of our anxieties can be attributed to something that we find difficult to confront. Rather than accept them as situations that demand resolution, we project them as external threats, like robbers pursuing us or an unknown enemy stalking us in a dream. Anxiety is, often, not amenable to reason, and the accumulation of free-floating anxieties slowly turns into an unidentifiable fear. An anxiety may subside when the associated threat recedes, but only temporarily. When a little more entrenched, the anxiety can resurface with greater vehemence than before. Dreams provide one of the most effective ways to confront an anxiety or fear.

This is exactly what the Senoi people, a 12,000-strong community living in the mountainous jungles of Malaysia, do: they teach their children the art of dreaming.[9] Dreams being central to the community, every morning, each member of the family from the youngest to the oldest relates his or her dreams. Among other things, these dream sessions are thought to help the children to confront their fears.

Suppose one of the children recalls a dream of being chased by a tiger and he is fleeing in terror. The father would invariably urge his son that the next time he is chased by a tiger in a dream, he is not to run. He has to learn to stand his ground, and not only that, but to slowly turn around and face the tiger. His education does not end after confronting the menacing dream figure; he is then told to look directly into its eyes and ask: Who are you? What do you want? The Senoi are said to teach their children that nocturnal adversaries are hostile spirits that transform into helping spirits if they are confronted and overcome.[10]

This aspect of the Senoi theory has come under strong criticism in recent times. Their dream culture was brought to the attention of the Western world by Kilton Stewart. However, it has been subsequently established by other anthropologists[11] that Stewart had blurred imagination with his field notes. Although its anthropological origins are suspect – even fabricated – I have touched upon this dream technique due to its psychological relevance. One may or may not believe in hostile or helping spirits, but a very important psychological truth is, perhaps, embedded in these simple practices. They force the dreamer to confront a fear at its roots – the unconscious. The hostile spirits have been reborn as the anxieties and fears of urbanized people and if left unchecked they can devour them. If the tiger is faced in the dream, the dreamer may find that he or she is able to confront the threat in waking life, be it a difficult boss, a messy relationship, or a debtor at one's doorstep. If our dream figures represent internalized ideas about others and ourselves, then the effort we make in changing our reactions to them in our dreams may alter the way we interact with our waking environment, thereby transforming our ideas about our self and the world. Once one fear is faced, it strengthens the dreamer's capacity to cope with other fears.

Falling

In a falling dream, the dreamer experiences a steep fall through space – from a cliff, from the top of a high-rise building, or from a window – this being attended by an acute sense of panic or fear. An abrupt awakening on the part of the dreamer before hitting the ground usually terminates such a dream.

There are different schools of thought on what these dreams could symbolize. The physiological school explains them simply as the transition from wakefulness into sleep. As we fall asleep, the brain produces a steady alpha rhythm that characterizes a state of deep relaxation; the pulse and breath rate slow down, the body temperature drops, and the sleeper enters fully into Stage 1 of sleep. This school believes that no metaphorical meaning should be attached to these dreams since they represent the bodily sensation of releasing control during the onset of sleep. 'Falling asleep' or 'dropping off to sleep' are common expressions that factually describe this process. Research indicates that women report falling dreams more frequently than men, when falling asleep.[12]

Frederick Myers, one of the pioneer British explorers of the unconscious, gave the term *hypnagogic* to dreams that precede sleep and *hypnopompic* to dreams that come just as we are awakening. Falling, tripping, or stepping off a curb accidentally are all images associated with hypnagogic dreams that come as we drift from waking into sleep.

Freud disagreed with the somatic explanation. He felt that falling dreams are the reproduction of childhood games involving movement, which are very attractive to children. He believed that in childhood there cannot be a single child who has not been held aloft and made to 'fly' across the room, or who has not been thrown up in the air and then suddenly dropped and caught again. Children are delighted by such experiences and never tire of having them repeated. Freud says, 'In after years they repeat these experiences in dreams; but in the dreams they leave out the hands which held them up, so that they float or fall unsupported.' He adds, 'These games of movement, though innocent in themselves, give rise to sexual feelings. Childish "romping", if I may use a word which commonly describes all such activities, is what is being repeated in dreams of flying, falling, giddiness and so on; while the pleasurable feelings attached to these experiences are transformed into anxiety. But often enough, as every mother knows, romping among children actually ends in squabbling and tears.'[13]

In complete contrast to the physiological theory and Freud's kinetic-sexual basis of falling dreams is the theory where falling is treated as a symbol and interpreted as such. Downward motion often has negative connotations: we *fall* short on a job; we *fall* into the enemy's hands; we *fall* upon hard times; we *fall* into bad ways; or we *fall* from grace. In a falling dream we have 'lost our balance'. Falling dreams are thus generally considered to represent situations in which the dreamer feels a loss of control, is helpless, is in danger of losing his or her status in someone's eyes, or fears the loss of security or emotional stability.

Flying

In this kind of dream the person is flying unaided through the air. In contrast to falling dreams, flying dreams bring a remarkable sense of exhilaration. Rarely are flying dreams experienced as unpleasant or fearful, for they bring with them a sense of freedom and exultation wherein dreamers feel empowered and in complete control of their actions. Some dreamers speak of a strange recognition, as if flying is a skill that they have always possessed, yet for some reason have forgotten how to use.[14]

These are not restricted to solo flights; there can be other people – strangers, friends, or guides – accompanying the dreamer. You may find that you are running hard in a dream and then suddenly, without any warning, you are airborne and flying. Or from the start of the dream you may be in the air flying like a bird; or cutting through the air Superman-style with arms straight out; or just floating high above the rooftops, sailing in the air as you observe the world below.

Flying has connotations of 'flying high', of being successful, of feeling elated, also of being ambitious and achievement-oriented. Many people have reported that the 'high' from a flying dream can last for several days. The sky, literally, is the limit and sometimes even beyond, into space and among the stars. Anjali Hazarika, a corporate consultant who uses dream work in her training programmes for managers, says in her book, *Daring to Dream*, 'I flew for days in my dreams after I got a first class first in my postgraduate degree course in Psychology.' [15]

In Freud's phallocentric universe, flying dreams are associated with an erection, but although women's experiences of sexual arousal are different, they report as many flying dreams as men do.[16]

The symbolic implications of flying may be that you are feeling satisfied or exhilarated about something. You are feeling effective or competent in relation to a recent event in your life. You may have discovered an unusual ability, may have fallen in love, or you may be feeling that you have overcome a great obstacle. Flying dreams may also afford the dreamer new perspectives on situations that may seem overwhelming when viewed from ground level.

Examinations

I am sitting for an examination and the invigilator hands me the question paper. I read through all the questions. To my complete horror I do not know the answer to any of them.

This was 'Arvind Mehra's' dream on the eve of a presentation he had to make for an advertising campaign that he had been working on for days.

It is amazing how many people have complained of the obstinacy with which they have been pursued by the dream of failure in an examination. There are many variations: the dreamer arrived late for the examination, the wretched pen would not work, the dreamer studied for the wrong exam, or could not finish the exam in the allotted time. The irony is that many of the dreamers have successfully negotiated their school and college examinations, and are now themselves doctors, university professors, or top executives.

The term 'examination dream' is also used to describe situations in which the dreamer had to deliver a talk and was suddenly speechless; was cast in a play and could not remember the lines; or said something utterly inappropriate to what was being asked. The commonality in all these dreams is that the person feels inadequate, ill-prepared, and fears failure or the disapproval of others.

The anxiety in these dreams is reminiscent of our school and college years when we were straining to perform, but were uncertain of the outcome. Examination dreams may coincide with phases in our life when we are judging our professional competence, when we feel unready to meet personal challenges like shifting house, becoming a parent, or even qualifying for a driving licence. I was told an examination dream by a man who was preparing for his daughter's forthcoming marriage, which given the circumstances in India is indeed a trying experience!

These are not veridical dreams, warning or predicting a particular outcome. It was understandable that on the eve of an important presentation Arvind Mehra was anxious about how it would be received. However, his inability to perform in the dream was not a comment on his presentation. All it recorded was his anxiety about an impending situation. In fact, Wilhelm Stekel, who moved away from Freud and developed his own 'active analytic therapy', says that 'dreams of Matriculation only occur in people who have successfully passed it and never in people who have failed in it'.[17] It seems that the anxious examination dreams appear when the dreamer has some responsible act to perform and is afraid it will end in a fiasco. The dreaming mind, in order to reassure the dreamer, searches for some experience in the past in which the anxiety turned out to be unjustified and had been contradicted by subsequent events. That dreams of examinations are often dreams of reassurance is a point that Freud himself testified to. He mentions how he had failed in Forensic Medicine in his finals, but had never dreamt of that particular exam. He says in *The Interpretation of Dreams*, 'In my dreams of school examinations I am invariably examined in History, in which I did brilliantly.'[18]

Missing a train

Similar to the examination dream is the dream in which a person misses a train, or any other mode of transport. This is frequently reported and thus warrants separate treatment.

> *I am running down the steps that lead to the railway platform.*
> *Halfway down the staircase I see the train pulling out of the platform.*
> *I charge down two stairs at a time, trying desperately to weave my*
> *way through the throngs of people. By the time I reach the platform*
> *I can see the last coach ahead of me. I run as fast as I can. The train*
> *gathers speed, leaving me standing breathless and anxious on the*
> *platform.*

A familiar dream for many of us. It could be a bus, boat, or aeroplane that has been missed – but the theme remains the same. It could even extend to missing an appointment, or misplacing your luggage.

These dreams of arriving too late may be seen as frustration dreams. They may, at times, occur in people who harbour contrasting desires that neutralize each other and make both desires ineffectual. These contradictory impulses may induce the dream image of not reaching in time.[19] In general, these dreams may alert the dreamer that some resource is being depleted and the effort to find a proper adaptation to the external circumstance is being missed.

Dreams may also employ these transport metaphors to tell us something about the attainment of our immediate goals. Missing a train, a bus, or a plane could signify the fear of losing an opportunity;

the anxiety of not being there for an important meeting or feeling that life is passing us by.

> *Having waited for what seemed hours I turned my back for just a moment and during that time I missed the bus I was meant to catch. I run after it, shouting and gesticulating to make it stop, but it disappears down the road in a haze of dust.*

This was 'Meenakshi Sinha's' dream, who still single at 36, felt she had 'missed the bus'. Her long wait for the bus and then its departure without her was a metaphor for her dwindling hope of marriage.

Sex

> *I am having sexual intercourse with a stranger in the back of the bus, completely oblivious of the other passengers.*

Many people are alarmed by explicit sexual dreams because the subject of sex is overarched by social and moral constraints. These dreams are dominated by overt sexual content and mostly have a singularity of focus. Frank sexual dreams are common to both men and women, especially in adolescence. Although sometimes the sexual content of male dreams is openly manifest in the wet dream, women are equally prone to sexual dreams.[20] One study, for example, found that women's dreams are influenced by the menstrual cycle. They tend to have erotic dreams during the first half of their cycle, when the sex hormone is most active. 'During the second half of the menstrual cycle when the maternal hormone comes to the fore, their dreams become maternal in character.'[21] According to the Kinsey study, about 85 percent of males will experience one or more wet dreams during their life.[22] Men often feel that erections during sleep are a give-away of the erotic content of their dreams, but that, perhaps, is not strictly true. Researchers have discovered that genital arousal during sleep has a physiological explanation.

We already know that certain physiological changes in a sleeping subject alert laboratory researchers to the onset of a dream. The most prominent are the rapid eye movements and muscular atonia. However, there is one other physical phenomenon that has been observed time and time again: REM sleep is very strongly connected with genital arousal.

A very ambitious programme undertaken at the Baylor College of Medicine in Texas studied 125 males, ranging in age from three to seventy-nine. All the subjects exhibited erections during sleep: The ten-to-twelve-year-olds spent more than three hours of their sleep in tumescence, and this gradually declined to a minimum time of an hour and a half for men in their sixties and seventies. Even little boys in the age group of three to nine spent an unusually long period in penile tumescence.[23]

A similar study was performed with women to measure genital arousal during REM sleep, and the results confirmed that they also experience genital arousal while dreaming, except that it was not as evident as with men.[24]

It must, however, be pointed out that nocturnal genital arousals are triggered by neurological activities and may not be directly related to the erotic content of the dream. In fact, regardless of the content, every time men experience a dream they will have an erection. This is confirmed by another study that tried to ascertain the effect of pre-sleep or recent sexual outlet on genital arousal during REM sleep. Fewer erections were found during periods of abstinence in comparison to those following intercourse.[25]

An interesting and very useful observation emerged from these studies of nocturnal erections. People with a physical basis for impotence, such as severe diabetes or nerve damage, showed no erections during sleep, while those whose impotence stemmed from psychological causes displayed full erections during sleep. The psychodynamic conflicts that contribute to erectile dysfunction in waking life are bypassed in sleep.[26] Could this be because we enjoy sexual gratification in dreams without feeling responsible, guilty, or condemned?

Sleep researchers have identified the physiological realities in the dreaming process, but that is not a comment on the meaning of the images we see in dreams. The discovery of genital arousal during REM sleep, irrespective of dream content, is certainly provocative and would surely have gladdened Freud's heart. This finding pushes us to ask whether Freud had actually voiced a great truth when he said that our dreams have a sexual substratum to them. To Freud, every innocuous dream image, even if it has no sexual content, is a disguise for repressed sexual impulses. Further, dreams prevent these sexual desires from disturbing sleep. Perhaps this is true for many dreams – if we dig around them we may be able to uncover their sexual foundations. There are, however, some dreams that would make us question Freud's thesis: If dreams are a disguise meant to preserve sleep, then how do we understand dreams that do not use any symbolic disguise, but are a realistic portrayal of the sexual act and yet do not awaken the dreamer? What, possibly, could be the message of dream images replete with overt sexuality? Are they alluding, perhaps, to even more forbidding sexual impulses?[27]

We might be able to answer this simply: explicit sexual dreams imbue the dreamer with a compelling desire for sexual gratification and, perhaps, that is all the meaning we can derive from their imagery – a physiological tension is being released in a straightforward manner. However, sex dreams are rarely so simple and unembellished. Often the 'sex impulse is framed in a larger, more complicated picture, the analysis of which yields considerable knowledge about the dreamer's total conception of sexuality and all of its ramifications in his personality'.[28] Everyone has this basic sexual impulse, but if we need to understand a person's behaviour we need to find out how this impulse is viewed. For it is one's idea of the impulse that determines behaviour, not the impulse itself.[29] If the person conceives of sex as something to be ashamed of then the dream imagery, like in the bus dream above, will be consonant with this idea. She was surprised that despite people watching her she indulged in the sexual act. If viewed as a dangerous alien force, like Manish did, it appears so in his dreams as a battle. To take another example, a woman dreamt:

> My school teacher is making passionate love to me in an unhurried way. He gradually builds it up, so that every gesture is an invitation which culminates in a refined eroticism. Slowly, not only our sexual communion, but the whole room is aglow with a marvellous radiance.

Her dream may be indicative of her personal sexual predilections, however it is not restricted to that alone. The dream is also suggestive of discovering that particular glow which can inform sex, but which goes far beyond the act itself. Jung felt that sexual themes symbolize a higher creative process, as seen in the erotic sculptures that adorn the exteriors of many Hindu temples. These do not simply refer to the sexual union of male and female, but to the wholeness within the Self and to the marriage of opposites – between earth and sky, mortal and divine, spirit and matter.[30] The 'ancients considered the phallus primarily as the source of fertility and did not attach any immoral meaning to it'. In all ancient religions, procreation was considered as that sphere of human activity that made them holy, godlike creatures. Through the sexual act they believed they participated in the divine process of creation.[31] Mystics in virtually all religions have used sex as a metaphor for divine union, where 'ecstasy' is viewed as 'the state of being beside oneself'. In fact, descriptions of mystical ecstasy are so reminiscent of sexual ecstasy that many traditions hint at a connection between them. For example, Tantrism allegedly derives its charge of mystical bliss from sexual ecstasy. Also, in many of the finest devotional poems from India 'the sexual and the mystical are so intertwined that it is difficult to separate the two'.[32]

This leads one to speculate that some of these dreams may not necessarily be sexual. Are they, perhaps, religious? Can the sexual experience be a euphemism for god?[33]

Being naked in public

Contrary to what is widely believed, dreams of being naked in public have nothing to do with sexuality, but often have to do with feeling exposed, embarrassed, or ashamed.[34] They usually allude to some circumstance in the dreamer's life that makes him or her feel stripped of normal defences. Strangely, it is mostly only the dreamer who is aware of his or her nudity – other people in the dream appear to be oblivious to it. Perhaps the dream is cautioning the dreamer that his or her vulnerability is more an internal notion than an external reality.

Clothes, it may be pointed out, can represent our identity. A policeman's clothes are different from a factory worker's, a business executive's from that of a doctor's. Clothes can represent not only our occupational status, but also our social status. We often judge people by the clothes they wear, and so seeing yourself naked in a dream may be a way of asking, 'What will people think of me if they see me for what I really am?'

However, dreams of nudity can also indicate honesty, where the person stands exposed, open, and vulnerable towards another as an expression of trust in the relationship. Also, the discarding of clothes may represent a violation of the social code and thereby could indicate that the dreamer wants to rise above social restrictions.

Freud believed that in the innocence of infancy we have no shame in our nakedness. In fact, children love to laugh and jump and slap themselves in their nakedness, enjoying this intoxicating display, which is often met by their mothers' disapproval. He believed that the childhood desire for exhibitionism resurfaces as dreams of nakedness in adulthood – this being an expression of the original infantile self-display that was repressed due to punitive parental attitudes. The censure expresses itself as the distress or shame experienced in the dream. Thus, to Freud, these dreams are also an example of wish-fulfilment.[35]

Teeth falling out

The biographers of the Indian emperor Ashoka (third century BC) tell us that the king dreamt one night of his teeth falling out. He summoned his dream interpreters and asked them what his dream portended. They said:

> One whose teeth decay
> And fall out in a dream
> Will see his son's eyes destroyed
> And the death of his son as well.

Hearing these words, a distressed Emperor Ashoka began making salutations to the deities, imploring them to protect his son Kunala.[36]

The belief that falling teeth are an ominous portent was not only the preserve of Buddhist oneirology, but also a view held by many cultures. The ancient Hindu Puranas warn that 'one whose teeth are broken or fallen meets with the loss of wealth besides suffering bodily disease'.[37] In the Talmud, teeth were interpreted as members of the dreamer's family, and death was foretold for a particular member after such a dream.[38] Artemidorus, in the second century, laid down guidelines on how to distinguish who would die after such a dream: 'The upper teeth represent the more important and excellent members of the dreamer's household; the lower, those who are less important ... Furthermore, the so-called incisor teeth or front teeth signify the young; the canine teeth, the middle-aged; the molars ... old people. Therefore the type of person he is to lose is indicated by the type of tooth he loses.'[39]

Modern-day interpreters hold a diametrically opposite view. They argue that since research has indicated this type of dream to be more frequent among women, it refers to giving birth – a small object is expelled from an orifice of the woman's body, resulting in pain and bleeding. This also dovetails very neatly with the folk belief that a woman loses a tooth for every baby she bears.[40] Freud would as a rule interpret a dream of someone else pulling out a tooth to mean fear of being castrated. Stekel even included dreams of having one's hair cut in this category.[41] The common element in these interpretations (castration and birth) is the separation of a part of the body from the whole. Freud, however, made a distinction between these dentist dreams and dreams with a dental stimulus; he felt the latter were dreams of masturbation.[42]

At a symbolic level, losing teeth could be alluding to the inability to 'chew' on a particular experience, finding it hard to grasp or to comprehend it. We are toothless at two stages of our life – in infancy and in old age. Both are characterized by helplessness and dependence. Losing teeth could be a concern with aging, the general diminution of one's powers, and the attendant feelings of embarrassment and weakness. Most people who recount dreams of falling teeth feel anxious and distressed in the dream. When asked why they felt anxious many would say, 'But I'll look awful! And how am I supposed to speak without my teeth?' Such unease is often created in the dream from some waking concern that triggered it.

Recurrent dreams

Typical dreams are those that most people experience at some stage of their life. A recurrent dream, as the term implies, is one that repeats itself again and again. These recurrent dreams may involve a typical dream theme of being chased, taking an examination, flying or falling, but not necessarily so. Also, recurrent dreams need not be repetitive in their thematic content, but a symbol, a character, or an emotion may repeat itself for many years. Approximately two-thirds of adults experience some form of repetitive dreams and most of them seem to be associated with stressful events.[43]

Functional efficiency demands that we identify our problems, understand their psychodynamics, and resolve them through discursive reasoning. This may not be entirely applicable in life; we do dwell on our problems, often stating and restating them over long stretches of time, repeatedly wanting to discuss them like a recurrent dream. A close parallel to this is a child's fascination with fairy tales, which parents usually read to them at bedtime. Bruno Bettelheim, who distinguished himself with his psychoanalytic work with children, studied the meaning and importance of fairy tales. He wrote, in *The Uses of Enchantment*, 'Soon he [the child] will indicate that a certain story has become important to him by his immediate response to it, or by his asking to be told this story over and over again.'[44] Bettelheim believes that this repeated interest in a particular fairy tale is because the child is attempting to come to terms with 'the psychological problems of growing up – overcoming narcissistic disappointments, oedipal dilemmas, sibling rivalries; becoming able to relinquish childhood dependencies; gaining a feeling of selfhood and of self-worth.'[45] The child subconsciously grapples with a current problem through the aegis of the fairy tale; the adventures and final resolution in the fairy tale become the symbolic matrix through which the child imaginatively journeys in an attempt to try and come to terms with the current problem. Similarly, by repeating themselves our dream images make us aware of an issue that is seeking resolution.

Jung attached great significance to recurrent dreams and believed they were 'of specific importance for the integration of the (overall) psyche'.[46] In his view, recurrent dreams indicate that some focal conflict remains unresolved. It is as if the psyche is periodically reminding the dreamer that a pending matter is awaiting settlement. He wrote: 'There are cases in which people have dreamed the same dream from childhood into the later years of adult life. A dream of this kind is usually an attempt to compensate for a particular defect in the dreamer's attitude to life; or it may date from a traumatic moment that has left behind some specific prejudice. It may also sometimes anticipate a future event of importance.'[47]

'Anil Ahuja's' recurrent dream is one such example:

I am fleeing in absolute terror from something that is pursuing me. I cannot even turn around to see what it is. I have to cross a river but as I try to do so, the water turns into thick rubber sheets, which clamp my feet down. I struggle again and again to extricate my feet but cannot, all the while fearing that my pursuer is gaining ground and I will not be able to get away.

If Anil had dreamt this once or twice, we may have treated it as a typical anxiety dream of being chased. The sheer repetition of the dream over many years alerts our attention to something more powerful, something more significant. The dominant metaphor is of getting stuck; the dreamer appears to be getting away from his pursuer (the challenge) only to be unexpectedly hampered midway through the river.

And curiously enough Anil had tried his hand at many things without feeling successful at anything. He had a degree in Fine Arts from Paris, but had not painted for the past twenty years. He had tried his hand at rural education, but then switched to handicrafts. Later he attempted to write a book. When he related this dream to me, his current business enterprise, a modest one, was facing the threat of closure, and he and his partner had fallen out with each other. Anil was convinced that every project he undertook was doomed to remain incomplete. Chased by the demons of frustration, he felt paralysed, unable to progress in any venture he undertook. He found himself trapped in a repetitive cycle of failure.

Not all recurrent dreams have an anxious theme like those of Anil's. Some have much more frightening content, and these have the potential for becoming nightmares.

Nightmares, night terrors, and post-traumatic dreams

These dreams are associated with an overwhelming state of anxiety, which often awakens the dreamer. They are very different from the anxiety dreams we have been discussing till now. We may label them as 'bad dreams' or as nightmares. Researchers distinguish among a variety of experiences generally referred to as nightmares. The difference between a nightmare and a night terror is that there is a very detailed recall of the dream events in the former, while the latter often leaves people with a short, single frightening image, for example, of being choked or crushed. A scream frequently precedes awakening from a night terror, and is followed by temporary disorientation. In addition, clinically a nightmare is associated with the later part of REM sleep, usually early in the morning. A night terror, on the other hand, occurs during the first two hours of sleep and is associated with NREM Stage 4 of the sleep cycle.[48]

Post-traumatic dreams replay traumatic events of our life, such as combat scenes, rape, natural calamities, accidents, and loss that the dreamer may have been unfortunate enough to experience. In such dreams the dreamer relives the traumatic scene, or a variant of it, over and over again, sometimes for many years. They are a mixture of nightmares and night terrors – they can occur both during NREM sleep, when night terrors occur, and during REM sleep, when most ordinary nightmares arise.[49]

Nightmares

Almost everyone has had a nightmare at some time or other, most likely in childhood. Some are so powerful that they are vividly remembered throughout our lives.

Nightmares commonly occur between the ages of three and six. While they become less frequent after the age of six, their incidence may increase again in adolescence between the ages of thirteen and eighteen.[50]

Ernest Hartmann, the director of a sleep laboratory at Lemuel Shattuck Hospital in Boston, has extensively researched nightmares.

He believes that average nightmare-sufferers have certain personality features that make them prone to such dreams. They are typically the kind of people who are open, easily hurt, self-disclosing, and vulnerable. He characterizes them as having 'thin boundaries' so that they often merge thought and feelings, and sometimes have vivid fantasies that are difficult to tell from reality.[51] It has also been found that people in the arts or other creative pursuits are more prone to nightmares than the blue- or white-collared worker.[52]

Nightmares, though relatively rare for adults, may provide insights into areas of our life that may have been ignored because they were painful. If we can understand these dreams and locate the problem, we may loosen their grip on both our waking and dreaming selves. Daytime events and feelings that trigger nightmares and bad dreams are often linked to some deep fear, frustration, or resentment, which may be a lifelong trouble spot that the dreamer has avoided confronting. Such dreams may then serve the very useful function of turning the spotlight on the ignored problem. They can point to the source of the problem and help the dreamer take the first significant step to resolving it. The Senoi method of facing the danger in the dream and then conquering it consciously can be very useful in dealing with nightmares.

Not all nightmares originate in psychological causes; physiological issues may sustain their roots. Hartmann describes several physiological causes of nightmares, the most common being drug-related. If you suddenly begin to have frequent nightmares, for the first time in your life, then your first step should be to talk to your doctor as some forms of medication are known to cause them.[53]

Night terrors
Night terrors, like nightmares, are most common in children. The frequency of these decreases as the child grows older. Many researchers are hesitant to refer to night terrors as a genuine dream, but view it as the effect of sudden shifts in the physiological status of the body during sleep, rather than the attempt by the unconscious to highlight psychological conflicts, as in a nightmare. In a night terror tremendous changes in the autonomic nervous system take place very rapidly – the pulse and respiratory rates sometimes double in the process. As the awakening is so abrupt and involves such dramatic shifts in the nervous system, night terrors have been classified as 'disorders of arousal'.[54] Sleepwalking sometimes follows the onset of a night terror. Unlike nightmares, where a symbolic dream narrative is being unfolded, which

gradually awakens the sleeper, in a night terror the awakening is very abrupt with no recall of the dream.

Post-traumatic dreams

Any trauma leaves a scar on our psyche, which may be reflected in dreams. Almost every traumatized individual experiences some kind of nightmare incorporating the trauma. After a severe accident, a fire, or the death of someone close, dreams may continue to reflect this in one way or other for a few weeks. However, for some individuals these continue to recur over many years. Clinical researchers tend to treat this not at the level of an 'ordinary' nightmare. Hartmann and others, after studying Vietnam veterans, treat them as *memory intrusions* into dreams.[55]

We know the devastation that wars inflict, but its cost in human terms – the scars carried by the survivors, the personal hells these survivors undergo in their private worlds at night – is rarely discussed or understood.

Ramesh Khanna, a marine engineer, was on a merchant ship off the Cape of Good Hope, near Durban, when a German submarine torpedoed his ship. This was in January 1943, during the Second World War. He was lucky to jump into the water and scramble onto a lifeboat. More and more survivors got onto the boat till it could hold no more and sank. Ramesh soon found a buoy and clutched onto it, but so did ten others. Predictably, it also sank, and Ramesh had to keep afloat unaided. Sixteen hours elapsed before he was picked up by an Allied warship. He was hospitalized for three months in Durban, and heavily tranquillized to enable him to come to terms with the trauma. He was a courageous man. Before the end of the year he was sailing again on another merchant vessel. History repeated itself in 1944 when his ship was sunk once again, this time in the Pacific Ocean. After recuperating, he still continued to sail. He, however, was prescribed mild sedatives every night to protect him from his trauma.

After the war, he was travelling home on leave from Bombay to Lahore on the Peshawar Frontier Mail train, when his traumatic memory intruded his sleep. He was sleeping on the upper berth of a first-class compartment. While completely asleep, he jumped down and leapt for the door, ready to jump out of a moving train as though it was a sinking ship. Luckily, the person sleeping on the lower berth held on to Ramesh before he could jump off the train. The gentle rocking of the train must have rekindled the experience of a rolling ship. Perhaps a jerk in the rocking of the train triggered the memory of being torpedoed. He instinctively lunged for the door to bail out. For many years afterwards, he needed to be protected from this intrusion of memory by ensuring that someone travelled with him, just in case. With the passage of time the intensity of the trauma gradually diminished, but not without the help of sedatives, which he continued to take for many years.

We said earlier that during dream sleep the muscular tonus is reduced, foreclosing the option of movement while dreaming. Ramesh Khanna did exercise muscular control in jumping down and opening the door, probably indicating that his memory intrusion was not experienced during REM sleep, but during non-dreaming sleep.

In an 'ordinary' nightmare the dream is trying to highlight a fear, or a conflict, in its attempt to absorb it. The unconscious is trying to heal the wound, by presenting it in various forms for it to be wholly accepted or ingested. However, the post-traumatic repetitive nightmare sometimes fails to do this. The unabsorbed traumatic material continues to haunt the dreamer's psyche. Hartmann says, 'It is branded or etched into memory. It is "encapsulated" somewhat like an abscess, separated from the body by a wall and yet tender to the touch.'[56]

In a world where we have to cope with many kinds of stress, it would be rather unusual if our dreams did not reflect them. Dreams often dramatize images to make a point, but typical dreams are perhaps a way to deal with the general strains of everyday life. Unless the dream is recurrent or nightmarish, most typical dreams are a scan of what we have had to cope with recently. Sometimes we know we are anxious or tense, and at other times we may be entirely unaware of our fears. Regardless of whether we are aware of our situations or not, dreams faithfully record what we're going through, so that small neglected worries, a bruised self-image, anger we could not express, struggles we dare not name, surface to be ingested bit by bit. But even though many of our dreams portray and comment on our everyday concerns, such is the range of the dreaming mind that it is not limited to the humdrum issues of our lives. Standing at an important crossroads, where the direction we take could alter the course of our lives, dreams become all-important pointers to the path best suited for us. Kavita Nayar's dreams in the next chapter are one such story.

Chapter 12

ARCHETYPAL DREAMS
AT A CROSSROADS

A dream which is not understood is like a letter which is not
opened.

Talmud

Kavita Nayar, an established Indian painter whose work has been
exhibited in Europe, the US, and Japan, recounted a powerful
dream she had over sixteen years ago, a dream that altered the course
of her life. We sat in the living room of her three-bedroom apartment-
cum-studio in New Delhi, where on the ground were two mattresses
covered with colourful red and yellow Rajasthani bedcovers, and an
assortment of cushions. A low table in the centre and two wickerwork
stools completed the functional necessities of the arrangement. Yet
everything diminished, receded, almost became non-existent in the
overwhelming presence of the paintings that met you on the walls of
the house, in the corridor, outside the kitchen, in one of the bedrooms.
Stilled and held on canvas, these images had not lost their swelling
vibrancy, despite being imprisoned moments of imagination. In one,
a pensive woman was sitting on a windowsill, as another walked away
into the distance while her red scarf swelled in the wind. In another
painting the trunk of a gnarled tree transformed into a hand reaching for
the sky. It bespoke of a belief that took its birth in reality, yet belonged
to a realm beyond it.

'Sixteen years ago, one single dream changed everything for me,' Kavita said.

'That's a long time to hold the memory of a dream,' I commented.

'True, but it came after I had struggled long enough with a conflict that defied solution.'

'Did your dream suggest a way?'

'Yes, that's why I remember it.'

'What made you follow its advice?'

'It addressed my dilemma directly. More than that, the power of the dream was such that I felt assured, at a much deeper level, about the choice I had to make. You see, my personal situation had become so charged that when the dream came I felt a sense of relief, a handing away of a burden,' Kavita said, her large eyes softening with remembrance.

'What was the burden?' I asked.

'I was being pushed to marry when I did not want to. My parents and I were at loggerheads on the issue. They felt I was going to miss the bus.'

'Were you in love with someone else?'

'Not at all. If I were, it would have resolved the issue. Marriage itself did not hold any attraction for me.'

I wondered if this was the normal reticence of a girl on the brink of marriage. Marriage is an important transitional point, where the focus of life will redirect itself, especially for an Indian girl bound to the 'arranged' marriage system. Could this have been the source of the problem that was consuming Kavita?

Maybe marriage entails a different set of anxieties for a woman in India than it does for the man. It is certainly true that it brings about a far greater change for her than for her spouse. Puberty registers strongly for boys, as it had done for Manish; possibly marriage is the equivalent potent transition for the girl, and I wondered whether Kavita's angst could be understood against this background. For her male siblings puberty signals an expansion, an opening out of vision that urges them to explore their emerging masculinity, while for the Indian girl it limits her to the house, accelerating her training in service and self-denial, in preparation for her imminent twin roles of daughter-in-law and wife. She learns that the 'virtues' of womanhood that will reliably help her negotiate her life are submission and docility – submission to the husband and docility towards the mother-in-law – as well as skill and grace in the various household tasks.[1] The price she pays for this ideal is self-effacement. However modern or Westernized her upbringing may have been in the cities, somewhere in her psyche linger her mother's words: 'It's up to you to keep the family together ...'

An Indian girl is often aware that she is her parents' second choice in comparison to her male sibling. It is around her brother that parental expectations centre, for he will grow up to enhance the family income, look after his parents in their old age, and on their death he will be the one who will perform their last rites. On the other hand, the girl will be reminded time and again that she is a 'guest' in her parental home; that her 'real' family is her husband's family.[2] Thus, puberty for Manish was the beginning of his larger involvement with his family, and for the girl it is a strong reminder of her ultimate exit from it.

What her marriage could bring – from the lonely struggle in an alien environment and coming to terms with a man who is a virtual stranger, to the demands of sexual intimacy without the foundation of an emotional relationship – she must face and cope with all alone. She is not allowed backward glances, she cannot return to her parental home in any permanent sense ever again. And if through all this she finds that her husband is unworthy, she still has to continue to live with him, performing a role that holds no promise of personal fulfilment.[3]

Under an umbrella of such uncertainty about her future it comes as no surprise if internal panic turns to resistance, and resistance to the denunciation of marriage itself as a defence against future disappointments. Was this what Kavita was subliminally facing? Was she fighting for her own voice, which must perforce only end in silence? Did she have any real choice?

There are periods in life when a single issue, or conflict, dominates the landscape of the mind for months, maybe years. Kavita was unsure which road was hers to take, the very contrariness of the issue pulling her apart. At such points a dream may emerge from the profound depths of the psyche, compelling us to take a particular path that is meant for us. The figures that typically appear in such dreams stir up emotions that are not ordinarily experienced in everyday life, symbolically portraying a truth that has no conscious equivalent. It is not unusual to see gods and goddesses or mythological figures in these dreams, which leave the dreamer feeling that wisdom from an outside source has been received. These are archetypal dreams, or what Jung called 'big' dreams.

An archetypal dream addresses a personal dilemma and yet transcends it. The solution shines through because it is intertwined with the numinosity of a transpersonal dimension, where we feel privileged to have glimpsed the mysterious powers of the universe. Manish's dream had hinted at a power that was beyond his personal sense of self. Further maturity allows a more direct allusion to the transpersonal in dreams, as perhaps experienced by Kavita. In fact, every subsequent negotiation of a transitional phase may signal a greater exposure to this power.

The conflict in Kavita's life arose between her all-consuming passion to paint and her parent's view that it was but an escape from the demands of marriage. Could it be that she genuinely had a calling that her middle-class parents and society – steeped in conformity – could not comprehend? Never having allowed passion to be the rule of life, they knew nothing of its dictates.

In the course of our conversation Kavita recounted two other dreams that she had had earlier. Although these dreams occurred at varying intervals of time, I have treated them as a series – a dialogue started by the first is continued by the second and culminates in the final 'big' dream.

From her childhood Kavita felt the need to protect and keep inviolate her urge to paint. Her parents wanted her to study the Sciences instead of Fine Arts, her mother constantly reminding her that painting, at best, was a hobby for a well-brought up girl, never a profession.

But Kavita quietly persisted. Hungry to learn more, she would visit the British Council Library after school to read about and absorb the paintings of the masters. One afternoon when she returned home, her mother opened the door and chided her: 'You're late everyday. I suppose you loiter around on the streets with your friends.'

Kavita walked past her mother too wounded even to voice an explanation. For a week she did not speak to her. Everyday she would come home straight from school and just sit on the windowsill, feeling desperately misunderstood. She was about sixteen at the time and had this dream:

I am standing on the terrace of my house. Everything around me is being bombarded, razed to the ground. No neighbouring house remains, no maidan, no buildings. I realize that only my house has remained intact in all this debris.

Years later, Kavita and I tried to understand this dream in the context of her adult life. It seems that 'her house' is the lead metaphor, an attention-grabbing device, given that it is the only structure that remains intact in the dream. We can get a clue to the dream if we understand what the house could represent. Among other things, our house is our abode, and a reflection of what we house at physical, emotional, and mental levels.

'What do you think stayed intact within you, even in your teens?' I asked Kavita.

'My resolve to paint,' she replied promptly. 'It was an urgent need even then.'

This helped make the bridge from her house in the dream to her art. That her urge was strong even in her youth then becomes evident in the dream. Everything else in the scenario is razed to the ground, lying in a heap of insignificance, in a brutally ravaged environment. This could symbolize that no one else's opinion counted. Her yearning to be an artist stayed unaffected, even if that meant being isolated from her environment. A stubborn desire, by its very nature, tends not to count the cost of all that it is compelled to ignore, in order to remain focused.

At first glance the dream seems only to reflect the reality of her situation. The dream can be left at being a comment on a primary need, holding its own, in spite of difficulties. However, a deeper look at the dream made me believe that it was not just faithfully mirroring the reality of Kavita's situation, but was also posing a question that the young Kavita at the time she had the dream may not have known. The dream, ironically, seemed to be asking: If you erase everything around you, how could your art flourish in such conditions?

The dream, while expressing her main urge, also highlighted the dilemma of existing in a state of defensive isolation. Artists render their perceptions in relation to the world they inhabit. What we express cannot be independent of the world it is poured into. Our ability to engage with the ambiguities of experience often can be the soil in which our creativity grows. Moreover, the dream seemed by its very starkness to suggest that no creative impulse, however powerful, can flourish in isolation, for it has nothing to compare itself with if the reference points around have all been ignored or obliterated.

So painting was the very cornerstone of Kavita's existence and she had struggled for years to centre everything in her life around it. When she entered her twenties, her parents, like most Indian parents, began to put pressure on her to get married. Their demands grew stronger and more persistent, but she remained resistant, fearing that no man would be able to understand her passion to paint, and would inevitably try and suffocate her with the demands of domesticity. She felt that marriage would be the death of all that gave her meaning in life. If her own parents could not understand how important it was for her to paint, how could she expect a complete stranger to do so?

The conflict with her parents peaked when one morning she found out that yet another stranger, another prospective husband, was being thrust on her.

'You do remember that Pawan and his parents are coming for tea. Please be back on time,' her mother said in a peremptory tone as Kavita was about to leave the house.

Kavita left for Garhi, the artists' colony in New Delhi that she worked in, with a dull sense of dread. She wondered how many times she would have to go through this before her defences crumbled and she would submit to a decision she would live to regret for the rest of her life.

No sooner had she reached the gates of Garhi and walked through the entrance of the old monument that now housed artists' studios that all her worries faded, leaving behind a blanketing sense of peace. As she walked through the large compound shaded by trees, she saw someone throwing a pot on a wheel, another firing a kiln, and further down an artist contemplating a sculpture. 'Mohini', a colleague, was engrossed in her canvas below the old banyan tree. Kavita's heart surged with pride at belonging to such a world where the act of creating seemed as quiet and consecrated as prayer.

'All this would be snatched away from me, if I agree to marriage,' she said to herself.

Kavita worked peacefully at Garhi all day, but as the shadows of dusk lengthened, laying claim to the day, her thoughts swung back to Pawan and his parents awaiting her arrival at home. She lingered on, delaying the inevitable meeting.

Kavita arrived home deliberately late in a pigment-stained khadi kurta-pyjama and rubber slippers, trying to look as unappealing as possible. She had hoped that, tired of waiting for her, Pawan and his parents would have left by the time she returned. But fate would not have it so – the guests were delayed and had arrived only minutes before Kavita did.

'You must have liked him,' her mother said eagerly after they left. 'He's tall, good-looking, and has a very good job.'

Her mother's criteria for a suitable husband always amazed her. If once, only once, she would say, 'You know, this man you've just met is the sort who would support you in becoming what you most desire to be,' Kavita may have felt that her mother at least understood who she was, and what she needed. But this blind pairing of two people for no reason other than financial security and social conformity seemed a ritual all too familiar to her.

On the last such occasion, during her third year at university in Shanti Niketan near Kolkata, Kavita's father had arrived with a prospective bridegroom in tow, ambling two steps behind him. He took her aside and in a hushed voice told her about the boy, his eyes gleaming in anticipation at the prospect of such a good match.

She didn't reply except with anger flaming in her eyes.

'Kavita, I really don't know what you want. I'm getting old. Am I being perverse if I hope that you're married before I retire?' Her father asked rhetorically, shaking his head in frustration.

She knew that if she refused this boy another would be produced until she said yes. After a while her anger subsided, replaced by a weary acceptance of the inevitable. She got engaged, but without the slightest inclination to get to know her fiancé. He wrote her long letters of love and longing, provoking the only emotion Kavita could muster – that of distant disdain.

She always blamed her phoney engagement for what befell her work at Shanti Niketan. Suddenly the full flow of her creative stream just dried up. The abundant images of her imagination would vanish the moment she tried to actualize them. She would sit in the garden with her sketchpad, but neither nature nor her intent helped. Gone was the creatively active period of the previous two years when amidst the evening power cuts, crouched before the light of a hurricane lamp, she had begun her journey of drawing surrealistic images – forms taken from trees, images evoked by the leaves pirouetting in the wind, or reflections bouncing off the white-washed walls in her room. All that just vanished. There was a silence, a blanketing fog that she could not penetrate.

Around this time, she had another dream that lingers in her memory:

> I am travelling in a bus that meets with an accident. In the accident I lose my left arm. Panic-stricken, I frantically begin to search for it in the mass of bodies strewn on the road. Some are dead, and others are dying, as I pick my way through, searching for my lost left arm. I finally find it and go to a local village doctor and ask him to stitch it back. He stitches it back but it falls off. I then go back and ask him to stick it with Fevicol [adhesive]. He does that.

The central metaphor around which the dream drama revolves is the loss of a limb. The dream seems to suggest that something in her life has been severed – a relationship, perhaps – and she may be feeling 'cut off'. We see once again that the drama of both the earlier dream and the current one is being enacted against a background of destruction. That the theme of both the dreams is the same necessitates treating them as part of a single series. In the previous dream, buildings were razed to the ground, while in this dream human beings lie injured or dying all around. There is a movement from inanimate objects of the previous dream to human beings, that is, from her external environment to something within her. In spite of this apparent progression, the previous problem still remains unaccepted or unresolved. We discover this by the acute anxiety that the second dream conveys. What the exact nature of the difficulty is, only Kavita could explain. Since the lead metaphor in the dream is not just an arm but the left arm, it seems to be drawing attention to itself. So I asked Kavita about her associations with 'left' and 'right'. She said that the majority of people are right-handed, and she felt that 'right' signifies the accepted way, the mainstream, the reasoned approach. On the other hand, 'left' for her is where the heart is, the centre of emotions and affections, from where arise the capacity for sympathy, courage, spiritedness, and enthusiasm. With the loss of her left arm she was feeling severed from these positive emotions.

The dream was once again mirroring her emotional state at the time. It seems that the emotional resistance she had to put up against her father's demands and her subsequent engagement had left her drained, leaving her with little energy to invest in her paintings. Her art had dried up, her creativity amputated.

The dream follows three metaphorical sequences: loss, search, and renewal. The metaphor of loss only mirrors her predicament, while the second metaphor is asking her to search for solutions, to recover from the loss. Once this is done only then can renewal take place. This dream is different from the earlier one; it is a step forward because it hints at renewal, while the previous one showed a stark view of destruction with no overt indication of Kavita seeking a change.

In this dream Kavita goes to a village doctor, a man who represents a traditional form of healing. He sticks her arm on, but it falls off. This could be understood in two ways. It may mean that a conventional, role-oriented approach of relating to her own emotions may not work for her. The traditional path was exemplified by her parents and environment, where she was expected to be subservient to duty, fall into set roles and prevailing stereotypes. She may have attempted to 'stitch' her feelings (arm) in the conventional way – she had, in fact, agreed to the engagement. But the arm drops off – her emotions seem unable to function through that medium. So she tries another method. She asks the village doctor to stick her arm back with Fevicol, a brand of adhesive used for gluing wood. Naturally, it cannot bind living tissue. Could the dream be suggesting that the engagement was bound to break? We know that her deep-rooted desire to paint would not brook any compromise. But this also meant an amputation of her emotions. At another level, the dream could be suggesting that Kavita, having severed emotions (left hand) from her life (body), is now resorting to solutions that do not deal adequately with the loss of emotional flow in her life; an inappropriate quick-fix (glue) is being used, instead of a more relevant 'solution'.

Our emotional energy produces the flow of activity in our life. If it is blocked or cut off, every aspect of life suffers – relationships, work, and creative endeavours. Maybe Kavita could not paint in this phase because she had to relocate the emotional self that engages with other people as a natural and fulfilling function of life. As her earlier dream had suggested, her house stood alone, unrelated to everything around her. At that stage the psyche allowed that house to remain alone, so that her urge to paint was granted the space it needed to emerge. But later the dreaming intelligence showed that a vital part of herself had been sacrificed in the process, and it was now in need of urgent attention. If she avoided relationships because they distracted her from her art, she also ran the risk of amputating her feeling self; that which is of utmost significance to art.

The dream was suggesting something quite contrary to what Kavita was feeling at the time. She believed that her engagement was what caused the drying up of her creative impulses. The dream was telling her otherwise: that this 'drying up' was due to her persistent emotional isolation from herself and others.

However, following her conscious intent to its conclusion, Kavita moved to Delhi after she graduated from Shanti Niketan and began to share a flat with a friend. The first crucial step was taken towards a life she had always dreamt of. Soon afterwards she began to work at the Garhi studios.

Shocked by such unconventional behaviour, Kavita's fiancé's parents started to whisper among themselves:. If their future daughter-in-law could take such a 'bold' step before marriage, how many more such independent steps was she capable of taking after she got married? She did not seem the homely, submissive creature they had hoped for. Kavita's fiancé tried to dissuade her from living independently in Delhi, but Kavita ignored his protestations. The engagement was called off. Kavita wept in sheer relief.

Destiny had intervened on that occasion, but now, presented with a new man, Pawan, Kavita felt she would have to tackle the situation herself. She would have to take strong measures to stop Pawan from marrying her, so she asked to meet him alone. Kavita's parents were overjoyed since this was the first time she had taken the initiative to meet any of the young men they had suggested.

Pawan and Kavita met the following evening in a restaurant. She came straight to the point: 'I must tell you from the start that painting is my life, and everything else is secondary to it. I may never earn anything from my paintings and yet I expect my future husband to support all the expenses my art demands. Besides which I will need a studio to work in.'

Pawan kept silent.

'I doubt if you know that I've already broken one engagement, and the fault was mine.'

Pawan stared at her, but still kept silent.

Kavita felt her plan was working. She would push him into rejecting her.

Finally Pawan asked, 'Were you emotionally involved with this man?'

'Not at all. That was the crux of the problem. I felt nothing for him.' Left unsaid, hanging in the air was the next sentence: *And, if I'm engaged to you, I'll feel nothing for you either.*

More silence ensued as he tried to digest what she said.

'Also I do not want children for a very long time. In fact, I may not want any of my own but, instead, adopt a child.' Kavita had played her trump card, which she thought would daunt every traditional man.

Pawan looked at her with pensive eyes. He realized she was on edge. Instead of reacting to her declarations of war he asked gently, 'This desire to paint ... was it there from very early on?'

Kavita was nonplussed. She had not expected him to come up with a question like this out of all the bombshells she dropped. 'I think I felt its first stirrings when I was eight. Over the years it just grew, till it became the only thing I wanted to do.'

'And you feel marriage will come in the way?' Pawan probed.

'How did you know?'

'From the word go you've done everything to dissuade me from marrying you.'

Kavita laughed and then looked at Pawan as though for the first time. 'I must match your perceptions with honesty. I do not want to get married. I'm just being pushed into it all the time.'

'Are you involved with any other man?'

'Oh, God! No!' Kavita said sincerely.

'Have you ever thought that your husband could be proud of you and may want to support what you are doing?'

'I don't live in a dream, Pawan. Very few men would understand the long hours I need to be totally alone to paint. In those moments the world does not exist. What will happen to the simple daily chores – buying vegetables, getting food on the table, mending buttons? Which man could tolerate that?'

'Artists do marry. They manage.'

'But I must feel the need to marry. If that is absent I'm being unfair to myself and to the other person.'

Two days later Pawan's parents rang up to say that Pawan wished to marry Kavita. Kavita was stunned. What was wrong with the man? Hadn't she told him in plain English that she did not want to marry? Her parents were overjoyed. Her father would never entertain a 'no' from her now. She was trapped.

A deep depression swept over Kavita. Like the fading light of day she felt the darkness of domesticity engulfing her. Just to get away she went to Shanti Niketan. There she had the dream that changed the course of her life.

In front of Society cinema in Kolkata there is a pavement temple with zigzag black and white marble flooring. Instead of the image of Kali [a Hindu goddess] in it, there stands the figure of Shiva. I have to cross the street and get to this temple but I'm unable to do a simple thing like that. I stand at the edge of the street with tears flowing down my cheeks because I'm rooted to the ground and cannot cross. Suddenly the image of Shiva comes to life as he beckons me to cross the road and come to him. I protest by saying, 'How can I cross? Hanuman is lying there.' Hanuman [the monkey god] is lying across the street.

Hanuman simply gets up and moves away, saying, 'Go, the path is clear.'

I look up, only to see Shiva smiling, and he says, 'Cross, and it will be all right.' He beckons me, as I take my first step towards him. His eyes are compelling pools of light, drawing me, inspiring me to cross the road.

What does one do with a dream like this? Kavita was not familiar with Jungian dream theory that would look at Shiva, who stands high in the pantheon of Hindu gods, as an archetype. For Kavita, Shiva's appearance in the dream was real. It was not an archetypal image, emerging from the collective unconscious to make a symbolic appearance in a dream. Kavita believed she had been graced with Shiva's actual presence – the dream did not need interpretation. It was a message from the gods: marry and it will be all right. Shiva and Hanuman themselves would bless the union.

Maybe it is important to reflect that in South Asian texts there is the consistent use of the verb 'seeing' (*darshana*) rather than 'having' a dream. Such language points to the conviction that dreams are *given* to the dreamer as opposed to being *created* by the dreamer, and emphasizes the external origin of the dream, thereby lending them divine or demonic authority. 'To say one has "seen" rather than "had" a dream is to suggest that the dreamer is the passive recipient of an objective vision.'[4]

It may be difficult for many of us to subscribe to the idea of a dream *darshana* – of 'seeing' a god – and so we may need to fall back on the concept of the unconscious speaking to us in the highly charged dream symbols of Shiva and Hanuman. Even if the dream is looked at through the prism of archetypes emerging from the collective unconscious, the potency of the dream is in no way diminished.

The lead metaphor in this dream is that of crossing the road. The bridge from the dream to Kavita's life is obviously her dilemma about Pawan's marriage proposal and the indecision from which she suffers. Two powerful dream symbols are part of the story – Shiva, the great cosmic dancer and the erotic ascetic, and Hanuman the god who, as Kavita described him, removes obstacles. They are both assisting her in crossing the road.

Crossing the road is a significant metaphor for abandoning indecision. But Kavita is weeping and seems unable to cross the road. She is paralysed with indecision despite Shiva beckoning her. It is interesting to note how a simple manoeuvre like crossing the road – an action we perform without any thought – can fill us with such anguish in a dream. She pleads for understanding by saying that Hanuman, the god who never married, is lying on the road, and so how can she possibly step over him? – thereby signifying her intent to remain single. However, Hanuman, by rising, removes the obstacles to marriage and says, '*Go, the path is clear.*'

Shiva, in Hindu mythology, represents the paradox of the erotic ascetic. The great ascetic is also the god of the creative force, symbolized by the phallus (the *lingam*). Certain sects have attempted to separate Shiva's asceticism from his erotic aspect, but the greatness of the myth is that the two opposing strands have been fused into one. We see this fusion of his paradoxical sides within Kavita's dream symbol. On the one hand, Shiva the ascetic beckoning her may signify that she should remain celibate. Yet Shiva in Hindu mythology is not only an ascetic with matted locks and an ash-smeared body, he is also a householder who married Parvati and fathered children through her. So, is the beckoning Shiva inviting Kavita to cross the threshold (road) of asceticism, thereby inviting Kavita to experience conjugal union like he himself did?

Perhaps Jung is right when he says that dreams of numinous figures and gods represent not mundane answers but attempt the reconciliation of opposites that defy resolution to the waking mind. Kavita's single-mindedness with regard to her art would not admit any space for marriage. Yet, as her previous two dreams had hinted, her art and her sense of self stood divorced from all 'others' – all relationships. This dream, through the sacred marriage (*hieros gamos*) of Shiva and Parvati, was beckoning Kavita to unite these disparate strands of her life. Shiva had brought the heat of *tapas* (a burning dedication to a single aim) into the folds of marital life, while Parvati brought domesticity (the function of interrelatedness) into the world of asceticism, both figures enlarging and augmenting each other by their union.

Shiva, in this dream, does not represent a negation of marriage, but symbolizes a reconciliation between the creative urge (Kavita's need to paint) and its relational aspect to life or experience. Unmarried, Kavita's art may not only have lacked the grounding necessary to mature its expression, but also may have left her emotionally stultified.

Kavita felt that this dream was a turning point for her. She had awoken from the dream with an overwhelming sense of relief. As the days passed she felt a burden had been lifted from her shoulders. It was as if something of vital significance had been communicated, which had bypassed reason and touched her heart. She returned to Delhi and found herself calling Pawan without knowing why or what to say to him. All she did was to narrate her dream as though it was her answer to him.

Kavita married Pawan, who not only grew to appreciate her art but also actively supported her in her work. Years later, when Kavita recounted the dream, she firmly believed she had taken the right decision. Even though they lived in a joint family, Pawan never expected her to assume the role of a traditional Hindu wife. And though he himself had never been exposed to painting, music, or the arts, he wanted to learn, so that in the evenings he accompanied her to art exhibitions and concerts. And most unusually for an Indian male, he looked after their four-year-old child when Kavita got a year-long scholarship to study lithography and etching in Paris.

Of course, Kavita does not call it a fairy-tale marriage; it went through its share of upheavals. But what she desired most she got – a supportive environment in which she could pursue her work. Kavita said, 'I know now, what I did not know then. I discovered that one actually does not create anything in isolation. More than one's art, there is a human dimension that gets satisfied, which I had refused to acknowledge earlier.'

That is precisely the line of argument her dreams had taken throughout. Against her conscious wish, her dreams were pointing out an area of neglect, saying, 'Don't fear involvement. If you do, you will cut off the very roots of your sustenance.' Dreams gave her a clue to her own developmental cycle. They unmasked areas in her life in order to provide a counterpoint to her consistently one-dimensional view on things. Perhaps, by learning to appreciate the multiple dimensions of a situation, she began to discern what is truly right for her.

This reflected in Kavita's art. By the time I met her, she had created more than 500 individual works, all of which were held together by an underlying theme of exploring human aloneness. In fact, her work could be classified into four distinct stages. 'Beginning with the *Me Alone* works depicting the primal state of loneliness, this is followed by the *You and Me* series, where loneliness is partially offset by the presence of the other, and more fully offset in the *We Together* series, where emotional union is achieved, to the crescendo of the *Entwined* series which celebrates the joys of union'[5] – a progression we have been following through her dreams. Fittingly, Suneet Chopra, an art critic who wrote about her work in the major Indian newspaper *The Economic Times*, commented: 'It is interesting to observe how Kavita has moved from expressing feelings of alienation to reaching out and evoking relationships and harmonizing them with an environment that has been domesticated yet has a life of its own. This is essentially different from the existentialist position of being the outsider looking in.'[6]

Later, Chopra reinforced her dream theme when he reviewed Kavita's exhibition of prints and mixed media works at the Galerie Romain Rolland in New Delhi: 'The quest that began as a lonely one in her early work, has expanded to include other humans ... The problems of existence can only be solved in the context of human relations and in relation to the wider natural environment.'

Perhaps Kavita had actually found 'love'. And her dreams helped her settle for nothing less.

Given Kavita's experience, are we to assume then that every time a god or goddess, a holy person or guru appears in a dream it augurs well for the dreamer? Are these appearances manifest signs of benevolence, of good fortune? This would be a misrepresentation of the role of myths in dreams. Mythic figures are universal archetypes, rising from the dreamer's psyche as a response to the need of the hour. They contain no moral judgment of 'good' or 'evil', no aesthetic pronouncements of 'beautiful' or 'ugly'. They are simply representations of the core issues in the unfolding patterns of a dreamer's life, and are aligned almost dispassionately to help the dreamer negotiate significant transitions. And so, in one instance Shiva may beckon Kavita to cross the road and marry, and in another instance the god may caution the person against marriage, as seen in 'Megha Kashyap's' story.

Lord Shiva appeared, once again to a young girl ready for marriage, but this time the ending was very different. Megha was eighteen when she met 'Suresh', a man who personified all she desired – talent, good looks, and money.

'He became my obsession. I prayed every night that he would ask me to marry him,' Megha reminisced.

What she desired most came to pass. Suresh did ask her to marry him, and Megha lived in a delirium of joy. On the night of her engagement she dreamt:

Lord Shiva is sitting cross-legged opposite me. I see him with his hair in a coil of matted locks, adorned with the crescent moon, and a trident in one hand. I am overwhelmed by his presence and bow my head. He asks me to extend my hand. When I do so he places a small but heavy object wrapped in a red cloth into my outstretched hand. Lord Shiva says somewhat sternly: 'Do not open it till I tell you to.' But I am so overwhelmed with curiosity that I open it. Much to my delight it is a gold necklace, which I promptly wear around my neck.

Megha felt blessed: Lord Shiva himself, to whom Hindu women pray for a good spouse, had appeared before her with a gift. Despite Shiva's injunction, she opened the bundle. The gold necklace confirmed her belief that fortune was on her side. Unfortunately, her fairy tale ended soon after the wedding. The 'most eligible' bachelor turned out to be a narcissistic womanizer, who flaunted his numerous affairs in her face without remorse.

The Megha that I met, a saddened woman, who had lived through a loveless marriage, said, 'Everything turned to ashes. I lived in a haze of humiliation and pain. I could not believe this was the man I had married – the same man I had met when I was eighteen. I forgave him his first affair, but when affairs followed one after another, I felt broken.' She looked straight into my eyes and continued with conviction: 'I now believe I had been given a warning when I was told not to open the "gift".'

'Why do you feel that?' I asked.

'I wanted to marry Suresh so much that I was not prepared to listen to anybody. Lord Shiva was telling me not to go headlong and open this so-called "gift" of marrying Suresh.'

The whole issue was so imbued with desire – symbolized by the gift being wrapped in a red cloth – that she ignored the warning and opened it.

'And how did you understand the gold necklace?'

'What else, but the Shakespearean warning, "All that glisters is not gold ... Gilded tombs do worms enfold ..."' Megha quoted forlornly. 'What I thought was a golden opportunity was nothing of the sort.'

Was the god who appeared to the love-struck Megha an apocryphal figure? Was it a deceiving god bestowing gifts of gold, which turned to dross? Or was it Megha's strong desire that obscured the meaning of the dream?

For the young, besotted Megha to comprehend the full implications of the dream at the point it occurred was well nigh impossible. Only in retrospect could its intent become clearer. The lead metaphor in Megha's dream is the gift. The necklace is not a wedding gift from Shiva. The obvious reference is to Suresh. Shiva is cautioning her to leave the gift, or Suresh, alone. But it can't be expected that Megha will not fall prey to her fate, and open the bundle and adorn herself with it. In other words, the dream shows that she will marry Suresh.

Many myths and folk tales abound with stories of how when a command given by a god or goddess is disobeyed, it leads to pain and suffering, as, for example, in the biblical story of Adam and Eve. In Greek mythology, Prometheus, who stole fire from the gods to bring it to man, outraged the gods by his act. Zeus sought revenge and sent Pandora to wreak havoc. Despite being warned Prometheus's brother, enchanted with Pandora's beauty, welcomed her into his house. Pandora had brought in her arms a box and when she raised its lid, the terrible afflictions contained in it escaped and spread across the earth. To think that these are stories of some vengeful god who, feeling slighted, hurls thunderbolts of misfortune on the person, is to read mythology wrong. Myths are symbolic stories depicting an underlying truth.

In each of these tales the person is cautioned not to do something and invariably the person disobeys, almost as though the disobedience is necessary – necessary in that the events that unfold thereafter catapult the person through a cycle of experience that inevitably results in his or her being confronted with the consequences of the choice made. In such a confrontation, lessons are learnt. Megha had to disregard Shiva's words of caution and play out her fantasy-dominated romance to see the vacuity of the values that had earlier driven her.

Joseph Campbell says in *The Hero with a Thousand Faces*, 'It has always been the prime function of mythology and rite to supply the symbols that carry the human spirit forward, in counteraction to those other constant human fantasies that tend to tie it back.'[7]

From such life circumstances comes the recognition that every time we dream of a god, it does not necessarily portend beneficence. It could, however, signify an important transition point where a critical choice has to be exercised. Shiva's personality brims with contrasts; he appeared as the compassionate god who asked Kavita to cross the road and marry, while in Megha's dream he cautioned against it by presenting himself as the great destroyer of illusions.

As Jung said, 'To be effective, a symbol must be by its very nature unassailable. It must be the best possible expression of the prevailing world-view, an unsurpassed container of meaning; it must also be sufficiently remote from comprehension to resist all attempts of the critical intellect to break it down; and finally, its aesthetic form must appeal so convincingly to our feelings that no argument can be raised against it on that score.'[8]

That is the power of the archetypal dream. At one level we can say that Shiva is merely a symbol clothed in a god-image, which appeared in both these women's dreams at significant junctures of their lives. Yet on the other hand, how else does the human psyche reach an infinitely far away and inaccessible Truth, if somewhere, sometime that same Truth does not convey its nearness and immediate presence? Both Kavita and Megha felt this as an uncanny numinous power that conveyed a powerful sense of meaning directly in the dream. It is often in archetypal dreams that confusion gives way to clarity. The dream becomes something more like a vision – the direct apprehension of the ineffable.

Chapter 13

CALVIN HALL AND
THE CONTENT ANALYSIS OF DREAMS

It is only by reading a number of books by the same author
that we can discover the characteristic and essential traits of
that author.

Marcel Proust

Why another approach?

*F*reud and Jung had proposed that the dream is born from the
unconscious, from motivations that are hidden from the dreamer's
waking thoughts. Other analysts had largely concurred with this thesis,
even though they differed on a few matters of detail. To all of them
it was the job of the analyst to elicit the dreamer's associations to
various elements of the dream to arrive at its interpretation. Perls and
Ullman had taken the dream out of the clinic and relocated it within
an encounter group. Here the analyst was replaced by a facilitator (or
a member of the group), who suggested the meaning of the dream,
but left it to the dreamer to accept or reject the suggestion. What is
evident is the level of subjectivity in these various approaches. Can this
subjectivity be weeded out?

Freud and the psychological school had demystified dreams, but they
had been unable to provide a quantitative method of eliciting objective

knowledge from dreams. Since most of these methods tend to embed the dream within their own interpretational agenda, their analysis becomes subjective, and they sometimes yield conflicting results. Perhaps these theories and methods would have to be put aside if we want an objective, scientific investigation into the nature and meaning of dreams.

Calvin Hall

A totally different approach to dreams, in fact a complete redefinition, was proposed by American psychologist Calvin Hall, who actively studied dreams from the 1940s till his death in 1985. He argued that what we are interested in is the content of dreams, and what they tell us about the dreamer and his or her behaviour, not the process of dreaming – why we dream and the function or purpose of dreaming – as most other dream theorists have focused upon. Freud claimed that dreams fulfil wishes that have been repressed, while Jung believed that dreams are compensatory of the underdeveloped facets of the personality. Both had attributed a function to dreams. This, Hall felt, is speculative and short on tested knowledge. Since Hall had no theoretical axe to grind, he approached the study of dreams without any such preconceptions. He started by amassing a very large databank of dream reports of people from very diverse backgrounds. He found a close correspondence between what people dream about and what they do and think when awake. Teachers dream of classroom situations, bankers of banking activities, alcoholics of drinking, and so on. Based on his findings, Hall was forced to question the relationship between dreams and waking behaviour that had been so far postulated: the ancient world had believed that dreams portray the opposite of what will occur in waking life; for Freud dreams satisfy what is denied in waking life; and Jung asserted that dreams give expression to those aspects that are neglected by the conscious personality. All of them explore an inverse connection. Hall's evidence indicated that a large number of dreams reflect rather faithfully the daytime activities and preoccupations of the dreamer, and he concluded: 'The dream world is neither discontinuous nor inverse in its relationship to the conscious world.'[1]

Rather than conceive the dream as a product of the unconscious, Hall believed that it is a projection of what dreamers think about themselves, other people, and the world they live in. Dreams are a cognitive process and dream images are 'the embodiment of thoughts'. Nothing appears in the dream that the dreamer does not put there. If dreamt, it must have been thought or felt by the dreamer. The dream, according to Hall, is an objective and clear report, a mirror to the dreamer's waking life. There is nothing hidden, nothing obscure that needs to be unearthed in a dream. The meaning of the dream rests solely on what appears in it. With this new metaphysic in hand Hall countered that the dream alluded neither to a Freudian unfulfilled, infantile past nor to a Jungian-directed unfoldment of the personality in the future. Dreams, Hall stated, are the continuation of thoughts from the waking mind, which reveal the current preoccupations of the dreamer. The unusual features of the dream, its bizarreness, may be the product of figurative thought, similar to the figures of speech and metaphors we employ while conversing when awake.

Hall's technique was not to focus on a single dream but to collect a number of dreams – a series of them – from a dreamer, and then examine them as a whole, without eliciting any associations. Each dream in a series, he felt, complements or supplements the other dreams. What may have been ambiguous or hidden in one dream is revealed in another dream. His method is not unlike that used in putting together a jigsaw puzzle, where one usually starts with a prominent piece and then fits the rest of the pieces around it. A prominent or *spotlight* dream with obvious significance becomes the starting point in his method. According to Hall, anyone who can look at a painting and say what it means ought to be able to look at a spotlight dream and understand its significance because its meaning is usually right out on the surface of the dream. However, 'the interpretation of any one dream is a hunch until it has been verified by falling in place with interpretations made of other dreams'.[2] The elements from other less obvious dreams are then fitted around it, as consistently as possible. If the interpretation of the spotlight dream is not supported by other dreams, then another hypothesis is formulated for what the conflict could be, and then tested for consistency with other dreams of the series. How well the pieces fit together and whether they make a meaningful picture are the main criteria for this approach; the degree of internal consistency of the dream series is important.[3] Once the basic features of any series have been identified they, in turn, will help determine what any single dream might mean. Thus, by stepping from the simple to the more complex, even the most obscure dream will divulge its meaning.

The difficulty with associations
Hall was forced into this reformulation because he felt frustrated with the theories of Freud and Jung. Besides being subjective, they were difficult

to apply and their interpretative technique was time-consuming. He felt that when the dreamer free-associates or amplifies a dream, something external to the dream has been introduced into the analysis, which is beyond the information provided by the dream itself. In Freud's method the dreamer alone produces the associations, while in the Jungian technique of amplification the analyst also contributes associations to various dream elements. And once that is done subjectivity enters the process, leaving behind the actual dream and what it can reveal of its own accord. This inadequacy, Hall believed, was due to some inherent difficulties in the methodology adopted.

Consider, for example, Freud's method of free association. People vary a great deal in their aptitude to freely associate. Some dreamers do not easily provide their associations and tend to be monosyllabic; others, if prodded by the analyst, prefer to explore their associations only in the direction suggested by the therapist. Yet another kind of difficulty presents itself when the person is young, as in the case of Manish Chawla, who was unable to bring forth any associations to his dream, so that phonetic metaphors were employed to cull its meaning. The significance of the dream is thus directly bound to how articulate the dreamer is. This should hardly be the case.

In addition, analysts may also differ in their ability to elicit associations. Some may be more proficient than others in coaxing out associations from the dreamer. Also, some therapists may be better equipped in dealing with certain kinds of dream elements, say, Freudian imagery over Jungian archetypes, and their own inclinations and biases inform the process. Moreover, Hall believed that therapists are 'prone to project into dreams conflicts of whose existence they already possess knowledge'.[4] A therapist conversant with the dreamer's circumstances and difficulties may unwittingly read the dream in terms of prior knowledge about the dreamer, and then be inclined to view it as a validation of his or her beliefs. Hall suggested that this 'fallacy of pseudo-validity can be avoided by analysing the dreams of anonymous subjects'.[5] This premise works fine if only one dream of a person is to be analysed, but if the therapist is given a series of dreams to analyse, or is regularly analysing the dreams of a particular individual then the anonymity of the dreamer dissolves.

In the approaches taken by Freud, Jung et al., the meaning of the dream does not rest only in its content, but involves three key constituents: the dream, the dreamer, and the interpreter. As opposed to this, Hall felt a dream should be self-evident from its content and should require neither associations nor a special analyst to understand its meaning.

In Hall's view, if dreams are to be used to understand the character and personality of a large number of people, we would need to establish the norms in dreaming. Only in relation to the norm can we point out the differences and similarities in an individual's dream, and thereby define the uniqueness of the dreamer. For example, if the norm is that young men between the ages of twenty and thirty dream of failure in 13 out of every 100 dreams, then if we find that a twenty-six-year-old man dreams of failing 26 times in 100 dreams, we would surmise that he is more preoccupied with failure as compared to other men in his age group.

To make such assessments we would need dreams from a wide cross-section of people with considerations of gender, age, and status. Only then can we compare the dreaming habits of males versus females; children versus adults; Hindus versus Christians; and so on. Needless to say, these norms cannot be identified on the basis of just a few dreamers. Thousands of dreams are needed to ascertain an accurate norm.

Calvin Hall's method is able to do just this: it fulfils all the above criteria. Fifty thousand dreams, recorded under both laboratory and home conditions, were collected from all walks of life and from all around the world: Australian Aborigines, Argentinians, Zulus, Americans, Mexicans, Peruvians, school children, college students, alcoholics, transvestites, blind men, criminals, people undergoing psychoanalysis, factory workers, professors, psychologists, businessmen, engineers, school teachers, celebrities, and more. From this he developed an objective and quantitative method. When used by different investigators to understand dreams, his method yielded similar results. These results could then be mathematically computed and statistically verified for their authenticity, unlike other dream-interpretation theories, which were subjective and qualitative, and yielded conflicting results under different analysts.

The content analysis of dreams

Hall's method – content analysis – consisted of taking written reports of series of dreams from a large number of people and then deconstructing the contents into certain categories. Though there is a great variety of content in dreams, almost always there are people in them. People constitute one of Hall's basic categories. Anyone who has kept a dream journal will agree that the people we dream about most frequently are those with whom we actually have the closest relationships. Husbands dream about their wives, children about their parents, and lovers about each other. The frequency with which a particular person appears in dreams is also indicative of the intensity of the relationship. Barring a few exceptions, when a relationship with someone is broken, gradually that person disappears from our dreams. The exceptions are our parents and spouse. They never seem to vanish completely from our dreams. Hall also wanted to investigate which characters frequent our dreams. Are they strangers or familiar people? A large number of strangers would suggest that the dreamer feels isolated from people in waking life. If familiar characters appear in dreams we would have to identify whether they are family, friends, or work acquaintances. If, for example, a man dreams more often about his wife than any other person, we can be certain that his wife has a central position in his life. In what way she is important would be determined by analysing the different types of interactions that he has with her in his dreams. If admonitions and aggression predominate over friendly and helpful gestures, we may immediately infer that there is antagonism between the couple.

Another of Hall's basic categories is the setting of the dream. A dream, like a play, nearly always has a setting. It may be one that is unfamiliar or somewhat familiar to the dreamer, but it is only in very few dreams that the dreamer is not aware of the setting. There are many dreams where the dreamer is in some form of transport – car, plane, boat, etc. – and this may signify something about the dreamer's conception of his or her self. As a passenger the dreamer plays a passive part and this may indicate a dependence on others. As a driver, the self-image is of independence and mastery. The following dream of a young woman demonstrates this:

> *I dreamed that my father and I were in an old Chevrolet. I was driving but I could not seem to make the car go up a very steep hill, so my father took the wheel.*[6]

Hall believed that the dreamer is attempting to view herself as an independent person, but when confronted with difficulty she reverts to a dependence on her father. Then there are a few dreams where the dreamer is walking along a road. This by itself may not have direct significance, except for those in which the dreamer is crossing a bridge or a street – indicative of a transition that the dreamer is negotiating. However, the most popular setting in dreams is a house or a room within it, like the living room, bedroom, kitchen, or the stairway.

The particular room will have some special symbolic significance. Besides houses, outdoor settings are also fairly common in dreams. It is interesting to note these are more common in the dreams of men than of women, who have more dreams of being inside a building. 'This finding is consistent with the belief that men find more satisfaction in freedom from confinement whereas women prefer the security of enclosed places.'[7]

The third basic category is the objects in the dream, like buildings, household articles, vehicles, clothing, and implements. If a particular class of objects repeats itself in a dream then that indicates the dreamer's preferences for it. In a study of the writer Franz Kafka's dreams, Calvin Hall found many references to clothing. In waking life, Kafka displayed the same preoccupation with clothes. Later it was discovered that this preoccupation was motivated by a desire to hide his body, of which he was ashamed. He compensated for feelings of physical inferiority by wearing fashionable clothes.[8]

The fourth basic category a dream report usually includes is the activities performed in the dream. These activities may or may not involve other characters. We may walk, sail, or ski; talk, laugh, shave, or think; eat or play the piano – these are all activities. Usually people dream about those activities that interest them in waking life. A businessman rarely dreamt about his work but frequently dreamt about stamp-collecting activities, which turned out to be his favourite pastime. A psychologist-member of a Mount Everest expedition noted that climbers had numerous dreams about climbing mountains.

The last basic category is emotions in the dream. Here we must be careful not to link emotion with activity. Hall found that in many instances when the dreamer is in danger of drowning, or is fighting invaders, or making love, these experiences do not necessarily produce emotion. However, enough emotion is felt in dreams and Hall found that happiness, anger, apprehension (fear), sadness, and confusion are the dominant ones experienced. Anxiety and guilt (both are a part of apprehension) are the commonest emotions, while sadness is the least felt. It was also found that women experience more emotions than men do. All this helps sketch a portrait of the dreamer.

After breaking down a dream report into its constituent elements, the investigator tabulates the number of times each element occurs. In 100 dreams, for example, there will be numerous characters, objects, settings, a variety of emotions felt, and a range of interactions the dreamer has with other characters in the dreams. The end result of the content analysis of these 100 dreams will be a set of frequencies (numbers) within each category, and this will provide us with valuable information about the dreamer. Armed with these frequencies, the investigator would be able to assess the dreamer's preoccupation and interest in direct proportion to their occurrence. The associations of the dreamer to particular dream elements would thus no longer be necessary. Complete anonymity could be maintained and with that objectivity is assured. No longer did analysts project onto dreams conflicts that they had prior knowledge of, nor seek validation of their own theory in the reported dreams. Content analysis universalized dream interpretation, creating a system in which across cultures an objective method of assessment could be used to assemble the personality profile of an individual with his or her current conflicts. This method treats the dream as a 'fully knowable object', subject to scrutiny by aggregate statistical research. Thus an objective, statistical method of scoring and understanding dreams had been founded.

An example would best describe this process of scoring. A twenty-one-year-old unmarried college student, who worked as a part-time salesman, reported the following dream:

> I was in a classroom teaching young women several things about cosmetics, hair care, etc. I remember getting into a big discussion on the virtues of natural hair brushes vs. nylon ones and the correct way to brush hair. The class was about 30 women about age 18 in a classroom much like we had in high school (fixed desks, and old building). The women all paid attention and discussed things well.[9]

Hall's system of content analysis would score this dream in the following manner: The characters in the dream are the dreamer and a group of adult females, unfamiliar to the dreamer. There are seven objects in the dream: the classroom and the old building (two architectural objects of a vocational nature); cosmetics, natural hairbrushes, nylon brushes, and desks (four household objects); and hair (a part of the body, specifically the head). The setting of the dream is indoors, in a place of uncertain familiarity to the dreamer. The only interaction in the dream is a friendly one, with the dreamer teaching the women about personal grooming. The only activity in the dream is a verbal discussion between the dreamer and the group of women. The dream does not exhibit any emotions like anger, apprehension, happiness, sadness, or confusion.[10]

The reader may well ask: how can all this tabulating help a dreamer understand his or her own dreams? No doubt such an exercise is a valuable contribution to the vast corpus of statistical information, and may even help establish norms of dreaming, but how does it touch a dreamer at a personal level? Perhaps two examples may illustrate the bearing of this method on the individual life of a dreamer.

A mother of a nine-year-old boy told me with some measure of concern that her son often had frightening dreams of animals, and she was worried if this was normal. I immediately reassured her that such dreams were very natural, that many young children report similar dreams at his age. He was far from odd; in fact, he was following the norm on the pattern of dreaming in his age group. I asked her whether his dreams over the past few years had changed from wild creatures and monsters to more domesticated animals; from larger to smaller ones; from more to less threatening episodes. With each affirmation her eyes registered amazement as though I held the art of divination in my hand. The look of relief on her face was transparent as she realized that her son was following a pattern of dreaming common to many boys of his age.

I could make this statement because Hall and other researchers had systematically built up a database that found that animal figures are present 40 percent of the time in the dreams of four- and five-year-old children. This steadily decreases to below 10 percent by the time they finish school. Typically one in every three dreams of a nine-year-old will have an animal in it. Bears, lions, tigers, gorillas, dinosaurs, dragons, and monsters will figure in fewer and fewer dreams as the child reaches adulthood. Women and girls report significantly more mammals in their dreams, while males dream considerably more about non-mammals.[11]

Besides establishing the norms of dreaming, content analysis is an excellent means for pinpointing the current conflict in an individual by breaking down the dream into various elements and then tracing the correlation between them. Consider the following dream reported by a young man:

My mother was told by my aunt with whom I stay that I had wasted my money buying a book on human anatomy. My mother was very angry, stating how bad it was and how the pictures inside were dirty because they showed naked people. As she was protesting, my father and brothers came to my rescue, stating it was the best thing I ever did. My father said he was proud of me and it showed I was really

going to become a great man. The dream ended with my father and
brothers siding with me and my mother was left stranded with her
own thoughts of the uncleanliness of an anatomy book.[12]

Along with the dreamer, the characters in this dream are the mother, aunt, father, brothers: family members. The interaction between the dreamer and the others is distinctly polarized. The aunt and mother disapprove of the dreamer's purchase of an anatomy book, while the father and brothers are supportive of it. The dream characters perform two actions: buying a book and talking. The objects in the dream are money, book, and pictures. The emotions in the dream as expressed by the characters are both negative (mother and aunt) and positive (father and brothers).

It becomes apparent from this that the women in the family are opposed to the dreamer's interest in the human anatomy (sex), just as the men of the family are encouraging of it. The dream suggests that the young man is suffering from a conflict about his interest in sex and is seeking the support of his father and brothers to resolve his dilemma. In the process he is realigning himself to the male members of the family and rejecting the feminine values: '*mother was left stranded*'.

This is a radically different method of dream interpretation. Freud would have needed free associations to elicit the latent content of this dream, while Jung would have used amplification to coax its meaning. Hall used no such tools to decipher the dream. The dream was by itself a self-evident document that could be read like an anonymous letter. Its contents told its own story. The process of dream interpretation was to convert the dream images back to the ideas and thoughts they were referring to.

Hall's extensive work in content analysis led him to formulate the continuity hypothesis, the central axiom of his approach. It states that 'dreams are continuous with waking life; the world of dreaming and the world of waking are one ... We remain the same person, the same personality with the same characteristics, and the same basic beliefs and convictions whether awake or asleep. The wishes and fears that determine our actions and thoughts in everyday life also determine what we will dream about.'[13]

Hall fashioned this understanding by arguing that dreaming is a form of thinking and thinking is a process of conceiving, the end-product of which is a conception or an idea. A conception is thus a formulation of experience, which has meaning for the person, but is not dependent upon the input of sensory impressions from the external world. Perception, on the other hand, is a process that is dependent on the stimulation of the senses. We 'perceive' summer when we see a parched landscape, while we can 'conceive' of summer at any time of the year. Conceptions can be communicated through a variety of forms. Artists express conceptions in visual terms, writers use words, mathematicians employ numbers, musicians express them through sound, and architects through buildings.[14] It is our conceptions that we express through dreams. When we dream, these conceptions are turned into pictures. 'Accordingly the true referent of any dream symbol is not an object or activity, it is always an idea in the mind of a dreamer.'[15]

If dreaming consists of transforming conceptions into images, then dream interpretation reverses this process, translating images back to their referent ideas. To interpret a dream is to discover the conceptions of the dreamer, and these may be inferred from a number of lines of evidence. The dream itself will let us know of the dreamer's self-conceptions, impulses and inhibitions, and feelings about other people. Dreams are also an effective means for discovering the dreamer's conceptions of the problems and conflicts that confront him or her, and of the world he or she inhabits. This is where the scoring system introduced by Hall comes into play. The pattern of scoring content based on the five fundamental categories of dreams – character, setting, emotions, objects, and activity – will help identify the conceptions of the dreamer.

For Hall, the dream is primarily a mirror that reflects the self-conceptions of the dreamer. The repertoire of characters the dreamer plays in a series of dreams sheds light on the dreamer. In one dream series, for example, the dreamer was pictured consecutively as a great general, a rich and influential man, and an important steel manufacturer. In each case, however, he loses his power by being disabled in vigorous combat by a superior force. Here we see that a self-conception of strength and potency cannot be maintained.[16] In many of the dreams Hall analysed, the dreamer is more often the victim than the aggressor. In an interaction between a person who initiates the aggression and an aggrieved party, it is inevitably the dreamer who is the victim, highlighting people's basic self-conception of vulnerability. The incidence of this, Hall found, is higher in children's dreams and adult female dreams.[17]

This method of interpretation allows the analyst and the dreamer to get a very clear picture of what the person thinks of him or herself. No other medium can provide as clear a self-portrait as dreams do. Perhaps that is why Emerson wrote: 'A skilful man reads his dreams for his self-knowledge.'[18] They also reveal what the dreamer thinks about other people – parents, siblings, spouse, and associates. In accordance with the continuity hypothesis, if the dreamer thinks of his or her mother as uncaring, then she will play the same role in the dream. Young men often dream of being attacked by other men, clearly indicating the common conception of enmity and antagonism that exists in males towards their own gender.

It is apparent that Hall conceived of the role of the ego very differently from Freud. For Freud the ego relaxes its hold at night, but is periodically provoked when tensions mount within the unconscious. At this juncture the ego seems to rouse itself and intervenes, censoring the satisfaction of the instinctual impulses. The dream is then a resultant compromise, in which the ego's role is limited to policing the conflicting urges. Hall, on the contrary, felt that the ego is not supine during sleep or a mere mediator in quelling threatening impulses, but continues the work it performs during waking hours. It is thus an active participant in the dream, expressing its conceptions and ideas, instead of merely being an arbitrator for the steamy, instinctual uprisings of the unconscious. Since it is the ego that is in control during both waking and sleeping, for him dreams became a clear route in comprehending the dreamer's personality.

Hall and his colleagues used content analysis in a particularly interesting manner to understand the personality of two famous people. They applied its methodology to analyse the published dreams of Freud and Jung. There are many similarities in their dreams, but there are also clear differences. Freud's dreams have more characters than Jung's, attesting to Jung's predilection for spending time alone at his retreat in Switzerland. Of the characters present in his dreams, Jung dreamt more of his family members than did Freud, confirming that Jung's social life was centred on his family.

References to food and eating are more prolific in Freud's dreams than in Jung's. Freud smoked an enormous number of cigars, to which was attributed his mouth cancer that afflicted him in later life. Hall concluded that Freud's high number of oral dreams reflect an infantile wish behind an adult fear. Freud himself had pointed out that usually behind an intense fear lurks a wish for the very thing one is afraid of. Freud's dread of being dependent was, applying his own hypothesis, a reaction to an unconscious wish to be taken care of. This desire develops during the 'oral' stage, when the baby is dependent upon the mother.

Perhaps one of the most interesting patterns in Freud's and Jung's dreams is the type of interaction with characters of different genders. Most men have aggressive interactions with other males in their dreams and friendlier ones with female characters. Jung's dreams followed this pattern, while Freud's dreams manifested the opposite, displaying greater aggression towards women and more friendliness towards men. Based on Freud's own writings, it has been said that he was hostile towards women. Ernest Jones, his friend, fellow psychoanalyst, and biographer said Freud's attitude towards women was 'old fashioned'. He considered their main function 'to be ministering angels to the needs and comforts of men'. Other biographical material supports the notion that Freud had intense friendships with men and had a negative attitude towards women.[19]

The most impressive analysis that Hall conducted did not involve a famous person. Anonymity, in fact, was its basic condition. A psychologist, Alan Bell, had been working with a patient called Norman and in the process had obtained 1,368 dreams from him. Hall was given all these dreams and provided no other data on Norman except his age and sex. Based on these, Bell asked him to sketch a profile of Norman's personality. Hall compared the elements in Norman's dreams with the norms for male dreamers of his age and then noted the frequency with which a dream element or a theme occurred in the series. The presence of women with beards and penises led him to conclude that the dreamer suffered from gender confusion. References to internal organs and the genitals in numerous dreams were highly unlike the norm for most dreamers, who focus more often on the extremities and the head.[20] Hall not only charted the frequency of a dream element, but also noted the lack of certain elements that are expected to occur in a male dreamer of Norman's age. Not even in one of the 1,368 dreams was his father present. From this Hall speculated that Norman's father was either absent or had caused him some trauma. From other elements in the dreams he predicted that as a child Norman had been sexually abused by his father. After Hall had completed the analysis, Bell provided the biographical information of Norman's life, while Norman himself communicated additional information in response to Hall's queries. It was found that the statements based only on dream material were in striking agreement with the biographical data that was later given. Hall had correctly predicted that Norman was a child molester who had been institutionalized.[21]

This was an impressive validation of Hall's continuity hypothesis and his mode of interpretation employing statistical comparativist data while maintaining objectivity.

A remarkable feature in the data that Hall gathered is the relative absence of concerns for the outside world in dreams. Dreams are 'relatively silent regarding political and economic questions; they have little or nothing to say about current events in the world of affairs'. Even the last catastrophic days of the Second World War, when the first atomic bomb was exploded, did not register in a single dream of students from whom Hall was collecting dreams daily. 'Presidential elections, declarations of war, the diplomatic struggles of great powers, major athletic contests, local happenings that make the headlines, all are pretty largely ignored in dreams ... Nor are intellectual, scientific, cultural and professional topics or the affairs of finance, business, and industry the subject matter of dreams.'[22] If such a large chunk of experience is overlooked, what remains? Dreams, Hall found, are involved with what is personal and intimate; they are also concerned with factors that generate conflict in the dreamer's life. 'Since it is the way in which a person conceives of his conflicts that determines his behaviour, the inside view is a prerequisite for clear understanding of human conduct ... the delineation of a person's conflicts may be made by analysing a dream series.'[23]

Hall felt that his methodology was much more effective and best suited to the study of dream series rather than a single dream. He observed that in a series, 'the dreams read like chapters in a book. When put together in order as we have done there is organization, unity and coherence among the dreams. Each dream complements or supplements the other dreams of the series. There is very little left to guesswork since what may seem ambiguous or hidden in one dream is revealed in another dream. Dream interpretations based upon a series of dreams can be very precise and objective if one approaches the task in a scientific manner.'[24]

Kavita Nayar's first dream came when she was sixteen, the next when she was twenty-two, and two years later the culminating dream of Shiva occurred. Despite the obvious and relatively long intervals between the dreams, they were still looked at as a single series on the basis of one central conflict running through all of them. Normally, what would be considered a dream series occurs at much shorter intervals – on subsequent nights, a few days, or maybe a month apart. Also, the numbers of dreams that are studied in a series are far greater and can span months and years so that, as William Domhoff says, '75 to 100 dreams from a person gives us a very good psychological portrait of that individual. Give us 1,000 dreams over a couple of decades and we can give you a profile of the person's mind that is almost as individualized and accurate as her or his fingerprints.'[25]

Chapter 14

A DREAM SERIES:
A CHAPTER IN A LIFE

The psyche does not merely react, it gives its own specific
answer to the influence at work upon it.

C. G. Jung

*I*n the dream series that follows, we will try and use Calvin Hall's
method of content analysis without using the scoring system of
breaking down each dream into its various contents, since many more
dreams would be required to do that. But we may get a flavour of Hall's
methodology from the few dreams we apply it to. I will treat the dream
series like a jigsaw puzzle, not necessarily dealing with each dream in
a chronological order, but at times clubbing two dreams together that
may not have followed sequentially. I will also pick similar elements
from different dreams to build a larger picture. This will allow us to
move back and forth from the dreamer's outward circumstances to her
dream-dictated aspirations, to discover the complexity of the issues
involved, some apparent some implied. Through the process, Hall's
spotlight dream will need to be identified, to understand what the
central conflict is, reinforcing Hall's continuity hypothesis of how our
waking predicaments are reflected in our dreams.

The following dream series belongs to 'Akansha Mishra', a thirty-
eight-year-old woman married to 'Abhishek', a management consultant.

Their two children 'Neha' and 'Arjun' complete the family picture. The good days peaked when Abhishek was offered a lucrative assignment in Australia and the family moved there from India. What happened to them subsequently, Akansha's dreams will tell.

The artist

An artist is performing with her puppet, and the audience is clapping and marvelling at her. She is like a street performer, performing everywhere. Then at some point, she begins her performance at a place that feels threatening to her (she is now part of the audience). It is full of these neo-Nazi skinheads and she feels she shouldn't perform for them – it's a hostile audience. She begins her performance and they all watch in cold silence. I want to tell her not to perform because she will be harmed. She seems unaware of the danger. And sure enough, a huge, monstrous woman in the audience lies down on top of her. The artist tries to move, and is crushed to death. I know that if she had allowed the grotesque woman to lie on her without moving, she would have survived. But she moves in protest, and so dies.

I say to the audience in anguish, 'We all allowed her to die, we did nothing.'

And one of them says to me, 'There was nothing we could do.'

Now the artist's friend gives life to the artist's puppet. She gives the puppet the artist's voice and the puppet performs superbly. It seems to have a life of its own now, and as the dream ends, the puppet is flying up, up, and away to seek vengeance for the artist's death. And I know it will be successful in its mission. Everyone is clapping and cheering it on.

A performance in the dream begins in an atmosphere of appreciation and ends in hostility. Where once the audience and artist were in tune, now conflict has arisen to such an extent that the death of the artist ensues. Does this indicate that strife has overtaken the dreamer's life resulting in the death of something vital within her? An overwhelming situation, represented by the monstrous woman, overpowers her life. It appears that the dreamer is stricken with remorse at her inability to do anything about the situation – *'We all allowed her to die, we did nothing.'* What she could not do herself, she hoped would be done for her. The puppet seeking vengeance for the artist's death may signify that the dreamer is hoping that justice will be done. The dream clearly describes a sequence of events in which a state of well-being is overpowered by an unexpected threat, which the dreamer finds herself unable to cope with. She feels paralysed, unsupported by those around her, her sensibilities asphyxiated like those of the artist in the dream. Incapacitated by these conflicts, she needs to do something to rise from the morass of her situation. In the dream this occurs with the resurrection of the artist through the puppet. The conflict and her responses – feelings of guilt and injustice – are represented by her multiple identifications within the dream: first with the performing artist, then as a spectator, and finally as the resurrected artist. This dream makes a strong claim to being the spotlight dream as it highlights the various preoccupations of the dreamer's life. Let us see how the other dreams support this claim.

The ocean

> The four of us are holidaying near the sea and swimming in a vast ocean where we can't see the shore. When it's time for the next swim I prepare to dive, only to see that the ocean has become a swimming pool. When I look again, I find there is no water whatsoever. All I can see are the sand and rocks. I realize the sea is waning, so I walk on the dried-up seabed to find out when it will fill again. When I reach the boundary, I see a spring of water coming out of the mountains. It is flowing into the sea. But the trickle of water is so little, and the seabed so large, that I can still see the dry bottom with its rocks. I wonder how it will ever fill up again.

A relaxed family holiday ends with Akansha being alone as she explores and hopes for the impossible – that a mere trickle of water would fill an empty ocean. Like the earlier dream, this, too, begins with promise, only to end in disappointment and frustration. In fact, this dream also shows the process of gradual depletion, and the build up of a conflict, as did the previous dream. The vast ocean contracts to a swimming pool, and then finally dries up, indicative of circumstances closing in on her, in the process exposing the hard, 'rocky' problem in her life that can no longer be hidden. Rocks represent danger to a seafarer, and an allusion to them is suggestive not only of a problem that lies ahead, but of the intransigent nature of the problem that is surfacing. As in the previous dream, she wishes for a way out of the current impasse, hoping that she can go back to the point when the ocean was full and they were together as one happy family. But the dream informs us that this is an impossibility given the fact that the energy-giving, life-sustaining force of water is waning and the trickle from the spring is but a forlorn hope belying a return to former times. The death of the artist in the earlier dream and the empty ocean in this one indicate that the dreamer is aware that there is a major problem in her life, but she has yet to accept that the issue has come to stay, and will not simply vanish on its own. Clearly this dream is centred on the same theme initiated by the previous one, perhaps confirming that the first dream is indeed the spotlight dream.

Amen

> *An illustrated book of mine, which I had completely forgotten about, is going to be published – some European woman is going to publish it. She has a baby called Amen. He was just a baby when I last knew her. I do not know what has happened to the baby.*

The dream seems to suggest a connection between the book to be published and the baby. Amen would then describe the book in some way. Not knowing what happened is a statement more about the book than the baby; perhaps it failed to be published. Amen, the conclusion of a prayer, is also a statement of finality. So, a thing that had promise does not come to fruition, but ends prematurely. This dream concludes the previous two – a phase in the dreamer's life seems to be coming to a close.

A repetitive theme runs through all these three dreams: Things well begun end in death, dry up, or fail to fulfil the promise they started with. The audience in the artist dream suggests that the problem is concerned with people in her immediate environment, while the dream of the dried-up ocean attributes it to her family life and its gradual erosion. And with each dream there is a sense of powerlessness in dealing with the situation. The issues raised by the spotlight dream are now finding specificity in this dream.

To see how these dreams reflect Akansha's life circumstances, we may have to know what was happening to her during this phase. Two years after their move to Australia, things were going well just as her dreams had indicated. They were a happy, close-knit family. Then something new entered their life, which would soon tear them asunder. Disaster struck unexpectedly: Abhishek began losing weight, he found it difficult to eat, his stomach felt distended all the time, and he was always depleted of energy. Investigations revealed a blockage in the large intestine that they suspected was cancerous. Overnight their days began to be measured against the backdrop of this threat, which questioned their time together.

Their joint concern was soon polarized. Abhishek, characteristic of some cancer patients, went into denial mode. He began to doubt the diagnosis, choosing to consult another doctor, who he was confident would pronounce him well. Akansha, believing that time was of the essence, persuaded him, with the greatest difficulty, to have a colonoscopy. The biopsy confirmed the diagnosis. The tumour was cancerous. An immediate operation was suggested, but Abhishek was unwilling. He began shopping around for still more doctors, his anger rising as the diagnosis was repeatedly confirmed. Akansha and the doctors continued pressing him into an early surgical intervention; he maintained that the doctors were no good, their equipment archaic, and the prescribed medicines ineffective. He also complained that Akansha was just not cooking the right food for him and that was the actual reason for why he was not getting well. His expectations of her rose with his innumerable demands and their marriage was beginning to fall apart. The children were not spared either, so much so that Neha, a cheerful child, now cried all the time, while Arjun never seemed to be well enough to get out of bed. This led to further divisions. If Akansha tried to protect the children from his anger it upset Abhishek. If she indulged his desire to procrastinate over the surgery she believed it would greatly harm him, not only physically, but emotionally too, as evading it would make him fester further. If she pushed for the surgery her isolation from him would only deepen. As indicated in her dreams she was confronted with a multitude of problems. Both husband and wife now perceived each other as the hostile audience hampering their individual performances in life. Akansha did not know what would become of that baby called Amen that had once been born from the promise of their relationship.

She then had another dream.

The fall

We are in an arena, a kind of indoor stadium. It is huge, and there are seats all around, but we take the ones right at the top because the ones below are very expensive. Abhishek, his brother and wife, Neha, Arjun, and I are watching a performance. I'm not sure what the performance is – it might be a circus. Abhishek leans down to see more clearly and suddenly loses his balance. He begins falling down and I know then that he will die. In that instant three thoughts run through my head. One, that now he will die. Two, that maybe this kind of death is better than his having to suffer through a long, drawn-out illness. Three, that I haven't been able to sit down and have a conversation with him and tell him how much I love him. These thoughts flash through my mind as he falls. And just before he lands on the ground, he is caught by three people from the circus. I run down the steps to where he is. I can't believe that he's not dead. It's a miracle, against all odds. As I go to him he begins moaning and shouting like a madman and runs across the arena towards the door, and I run behind him, shouting his name and trying to catch hold of his arm. But he cannot be stopped. He cannot be contained by anyone.

The dream seems to unfold with a clear and simple narrative thread, wound around the spindle of the dream drama. Amidst an enjoyable family-outing, a calamity occurs: Abhishek has a precipitous fall from the top of the stadium. To find a bridge between this unexpected near-death fall to their life situation is hardly difficult. The threat of cancer often feels like plunging into death's lap. However, something unexpected happens. Abhishek's fall is checked, and by the time Akansha reaches him she realizes a miracle has occurred. Abhishek is not dead. This is the more difficult metaphor to handle; what could the bridge for this be? Is it Akansha's deepest wish for a miracle, which is being reflected in this metaphor, or are we to read this part of the dream literally – that it is anticipating his recovery? Could it be suggesting that despite the odds, Abhishek will not die?

If it is an anticipatory dream, then in some sense it has the flavour of what Jung calls the *initial* dream. In Jungian therapy, the initial dream is the first dream the patient brings to analysis. This dream may have occurred on the eve of the first session, or after the first session, it may be a recent one that the patient recalls or even a dream from childhood. It is considered of diagnostic and prognostic significance, pointing to the root of the problem and the likely outcome of the treatment.[1]

Technically this is not an initial dream, and nor is Akansha undergoing therapy. Yet it contains the essence of the initial dream, suggesting what may unfold. It may be prescient of Abhishek's recovery. If we assume the dream's prescience, then the dream's conclusion, where he runs around wildly like a madman, unreachable by anybody, has a fairly ominous ring. He may recover, but will their difficulties continue?

The pattern of interactions between Akansha and Abhishek persisted, as Akansha pushed for the operation and Abhishek sunk into a vortex of depression. Finally he underwent surgery, after which chemotherapy followed. Akansha left her job to become a full-time caretaker to Abhishek. After the first two cycles of treatment, he lost all his hair, was periodically nauseous, and the once handsome face appeared bloated and ravaged. This was a great blow to his self-image. Anger was the natural consequence. But over the next twelve months he recovered to the extent that he went back to work, and started to travel and consult on a regular basis. His cancer marker test also showed a considerable decrease in the spread of the disease. In tune with the anticipatory nature of the earlier dream, which occurred in their bleakest hour, the fall from the top of the stadium did not indicate an escalation of the cancer or result in his death. In fact, Abhishek had a new lease of life.

One would have imagined that with the abeyance of the cancer threat and Abhishek's return to normalcy, the relationship between husband and wife would improve gradually. But the conflict between them, which the earlier dreams indicated, steadily grew more entrenched. The problem again lay in their individual perceptions. Abhishek, even after his return to normal life, still considered himself a sick man who deserved special treatment for everything. For Akansha, his return to work and a social life was a sign that he would now be more participative in family life. If she asked him to mind the children in the evening, when she went to shop for groceries, the idea irritated him. Through many phases of his illness and after it also, he could not bear to be alone. So he constantly invited people to stay. Family came, friends came, and even acquaintances were asked with great enthusiasm to fill the house. The sapling of an attitude that was only just visible earlier in their marriage, turned into a full-grown nettle bush, where Abhishek became the traditional all-demanding male binding her to the treadmill of daily routine – cook, clean, drive the children to school and back, fetch groceries, take the guests shopping and feed them well, keep the children under control so that they do not disturb him, and always cheerfully extend herself to do more. When Abhishek's parents came to stay, during the illness and afterwards, the days seemed a blur of picking up dirty dishes from the dining table, constantly meeting demands for traditional Indian food in a land of beef and sandwiches, with teatime being yet another excuse for homemade *samosas* and *pakoras* (savoury). Once, when Akansha complained of fatigue and a backache, Abhishek responded wounded and bitter: 'You can't do this much for me, when my life could end any time?'

It was a marriage under duress, with one partner mired in self-pity and the other freighted with guilt. During the illness, Abhishek's temper worsened and Akansha learnt to keep quiet, inundated with guilt at standing up to a terminally ill man. Unfortunately, this persisted much after the illness. His temper now took the form of taunting and ridiculing her at any opportunity. When Abhishek's father insisted that Akansha keep *vratas* or weekly fasts for Abhishek's continuing well-being, Abhishek taunted her by saying, 'If she had kept these fasts earlier, I am sure I would never have got this dreaded disease. Since she was remiss in her duties, I had to pay for it.'

Before Abhishek's illness, Akansha had worked in a school as an arts and craft teacher, and had enjoyed her work immensely. Once when she was showing a guest a scrapbook of collages she had created with the children, Abhishek said, 'Trust Akansha to have chosen a profession that does not bring much money home.'

His cancer had gone into remission but his internal fears festered, and Akansha became the scapegoat of that putrefaction. So much so that one day when he lost his temper he shouted, 'This illness should have happened to you, not to me! I am the kind of guy who knows how to enjoy myself, but you don't. It would have affected you less.'

Something within Akansha died with those words. She realized the irreversibility of the situation. What she had hoped was just a phase and would pass with the illness, now seemed unlikely to end. A personality change had taken place in Abhishek, which is not unknown in people faced with terminal illness. But in many cases the depression, anger, denial, and self-preoccupation melts with the passage of time and is replaced by some kind of acceptance. In Abhishek's psyche, however, they had built a home. Deep down he acutely felt the injustice: everybody else, and his wife in particular, would enjoy health and life, while he was being denied them.

Calvin Hall stated that the dream not only presents the dreamer's self-conceptions, but also portrays the dreamer's conceptions of those closest to him/her. Moreover, the portrayal of that person in the dream will literally be the same as what the dreamer thinks of that person in waking life. Using this idiom, we can say that Akansha saw Abhishek as a man maddened by an unbridled neurosis. The falling dream depicts him as a *'madman'*, whom no one can stop or contain. At the end of the dream, Abhishek gets up *'moaning'* – indicating self-pity – and Akansha tries to reach him, but he rejects her overtures. Instead of alleviating his fears, his physical recovery only entrenched them deeper. The conflict that had emerged in the first three dreams, with its anticipated prognosis in the falling dream, had come home to roost. In the monstrous woman of the spotlight dream was embedded the intractable force of circumstances that had resulted in the death of something precious; the rocks jutting out of the empty sea were the unsuspected danger that had ripped her ship asunder; and the prayer and petition for hope and change had ended with a ring of finality – Amen.

Other dreams followed, providing important clues about the direction Akansha's life was taking.

The lock

I have to open a lock. Two numbers are flashing before my eyes, a complicated number and a simple one. The simple number will open the lock, not the complicated one. I am trying over and over again.

A dream series, according to Calvin Hall, expresses over and over again some basic conflict in which the dreamer tries now this solution, now that, in a trial-and-error fashion so typical of a person engrossed in problem-solving.[2] The above dream gives that impression. The lock symbolizes the obstacle encountered, the problem at hand. The repeated efforts to open it depict the frequent attempts to find a solution. The earlier dreams revealed the emotional climate in which the conflict arose between husband and wife. This dream shows the first stirrings in Akansha to try to solve the problem.

Hall believes that dreams vivify the person's conceptions and the obstacles that pave his or her path. 'These obstacles are often prohibitions emanating from his conscience and may be represented in dreams by such obstacles as walls, curbs, and locked doors.'[3]

In Akansha's dream the lock represents the obstacle she is facing. There are two ways to open the lock, one that is simple and one fairly complicated. The problem confronting her is actually quite universal; most marriages, if not all, encounter it in one form or another – dealing with resentment and self-pity on one hand, and guilt on the other. In Akansha's marriage the issue has been complicated by the overhang of a terminal illness – according to the dream, the complicated number of the lock. The dream informs her that the simple number will open the lock of her problems. In other words, the conflict will not be resolved, the lock cannot be opened, if it is not perceived in its fundamental dimensions – does she need to continue to feel guilty and thereby indulge Abhishek's self-pity?

Abhishek had actually recovered from his illness and was by then leading a normal life. He was interacting with clients, travelling, routing for work, and doing what his colleagues were doing. Was it then necessary for him to be indulged and treated as a sick person at home? Was it, in fact, advisable to meet his demands to be nursed emotionally and physically? The dream was unsentimentally voicing the truth of the situation: An excess of guilt will only confuse the solution for Akansha. She was torn between the guilt over her reluctance to fulfil his expectations and her own perceptions of his normalcy. If she continued to reinforce the sick-man syndrome, Abhishek would continue to enact his unhappy part, perpetuating the morbid atmosphere in the house. In some sense the dream was pointing out that unless she rid herself of this complication, she will not be able to reach the simple, rather basic problem that exists between them.

Food, cars, and gold

> *A glut. Too much of everything. Food, rooms full of food. A good friend presents me with a Mercedes Benz and I can't refuse because she is giving it to me with so much affection. But I don't want it. Someone else presents me with another car. A person who has no love for cars, now I have three (including my old one). In short, an abundance of things that I do not want. Another person gives me gold earrings. Again, I don't want it but take it out of politeness.*

Food, cars, gold – conventionally coveted items – are not what Akansha seems to want. She is receiving many gifts from different people. Also the glut of food tells us that Akansha is in the midst of a social situation like a wedding, where there is a surfeit of everything, including gifts. Who are these people that have entered her life? Are they relatives and close friends who are visiting the couple often, even spending a few days with them? Confronted with an illness people do flock together to express concern and solidarity (a social situation). But then what are the gifts that she is receiving? In such social situations it is normal to offer gifts of free advice (how to cope with the illness and its aftermath), just like she is being swamped by gifts in the dream – gifts she is unenthusiastic about, yet reluctantly accepts out of politeness. Perhaps the people around her are imposing on her their conceptions of how she should behave, and what her role as daughter-in-law and wife should be. Their intention is to make her conform, mould her by 'gifting' her the ways of their family – the traditional ideal of the all-giving, all-forgiving model Indian woman. The performance of the role is meant to be fulfilling enough, for by living up to this collective image, family and public opinions are satisfied, which in turn reinforces the person's own sense of identity.

Today, this may work in a traditional family in small-town India, but Akansha, who had a Western education, was now living in Australia, where individuality defines your worth. Still steeped in the value system of her country, where the ideal woman is judged by the extent of her self-sacrifice, by her submergence in the collective, by the dissolution of self-definition, she now stood at a strange juncture, where the conventional gifts of her dream may not be the answer to her problem. And perhaps this is the crux of the issue plaguing Akansha: Identity versus submergence.

The toilet

I am in this house full of people who have come to attend my friend Neera Khanna's wedding. I am planning to stay till the end of the wedding. Neera's parents and two other couples have an attached bathroom to their bedrooms, but the rest of us are not allowed to use those bathrooms. We have to use the public toilet outside the house, which has no walls, no door, nothing. It is an open toilet and you can be seen by all. In the morning I need to go and Neera says that I can go to the public toilet. I am appalled. I protest, but Neera simply says, 'It's the only place.'

I am by now quite desperate to go. 'How do you go to such a place?' I ask her.

She says, 'I just don't go.'

I am stunned and say, 'You don't need to go? But I can't do that.'

I ask another couple if I can use their bathroom. The husband is not forthcoming. Then I realize I have to leave the house and go back to my parents. I decide to go to them and return later for the wedding.

At some point I'm reading a book on herbal medicines for my health. It becomes clear to me that there's no point reading it unless I first clear up my system by going to the bathroom – that is the first priority before taking any medicines.

If we had any doubts about the meaning of the previous dream, this one puts them to rest. This dream is clearly stating that Akansha has a conflict, a basic problem – a toilet problem is pretty basic. Her friend advises her on how to solve it, perhaps continuing the theme of gifts of advice of the last dream. The solution that her friend offers has two components. Firstly, conform to tradition and ignore personal needs: go out into the open – a traditional Indian method, for which fields, open spaces, and jungles are considered appropriate, even if they lack in privacy. Secondly, if rebellious responses arise within you then restrain them. (Her friend says, *'I just don't go.'*) May we then presume that the spoken or unspoken advice of the guests (the 'others') in her own house (in her waking life) is the same: to play the customary role of wife and daughter-in-law? In the previous dream, she was unenthusiastic about these 'gifts'; now she cannot see the wisdom in this advice. Her resistance to heed this advice alerts us to the idea that she may be finding it difficult to play the role of the accepting wife and dutiful daughter-in-law.

However, the pressure of the conflict is building up within her. She needs to go to the bathroom to get rid of the toxins of the conflict; she feels that the problem raging within her can no longer be avoided or held back. The dichotomy between the role she is meant to play and her own need for something different becomes apparent in this dream for the first time. She expresses a preference for what she wants, instead of politely accepting what she doesn't. While earlier her problem was outside her, between her and Abhishek, now another facet of her problem surfaces – of who she is and what she wants.

This dream marks a watershed in the conflict. Akansha is now trying to look for solutions. She goes to her parents, that is, into her past to find the resources to deal with the conflict. The end of the dream finds her still looking for a solution. She does not use the toilet outside – holding out against traditionalism all the while aware that she has to psychically detoxify herself before the solution can be found. Stated in a single sentence, her conflict is traditionalism versus individuation.

As in her dream, so in her life: she began searching for ways to replenish her inner depleted resources. For a while she lived in the twilight zone of indecision, not knowing what would sustain her. One morning she found herself paying a visit to the school where she had once taught art and craft. She spent a very happy morning with the children and realized that she had consistently banished thoughts about restarting work. She talked to the principal of the school and asked if she could rejoin. There was no vacancy, but he promised to contact her whenever there was one.

Later she thought of starting weekend art-and-craft workshops for children from home. And in that process the dead artist of the spotlight dream was resurrected, the forgotten manuscript was perhaps ready to be published by baby Amen's mother.

In rather clear terms the following two dreams reflect the new direction that her life was taking.

The bugs

I need to take care of these seven adorable bugs. And I need to transport them to a safe place. So I do, through rain and storm. I am advised by a security guard to put them in a box full of water so that they won't get lost in the storm, and they will float safely in it. So I do, and take them safely to the Khanna family, my very close friends. And now that I've handed them over I know that the bugs are not mine. Even though I love them they're not mine. There is a sense of loss, yet certainty that this is how it must be.

This dream shows that despite the rain and storm of difficult circumstances she had transported something she treasured to safety. The next dream also has a very similar story to tell.

Exodus

There is an exodus. Streams of people walking in one direction including me. One of the women, who in the course of the dream becomes me, sees the floodlights of a car approaching and knows it is for her. She has to hide. So I run and hide behind a wall surrounding a large building. I have to crouch down because I am taller than the wall. The man following me has got out of the car and is searching for me. The torch flashes nearer and nearer till he is literally at the wall and I am now lying on the ground so that he can't see me. Later, hours later, I hear a sound and a woman comes out holding a proclamation that all is safe. The man has gone. I realize I am out of danger.

The dream shows her progression from hiding, crouching, and feeling threatened to feeling safe and secure. The end of the dream succinctly characterizes her real-life feelings: out of danger!

The reader may comment that Akansha's dreams are being interpreted in the light of the information we have about her life; that, in retrospect, we are reading into the dream what we know about her. However, let's try a content analysis of these nine dreams (including the spotlight dream) and see what it yields. No doubt statistically the number of dreams is miniscule, but even with this small number we may be able to highlight trends and personality traits that stand out distinctly as an index of her feelings and situation.

I am going to list these out as statements with their possible implications:

1. These nine dreams are predominantly peopled by characters who are not known to her, indicative of her alienation from the immediate people in her life.
2. Barring two dreams, Abhishek is conspicuously absent in all the other dreams. She perceives herself as estranged from him.
3. If we tabulate the gender of the characters appearing in these dreams, there are twelve females, seven males, and seven people of unspecified gender. The predominance of females is representative of the larger role women play in her world.
4. The dreams do not portray too many interactions between the dreamer and the other characters in the dream, signalling that the dreamer does not involve herself in the nitty-gritty entanglement of interactions, yet all the while maintains a cordial face whenever she interacts. Also conspicuous is the dreamer's consistent friendliness whenever she interacts with other people, and yet most of the dreams are underscored by ambivalence, puzzlement, confusion, difficulty, or disappointment. Further, these ambivalent feelings are not overt except in the spotlight dream of the artist performing with a puppet. This shows that though there is an inherent difficulty with others – and we know these to be mostly women – there is no demonstrable aggression from either side. The internal ambivalence is kept under wraps and an outward pleasantness is always maintained.
5. Out of all the male figures that appear in her dreams, if we ignore her father and Neera's father who are avowedly on her side, we are left with two men with whom she interacts: her friend's husband in the bathroom dream and the man from whom she is fleeing in the exodus dream. (The security guard's sexual identity is undisclosed.) Both these interactions are suspect. The friend's husband is unforthcoming, while the other man is downright threatening. Perhaps some male member in her household had exhibited naked aggression, leaving her with a feeling of being hounded by him.

6. Only in two dreams – the artist and toilet dreams – does she perceive herself as part of a group, and in both she feels marginalized. In the first she is the lone voice standing up for the death of the artist, while in the second one she is out in the cold, desperately seeking permission to perform a simple biological function – something we take for granted. It is obvious from this that she is not enthusiastic when people come in groups to her house, since she feels alienated from them.

7. She also appears to be unconnected with her environment; she is consistently dreaming of unfamiliar settings. Could this be due to the conflict in her circumstances, or is it because she is living in a country alien to her?

8. Eight out of the nine dreams feature difficulties of one kind or another that are external to her. In the first two dreams the difficulties are accidental and therefore beyond her control.

9. Five out of the first seven dreams show a failure to cope, indicative of the deterioration in her situation. It is only in the last two dreams that she succeeds in overcoming the difficulties encountered. She appears to have taken a decision and by standing up for herself she may have averted any danger to herself and her marriage.

Based on Hall's method we are now able to identify the brush strokes that form the picture of Akansha's life and conflict. An emotionally absent husband; Akansha, estranged from her home because of guests; the women not openly confrontational, but implicitly condemning; a father-in-law, not prone to exercising the restraint in speech and behaviour of the female relatives, demanding a traditional espousal of duty from her in an alien land; and Akansha, herself confused, with no solution to the situation. The rekindling of her creative interests perhaps provides hope and a way out of her hostile environment, epitomized by the last two dreams where threat capitulates to feelings of safety.

No doubt the idea of rekindling an old interest is a means for self-sustenance, as much as it is an exploration of who she is. Yet often the price of this journey is loneliness and uncertainty. The person is making a move from the known to the unknown, from the collective value system of conformity, to the dictates of living by a sensed inner reality. There are no maps in such a terrain, no familiar milestones, and as you look back you realize you are standing alone, apart from the crowd, and the loss of familiar anchors fills you with eroding anxiety. The next dream shows just this.

The skyscraper

I'm lying on my stomach on top of a skyscraper and can see the traffic below. I seem to have been here for some time, but now, as I look down, I'm terrified because I know I can fall. I want to get down, but suddenly the space on which I'm lying has shrunk and there's no place for me to move. I know I'll fall. Then I put my foot down, and step down – easily. For now I'm larger and taller than the skyscraper.

Her isolation atop a skyscraper, where she is far removed from the traffic of life – or from the societal norms that govern her life – is perceived by her as precarious and terrifying. Her move towards a measure of self-reliance leaves her feeling anxious and isolated. Her old definitions, which have imprisoned her, have to be discarded. Yet she is unsure whether she has the resources to sustain herself without them. The space shrinks, the pressure mounts, as she feels bereft of any support in venturing into this phase of her life. Maybe this is the beginning of the process of individuation. To quote Jung, 'Individuation cuts one off from personal conformity and hence from collectivity. That is the guilt which the individual leaves behind him for the world, that is the guilt he must endeavour to redeem. He must offer a ransom in place of himself, that is, he must bring forth values which are an equivalent substitute for his absence in the collective personal sphere. The man who cannot create values should sacrifice himself consciously to the spirit of collective conformity.'[4]

This comes about in a journey that takes us beyond familial and societal conditioning in our search to know who we are. Something within us demands expression, waiting for our personal recognition to come into being. And that 'something' has its own imperatives, for it makes us tread a path that is only ours to walk – where the rules may get reversed, so that collective conformity becomes the servant rather than the master of the house.

Some significant step has been taken in that direction, as Akansha literally and metaphorically puts her foot down in the dream. When she does that she feels equal to the task. She is not diminished by it, but enhanced. Her fears are unfounded, for when she decides to do it, it happens with ease. As easily as her rejoinder when Abhishek ridiculed her about her cooking in public. She did not do what she normally did – keep quiet. Instead, much to her own surprise, Akansha retorted, 'No I do not know how to make good chapatis. I only know how to clean your vomit and pee.'

It was not merely the replying back that was the point, but that she was finally able to manage her guilt and put her foot down against his transgressions.

Past and present

Abhishek and I are standing on the road outside the house I lived in when I was ten. Someone whom we know from the past passes by, and we say hello. Then another person from the past comes by, and then another, until there's a crowd of us standing on the road. Then, we realize that each of us standing here now were together in the past, standing on a road, when the very same people who passed us now, had passed us then. We are struck by the coincidence. Someone says, 'There is a one in a million chance of this happening.'

The matter concerns Abhishek and Akansha, as they are the chief characters in this dream, while those drifting in from the past and meeting them are unidentified people. Something from their past is intersecting with the present and influencing it. This is further reinforced by the fact that they are standing outside a house that Akansha lived in as a child. The past in Akansha's case could be her family values, inherent impulses, and moral upbringing, and they are now affecting her marriage. It could be the traditional notions of what a good wife and mother should be, and her constant measuring of herself against them, followed by feelings of guilt if her self-appraisal fell short of those deeply ingrained ideas. This creates self-doubt, which makes her revert back to a helpless passivity, a stance that ultimately fills her with inner turmoil, and the cycle repeats itself, much as we see a repetition in the dream of the same people, meeting at the same point now, as they did in the past.

Besides this, the past could be interfering in another way in Akansha's marriage. Alongside traditional conceptions, each of us picks up from our parents ideas of how we should behave, how others should behave towards us, how we should deal with conflict, and many other such issues. We may or may not realize that we are influenced by these beliefs, but if we were to observe ourselves and ask ourselves where a particular attitude comes from, we may be able to trace it back to one of our parents. The attitudes we develop may have been directly imbibed from a parent, or they may be reactions against a parent's views – both being two ends of the same continuum. Calvin Hall believed that 'prototypic conceptions have their origin in early life and that they are most likely to express themselves in dreams than through any other medium'.[5]

The exact nature of the conceptions from the past influencing Akansha's present are not specified, just as the people from the past in her dream remain unidentified. Yet their confluence with the present in the dream is significant and important enough to be noted. Each partner in a marriage comes with a bundle of preconceived ideas woven into his or her psyche. Often these beliefs interfere in seeing the spouse as he or she actually is. Instead we see the other through the filter of our expectations of what the other person should be. So, are Akansha's conceptions from her upbringing influencing the way she perceives the conflict between Abhishek and herself? If she were to view it without this filter, would it help her understand the situation better?

The next two dreams seem to be of a completely different genre. They do not go into the nitty-gritty of the problem, but give an overview of why her life took the course it did. The dreams suggest a design, a planned unfoldment, offering a view into the dictates of destiny whose true purpose can only be garnered in its living. These dreams seem to suggest that often struggle and suffering are the medium through which our personal biography is granted the precious gift of meaning.

The lifts

I have to go up in the lift to the fourteenth floor. Finally, two lifts come down together, and their doors open. One lift, to my left, is large and spacious. The other is tiny and is actually an Indian-style toilet, an untidy but clean one, with a frayed green carpet. I step into the toilet lift instead of the larger one. I don't know why it is so clear to me that I had to choose the toilet lift. Then as soon as I do, I regret it. As it goes up, the door doesn't open. I keep waiting but it refuses to open. I'm terrified.

The astrological chart

Two friends of mine are examining my astrological chart and telling me about the end of this year. The chart is like an old, tattered, rolled-up green carpet. One of my friends is kneeling down and looking at the frayed parts and telling me, 'Only that much is left for you to go through. It's not very much now.' Of course, I'm relieved that this terrible year is coming to an end.

The lifts dream presents an interpretational dilemma. By what method do we understand it? If we treat this dream simply as an expression of Akansha's waking conceptions and concerns, then we run up against a problem. In this dream her choice of the Indian-style toilet lift is reminiscent of an earlier dream where she is looking for a bathroom in her friend's house and does not go out in the open, thereby rejecting the choice of the traditional Indian way of dealing with her conflict. In this dream, however, she chooses the traditional Indian toilet lift over the spacious one. If we understand this dream by a similar symbolic rendering as in the earlier one, then we are faced with a contradiction. We would have to assume that after all her struggles the dream is suggesting that she is espousing a traditional approach. This would render all her earlier struggles meaningless.

We could consider this dream as a continuation of previous dreams. Earlier, whenever she had exercised a choice, like when she put her foot down, she had become as tall as the skyscraper. In another dream, she had taken it upon herself to return the seven adorable bugs to her friends – here also she had gained in her inner stature. Her dreaming life was encouraging her to believe that if she exercised her power of choice in confronting her conflict, she would be helped. Contrarily, in the current dream, exercising a choice makes her feel hemmed in; it is suffocating her. This leads one to conjecture that the dream seems to have stepped beyond the confines of the little details of her waking concerns, to a broad overview of her life. If that is so, it may be better to revert to a Jungian method of understanding the dream through amplification and searching for parallels.

The lift dream focuses on a choice. Akansha chooses the toilet lift against all good sense and reason, seemingly bound by a strange compulsion that prevents her from stepping into a more comfortable lift. The dilemma would be better understood if we knew what exactly this 'choice' is that the dream is alluding to. The clue may be sought in the number fourteen, which Akansha had associated with the number of years she had been married.

The dream seems to be alluding to her marriage, and her choice of Abhishek as her life partner. The toilet lift is a symbol for her life with Abhishek, which now feels cramped, isolating, and restrictive. However, the dream suggests that she cannot get out of the lift. She is gripped with terror, but the door of the lift does not open to let her out. This implies that however difficult her relationship has become with Abhishek, something prevents her from opting out. She may have thought of this option, but the dream suggests that she cannot bring it to bear.

None of us choose or opt for difficulties and reversals. They seem to just happen as part of the course of a life. Yet in Akansha's dream there is an awareness of deliberately making a choice that spelt difficult life circumstances. Two lifts came down, that is, two sets of opportunities were presented to her. One a large, spacious, comfortable one and the other a cramped Indian-style toilet lift, symbolizing restriction and difficulties. She notes the difference in the two lifts, yet opts for the more uncomfortable one. There is something utterly mysterious operating here, for the minute we perceive that a choice spells discomfort we generally avoid it. But Akansha did not.

The old green carpet – an object common to both dreams – perhaps affirms our decision to interpretationally sew these dreams together. In the lift dream it lines the lift she chooses, suggesting that it is the basis of the matter; in the next dream it is equated with an astrological chart. This, possibly, gives us a clue to the thematic content of the dreams: both these dreams are alluding to her destiny – what underlies her life. Something in her life is seen as predetermined.

When stated this way, the dream continues to appear meaningless. If her life is fated, if her choice of marrying Abhishek is predetermined, then why the struggle to understand her conflict or individuate? Just accept the fated event, follow the traditional approach, and abandon any hopes for change. This conundrum alerts us to the understanding of the symbol of astrology. Admittedly, it is a complex symbol and may need to be looked at closely.

The astrological chart is cast for the moment of birth and is supposed to be the signature of what will befall us during the course of our lives. It is therefore considered our fate or destiny. However, this may be a very limited rendering of the symbol for the purpose of Akansha's dream.

If properly understood the astrological chart is a blueprint of our personality traits and tendencies. It maps out how an individual's drives match or oppose each other and the way they seek expression in life's arena. This pattern of potentialities is what imparts uniqueness to any personality. Every mother knows that each of her children has a distinct personality from a very young age, and that this personality has nothing to do with conditioning. It is something the baby is born with. Each human being comes with an inherent or innate nature. It is this nature or axis of inclination that is mapped out on the birth chart.

Psychologists affirm that our inclinations propel us towards certain choices, and possibly these choices attract our life circumstances. Astrology, when viewed as the portrayal of the cluster of drives we are born with, becomes the basis of our predispositions. These predispositions draw us into specific circumstances, which become our destiny.

So astrology as a symbol in this dream is not a map of fate, but an explanation of why we find ourselves in a particular set of circumstances. We are impelled towards them, as is Akansha with her choice of the more formidable and arduous option. Sometimes we are, like Akansha, aware of the problems inherent in our choices. Yet at times it is clear to us that actually we would have made no other choice but that one. From the apparently diverse choices available to us we seem to hone in on just that one option, as though none else truly existed.

We cannot here succumb to the temptation of saying that her 'choice' of Abhishek as life partner – an option she had exercised fourteen years ago – is the central issue in the dream. Nor can we say that in casting a backward glance she was regretting her present option. This dream seemed to affirm the notion that even if she had known the difficulties, she may have still chosen the cramped lift – a turbulent life with Abhishek.

We can only conjecture that she 'needed' to choose that lift to fulfil some purpose. What that purpose is, we can never really be sure. Broadening the scope of Akansha's dream, we can but hypothesize that the psyche chooses those circumstances that may not necessarily be commodious and agreeable, but are perceived as essential for its individuation. The very obstacles and challenges it chooses in its life circumstances become the self-afforded opportunity for greater self-understanding.

If we are given any hint at all as to what Akansha has chosen to learn, then the toilet lift may give us a clue about it. In an Indian-style toilet the process of elimination is often faster because one is squatting uncomfortably on one's haunches, unlike the chair-like comfort of a Western toilet seat. Could it be that Akansha chooses the toilet lift because it would help her shed expendable psychic baggage faster? Akansha later told me that this phase (during and after Abhishek's illness) had transformed her, and pushed her into seeking meaning at an internal level. In this evolution she had to eliminate what was toxic, wasteful, and redundant in terms of emotional baggage – her sense of injustice, acute resentments, unbridled fear, and chronic anxieties. Like

Psyche's painstaking task, she had to sort and separate the emotions to discern the meaning of her tribulations.

The process of personal development involves an interplay between the outer and inner worlds of a person. If at the outer level, Akansha tried to be firm with Abhishek, resisting his bad temper, as the earlier dream had suggested, or tried to pick up the threads of her life and pursue an old interest, then that was one aspect of the process. However, the more demanding and strenuous task concerned her inner world, where she had to let go of her own emotional baggage that was impeding her personal fulfilment. In the spotlight dream at the beginning, Akansha realized that if the artist had 'kept still' instead of moving and protesting, the monstrous woman would not have been able to kill the artist. Because she moved and protested, she died. In other words, if Akansha's anger persists, then something essential within her will get crushed. The solution to a problem is seldom found in the stages of anger or depression. It comes when the situation is accepted in its widest sense. She had to separate the outward events from her own reactions to them. The monstrous situation may lie atop her, but if she goes quiet within, no harm will befall her. She would then fulfil the purpose of the conflict, which pays more attention to the way of acceptance and less to the things to be accepted. The situation does not alter, but our attitude to it does.

As the story goes: Two men looked into a pond. Said the one: 'I see a quantity of mud, a shoe, and an old can.' Said the second: 'I see all these, but I also see the glorious reflection of the sky.' When you allow acceptance to seep in, the mud of turbulence settles down and a growing clarity emerges.

The process of individuation is not an assertion of one's personal identity. It is the process by which we come to terms with the fact that the shadow that crosses our path is our own.

As Robert Browning said: 'When the fight begins within himself, a man's worth something.' And that is the one primary factor that impels Akansha to choose the toilet lift. For in it and through it she presented herself with the opportunity – seen as the designs of destiny – to recognize what is inessential, and then find the wherewithal to let it go. These two dreams reinforce Erik Erikson's insight: 'It is the acceptance of one's one and only life cycle as something that had to be and that, by necessity, permitted of no substitutions.'[6]

The last step

I'm climbing up this very narrow cliff or mountain that seems to touch the sky. There is nothing on either side of me to hold on to. I am almost at the top when I look down and feel I'm going to fall. I see how far I've climbed with no help, and feel the void that is all around me. I feel I can't take that one final step required to reach the top. I can't do it and I tell the people who are already there. They tell me I can. Someone gives me a hand and I hold it, take that one step, and reach the top. Even there I'm struck by the fact that I got this high without anything to hold on to.

Then the woman who has helped me says, 'Imagine, you did this when you were pregnant.'

I look down at myself and realize that it's true. I didn't even know it. She is full of admiration at my having done it in that condition.

It is apparent from this dream that Akansha has made a tremendous effort in facing the challenges of her situation. She has climbed the mountain of difficulty, fought each step of the way, and perhaps without any assistance. Further, it seems that she has momentarily paused to catch her breath, assessing how much ground she has covered. When she looks down the dream is showing her the enormous distance that has been traversed from the slough she was in. For a moment she is awed, as far, far below lies the valley of her old thoughts and preoccupations. It seems she now stands on the threshold of transforming her view of her former life. At this point there may be a moment of sheer terror as Akansha perched atop feels *'there is nothing on either side to hold on to'*. Gone is the secure familiarity of the old ways of behaviour, gone is the all-consuming focus of old fears, gone is the raging battle against fate. And then comes the quintessential moment, the pause at the brink, in which the old is dying and the new is on the verge of being born (pregnant without knowing it) in the unfamiliar mountain stillness.

Akansha had walked too long and too far from her earlier concerns to run back in fright. Yet the *'last step'* seemed the longest and hardest to take. Whether this last step was an internal one or referred to an external event is not clear from the dream. All that is apparent is that she sensed a void around her, and was uncertain of her ability to heave herself onto the last vantage point of stability. And then help comes – a hand is extended, mysteriously and with uncanny timing, pulling Akansha to the top.

The derailed train

I'm in a train at a station, and another train is in some kind of trouble. I get down and see people crowded in one of the compartments of that train. It seems to me that they are stuck, but it turns out they are not. Part of their train has got derailed, and they pull and pull the chain, all together, in order to lift that part of their train and put it back on the track. I think to myself, they can never do it, even if they all try to lift it together. It's just too heavy. But they pull and pull, and then, to my astonishment, the derailed part of the train slowly rises and is then put back on the track.

A theme similar to the one in the earlier dream: What Akansha thought was an impossible task has been achieved. She felt incapable of taking that last step to the top, but she managed it. Now a derailed train has been put back on the tracks with great effort. The struggle to *'pull and pull'* is perhaps an allusion to how Akansha fought with all her might to come to terms with her circumstances and managed to put her derailed life back on the tracks of normalcy. Akansha's life had got derailed because she was unable to manage her fears, guilt, and anger with the situation. Perhaps her dream is informing us that she has found the means to cope with these emotions. No doubt these feelings would continue to rear their heads from time to time, but these dreams marked the breaking of a cycle of emotional entrapment. In any cycle of struggle there are points when significant breakthroughs are made. The last two dreams mark such points. Often our conscious mind may not know that we may have crossed the Rubicon, but our dreaming mind does and, possibly, celebrates the event.

Akansha did not know how long or short her reprieve would be. She took each day as it came. But after the struggle, when life struck a more even note, she wondered what it all meant. After the battle, you survey the carnage and wonder what has actually been won. You may have gained in endurance, faced many a fear as you withstood the shelling, but did it amount to anything? Had she not in some fundamental way lost the security of her old relationship with Abhishek?

Prompt came the reply from her dreaming mind.

The dolphin

There is a bucket full of water in which a small mechanical toy is swimming. Suddenly it changes into a small baby dolphin who has come from the sea. The dolphin is unhappy at being confined to the bucket and longs for the open sea. Tears stream from the little dolphin's eyes. Then a strange and wonderful thing happens. Every time the dolphin cries the tears change to precious stones. She no longer weeps tears, but jewels. And stranger still is the fact that if she went back to the sea, she would not weep. And if she did not weep there would be no jewels either.

The creativity of the dreaming mind is perhaps at its expressive best in this dream. One is amazed at its appropriateness and meaning-rich content. The small mechanical toy seems to be an allusion to the mechanicalness of our habituated self, which, when confronted by difficulties and hardships, tends to get upset and shed tears. But it is the tears of real suffering that produce the jewels of wisdom. Transposing the symbol to Akansha's life, the dream is suggesting that a state of comfort and security, like the unhampered sea for the dolphin, will not yield the precious stones or the things of value. What produces the gems, according to the dream, are often the restrictive, isolating, and confining circumstances, which create the impetus for transformation and originality, and lead us to our source of inspiration. Real understanding is often the child of difficult circumstances, for it emerges as a need for an answer. As Ben Okri says, 'Often ideas of great beauty come to us when we are most constrained. You might think there is a kind of perversity to inspiration.'[7]

Akansha's struggle is a universal struggle. Each one of us at some point or the other in life finds ourselves in a set of circumstances that demands something more from us than simply living in a pattern of knee-jerk reactions and habitual responses. We may outwardly fulfil the responsibilities of the situation, but that is not the only demand life poses for us. Intertwined within the fabric of those circumstances is the thrust of an evolutionary drive seeking fulfilment. It demands that we live by the highest within us. We may lose sight of this, but not our dreams. They are moments of awakening, wherein we dip into the ink of inspiration to write more legibly the story of our lives.

To know the sequel to Akansha's life, with all its personal nuances, we would need another dream series. She did not, however, give me the next series of dreams she had, and all I know are some broad outward details: Akansha teaches; her children have grown; and Abhishek, even six years later, is busy in his consulting career. There has been no recurrence of cancer.

PART 4

THE DREAM: A WINDOW TO REALITY

God turns to good all our dreams
For one great mystery, to me it seems,
Is how it is that dreams are born
Whether at evening or at morn,
And why it is that some come true,
While others never do.

Why that's a dream of things to come,
Why this is revelation,
Why this is nightmare, that a dreaming,
Never holds for all men the same meaning.
Why this is an apparition, why these are oracles,
I know not, but if the causes of these miracles
Are known by someone better than I
Let him explain them ...

Geoffrey Chaucer, The House of Fame

Chapter 15

THE UNSOLVED MYSTERY OF DREAMS
AND THE HINDU VIEW

Dreams are real while they last; can we say more of life?

Havelock Ellis

The modern psychological paradigm views the dream as a comment on the emotional health of the dreamer. For example, Manish Chawla's dream was a comment on his internal landscape – his emotional difficulties during puberty, his concealed conflicts, and so on. In fact, the whole of the last section looked at the dream in terms of the dreamer's personality, of his or her psychological reality. In this scenario outer events are allowed dream space only in relation to their emotional significance on the dreamer. However, dreams need not restrict themselves to the dreamer's interior world alone. In direct contrast are dreams that comment on the actual waking reality of the dreamer. When such dreams occur, the psychological model appears inadequate because it has created a schism between the waking and dreaming world, which, according to it, can only be bridged by a one-way communication from the day world to the dream world, but never the other way round. Perforce, the dream can only be constructed from what is known, thought, or felt, and never from the imagination. Consequently the dream can only be a device that fulfils, compensates, or reflects waking life. Granted that more often than not what we dream connects with our feelings and our memories. But does the psychological paradigm encompass the entire range of the dreaming mind? For example, my dream that foresaw my Teacher's return to the hermitage two days earlier than planned was understood as a direct comment on his travel dates. There was no psychological component to it and the dream simply reflected real events, as they would unfold. Sometimes such dreams not only comment on our waking reality, but may also possess the power to alter it. However, before we take that road, we need to appreciate the need for a new paradigm related to the phenomenological. To do so, let's look at another dream.

The dreamer was a man of high education, about fifty years of age, and a fearless and passionate mountain climber, who would frequently escape work and family life for the mountains.[1] He was also involved in a number of shady affairs.[2] This man dreamt:

> *I am climbing a high mountain, over steep snow-covered slopes. I climb higher and higher, and it is marvellous weather. The higher I climb the better I feel. I think, 'If only I could go on climbing like this for ever!' When I reach the summit my happiness and elation are so great that I feel I could mount right up into space. And I discover that I can actually do so: I mount upwards on empty air, and awake in sheer ecstasy.*[3]

A psychological rendering would inform the dreamer that he is living above himself in a fantasy of fictitious assumptions and unrealistic opinions that fostered an overestimation of himself and his abilities. His involvement in clandestine affairs has made him develop an almost morbid passion for mountain-climbing as a sort of compensation. Clearly, the dream is about him trying to 'get above himself'[4] – perhaps as an avenue of escape from a life that had become intolerable.

A non-psychological approach would read this dream as predicting his death in the mountains: it is cautioning him against being over-ambitious while climbing. His sense of ecstasy in the dream and his climbing even higher than the mountain into empty space are transparent allusions to his imminent death.

Two months later, when out alone in the mountains, he was buried by an avalanche but was dug out in time and saved. Three months later, while climbing down a mountain with a friend, he fell on the friend's head and they were both dashed to pieces. A mountain guide watching them from below reported that they were letting themselves down on a rope at a treacherous stretch of the mountain slope. The friend had secured a temporary foothold on a ledge when the dreamer, following him down, suddenly let go of the rope. The guide described his last movement as though he was 'jumping into the air'.[5]

Perhaps this dream strongly suggests the need for locating a different dimension of dreaming, which allows the dream to comment on a phenomenological reality as opposed to merely an internal one. The dreamer had actually been warned in very frank terms by Jung that 'he was seeking his death in the mountains, and that ... he stood a remarkably good chance of finding it'.

'But that is absurd,' the dreamer had replied, laughing. 'On the contrary, I am seeking my health in the mountains.'[6]

It is tempting to conjecture that had he listened and been careful, the dream would then have had the power to alter reality.

My intention is not to suggest that we interpret every dream phenomenologically as above, but that such an approach should not be denied. Nor is this dream an isolated example. There are countless others of which some will be related in the next chapter – dreams that were heeded by their dreamers, dreams that even effected changes in the world. Yes! The real world of insulin injections and sewing machines. Other dream types that need space under a wider umbrella of dreaming are problem-solving dreams, which aid the dreamer in overcoming an actual problem confronting him or her in waking life. Besides this, dreams can also comment on the ailments of the dreamer, sometimes even cautioning him or her about death. It must be appreciated that we are not alluding merely to dreams about the future – future events, future illnesses, and death. There are other aspects to this larger dimension, which the psychological paradigm does not address. An example:

Dr Sandor Ferenczi, a disciple of Freud, was pestered by a clairvoyant that given an opportunity he would demonstrate the efficacy of telepathy. Ferenczi, after initially resisting the suggestion, agreed to an experiment. On a particular day, at a pre-arranged time, Ferenczi would think of something of his choice and the clairvoyant, some distance away, would pick up Ferenczi's thoughts and tell him what he was thinking about. It was a simple enough experiment, which, if successfully executed by the clairvoyant, would prove telepathic occurrences.

At the appointed hour Ferenczi, in the privacy of his consulting room, lay on his couch for ten or fifteen minutes, holding the statue of an elephant in his hands. A few minutes later he received a telephone call from his friend, Robert Bereny, recounting a terrifying dream he had just had in which he saw Ferenczi in a jungle, fighting with all sorts of wild animals, among them an elephant.

In due course, the letter of the thought-reader appeared, containing utter rubbish.[7]

The clairvoyant's failure and the friend's spontaneous dream success in telepathy did not fit the expected pattern, and this possibly highlights the idea that the most interesting results are often the most unexpected.

Perhaps the biggest stumbling block for followers of the psychological paradigm is the paranormal dream involving extra-sensory perception – premonition, telepathy, clairvoyance, and such like. Once confronted with this kind of dream, the debate immediately regresses into either/or correlates – antiquated conception versus modern understanding, superstition versus science, romantic philosophy versus rationalism. Typically, the argument concludes with: 'Some things we dream do come true, but many more do not. Those that come true stick in our mind while those that do not are quickly forgotten.'[8]

This was brought into sharp focus through dreams experienced by many people after the kidnapping of the two-year-old son of American aviator and hero, Charles Lindbergh. For a long time the child's whereabouts or what had become of him were unknown. It became a major concern of the national media. During that period, in March 1932, two Harvard psychologists, Henry Murray and D. R. Wheeler, conducted an investigation. Newspapers had made a request for dreams related to the kidnapping. This elicited over 1,300 dreams, which were compared with the subsequently established facts of the case. These were that the boy had been killed and his 'mutilated' and 'naked' body was discovered in a 'shallow grave', in some 'woods, near a road' several miles away from the Lindbergh home, and that his death had been instantaneous. Approximately 5 percent of the dreams had foretold the baby's death, and in seven dreams the actual location of the body, its nakedness, and the manner of its burial were more or less accurately described. Perhaps the most faithful of the seven descriptions was:

> I thought I was standing or walking in a very muddy place among many trees. One spot looked as though it might be a round, shallow grave. Just then I heard a voice saying, 'The baby has been murdered and buried there.' I was so frightened that I immediately awoke.

Was this dream prophetic or clairvoyant? (Prophetic if it had come before the death of the kidnapped boy; clairvoyant if it appeared after or during the event.) Hall argues that since 'only 5% of the dreams pictured the baby as being dead is itself a strong argument against the validity of prophetic dreams. It suggests rather that the desire to have the baby alive (wish fulfillment) is the determining factor for the 1300 dreamers.'[9]

Though the paranormal dreams looked at so far have been interpreted at face value, this should not lead to an assumption of what characterizes the various paradigms of dreaming: psychological dreams speak through symbols, while the other kind is a literal dream. The understanding of the paranormal dream should not be restricted to the literal truth, but figurative or metaphorical truths must also be given space within it. These will be dealt with in a later chapter.

The examples above make it fairly clear that the mirror of dreams not only reflects our psychological reality, but can also open a window to our outer reality. However, before we proceed to consider such dreams, we need to outline a framework of dreaming different from the one used for the psychological paradigm. Although the Jungian belief system perhaps comes closest to accepting this dimension of dreaming, other theorists find it embarrassing to share the same philosophical bed with paranormal dreaming. Freud went to the extent of saying that 'dreams which *make sense* and are at the same time *intelligible*, which, … can be inserted without further difficulty into the context of our … life … deserve little attention, since there is nothing astonishing or strange about them'.[10] In other words, a literal dream can be ignored! Since a literal dream has neither latent content nor does it employ dream work in its formation, Freud was not engaged by it. Not only Freud, but all modern dream theorists hiccup when confronted with paranormal dreams. Let us briefly consider some of the difficulties that are encountered in the theories of Freud, Jung, and Hall.

Freud
If every dream is a wish-fulfilment, as Freud said, then it becomes difficult to explicate anxiety dreams. Anxiety disturbs the sleeping mind and may awaken the dreamer. Freud conceded that anxiety dreams challenged his theory, but ingenuously claimed that they simply show that the censor had failed in its duty to disguise them! Are these anxiety dreams then cases of aberrant dreaming? The failed-censor argument would be permissible if there were only a few such dreams and not when every other dream is anxiety-riddled as dream-content studies have indicated. Hence this hypothesis becomes difficult to maintain.

Calvin Hall had also raised some simple questions about the sexual content of dreams that still need answering: When, on occasion, we do have explicitly sexual dreams, then why should there be need for an elaborate deception of sexual intent in other dreams? If the censor allowed the contraband images to be smuggled in one night, why camouflage or conceal sexual allusions the next night?[11]

Also, we are familiar in daily converse with the contrived symbolism of jokes and slang,[12] much of which are sexual in character. So why does the nocturnal censor take so much umbrage about sexual content?[13] In Victorian times it might have been relevant, but in today's day and age it is difficult to comprehend the bashfulness of the censor.

Further, Freud does not clarify what kind of material is being censored. Surely such material must be reflective of the ethico-moral standards of the dreamer's society. It cannot be assumed across the board that blatant sexual thoughts have to be censored because we believe that any unfettered expression of sexual impulses is against all that is good and right. What about people whose mores are not bound to this definition, for example, tribal societies where sexual restraint is not an ethico-moral issue. Will their censors allow sexual material to flow unimpeded into their dream life?

Besides these internal inconsistencies in his theory, Freud never acknowledged paranormal dreaming or the precognitive dream. Even though he had flirted outrageously with the telepathic component of dreaming and acknowledged it, he did not allow telepathy any theoretical space. He simply denied that it was a dream: 'Supposing, then, that we are brought face to face with a pure telepathic "dream," let us call it instead a telepathic experience in a state of sleep. A dream without condensation, distortion, dramatization, above all, without wish fulfillment, surely hardly deserves the name.'[14] Thus another paradigm, different from Freud's, would be required if paranormal dreaming is to be acknowledged in any way.

Jung

Among the modern theorists, Jung came closest to recognizing the paranormal dimension of dreaming, but he never whole-heartedly espoused this paradigm. Always hovering on the edges of a belief in the paranormal, Jung proposed that besides compensatory functions, dreams could also be prospective (anticipatory), telepathic, and prophetic. But he added that only when a compensatory interpretation is not valid should a prospective one be considered. What are prospective dreams?

Jung said they 'prepare, announce, or warn about certain situations, often long before they actually happen'.[15] In olden times this type of dream was regarded as a truth-telling oracle, but Jung believed that it merely 'results from a fusion of subliminal elements and is thus a combination of all the perceptions, thoughts, and feelings which consciousness has not registered because of their feeble accentuation'.[16] Jung said the dream originates in an unknown part of the psyche and prepares the dreamer for what may happen, 'like a preliminary exercise or sketch, or a plan roughed out in advance'.[17] Thus, prospective dreams may seem prophetic but they are no more so than a medical diagnosis or a weather forecast. They are merely an anticipatory combination of probabilities that coincide with the actual behaviour of things.[18] Jung even classified the mountain climber's dream as anticipatory rather than prophetic, evidently because he only acted out an inherent tendency that the dream was cautioning him against. Prophetic dreams, Jung warns his readers, are rare, and he cites only one example out of the estimated eighty thousand he had interpreted as truly prophetic.[19] He did not consider telepathic dreams as paranormal; they were based on something inaccessible to our present level of learning. A telepathic dream, he believed, often has a compensatory meaning also. Jung's delightful ambiguity about paranormal dreaming seems strange given the rich variety of his personal dream life. Perhaps he preferred to be called an empiricist rather than a mystic, a term later theorists labelled him with, and therefore when it came to paranormal dreaming he fought shy of calling a spade a spade.

Hall
Content analysis, though unencumbered by theoretical considerations, is also unable to grasp the entirety of dreaming. Hall's method probably works very well for normative dreaming – dreams that are generally encountered by us every night. Yet extraordinary dreams do occur. It is precisely the more infrequent variations – the fantastical ones where fierce dragons become friends, where gods descend from the heavens – that draw our attention to dreams in the first place and make them worthy of study. These are the dreams that are remembered and cherished. Although not everyday occurrences, they are certainly not rare. Any theory of dreaming must create space for them. Content analysis tends to gloss over any infrequently occurring dimension of dreaming. It therefore denies validity to the multiple approaches to dreams, sticking to a single aspect increasingly centred on cognitive

processes that can only cut, chop, and consolidate old memories and blend them with the inputs of the day.

Presumably these difficulties arise because each theory hopes to enunciate a single reason for why we dream. Such an approach tends to ignore the multiplicity of dream types. To attempt to ascribe a single reason for dreaming would be akin to saying that people talk for only one reason – to communicate ideas and experiences. Wittgenstein observed that 'there is no one reason why people talk. A small child babbles often just for the pleasure of making noises. This is also one reason why adults talk. And there are countless others.' Similarly, why confine dreams only to one paradigm? Why not acknowledge that dreams not only convey the psychological truth of the dreamer, but they can also warn, herald, congratulate, create, introduce, announce, guide, foretell?

Postmodernist views on dreaming

Releasing the dream from the shackles of psychological preoccupations and its scientific deconstruction in the laboratory, the postmodernist researcher steps into the domains of social anthropology, philosophy, and linguistics, among others, to comprehend the dream. Concentrating on dream experience, they question why dreams need to be trapped within the mental net of interpretation. Are we doing justice to the reality of the dream by viewing it only through a mental prism? Are we not restricting its significance to the spectrum of analysis, which in turn is informed by our beliefs? They point out that the dream is experienced in a visual language peculiar to the dreaming world, and any dream recall is actually an attempt to render the dream in a language that is appropriate to our waking reality. Also, it has been found that a dream first reported in the middle of the night by a subject awakened in the laboratory will be recounted as a more cohesive story when it is described again in the morning.[20] Which report is the 'real' description of the actual dream experience? The point is that a translation takes place – and it takes place not only at the moment of recall. Another translation occurs when the interpreter decodes the meaning of the dream for us.[21] If we think of poetry, doesn't a poem lose some of its flavour (significance) when it is translated into another language, howsoever good the translation? What then happens to the dream, whose interpretation is really a translation of a translation? This raises another important question: wherein does the meaning of a dream reside? Is it in the dream, in its narration, or in its interpretation?

This is where the linguistics theorists step into the debate on dream meaning, and they affirm that the dream is primarily an experience that is distorted by interpretation. Further, the dreamer tries to weave a narrative into the dream while recalling it, and in doing so attempts to infuse meaning, purpose, or function into his or her narrative through the theoretical orientation of the analyst.[22] May we not therefore ask, with apologies to T. S. Eliot: Where is that (dream) experience we lost in interpreting it?

This loss is perhaps best enumerated by comparing the dream to a text. Imagine you faithfully captured in words an interesting conversation you had with someone. The conversation, like any dream, is experience, while your memory of it, rendered in words, is equivalent to dream recall. But can the words adequately capture the significance of the conversation? The answer has to be in the negative, as words cannot reveal the intonation, the implied nuances. Sometimes meaning is conveyed more by the silences, in the pauses between the words, by the relationship between the conversationalists.[23] What the postmodernist states is that dream narratives are not dreams, and the meaning derived from them cannot be restricted to or equated with what is extracted from the dream consequent to its interpretation. Meaning derived on wakefulness by way of interpretation is in itself a 'new' meaning, and the dream itself is left behind in the act of conceptualizing it for waking understanding. Consequently, interpretation diminishes the dream, as a presence comes between the truth of the dream experience in itself and the rendering of it. In short, can we interpret experience (the dream) conceptually by breaking it up into its various parts and yet claim that we have not lost its essence in doing so? Perhaps Yeats understood this perennial conundrum of the organic relationship between the part and the whole, when he asked:

O chestnut-tree, great-rooted blossomer,
Are you the leaf, the blossom or the bole?
O body swayed to music, O brightening glance,
How can we know the dancer from the dance?[24]

The postmodernist view in no way discredits dream hermeneutics, but asserts that the full significance of a dream cannot be trapped within psychological messaging; its complete import is possibly untranslatable as it is a part of the phenomenological realm where experience is coeval with being. As Bert O. States, who adopts a phenomenological approach to dreams, argues: 'There is a colossal difference between saying, "My love is fresh, delicate, soft, beautiful, fragrant, etc.," and [Robert Burns'] "My love is like a red red rose," and the difference is that one is a string of qualities and the other is a sensory experience that calls up our felt memory of the world; one tells you what your love is, what sorts of things it is made of, the other tells you it is an ineffable feeling but that it has a certain character.'[25]

If we are honest, we will have to admit that we do not know the true purpose of dreaming, and possibly all that humankind has postulated till now may be an oversimplification. This does not mean that all significance we have attributed to the dream is untrue. What the ancient and modern theorists have 'read' into them are true and valid, 'but what is always left behind is the dimension of meaning that cannot survive translation. [Ultimately,] a dream is a dream is a dream.'[26]

The dream: A window to reality

What the above suggests is that the reality of the dream does not need bolstering by a theoretical framework to make it appear presentable in the waking world. Like any other experience, it has a self-contained reality, which is not entirely dependent upon interpretational intervention to establish its validity. The postmodernist theory in a sense restores the dignity of the dream by giving it an independent status. The dream need not depend on waking reality for its confirmation through a laborious system of interpretation, nor is it subservient to the material world.

Granting an independent experiential validity to the dream state throws open the entire debate on dreams to a much larger issue, which until now has been completely ignored in our discussion. Is the dream real or is it merely an illusion? This crucial question is not concerned with the meaning of the images, but is related to the importance accorded to the act of dreaming itself. The world of the dream is a completely different phenomenon from the waking world. Is it then more real, less real, or as real as the waking state?[27] The way this issue is addressed will determine the significance of the dream and thereby give (or deny) to it its persuasive force.

Dreams seem real as long as we are in the dreaming state, but once awake what reality can we ascribe to them? Possibly in earlier times human beings were so impressed by their dreams that they often gave them greater importance, believing them to hold superior knowledge to that found in waking reality. They believed that dreams are a privileged medium to access all that otherwise eludes objective consciousness – the world of divine invisible beings, the realm of the dead, the indications of fate, foreknowledge. Enough conceptual legroom was given to the dream, so that it is not merely a poor relative subsisting on the alms of waking reality, but an accepted state of consciousness that permits access to realms beyond the sensible world.

The ancient Hindus were more than comfortable with such a belief because they felt that knowledge is not limited to the gateway of the five senses, and so willingly included the dream into their reality. In fact, the Hindus believed that the state of dreaming has greater access to 'other' realities because it is a state of consciousness closer to the ultimate reality. For example, the ancient Hindu scripture Prasna Upanishad teaches that the only truth is *Brahman* (the Absolute) and that human beings experience four states or levels of consciousness – waking (*jagrat*), dreaming (*swapna*), deep sleep (*sushupti*), and, finally, transcendence (*turiya*). It further states that the sequence progresses towards greater reality, taking *turiya* to be most real. They believed that whatever is experienced when awake, is also experienced in the dream, and both these experiences impact our lives, though with one important difference: we become attached and bound to our waking experiences, while we remain unattached to our dream experiences. It is in this sense that the Upanishadic texts treat the dream state as being less binding than the waking one, and therefore closer to reality.[28]

The sophistication of the Hindu conception is that it saw consciousness as a continuum where waking, dreaming, and dreamless sleep are modifications of the foundational state of *turiya*, the latter unnoticeably informing each of them. This is quite contrary to the modern tendency to confer reality only to that which is known and intelligible. In fact, by allowing such an elasticity of operation within their belief systems, the Hindus further gained the confidence to question the very nature of reality.

The Hindu view of dreams

There was a fundamental difference between Freud's reason for studying dreams and that of the Upanishadic Hindu, and this was possibly due to their cosmogonic views. Philosophically, the latter considered the entire world as *maya* (illusion: in that it is not what it appears to be) wrought by the Creator for his *lila* (play); the whole universe, including you and me, is merely a dream of the Supreme Being Vishnu.[29] For the Hindu, nothing existed at the beginning of this *kalpa* (eon) but a vast ocean on which Vishnu sleeps on the coils of a great snake. As he sleeps, he dreams, and out of his navel grows a wonderful lotus, from which arises the universe. God's unfolding dream is the basis of all that exists. Thus it was believed that by entering the dream state one can enter into a direct relationship with God and his creative powers. Indeed, we all do just this whenever we dream, in that we create whole worlds out of nothing.[30] Dreams, therefore, in some inexplicable way, became a valid source of insight into reality. An archetypal story may be relevant as an illustration:

> One morning King Janaka summoned the royal guru and told him that he had dreamt, the previous night, of being a beggar. Perplexed, he implored his Guru: 'Tell me what is real? Am I a king who dreamt of being a beggar, or am I a beggar who is currently dreaming that he is a king?'[31]

The story forces us to explore the uneasy relationship between dreams and waking life, an uneasiness that, perhaps, demands a comparison between their ontological realities. It questions our view of conventional reality and asks which state is *really* real – dreaming or waking? Inversely, it asks which state is actually illusory – our daytime experiences or our nocturnal ones? Writing in a similar vein, the English philosopher Bertrand Russell (1872–1970) said, 'It is obviously possible that what we call waking life may be only an unusual and persistent nightmare.' He further added, 'I do not believe that I am now dreaming but I cannot prove that I am not.'[32] And therefore, can we know for sure which state is more real – dreaming or waking? How could the Vedic Hindu confidently assert that one state is more reliable than the other, when to him everything is *maya* (illusory)? This does not imply that he considered the world and himself as unreal, but that everything we normally consider real (rocks and roses) or unreal (dreams) is in fact *maya*.[33]

One of the most intense debates in Hindu philosophy is the question of what is real and what is not. It was argued that some aspects of the waking state are as unreal as dreaming because a false reality may be apprehended. For example, a shell being mistaken for silver[34] or the better known mistake of perceiving a snake for a rope. Hence, though some things may be real, they can be mistaken for something that is unreal. And, since it is difficult to know when such mistakes occur, it is impossible to ascertain the precise nature of reality. We perceive grass as coloured green and roses as red, while science informs us that they are really colourless; the different wavelengths of light bouncing off them provide the illusion of colour. Once again, on closer scrutiny we discover that we are prey to error when we trust only sense perceptions. Can we then consistently call the dream an illusion, and deem the waking state as always being incontestable? The Buddhists understand the rope-snake not only as a mistake but also as indicative of the illusory nature of reality. The Buddhist sacred text Lankavatara Sutra states that 'like fools who, not recognising the rope, take it for a snake, people imagine an external world, not recognising that it is made of their own thought'.[35]

The Hindu-Buddhists consider the waking state as unreal because its perceptions have their origin within us, primarily in the mind, which is subjective. For instance, my neighbour and I perceive the world differently even though we see the same trees and ride on the same bus to work. Furthermore, the reality of the waking state is chained to the weight of materiality, limited *only* to sensory perception, while the dreaming state is free of this bondage and can transcend it. Perhaps that is why the Hindu sage, in harmony with Vishnu's dream, could visualize all of life as a dream from which we awake only at death.[36]

It is not only Hindu philosophy that ponders over the nature of reality, but all other systems of philosophy as well. Special attention is given to 'the degree of reality that one may attribute to the dream',[37] since any assessment of 'what is real' depends largely on an understanding of the relationship between the dreaming and waking states. This is a dilemma that has puzzled human beings since antiquity. Descartes, the father of Rationalism, wondered what would happen to a sleeper who not only had coherent dreams, but continuity was preserved in them across nights. What if, night after night, dreams took the sleeper back to the same setting, to the same conversation with the same people he or she had interacted with on previous nights? What if, in essence, dreams on successive nights were thematically contiguous?[38] The dream may then acquire the permanence of reality, and it would become difficult to ascertain which was *really* real – dreaming or waking – akin to King Janaka's dilemma. In modern times, Freud considers 'whether we are to attribute *reality* to unconscious wishes' (and consequently dreams), and concludes without doubt, 'that *psychical* reality is a particular form of existence not to be confused with *material* reality'.[39]

Admittedly this mode of cognition provides a jolt to the rationality of our *common sense*, which typically takes for granted the distinctions in the dichotomy of real-unreal, or waking-dreaming. Although these dichotomies may be useful when trying to understand such distinctions, they may not exist in themselves. And when the lines of demarcation that support such dichotomies are probed deeper they tend to wobble, if not disappear altogether.[40] For example, science introduced us in the early years of school to the dichotomy of matter and energy. It is an elegant description of the temporal world, one that helps every student grasp the intricacies of physics (the study of energy) and chemistry (the study of matter through its elements), thereby enunciating a very intelligible model of the sensible universe. However, on deeper probing, the distinction in this duality is rubbed clean by Einstein's famous equation ($E=mc^2$), which mathematically informs us that the boundary between matter and energy is not inviolate. The universe is not composed of bits of matter on which energy acts, but that mass (matter) can be traded for velocity (energy), and this exchange rate is fixed by the equation. Today a conscious blurring of reality between fact and fantasy permeates our lives through the mass media, television, films, and comics. This porous boundary registers most strongly through the world of computers – virtual reality and cyberspace.

The current Western approach is that the existence and reality of dreams is ascertained through the scientific equipment found in sleep laboratories, and their meaning is established on the psychoanalyst's couch.[41] This is a corollary of their belief that dreaming is an adjunct of the waking state; a surreal footnote to the solidity of the waking world, its bumbling country cousin, unschooled and lacking in the sophisticated logic of reality.[42] These constructs push us to view the unconscious as the repository of banished impulses that threaten waking consciousness. It becomes but a matter of detail whether this cauldron is boiling over with forbidden sexual desires (Freud), the will to power (Adler), challenges of a particular life stage (Erikson), or focal conflicts (French). The actual solution of dreams, then, lies in the disclosure or acceptance of these discarded impulses by waking consciousness.

The ancient Hindus, on the other hand, viewed dreaming very differently – as one of three commonly experienced states of consciousness: *jagrat, swapna,* and *sushupti*. (We have excluded *turiya* as it is an intangible, foundational state of which the other three are modifications). The first is the waking state, wherein the senses are turned outwards and they overpower the field of cognition; the second is the dreaming state in which the organs of perception are in abeyance, thereby permitting the dream world to be cognized; and, thirdly, the state of deep sleep, during which the sleeping soul is temporarily one with the cosmic soul (*Brahman*)[43]. This threefold classification of everyday consciousness is consistent with laboratory observations, which also characterize it in three distinct modes. The ancient Hindu may have been forced to posit different forms for consciousness due to its loss in sleep. The consequent return of consciousness on waking suggests the dialectical Upanishadic question: 'When this man fell asleep thus, where then was the person who consists of intelligence (*vijnana*)? Whence did he thus come back?'[44]

This state to which our consciousness goes during sleep cannot be unreal, otherwise one would be forced to conclude that our consciousness, and therefore we, do not exist when we are asleep. Another argument considers the possibility of bringing back from the world of dreams a token that will be proof of the dream's reality. The mystic Sri Ramakrishna Paramhansa elucidates: 'A man dreamt of a tiger. Then he woke up and his dream vanished. But his heart continued to palpitate.'[45] Something tangible (the fear) survived, even after the 'illusions' of the dream had faded away, to attest to the unimpeachable existence of the world from which it had been brought.[46] If dreams are an illusion how can they create real emotions?[47]

Perhaps a more compelling argument is the reality of the wet dream. Central to our rationalism is the belief that real events have real causes. The hard evidence of semen – as real as getting wet in the rain – will not let us wash the dream away as mere illusion.[48] It may be objected that the semen is evidence of only a biological need. Then the counter-objection is if there was an insistent somatic need, why does it need to discharge itself only during the currency of a dream? Or do we believe that the stimulus of a dream is essential for this need to express itself? Whichever way we look at it, we cannot escape the conclusion that something we think of as unreal (the dream) caused a real event. Thus not conceding reality to the dream state leaves us in a position similar to finding ourselves in 'imaginary gardens with real toads in them'.[49]

The Vedic Hindus argued that the dreaming state, therefore, must be as real as the waking state. In their schema sleep is akin to death,[50] and waking to this world; both are real as well as unreal, and it is unnecessary to establish a hierarchy between them as both have their truths. Initially they did not distinguish between the sleep of dreams and deep sleep, as they believed that human beings have only two abodes – this world and the realm of death. Then, when asked if dreams are a part of this or the other world, they explained that they belong to neither; the dream state is at the junction of the waking state and deep sleep, at the junction of this and the next world. Like the junction of two villages, the place where they meet, though belonging to both, may be distinguished as a third place. Dreams, similarly, are the third state of consciousness. And just as a person standing at this junction can survey both the villages, the dream state too can have access to both the worlds.[51] Once this metaphysical framework was in place the process of dreaming could be understood, and consequently the meaning of dreams.

This framework, with the dream having access to both worlds, made it possible to conceive the dream state in two ways: Firstly, the spirit stays in the body and nightly fashions from itself a world of forms in dreams, using the materials of its waking hours; secondly, the soul forsakes the body to bring material from the other world to the dream state.[52] The Mediterranean world also held a similar belief: the soul separates from the body during sleep. Based on this view they perceived the sleeping state as dangerously close to death. During this roaming around the soul could pick up contaminants from which arise evil dreams. Incidentally, this latter conception is the basis of the belief that one should not jerk a sleeping person awake, the fear being that their soul may not be able to return to the body.

The elegance of this framework is that it permits an understanding of every type of dream, and it introduces the dreamer to experiences that are beyond his or her everyday reality. The dreamer is granted access to realms beyond the normal waking consciousness. The ancient Hindu treatise *Padartha-dharma-sangraha of Prasastapada*[53] states that dream cognition is of three kinds: due to disorders of the body; the strength of previous impressions; or unseen forces. At the most elementary level, dreams reflect the bodily condition of the dreamer – the Atharva Veda[54] says that if the dreamer is thirsty then he will dream of lakes and rivers. These are the prodromal dreams of the Hellenic world, which are discussed in detail later. Through them our body warns us of impending illnesses as well as any changes in it. The next category shows that the Hindus were aware that dreams can be a vehicle of wish-fulfilment: 'It often happens that when a man, having a strong desire for something and thinking constantly of that thing, goes off to sleep, that same series of thoughts and mental images appear again in the form of sense-cognition.'[55] The strength of impressions, according to the Ayurvedic text *Caraka Samhita*, pertains to things seen, heard, experienced, pictured from inner desires, or created by fancy.[56] Herein lies the entire range of psychological dreaming, allowing all the materials of the waking world, including Freud's day residue, to be availed of in the dream life. The Hindu philosophical text Brihad-Aranyaka Upanishad says that in the dream state: 'There are no chariots there, no spans, no roads. But he projects from himself chariots, spans, roads. There are no blisses there, no pleasures, no delights. But he projects from himself blisses, pleasures, delights.' [57]

This bears clear testimony to the fact that the Hindus were aware of the symbolic meaning of dreams, wherein the manifest images refer to something else. By allowing the boundary between dreaming and waking to be porous, not only do elements of the waking world invade dream space, but also perceptions from the dream world help fashion waking reality into a tangibly better world – a theory holding weight through centuries and valid in the modern world. We will cite examples of how dreams have changed the world of science, medicine, technology, politics, literature, and golf, among much else in the next chapter. The Hindus did not restrict the strength of previous impressions to only things current, but also saw in them 'glimpses of occurrences and experiences of previous existence'.[58]

The idea that the soul leaves the supine body gives the dreaming intelligence the possibility to freely roam the three worlds. Not only can it travel to places in this world (out-of-body experience or astral projection), but it has the ability to cross the boundary and journey into the other worlds, bringing back with it information about the 'other shore'. By allowing dreams to partake of both worlds, the Indian texts permit them to 'dissolve the line between waking and dreaming reality by dissolving the distinction between a shared waking world and a lonely dreaming world'. Or perhaps we can say that 'they make it possible to drag back across the still acknowledged border between the worlds those dreams that enrich and deepen the reality of the waking world'.[59]

This freedom, guaranteed by the philosophical framework of the Upanishadic Hindus, provides the rationale for the precognitive dream – discussed in detail later – since all prognostication is about being privy to information beyond the sensory world. It also authorizes the dream to comment on issues pertaining to human destiny and its meaning thereof – on death, on the afterlife, on things unknowable in the waking state,[60] on the domain of the gods and the transcendental beyond. This is the 'big' dream, the luminous vision into the ground of being – the mystical dream, which is considered at the end of this book.

It is not being suggested that we revert back to ancient beliefs and espouse those conceptions in their entirety. I have alluded to the Hindu conception only to highlight its ability to expose us to a far greater range of the dreaming mind. However, the biggest stumbling block posed by ancient theories – Hindu or Greek – is the notion that the dream is a product of the actual nocturnal journey of the soul. Incidentally, this was not a simplistic explanation, but could also account for the variety of dream types. This olden-day conception posited that when the soul stays close to the body, the sleeper dreams about the condition of the body (the somatic dream). If the soul travels slightly further, then the dreamer experiences dreams about current personal concerns, as well as concerns of the recent past (the psychological dream). When the soul travels still further away, it can survey the events that will meet the dreamer in the near future (the precognitive dream). For example, it may discover a long-separated friend journeying to meet the dreamer. This fact can then be communicated through a dream in advance of the arrival. And, when the soul moves the furthest away, it can even bring back tidings from the land of the dead, the realm of the gods, or the underworld. Archetypal dreaming is largely concerned with this type of dream experience.[61]

It is this mechanism of dream formation that really stretches our credulity, and we tend to reject the whole conception of dreaming in favour of a modern one. The modern paradigms, with their avowed allegiance to rationality rather than experience, are apt to dismiss anything that threatens waking intelligibility. The only reality acceptable to psychotherapists is the truth of the autonomous ego. They perforce sweep aside all extra-sensory perceptions, labelling them as pagan or delusional. Freud, when confronted with the reality of the precognitive dream, refused to acknowledge it as anything besides a wish aching to be fulfilled.[62] Perhaps his metaphysical beliefs inhibited him from stepping into the wider spectrum of the dreaming reality.[63]

The psychological approach may provide us with a rationally neat system, but it is at the cost of allowing the dreaming mind its full expression. Paranormal dreams do occur to many people, and our paradigm of dreaming must encompass them, even if it challenges our rationality. We cannot just wish them away.

If, however, we concede that even mysterious dreams need a framework, then we may be able to appreciate why the ancient world posited nocturnal travel. It is undeniable that anyone would be filled with wonderment when a dream has foretold the actual arrival of a friend (or any other event); they are baffled by its source of knowledge. How could a motionless sleeping body have been privy to this knowledge?

It certainly has not been sourced from memory or experience. Does the mind go elsewhere to seek this knowledge, or does the prognostication come of its own accord to the mind? It is then that the wanderings of the soul become an alluring metaphor to explicate the mystery of the prophetic dream. Perhaps our rational difficulty with nocturnal travel would be somewhat mitigated if, instead of treating this as a factual description of a journey, we consider it as a metaphorical journey (in psychical space) employed to explain empirical evidence presented by dreams. Psychology and Sigmund Freud do not doubt the reality of psychical space like the unconscious. Furthermore, this metaphor of spatial travel can also be reversed by making other souls come to the sleeper and hold conversations, as also to inform of events occurring in places geographically removed from the dreamer – the telepathic or clairvoyant dream. Ferenczi would certainly attest to the validity of telepathy. And if the metaphor's horizon is further extended, then its messages can include conversations with the dead – the visitation dream.

Just when I thought I had, at last, come to terms with astral travel by thinking of it as a metaphor, two events occurred, which confounded me further and consequently deepened the mystery of dreaming. The first: while researching this book I happened to meet a surgeon who told me about how two of his patients had reported back to him the conversations he had had while operating on them. This was perplexing, to say the least, as they had been anaesthetized, yet they had accurately recalled the details of what he had said. Further, both patients stated matter-of-factly that they had been floating near the ceiling of the operation theatre, from where they had not only been privy to their doctor's conversation, but had also witnessed the progress of their own surgery. Had their souls left their bodies?

These were not isolated cases. Experiences of this kind have been and continue to be reported, even to the extent that a vocabulary has developed to account for the variations in the experience. Researchers call an experience *ecsomatic* when the person appears to observe their own physical body from outside, as if it were the body of someone else. Not only that, but some researchers also draw a distinction between two different types of out-of-body experience – the *parasomatic* and the *asomatic*. In the former, the percipient seems to have another body through which he or she observes. In the latter type, the subject does not have another body, and, as it were, is temporarily a disembodied being.[64] Proof of this kind of experience is sometimes provided by the ability of these people to describe happenings and conversations occurring during the currency of their experience and which their normal sense-mind could not have been privy to. How may we explain these out-of-body experiences?

The other event was my first trip to Oxford and my deep sense of shock when I visited the Bodleian Library there. Many, many years earlier I had dreamt of walking outside a library, a dream already related in the second chapter. Unlike the above two cases of patients who could recall being exteriorized from their body, I have no such memory recall to explain my familiarity with the library. And it is only to account for the concordance between the library and the imagery in my dream that I find this metaphor of travel appealing. Another possible explanation could be telepathy. Or could it have been sheer coincidence? Just like Ferenczi's friend could have coincidentally dreamt of elephants while Ferenczi was thinking of them. Whatever may be the exact mechanism of these types of dreams, they remain an enigma. A great amount of research has been done on this subject – experiments done under controlled conditions to test the occurrence of telepathy and precognition – which is described in a subsequent chapter.

Fundamentally, at the heart of the dream there is a mystery, and Freud was not unaware of this, as evidenced by one of the most cryptic footnotes in *The Interpretation of Dreams*, where he states, 'There is at least one spot in every dream at which it is unplumbable – a navel, as it were, that is its point of contact with the unknown.'[65] It is interesting and telling that he visualizes the contact point with the unknown as the navel – precisely the point where the Hindu cosmogony states this world arose from: the navel of Lord Vishnu.

Dreaming and waking are not fully segmented or compartmentalized worlds, but rather overlapping experiences. The psychological paradigm does not recognize this fact; it believes that the day world has a monopolistic hold on reality and that the night world's perceptions are limited to comments on the psychological status of the dreamer. In the next few chapters we will present dreams that appear to step beyond their psychological brief and solve real problems in the waking world, depict actual events that will happen in the future, as well as comment on what is occurring in places far removed from the dreamer. They will inform us of impending illness as well as recovery, and even be presumptuous enough to converse about death. And, rarely, dreams may 'seek deathlessness with inturned gaze' to become the gateway to the Great Beyond.

Chapter 16

DREAMS THAT HAVE
CHANGED THE WORLD

The poet to come will surmount the depressing idea of the irreparable divorce between dream and action.

André Breton

A nation was in distress. It had been under foreign domination for far too long. The people wanted their freedom, but how was it to be won? One man meditated on this problem for weeks. Then he had a dream on the strength of which he initiated the nationwide *satyagraha* movement (a policy of non-violent political resistance) in India. The man was Mohandas Karamchand Gandhi. The year was 1919, when the harsh Rowlatt Bill was likely to be gazetted into an act that would give the British government powers to arrest any person on suspicion without a warrant.

Protest against the bill was unequivocal. Gandhi had earnestly pleaded with the viceroy, through public and private letters, arguing that the bill was not only harsh but also unjust. The British government, however, remained undeterred and the threat mounted of the bill becoming an act. Gandhi met Rajagopalachari, the great Indian statesman, to discuss what could be done. He wrote in *The Story of My Experiment with Truth*,[1] 'We daily discussed together plans of the fight, but beyond the holding of public meetings I could not then think of any other programme. I felt myself at a loss to discover how to offer civil disobedience against the Rowlatt Bill if it was finally passed into law.'

Gandhi was in a great quandary. How was he to offer resistance to a bill whose tyrannical powers had still not been brought into operation? What were the Indians to offer *satyagraha* against? Moreover, after his South African experiment he had tried *satyagraha* in a few local cases in India but had never practised it on a national scale. Besides addressing a few public meetings, how was he to galvanize an entire nation to resist tyranny without themselves succumbing to violence in the process?

While Gandhi was pondering over these questions, news came to him that the Rowlatt Bill had been passed as an act. That night he fell asleep, deeply perplexed about the issue. In his autobiography he writes: 'The idea came to me last night in a dream that we should call upon the country to observe a general *hartal* [a strike that calls for the closure of all places of business, courts of law, and schools, as a mark of protest or sorrow]. Satyagraha is a process of self-purification, and ours is a sacred fight, and it seems to me to be in the fitness of things that it should be commenced with an act of self-purification. Let all the people of India, therefore, suspend their business on that day and observe the day as one of fasting and prayer.'[2]

Gandhi declared 6 April as the day of the *hartal*. Both Hindus and Muslims responded to his call with great enthusiasm. Gandhi's message reached the four corners of the country and the whole of India, every town and village, observed a complete *hartal* on that day.

From an idea in a dream, a nation demonstrated a phenomenal collective will as 'soul' force won over brute force.

Was this one great man's isolated dream or is history replete with examples of people who have heeded their dreams and changed the course of human thought? In every field – from science, sports, literature, art, philosophy, and film-making, to the winning and losing of wars – the creative process of dreaming has offered revolutionary insights. Often the dreamer is consciously working on a problem (like Mahatma Gandhi) when a dream suddenly provides him or her with a crucial hint.

As a young man Albert Einstein had a dream of critical importance to the history of science. 'He dreamt he was speeding down a steep mountainside on a sled. He went faster and faster and as he approached the speed of light he noticed that the stars above him were refracting light into a spectra of colours that he had never seen before. This image impressed him so deeply that he never forgot it, maintaining that his entire scientific achievement had been the result of meditating on that dream. It provided the basis of the "thought experiment" through which he worked out the principle of relativity.'[3]

In another branch of science Friedrich A. von Kekule, a professor of chemistry in Ghent, Belgium, had been grappling for years with the critical problem of the molecular structure of benzene. One evening in 1865, he fell asleep in his chair next to the fire, and dreamt one of the most significant dreams of history. He relates: 'Again the atoms were gambolling before my eyes. This time the smaller groups kept modestly in the background. My mental eye, rendered more acute by repeated visions of this kind, could now distinguish larger structures, of manifold conformation; long rows, sometimes more closely fitted together; all twining and twisting in snakelike motion. But look! What was that? One of the snakes had seized hold of its own tail, and the form whirled mockingly before my eyes. As if by a flash of lightning I awoke.'[4]

The serpent biting its own tail gave Kekule the clue to a discovery that has been hailed as the 'most brilliant piece of prediction to be found in the whole range of organic chemistry'.

What is now taken for granted in chemistry was unknown then – that the molecular structure of benzene is in the form of a chain of molecules arranged in the shape of a ring. The benzene ring, as it is called, presented itself to Kekule in a dream in the form of a snake grabbing hold of its own tail. From this dream imagery he constructed a model of a closed ring with an atom of carbon and of hydrogen at each point of a hexagon. This discovery revolutionized organic chemistry. It was no surprise therefore that Kekule, relating his dream-discovered insight to a scientific convention in 1890, ended his presentation with an exhortation to his colleagues: 'Let us learn to dream, gentlemen, and then we may perhaps find the truth.'

Niels Bohr, one of the key figures in the genesis of modern atomic physics, had a vivid dream when he was a student in which he was standing on the surface of a sun composed of burning gas. Planets whistled past him, each of them attached to the sun by a thin filament. 'Suddenly, the gas sun cooled and solidified, the planets crumbled away.'[5] By 1913 this was the commonly held picture of the atom: a central, positively charged nucleus (the sun) around which orbit negatively charged electrons (the planets). This model, however, left some crucial questions unanswered. If the atom contained a concentrated positive charge at its centre, why were not the electrons drawn into its centre? The analogy with the solar system did not answer the difficulty because according to the laws of electrodynamics the electrons, unlike the planets, should continuously dissipate their energy while orbiting and follow a shrinking spiral path that would make them crash into the nucleus in a very short time.

Bohr had another powerful dream when he was puzzling over this problem that helped him formulate his famous atomic theory. 'He was at the races. The horses ran in lanes, which were clearly marked with white dust. They were permitted to change lanes provided they maintained a distance between one another. If a horse ran along a white line and kicked up dust, however, it was immediately disqualified.'[6]

When he awoke, this 'rule of the track' gave Bohr the clue to the structure of the atom. His theory states that electrons orbit the atomic nucleus in circular (or more generally elliptic) orbits. The electrons can orbit only in certain well-defined orbits, just as horses have to keep to the lanes. As long as the electron remains in a given orbit it emits no energy and continues to circle around the nucleus. They can change orbits only by gaining or losing energy, but they cannot travel in the intermediate space lying in between these well-defined orbits. The horse would be disqualified for running outside its defined lane.

Bohr had found this notion 'so exciting that he postponed his honeymoon to write what became a landmark paper'.[7] It was on the basis of this insight that Bohr was awarded a Nobel Prize in 1922. Perhaps quantum theory has much to thank the dreaming mind than it would care to admit!

On the night of 10 November 1619, at the age of 23, Rene Descartes, the founder of modern philosophy and scientific thinking, had three remarkably vivid dreams in quick succession. He considered them to be 'the most important affair of his life'. They involved a whirlwind; a clap of thunder and a multitude of fiery sparks; and two books – one a dictionary and the other an anthology of poems. Descartes believed that God sent the whirlwind to drive him forward; the thunderclap was a sign of the spirit of truth; and the books revealed that both philosophy and wisdom had a part to play in this truth. The dictionary represented for him the unity of mathematics and the sciences, while the book of poems signified the poet's ability to combine enthusiasm and imagination, thereby bringing out the seeds of wisdom much better than reason can.

The first of his dreams was full of anguish and terror. He was walking in the streets leaning heavily on his left side because he felt a great weakness in his right side. When he made an effort to stand upright, he felt a violent wind spin him around three or four times on his left foot. He feared falling at each step and sought refuge in a college chapel, where he hoped to pray, but realizing he had passed a man he knew, he tried to retrace his steps. However, he was driven back violently by the wind that blew towards the college. At the same time another person, in the middle of the courtyard, called him by name and told him that he had brought a gift of a melon from some foreign country. But what surprised Descartes further was to see that those who were gathered around this man were upright and firm on their feet, although he himself was still bent and tottering, and that the wind had greatly diminished. At this point he awoke.[8]

Descartes interpreted the melon to mean his instinctual (sexual) life and the chapel represented his religious life. Both he had rejected in his search for an exacting truth. The young philosopher was apt to doubt and question everything and rely only on the ability to reason to accept anything. The dream was suggesting that he had proceeded in an unbalanced manner – there is a conflict between right and left. He has to rely on the left (instinctive as opposed to the right, which stands for reason) to continue walking. Perhaps his limp was meant to remind him about the dissociated aspect of his life. At the risk of oversimplification, it seems that the task posed by his dream was to make him reconcile the domains of the body and the spirit, and to understand their interrelations in a scholarly context (the college courtyard). 'His eventual solution was to develop the philosophical theory of dualism; man's physical body functioned in a manner similar to that of other animals, but his mind operated on a nonphysical basis, under the influence of a soul.'[9] Descartes' dreams helped move his metaphysics away from its earlier rational moorings to reconcile religious faith and the advances of seventeenth-century science in the classical expression of dualism.

Now herein lies the apparent paradox. Descartes in the philosophy of science, Kekule in the field of chemistry, Bohr in the microcosmic world of atoms, and Einstein in the macrocosmic sphere of stars and galaxies: these were men who were the founders of modern science – a branch of knowledge whose entire basis and belief is objectivity, logicality, and verifiability. This entire scientific credo is reversed as we find these men are dependent on mental processes that are intuitive and irrational, and verifiable only after the event.

It would be natural to look at these men of science as ice-cold logicians, but if we read extracts from their autobiographies and letters without knowing who they are, we may be led to believe that the writers are a bunch of naive, romantic poets or artists. There are several remarkable qualities that underscore their work and run through each of their writings: the setting aside of logic and deductive reasoning except when verifying an insight; a deep aversion for the one-track mind; a distrust of the scientific demands for consistency; and scepticism towards an all-too-conscious thinking. This sceptical reserve is compensated by trust in intuition and unconscious insights.[10]

A whole industry owes its livelihood to Elias Howe's invention of the sewing machine, which was heralded by dream imagery. People had been trying to fabricate such a device for half a century in America and elsewhere without much success. Howe spent five years trying to develop a model of the sewing machine and repeatedly failed because he always made the needle with the thread-hole in the middle of the shank. Unsuccessfully he struggled with it day and night. Then one night he dreamt:

> He has been captured by a tribe of savages, who take him to their king.
> 'Elias Howe,' roared the monarch, 'I command you on pain of death to finish this machine at once.'
> Cold sweat poured down his brow as he saw himself surrounded by dark-skinned warriors, whose faces and chests are painted and who formed a hollow square about him as they lead him to the place of execution. Suddenly he noticed that near the heads of the spears which his guards carried, there were eye-shaped holes.[11]

He awoke from his dream realizing he had solved the riddle. What he needed was a needle with an eye near the tip, not at the top or the middle. He sprang out of bed, and at once made an eye-pointed needle. It worked.

It is fascinating how Gandhi, Kekule, and Howe awoke from their dreams with a clear perception that they had found the solutions to their problems. Gone was the confusion, the struggle inherent in trial and error; in its place was a conviction that an answer had been found.

Dream insights can occur in two ways: they can either provide the solution to a problem in its totality, in clear and literal terms, or they can furnish the symbolic idea from which the solution emerges. The discovery that was to give hope to diabetics came to Sir Frederick Banting in its totality when he awoke from sleep. Before the 1920s, diabetes was an incurable disease that spelt sure death. In those days, despite assuaging the great bursts of hunger and thirst, the diabetic suffered and slowly wasted away, became comatose and died. Thousands of people around the world, especially children, were afflicted with diabetes when Sir Frederick Banting began his research work on the subject. On the night of 30 October 1920, while preparing a lecture on diabetes, Banting fell asleep. At two o'clock in the morning, he woke up and scribbled these sentences: 'Tie up the duct of the pancreas of a dog. Wait for a few weeks until the glands shrivel up. Then cut it out, wash it out and filter the precipitation.'[12]

So far all attempts to isolate insulin had repeatedly failed. Banting put to test these sleep instructions in a laboratory. He tied up the pancreatic duct of a dog and waited for seven weeks, and then he opened the dog's stomach to see if the pancreas had shrunk in size. Since it had not, he repeated the experiment till the desired result was attained. He was able to extract insulin from the pancreas and inject it into a diabetic dog that was dying. The dog soon sat up wagging its tail.

On 11 January 1922, Banting injected insulin into a fourteen-year-old boy dying of diabetes at Toronto General Hospital. Almost immediately his blood sugar levels fell; within days, he was out of bed, and within weeks he was home, though dependent on insulin injections. The world applauded Frederick Banting, and he was awarded the Nobel Prize for his efforts.

Dream insights also helped Otto Loewi win the Nobel Prize in Physiology and Medicine in 1936. Loewi, like Banting, noted down an experiment that changed the perception of the functioning of the human body. Once again the solution appeared in his dream in its totality. Prior to Loewi's time it was assumed that nervous impulses in the body were transmitted by an electrical wave. Loewi, in a conversation with a colleague in 1903, conceived the idea that there might be a chemical transmission of the nervous impulse, rather than an electrical one, but he saw no way of proving his hunch and it slipped from his conscious memory, only to emerge again in 1920.

'The night before Easter Sunday of that year [1920] I awoke, turned on the light, and jotted down a few notes on a tiny slip of thin paper. Then I fell asleep again. It occurred to me at six o'clock in the morning that during the night I had written down something most important, but I was unable to decipher the scrawl. The next night, at three o'clock, the idea returned. It was the design of an experiment to determine whether or not the hypothesis of chemical transmission that I had uttered seventeen years ago was correct. I got up immediately, went to the laboratory, and performed a simple experiment on a frog's heart according to the nocturnal design ... Its results became the foundation of the theory of chemical transmission of the nervous impulse.'[13]

It appears that creativity, like dreaming, relies heavily upon the unconscious. Loewi's idea that there might be a chemical transmission of the nervous impulse gestated for seventeen long years because he saw no way to prove his hunch. The thought slipped from his conscious mind, but it seems that his unconscious kept working, as the design of an experiment crystallized in 1920.

The mathematician Henri Poincaré, who discovered the existence of Fuchsian functions, believed that mathematical talent is essentially dependent on unconscious processes. 'When one is working on a difficult problem,' wrote Poincaré, 'it often happens that at the start of the work one makes no progress. One then allows oneself a shorter or longer break for rest and thereafter sits down again at one's desk. During the first half-hour one again finds nothing, and then suddenly the decisive idea presents itself ... Probably unconscious work went on during the rest period, and the result of this labour is later revealed.'[14]

Similar experiences have been reported by other mathematicians. They seem to be the rule rather than the exception. One of them is Jacques Hadamard: 'One phenomenon is certain and I can vouch for its absolute certainty: the sudden and immediate appearance of a solution at the very moment of sudden awakening. On being very abruptly awakened by an external noise, a solution long searched for appeared to me at once without the slightest instant of reflection on my part – the fact was remarkable enough to have struck me unforgettably – and in a quite different direction from any of those which I had previously tried to follow.'[15]

The psychology of creative insight seems to follow a progression that begins with a conscious perplexity about the problem, followed by a period where it recedes from conscious thought, sinking into the fertile underground layers of the mind. There the unconscious, perhaps, appraises one solution after another until it hits upon something that may be the answer, pushing it upwards into consciousness as that sudden and spontaneous insight.

In 1869 the Russian chemist Dmitri Mendeleev, who had been working for years to discover a way of classifying the elements according to their atomic weight, fell into an exhausted sleep after devoting long hours to the problem. Later that night, Mendeleev 'saw in a dream a table where all the elements fell into place as required'.[16] Upon awakening, he immediately wrote down the table just as he remembered it in his dream. Amazingly, Mendeleev reported, 'Only in one place did a correction later seem necessary.' The solution to his problem was dream-delivered in its totality, and this was the genesis of the periodic table of elements, a fundamental discovery of modern chemistry.

The freedom-fighter dreams of non-violent resistance, the scientist of his laboratory experiments, and the poet Coleridge dreamt the poem 'Kubla Khan' in full and finished form one lazy summer afternoon in his English countryside cottage.

Samuel Taylor Coleridge (1772–1834) was turning the pages of a history book called *Purchas, His Pilgrimage*, where he read the words, 'Here the Khan Kubla commanded a palace to be built ...' His addiction compelled him to take opium, which induced sleep. When he awoke, three hours later, the stately passages of 'Kubla Khan' were firmly in his mind. In his sleep he composed not less than 'two to three hundred lines' in which all the 'images rose up before him as *things*, with a parallel production of the correspondent expressions, without any sensation or consciousness of effort'.[17] On awakening he had a distinct recollection of the whole poem and he seized pen, ink, and paper and began writing. Unfortunately no sooner had he begun, than a person on business intruded and detained him for over an hour, so that much to his mortification except for the fifty-four lines we know today 'all the rest had passed away like the images on the surface of a stream into which a stone has been cast'. However, what remains of Coleridge's masterpiece is still soaked in the inspiration of his dream state, where he 'had drunk the milk of Paradise' so that the poem is still 'a miracle of rare device'.

For Coleridge, 'images rose up ... as *things*'. The pictorial representation of thought is the hallmark of the unconscious – the dream, the hypnagogic half-dream, the artist's imaginative vision all encapsulate thought into visual images. The scientific counterpart to Coleridge's experience was Kekule's vision of the serpent biting its own tail.

The famous book *The Strange Case of Dr. Jekyll and Mr. Hyde* is an example of British author Robert Louis Stevenson's reliance on the creativity of his dream life. He had long been trying to write a story on man's dual nature, in which the irrational side can overwhelm the mind. Dissatisfied with an earlier manuscript on this topic, he had destroyed it. Then pressed for money, he resumed thinking about the theme: 'For two days I went about racking my brains for a plot of any sort; and on the second night I dreamed the scene at the window, and a scene afterwards spilt in two, in which Hyde, pursued for some crime, took the powder and underwent the change in the presence of his pursuers. All the rest was made awake, and consciously, although I think I can trace in much of it the manner of my Brownies.'[18]

Stevenson's 'Brownies' were the little people of his dreams who would 'bestir themselves ... and labour all night long' to produce 'truncheons of tales upon their lighted theatre' of the night. So vibrant and alive were these tales for Stevenson that with a 'jubilant leap to wakefulness, with the cry, "I have it, that'll do,"'[19] he would immediately set pen to paper and write down the tales his little Brownies had enacted. So real were the dream-Brownies that according to him 'they can tell him a story piece by piece, like a serial, and keep him all the while in ignorance of where they aim'. He confessed that they gave him 'better tales than he could fashion for himself'.[20] Do we trace a Greek influence here? To the Greeks dreams were peopled from the village of dreams (*oneiros demiros*), while Stevenson calls these people 'Brownies'.

Charlotte Bronte, whose novels contain perfect descriptions of states she possibly could not have experienced owing to the restrictive circumstances that women of her time lived in, took the aid of her dreams to do so. Her description of an opium-induced state in *Villette* is so startlingly true to life that she was asked if she had ever taken opium. Charlotte Bronte replied 'that she had never, to her knowledge, taken a grain of it in any shape, but that she had followed the process she always adopted when she had to describe anything which had not fallen within her own experience; she had thought intently on it for many and many a night before falling to sleep – wondering what it was like, or how it would be – till at length, sometimes after the progress of her story had been arrested at this one point for weeks, she awakened in the morning with all clear before her, as if she had in reality gone through the experience, and then could describe it, word for word, as it had happened.'[21]

Dreams have also inspired writers today. In a Discovery Channel show entitled 'The Power of Dreams' (aired in 1994), Isabel Allende talked of how she had been struggling with the end of a story that she was working on, and which was later to become her bestselling debut novel *The House of Spirits*, when she had a dream that roused her creative imagination. She dreamt that she was sitting beside the corpse of her grandfather, which was draped in black, in a room with black furniture, telling him about the book she had written. These images inspired her to conclude the story of her family's life with the grandfather's passing;

it was as if she were keeping vigil by his body, waiting for the moment when she would bury him.[22]

Other writers who claim their work was inspired at times by their dreams are Sir Walter Scott, John Keats, Mark Twain, Edgar Allan Poe, H. G. Wells, Katherine Mansfield, Graham Greene, and J. B. Priestley.

Creative dreams have also inspired some of the greatest artists of all time. William Blake, the English artist-poet-engraver, illustrated his poems with his own engravings, but the technique was expensive, and he found himself 'intensely thinking by day and dreaming by night' of how to come by a cheaper alternative, but with no success. At long last he had a dream one night, in which his dead brother Robert appeared to him and 'revealed the wished-for secret', namely a process of copper engraving.

The next morning Blake sent his wife out with their last half crown to buy the simple material 'necessary for setting in practice the new revelation', and henceforth engraving for Blake became the principal means of his livelihood.[23]

Such is the power of our sleeping mind that if we wish to know the answer to something and think 'intently on it for many nights before falling asleep' we may wake up one morning with an answer. In fact, Charlotte Bronte seemed to have unwittingly followed what the ancient Greeks called incubation – the sought dream.

Writers, musicians, painters, performers seem much closer to the workings of the unconscious, instinctively realizing that it is the fount from which creativity springs. Salvador Dali, the famous painter, formed a bridge between his dream imagery and his paintings. His fascination with dreams was stimulated after he read Freud's *Interpretation of Dreams*, and like some other surrealists, Dali attempted to preserve dream imagery on canvas and to enhance the mood that permeated his nocturnal visions. Dali referred to his work as 'hand-painted dream photographs', and to heighten the visual intensity of his dreams, he liked to sleep with an intense light on.[24] The surrealist's goal, according to French poet André Breton, was, 'the future resolution of these two states, so contradictory in appearance – dream and reality – into a kind of absolute reality, or surreality'.[25]

The painter draws 'still' pictures while the film-maker produces moving visual images, sharing a commonality with dreams. Films, like dreams, change characters and setting, have flashbacks, can produce time distortions and yet project a reality. Ingmar Bergman, the well-known Swedish film-maker, who reproduced episodes from his dreams as accurately as possible in films such as *Naked Night* and *Wild Strawberries*, said in an interview, 'I discovered that all my pictures were dreams. Of course I understood that some of my films were dreams, that part of them were dreams ... but that *all* my pictures were dreams was a new discovery.'[26]

Dr Marie de Manaceine, a nineteenth-century Russian physician from St Petersburg, drew up a list of many creative people who found inspiration in their dreams. She says, 'A great many men of science, poets, philosophers, musicians and others have declared that they received important ideas and suggestions in dreams ... Much that we honour in literature, science, and art is the direct result of mental work during sleep, and due to unconscious cerebral activity.'[27]

Unconscious cerebral activity is a scholarly way of referring to dreams. Dreams are not mired in the dos and don'ts, the taboos, the mechanical modes of perception that the conscious mind is subject to. The unconscious has this amazing ability to mix and match the oddest things, people and situations; to roam freely between past, present and future; to free associate between unrelated situations, juxtaposing 'kings and cabbages' with its own inimitable logic. This uncanny ability to sift through a plethora of detail and come up with something utterly pertinent to the dreamer's preoccupation is a highly creative act. Goethe wrote: 'Man cannot persist long in a conscious state, he must throw himself back into the Unconscious, for his root lives there ... Take for example a talented musician, composing an important score: consciousness and unconsciousness will be like warp and weft.'[28]

Dream creativity is not restricted only to mental enigmas or artistic inspirations. Jack Nicklaus, the famous golfer, saw the solution to a problematic golf swing in a dream. After winning a number of championships, he found himself in an embarrassing slump. When he regained his championship form seemingly overnight, a reporter from the *San Francisco Chronicle* (27 June 1964) asked him how he had done it. He replied, 'I've been trying everything to find out what has been wrong ... But last Wednesday night I had a dream and it was about my golf swing. I was hitting them pretty good in the dream and all at once I realized I wasn't holding the club the way I've actually been holding it lately. I've been having trouble collapsing my right arm taking the club head away from the ball, but I was doing it perfectly in my sleep. So when I came to the course yesterday morning, I tried it the way I did in my dream and it worked ... I feel kind of foolish admitting it, but it really happened in a dream.'[29]

Why didn't this dream come earlier to Nicklaus? Why did it wait till his game was down, and he was in a slump? What would have happened if Banting had received his instructions in a dream ten or fifteen years earlier? Wouldn't many more people have been saved the suffering inflicted by diabetes?

Before answering this question we may have to ask if these people were prepared to heed their dreams had they come earlier. When Nicklaus was winning tournament after tournament would he have paid attention to a 'silly' dream commenting on his swing? Probably not. But if the dreamer has been grappling with the problem for a long time and has exhausted all consciously reasoned avenues, then he or she may be tempted to try the dream's instructions. Questions like these are of great interest to researchers while they study the 'why' and 'how' of creativity. In fact, the process behind dream insights noted earlier resembles the well-known steps of the creative process itself – both being inexorably linked to the unconscious.

It seems that the prerequisite for a creative insight is complete *immersion* in the problem. The data has to be collated, organized, mulled over, and absorbed: all logical possibilities have to be explored and tested out again and again. Creativity is most likely to be activated when in waking life the conscious mind is totally focused on a single issue. The problem may be just a few days old or may have stretched over months and years. Banting, in his research on diabetes, had been thinking over the problem 'for many months', as had Kekule. Howe had spent five years working on the sewing machine, while Mendeleev had 'been working for years' to discover a way of classifying the elements according to their atomic weight. Mahatma Gandhi only approached a solution after 'weeks of meditation on the problem'. There seems a minimum time interval during which the person must soak him or herself in the problem, often without any success. Usually in the immersion stage the experience is frustrating and seemingly unproductive.

It is during the second phase of *incubation* that productive ideas are generated. The conscious mind in this phase may be focused elsewhere, on other problems, other projects. Yet one's mental faculties do not remain idle with the cessation of conscious thought about a particular issue. This is a state of active passivity, when the deeper substratum of the mind keeps trying one possible solution after another, sifting, searching, screening – though finally how the insight is arrived at remains a mystery. Wilhelm Wundt, the pioneer of German experimental psychology, encapsulated the dilemma aptly when he said, 'Our mind is so fortunately equipped, that it brings us the most important bases for our thoughts without our having the least knowledge of this work of elaboration. Only the results of it become conscious. This unconscious mind is for us like an unknown being who creates and produces for us, and finally throws the ripe fruits in our lap.'[30]

Characteristically the actual moment of *illumination* is compared to a flash of lightning. It is that spontaneous moment when the person knows with certainty that a solution has been found. Kekule awoke 'as if by a flash of lightning' and Stevenson arose 'with a jubilant leap to wakefulness' at the decisive point of illumination. The force of shock of the sudden and unexplained illumination gives the dream, for that moment, a kind of kingly privilege in this domain, overshadowing the timid claims of mundane reality.

The joyous cry of Eureka, the sudden flash of insight inevitably needs to be verified by the conscious mind. What the unconscious creates, consciousness has to assess. The fact that a dreamer has had an unusual dream by itself does not imply that it will be a correct solution. The final step of *verification* of the dream idea is essential.

Creativity, then, is a process marked by stages of immersion, incubation, illumination, and verification. Verification, of course, demands the hard work of experimentation, and finally its appropriate application. Immersion and verification depend predominantly on conscious, logical processes, while incubation and illumination depend more on unconscious processes.

Possibly, we ordinary dreamers – those of us who are not novelists, scientists, musicians, and inventors – can use dreams for solving problems that concern us in our everyday lives. Twenty-three-year-old Sangeeta Kaul, who was developing a computerized network of libraries (Delnet) at the India International Centre in New Delhi, recounted that while working on a particular software program, she was unable to access one particular section of it. She wanted online information on how many libraries accessed her company's data. For three months she had tried but could not find the right command. Then one night she dreamt of the command that would execute the program. Even in the dream, she knew that the command was the right one. Sangeeta was at her office at seven thirty the next morning. She punched in her dream-dictated command and, sure enough, it worked.

Nita Berry writes books for children. While holidaying in Goa she was horrified at the extent by which the sea was polluted by industrial waste. The fish fed on the waste, gradually became resistant to it, and the catch had harmful toxic effects on those who ate the fish. Deeply troubled by the issue and wishing to write a story around it, she fell asleep. Quite like Stevenson, Nita's little Brownies set to work and she dreamt the entire plot of her story. Nita awoke from her dream drama and in one continuous stretch wrote the story out – a story that won her India's prestigious Shankar's Award.

One of the most striking uses of the creativity of the dreaming mind is made by Dr Francis Menezes – director of the Tata Management Training Institute, in Pune, near Mumbai – in the tough world of business and management. He has done pioneering work in developing and conducting dream workshops at the institute for corporate executives, besides introducing dream work into mainstream management education in India in the mid-eighties, with the view to stimulating creativity and problem-solving through dreams.

I went to Pune to meet him, curious to know how he was introducing the romantic world of dreams to the hard-nosed realm of business. The evening I arrived I had dinner with over forty engineers and corporate and management executives, who had come to attend Menezes' workshop. After dinner Menezes, a frail man with a disarmingly gentle smile, ushered us into a large room where he spoke about the power of the unconscious to solve knotty interpersonal problems, enhance performance, and give a new surge in accomplishing goals.

He said, 'I am not here to ply you with dream theories, but I want you to do one thing tonight. Take a piece of paper and think of a problem that has been bothering you. It may be a work problem or an interpersonal dilemma. In a single-phrase question, write it down, insert the paper into an envelope, and put it under your pillow. Just before going to sleep, ponder over your question. When you wake up the next morning try and remember your dream, and write it down immediately. We will then see what the problem and its solution are.'

'Single-phrase questions' could be: Why am I stuck in my project? How do I redesign the machine I am working on? Why is it so difficult to get along with my boss? How do I quit smoking?

A somewhat bemused gathering of executives left the room that night. They had expected talks on motivation and how to enhance their creativity. They did not expect to be told to go to their rooms and dream!

Menezes has conducted many such workshops over the years with gratifying results. Within the space of a three-day workshop, he said, he opened the way for over 70 per cent of the participants to a method of tapping into their own resources to find solutions to their dilemmas, instead of relying on imposed ones. You may notice that Menezes' programme followed a certain order that many creative dreamers had followed unwittingly. He led the participants through the process of deliberate immersion by asking them to focus clearly and single-mindedly on an issue for which they wanted an answer. Writing it down and putting it under the pillow was a way of 'priming the pump' for the process of incubation to take place during sleep.

Menezes demonstrated the efficacy of his programme when he was hired by a gigantic chemical manufacturing firm owned by the Government of India to solve a morale problem in its research and development wing. He invited fifty-two scientists from the department to spend three days and nights at Pune. Each evening, after dinner, he asked the scientists to think of a persistent, nagging workplace problem, then write it down in a single phrase and think about it before going to sleep.

The results were startling. After the first night each of the scientists, including the sceptics, announced that they had dreamt surprisingly relevant dreams about their work-related problems. One scientist, for instance, found himself haranguing one of his most competent co-workers; another scientist found himself pelting his unappreciative boss with lab equipment! Based on the analysis of the dreams, Menezes gave his recommendations to the firm's top brass. So impressed was the management that they took note and initiated a number of changes. Dreams of a large number of the participants revealed that they were working in an atmosphere of fear and suspicion. Taking note of that the management introduced and promoted better internal communication, productive teamwork, and more flexible working conditions.

Perhaps what was more impressive was that independent of the workplace, most of the scientists who had participated in the dream workshops made it an ongoing process, and started their own weekly meetings to discuss their dreams and review the week's outcome.

The real power of dreams lies in their ability to change the habitual way we look at the world. As children our imagination is vivid. The world is full of mystery and wonder, and we have an unjaded curiosity about it. As we grow older we learn to behave and respond in acceptable ways. Environmental, social, and educational determinants may stultify the

imagination, circumscribe the vision. Originality and creativity get
smothered. The order and discipline of conventional thought hardens
the fluidity of imagination. We tend to lose our ability to discern new
patterns, spot interesting analogies, and make insightful leaps.

Luckily our dreams remain untainted; they are spontaneous and
autonomous expressions that can be closely linked to our waking
concerns. They combine elements in extraordinary ways, seeing
correspondences and connections where none existed before. In each
of the dreams discussed above none of the images were random or
bizarre, but had specific relevance to the dreamer's preoccupation. Each
dreamer was able to see the dream images as an answer to his or her
waking concern, like the snakes in Kekule's dream.

It is noteworthy that in these varied examples there seems no
question of looking for any hidden significance in the dream images.
The dreams are taken literally. Howe's dream had all the symbolic
imagery to unravel it within a psychological framework. A tribe of
spear-wielding savages leading a hapless victim to death could be
treated by a Freudian therapist as an expression of the uprising of the
primitive sexual (spears) urge under whose sway the dreamer feared
being overwhelmed. Even Stevenson's dream of Hyde being pursued
for a crime and changing his persona in the presence of his pursuers
could have been interpreted as the 'splitting' of the many selves that
reside within us, depending upon circumstantial provocation. Bohr's
dream of horses running in lanes that were clearly marked by white dust,
which if transgressed disqualified the horse, was not interpreted by him
as a psychological truth even though it was couched in metaphorical
language. None of these dreamers believed that these dreams were
symbolic commentaries on their psychological state of being; they
were taken literally and granted the same validity as any significant
waking perception.

What emerges from many of the examples cited is that dreams are
not merely a private realm or, as Freud stated, 'completely asocial'. He
wrote that the dream 'has nothing to communicate to anyone else; it
arises within the subject as a compromise between the mental forces
struggling in him, it remains unintelligible to the subject himself and is
for that reason totally uninteresting to other people'.[31] But the dreams
we've just considered are not mere compromises between warring
mental forces. These dreams are intelligible, and carry an import for the
dreamer. In fact, they often hold enough potency to transcend private
experience and change the world.

No doubt we cannot bring back from the world of dreams some physical object that would serve as proof of the dream's reality – something solid and tangible like a ring or a photograph, to attest to the existence of the world from which it has been retrieved, long after the dream has faded. Yet something that outlasts the dream is carried across the threshold of the dream world. They are the insights, ideas, facts that will compel waking reality to reproduce or imitate them. With this the dream begins to change outer reality. It directs it as though it knows how it is designed to unfold. 'The future is unknown, diverse, indeterminate. Once dreamed, it becomes immutable. This is the power of the dream: to twist reality after itself.'[32]

We do not know from where dreams gain their secret authority wherein they become imperious commands of the night; commands that the dreamer cannot disregard. Previously the dream had been granted secondary status as it was nothing more than a reorganization of memory – of events, thoughts, and emotions experienced in waking life and preserved in some part of the brain. At night, according to the psychological theorists, the sleeping mind either by design or chance condensed and displaced the stored information to generate a dream. In other words, waking reality caused the dream. However, in these dreams it would be truer to say that 'the dream is the beginning of a chain of causes, not the result of such a chain'.

If these dreamers had not recalled their dream, then reality would have remained unchanged. By itself no change would have occurred. The dream became the cause of the outer event. It then becomes difficult to define which half of the experience is more significant: the dream as the dark womb that seeds the idea, or wakefulness that nourishes its growth.

We have to be careful to distinguish these dreams from those that simply reveal an event about to happen: the prophetic dream. The precognitive dream often reflects a future event, without being its cause. The event was bound to happen with or without the dream. However, both these dream types – those that can reflect reality and those that can change it – remain outside the realm of the psychological dream. These kinds of dreams have their own phenomenological reality and they often blur the distinction between reality and imagination, waking and sleeping, necessitating them to be treated separately from the emotionally therapeutic or psychological dream. The rationalist may be prepared to accommodate the problem-solving dream as a part of our creative expression, but our cultural beliefs find it very difficult to make space for the precognitive dream. How can you hear the echo before the sound?

Whatever dreams may be, occasionally a dream carries such a strong impact that its vividness is remembered long after. When this happens cultural belief wavers, allowing the dreamer to speculate that this dream may, after all, cause or reflect reality.

Needless to say that millions of diabetics are grateful that Banting's cultural belief had wavered.

Chapter 17

PARANORMAL DREAMS: THE ECHO BEFORE THE SOUND

There can, indeed, be no doubt that there are such things as prophetic dreams, in the sense that their content gives some sort of picture of the future; the only question is whether these predictions coincide to any noticeable extent with what really happens subsequently. I must confess that upon this point my resolution in favour of impartiality deserts me.

Sigmund Freud, *The Occult Significance of Dreams* (1925)

*U*sha' jerked into wakefulness. Slowly she unclenched her fists and tried to even her breathing. She lay in bed, trying to locate the reason for her discomfort. Her body coiled with tension as the early morning dream came back to her:

The door of my cupboard had been prised open and all my jewellery stolen.

The dream recall was so vivid that she could still feel her hand going into the safe only to contact the implacable, cold emptiness of steel. Her hand had grown clammy as she groped around for any kind of reassurance that some trinket still remained. But there was nothing there. Horror had filled her and startled her awake.

Usha sighed with the relief that wakefulness brings after a bad dream. Yet she could not shake off the sense of foreboding. Repeatedly she told herself it was only a dream; it cannot come true. I cannot possibly be robbed after all I have been through. Her mind tried to dismiss what her heart could not reconcile to. Why don't I go and check my cupboard? she thought. Just to be on the safe side.

She continued to lie in bed, the dream's familiarity haunting her. Usha was convinced she had had the same dream earlier with the same doomed feeling of calamity on waking. As daylight dappled the room, her fear persisted, but doubt crept in whether she had heard the dream elsewhere. Then suddenly it struck her that it was 'Nidhi', her closest friend, who had had exactly the same dream. Four days ago, she had rung up to tell her about an awful dream she had, 'in which my cupboard had been forced open and all my jewellery and money was missing'.

How strange that I should have an identical dream to Nidhi's, Usha thought. But how can this happen? I scarcely paid any attention when she related it. Now my own dream has drawn it out of memory like a magnet. Could our emotional closeness have provoked similar dreams?

Dreams of jewellery ... dreams of loss. She did not know the source of Nidhi's dream, but her own was not so difficult to trace. Her thoughts clustered around the time when, with all the vulnerable hopefulness of a young bride, she had entered the unknown arena of 'joint-family' life. Initially, she did not question her mother-in-law when she took custody of her jewellery and put it into the family safe-deposit locker. Usha's first surprise came when, for a family wedding, her mother-in-law did not allow her a choice of jewellery. Instead, she brought from the locker what she thought Usha should wear, taking it back soon after the wedding was over. This ritual was repeated many times till the lines of ownership were completely blurred. The mother-in-law slowly divested Usha of her claim on what was hers. Her protests were seen as rents in the fabric of family life, so that slowly she had to convert her outrage into a show of acceptance. But she never truly submitted to the injustice, hoping that one day her jewellery would be restored to her along with her ruptured self-respect. This hope was rekindled when years later her mother-in-law died. The passing away of the dominant matriarch left a window of opportunity for the issue to be reopened. However, the debate suddenly went into abeyance when, to the shock of the family, her father-in-law announced his decision to remarry.

Usha got out of bed, made herself a cup of tea, and sank into her favourite armchair, wondering how the issue of her jewellery had even managed to embed itself in her dreams like a nail driven deep into her psyche, hammered in further by her father-in-law's second marriage to 'Shanta'.

Dogged by a repetitive fate whose spell could not be broken, Usha helplessly watched Shanta follow in the footsteps of her dead mother-in-law. She took possession of the family locker and all that it contained. Usha and her husband tried to lay claim to what was theirs, but this time a sternly wagging patriarchal finger silenced them.

Usha smiled to herself as she thought: Justice is finally done, what belongs to you will come back to you. I know that better than anyone else. The ringing of the phone interrupted her thoughts. She looked at the watch – it was seven thirty – too early for anyone to phone her. Who could it be? she wondered as she reached for the phone.

A distraught Nidhi was on the line: 'Usha! I was robbed last night. They got into my steel almirah and have taken all my jewellery and the money. We have rung up the police.'

Usha was too stunned to say anything.

Nidhi paused before continuing, 'You remember I had told you about that bad dream? It was a warning. Everything was exactly the same as the dream. I feel so awful – could I have done something? Kept the jewellery in the bank locker? Thank god everyone in the house is safe.'

Usha put down the phone and decided to go over to Nidhi's house immediately. Yet for a while she was rooted to the spot as alarming thoughts coursed through her mind: Nidhi had a dream of being robbed and it came true. I dreamt the same dream. Will it also happen to me? Usha then walked purposefully towards her own cupboard. The jewellery was all there. How superstitious of me, Usha thought as she relocked her cupboard – especially after the amazing manner in which the one boon I had asked for was granted. After all I was given back what was mine. How can it be taken away now?

The reels of memory rewound and stopped at the point when the father-in-law's death brought the inevitable split in the family. Yet before dying, unwittingly he did Usha and her husband a favour. He had declared the jewellery in his last wealth-tax return, specifying each piece.

Shanta had moved out of the family house after her husband's death to stay with her sister 'Anjali'. Constant ill-health dogged Shanta thereafter so that she started relying more and more on Anjali, even naming her the joint operator of her locker – in which Usha's jewellery still remained.

The story took an unbelievable turn when a guilt-stricken Shanta, who, as she lay dying, called Usha and her husband to say, 'For years I have kept what belonged to you. I can't die with this burden.' Turning to her sister Anjali she said, 'Please return Usha's jewellery, or my *atman* [soul] will never be granted peace.'

Shanta died soon afterwards, but Anjali never honoured her dying sister's request. She kept Usha's jewellery.

Usha saw the police vehicle leaving as she reached Nidhi's house. A sense of unease hit her again – for herself, for her friend – as though the unknown lurked menacingly around the corner. Nature, they say, provides warnings before an event ... it leaves signs; it speaks in various ways, maybe even through a dream like mine, Usha thought. Yet Nature never prepared me for its benevolence when Anjali's husband had an income-tax raid at his nursing home, and all their bank accounts and lockers were sealed. Justice was served when the income-tax officers opened Anjali's locker and found large amounts of unaccounted-for jewellery. On being questioned, Anjali was forced to admit that the jewellery belonged to Usha and 'Rakesh Sahay'.

Usha still remembers that hot June evening when there was a knock on their door. Two men identified themselves as income-tax officers. In the taller man's hand was a large wooden box. Her breath caught as she opened the lid and saw her jewellery – the gold set, the emerald necklace, her *kundan* earrings, and much more – lying before her. The senior officer asked if they could prove that the jewellery was theirs. Rakesh immediately produced the list in which his father had declared the family heirlooms. After a few months of paperwork, nearly thirty-five years after her marriage, Usha finally had her jewellery returned to her. And that was only six months ago. It was a momentous occasion. Her mother, who believed that the contentious history of the jewellery had tainted it, and disregarding its value, had urged her to give it all away. 'It will only bring trouble!' she had said.

Usha entered Nidhi's house. The two women were now bound together not only by the bonds of friendship, but also by a common dream. For one woman the nightmare of her dream had been enacted by an actual robbery, while the other dreaded its occurrence. Was Usha's dream also foretelling a coming event?

I met Usha shortly afterwards. She told me her dream, its backdrop, and wanted an answer to the question uppermost in her mind. 'Am I being warned that my jewellery is going to be stolen?'

Her question was fuelled by an earthy logic: 'Nidhi and I had identical dreams. Her jewellery has been stolen. Will mine also be stolen?'

Are we back to the ancient belief of our ancestors that the main power of dreams resides in their oracular content – a belief that dream images literally forewarn us of an impending event? In doing that aren't we ignoring the strides modern psychology has made in establishing dreams as a mirror of our inner thoughts and motives, instead of being signs and omens for the future? My first instinct was to wonder whether Usha, through this dream, was reliving a trauma that had not been fully digested by her emotionally. The pattern of years, when the sense of loss and injustice had been acute, was still echoing in the night; the dream theme of loss could be indicative of a wound that had not yet healed. By making an allegorical reference to a robbed safe, the dream was helping her bridge the gap between the past, in which she was to some extent still emotionally located, and the present where her circumstances had moved ahead.

Treating the dream as a metaphor for an unhealed wound does not exhaust all the symbolism inherent in the dream. The main metaphor of the dream refers to something of value, something precious being stolen. Attempting to form a bridge, I asked Usha if she felt that something of deep value was being taken away from her.

We discussed growing old, with its attendant loss of energy as a possible metaphor of something precious being lost, but I let it slide when Usha looked unconvinced. To change the conversation I asked about her children and she said, 'My daughter is getting married next month.' It immediately struck me that this could be the bridge between the dream and her life. Something precious, kept safe and protected – her daughter – was being taken away from her. The marriage of her daughter may perhaps prove to be a defining point for Usha because she would have to let go of a part of herself – a very precious part – that no longer belongs to her, but has a life of its own. This wrench may be depicted in dreams as a forcible intrusion, a prising open, a taking away of something valued.

My attempts at a psychological interpretation left Usha unmoved. After probing her for a considerable length of time, all she asked me was, 'Are you sure my jewellery will not be stolen?'

I really did not know the answer. I was viewing her dream as being born of anxiety, but could I be certain that it was definitely not a predictive dream, especially after Nidhi's dream had strongly registered its precognitive content? Had I unwittingly succumbed to the belief that paranormal dreaming is either delusional or fraudulent, and was thus excluding precognition as a possibility? How does one discern whether a dream should be interpreted psychologically or prophetically?

Usha's confusion was not peculiar to her; it has been humankind's dilemma every time a dreamer awakes from an enigmatic dream. Since antiquity it has been assumed that the sleeper occasionally transcends the boundary of that which is known. Whenever this happens it is accompanied by mystery and awe on the part of the dreamer. However, one problem remains: how does one distinguish this special dream from the normal dreams that visit the sleeper every night? We have already witnessed the earliest attempts at dream understanding, wherein precognition of the future is inextricably linked to a divine will. Later efforts endeavoured to distil other attributes, which would alert the dreamer (or the interpreter) to the nature of a prophetic dream. Artemidorus had distinguished between the mantic import of the theorematic and allegorical dream, the former literally foretells events to come, while the latter couches its prediction behind symbols. Penelope, in Homeric times, would have had us believe that both these types of dream emanated from the 'gate of horn', through which only those dreams pass that are prophetic. We do not reliably know what feature or aspect of the dream would make Penelope relegate a dream to the 'gate of ivory', or Artemidorus declare it a mere *enupnion*, empty of prophetic value. In other words, we do not know the touchstone for determining whether Usha's dream is predictive or not. Nor does Macrobius unambiguously clarify the issue for us. It seems the attempt in the Greek world was largely to look towards the enigmatic content – the strange or vivid elements woven into the narrative of the dream. Plato clearly defines in *Timaeus* the state conducive for precognition: 'No man, when in his wits, attains prophetic truth and inspiration; but when he receives the inspired word, either his intelligence is enthralled in sleep, or he is demented by some distemper or possession.'[1]

The Hindus had independently developed their own criteria by which they assessed this type of dream. Caraka, the father of Ayurvedic medicine, classifies dreams into seven kinds: dreams that reflect what has been seen in the waking world (*drsta*) and what has been heard while awake (*sruta*); those that emanate from waking experience (*anubhuta*); dreams that are sourced from the imagination of the dreamer (*kalpita*) by the combination of two objects, like a golden cow, which is a combination of gold and cow; dreams that are wish-fulfilments (*prarthika*), gratifying desires that have remained unfulfilled in waking life; and the fault-born dream (*dosaja swapna*), which is attributed to some disorder within the organism, like the wet dream. If a dream cannot fit into any of these categories then, perhaps, it could be a prophetic (*bhavika*) one.[2] This simple classification also does not reliably identify a precognitive dream; further caveats are needed if we are to link prophecy with dream. Caraka advises, 'Dreams one sees during daytime, and all dreams that are exceedingly short, and those that are exceedingly long, should be regarded by the intelligent physician as not likely to be realised.'[3] Such severe criteria would render most dreams, if not all, as incapable of fulfilment. If Caraka is to be believed, then the brevity of Usha's dream should certainly assure her that her jewellery would not be stolen. Also, since it is based on something heard by her (*sruta*), it is further disqualified from having any prophetic content.

Other cultures believed that the best way of judging the prophetic content of any dream is by the level of excitement experienced by the dreamer. In the *Pitron Chalomot*, a sixteenth-century treatise on dream interpretation, the Jewish scholar Solomon Almoli states that 'if one dreams of powerful fantasy images that cause him to be excited or to feel anger during the dream itself, this is a true dream; but if the images are insipid and arouse no strong feelings, the dream is not true. The reliability of any dream is thus in proportion to its level of excitement.'[4] Usha's dream had invoked strong feelings that persisted within her and by this token her dream would be considered prophetic.

Nevertheless, Usha's dream remains enigmatic because it falls within the parameters of a *shared* dream. When two or more people have a dream with the same meaning on the same night, it becomes a shared or *parallel* dream. The parallel dream was dramatically exemplified when the Buddha was about to leave home forever. Three members of his household experienced the same dream. The Mahavastu, a composite text on the life of the Buddha that dates back to the second century BC, says that the 'Buddha's father dreams of an elephant leaving the city, his aunt dreams of a white bull leaving city, and his wife dreams of a great cloud that pours rain.'[5] Although they contained different symbols, the fact that three members of the future Buddha's household shared the same dream theme was a powerful testimonial to their prophetic content. The shared dream is not the preserve of religious or mythological texts; it visits many people even today, as I know from personal experience.

One morning my husband mentioned to me that he had dreamt of a friend, who lived in Mumbai, looking very depressed. I was extremely surprised since I had had a similar dream – of the same friend in the same kind of mood. Without trying to interpret either dream, I called this friend only to learn that the previous night he had got news of his father's death. An ordinary dream had assumed a different tenor by virtue of it being a parallel dream; the authenticity of its communication seemed beyond doubt because two people had shared the same dream. Our friend's condition had somehow been communicated to both Rajeev's and my dreaming mind. One of us dreaming of him may qualify as a chance occurrence, but what are the chances that the same theme would invade the content of both our dreams?

Another variant of the shared dream is the *repetitive* dream. Unlike the parallel dream, where the content is repeated to different people on the same night, the repetitive dream is shared across time. By transcending time it becomes a (trans-temporal) shared dream. The Bible has already told us how Joseph's supremacy over his family was powerfully confirmed because two dreams had shared an identical message, albeit through different symbols and on different nights. In Buddhist literature the conception dream of the Buddha's mother, Queen Maya – she sees a magnificent white elephant, which, by striking her right side with its trunk, is able to enter her womb[6] – is the same dream as the one dreamt by the mother of the preceding buddha Dipamkara.[7] A similar understanding of the shared dream exists in the Jaina texts when a hero is about to be born. According to the Kalpa Sutra (a religious Jain text dealing primarily with the lives of the founders of Jainism), on the night that Mahavira, the twenty-fourth *tirthankara* (enlightened soul) in the Jaina tradition, entered Queen Trisala's womb, she had fourteen sequential dreams in which she saw fourteen different things. When her dreams were related to the royal dream interpreters, citing the authority of dream books, they highlighted that there are thirty great dreams set to a formula whenever an exemplar is born. If a mother has fourteen of these, it heralds that a *tirthankara* will be born.[8] The birth of a *tirthankara* is always marked by similar dreams being experienced by the expectant mother. Though these dreams are separated in time by many years, whenever a pregnant mother shares the same dream content it becomes a prophecy heralding the advent of a world saviour.

Usha's and Nidhi's dreams are also shared dreams with identical content. Will they, then, herald similar outcomes? Shared dreams even frequent the consulting rooms of psychotherapists. Jule Eisenbud, an analyst in the late 1940s, was intrigued by paranormal dreams and attempted to verify them by sending telepathic messages of a three-digit number to his patients, which he hoped might surface in their dreams. He did not meet with any spectacular success, the sort that would substantiate thought transference, but he did come across what he calls *rêve-à-deux*, or a pair of dreams, that in some sense is a shared dream. To cite one example, Selma, his patient, dreamt:

> *I was walking the street in a very heavy downpour and came to the house of a next-door neighbor where I decided to ask for shelter. The house seemed to be a palatial mansion. I was a little afraid to go in because these people were very snobbish; but I reasoned that they couldn't refuse me shelter from such a downpour. When I came inside I was very conscious of my clothes which were not only soaked and dripping but very shabby besides.*[9]

This is a perfectly innocuous dream, except that Eisenbud was very surprised when the next patient related the following dream:

> *I was living in an old shack. Outside there was a heavy downpour. Some neighbors came in from the rain, of whom the only one I could identify was Selda X. Although she had just come in from a heavy rain she was absolutely dry and seemed faultlessly and even glamorously dressed. She was saying that she always had her things done at the Chinese laundry because they were returned so white and clean. She also said that she had a reciprocal arrangement with another neighbor whereby if she were out when the laundry was delivered, the neighbor took it in, and vice versa.*[10]

Though these two dreams are not identical in the way that Usha's and Nidhi's are, even a cursory examination of them reveals interesting coincidences. Both dreams are set in a background of heavy rain and in both a woman seeks shelter from the rain. Strangely in both dreams the woman, rather than brave the few extra yards and seek the security of her own home, takes refuge in a neighbour's house. In the first dream, Selma takes shelter from the rain, while in the second dream the woman who takes shelter is Selda. Their names are so similar – the 'm' has been replaced by a 'd' – that it becomes tempting to conjecture whether the person taking shelter could have been the same woman in both the dreams and that the second dream might have merely mispronounced her name. The issue in both dreams appears to be the clothes worn by Selma/Selda. In the first dream they are dripping wet and a matter of embarrassment, while in the second they are dry and a source of pride. In fact, one wonders whether the second dream could actually be a continuation of the first. In the first dream Selma is awed by the palatial house and embarrassed about her shabby clothes. These have been exchanged for the non-threatening shack and enviably glamorous clothes in the second dream, as though in the second dream Selma / Selda had compensated for her embarrassment in the first dream. There also seems to be some internal evidence in the second dream that supports the assumption that these dreams are a pair. The last sentence informs us that there is a *'reciprocal arrangement'* with the laundry, which enables a neighbour to take delivery when Selda is not around. The allusion to the laundry – dirty or clean linen – is symbolic of psychological cleaning during analysis. Further, the reciprocal arrangement suggested in the dream may be indicative of some form of sharing (telepathic) that will enable a patient to receive a message intended for another.

These two dreams occurred on successive nights to dreamers who did not know each other, though they recounted them to their analyst on the same day, one after the other. The second dream seemed to expand upon the dialogue of the first dream. Even after Eisenbud had elicited their individual associations, the problem of the two dreamers dovetailed beautifully into each other, so that one dreamer appears to be dreaming out the other's problems and symptoms, and vice versa. For example, the central point of the emotional life of the first dreamer (Selma) is alluded to in the symbol of *'walking the street in a heavy downpour'*. The first dreamer's associations disclosed that this represents her sense of loneliness and isolation, which she superficially cloaks by her extensive relationships. In fact, she further revealed that her compulsive need for love and acceptance had led her to have intimate sexual relationships from the age of eight, when she became the sex toy of a neighbourhood gang of boys. The second dreamer's association to Selda X. – the one neighbour she recognized in the dream – was most striking of all. She, it turned out, was not a neighbour, but a woman she had met at a summer resort, who was known as the 'whore of X. Beach'. In other words the second dreamer's association to Selda fit the description of the first dreamer's personality.[11]

The symbols in both the dreams fit very neatly and appear to be equally applicable to the life context of both the dreamers. One patient's association to a dream symbol when told to the other patient helped her understand her conflicts better. This leads us to believe that presentiments of one patient may find fulfilment in the dream of another. It further appears that neither dreamer has proprietary right over her own dream: both dreams appear to belong to a common substratum. Their interpretational reality also blurs the fact that these dreams belong to two total strangers, whose lives have never intersected.

The above goes to show that the shared dream represents a conundrum that does violence to our common-sense conception of dreams. We believe that nothing is more personal than a dream; 'nothing else is as stubbornly resistant to being shared. In the world of reality everything is experienced in common. The dream, on the other hand, is an adventure that only the dreamer himself lived and only he can remember; it is a watertight, impenetrable world that precludes the least cross-checking.'[12] However, because two people have experienced the same dream, it sets up a strange bond between the dreamers similar to a connection between two people meeting in the waking world. These dreams suggest that the dreamer shares a common psychic substratum that is permeable to other people. To the Upanishadic Hindu this sharing is possible because we, and the world we inhabit, are all part of the dream being dreamt by Lord Vishnu. This mythical bond might have been an acceptable explanation in times past, but for the modern mind, with its reliance on an autonomous individuality, it is very difficult to acknowledge this underlying linkage. What has been observed is that a strong binding emotion may provide the soil for the shared dream to flourish. This connection can help one person to leap across the chasm of individualness and communicate with the other, defying spatial limitations. Indian texts also describe shared dreams where two people, totally unknown to each other, dream the same dream of falling in love with the other and then find each other in waking reality.[13]

However, in Eisenbud's *rêve-à-deux* the communication is not from one person to another but directly from dream to dream without the intercession of waking reality. Had these dreams arisen from the same person, we may have felt that the second dream had compensated for the sense of inferiority experienced in the palatial house in the first dream. The dream character had exchanged her shabby clothes for glamorous ones. However, since these dreams belong to two people unknown to each other we can only conjecture that the communication of inferiority and its compensation had been communicated directly from one dream to the next. We cannot invoke telepathy, which by and large is instantaneous, to explain the common material of these two dreams as they were dreamt on successive nights. By what mechanism can we explain this dream sharing? Jungians, of course, would readily attribute this sharing to the common substratum they term the collective unconscious.

Rahul Verma was studying for his engineering examination. Late at night he put his books aside and went to sleep and dreamt:

> *I'm sitting in the examination hall and the invigilator hands me the question paper. I read through the ten questions listed there and debate which one to tackle first.*

The following day Rahul was stunned when exactly the same ten questions appeared on the exam paper handed to him by the invigilator. This is not an isolated case; I've had many such accounts related to me, including one from a retired chief justice of the Supreme Court of India, of the dreamer 'seeing' the exam paper or a part of it in a dream.

Susan Verghese is a twenty-four-year-old nurse working at Lyon's Hospital in Delhi. Previously she had worked for three years in a Methodist hospital in Madurai in the south of India. Once on night duty, exhausted after the day's rush of activity, Susan was overcome by sleep. At about four o'clock in the morning she told the other two nurses that she needed to take a short nap. She then dreamt:

> *I see a patient being rushed into the emergency, with severe bleeding from the mouth. The man has a dark, thin, long face and I feel I need to attend to him immediately.*

Susan awoke from the dream, automatically put on her cap and glided silently through the dimmed corridors of the hospital towards the emergency ward, even though her night duty was in the general wards. To her amazement, she was confronted with the same dark, thin, long face she had just seen in her dream, being rushed into the emergency. It was a case of severe bleeding from a rare gum infection. The doctor on duty needed a nurse who had dealt with such a patient before. None of the nurses, with the exception of Susan, were familiar with this kind of infection. And there stood Susan, assisting in the dressing, wondering at the unreality of it all; at the strange synchronicity of the dream, the patient, and her arrival just when and where she was needed. Many years later she still continues to wonder about this unknown face that had unwittingly propelled her into the emergency ward: How did I see this man through walls, darkness, and closed eyelids? What power made me walk straight to where I was needed?

Yes, what power is it within us that not only directed Susan to where she was needed, but can also accurately predict the date of a person's death? However incredible it might seem, it happened to my husband's grandfather, Balraj Bhalla. He noted a dream in his diary in June 1956, which he also mentioned to his wife. The dream was:

> *I am reading the newspaper. I turn to the section on obituaries and read, 'Balraj Bhalla died on the 25th of December 1956. The prayer ceremony will be at 3 p.m. on ...'*

Six months later, Balraj Bhalla died on Christmas day, as his dream had foretold. Was it a fantastic coincidence or was it that something within him 'knew', and found its voice within a dream?

Balraj Bhalla is not an isolated case of foreknowledge of death. Keki Daruwala, a poet and writer based in New Delhi, recounts that his wife awoke one morning from a very disturbing dream. In the dream she saw Keki, their grandchild, and herself meet with a terrible road accident near traffic lights.

Keki and his wife were due to go to the U.S. to meet their daughter and grandchild, and Mrs Daruwala was looking forward to the visit. However, as the date for departure came closer, an unexplained reluctance to go seized her, so much so that she wanted to cancel the trip. Finally she dismissed her forebodings and they decided to go ahead with their plans. Four months after her dream, Keki was driving the car with Mrs Daruwala beside him in the streets of Austin, Texas. Just as they approached a traffic light, a speeding paramedic pick-up hit their car broadside with great force.

Mrs Daruwala died in the accident. Unlike the events in the dream, their granddaughter was not in the car. In hindsight Mrs Daruwala's reluctance to go abroad was not unfounded. She had a strong sense of what was to happen, contrary to everything else that suggested a pleasant trip. Her dream uncannily depicted the manner of her death.

If one were to suggest to any of these people that what happened was a mere coincidence and that their dreams held no foreknowledge of coming events, they would probably look at you with disbelief. Anyone who has experienced a predictive dream that has come true is staunchly convinced about precognition. They may not be clear about the hows and whys of it, nor about its philosophical implications, but they do not doubt its reality.

A small incident happened to Rajeev on his way to catch a train from Delhi to Jalandhar in the north Indian state of Punjab. He was running late, and there was the usual traffic jam at the entrance to New Delhi Railway Station. With his small overnighter, he rushed to the platform to buy a ticket for his journey. As he wove his way through the throng of people at the entrance to the station, he suddenly remembered his dream of the previous night: his bag had been stolen at New Delhi Railway Station. He shrugged the dream aside as one of anxiety about the impending business trip to Jalandhar, but soon after, he thought again and asked himself: What will I miss most if my bag is stolen?

The question remained unanswered as he negotiated his way through the crowd. He reached the ticket counter and put his bag down beside him while he paid for the ticket. Within the space of collecting the ticket and his hand reaching down to pick up the bag, it was gone. Stolen.

Later Rajeev could only lament, 'If only I had paid attention ...'

Was it an anxiety dream or a nocturnal prompting that had warned him to be careful? In hindsight its precognitive content is difficult to deny. It also raises the question we had touched upon in the last chapter. Was his dream, then, reflective of reality as it was to unfold? Or did it have the power to alter it? After all, had he heeded its prompting his bag possibly may not have been stolen.

Perhaps there are few incidents of mysterious occurrences that have had more influence on psychoanalysis than the explosive noises that occurred in 1909. These may also have signalled the break between Freud and Jung. Both of them were heatedly arguing about paranormal phenomena, especially precognition, which Freud forcefully rejected. At that moment both of them were alarmed by a loud noise from a nearby bookcase, which they feared might topple over on them. Jung felt it vindicated his position and said, 'There, that is an example of a so-called catalytic exteriorisation phenomenon.'

'Oh come,' Freud exclaimed. 'That is sheer bosh.'

'It is not,' Jung retorted. 'You are mistaken, Herr Professor. And to prove my point I now predict in a moment there will be another loud report!'

No sooner had these words been spoken that another loud bang was heard from the bookcase. Freud only stared aghast at Jung.[14]

All over the world, from time immemorial, some people have been called gifted with what is variously known as the second sight, the third eye, the sixth sense; with powers of the mind that seem to bypass the usual sensory channels and transcend mundane reality. Shamans have communed with their gods, saints have seen visions, and oracles have foretold the death of kings. The ability to 'sense' the future is not uncommon. In one study questionnaires were given to approximately twenty-five hundred eighth-grade students in northern India, two hundred university students in West Africa, and three hundred students at the University of Virginia, in the U.S., asking them if they ever had had paranormal dreams. About one out of every six of the eighth-grade students and one out of every three of the university students indicated that they had experienced a paranormal dream at some time during their life.[15]

This confronts us with a problem. Despite the widespread prevalence of paranormal dreams, there is a deep scepticism about them in the modern mind. How then do we rationalize them to ourselves? There are some inherent difficulties involved in paranormal dreams in general and in precognition in particular, which need to be addressed. Suspicion arises in our minds primarily because many of the dreams we dream could be understood to anticipate reality, but events belie their being prophetic. These failed dreams heavily outnumber the truly prophetic ones. Yet when a dream fulfils its promise we attach a great deal of significance to it and do not dismiss it as mere chance. Moreover, the field of paranormal phenomena has had a long-standing association with people who are delusional. Many mentally disturbed people exhibit paranormal tendencies like telepathy – of influencing and being influenced by minds at a distance – and the ability to make predictions about future happenings. All these abilities disappear once the patient regains mental health. As the patient's hold on reality returns these paranormal phenomena occur less frequently, suggesting that they were directly related to the person's delusional state, and are therefore to be considered inherently unreliable. Adding to the burden of disbelief are accounts of normal people who for want of fame or attention invent episodes involving paranormal phenomena. While others who are not fraudulent subject their genuine experiences to retrospective falsification, usually done unconsciously. This last aspect a rather subtle and complicated issue, which raises many questions ut paranormal dreaming. Let us suppose that a man dreams about geing father; when he awakes his belief that his ailing father may ve long to live fastens onto the dream. Thus 'I dreamt about my r' may unwittingly transform into 'I dreamt my father is dead.'

And if the father does die soon afterwards, was the dream actually a precognition or was it subject to retrospective falsification? Since in most of these cases there is no intention to defraud, no useful purpose is served by highlighting the difference to the dreamer.

I could, however, confront Rajeev that he had retrospectively falsified his dream about his bag being stolen. I questioned him, suggesting that he may have experienced a simple anxiety dream that contained a vivid image of New Delhi's railway station. And, perhaps, the next day his unbidden thought of losing his bag had got superimposed on the previous night's anxiety dream, leading him to believe he had had a precognitive dream. He conceded that this could be a very alluring explanation. But then he countered: 'Granted, it may not have been a prophetic dream, but then how do you explain my thoughts just before the bag was stolen? If it was not a precognitive dream, then it certainly was a precognitive thought!'

Then there is another type of difficulty: if the dream does not predict the outcome exactly, does it still qualify as a prophetic dream? To illustrate: a man may dream that his ailing father died on the twelfth of September, and his father actually passed away on the ninth of December. Is the dream a hit or a miss? After all, the two dates – 12/9 and 9/12 – are transposable and liable to be muddled in the dream.

There is yet another kind of difficulty, one which Freud himself experienced. Soon after he received the title of professor, Freud was walking down a street one day when he found that his mind was inundated with negative thoughts about a couple whom he felt had been disrespectful to him. He could characterize his thought only as 'childish revenge fantasy' as they revolved around him snubbing them if they now asked him to take a case. He was interrupted from his reverie by that very couple wishing him, 'Good evening, Professor.'[16]

At first glance this seems to be a remarkable coincidence – his thoughts had anticipated their appearance. Freud thought otherwise, believing that he must have subliminally noticed them approaching and that had triggered the fantasy. If this subliminal stimulation had actually occurred, then it becomes a pseudo-paranormal phenomenon. This could also explain why that unbidden thought had crossed Rajeev's mind as he neared the ticket counter – notices warning of pickpockets may have been peripherally perceived without them registering consciously on him and triggered his thoughts.

These are some of the reasons that lead to doubt and ambiguity when confronted with paranormal phenomena. But this does not mean that all paranormal happenings can be denied outright; it only cautions us not to be credulous and to proceed with circumspection. Rather than rely on anecdotal evidence let us explore paranormal dreaming through the reliable and objective gaze of psychologists, who are aware of the difficulties involved. If paranormal dreams are a dimension of dreaming, then people undergoing therapy must also be experiencing these extraordinary dreams. To explore the issue further it may perhaps be profitable to start digging in Freud's own backyard. Apparently he had many occasions to confront these dreams, the following being only one example.

An intelligent man, not in the least 'inclined towards occultism', related a remarkable dream to Freud. He had dreamt that his second wife had given birth to twins. The dream apparently could not be ascribed to wish-fulfilment since the dreamer had long ceased to have sexual relations with his wife and also believed she had no aptitude for bringing up children sensibly. Nor was he afraid that this unwished-for event might occur. The dream was remarkable because the following day a telegram announced that his daughter, from the first marriage, had given birth to twins on the same night as his dream. He knew his daughter was pregnant, but she was due to deliver a month later and there had been no suggestion of twins. The dreamer asked Freud whether the coincidence between dream and event was accidental.[17]

Freud had noted that the man, to his own admission, was dissatisfied with his second wife and would have preferred his wife to be like the daughter of his first marriage. All that his unconscious did was to drop the 'like'. Unlike the earlier example of the revenge fantasy, Freud, by the time this dream was related to him, was willing to entertain the phenomenon of telepathy. He interpreted the dream by proposing that a telepathic message had been received communicating that his daughter had given birth to twins. His interpretation, however, also managed to preserve his wish-fulfilment theory. The dreamer's fondness for his daughter when taken to its conclusion would have wished him to father children from her rather than his second wife; a wish that psychoanalysis has found to be very common on the part of middle-aged fathers. The dream work took control of the news, allowed the unconscious wish by replacing the daughter with the second wife, thus disguising the wish and distorting the message to produce the dream. Psychoanalysis, Freud proudly stated, had discovered and pinpointed a telepathic event.[18] Ordinarily we would have glossed the telepathic content of the dream because it had been inaccurate – the daughter and not the wife had given birth to twins. This generalization of Freud possibly marked a change in the way we investigate and accept paranormal dreams. Till then errors and near-misses, in fact, any departure in accuracy of the paranormal perception, had rendered it false and unacceptable. This had become the bugbear in collecting and investigating spontaneous occurrences. What Freud had said in effect was: 'Distortion of perception is one of the characteristics of mental functioning dominated by unconscious needs ... There is no reason to suppose that telepathic perceptions should be free from this universal effect.'[19] The implication was that we need not look only for dream material that corresponds exactly with events, but distorted correspondences are permissible in identifying telepathic communication. Thus, the dream about the father dying on 12 September can be considered to be precognitive.

Freud's ambivalence towards the paranormal, however, did not permit him to leave the explanation at that, but he attempted an alternative rendering that denied thought transference. He argued: the man may have believed that his daughter had miscalculated her confinement by a month, and the idea that the actual day she would deliver would be that night might have been the stimulus for his dream. And this belief could have also been fuelled by a subliminal feeling that his daughter looked as though she may deliver twins when he had last seen her. Also, his dead first wife was fond of children and she might have wished that their daughter gave birth to twins. A combination of these wishes and beliefs may have provided the stimulus for the dream and not telepathic thought transference.[20]

In proposing these conflicting mechanisms Freud had carefully refrained from taking a position one way or another on the reality of telepathy. The reason for this is not hard to identify as he himself admits that he had never had a telepathic dream,[21] besides which he also felt that by accepting telepathy he would compromise the scientific underpinning of his work. His earlier dismissive attitude had given way to an open-minded scepticism. Despite reservations he nevertheless returned to the subject of telepathy three years later, in 1925, with a somewhat changed attitude. Rather than subscribe to cumbersome mechanisms to obviate telepathy, like in the above case, he now admitted that reports of telepathic events could not be easily ignored, even though they may not be sufficient to carry an assured conviction.[22] Freud's simple observation that psychoanalysis is capable of unmasking a telepathic event had opened the door of the dreaming world to telepathy.

He then took another step towards accepting paranormal dreams: 'If there are such things as telepathic messages, the possibility cannot be dismissed of their reaching someone during sleep and coming to his knowledge in a dream. Indeed, on the analogy of other perceptual and intellectual material, the further possibility arises that telepathic messages received in the course of the day may only be dealt with during a dream of the following night. There would then be nothing contradictory in the material that had been telepathically communicated being modified and transformed in the dream like any other material.'[23]

This opened the door even further. All along it had been argued that for a communication to be considered telepathic it had to occur simultaneously. A time-gap was not admissible. Now Freud was suggesting that telepathy is not restricted to simultaneity; the message may have been received during the day and may have registered only at night through a dream.

Freud then maintained an eight-year silence before opening a new dimension of telepathic communication – in the interaction between the analyst and the patient. The suggestion was that the psychological consultation provides the soil in which telepathy could flourish. We know that while interpreting a dream the analyst has to become passive and uncritically receive the free associations of the dreamer. These associations do not automatically lead the analyst to the underlying desires seeking expression. He or she has to make an intuitive leap in order to arrive at the meaning of the dream. What the patient has offered is only an obscure betrayal from which the analyst imaginatively creates insights into the hidden depths of the dreamer. This process, it must be appreciated, is outside the domain of our conscious faculties. Freud recommends the analyst to be intuitively empathetic while listening; to transcend him or herself and aim to become one with the dreamer's unconscious.[24] This ability can only be described as 'analytic intuition', for the analyst is not dealing with concrete happenings, but with his or her own unconscious perception. Only subsequently does conscious knowledge tame this unconscious perception and order it into harmoniously connected thought sequences. In other words, he intuitive element is transformed into insight. Usually we fail to rceive these occult features because they occur within the confines scientific process – psychoanalysis.

was this communication outside the conscious channels that iighlighted: 'I have often had an impression, in the course of nts in my private circle, that strongly emotionally colored [sic]

recollections can be successfully transferred without much difficult
On the basis of much experience I am inclined to draw the conclus
that thought transference of this kind comes about particularly ea
at the moment at which an idea emerges from the unconscious ...

Perhaps every person who has undergone analysis will recall instan
when he or she felt that the analyst was a 'mind-reader'. Outside t
analytic arena this phenomenon is also visible between a husbar
and wife or in close friendships, though it never shows up in obtrusiv
ways. It is an often-observed fact that women in love know when the
beloved is betraying them. In psychotherapy, if this analytic intuitior
becomes intense the analyst may experience telepathic perception.
'When such intuitively perceived material erupts from the deeper layers
of the psyche and intrudes into the sphere of consciousness, it tends to
acquire the appearance of an "occult phenomenon".'[26]

If the analyst has access to the telepathic doorway, it can, under
special conditions, also be used by the patient to delve into the analyst's
personal world. This contact between the therapist and patient is best
described by the following excerpt from a dream reported by 'Ruth' to
her analyst, Dr Ehrenwald, on 10 March 1948:

> The apartment was to let. We looked at it. It consisted of a beautiful
> long, well-shaped living room, spacious, with high ceiling. It opened
> out to a nice open terrace where the sun shone. It was long; it stretched
> along the whole building across the front ... some 50 feet or so. It had
> a brick wall and the floor was made of planks with cracks in between.
> There was not much furniture in the room, not so much as you would
> have if you would furnish it yourself. There was quite a lot of space
> left between the things. It was not a cluttered room. There was no
> carpet, only oriental rugs, a big one in the middle with figures like
> the one you have here in the office. There were smaller rugs at either
> end. But they covered only part of the floor, much of it was showing.
> There were also a few mahogany chairs and an open fireplace. A
> french door and two french windows opened to the terrace. A dingy
> little hall led into the bedroom and into a bathroom.[27]

This does not seem to be a dream; it is more like a sensitive depiction
of a house in a novel, where the author is taking the utmost care to
bring alive every room and communicate its flavour for the benefit of
the reader. Ehrenwald, however, was not surprised with the delicate
artistry of his patient's description, but what startled him was how she
had accurately detailed his own flat that he had barely moved into a

ek earlier. Perhaps the only feature she had omitted was the rent he
s paying for it! Incidentally, Ehrenwald, on the same night as the
am, was proudly showing his relatives his new lodgings. May we
njecture that Ruth was telepathically eavesdropping on her analyst's
ur through his apartment?

As Freud boldly claimed, 'It no longer seems possible to brush aside
e study of so-called occult facts; of things which seem to vouchsafe
e real existence of psychic forces other than the known forces of the
uman and animal psyche, or which reveal mental faculties in which,
ntil now, we did not believe.'[28]

If Freud was right, then the five senses are not the only possible
modes of perception; 'knowing' may have wider gateways and
thresholds. Beyond human sight there may be another way of 'seeing'.
Researchers, since the nineteenth century, have started to codify such
'seeing'. Unlike in early times, when it was supposed that only a select
few were gifted with this special power, it is now believed that ordinary
people, in fact, the whole human race, has a latent extra-sensory power,
which manifests most often through dreams. These paranormal dreams,
rather than be treated as supernatural indications of certain critical
events, are now being distinguished into various types of extra-sensory
abilities: clairvoyance, telepathy, and precognition. Clairvoyance is
the ability to see objects or events that by their remoteness in space
or time cannot be seen by ordinary vision; telepathy is the ability to
transmit and receive thoughts without recourse to any known form of
communication; and in precognition information is known before the
event has occurred. The difference between clairvoyance and telepathy is
that the former is witnessed, while the latter is a message communicated,
though admittedly, the boundary separating them is sometimes thin
or difficult to define. Precognition alludes to foreknowledge and is
different from both telepathy and clairvoyance as the event has yet to
happen. It is like hearing the echo before the sound. In both telepathy
and clairvoyance, the event is already existent in time.

Clairvoyance can take place either while one is awake or asleep. In
its most dramatic manifestation, it may involve a prolonged vision,
say, of a fire, an accident, or a murder taking place; more often it is a
quick mental picture. One of the better-known cases of clairvoyance
involved the Swedish philosopher Emanuel Swedenborg. It is reported
that on the evening of 19 July 1759, without any explanation, he left
in the middle of a party in Gotenborg. He returned a short while later,

looking pale and shaken, and pronounced that a fire was raging, that it had already destroyed a friend's house and now threate his own. The guests exchanged startled looks because they all kr Swedenborg did not live in Gotenborg, but in Stockholm, which almost three hundred miles away. Could he have 'seen' that a fire rag there? An answer came the following night when an express messeng arrived from Stockholm with news of a great fire, followed by a secor messenger who brought more details. They matched Swedenborg account of the blaze and confirmed that it had halted only three door away from his own house, and had ended, just as he said, at 8 p.m Swedenborg's clairvoyant vision psychically saw what the eye possibly could not have perceived.[29]

Vinay Mehta, the captain of a merchant vessel, had embarked on a voyage from Portland to Japan. It was a clear night as the ship sailed peacefully in the North Pacific Ocean. Captain Mehta came to the wheelhouse where he was smartly saluted by the second mate, who was on duty. The captain looked out into the night and noted with satisfaction that the visibility was good and the sky, sprayed with stars, was unclouded. He told the second mate that he was going down to his cabin to sleep.

While asleep, Captain Mehta dreamt that his ship was in grave danger and was about to crash into another ship. He awoke with a start and checked his watch. It was two thirty in the morning. He looked out of his porthole to see the light of another ship nearby. Instantly he realized the ship was too close and that they were on a collision course. He rushed to the wheelhouse to discover that the ship was on autopilot and the second mate was nowhere in sight. He released the autopilot and changed the course of the ship, thereby preventing a major disaster. Needless to say, the second mate was charge-sheeted for dereliction of duty and signed off the vessel.

Dream clairvoyance was operating in Vinay Mehta's case, as was Susan's experience of 'seeing' a man with a severe case of bleeding in the gums. Rahul Verma had also 'seen' the exam paper by 'second sight'.

Telepathy is the most common of the three kinds of extra-sensory perception, but we are not always aware of its occurrence. The Egyptians held that homeless spirits carried the telepathic message. Other cultures believed that the dreamer's soul could quit the body and thus gather information external to the sleeping person. During its excursions the soul could visit other dreamers and communicate messages to them.

t was Democritus (460–370 BC) in Greece who provided us with the first explanation of telepathy, which did not involve the supernatural. Everything, he believed, is made of atoms – indivisible minute particles. These atoms constantly emit images of themselves, and an image imbued with sufficient emotional charge could be transmitted to a dreamer, these atoms entering the dreamer via the pores of the skin. Modern findings confirm that emotion does play a large role in telepathic transmission. Aristotle felt that paranormal dreams are transmitted in the same way as a ripple. Subtle waves are being generated around people and events all the time but they are dissolved by the disturbances present in the day, while the tranquillity of the night allows them to reach the dreamer.

In modern times Freud suggested that telepathy might be 'the original, archaic method of communication between individuals and that in the course of phylogenetic evolution it has been replaced by the better method of giving information with the help of signals which are picked up by the sense organs. But the older method might have persisted in the background and still be able to put itself into effect under certain conditions – for instance, in passionately excited mobs.'[30]

Whatever be the mechanism of telepathy, enough evidence has been accumulated to postulate some conditions that are conducive for it. It is now believed that telepathic dreams usually occur between persons closely bound to each other by strong emotional ties, like the father and his daughter who gave birth to twins. Telepathy is normally accompanied by an event occurring in conditions that are adverse to communication, like geographical distance, helplessness, inhibition, or repression. Since the birth of the twins was premature and sudden the good news could not be communicated immediately to their grandfather. There must also be a need to overcome this barrier – which usually happens during sleep. All these conditions are fulfilled in the telepathic dream produced in the psychoanalytic setting. Many patients, like Ruth, feel neglected by the analyst when he or she is self-preoccupied or when other patients consume his or her attention. The neglected patient, so to say, senses that a barrier has been erected, which needs to be overcome. In an effort to re-establish the full flow of attention from the analyst, the patient telepathically unmasks personal psychological material belonging to the analyst, which is exactly what Ruth had done. Her entry into the corridors of her analyst's personal flat had certainly re-established Ehrenwald's attention towards her!

By understanding a little more about paranormal dreams, are we better equipped to interpret Usha's dream? We can rule out clairvoyance, since Usha's jewellery is still very much with her. Had she awoken to find her jewellery stolen, then it would be a clear case of clairvoyance, since her dream would be a mental image of seeing the robbers prising open her cupboard. Nor can we treat Usha's dream as telepathic because Nidhi had already related her dream – four days earlier. However, we cannot rule out the possibility of Usha's dream foretelling future events.

The Atharva Veda and other Indian texts suggest a connection between the time of night when a dream has occurred and its possible time of fulfilment. A dream from the first quarter of sleep will come true within a year, those dreams arising in the second quarter of the night within eight months, those from the third quarter within three months, while those that come in the last part of sleep, or early morning dreams, are indicative of events that have already been set in motion.[31] Presumably this would only apply to a dream that has already been deemed prophetic and does not apply to all dreams.

We have, however, not been able to identify any single element of a dream that can alert us to its precognitive content. It seems that only in retrospect can we be sure that a dream is precognitive. Yet some people, like Balraj Bhalla and Mrs Daruwala, felt uneasy when confronted with an unusually vivid dream.

This is not to suggest that precognitive dreams predominantly concern the death of someone, or dwell on distress or danger. Both examples of precognition, cited above, are about death, and even the other dreams – Susan's and Vinay's – concern an emergency. Precognition may also focus on other matters too.

The disaster that 'Geeta Prasher' was heading towards seemed to be an emotional one. Her marriage had been eaten away by incompatibility, and all she was left with was the hollow sound echoing within the empty corridors of parallel lives. Then one night she dreamt:

I see my husband going to someone's house. He rings the bell and a woman opens the door. They embrace each other as lovers would. I cannot see the woman's face but I realize she is someone I know very well. I'm struck by the fact that my husband knows this woman only through me.

Geeta could not bring her dream's suggestion to any conclusion. Only after a month-and-a-half, when she unexpectedly went over to her closest friend's house, did she realize who the woman was. It was her best friend, and she was in her husband's arms. In one shattering moment she lived through dream and reality simultaneously. The dream was actually a warning.

No doubt many an anxious husband or wife may dream of their spouse's infidelity. And, of course, not every anxiety dream is a warning dream. Yet Geeta felt her dream was a warning perhaps because it was so vivid. Also, it had a particularly tenacious quality. Most dreams dissolve like mist, evaporating when the dreamer awakens. This dream continued to plague her long after it occurred.

It was a similar insistent quality in a later dream that alerted Geeta to another change in her life. The affair between her husband and her friend continued, despite Geeta's violent protests. Crushed by her husband's remorseless infidelity, she moved out of the house with her two children. Her friend and her husband began living together and a year later announced their intention of getting married. Two months after learning of this news she had another dream:

A preparation for a marriage is underway. I see my friend dressed in bridal clothes, getting ready to marry my estranged husband. Relatives from both sides are laughing and singing and they wait for the bridegroom to appear. I am going from one relative to another saying, 'He will not turn up for the wedding. He's not going to come, believe me.' No one listens to me – it is as though I'm invisible. I'm like a ghost who feels the reality of its own presence and thoughts, without anyone else relating to it.

The dream could be read as Geeta's intense wish to stop the wedding by convincing herself that the bridegroom was unwilling to marry, or, contrary to the news of the forthcoming wedding, the dream was predicting an unexpected end to the affair.

Events substantiated the latter interpretation. Soon afterwards, Geeta's estranged husband called her to say he was not marrying her friend; they had parted ways for good. He asked Geeta if she would consider allowing him back in her life.

If paranormal dreams warn the dreamer about emotional danger, can they also warn us about large-scale calamities? Two surveys were conducted in which people were asked about precognitive warnings related to impending disasters. The first concerned the tragic accident of the *Titanic*. These were cases about people who had somehow not boarded the ill-fated ship. For example, J. Connon Middleton, for two nights in a row, dreamt of seeing the *Titanic* wrecked beyond redemption and seeing 'her passengers and crew swimming around her'. He was deeply concerned, since he was due to sail to New York on the *Titanic* for a business conference. Feeling uneasy and oppressed he told his friends and family about his dreams, but did not cancel his trip to America until a few days later when he received a cable from New York urging him to delay his journey and take passage on another ship.[32]

Colin MacDonald, a marine engineer, had a strong premonition about the *Titanic* meeting with disaster and declined the position as its second engineer. The *Titanic* went down on 14 April 1912.[33]

After carefully analysing the *Titanic* premonitions and discarding all vague forebodings, as well as after-the-event claims, at least ten impressive cases of precognition remained, out of which eight pertained to dreams. I have listed only two. Precognition of large-scale calamities was similarly affirmed in an incident in a little-known mining village in South Wales called Aberfan.

On 21 October 1966, a massive coal-tip slid down a mountainside and engulfed Aberfan, killing 144 people, mostly school children. The following week, in response to an appeal in a national newspaper, an English psychiatrist, Dr J. Barker, obtained a large number of reports from people who felt they had received precognitive information concerning the tragedy. After all claims were scrutinized thirty-five cases remained that Dr Barker considered reliable. In twenty-four cases the person had related the information to someone else before the landslide occurred. Dreams figured in twenty-five of the accounts.[34]

But why do precognitive dreams not happen to everyone? Are they the preserve of the gifted few? This belief was entirely refuted by J. W. Dunne, a military engineer, in his famous book *An Experiment with Time*. Its publication in 1927 caused a sensation with its suggestion that everybody has precognitive dreams, but most people fail to notice them. His great interest in dreams was sparked off by a particularly impressive disaster dream. In the spring of 1902 he was encamped with the 6th Mounted Infantry in Orange Free State in South Africa. There he had had an unusually vivid dream, where he saw himself standing on an island that he had dreamt of before:

> ... an island which was in imminent peril from a volcano. And, when I saw the vapour spouting from the ground, I gasped: 'It's the island! Good Lord, the whole thing is going to blow up!' For I had

memories of reading about Krakatoa, where the sea, making its way into the heart of a volcano through a submarine crevice, flashed into steam, and blew the whole mountain to pieces. Forthwith I was seized with a frantic desire to save the four thousand (I knew the number) unsuspecting inhabitants.

In the dream Dunne then tried to warn the French (he was sure they were French) authorities that the volcano was about to explode and that 4,000 lives were at risk.[35]

When the next batch of newspapers arrived from Britain a few days later, Dunne found a major story in the *Daily Telegraph* on the eruption of Mount Pelée on the French island of Martinique, with the 'probable loss of over 40,000 lives'. In another column of the same paper a headline read: 'A Mountain Explodes' – exactly as he had witnessed in his dream. Clearly the dream was precognitive, but one small mysterious detail remained unexplained and which came to his attention after the next batch of papers had arrived from Britain, giving more exact estimates of the actual loss of life. The true figure of loss of lives had nothing to do with the number in his dream, or with any combination of fours and zeros. The first reports had made one assume that the dream had neglected one zero and therefore announced the loss of lives as 4,000. Incidentally, Dunne admits that while reading the newspaper account he had, in fact, misread 40,000 lives as 4,000, and it was not until much later that he realized his mistake. Freud, we know, would have attributed this mistake to the deception of the dream work and dug into the dreamer's associational network to identify the latent content of the dream. Dunne, instead, argued otherwise: the erroneous number suggested that the dream had obtained its precognitive information not from the actual events themselves on the island of Martinique, but from the misread newspaper article.[36] He then honestly questioned himself about whether the whole thing was, what doctors call, a case of paramnesia (recall of events that never have happened) – that he had never really had any such dream, but after reading the newspaper report he had imagined that he had previously dreamt all the details given in the paper. This distortion of memory appears to be a close cousin of retrospective falsification, which we had encountered earlier; both engender false memories.

If true, this mechanism of paramnesia would render all precognition or even all paranormal dreaming as false or deluded. And so in the case of Usha, we would now have a definitive answer to her question: Was her dream prophetic? It would be a most emphatic no! She had not experienced the dream, but her identification with Nidhi was so strong that when told about the robbery she had imagined she had a similar dream.

Luckily or unluckily for Usha, another of Dunne's dreams completely shattered the paramnesia theory. The dream occurred in the autumn of 1913, wherein Dunne repeatedly saw a high railway embankment in a place that was just north of the Firth of Forth Bridge in Scotland. The last time he witnessed this scene in his dream, a train going north had just fallen over the embankment, with several carriages lying towards the bottom of a grassy slope. He gathered that the date of this occurrence was in the spring of 1914. When he awoke – and this is crucial to dispel paramnesia – he told his sister about the dream. They joked that they should warn their friends from travelling north to Scotland in the spring.

Exactly two years after the *Titanic* tragedy, on 14 April 1914 the *Flying Scotsman*, one of Britain's most famous mail trains, jumped the parapet near Burntisland Station, about fifteen miles north of the Forth Bridge, and fell on to the golf links twenty feet below.[37]

Dunne had many other clearly precognitive dreams, which led him to believe that dreams – everybody's dreams – are a blend of images not only from past memories but also of future experiences. Thus precognitive dreams are a part of normal dreaming as opposed to the belief that they are an extraordinary aspect of dreaming, the prerogative of a few blessed individuals. The majority of the images that have prophetic value may not be distinct and separate, but, on the contrary, are so blended and intermingled that it is difficult to distinguish them as precognitive of any waking event. Dunne contended that we all too easily recognize a past event in this blend of images and fail to cull a future event from the menagerie of images within the dream, as the following example reveals.

I was very surprised to see Rajeev come home after work one day without the car. He explained it had been sent for routine servicing when a mechanic discovered a tiny pinhole in one of the brake pipes. The entire piping had to be changed and the car would only be ready the following day. Strangely this mundane conversation made me remember an anxiety dream I had the previous night.

I am in a bus en route from Chandigarh to Delhi. The bus needs to brake as we are fast catching up with the truck ahead. I wonder why the driver is not slowing down the bus, as he is very close to the truck.

I then notice that he is pumping the brakes again and again. All the
while we are drawing ever closer and closer to the truck. Suddenly
all this pumping bears fruit – the bus slows down.

I was convinced that the dream had sourced its images from a past
experience. Many years earlier while returning on that same highway in
a van driven by Rajeev, the brakes had failed. Similar to the dream, we
were rapidly approaching a slow-moving truck ahead. I had indignantly
looked at Rajeev, as I had looked at the bus driver in the dream. Rajeev
had attempted to brake but a copper brake-pipe had burst, rendering the
brakes inoperative. Luckily we had managed to swerve off the road and
narrowly escaped an accident. Dunne asks the question of us, and quite
rightly: Why do we assume that the dream utilizes only past imagery and
not a future one? Sure my dream imagery was reminiscent of an earlier
memory, but it was equally reflective of what may have happened if
the pinhole in the brake-pipe had gone undetected – the brakes would
have failed as in the dream. Dunne's conclusion that dreams not only
pick imagery from the past, but also from what may be discovered the
following morning is reiterated by my dream. After all, there must have
been some connection between the mechanic's discovery and the dream
for me to recall the latter on being told the former!

An important point to note when identifying future images, Dunne
cautions, is that one must not expect to come upon a complete idea or
scene that may relate to a future event. Often it may only be one part
or one image of the dream that is related to the event – the rest remains
unconnected. This dissimilarity of the adjacent parts of the dream plot
often becomes the excuse for not accepting the association between the
dream and a subsequent event, like I had done in the above example.
Sometimes this connection eludes us because of a failure to take note
of all the details in the dream.

One day Dunne was blowing a wood fire with a pair of bellows,
and, while doing so, he brought the nozzle of the bellows into contact
with the red-hot surface of a large log. A dense shower of very brilliant
sparks leapt at him from the fire. This made him recall the previous
night's dream where precisely such a shower of sparks flew past him.
In his dream diary, however, he had not recorded his immediate dream
impression. Instead he had only noted that a crowd of people in his
dream were throwing cigarette ends.[38]

Another critical point that must be kept in mind is that there has
to be something odd or unusual about the image or incident for us to

acknowledge it as a future correspondence. A dream contains many images and during the day we gather many more impressions. In our hunt for future correspondences with individual images we would have to guard against ordinary laws of chance operating. For example, dreaming of a combination lock and then coming across one the next day may perhaps not constitute precognition.

Yet another reason why we fail to see the precognitive content in dreams, besides lack of detail, is that we are not on the lookout for it. Even though we may have kept a meticulous record of our dreams we are apt to let slide the connections with waking events. It is possible that we instinctively reject this correlation because the connection is the wrong way round. My above dream would perhaps have been more appropriate after the discovery of the pinhole with its potential danger of brake failure. It would have triggered my fears, evoked past memory, and precipitated the anxiety dream. This sequence is plausible to our way of thinking. But the dream had come the other way round – the dream was one day too early! It is for these reasons that Dunne cautions us to look closely for these resemblances that we often miss at first glance.

One day, while out shooting, Dunne realized he was trespassing on someone else's property. He heard two men shouting at him from different directions. Moreover, they seemed to be urging on a furiously barking dog. Dunne made towards the nearest gate in the boundary wall. The shouting and barking came nearer and nearer, but Dunne managed to slip through the gate before his pursuers could see him. This was a small insignificant incident. We are prone to forget such incidents easily. While reading his dream diary that evening Dunne noticed nothing at first, but then came across a dream snippet recorded some two weeks earlier: 'Hunted by two men and a dog.' Not only could he not remember the dream, he could not even remember writing it down, though it had been recorded only two weeks earlier.[39]

Dunne persuaded friends and relatives to try out his experiments with dreams: of carefully noting dreams and subsequently going through them to relate waking events with dreamt images. They met with much success. A cousin of his had a precognitive dream only eight days after she started using Dunne's dream-recall process. Before this she had rarely even remembered her dreams and was positive she had never had precognitive experiences of any kind. This kind of precognition was noted not only by Dunne's friends and relatives but also by other people much earlier. Charles Dickens describes in his journal: 'I dreamed that I saw a lady in a red shawl with her back towards me ... On her turning around, I found that I didn't know her and she said, "I am Miss Napier."'[40]

Dickens could not help but muse, the next morning: 'What a preposterous thing to have so very distinct a dream about nothing! and why Miss Napier? For I have never heard of any Miss Napier.' After his next public reading, while he was in his retiring room, he was visited by Miss Boyle and her brother. With them was the lady in the red shawl whom they presented as Miss Napier!

Contrary to the general belief that parapsychologists have a vested interest in pushing paranormal happenings, the psychical researcher would be sceptical of this account. Although Dickens testifies that 'these are all the circumstances exactly told', researchers would not use his dream as evidence because it had been written only *after* his introduction to the red-shawled Miss Napier. After all, the memory of even a famous author is prone to play tricks – retrospective falsification or paramnesia. Parapsychology would require much more rigorous proof.

From Dunne's personal experiments extra-sensory perception was scrutinized in research laboratories. Anecdotal accounts of paranormal dreaming have been handed down to us since antiquity, but researchers and rationalists alike have doubted their veracity on one ground or another. Some of the real difficulties with these kinds of spontaneous accounts have already been enumerated. Validation would require controlled conditions and the elimination of all other factors. Here we are confronted with a genuine problem: the very attempt to contain this phenomenon, to measure or verify it, may destroy it. However, some researchers managed to do this by devising ingenious experiments that would withstand the rigorous analytical glare of parapsychology. Initially the way was opened by the pioneering genius of Dr Joseph B. Rhine (1895–1980), whose statistical experiments transformed psychical research into scientific parapsychology. He developed many experiments to test clairvoyance, telepathy, and precognition using a special set of cards, called Zener cards, at Duke University in the United States. His wife, Dr Louisa Rhine, worked alongside and over twenty years collected data on 7,000 spontaneous extra-sensory episodes.[41] Her analysis showed that 65 percent of them occurred in dreams.

Meanwhile the 'bug' of paranormal dreaming having infected the Freudian analysts was now threatening to become an epidemic. Jung and his prospective function of dreaming needed no convincing. Calvin Hall was also susceptible to the same infection. One night his co-worker Robert Van de Castle dreamt that he was walking across a university campus when he felt himself strongly impelled to enter the basement of a particular building, where a boxing match was in progress. He became deeply engrossed in the match and began to root for the underdog. Hall was shocked when he heard the dream because without telling anyone he had decided to send a telepathic message and see for himself the truth about ESP in dreams. The target stimulus that Hall was beaming out was the recently concluded boxing match between Cassius Clay and Sonny Liston, where the underdog had recorded a convincing victory.[42]

The 'epidemic' of paranormal dreaming was taking firm hold. Soon Hall was to conduct (successful) studies about telepathic dreaming. He published his statistically significant results of a study involving six male subjects in a German journal.[43]

Barely had the excitement over the discovery of REM dreaming settled down when Montague Ullman and his associates initiated a very systematic study of paranormal dreaming under laboratory conditions. In 1962, he established a dream laboratory at the Maimonides Hospital in Brooklyn, New York. Another psychologist, Stanley Krippner, soon joined him and for ten years the two specialists studied the parameters involved in paranormal dreaming. They published a number of scientific articles and their findings are summarized in their book *Dream Telepathy*.[44] Their experiments were designed to weed out any factor, except telepathy, which could influence the results of their study. This meant that all sensory leakage through inadvertent behavioural or subvocal clues would have to be blocked. Admittedly these may appear very trivial and none of them may be significant by themselves, but taken together they could provide an avenue of subliminal perception.

If you were to conduct an experiment to establish whether two people can communicate telepathically, what would you do? You would probably ask a friend to think of something and you would attempt to pick up the thought. If you were successful, then a critic would object that since all communication is not verbal, the message was transmitted by body language. At the Maimonides Laboratory, Ullman and Krippner tried to remove these valid objections by keeping the 'sender' (your friend) of the message and the 'receiver' (you) in different rooms. The next objection could be that you know what your friend's current preoccupations are, and can thus infer his or her thoughts. Your answer would really be an educated guess and not a telepathic pick up. It's a subtle objection, but nevertheless a valid one, and even this was weeded out. The experiments at Maimonides were designed as follows:

The 'sender' and the 'receiver', as well as two other people, were involved in the experiment. The 'receiver' was not to pick up the message when awake, but only while dreaming, and would be asleep in a sealed room where no sound could reach him or her. Initially the 'sender' was kept in the room next to the 'receiver', then moved to the adjoining block, and finally kept fourteen miles away. The message to be communicated would not be of the 'sender's' choice. A third person would choose eight coloured reproductions of paintings or sculptures (to eliminate personal messages) and put them in envelopes. This third person would then be taken away and locked in a room for the night, before the 'sender' chose one envelope to communicate its contents to the 'receiver'.

The whole procedure ensured that the choice of the message to be transmitted was random and that absolutely no one knew the subject matter to be communicated. Meanwhile the 'receiver' would go to sleep wearing (EEG) monitoring equipment. No sooner did the 'receiver' enter the REM phase, a 'monitor' (the fourth person in the experiment) would alert the 'sender' by means of a buzzer. The 'sender' would then concentrate on the chosen art print, in an attempt to convey it to the 'receiver'. Towards the end of each REM period the 'receiver' would be awoken by the 'monitor' and any dream experienced was recorded via an intercom. This went on for the full night, with every remembered dream being recorded. Incidentally, the 'monitor' was also not aware of the subject matter of the intended telepathic communication, otherwise there was a chance that he or she could, by some subtle means, influence the result. Could there be any further objections to the methodology used in the experiments? Apparently, yes! Maybe all the people involved in this experiment were willing to believe in telepathy and were therefore prone to read the telepathic message into the dream, thereby evaluating the dream communication to be a 'hit'. Ullman and Krippner, to leave no stone unturned, sent the recorded dreams and all the eight prints to external judges, asking if they could find a match between any of the prints and the dreams. They were not told which dream the 'sender' had attempted to communicate. Could there have been any other subtle factor left out which could have aided the communication? And what would you say if this procedure was followed for a series of eight nights, and thirteen such studies were carried out; that nine out of the thirteen studies showed statistically significant results? Do these experiments convince you that telepathy, dream telepathy, exists?

Of course, the 'receiver' may not have relied on telepathic sensitivity, but may have clairvoyantly 'seen' the target picture without the mediation of the 'sender's' thoughts or efforts. For this reason it may be more appropriate to call this communication extrasensory perception rather than just telepathy. But, what about precognition? Are there any experiments validating this phenomenon?

Two studies were done with an Englishman, Malcolm Bessent, whose training in London had developed his psychic 'sensitivity'. He had a history of spontaneous precognition. In late November 1969, while staying in Brooklyn, he experienced a series of images that he felt were predictions of the future. He was urged to write them down. He sent them on 7 December 1969 to the Central Premonitions Registry (Box 482, Times Square Station, New York, NY 10036). In this he made three predictions: an oil tanker would be involved in a disaster of international significance within 4–6 months time; Charles De Gaulle would die within a year; and Prime Minister Wilson would be involved in a change of government in England. All three proved to be true. In February 1970, Onassis's oil tanker, the *Arrow*, ran aground and met with disaster off the coast of Nova Scotia. Its cargo of oil spilt, causing an oil slick that was of 'international' concern. General De Gaulle died eleven months afterwards on 10 November 1970. And, contrary to the expectations of all political pundits and the polls, Edward Heath ousted Wilson from the British government.

Impressive though this may be, Bessent was now to accomplish a far more challenging feat. Rather than naturally experience spontaneous precognition, he would have to perform on demand. After all, a controlled experiment cannot wait till inspiration is upon the subject. Not only that, he would have to perform on successive nights in a long experimental series.

In these experiments Bessent would go to sleep with the monitoring equipment, then would be awoken at the end of each REM period so that any remembered dream could be recorded.[45] In the telepathy experiments, the choice of target was made before the dream had commenced. Now, the target would be selected the next day, *after* the dream had been dreamt. Every care was taken that no sensory leakage through behavioural or subvocal clues took place between the dreamer or the recorder of the dream and anyone involved in choosing the target. The morning after Bessent would leave the laboratory, a sealed envelope containing a page number in Hall and Van de Castle's book *The Content Analysis of Dreams* would be selected by someone who had had absolutely no contact with the dreamer. A second person would randomly select another number. Both these numbers would be presented to still another person who with their aid would locate a content item in the book. Using this item as the 'keyword' he would then select an art print (from a pool of several hundred), which portrayed this word. This was the target about which the dreamer should have already dreamt the previous night.

The design of the experiment was such that the choice of the target was absolutely random and there was no way that the dreamer or the monitor could have inferred it based on the knowledge of the people who chose it. Care was also taken of the next potential pitfall. The assessment of whether the dream was a hit or not was left to external judges – people who were not involved in the experiment. To see how exactly this worked it might be useful to follow one night's dreams and the target art print chosen the next morning, about which Bessent was to have precognitively dreamt: Bessent's first dream was an 'impression of green and purple ... Small areas of white and blue.' In the second dream of that night 'there was a large concrete building ... But it was architecturally designed and shaped ... and there was a patient from upstairs escaping ... She had a white coat on, like a doctor's coat, and people were arguing with her on the street.' The third dream made him 'aware of an impression of hostility ... It had to do with my work, and I think all the people were medical ...'

In the morning the two numbers randomly selected led to the word 'corridor' in the Hall–Van de Castle book. From this a target picture was selected (the person making the selection was not aware of the content of Bessent's dreams) and this was Van Gogh's *A Corridor in the Asylum*. The picture portrays a lone figure in the corridor of a mental institution that is constructed from concrete. The predominant colours are orange, green, deep blue, and white.[46] Needless to say, Bessent had correctly divined what would be chosen the following morning.

The scoring was done along a graduated scale. For five out of the eight nights the judges scored direct 'hits' and on the other three nights the rating was close to a 'hit'. A second study, with some changes in the procedure, was also done with comparable results.[47] This suggests that even so elusive a phenomenon as precognition may be trapped within the net of laboratory experimentation.

The degree of success that these experiments enjoyed is almost unparalleled in the history of parapsychology. Perhaps it might just be possible to catch the echo before the sound. And in the mysterious reverberations of this echo, we hear the untold story of a human endowment that pushes the frontiers of ordinary human consciousness to reach far beyond it.

The anecdotal as well as experimental evidence suggests that precognition is a human faculty that has as much of a reality as the data we gather from our other sense perceptions. Yet it is always difficult to ascertain whether a particular dream is precognitive or not. Often it is only in retrospect that the prophetic content of the dream is proven or disproved. And the same can be said about Usha's dream. We cannot say with any degree of certainty that her dream is precognitive. Till very recently she had not been robbed; she still possesses her jewellery. I reckon that if her dream had been a premonition, subsequent events would have substantiated its prophecy by now. However, the difficulty in determining whether a dream is precognitive or not in no way detracts from our ability to 'know' things before they actually become known.

In 1935, three years before his death at age 82, Freud was asked by the Hungarian writer Cornelius Tabori about his views on paranormal phenomena. Freud said, 'The transference of thoughts, the possibility of sensing the past or the future cannot be merely accidental. Some people say,' he smiled, 'that in my old age I have become credulous. No ... I don't think so. Merely – all my life I have learned to accept new facts, humbly, readily.'[48]

Chapter 18

PRODROMAL DREAMS
OF ILLNESS AND HEALING

> For this is the great error of our day ... that physicians separate
> the soul from the body.
>
> Plato

*I am standing on top of a tall building. Suddenly an eagle dives
straight towards my face. I am afraid of its sharp beak and get to
my knees, crouching against the parapet to protect myself.*

The dreamer, an eighty-year-old man, awoke to find that he had
fallen off the bed and was crouching against one side of it. He
had stubbed his toe and was bleeding from the forehead. He had had
a frightening dream and while protecting himself against a swooping
eagle the sleeper had fallen from his bed and hurt himself in the
process. However, there is a difficulty with this explanation: we know
that during a dream the body becomes immobilized due to muscular
atonia. Therefore, his dream could not have made him fall off the bed.
Are we then to presume that he had started moving in his sleep (NREM)
and the sensation of falling had elicited an image of an eagle swooping
down on him? The impact of his forehead against the edge of the bed
had been converted to fright in the dream, making him take evasive
action to protect his head from the sharp beak of the eagle. If this was

the sequence then it would mean that bodily sensations – of falling and pain – had triggered the dream. Needless to say, the dreamer was convinced that this is what had transpired. He was all the more certain because only a few months earlier he had dreamt that a German dive-bomber was coming at him, and he had sought the safety of the parapet of the building by doubling up against it. Then too he had awoken from the dream to find himself lying on the ground, having rolled off the bed while asleep. The dreamer was stressing to me the power of the repetitive dream. This time the implication was not prophetic but somatic – the sensation of falling had initiated the dream. Does this mean that the popular belief that dreams are stimulated by indigestion (an internal event) holds some truth? Are the ideas that arise in dreams due to sensory stimulations?

We are not restating the Hobson-McCarley thesis, where the brainstem triggers random images, but asking if the excitation or activity of the sensory functions stimulates dreams. We have observed that external stimuli can affect the content of dreams; the favourite example is the shrill of the alarm clock perceived as the ringing of church bells in a dream. Monitored under laboratory conditions it has been observed that brief external stimuli such as applied heat, sprays of cold water, or even the recording devices attached to the dreamer's body are sometimes incorporated into a dream. A jet of cold water may be experienced as drowning in an icy sea, the application of warmth as an inferno in a dream. A peal of thunder may set us amidst battle; the creaking of a door may produce a dream of burglars; dangling feet over the edge of the bed may produce dreams of falling over a cliff; and if our head happens to be buried under the pillow, we may dream of being beneath a huge overhanging rock.[1]

But could this stimulus for a dream, instead of originating from an external source, come from an internal organ of our body? The reasoning of Schopenhauer, the philosopher, has had a decisive effect on this question. He argued that during the day the mind is totally occupied with external stimuli and our responses to them, so that any stimulus coming from within the body is all but drowned. At most, it registers as a diffused awareness, reflected as merely a vague quality of our mood. But at night when the deafening impressions of the day are mute, then our attention may be attracted by stimuli emanating from the organs – just like at night we can hear the murmuring of a brook that is drowned by daytime noise.[2] Thus, a change in respiratory rate can lead to dreams of suffocation or drowning; laborious breathing may produce a vision of a blazing furnace; changes in the middle ear can trigger an image of a shouting demagogue. Like a barometer, imperceptible bodily fluctuations are recorded. The dream can incorporate into its imagery any stimulus, despite it being indistinctly perceived.

Perhaps it has been every dreamer's experience of eating a scrumptious meal in a dream and awakening to find you are ravenously hungry. Had the dream banquet titillated feelings of hunger, or was the stomach experiencing hunger pangs as you slept, and the brain, registering these sensations, conjured up images of food? The former would imply that the dream is the cause of the wish, while the latter indicates that a somatic stimulation had evoked a dream.

Freud unhesitatingly accepted that somatic stimuli derived from the internal organs of the body find their way into the dream. He believed that somatic sources of stimulation during sleep, unless they are of unusual intensity, play a role similar to the day's residue in dream formation.[3] It is only a small step from Freud's belief to the thesis that dreams can warn us of impending illness, as also of recovery from illness. Internal organs may register indistinctly when we are in a healthy state. However, they can send more urgent intimations when they are malfunctioning. Since normal bodily processes create sensations that are converted into dream pictures, we should not be surprised when abnormal body processes – those that occur in illness or injury – also find a voice in dreams. In fact, each organ in the body has a voice in our dreams. When the harmony of the bodily process is disturbed, our dreams are often the first to know, and are capable of indicating silent, undetected changes occurring below the thin mantle of our skin.

A poignant case is of a woman in early pregnancy who dreamt that much to her horror her green carpet had turned red. Next day she began to haemorrhage and lost her child. Was the dream warning her that green, the colour of life and growth, as seen in plants and trees, had transformed to red, the colour of blood?

A friend of mine dreamt that she was brewing a herbal mixture, the kind her mother used to administer for coughs and colds when she was young. Three days after this dream she came down with an attack of bronchitis. It is noteworthy how the dreaming mind chose a symbol specific only to the dreamer, so that it could depict a very specific area – the throat and chest – for which some form of medicine or healing would be required. In another instance 'Mandira Mukerjee' dreamt:

I'm driving my car and suddenly realize that I have run out of fuel.
I find myself stranded in a remote village.

Five days later, quite unexpectedly, Mandira's blood pressure dropped and she was advised complete rest. The car, a symbol of her body, is brought to a sudden halt as it ran out of fuel, the car's fuel being analogous to the body's fuel. The feeling of being stranded in the dream is a metaphor for her inability to temporarily lead a normal life.

It is unfortunate that the notion that dreams can warn the dreamer about impending illness has not been explored in modern times. Scientific researchers are all too keen to study the effects of biochemical and physiological factors on dreaming, but the influence of malfunctioning organs on the content of dreams is not considered. Also, there is hardly any literature available on this aspect of dreaming. This, despite the personal experiences of prominent dream researchers that confirm this kind of dream, as the following two examples show.

A former president of the Association for the Study of Dreams (ASD), Alan Moffitt, was allergic to cats; whenever he petted a cat his eyes and sinuses would swell up and he would experience difficulty in breathing. When he was nine years old he had a dream in which a cat had been rubbing itself over him. In the morning he experienced a full-blown allergy attack.[4] Though his dream did not contain a direct allusion to his ailment, the imagery was intimately associated with his previously known allergy to cats. William Dement, a pioneer of REM research, had an exceptionally vivid and realistic dream of suffering from inoperable lung cancer. He saw the ominous shadow in his chest X-ray and realized that the entire right lung was cancerous. A colleague conducted the subsequent physical examination and detected widespread metastases in his lymph nodes. On learning this he experienced a deep anguish that his life would soon end, as also profound regret that none of this would have happened had he quit smoking. On awakening his relief was immense. He felt he had been reborn and given a chance to alter his life. He immediately stopped smoking. The dream had both dramatically cautioned him about an ailment and wrought preventive measures in a manner that is the unique privilege of dreams.[5]

Fortunately, Russian psychiatrist Vasily Kasatkin, at the Leningrad Neurosurgical Institute, had not disregarded the somatic basis of dreaming. His book, *Theory of Dreams*, relies on the most comprehensive research on the relationship between dreams and bodily ailments, and describes his findings based on 10,240 dreams obtained from 1,200 subjects.[6] It impressively elaborates upon connections between dream images, the diseased organ, and the possible time span for the onset of illness.

Kasatkin called dreams the 'sentries that watch over our health. There are nerves coming to the brain from every part of the body – and they relay the signals of impending illness that the subconscious translates into dreams.' He observed that changes in dream content begin occurring shortly before the onset of an illness or the appearance of any clinical symptoms of the disorder. Illness is associated with increased dream recall, and dreams caused by illness are longer than dreams caused by ordinary annoyances. He found that, in general, dreams announcing illnesses were distressful and included violent images of war, fire, blood, corpses, tombs, raw meat, garbage, dirty water, spoiled food, or references to hospitals, doctors, and medicines. Gloomy thoughts and feelings of fright were associated with these images in 91 percent of the dreams, but pain was experienced in only 9 percent.[7] These dreams paralleled the course of the disease. As symptoms worsened, so did the dream content; as the symptoms abated, the dream images grew less unpleasant.

One of Kasatkin's most dramatic conclusions was that in almost every case, the patient's dream images involved the appearance of the affected organ or body part, indicating its location, the sensation it undergoes, and its malfunctioning. Patricia Garfield confirmed this in her book *The Healing Power of Dreams*, where she says our dreams even reflect the onset of something as ordinary as a headache. 'I have examined over forty dream reports from people who awoke with headaches they did not have before they went to sleep – some from my own collection of people's dreams, others from research studies.' She found various dream images typical of headaches, where the dreamer is hit on the head either with an axe by an assailant, or with books, or by falling material as a building collapses. In each of the dream images the sense of violence to the head is prominent.[8]

Kasatkin came to believe that recurrent dreams of bodily wounds 'are amongst the most serious and they invariably indicate a very dangerous illness such as cancer, liver trouble, kidney or heart disease.'[9] For instance, repeated dreams of a chest wound are indicative of a possible heart attack. Recurrent dreams of stomach wounds may suggest liver or kidney disease.[10]

He reported the case of a recently widowed woman who dreamt that she was in the cemetery, sitting on her husband's grave, 'when two skeletal hands came out of the grave and grabbed her. One grabbed her at the throat, and the fingers of the other hand pierced deep into her flesh near her heart. She awoke choking and had a mild cardiac arrest.'[11]

A forty-year-old man who had a recurrent dream of a rat gnawing at the lower part of his abdomen was later diagnosed as having a duodenal ulcer.[12]

Kasatkin wanted to develop a system of early warning of disease through dreams, especially for people who had recurrent dreams about a specific body part. Numerous reports of dreams preceding the onset of cancer have been published. 'One author traces a link between dreams, disturbing emotions, lowered functioning of the immune system, and increased susceptibility to cancer. He claims that the images in dreams can symbolize the type of cancer and its location and gives the example of a woman who had recurrent nightmares of dogs tearing at her stomach a few months before she was diagnosed with stomach cancer.'[13]

Bernard Siegel, a cancer surgeon at the Yale University School of Medicine, described the case of a journalist who had a dream in which torturers placed burning hot coals beneath his chin. He felt the heat sear his throat and screamed in pain as the 'coals gnawed his larynx'. The journalist felt sure that this dream indicated some malfunction in his throat even though he had a tough time persuading his doctor to take him seriously. A physical check-up confirmed the presence of cancer in his thyroid gland.[14]

In 1975, a newspaper article quoted Kasatkin as saying, 'By correctly interpreting dreams we've been able to discover and treat serious illnesses long before they would be diagnosed by any traditional means. We have been able to save many lives.'[15]

His dream diagnoses covered a wide range of diseases from minor tooth and skin problems to brain tumours. Kasatkin felt that the time span between a dream and the actual appearance of the disease varied. He noted it might be two weeks for a heart attack and a year or more for the manifestation of mental illness.[16]

The dream viewed as a diagnostic tool that monitors our health was an idea I wanted to explore further and cross-check with doctors in hospitals. I met over a dozen doctors but their responses ranged from downright disbelief to amusement and condescension.

'How can dreams tell you about illnesses? Only physical examination and tests can do that. Nothing else.'

When I quoted Kasatkin's long years of research to them they shrugged it off as something they had never heard of. Then I met Dr 'Trehan', a surgeon at Apollo Hospital in Delhi, who seemed interested in discussing the subject.

'Well, I have had some rather inexplicable things happen to me in my long career as a doctor. I deal with life and death all the time. Those are unusual conditions to be under. Maybe that is the reason I sometimes get unusual responses from people I am treating.'

'In what way?'

'It's happened to me twice. I was operating on patients, who obviously were deep under anaesthesia. Later, in both cases, they recounted conversations I'd had with either a colleague or an assistant during the operation. How could they have known? I can't understand it at all,' Dr Trehan said, shaking his head in perplexity.

'We probably have other ways of "knowing" besides what we gather from our five senses,' I ventured.

'Maybe. Both of them told me that they had floated up to the ceiling, from where they had observed the operation being performed on their inert body and had heard everything from there.' His eyes travelled towards the ceiling. 'I didn't know what to make out of their experience, so I didn't quiz them about it. But I've not forgotten it.

'On the subject of dreams there was another man – a simple, rather poor man who told me he had seen me in a dream and therefore claimed to recognize me. I had never seen him before yet he insisted only I should operate on him because of this dream. It did occur to me that it was a very clever way of pressurizing me to agree to his demand. Then he looked at me and asked, "You do not believe me, do you?" "How can I?" I said to him. The man shook his head and said, "In the dream you also told me the date you will be operating on."

'He gave me the date as being a month away. I smiled, checked my appointment diary, and gave him a date, fourteen days hence for his operation. I said to him, "Well, you may have seen my face in a dream but you have got the dates all wrong. Anyway, you need not worry. I'll operate on you – dream or no dream."

'Then something odd happened. I fell ill and did not go to work for a week. My appointments had to be rescheduled, and this man's operation had to be postponed. Two days before the operation, he was admitted into the hospital for preoperative care. I checked in on him on my rounds. The first thing he said was, "My dream was true. Day after will be exactly a month since I met you."'

'So do you now believe that he saw your face in a dream?' I asked Dr Trehan.

'He may have. But since I cannot find a reasonable explanation for it, I continue to be baffled.'

'Have any of your other patients ever mentioned a dream that may have provided a clue for the onset of their illness?'

Dr Trehan asked me to accompany him into the ward and talk to any of the patients who were willing. Needless to say, most of the patients were not interested in what I had to say. They looked disbelievingly when I told them that I was not a physiotherapist or a nutrition expert, nor a doctor assisting Dr Trehan, but a person researching dreams! Their expressions seemed to say, 'We are in hospital to be cured, not to dream!' However, a girl in her late twenties seemed interested. Her large eyes followed me keenly. 'Pushpa Bansal' was just twenty-five when her troubles began with persistent headaches. She remembered a dream from that period, which she related within minutes of our introduction:

I am in a computer factory where small fires are flaring up from the walls and leap out in threatening clusters from the centre of the factory. I'm trying to get out but the workers in the factory are not letting me.

This is an interesting dream because it depicts her condition faithfully. The brain has often been compared to a computer. The fires in the computer factory could be understood to represent her headaches. Her desire to get out is probably indicative of the effort she was making not to let her headaches bog her down. She appears not to have succeeded – the workers in the factory, or the cells in her brain, are not operating normally, and holding her ransom to the dysfunction.

The passage of months saw her condition deteriorate; the headaches became more and more intense with sharp pains shooting down her neck. One day, while watching television, she fainted. When she came around, she began to vomit. She was rushed to hospital where medication controlled the vomiting, but a dull headache still persisted. The doctors suspected a tumour in the brain to be the cause of her problems, but a confirmed diagnosis could not be given till a CT scan was done.

Often a patient isn't told about a life-threatening disease in an effort to protect him or her from morbid apprehensions. Nobody had told Pushpa about the suspicion of a tumour, but she had overheard her father whispering to her mother about what the doctor had feared. Surprisingly, the gravity on their faces made her more concerned for their suffering than her own condition. However, everyone maintained an optimistic facade, chatting about everything except the one subject uppermost in their minds. I feel that this secrecy was what made her open up to me so quickly. I was a stranger with whom no pretences were required, and she obviously needed to talk. She remembered a dream from the previous night, which she excitedly related to me:

> *I have been given a large watermelon. I cut it open to find, to my utter amazement, that it is seedless! I shape it in the form of a lotus.*

'Is it a good dream?' she asked, and then continued before I could answer: 'After all the lotus is a sacred flower. Maybe if I pray God may make me well.'

I didn't know what to say. It isn't uncommon to have wish-fulfilment dreams when you are confronted with the prospect of a life-threatening illness. Yet I felt there was something strange about the dream. Watermelons are full of seeds but this one is seedless. I felt that this could be the lead metaphor of the dream. However, try as I would, I could not interpret the dream beyond this initial observation. Perhaps my concern made her continue to chat with me.

'If there is a tumour in my brain my life will change, even before it has begun.'

'When is the CT scan?' I asked.

'Tomorrow.'

Two days later Pushpa still filled my thoughts. She had looked so bewildered and lost, yet so utterly brave in her struggle not to let despair overwhelm her.

On the third day I was back at the hospital, but Pushpa's bed was empty. I was worried and wondered if she was being operated upon. I went to see Dr Trehan.

'Oh, Pushpa!' he exclaimed. 'She has been discharged. Her CT scan was clear of any kind of tumour. Her problem was traced to excessive water retention in the brain.'

I was deeply relieved. As I walked out of the hospital my mind went back to Pushpa's dream. The watermelon could be taken as a symbol for the brain – its globular shape similar to that of the brain. The watermelon was seedless. A tumour would have appeared like a black shadow in the CT scan, akin to the seeds of a watermelon. There are no tumours! the dream seems to have told Pushpa.

The dream's choice of symbol was truly amazing. Perhaps it was an utterly spontaneous creative act that not only depicted the situation but pointed towards a prognosis as well. A watermelon is an excellent symbol as it is a fruit that retains water. The lotus symbol was also important since it grows in water. Both symbols were alluding to the problem of water retention that Pushpa was facing. In the dream she shapes the watermelon into a lotus – a positive symbol of healing, since the lotus lives and thrives in water without being swamped by it.

Once the problem was diagnosed the doctors found the right drug to dry the excessive fluid in Pushpa's brain. Pushpa got her life back and I was beginning to see that dreams could be a voice for our body. No doubt Pushpa's dream found its interpretation after the event. Yet in hindsight, it was evident that the dream imagery was like a CT scan before it had actually taken place, confirming Kasatkin and Garfield's research, which demonstrated that the affected body part is often highlighted in dreams.

A definite connection appears to exist between the condition of our bodies and what appears on the monitoring screen of our dreaming mind, and this concept did not originate with Kasatkin. This idea has ancient roots in history and has been practised by many civilizations with very effective results. In Greece the cult of the healing god Aesculapius flourished for nearly a thousand years, from the end of the sixth century BC until the end of the fifth century AD.[17] Such was his fame that shrines dedicated to him quickly sprung up all over Greece and the Roman Empire.

People in need of healing thronged from all over Greece to these temples to incubate their dreams and seek cures for bodily ailments. Dream incubation, or the art of inducing specific dreams to elicit advice about health-related problems, became a highly developed process with the Greeks. The person seeking a healing dream went through sacramental ceremonies and purification rites in the temples dedicated to Aesculapius. A sick person would enter the sanctuary, bathe, and perform various ceremonies. The supplicant, purified by lustration and massage, and surrounded by the fragrance of incense, would lie in a state of exaltation on stone slabs covered with the skin of a sacrificed ram. It was expected that they would drift into sleep with the question they sought an answer to uppermost in their mind. Once asleep they would dream of the remedies for their illness. These would be revealed in their natural form or in symbols, whose significance would afterwards be interpreted by the priests. Sometimes Aesculapius himself appeared to them in a dream and revealed the cure. Similar practices took place in some Hindu temples, for example, the Shiva temple at Tarakeshwara (in West Bengal, India).[18]

The ancient Greek physician would also pay close attention to dreams, believing that a particular kind could predict the onset of illness. This was called the *prodromal* dream, from the Greek word *pro* meaning 'before' and *dromos* meaning 'running', thus a forerunner. Today 'prodrome' in medical terminology refers to a symptom – an indicator of the onset of a disease.

Hippocrates, the acknowledged father of Greek medicine, believed in diagnostic dreams and felt that specific dream images prognosticated future ailments. In a long essay titled 'On Dreams', he said that dreams of overflowing rivers meant an excess of blood, dreams of springs indicated bladder trouble, and dreams of barren trees are associated with insufficient seminal fluid. Hippocrates referred to dreams that reflected or were connected to the events of daily life as regular dreams. However, if the dreams were totally unrelated to or discordant with the pattern of our waking life, then bodily malfunctioning may be indicated. 'When dreams are contrary to the acts of the day, and there occurs about them some struggle or triumph, a disturbance in the body is indicated, a violent struggle meaning a violent mischief, a feeble struggle a less serious mischief.'[19]

In other words, Hippocrates saw dreams that reproduced recent experiences without distortion as a mark of health. Physical ill-health was indicated when the soul no longer 'abides by the purposes of the day'.[20]

It is important to notice and pay attention when dreams deviate from their normal course; unusual or bizarre dreams that wander away from normal expression. For this bizarreness is the dream's way of drawing attention to sensations and bodily changes that are still too feeble in their manifestation to have registered as symptoms in consciousness.

Once again, dream bizarreness appears to hold the key. In illness-healing dreams this bizarreness is an expression of 'some struggle or triumph' in somatic functioning. For example, the somatic struggle could express itself in dream images that depict dramatic transformations of various phenomena in nature: the sun drying the earth could signify inflammation or fever; a cold air blowing through the window, turning the house and garden into ice and snow sculptures, could indicate an excess of white phlegm or poor blood circulation. The dramatic and bizarre nature of the imagery then becomes the indicator of the specific organ or area that is somatically under siege.

Hippocrates' *illness-axiom* was echoed by Kasatkin's conclusion that special attention must be given to dream content that becomes nightmarish.

Building upon Hippocrates' belief, the Greek philosopher Aristotle observed that the awareness of external stimuli is reduced during sleep, thereby amplifying the presence of even minimal internal sensations occurring within the body. He wrote that the 'beginnings of diseases and other distempers which are about to visit the body ... must be more evident in the sleeping than in the waking state'.[21] He rightly believed that the sensory organs continue to be active during sleep, reverberating with what they sensed whilst awake and reacting to what is currently happening.[22]

With Galen, one of the most illustrious second-century Greek physicians, a great leap forward was made to unravel the unknown wonders of the human body. Even Galen's vocation was dictated by a dream: the god Aesculapius had appeared to his father, Nikon, and commanded him to raise his son as a physician. In the following years Galen made several important discoveries. He established that the arteries carry blood not air, a belief that had been prevalent for the previous four hundred years. He also showed how the heart sets the blood in motion. His discovery may have influenced later medical researchers, perhaps even William Harvey, the British physician who discovered the circulation of blood.[23]

When Galen was twenty-seven, he fell gravely ill with an abdominal abscess. He went to the incubation shrine of Aesculapius, where he was shown in a dream how his ailment may be cured. He should open an artery in his hand between his thumb and forefinger, letting it bleed spontaneously until it stopped. His faith in dreams was such that he performed this operation on himself and was cured.[24]

Like Hippocrates before him, Galen believed in using dreams as a diagnostic tool for medical conditions. He stressed the ability of dreams to foretell impending illnesses. In his book *Prophecy in Dream* he mentions the case of a man who dreamt that his leg had turned to stone. The man developed a paralysis of the leg a few days later.[25]

Arnold of Villanova, a physician in the Middle Ages, compared dreams to magnifying glasses, which could detect the small beginnings of physical illness. He describes the case of a man who dreamt on two successive occasions that his one ear was being beaten with a stone. Soon afterwards, he developed a serious inflammation of the same ear.[26]

The Hindu-Buddhist genius for classification becomes evident when dealing with somatic dreams. Though there are some differences between the Hindus and the Buddhists, they have much in common. A set of appendices to the early Hindu text Atharva Veda, the Parisistas of the Atharva Veda, goes deeper into the problem as it attempts not only to trace the origin of dreams to bodily afflictions, but tries to relate them to other things as well. Some of us are familiar with the threefold division of temperaments: bilious or windy (*vata*), choleric or fiery (*pitta*), and phlegmatic or watery (*kapha*). Physicians would gauge the temperament of a person by considering their physical characteristics. (It is interesting to note that astrologers believe that it is the planetary positions in the sky at the moment of birth that determine a person's temperament.) The beauty of the Hindu-Buddhist texts is that they were able to relate these temperaments to the dream life of the person, underscoring the idea that not only does the physical world (sky and body) reflect this temperament, but that it finds its resonances in the dream world as well.

The sixty-eighth appendix of the Atharva Veda states that human beings dream according to a specific individual pattern. Current research has confirmed that indeed the dreaming pattern of people does not vary much over the years. The Hindus attribute this pattern to the temperament of the person. Hence 'fiery' personalities dream of arid land and forest fires; 'watery' personalities dream of cool rivers, clear skies, and nature in splendour; and 'windy' personalities dream of flocks of birds, racing clouds, and mountains whipped by the wind.[27]

This is not only a method of classifying dreams according to the temperament of the dreamer, but it can also reflect the psychosomatic condition of the dreamer. For example, when a particular bodily sense is disturbed, the dreamer will dream of objects of that sense.[28] This could be of immense significance when diagnosing the health of the person through dreams. Indian medical texts go on to make much more specific diagnoses based on dreams. Dreaming of friendship with a dog means that the dreamer will become feverish; friendship with a monkey, consumptive; friendship with a demon, insane; friendship with ghosts, amnesiac.[29] Similarly, according to Vaisesika philosophy, one of the six schools of Hindu philosophy, a man may dream of flying when wind predominates his body.[30]

It may be relevant to point out that homeopathy also seeks to understand and embed the symptoms of a patient guided by his or her dreams.[31]

Dr 'Geeta Mangatram', head of the microbiology department in a leading Delhi hospital, told me about an amazing dream she had. The story that follows is an incredible account of a wife's dream portending her husband's medical prognosis. Dreams, as mentioned earlier, could either directly refer to the body part that is affected or portray illness through a sense of impairment, loss, or damage.

Geeta's husband, 'Mahesh', suffered from diabetes and hypertension at the age of forty-five. These diseases, if controlled, do not pose a life threat, but in 1989, in a recorded entry in her diary, Geeta relates the following dream:

> I'm standing in my lawn and overhead are flying, golden, rocket-shaped fish. I catch one of them and am able to throw them further. There is a sense of exhilaration in the fact that I can throw these fish so far. My son comes in and much to my pleasure is able to do the same.
>
> However, when Mahesh enters and tries to catch the fish he cannot. He becomes alarmed and frightened, and says, 'I'm losing my limbs,' and begins to cry. I look at him and try to save him but he begins to shrink before my eyes. Very quickly he takes on a little boy's shape. His clothes are too large and hang loosely on his limbs. I realize that he is not losing his limbs but is getting smaller and deformed.
>
> Each time he tries to touch the fish-rocket he gets smaller, till he becomes a little baby. I pick him up in my arms, but panic grips me as I feel he is disappearing, dying ...

The symbols of loss are far too insistent in this dream. Geeta and her son are able to catch the 'flying, golden, rocket-shaped fish' and throw them, but Mahesh cannot. I asked Geeta what her association with these fish was. She said, 'A healthy participation in life. A fish swims through water as we do through life. In my dream the fish are healthy, golden, active, and therefore there is a sense of exhilaration in catching them and making them go further.'

It's always worth noting if any of the dream characters, including the dreamer, have a physical illness or infirmity in the dream. What kind of abnormality is it? Which body part is particularly affected?

In the dream in question a sharp contrast is drawn between Geeta and her son's enthusiastic participation in throwing the fish and Mahesh's helpless inability to do so. Moreover, there is a repetitive emphasis in the dream on growing impairment. First, it is Mahesh's loss of limbs. Then he shrinks to the size of a small boy, another image of dependence. His clothes hang large and loose – an image of emaciation due to loss of weight or illness. He begins to appear 'deformed', a word that literally means losing your original form. Finally Mahesh changes into a baby – a baby whom Geeta has to pick up in her arms and nurture – embodying a state of complete dependence. The last sentence of Geeta's dream is truly poignant as she feels Mahesh is disappearing from existence – a phrase we only use when someone is terminally ill and close to dying.

What followed over the next few years is an unbelievable story of the ravages that repeated illnesses left on Mahesh and Geeta's life. A year after this dream, in 1990, Mahesh had his first heart attack after which an angioplasty procedure was performed. Two years later a carcinoid obstruction was found in the intestine, resulting in surgery. In 1996 Mahesh had a stroke and his power of speech and right limbs were affected – an uncanny resonance to Geeta's dream. After a month, however, the symptoms cleared.

Two years later in 1998 a brain tumour was discovered, which was operated upon. After a prolonged spell in hospital, the day Mahesh was brought home he suffered another heart attack. He was rushed back to the hospital's intensive coronary care unit. The doctors were now faced with a serious dilemma. A blocked artery in his heart indicated that he needed blood thinners, but that would result in the thinned blood collecting in the recently operated area of the brain – the bandages of which still bound his head. However, under the most careful monitoring of blood thinners, heart surgery was performed and the blocked artery opened. Unfortunately six months later, the enlarged artery collapsed again and a bypass surgery had to be done.

One intestinal obstruction, a stroke, brain surgery, and two heart surgeries. As Geeta's dream had warned, Mahesh began shrinking in size; he grew thinner and more frail, and his clothes hung on him loosely as his capacity to touch the *'flying, golden, rocket-shaped fish'* of a healthy, participative life diminished. It was almost as though in essence Mahesh's life was following the symbols of the dream. Each time the family felt they had fought an illness and believed Mahesh was on the road to recovery, another life-threatening illness vanquished him.

Unfortunately, the final part of Geeta's dream had still to be enacted. By November 1998 Mahesh could no longer retain food. A CT scan revealed another obstruction in his intestines. He was operated upon. The doctors discovered a tumour and a further twelve inches of his intestines were removed. Further weakened and diminished, the recovery was painfully and traumatically slow. He still could not retain food and was either vomiting or had diarrhoea. Geeta looked after him with total devotion. He was the babe in her arms, whose life she feared for.

'I felt I was watching him day by day, disappearing from existence,' Geeta said with eyes welling up with tears.

What is particularly amazing is that Geeta had this dream in 1989. Mahesh's illnesses unfolded progressively over the next nine years, till his CT scan in November 1998. Was the dream capable of knowing what Mahesh was going to endure in the years to come? Moreover, the dream did not come to Mahesh, whose body may have known what it was susceptible to. The dream came to Geeta. Maybe a strong element of precognition was operating here, since Mahesh's illness would dramatically change their life, and Geeta was being forewarned about it. Jung believes that in certain cases 'a dream, of visionary clarity, occurs about the time of the onset of the illness or shortly before, which imprints itself indelibly on the mind and, when analysed, reveals to the patient a hidden meaning that anticipates the subsequent events of his life'.[32]

I have come to believe that when a major change is upon us our dreams mark that shift. We may or may not be aware of it, but our dreams register this movement, portray the nature of the change, and are often the first indicators that the road ahead is going to be different from the one we have been travelling on so far.

How true this was of 'Manjula Mehra' who carried the burden of a family history of cancer, her mother's elder sister, her grandmother, and two aunts having died of cancer. Manjula had felt specially branded when her mother succumbed to carcinogenic tumours in the stomach two years earlier. Doctors reassured her that cancer was not hereditary, yet they advised her to undergo regular check-ups, which she began. A few months after her mother died she noted physical symptoms like hot flushes, an irregular menstrual cycle, and pain in the lower back. She simply dismissed them as premenopausal signs even though she was only forty-three. Yet somewhere, somehow a deep-rooted fear bound her, for she began avoiding her routine cancer check-up, always finding a reason to postpone it. Then one night she dreamt:

An old college friend who had been very fond of me says, 'You know I had wanted to marry you.'

I reply, 'To tell you the truth I had been rather fond of you myself, but that is all history since I am very happily married now.'

The man says, 'That's the problem with you. You cannot face the truth. You keep everything inside you. Please let it out, otherwise you'll hurt the people you are close to.'

I suddenly think, I have to face the truth of the coming check-up.
If I don't I'll hurt my family by avoiding it.

Manjula awoke startled by the dream. It had been a very long time
since she had thought of this particular friend, whose reappearance
in the dream brought an unexpected emotional charge to it. It was as
though the dreaming intelligence was evoking through the repressed
potency of an unexpressed relationship with an old admirer, the
emotional charge of the present issue – the cancer test. Could we apply
to this Hippocrates' rule that an unexpected dream, unconnected to
the day's residue, different from our normal run of dreams, can be
particularly significant?

The following week Manjula went for a check-up. A lump was
discovered in her uterus. She underwent a radical hysterectomy in which
the ovaries, fallopian tubes, and uterus were removed. The lump in the
uterus was found to be malignant.

Manjula said, 'When the dream came I knew it was saying: Face up
to the truth, which meant the strong possibility of my having cancer.
The friend in my dream cautioned me not to keep everything inside me,
but to let it out. I felt certain I would be undergoing surgery to remove
the cancerous part within me – expelling it, as the dream suggested.
If I didn't do it quickly I would be hurting my family by letting the
disease spread further.'

The tidings the dreaming intelligence brought were urgent and
frightening, and so it might have used the symbol of an old admirer
to cushion the shock. Unpleasant facts are more palatable when told
by someone who cares for us.

It is interesting to note that nothing in the dream actually pointed
to a medical problem – it was only Manjula's gut feeling during the
course of her dream and on her awakening that made her believe that
the dream carried a warning. Unfortunately, events also proved her
right.

Besides warning us about imminent illnesses, dreams signal our
return to health as well. Slowly, among the unpleasant images of loss,
impairment, and weakness, new elements arise. Although negative
dream content may continue for sometime, positive images signal
the beginning of our return to health. The two may intermingle for a
while.

Those who have undergone surgery may have dreams of meat
being chopped, or blood oozing – a symbolic depiction of surgery.
Immediately after a hysterectomy a woman dreamt of being raped by

strangers, characterizing the sense of violence inflicted on the body. However, within these violent dreams a different image may occur indicating recovery. Hippocrates put it succinctly: 'New objects indicate a change.'[33]

Patricia Garfield shares a few examples of dreams that arise as healing begins. The dreamer may see a beautiful view from a window, or green grass, lush fields, blossoming trees. He or she may walk into a new house, find new clothing or a restored watch. The birth of an animal or the growth of plants could also be metaphors of healing. Dreams where a car crash is prevented, or of manoeuvring a car successfully over a hazardous road, could well be metaphors that express the dreamer's returning sense of control over life. In other healing dreams a revered or wise person may be giving advice, or the dreamer is being hugged and held by someone he or she loves – symbols of feeling supported and accepted.[34]

Manjula Mehra, as mentioned earlier, had a radical hysterectomy to contend with. She also underwent two cycles of chemotherapy. Six months later she was due for her cancer marker test, which would determine whether the cancer had been arrested or not, when she had the following dream:

> *Some ruffians are chasing me and I'm running to save myself. The ruffians overtake me and pull at the shawl I'm wearing. The tug-of-war is so intense that at one point I feel I've lost the battle. Suddenly, I manage to extricate myself and escape. A great sense of relief floods me as I look at the shawl and find that it is totally intact. I had feared it would be torn or damaged, but it is whole and in one piece.*

The shawl symbolizes Manjula's body (many religions refer to the body as the raiment or clothing of the soul) and this raiment is being ravaged by ruffians, like the cancer ravaging her body. The initial part of the dream relives the trauma of the invasion of cancer and surgery from which she tried to escape. The tug-of-war was intense, and at times she felt she had lost the battle.

As we saw earlier, the woman who had a hysterectomy dreamt of rape, while Manjula dreams of ruffians violating the integrity of the body – powerful symbols of how these women felt, and what they had to come to terms with. In Manjula's case, however, in spite of her encounter with the ruffians or cancer, the shawl or the body is intact. The symbols of wholeness, of lack of damage, are embedded within the dream as pointers towards healing. Despite the earlier ravages, the dream reassured her that her body was moving towards recovery.

A few days later, the cancer tests confirmed this. The cancer marker in her blood had dropped from 390 to 10 (30 is considered the normal count). As Manjula said, 'The confirmation of this dream brought the bounce back into my steps.'

Depending on the dreamer's religious preference and cultural background, Aesculapius, the Greek god of healing, appears in many forms in dreams. He may be a helpful figure in a dream, a guru, a god, or a goddess who has a positive emotional significance for the dreamer. A powerful dream figure may signal the turning point of an illness.

Ritu Gambhir developed a cancerous lump in her breast at the age of twenty-five. Despite the initial shock she remained full of youthful hope as she resumed the care of her three-year-old daughter and two-year-old son after the operation. Five years later a persistent cough led to lung X-rays, where cancerous patches were found, and a bone scan revealed that the cancer had begun to gnaw at the bones as well. Waves of despair overcame Ritu, as the autumn of life seemed to engulf her even before spring had been fully lived. She began chemotherapy, but three cycles later she felt much worse. She couldn't get out of bed, a persistent nausea overwhelmed her, and the weakness in her limbs was frightening. Another CT scan revealed that the cancer had increased. She was just not responding to the chemotherapy.

It was at this point that a strong feeling entered Ritu, that she must fight the disease for the sake of her husband and their two small children. She had no idea how she was going to do this. She said, 'I did not even know whether it was possible to alter the course of a deteriorating disease like mine. But I felt I had to try. For the first time I truly prayed to be given a few years to bring up my children.'

Meanwhile, her doctors decided to alter the course of treatment and administer Texol and Carboplatinum injections. Once again she was back in hospital. At dusk one evening the doctor adjusted the drip and said, 'You may feel a bit drowsy.' He then gave the injection and left her alone. Drifting between sleep and wakefulness she dreamt:

The saint Shirdi Sai Baba is standing near my bedside. I try to get up, to touch his feet, but find I do not have the energy to do so. I lie back and bask in his presence, which brings me an overwhelming sense of joy. Peace surrounds him as he smiles at me, and with utter tenderness he passes his hand over my head and then blows on his palm as though he was blowing away something invisible. He continues to stand by my bedside and then I fall into a deep dreamless sleep.

'When I awoke,' Ritu said, 'my first thought was that Baba came and gave me time. He blessed me and blew away my illness. I will improve now.'

Strangely enough she did. Whether it was the change in medicine or the blessing of Shirdi Sai Baba, the much-revered Indian saint of miracle healing, she couldn't tell. Significantly, his appearance in her dream and the remission in the disease occurred almost simultaneously. From being bedridden she began moving around, gradually resuming the care of her children, returning to a more or less normal life. A year later the CT scan showed no increase in the cancerous growth.

For both Manjula and Ritu, their dreams brought faith, hope, or the human ability to inadvertently tap something deeper through suffering. Though their dreams were healing dreams, for them they were actually far more than that.

Bernie Bell's troubles were not as serious as Manjula's and Ritu's, but her experience is a clear-cut example of a dream portent followed by an exact unfolding of events:

I'm lying in bed and have been bleeding for three days. I don't know where I am bleeding from. A black cloud settles over me as I see blood all around. The doctors hover over my bed and are shocked that the bleeding is so profuse. After a while the cloud lifts and the peering, anxiety-ridden faces of the doctors suddenly appear calm as one of them says, 'There is nothing to worry about. It has passed.'

A few days later Bernie began to bleed profusely from the nose. The bleeding wouldn't stop. To find the cause, doctors performed all kinds of tests, but they found nothing. True to her dream she bled for three days and then as suddenly as it had appeared the bleeding stopped spontaneously. The attending doctor said, 'I think the problem is over. We do not know why it happened, but you are fine. You can go home tomorrow.'

Bernie recalled, 'When the bleeding stopped I felt the problem had passed, for in my dream the doctors had first looked worried and then calm – just like it actually happened.'

No doubt the exact problem area was not highlighted in the dream, even though the symptom of bleeding was. However, inbuilt in the dream was the reassurance of healing. Now not all dreams are as clear-cut as Bernie's. So the question remains: How do we differentiate a psychological dream from one that is warning us of an upcoming illness?

We may take a cue from the ancient wisdom of Hippocrates, who said that if the pattern of our dreams changes suddenly from our regular dreams to those that are dramatically different, then we may presume that we are being alerted to an unusual occurrence. He suggested that we give special attention to dreams that contain excessive or deficient heat and moisture, like dreaming of the earth being scorched, great fires raging, or drowning in water. Although these ideas may seem strange to us now, modern-day researchers have, for example, observed dreams of drowning among heart patients whose water retention is excessive.[35]

Garfield shows us examples of how dysfunctions in the body appear in dreams: A stairwell painted pink, covered with scratches could depict a sore throat. A dreamer impaled on a sharp pole in the anus could suggest haemorrhoids, while the dreamer's house being on fire could point to peptic ulcers. Images of the dreamer drowning in yellowish, dirty water could suggest bronchitis, a man holding the world standing on the dreamer's chest could point to pneumonia, and being shot or wounded in the stomach could be an attack of appendicitis.[36]

Kasatkin's research carried Hippocrates' point further by stating that we all have distress dreams, but those caused by illness are longer in duration and often persist throughout the night. Images of war, fire, blood, and corpses, if they persist, may have a warning element to them. We should take note of recurrent dreams that highlight particular body areas. For recurring images suggest not only persistent patterns of thoughts and emotions, but also recurring sensations in the body.

Chapter 19

DREAMS OF MORTALITY:
IS DEATH OUR ONLY DESTINY?

Merely, thou art death's fool;
For him thou labour'st by thy flight to skim,
And yet run'st toward him still

William Shakespeare

*I*n the Indian epic Mahabharata, a *yaksha* (nature spirit) asks Yudhishtra, one of the principle characters, a series of sphinx-like questions as a precondition for drinking water from his lake. These concern metaphysical speculations on death and mortality. One of the questions is: What is the greatest wonder in this world? Yudhishtra answers: Day after day people enter the Temple of Death, yet those that are left behind watch this spectacle believing themselves to be permanent, immortal. Can anything be more wondrous and puzzling than this?

We often witness the presence of death in life, but we are barely cognizant of it when a plant dies or when we encounter the carcass of an animal along the road. Death begins to register with the demise of a pet, and much more intensely with the passing of a loved one. Yet, we seldom think of death and dying as a personal reality.

This unfaced and obscure fear has darkened the whole subject, leaving people puzzled when their dreams centre on the theme of death.

They could have dreamt about their own death, or of losing someone emotionally close to them, and they wonder whether such dreams have an ominous meaning.

If I were asked to identify any particular class of dreams that interests people the most, I would say it is dreams about death. In an effort to understand them I have divided death dreams into three broad categories. Firstly, there are dreams in which a living person dies. Most of these dreams are what I term as *psychological* death dreams, although a few of them may be precognitive or augur an impending death. Usually these dreams should not be taken literally as harbingers of death, unless there are some very strong indications of this, which are discussed later in this chapter. In the second category of dreams, the dreamer sees dead people come alive. These I call *bereavement* dreams. Such dreams come after the death of a loved one. In the period of grief the emotional loss is accompanied by a disturbed dream life, and frequently the deceased person lives on in the dreams of the survivors. The dreamer yearns for the deceased, and agonizes over his or her departure.

In the third category of death dreams someone dead also appears, but the difference is that there is a tactile quality to the dream and the dreamer strongly believes that an actual contact has been made with the deceased. So strong is the belief, and there were more than just a few such dreams, that I simply could not sweep this category of dreams under the carpet; I could not ignore their belief by considering it as merely altegorical or delusional. If precognition is accepted and researched, then we must also be able to discuss these dreams. Let us call them *visitation* dreams.

This is a very broad categorization and an overlapping can occur, leading to a great complexity in understanding a dream concerning death. Take, for example, a dream I had more than twenty years ago:

> *I see my mother-in-law standing in front of me, dressed in a white saree. She says, 'I just came to say goodbye.'*
>
> *I walk with her a distance, and then we encounter a tunnel. I know I cannot enter the tunnel but my mother-in-law does. As she goes into the tunnel she waves, knowing I cannot follow. My last recollection of her is of a white saree-clad figure becoming more and more hazy as she disappears into the tunnel.*

This I learnt is not a very unusual dream; in fact, similar dreams – of entering a tunnel – are commonly reported. Apparently no actual death occurs in the dream, but many elements and symbols point towards it – a white saree, the traditional colour of mourning in India; a tunnel, connecting the living world to that of the dead. My mother-in-law can access the tunnel, while I am denied entry: only they enter it whose time has come. If this is not a death dream then how may we interpret it?

A dream referring to death is often indicative of a psychological process the dreamer may be undergoing. The dead person dreamt about may depict an aspect of the dreamer's psyche, a habit, or a fault that may be dying. It could be drawing attention to significant events such as retirement, losing a job, moving house, or the collapse of a close relationship. At a subtler level, it could represent the death of feelings or the death of hope, or it could indicate the need to let go of some old, outmoded image of oneself and create room for a new one.

I was living in my Teacher's hermitage when I had this dream. It came at a stage when I was finding it very difficult to relinquish the ways of the city for the rural life that we were now leading. This dream could thus have been alluding to the death of an old way of life. My mother-in-law could then be interpreted as representing another part of myself that was moving ahead into a changed lifestyle. Since the farming life was unfamiliar to me, the dream symbolized it as a tunnel – an area of darkness. The dream could then have been cautioning me to leave my city persona (symbolized by 'me' in the dream) behind in order to cope with the changed circumstances.

Meanwhile, other events brought new dimensions to the dream. My mother-in-law, unfortunately, had been diagnosed with cancer. Having undergone a radical mastectomy, it was now discovered that the cancer had spread to her lungs. When I had this dream she was going through a particularly difficult round of chemotherapy. Given this, one would be inclined to treat this dream not as a symbolic one but as a literal one. Research has shown that many of us dream of the departed saying goodbye to those who survive them. Thus, could this dream be treated as a bereavement dream? A mother, aware that her end was imminent, had wished to bid farewell to her son. We will discuss this type of dream in greater detail later. For the moment it should be stressed that Rajeev's mother was still alive, and I couldn't treat my dream as one of bereavement.

Commenting on the dreams of dying people, Marie-Louise von Franz, the Jungian analyst, said that these 'are not about death, but generally about a journey. They have to get ready for a journey, or they have to go through a dark tunnel and be reborn into another world.'[1] My dream has all these elements – journey and tunnel – indicators of the impending transition we call death. There was one difference: *journey* dreams come to dying people, and the dream had come to me and not Rajeev's mother. As I mentioned earlier, we could say that knowing of her impending death she had 'come', but not finding her son open to such communication, she did the next best thing – say goodbye to his wife. However, I couldn't treat it as a typical visitation dream because she was alive when I had the dream. At best it could be treated as a prognostication – it would certainly be a more rational explanation than believing that she had actually 'come' to say goodbye! Subsequent events proved that the dream-dictated indication was correct. My mother-in-law succumbed three months later to cancer, which had by then spread to her brain.

I have intentionally related this dream to show the difficulties of understanding death dreams, and the number of issues that came up in the process. They can be treated as a psychological indicator of an emotional process; or as bereavement dreams attempting to help us accept the reality of the loss and thereby work through the grief; or, in a few rare cases, they could be a visitation where contact with the departed, at some level, is established.

Death dreams activated by a psychological process are best exemplified by 'Vidya Sagar's' dream. I met her at a friend's house where she recounted her dream to me:

> *I am standing outside an operation theatre and suddenly the surgeon comes out and says to me, 'I am sorry, your husband has died of a heart attack.'*
>
> *I am stunned, disbelieving the news. I don't even cry because I feel so numb.*

'I woke up feeling very anxious. I hope it doesn't signify any bad news?' Vidya asked, a tinge of nervousness still lacing her voice.

'No, I don't think so,' I said. 'But I wonder what provoked the dream. Any recent ill health that may have caused you to worry?' I asked, trying to eliminate the most literal rendering of the dream.

'Thank god, no,' Vidya said.

Vidya had lived for over ten years in a large joint family that included not just her husband's parents, but also his two brothers, their wives, and children. They all shared a common kitchen and the inevitable tensions that arise with it. Vidya felt that her husband shouldered the maximum responsibility in the family business, but was not given due credit for it. She had been trying to persuade him to move out of the joint family to a house of their own. Finally, her husband agreed to talk to his father about their move. She was horrified and utterly bewildered when she learnt what her husband had said to his father: 'I know there are tensions in the house, but I don't want to move out. Basically it's the women's problem, not ours.'

The dream symbol of the dead husband was a potent one, for in its folds the dreaming mind had encapsulated a phase in their relationship. The hope of a new life, a home of her own, and the desire that her husband's loyalty would primarily be for his nuclear family instead of the joint family 'died' when she heard his reaction. The emotions most prominent in the dream were of numbness and shock, a very close echo of Vidya's emotional state. It is fairly apparent that Vidya's dream about her husband's death was in no way foretelling it.

Besides our physical death, we encounter emotional, mental, and psychological 'deaths' in the course of our lives, which dreams often mirror. In fact, dreams rarely foretell death by a direct allusion to it. If death is indicated in a dream, then it is generally couched in symbols, rather than a straightforward portrayal of the person dying, like in Vidya's dream. A precognitive death dream may centre around funerary or mourning symbols, which, it must be emphasized, tend to be culture-specific. For example, the Christian colour of mourning is black, while for the Hindus it is white – white being the preferred colour of bridal attire in the West. Also, the dream need not be couched only in *memento mori* (reminders of mortality), but can be dressed in other symbols. To the psyche, death is a transition and not an ending, thus it is seen variously as a journey, a crossing over, a barrier, a tunnel, an hourglass, the stopping of a clock, a wall (death being the great barrier), white birds, flower-filled villages, a dead tree, and other such images. However, it is important to remember that this does not mean that every time you dream of, say, a wall, it represents the death of someone. It is largely a question of having a feel for such dreams. It is probably safer, and more often correct, not to interpret a dream as an indication of death, unless many elements suggest it.

Our dreams not only depict someone dying, but, under certain circumstances, they bring alive a dead person in a strange reversal of reality. People are perplexed by such dreams. It is not surprising then that a dream about someone who has died is likely to be remembered with a sense of wonder. These dreams fascinate us, but they also torment us deeply; we are never sure whether we are actually communicating with the departed or not.

A balding, bespectacled man in his late fifties approached me in the library where I write, and whispered, 'May I talk to you about something?'

The man looked down at the floor gravely, recollecting his thoughts, and said: 'My dead father has come twice to me in the last week.'

Left unsaid was that he had *dreamt* of his deceased father. He was in a quandary. His dream must have been too real for him to simply ignore, and yet his rational side didn't know how to understand it.

I tried to calm his troubled mind by asking in a matter-of-fact manner, 'And what does he say in the dream?'

'That's the problem!' the man exclaimed. 'He just stands at the foot of my bed and keeps on looking at me.'

'What is the expression on his face?'

'It's as though he wants to say something to me, but is not able to.'

This is not a very unusual dream to have after bereavement. One half of this gentleman believed that he had seen his father's ghost and the other half was afraid that he might be hallucinating. My suggestion that it was a normal bereavement dream helped him to relax a little.

'How long ago did your father ...?'

'Three weeks. He died in his sleep. Our family physician said it was a silent heart attack.'

'What do you think he wants to say to you?'

'Probably, just goodbye. We could not manage that with the suddenness of his death. We had dinner together the previous night and the next morning he was no more,' the man said softly.

Many causes for regret haunt us when someone close to us dies, especially if the death is sudden. Death has such a finality to it that if we are to accept the parting as real, then some form of closure is required. In these situations a dream such as this one can be very effective in the healing process.

Many of the people I met reported similar dreams after bereavement. These dreams of dead parents, spouses, siblings, uncles, aunts, and friends never quite leave the dreamer. Outwardly the survivor is forced to confront the death, but inwardly the psyche is still dealing with the emotional trauma, and dreams reflect the process of bereavement. Studies have shown that after the death of a significant person in our life our dreams go through various phases, depending upon the stage of mourning, the recentness of the loss, and the nature of the death. Researchers describe at least three phases of mourning.[2]

Initially there is *numbness*, which is characterized by shock or denial of the death, where the bereaved person usually feels that the events are unreal. A phase of *disorganization* follows, in which there is emotional chaos, including grief, anger, fear, guilt, or anguish. Restlessness and a desire within the survivor to somehow emotionally locate the deceased are paramount. The survivor feels distanced from life; many questions arise, and he or she gropes for answers. In the last phase of *reorganization* the survivor slowly learns to cope with an environment where the deceased is absent, readjusting him or herself to this absence, and treasuring memories of the departed. He or she is now able to emotionally reinvest in life again.[3]

This does not mean that everyone's season of grief registers in such clear-cut stages; often they oscillate between them. Yet in each of these phases certain characteristic dreams emerge, as Patricia Garfield has outlined in her paper on 'Dreams in Bereavement'[4] from which I generously quote.

Immediately after the death of a loved one, when the survivor is dazed, a typical class of dreams is experienced, which Garfield calls *dying-again* and *alive-again* dreams. Their purpose seems to be to help in the acceptance of the loss. In this phase, dreams often reflect the deceased once again suffering the symptoms that caused the death. Equally common are dreams that suggest the reverse, those in which the deceased is alive and the survivor is surprised to see him or her. Frequently the death is explained away as a mistake.

Mrs 'Sharma', a sixty-five-year-old widow of an army officer, recounted her dream:

I walk into the house to see my husband sitting quietly on his favourite armchair, smoking his pipe and reading the newspaper as he normally did. I run to him overjoyed that he is alive. I am full of questions, which I ask with machine-gun rapidity: Where have you been? What took you so long? Why did you not try to contact me? I am not really interested in his answers, but repeatedly go on saying, 'Thank God! Thank God! You are back.'

During the dream, she was overjoyed to find her husband alive, believing that some sort of mistake had been made. I have often wondered whether these alive-again dreams intensify the sense of loss when the dreamer awakens. For a brief 'real' moment the departed one is alive again, but does this not reopen the wound every morning? It seems not. Mrs Sharma told me that she looks forward to sleep, in case he comes again. Perhaps the psyche needs to gradually digest the finality of the separation, and to momentarily believe that the beloved is alive again somehow helps in the acceptance of the parting.

Like alive-again dreams, dying-again dreams may also assist the dreamer in accepting the reality of the loss. They revivify the trauma of the person's death, highlighting the suffering and the symptoms that caused it, either faithfully reproducing them or exaggerating some aspects.

> *My husband is not able to breathe. He clutches his chest. I run to call the doctor, but no one answers the phone. I grow frantic and try to put him into the car, but suddenly there is blood everywhere – on my hands, on my clothes, on the car seat. I try to feel my husband's pulse, but his hand begins to shrink and I am filled with panic and despair. I feel he will die before we reach the hospital.*

This is the dream of a woman whose husband died of a heart attack. Actually there was no bleeding as portrayed in the dream, but the trauma of the death, with all its horror, was dramatically being replayed. Our dreams, by re-enacting the event, help us to come to terms with what the waking mind finds difficult to endure. When there is no movement towards the resolution of grief, dying-again dreams may continue for a long time.

Once the period of numbness wears off somewhat, the survivor will in all likelihood experience a phase of chaotic emotional responses. There are intense feelings of regret, confusion, incompleteness, which dreams then help express. My library acquaintance's dream fits very neatly here. Patricia Garfield calls them *saying-goodbye* dreams. This type of dream appears to bid a final farewell, irrespective of whether it is initiated by the survivor or the deceased. It may signify the end of the disorganized phase and the beginning of the bereaved person's return to everyday life.

Dr 'Toshi Talwar''s husband died of an ulcerated intestine, largely due to errors made by the doctors operating on him. Dr Talwar had watched her husband die in considerable pain, leaving her, in her late twenties, with their four-year-old daughter. Besides the anguish of losing her husband, she had to deal with the anger she felt towards the doctors who had operated on him. Added to this was her own sense of helplessness in being unable to save her husband despite being a doctor.

Six months later, on the eve of her birthday, she saw her husband in a dream: 'It was the same smile, the same look that he had in life, and he said to me, "You think I could forget your birthday?" Unlike my last memory of him, when pain had ravaged his face, in my dream he looked younger, without a trace of pain. In fact, much to my surprise, he looked totally at peace. He hugged me and then said goodbye. I was so happy to see him that I awoke with tears in my eyes.'

Dr Talwar's dream meant a great deal to her, for she had an inexplicable sense of having met her companion. The birthday greetings, his being at peace, and saying goodbye were all important stages in her accepting that which had earlier seemed impossible.

'The incident did not end with the dream.' Her eyes still held the wonder of that encounter even though she was much older now. 'Not only did he remember my birthday, he also sent me a gift!'

By a very curious turn the cheque for her husband's life insurance policy arrived the next day – on her birthday. It is very easy to dismiss such events as mere coincidences, but does it explain such matters more intelligibly? For Dr Talwar, it was immensely reassuring: her husband had not deserted her.

Telephone dreams, like saying-goodbye dreams, have a strong impact on the dreamer. Here, instead of meeting the deceased, the bereaved person dreams of receiving a telephone call from the dead, or of making a call to the deceased person. In both these kinds of dreams they talk about what is happening to the other. In another variation of the same theme, there is communication through a letter, and usually it is the deceased who writes to the survivor.

Another category of dreams characteristically appears as the survivor begins to adjust to the changed environment and journeys on to the last stage of mourning. Garfield calls these *young-well-again* dreams.

Deepa Nag's mother died of cancer. For months what was uppermost in Deepa's mind was the suffering her mother had undergone in the course of the illness. Yet Deepa, a year later, dreamt of her mother looking radiantly beautiful and much younger than when she had died.

Many of my family members are gathered together. We are in a garden where the table is set for tea and we are all waiting for my mother to come. She finally arrives, with flowers in her hair, the way she wore them when she was young. Her smile is so happy and free that I run and embrace her. As I walk her towards the tea table I am very conscious that she has come from afar for a short time.

Such dreams produce a very positive feeling in the dreamer. The general feeling of health and vibrancy in the dream helps the dreamer feel that the deceased is well and at peace. There are many variations to this theme. In some, the deceased comes and comforts the survivor by saying, 'Don't worry, I'm fine.'

The survivor may also receive advice about mundane matters. In some instances the departed can also criticize the living or strongly commend an action that the survivor is contemplating. The British writer Virginia Woolf had an ambivalent relationship with her father, both admiring him and resenting him for his treatment of her sister. Four years after his death, she dreamt of showing her father the manuscript of a novel she had begun to write. Her father read her work, snorted, and dropped it onto a table. She awoke melancholic and discouraged.[5] Garfield calls these *approval-disapproval* dreams.

Another class, *advice-comfort-gift* dreams are among the most pleasant for the survivor because it helps him or her accept the reality of death, while still feeling that communication with the dead person is possible. They signal the survivor's return to 'normal' life. The grief is greatly eased and there is a sense of comfort. Sometimes this is depicted in the dream as receiving a gift, which could be the teaching of a skill, as in the case of William Blake who was greatly aggrieved on his brother Robert's death. We touched upon this dream earlier: Blake dreamt that Robert appeared and taught him an innovative method of engraving.[6] Blake did try out his brother's suggestions and found they were an ideal way to inexpensively engrave his illustrations.

When someone dies, besides the acute sense of loss and separation, there is an urgent need to know what has become of them. Where have they gone? Have they been reduced to nothing, or are they living in another place or another kind of life? We must emotionally 'relocate' the deceased if we are to reinvest our energies back into life and to our new environment, which is now bereft of them.

Sukhvarsha Roy was forty when she had lost not one but both her parents in quick succession. Although she was at an age at which the world expects you to bear with equanimity the loss of your parents, for Sukhvarsha, and many others like her, it wasn't so simple. The days went by but the anguish did not recede. The normal demands that life made on her did not fill the vacuum left by the loss of her parents. Grief overwhelmed her. It was when she was at her lowest that Sukhvarsha had this dream:

> *I am sitting under a banyan tree that has a cement block around it. Somebody comes up to me and hands me two leaf plates on which are two* ladoos [sweetmeats]. *Then the person says, pointing to the sweets, 'This is your father and this is your mother. Now, eat.' I begin to eat, thinking of my father and mother.*

The dream seems to have a macabre element: she is being asked to eat her parents! An odd dream, indeed. But for Sukhvarsha it became a turning point. The symbolism of the dream spoke to her more convincingly than any advice offered by friends and family. Reflecting on the dream she felt that she was being urged to come to terms with the death of her parents. She needed, as it were, to ingest the experience. To accept it. Acceptance does not happen by discursive reasoning, but is the result of an internal shift in perception. The dream was nudging her towards making this transition.

As Sukhvarsha went through the ups and downs that accompany any process of resolution, she had another dream:

> *I see my mother come towards me with the gentlest of smiles. In her hand is a sunflower, which she lovingly gives me. The image then fades.*

The way her mother smiled and the gesture of giving a flower was so characteristic of her that Sukhvarsha felt that what she had witnessed in her dream was no mere symbol. Her earlier dream was about the acceptance of her loss, but this one convinced her that her mother was well and their connection was still unbroken.

This emotional relocation of the deceased is dependent on our cultural beliefs. Throughout history and across the globe, most cultures have believed in survival after death in some form or another. The progression after death to another kind of life is also taken for granted in most religions. The belief that something survives death is based on the supra-temporality of the soul. This is not to be confused with the Hindu-Buddhist belief in reincarnation. The Semitic religions do not believe in rebirth, but they teach that the soul journeys in the afterlife to Heaven or Hell. Hence all manner of ceremonies are prevalent for the dead. Mass in the Catholic Church is said to be for the benefit of the soul, which is something apart from the body.

It is only modern-day rationalists who question an afterlife – even though science can neither support nor refute their claim as the afterlife has not been investigated in order to comment on it. However much the sceptic within us may eschew the belief in an afterlife, when confronted with the death of a spouse, parent, or any loved one, even the most rational amongst us, irrespective of the religion we follow, will feel the need for some ritual that honours the onward journey of the departed soul.

May we then not ask what happens to the life that once animated the now dead body? What happens to the human consciousness that once shaped the living human being? There is an intangible, living, conscious component to human life; does that disappear after death? For those who consider consciousness to be merely an epiphenomenon, an outgrowth or by-product of the body's enzymes and proteins, this question is irrelevant. However, not every one subscribes to this belief. For those who believe otherwise, further questions arise. If some part of us survives the death of the body, then are these two phases of life and the afterlife mutually exclusive, so that there is no possibility of communication between them? Or is the demarcation we call death a veil through which we can sometimes glimpse the other side?

Is it possible that the people whom we have loved, and who are no more, can visit us through the medium of dreams? For most of us today the appearance of a dead person in a dream would be understood to psychologically represent an aspect of the dreamer's own psyche. The dreamt figure would be treated as a symbol of an internal process that is seeking resolution. This kind of dream is thus not considered a visitation, and probably Sukhvarsha's dreams would be seen as symbolic expressions to aid in her healing process. However, should all dreams about dead people only be interpreted at a purely psychological level? There are many cases where the belief in visitations from dead relatives cannot be easily dismissed.

Colonel Surinder Sikand's mother suffered a coronary thrombosis and lapsed into a coma at the age of 52. On the tenth night of her coma, he dreamt:

> *Strangely I find my mother sitting on my bed and she says, 'I'm going Surinder. My time is up. But I am concerned about your father. Please look after him after I am gone.'*

Surinder Sikand awoke, switched on the light, and, rousing his sleeping wife Sarla, pronounced, 'Mother has gone. She is no more.'

Half an hour later the phone rang to confirm the news of his mother's passing.

Surinder reminisced: 'I think she was concerned about my father and how he would handle life without her. They were very close to each other.'

'You believe she came to tell you to look after him,' I ventured.

'What else could it be?'

Silence filled the room as we realized we were treading on unknown ground; a terrain where personal experience and belief is all the proof there is to map the way.

'Did you somehow know she would never come out of the coma, so that the dream was more of a confirmation than a visitation?'

'Yes, we knew her condition was critical. But I knew that on the previous night too. Why didn't I have the dream one night earlier? Was it not rather coincidental that I dreamt about her more or less at the exact time of her death? Her "coming" and then my father immediately confirming her death over the phone is uncanny.'

Besides Colonel Sikand's own conviction I also knew that his dream did not fit into any of the categories of bereavement dreams. Initially it seemed to be a straightforward case of a saying-goodbye dream, except that he did not know his mother was dead, so the question of bereavement did not arise. It looked as if we were in the same dilemma as with the dream I had about my mother-in-law entering a tunnel. Then we tried to take recourse to precognition to detract from the possibility of visitations. Since the dream and his mother's demise were roughly concurrent, precognition may not be that appropriate an explanation. Perhaps telepathy may be a more plausible one. But does that make it more rational?

However, if we grudgingly concede to visitations, then we are seized with a further difficulty: Who is it that visits? The soul? Or is it the person without the body, but complete with personality traits and memories, as was apparent in this case? Surinder instantly recognized his mother. More than that, she seemed very much the same person as she was in life: Her affections, primarily for her husband, were still clearly evident as they had always been throughout her life. So another mysterious aspect about such visitations is that the dead seem to live on as more or less the same people we knew them to be when they were alive. Their personality, with its memories, affections, and inclinations, seems to exist somewhere, except it is not entombed within a visible body.

This became even more apparent when Surinder's mother made another visit soon after. His father, Dr B. K. Sikand, was a tuberculosis specialist, who after having trained in England had headed the Lady Linlithgow Tuberculosis Centre in New Delhi.

'His mother *came* one and a half months later to Mr Goel,' Surinder's wife Sarla informed me.

'Who is Mr Goel?' I asked.

'He was the accountant at the TB Centre. He dreamt that Surinder's mother told him:

In the large steel trunk which has all the blankets and quilts, under the green quilt right at the bottom, there are a thousand rupees which I had saved. Could you inform Dr Sikand about this money as I had never told him or anyone else about it?

Mr Goel mentioned the dream to Dr Sikand. The old man became emotional and immediately went to the store adjacent to the kitchen to open the steel trunk. Narinder, his younger son, seeing that his father was getting rather upset, tried to distract him by saying, 'Daddy, you know that Mother was not the kind of person who could save money. She enjoyed spending it, and tucking a thousand rupees under some quilts seems not only out of character for her, but impossible.'

Dr Sikand was not to be stopped; he opened the trunk and started hunting for the money. Barely had he gone through the top three or four layers when Narinder intervened: 'There is nothing here. You believe a mere dream! Why are we upsetting ourselves by going through with this?'

Narinder managed to persuade his father to leave the storeroom. None of them really believed Mr Goel's dream, except Dr Sikand. Narinder did not let his father search the trunk again, and it seemed that the matter had ended. Evidently not, for old Dr Sikand was biding his time, waiting for Narinder to leave town. He then insisted on taking Surinder's wife Sarla back to the storeroom and to the large trunk.

Sarla felt a little uncomfortable that her father-in-law's loss had made him vulnerable enough to act upon Mr Goel's dream in such an insistent manner. Yet she felt compassion for him – for his grief, for his restless search for anything connected with his wife. She found herself in the storeroom with her father-in-law, lifting the heavy lid of the trunk.

'I still remember the moment I opened the trunk,' Sarla recalled, 'and how the smell of dried neem leaves, which my mother-in-law used as an insect repellent, hit me. The trunk held layers of blankets and quilts. Oddly enough a strange expectancy filled the room as I began lifting the quilts out of the trunk, to reach the lower layers. When I neared the bottom layers my father-in-law gently placed his hand on my elbow and said, "Please, let me check."

'Daddy*ji* paused when he uncovered the last layer to reveal a green velvet quilt. He looked at me and said in wonderment, "Exactly as she said!" I stood there amazed. Mr Goel couldn't have known this! Daddy*ji* lifted the quilt first from one side, then from the other. Sure enough there was a wad of currency notes of all denominations. I was stunned. Very slowly he took the money out and began counting it. It was a thousand rupees!

'What can I say except that for more than a long moment we both stood there, in utter silence. I did not know what to think. Had my dead mother-in-law actually come to Mr Goel? There was no way Mr Goel could have known about the money. And why just him? None of us knew anything about the money. She had sent a straightforward message to her husband, and he had acted upon it.'

It seemed as if Sarla Sikand's last remark was aimed at my persistent rebuttals that began with 'Could it be that ...' I must confess that all my objections were silenced. My only question was, 'I wonder why she *came* to Mr Goel, and not to a family member?'

'I don't know. Except that she often relied on Mr Goel for small errands like getting a plumber, buying train or movie tickets, paying bills ...'

'You mean as in life so in death,' I said.

'What do you mean?' Colonel Sikand asked.

'Your mother depended on Mr Goel for some of the nitty-gritty details of everyday life. Probably, this money fell under the same category.'

The 'message' of Mr Goel's dream can hardly be thought of as symbolic since the money was found exactly as Mrs Sikand had told him in the dream. It would have been a symbolic dream only if the money had not been found. For the Sikands, the reality of hard currency notes was evidence of her 'visit'.

It is said that the memory of anything we see or hear, even subliminally, is stored in our brain. The theory of cryptoamnesia suggests that the number of flagstones that paved the walk I took with my mother at the age of six still resides somewhere within my mind. Nothing we experience in life either directly or indirectly is ever forgotten. Like in a computer, everything is stored in our memory as data to be accessed when needed. Could dreams be one mode of spontaneous access? In Mr Goel's case there was no means by which he could have known that Mrs Sikand had saved this money and hidden it in the trunk. So from where did his dream access this information?

It may be pointed out that this is not an isolated dream; there are many other such accounts. Perhaps the earliest reference to a visitation dream is from the *Iliad*: the spirit of the slain Patroculus appears before Achilles and demands burial.[7] There is also the curious account of two dreams in a letter written by St Augustine (in 415 AD) while arguing for the possibility of having experiences after death when the physical senses no longer function. Gennadius, a physician of Carthage, was troubled by doubts about the existence of the afterlife. In a dream he had, a youth of 'remarkable appearance and commanding presence' takes him to a city where Gennadius heard, 'sounds of melody so exquisitely sweet as to surpass anything he had ever heard'. On the following night the young man appeared again in a dream and enquired whether Gennadius recognized him. Gennadius replied in the affirmative. The youth then asked whether the events of the previous night had occurred in sleep or wakefulness. Gennadius said it was in sleep and further confirmed that his body during those moments was in bed. The youth investigated further: 'Do you know that the eyes in this body of yours are now bound and closed, and that with these eyes you are seeing nothing?' Gennadius replied, 'I know it.' The young man concluded by asking, 'What then are the eyes with which you see me?' When Gennadius could not answer, the youth then explained what was happening: 'Asleep and lying on your bed, these eyes of your body are now unemployed and doing nothing, and yet you have eyes with which you behold me, and enjoy this vision, so after your death, while your bodily eyes shall be wholly inactive, there shall be in you a life by which you shall still live, and a faculty of perception by which you shall still perceive. Beware, therefore, after this of harbouring doubts as to whether the life of man shall continue after death.'

We can only presume that after this dream Gennadius no longer doubted the afterlife.[8]

Frenny Bilimoria was in her late fifties when I first met her, but her peaches-and-cream complexion exuded youthfulness. Above where she sat was a rather compelling portrait sketched by her, in which the interplay of light and shade was a reminder of the persisting dualities of life – all co-existing at any given moment. And that is exactly how

Frenny viewed what happened to her daughter, Nilufer. She was full of life, bursting with ideas, when suddenly, at the age of eleven, she was diagnosed with juvenile diabetes. Overnight Nilufer's life changed. She was put on a carefully controlled diet and had to take three insulin injections a day.

Perhaps the acute deprivation in her diet made Nilufer opt for a profession in which she could at least cook food, even if she couldn't eat every kind of it. She went to England to train as a chef, and began working in a hotel. After she had turned twenty-four, Nilufer came home to her parents for a month's vacation. It was a very difficult holiday for both Frenny and her husband; they sensed a marked deterioration in Nilufer's appearance. It turned out that her eyes and legs were beginning to get affected by the diabetes.

It was then that Frenny had a dream. Her father had died some time earlier, but that night she felt he was communicating with her. Recounting her dream she said:

> My father was shouting at me. Not out of anger but as though to make me hear something. He said, 'We will lift Nilufer very gently. There will be no pain. Salome [their maid] will find her at nine o'clock on Sunday morning.' There was a short pause, and then he repeated the message, 'Remember we will lift Nilufer very gently. There will be no pain. Katie [Frenny's sister] will come from Calcutta and it will all pass very peacefully.'

Frenny said that the sentences were spoken like a telegraphic message and though her father was shouting to make himself heard, he enunciated the sentences as though he was explaining them to a child.

Frenny woke up very depressed and tried to banish the dream from her thoughts. Nilufer was a little worse than before, but her condition didn't seem life-threatening. After a few days Frenny told her husband the dream and said, 'I don't know why I am feeling so depressed. There seems to be no reason. Nilufer is here, she isn't that unwell, and the important thing is that she is happy. She's going out every day and enjoying her holiday, so I don't know what my dream is about.'

Nine days after Frenny's dream, on a Saturday night, Nilufer had gone out with her friends to a restaurant and returned late. Frenny and her husband came back later than Nilufer. Frenny peeped into her daughter's room and was reassured to find Nilufer sleeping peacefully.

Frenny's taut body relaxed as she gently closed Nilufer's door. The next morning Salome, the maid, went to wake Nilufer and found that she would not wake up.

She rushed to Frenny saying, 'Nilufer *baba* is just not getting up.'

A chill shook Frenny's body as she ran towards Nilufer's bedroom. They touched her and found her cold. There was no pulse and she looked lily-white. She had died in her sleep. Frenny looked at the time. It was a few minutes past nine o' clock.

Frenny said that despite the devastating grief they felt, amazingly there was a sense of quiet and peace surrounding Nilufer's death, even at the funeral. Nilufer had slipped out of her body in the most peaceful way possible.

This is a very startling dream, raising many questions. Did Frenny's father actually visit her and warn her about his granddaughter's imminent death, or could this be taken as a precognitive dream in which Frenny saw a future event, and the father was just a symbol who conveyed the message? Even if it is a precognitive dream where does this kind of information come from? And by attributing precognition to it, we are still in the realm of the inexplicable.

I asked Frenny, 'Do you think your father actually came across the barrier that separates us, the living, from the dead?'

She replied without any trace of doubt, 'Of course! Yes.'

'You don't think it was a dream telling you about a future event in which your father appeared without actually being there?'

'No, not at all! He was there. I cannot give you any other explanation, besides my own feeling of certainty that he was there. I will, however, say one thing: The people we love can and do come from the other side. They come because they feel we need them. I believe that many times, before actually appearing, they give signals to tell us they are nearby. It could be something typical of that person – a way of coughing, their footsteps or a scent of their favourite perfume ... enveloping you suddenly. This time, my father didn't give any indication before he came in my dream. However, the way he presented himself was so characteristic of him. Haven't you said to someone, "That's typical of you," without being able to quantify what it is?'

In a visitation dream what the dreamer feels after he or she awakens is important. Frenny's absolute certainty that it was her father is hard to discount, since the feel, or sense, of an actual visitation is very different from a mere symbolic dream. Frenny felt that her father was shouting as though being heard by the living is not a simple matter, and it requires great effort to gain our attention, especially under such circumstances.

But why do the dead appear to us in dreams? After all, one phase of human existence is over, death has cast its veil, and the edict should not be tampered with by backward glances. Yet it happens.

With visitations, it isn't only unfinished business that brings the departed to us, as in the case of Mr Goel's dream, but equally a need to reassure the living of what has become of them. Sometimes they may come out of concern for us, in our hour of need, as did Frenny's father.

Some people believe that when a person is about to die, a loved one comes to help make the transition from this world to the next. If true, Nilufer would be assisted by her grandfather, and my neighbour's father by his brother. We will have occasion to briefly touch on this aspect in the next chapter. It is further believed that if we (the living) are open enough, we would be able to sense the presence of a dead relative or friend about a week before someone is about to die. True or not, this is what some believe.

In 1944, Edmund Gibson, a Michigan-born engineer and parapsychology researcher, attempted to answer the question of why the dead visit the living. He culled his 313 cases from the earlier work of London's Society for Psychical Research and published his findings in the journal of the American Society for Psychical Research. He concluded that on average the dead appeared unexpectedly, when the person was either asleep or thinking of anything *but* the deceased. And when a message of some kind was delivered, it was generally of greater importance to the dead person than to the living. Like in Mr Goel's dream, it seems that it was more the mother's need for communication than it was any living person's. This doesn't mean that everyone who has passed into the other world will try and communicate with the people they loved, despite our remembering them.

Some people, in an effort to personally confirm the truth of the afterlife, make a promise to a close friend that whosoever goes first will try to communicate with the person still living. Jung and a friend of his made such a promise. The friend died and apparently tried to make contact with Jung. Laurens Van der Post has given a detailed account of this experience in *Jung and the Story of Our Time*.

At some point or the other each of us has to face our own mortality and enquire whether our end is merely in the dissolution of the body, or whether we will survive its death. My own belief about this question is born out of the dreams I had on the subject. I share some of them in the next chapter. I cannot be sure whether these dream-born insights reflect reality. I leave that to the reader's discretion.

While the hemlock was being prepared, Socrates was learning a tune on his flute. It is said that his friends who were with him on his last day were bewildered by this, and asked him: 'What good will it do you, to know this tune before you die?'[9]

Perhaps we can respond to this by narrating the experience of Dr Jay Dunn, a British psychoanalyst. Dunn was attending a hospitalized patient, 'Margot', an elderly woman suffering the final stages of a terminal ailment. She reported to her doctor a dream whose metaphorical image is as simple as it is profound.

> *She sees a candle lit on the window sill of the hospital room and finds that the candle suddenly goes out. Fear and anxiety ensue as the darkness envelops her. Suddenly, the candle lights on the other side of the window and she awakens.*

That same day Margot died, and in Dr Dunn's words, 'completely at peace'.[10]

PART 5

THE DREAM:
A GATEWAY TO TRANSCENDENCE

There are more things in heaven and earth ...
Than are dreamt of in your philosophy.

William Shakespeare, Hamlet

Dreams have, indeed, often been regarded as the gateway into the world of
mysticism, and even today are themselves looked on by many people as an occult
phenomenon. Even we, who have made them into a subject for scientific study, do
not dispute that one or more threads link them to those obscure matters.

Sigmund Freud, 'Dreams and Occultism'

Chapter 20

DREAMS AND KARMA:
DO WE LIVE BUT ONCE?

'Many lives, Arjuna, you and I have lived,
I remember them all, but thou dost not.'

Sri Krishna in The Bhagavad Gita, (IV:5)

*T*hus far we have looked at dreams that are in one way or another connected to our waking experience, whether they belong to the psychological or phenomenological paradigms. However, there are some dreams that do not arise from memory alone, and nor are they explicable in terms of the dreamer's experiential framework. Sometimes our most terrifying and blissful experiences come from dreams, the heights and depths of which we have never experienced in waking life. These dreams are not explained by either the psychological or paranormal paradigms. They are not expressive of the dreamer's personal or external landscape, but reflect the relationship of the self to something beyond itself. At times they may provide glimpses of an eternal order. To perceive this order the senses are not needed; to know it, the mind is not required. It can only be intuited, and in doing so the images of dreams can reflect the interrelationship between human beings and their transpersonal origins. Such dreams release the dreamer from the clutches of analysis and discursive reasoning. The dream becomes a state of consciousness, an experiential epiphany that transports the dreamer to an altogether different level of being. It connects the sleeper to a sense of the sacred. These can only be alluded to as transpersonal dreams.

It could be said that my interest in the transpersonal dimension of dreaming was the result of the years I had spent in an ashram and the fact that the foundation of my dream life had been inspired by a *sadhu* (monk). My only justification in presenting this dimension is because many people have dreams that shine with great clarity and elevate the dreamer into a heightened state of awareness against which their everyday integration can only be considered banal. Surely such dreams cannot be reduced merely to threads of memory or habit.

Upon finishing the last section on visitations, I felt that I had reached a watershed in many areas of my life. On the book front, there was a sense that my work on dreaming was somehow incomplete. Its natural progression from the last section would take me into the realm of the great enigmas of human existence – death and the after-life – and their possible reflections in our dream life. In my personal life, too, I was at a crossroads. My efforts to hold on to what I believed was 'real' and meaningful repeatedly drew me back to the thought of living in the hills, to living as we had during our seven-year stay in our Teacher's mountain hermitage. There my inner search had found a meaningful expression in the outer life. I felt that city life essentially offered an outwardly turned existence, where my energies succumbed to being soaked up by and dispersed in inessentials. For long I believed that the quiet of the hills was its antidote, and that it would be more compatible with my aspirations. But however much I yearned for this move, something held me back.

The meanderings of my surface mind attributed my indecision to relocate to the hills to the lack of medical facilities there, even though we had made a similar move when we were younger without any such concern. Possibly, the middle years of life provoke questions about illness and death; the illusion of an always-healthy body – one of youth's naive assumptions – no longer holds. The scent of mortality, so to say, had begun to assail me. As it usually happens, an inner dilemma (thoughts about death) had affected an outer decision (to relocate).

It was around this time I was asked by my dream life: Who are you? I am referring to the last dream mentioned in chapter 2. Despite its metaphysical component, the question in the dream was not an isolated enquiry. It was directly related to the concerns of my life. At the time I was going through several transitions, both internal and external, and the dream, with its impeccable sense of timing, had brought together these different strands and directed my gaze towards what was most essential in them. As I grappled with the import of the dream, I began to see that my ability to seek an answer to the dream's question would also affect my book and my personal life situation. The dream was a reminder that my manuscript would remain incomplete if it did not address what I considered fundamental to dreaming: the dream as a gateway to the transpersonal beyond. If the individual survives the annihilation of death, then in what realm and in what form does he or she exist? These and similar questions are beyond the purview of the two paradigms of dreaming already enunciated. Another dimension of dreaming, which penetrates the after-death state and soars to a domain even beyond that, would need to be explored.

My dream also made it clear to me that my decision to move to the hills would remain a mere outward shift; it would at best represent a restless, nomadic tendency, unless it was informed by the search for my essential identity. The dream had sought an inner clarification from me: What should be the focus of my life. That, it tacitly said, would depend on who I perceived myself to be. Is my 'I' restricted only to memory and experience – my ego – or is there an essential core beyond that, towards which the dream was drawing my attention – an essential core, which, if identified with during one's lifetime, would hold true even across the barrier of death? It seemed the dilemma confronting my life was more about 'how' I lived than 'where' I lived.

There was yet another reason that sparked my interest in transpersonal dreams, and especially those concerned with death and the after-life. A close friend and an aunt were diagnosed with cancer and I was confronted with the possibility of losing both of them. All my hidden doubts about illness, pain, death, and annihilation surfaced as I watched them battle for their lives. Adding to my confusion was the strikingly different responses they had to their illness. My friend, in her forties, was a bewildered hostage at death's door. My aunt, on the other hand, seemed to meet death with a measure of peace and fearlessness, as though death was a natural corollary to life, its fair and just progression. It then struck me that perhaps we have a choice when challenged by death, which depends on what we perceive death to be – a termination or a cross-over to another kind of existence. If the former, then death becomes the dreaded and feared unknown; otherwise death becomes a punctuation mark, a pause before continuing on to another state.

It was a strange phase of life where one way or another, through my writings, personal circumstances, and current relationships, I was being confronted by the same question: annihilation and survival. I thus found myself reading books on dying, on near-death experiences, and on life after death.

Sometimes dreams can give us hints that may help build a conception of this enigmatic transitional realm – the border between life and what lies beyond it. I had two dreams that seemed to have a bearing on these issues, and they influenced my beliefs about death. I include these dreams because they seemed to posit an inexplicable continuity between the question of dreams of death discussed in the previous chapter and transpersonal dreams that will be dealt with in the next chapter.

I now telescope time so that the dream I recount appears as an immediate consequence of my ruminations on death, whereas it actually occurred after a prolonged period of interest in the subject.

My dead body is lying on a cement floor in the crematorium. All my relatives and friends are standing around it in a circle. I am looking down on my body, which is covered with a white sheet with marigold flowers strewn over it. The priest lights the funeral pyre, starting at my feet. I tense up, anticipating the pain I will feel. But nothing happens as first my feet catch fire, then slowly the rest of the body is in flames. There is no feeling of discomfort. I am amazed and relieved, suddenly realizing that this is what death is – the painless burning of a body from which the person standing outside it can be as unaffected as the one lying on the funeral pyre.

After the cremation, all my relatives leave and go back to my aunt's house. I follow them, but they are totally unaware of my presence. Rajeev and my parents are sitting on the dining table. I can feel Rajeev's grief, as I can see that tears are still streaming down my mother's face. The others have resumed the business of living as the television is switched on and preparations for the evening meal begin. I realize as I stand there what a one-way street death is. It's curious that I seem to know each person's state of mind, even feel their grief or the lack of it, but for them I no longer exist.

Soon the conversation casually gravitates towards how my nephew's birthday should be celebrated, as though death and birth are a natural continuum. I just stand there uncertainly, not knowing whether I belong to them or what to do next. Through this confusion I suddenly have a moment of great clarity. I realize someone has come

to meet me. Someone who understands my plight. Who? A relative,
a friend, or a guide, I don't know.

This dream can be read at many levels. A purely psychological reading would focus on the prevailing conflict of my life, the dream imagery being responsive to my dilemma: should we move out of the city and live in the quiet of the hills? The anticipated discomfort of the priest torching my body in the dream may have symbolized my worry that my withdrawal from city life could prove to be painful. The dream contradicted that belief, showing me that I could 'die' to my former life, without regrets; that my new world would meet me with different, though unknown, kinds of stimuli.

Another way of viewing this dream could be that it was counselling me about the pain and fear attendant to death and dying. In fact, my first perception when I awoke was to treat the dream as though it was a reality: this is what it feels like to die. Given my intense preoccupation with the subject of death, a phenomenological exploration of it by the dreaming mind would not have been inappropriate. The dream was showing me that death in itself is not painful. What is painful is its anticipation.

What stood out was the accompanying realization that the body was quite separate from the entity that observed it. What burned on the funeral pyre was in no way 'me'. I still existed as I viewed what was happening. I was very much the same personality I knew myself to be, only now without a body. This dream certainly seemed to have stepped beyond a psychological exploration. But by which paradigm should we understand this dream? I was certain it did not contain a prophetic message about death – someone else's or mine. Was my dream then an out-of-body experience (OBE), a paranormal dream similar to the experiences of Dr Trehan's two patients who had exteriorized from their bodies while under anaesthesia for surgery? Later they had recounted the conversations between the doctors and nurses in the operation theatre.

OBEs are not a rare occurrence, as established by researchers after conducting a survey in Britain in 1966, in which more than 400 people responded with authenticated accounts.[1] In fact, the OBE has been known all through recorded history and there are marked similarities in this experience among people who are culturally very different. It is generally a once-in-a-lifetime experience, seemingly brought about by 'accident'. Sometimes great stress – physical or emotional – brings it about. In many cases it has been known to simply happen during sleep without the person being aware of what may have caused it. It is usually one of the most profound experiences of a person's life, even radically altering existential beliefs.[2] Prominent is the feeling that 'I am not the body'; a 'second body' (known as the *etheric* or *astral* body of the occultists, and the *parasomatic* body of modern researchers) becomes temporarily separated from the physical body and serves as an independent vehicle for consciousness. This experience often leaves the person with a strong conviction that something survives the death of the body.

It must be highlighted that during a normal dream very rarely is there any sense of separation from the physical body, whereas the OBE is always typified by this. In my dream I was released from my physical body, even though the senses and other perceptions continued to function. However, I cannot treat my dream as an OBE, since in an OBE the facts that the person recounts can be later authenticated. In contrast, my supine body was in no way actually lying in or near a crematorium, but in a comfortable bed. Nor was I in any kind of medical emergency that my dream was describing. It merely replicated the sensation of an OBE. If my dream cannot be treated as a paranormal one, I would like to take it at face value as a description of the phenomena accompanying death.

It may be argued that I am reading too much into this dream, that my personal proclivities had made me understand the dream in this manner. But my dream is not unique; its theme is fairly common. So let us briefly look at another dream. The following is the dream of 'Rahul', a forty-nine-year-old man who had recently suffered a heart attack, but had recovered after undergoing an angioplasty procedure:

> *I feel my body stiffening; my limbs are getting rigid, the breathing is getting harder and difficult. All of my family members are lamenting that I am dead despite my repeatedly telling them, 'I appear dead but I'm all right.'*
>
> *But no one can hear me. I can see and hear everything but cannot move my arms or legs. I am not frightened at all as I am sure that I am alive. The family takes my body and puts it on a pyre to burn it. Soon the body turns to ashes and I feel freed. I jump off the pyre and tell everyone, 'Why are you crying? I'm alive. I never was dead.'*

The dream appears to reflect the contrary strands running concurrently in his life. On the one hand, he had resumed work and was attempting a return to normalcy. On the other hand, his immediate family's continuing concerns about his health were a reminder that his life now was not what it had been earlier. This divide may not have been merely an external tug-of-war, but an indication that emotionally he still had to come to terms with his brush with death. However, the dream need not be restricted to this obvious dichotomy. Given his circumstances it may not be inappropriate to attribute a deeper significance to his dream.

There is a great similarity between his dream and mine. The dreamer feels alive despite the destruction of the body, and in both dreams the family is unaware of the presence of the survivor of the body. Rahul never shared the deeper impact that his dream may have had on him. Perhaps, like my dream, it may have reminded him of a profound existential truth – that death only applies to the annihilation of the body.

The power of my funeral dream was such that it refused to be straitjacketed within an external or internal experiential reality. It seemed to be closely linked to my earlier dream that asked me: Who are you? Both dreams seem deceptively straightforward – one raising questions about the identity of the person and the other about the survival of that person. Despite their surface simplicity, they are dreams whose main concern is to address the larger mystery of my own individual existence – its origins and its cessation. These dreams subtly questioned my beliefs. The earlier dream led me to a search within myself to find my essential identity, while in the funeral dream I witnessed for the first time an essential separation take place between what 'survives' and what 'dies'. This second dream provided a snapshot of a state that contradicted my assumptions about death and the after-life – a state I could have never imagined. To me, the message of the dream was more philosophical than psychological or even phenomenological: Shorn of fear, in one powerful moment, I was shown that 'I' am not only the body.

Anyone who has experienced an OBE or a dream like my funeral dream is certain that it not only seems to answer questions about pain, suffering, and death, but more significantly it opens up the road to something else – the after-life. If 'I' am not the body, then the death of the body does not mean that 'I' am also extinguished. The 'I' remains even after the body is destroyed. My dream had somehow provided me with a personal confirmation that there is survival after death. In an intense and forceful dream moment I felt I had actually died, and simultaneously surveyed life from the *other* side. Admittedly, it had offered me only a momentary glimpse, but it seemed to beckon me to explore what becomes of the 'me' that survives bodily death.

This dream was not a bizarre concoction of a sleeping psyche preoccupied with death; in fact, my dream was an almost exact replication of the description of death in the ancient Indian text of the Puranas: 'When he leaves the dead body, for a brief moment he weeps, and then he turns his face away and departs [alone].'[3] Then, 'his relatives turn away and depart ... but the karma he has done goes with him'.[4] In my dream, I was in a subtle body (*linga sarira*), which the Puranas believe is the carrier of karma in the transfer of merit from one life to the next.[5]

It could once again be objected that this unverifiable statement on the dream was fashioned by my cultural and religious background. But I was struck by another dream dreamt by a Westerner who did not share my cultural proclivities. He was a man well steeped in the rationalist tradition, yet he gave enormous credence to his prolific dream life. I am referring to C. G. Jung and the amazingly objective account of his experience with death in a dream he had while he was critically ill. The power of his dream, or vision, call it what you will, lies in furthering our understanding of what possibly happens to us at death and even beyond that.

> *It seemed to me that I was high up in space. Far below I saw the globe of the earth, bathed in a gloriously blue light ... My gaze was directed chiefly towards* [the Mediterranean] *... I could also see the snow-covered Himalayas, but in that direction it was foggy or cloudy ... I knew that I was on the point of departing from the earth.*
>
> *... I had been standing with ... my face to the north. Then it seemed to me that I made a turn to the south ... A short distance away I saw in space a tremendous dark block of stone ... It was floating in space, and I myself was floating in space.*
>
> *I had seen similar stones on the coast of the Gulf of Bengal. They were blocks of tawny granite, and some of them had been hollowed out into temples. My stone was one such gigantic dark block. An entrance led into a small antechamber. To the right of the entrance, a black Hindu sat silently in lotus posture upon a stone bench. He wore a white gown, and I knew that he expected me. Two steps led up to this antechamber, and inside, on the left, was the gate to the temple. Innumerable tiny niches, each with ... small burning wicks, surrounded the door with a wreath of bright flames.*

As I approached the steps leading up to the entrance into the rock, a strange thing happened: I had the feeling that everything was being sloughed away; everything I aimed at or wished for or thought, the whole phantasmagoria of earthly existence, fell away or was stripped from me – an extremely painful process. Nevertheless, something remained; it was as if I now carried along with me everything I had ever experienced or done, everything that had happened around me. I might also say: it was with me, and I was it. I consisted of all that, so to speak. I consisted of my own history, and I felt with great certainty: this is what I am. 'I am this bundle of what has been, and what has been accomplished.'

... There was no longer anything I wanted or desired. I existed in an objective form; I was what I had been and lived. At first the sense of annihilation predominated ... but suddenly that became of no consequence. Everything seemed to be past; what remained was a fait accompli ... There was no longer any regret that something had dropped away or been taken away. On the contrary: I had everything that I was, and that was everything.

Something else engaged my attention: as I approached the temple I had the certainty that I was about to enter an illuminated room and would meet there all those people to whom I belong in reality. There I would at last understand – this too was a certainty – what historical nexus I or my life fitted into. I would know what had been before me, why I had come into being, and where my life was flowing. My life as I lived it had often seemed to me like a story that has no beginning and no end ... and many questions had remained unanswered. Why had it taken this course? Why had I brought these particular assumptions with me? What had I made of them? What will follow? I felt sure that I would receive an answer to all these questions as soon as I entered the rock temple. There I would learn why everything had been thus and not otherwise. There I would meet the people who knew the answer to my question about what had been before and what would come after.

While I was thinking over these matters, something happened that caught my attention. From below, from the direction of Europe, an image floated up. It was my doctor, Dr. H. ... framed by a golden chain or a golden laurel wreath ... he is coming in his primal form ...

Presumably I too was in my primal form, though this was something I did not observe but simply took for granted. As he stood before me, a mute exchange of thought took place between us. Dr. H.

had been delegated ... to tell me that there was a protest against my going away. I had no right to leave the earth and must return.[6]

The moment Jung heard this, the vision ceased. Subsequent events that transpired raised this dream/vision to prophecy. It would take three weeks before the ailing Jung turned the critical corner. Curiously, the day he sat up in bed, Dr H. took to his bed and never treated anyone else again. He died of septicaemia. The doctor had appeared in his primal form in the dream, naked of all earthly embellishment, an indication that he was about to die. In the language of the dream, Dr H. would enter his rock temple to learn the answers to the fundamental questions that had woven his life around his personality.

The prophecy did not end with Dr H. The vision also foretold Jung's recovery. Jung was also in his primal form – a candidate for death – but he was recalled back to earth. This dream/vision, however, cannot be restricted to a premonition; it is significant at many other levels. Since it describes Jung's death experience it is therefore open to a phenomenological exploration. Notably, it is also a near-death experience (NDE), for it marks the stages in the process of dying. We do know that, medically, Jung was critically ill, hovering between life and death. That this was an NDE was also substantiated by the nurse attending to Jung, who afterwards told him, 'It was as if you were surrounded by a bright glow' – a phenomenon she had sometimes observed in the dying.[7]

Many allusions in this phenomenological account alert us to Jung's deteriorating condition. At the beginning of the dream, Jung found himself high above the earth, at the point of departure from it. Life ebbing from his body is symbolized in his onward journey away from earth in a non-corporeal form – a literal rendering of 'something' leaving a dying body.

Other symbols and indications that this is a death experience abound in his description. High up in space he made a turn to the south, perhaps indicative that Jung, the patient, had taken a turn for the worse and was slipping towards death, since south is often considered the direction of death.[8] In the vision, the discarnate Jung then encountered a rock temple, the temple of death. Had he entered it, his death was certain. Later we will return and discuss the symbolism of the temple and the Hindu yogi. Fortunately for Jung, just as he was about to enter the temple he was recalled to earth by Dr H.

Furthermore, his approach to the temple was characterized by the feeling that *'everything was being sloughed away ... Nevertheless, something remained.*' This symbolizes that the personal identity of the man called Jung was being stripped – the concerns and characteristics distinguishing his life were being taken away. The dream also informs us that contrary to our belief that death represents annihilation, despite this sloughing, something does remain.

The dream is replete with symbolic descriptions of death, similar to Rahul's and my dreams, which also attempted to portray the death process. However, Jung's vision penetrates deeper into the death experience than either Rahul's or mine. Ours was but a surface view, and justifiably so. Death was hovering over Jung, while we were asleep in our beds. More significant differences are that we had dissociated from the body, but we had not shed our earthly concerns. Both of us still identified with our recent life, suspended in what seemed to be a transitional zone. My perplexity as to where I should go after the body had been burnt allowed me to sense a presence that might guide me onwards. Probably, my experience could not go beyond this preliminary stage because there was no physical distress to the body. Perhaps one has to be sufficiently close to death for the dreaming mind to have the freedom to dwell on it. Jung's vision glosses over this initial stage by a cursory allusion: '*at first the sense of annihilation predominated*'. He transcended this first shock and the subsequent withdrawal from earthly concerns by realizing that this apparent sense of annihilation was of no consequence. It seemed a thing in the past, and so it had to be. All this clearly indicates that the dream had taken him much further into the process of death.

The power of Jung's dream resides not only in its description of the death process, but also in what it leaves unexplored. The dream can be viewed as a significant interior encounter. Without actually dying, Jung reached the outer-most limit of life and stood in the awesome presence of death to encounter its mystery. The imagery can be understood both as a metaphorical as well as a literal account of what happens to the individual after death. What is remarkable in this account is that it is not expressed through culturally comfortable symbols, but is abounding with imagery that is at variance with Jung's Western paradigm.[9] It may be interesting to explore the imagery in greater detail to discover what can possibly remain, or can happen, after the personality of the discarnate Jung has been peeled off.

It is significant that the dream resorts to predominantly Hindu imagery, culminating in the image of the Hindu yogi sitting in the lotus posture outside the temple, waiting for Jung. We will take recourse to the dreamer's associations to India to suggest how these images may be interpreted. Jung believed that it is only in India that the conception of the hereafter exists, 'formed by the ideas and images centring on reincarnation'.[10] To him, the idea of rebirth is inseparable from that of karma.[11] The dream then seems to be centred on the Hindu conception of the hereafter – rebirth and karma. The Hindu is appropriately dressed in white, the colour of mourning in India; this, after all, is an exploration of death. But more importantly, the images of the temple and the meditating yogi alert us to the fact that what Jung was about to encounter within the precincts of the rock temple would be akin to the Hindu conception of life after death.

We find confirmation of this theme by amplifying Jung's personal associations to the imagery. The rock-cut temple reminded him of the temple in Kandy, where the Buddha's tooth is preserved. Teeth are the hardest part of the body – extremely difficult to decay or dissolve, and often long outlast the death of the body. The temple therefore alludes to something old and sacred within the individual that continues to exist, long after the body dies. The granite of the temple is another allusion to something ancient that endures. The temple, it seems, has preserved a relic from Jung's past, similar to the Hindu view that reincarnation preserves the experiences of past lives. This preserved past does not dissolve, but continues to exist, as karma, somehow carried through the barrier of death; it survives and exerts its pull through lives.

If we were to understand the dream as making a statement about rebirth and karma, then Jung's feeling that everything had been sloughed away would represent the stripping of his surface personality. Naked of the identifications and preoccupations that had clothed the life just lived, the discarnate Jung would enter the temple. Importantly, despite feeling bereft of his personality, Jung realized that something essential remains – perhaps that which transfers the karmic imprint from one life to the next? *'It was as if I now carried along with me everything I had ever experienced or done, everything that had happened around me ... I consisted of my own history, and I felt with great certainty: this is what I am.'*[12]

This awareness of his own history obviously alludes to something far beyond the concerns of his present life, since those had already been shed. Unless this history comprised experiences gathered earlier, in lives lived before this one, his statement would become meaningless. Possibly, what remained with him represents the essence of all his past lives: the condensed historical learning of all that he had garnered through the chain of lives he had lived before, including the present one. Each oil lamp encircling the temple door, perhaps, represents a life lived; an ever-growing garland at the altar of death and rebirth.

As Jung approached the temple he felt certain that if he entered its illumined room he would meet all those people whom he belonged to in reality. This is quite an intriguing statement. The key to the dream rests in comprehending who these people could be. He was equally certain that they would finally solve the enigma of his existence: *'What had been before me, why I had come into being, where my life was flowing.'* These are basic existential questions that have puzzled human beings about their life from time immemorial. Yet Jung felt that the people in the temple would unravel these mysteries for him.

Jung was called back to earth before he could enter the temple, and so we can only speculate who these people were to whom he felt he belonged and who held the answers to his questions. By dovetailing his feelings and perceptions with the symbols hewn by the dream, we can imagine what Jung would have discovered had he actually entered the cave-temple. Inside the illumined interior of the cave he may have found, not other people, but 'the animated images of his previous lives, seen as distinct personalities with whom he was strangely familiar, a "group soul" united in the search for the meaning of life'.[13] Each 'person' in that cave was the embodiment of a life lived before the life known by the name Carl Gustav Jung. The cave was, thus, the conclave of his collective past where he would finally meet all those erstwhile *people* that had been Jung in previous lives – what the Hindus call the *Sutra-atman*, the individual flowers threaded in the garland of lives. Understandably Jung felt a strange familiarity, a sense of belonging, to them. The incarnation known as Jung was reuniting in death with all those people who were in a way responsible for him being 'Jung'. In the past, the common search of these people had inspired them to send a *representative* to earth to find answers to the questions that perplexed them. He was that representative, as much as they represented him. Had he entered that illumined room he would have apprised them of all that had transpired in his life, which in turn may have raised fresh questions. Together, once again, they would decide to send yet another representative to earth to continue the search, just like the representative currently incarnated as Carl Gustav Jung had come to birth in this life.

Perhaps this is the reason why the discarnate Jung felt with such utter certainty that had he entered the rock-cut temple he would come to know 'what had been before me, why I had come into being, where my life was flowing'. In that cave existed the psychic and emotional patterns from his past that had impelled this life: the assumptions and thoughts that had preceded and influenced him; the reason why his life had taken the turns it did; the explanations for why certain questions had assumed importance; and finally how all this together contributed to shaping the phenomenal biography that was Jung. Viewed thus, Jung's remarks make complete sense: 'My life as I lived it ... seemed to have been snipped out of a long chain of events, and many questions had remained unanswered. Why had it taken this course? Why had I brought these particular assumptions with me? What had I made of them? What will follow?'[14]

We are given further clues that these 'people' represented Jung's previous lives through other dreams, thoughts, impressions, and associations of Jung. He describes an earlier dream:

> I was in an assemblage of distinguished spirits of earlier centuries; the feeling was similar to the one I had later towards the 'illustrious ancestors' in the black rock temple of my 1944 vision. The conversation was conducted in Latin. A gentleman with a long, curly wig addressed me and asked a difficult question, the gist of which I could no longer recall after I woke up. I understood him, but did not have a sufficient command of the language to answer him in Latin. I felt so profoundly humiliated by this that the emotion awakened me.[15]

Jung's correlation of this dream with the later 1944 vision of the rock-cut temple permits us to marry the symbolic imagery of this dream with the later vision. The assemblage of distinguished spirits may be equated to the conclave of people in the rock-cut temple. He also says that 'the bewigged gentleman was a kind of ancestral spirit, or spirit of the dead ...'[16] He goes on to clarify that these ancestors are also his spiritual forefathers. May we then treat them such that they signify not only his biological bloodline but the lineage of past lives that he had come from, and to which he was returning as its newest son in the vision of the rock-cut temple? On awakening from the above dream, Jung believed that by working on his book he would be answering the question that had been posed to him by the bewigged man in the dream. Does this not show that Jung perceived a direct connection between his life and his work, and the question? Just like the 1944 vision suggests a connection between his life on earth and the conclave in the rock-cut temple. The assembly expectantly awaited his arrival so that he could apprise them of the manner of his life. Jung further clarifies that the above dream's question had been asked in the hope and expectation that they (his spiritual forefathers) would learn what they had not been able to find out during their own time on earth.[17]

Later, when he wrote the *Septem Sermones ad Mortuos,* once again it was the dead who addressed crucial questions to him. Contrary to the traditional view of the dead being the possessors of great wisdom and knowledge, we see that the dead, out of necessity, have to rely on the living for answers to many of their questions. According to Jung, the souls of the dead seem to 'know' only what they knew at the moment of death, and nothing beyond that. Hence their dependence on those who have recently returned from among the living for receiving the answers.

The reader may feel that my imagination, aided by my Hindu upbringing, has got the better of me! In support of my position I can only quote another dream to which Jung attached a great deal of importance. Two months before her death, a sixty-year-old female student of his had a dream, which Jung penned down:

> *She had entered the hereafter. There was a class going on, and various deceased women friends of hers sat on the front bench. An atmosphere of general expectation prevailed. She looked around for a teacher or lecturer, but could find none. Then it became plain that she herself was the lecturer, for immediately after death people had to give accounts of the total experience of their lives. The dead were extremely interested in the life experiences that the newly deceased brought with them, just as if the acts and experiences taking place in earthly life, in space and time, were the decisive ones.*[18]

Just like the conclave (the selves of former lives) awaited Jung's return in the rock-cut temple to learn from him what had been left incomplete in their sojourn on earth, this dream also suggests that the departed eagerly hope to hear and assimilate the experiences harvested in the life of the recently deceased. Eagerly they await, in the illumined interior of the rock cave, the return of their representative. Each return to death's door is not empty-handed. It is rich with life's spoils that death not only acknowledges but is also transformed by. The absorption of Jung's experience may effect a reformulation in the gathering. Perhaps another lacuna will be perceived. In other words, the conclave, driven by their incomplete experience, will send to earth a representative who embodies the questions that mystify the group soul. Their questions, after all, can only be the compulsions of the life previously led by the representative, its karmic dictates. The people in the cave are the per-sonifications of his past lives; the temple, the preservation of his deeds – his karmic storehouse. On his return, the representative would be reunited with the repository of his karma.

Jung himself mused along similar lines: 'Have I lived before in the past as a specific personality, and did I progress so far in that life that I am now able to seek a solution? ...

'I could well imagine that I might have lived in former centuries and there encountered questions I was not yet able to answer; that I had to be born again because I had not fulfilled the task that was given to me. When I die, my deeds will follow along with me – that is how I imagine it. I will bring with me what I have done. In the meantime it is important to ensure that I do not stand at the end with empty hands.'[19]

It is interesting that Jung perceived the continuity of lives as a process of evolution, where the incomplete tasks of one lifetime become the enigmas and challenges to be taken up again in the next life, so that they can be addressed more fully. As Jung said, 'The idea of rebirth is inseparable from that of karma ... But if a karma still remains to be disposed of, then the soul relapses again into desires and returns to life once more, perhaps even doing so out of the realisation that something remains to be completed.'[20]

And possibly this is how the conclave in the rock-cut temple of death chooses a new representative. It confers with the past and acknowledges the present, and then decides what still remains incomplete in their collective repertoire. This becomes the *task* for the new representative. To illustrate,[21] let us presume that the last life of a particular individual had been spent as a university professor who, absorbed in a theoretical framework, had strongly felt the lack of practical experience. If this is a deep driving desire, then it may influence the professor and his group soul to choose for the next incarnation a representative who will gravitate towards a practical, hands-on kind of life. The professor may be reborn as a farmer!

Each life then becomes an exploration, a search for understanding of some facet of the questions left unanswered in earlier lives. For Jung sees karma and rebirth in terms of a 'motivation towards knowledge',[22] and that becomes the explanation for this life[23] and the causation for the next life. Death, he believes, asks us a categorical question and we are under an obligation to answer it.[24]

It is but natural to ask at this stage that if the representative had set forth with such clear-cut directions, how come, after birth, it has no memory of that task? Why does it seem that most of our life is a process of trial and error, a stumbling towards direction, a groping for meaning and understanding, rather than a determined course towards our goal?

Much earlier I had had a dream that I had put aside, thinking of it as strange and entirely out of context in terms of my concerns at that time. To start with I had treated it perfunctorily as a psychological dream, but having got no further in understanding it, I lost interest. Looking back I think the dream came before its time. My interest in the subject it pointed towards had not grown sufficiently for me to be able to grasp its meaning. Now when I was grappling with the subject of death, rebirth, and karma, the dream suddenly had a context in which it could be understood. Strangely it had a link to Jung's vision. How does the karmic repository of any individual dictate his or her life circumstances? What is the basis for this rebirth? Who or what determines what will be essential to the life that will follow? My dream also suggested a reason why we forget what we've come for even while everything in our life seems to conspire to help us remember our original intent.

The dream revolved around Uma, my mother-in-law, who had come in a dream earlier to bid goodbye, and had now been dead for more than ten years.

> She knocks at my door and beckons me out. We get into a car, which she is driving. We travel for a long distance till we hit a dirt track that has deep grooves made by a previous vehicle, and we find the going bumpy. We pass through countryside; on one side of the track are fields with tall sugarcane, while rice is growing on the other side. After a while she stops the car and points towards a sludgy, soft brown mass of mud on the road. At that moment, a country-made machine appears and starts to compact the soft mud into a block, and Uma says to me, 'This is how karma is crystallized into a definite pattern. Like this amorphous soft mud, our desires – though they may be unrelated to each other – are compacted, and this becomes a life, a destiny, the joys and sorrows of a particular human being. When soft and amorphous, it is nothing; when compacted and solidified it becomes a particular set of circumstances – karma.'
>
> Next, I see a potter on his wheel, and it strikes me as he is throwing a pot that whatever one's karma is, it is finally just a role. Nothing more than that.

At first glance the dream appears odd, making a tenuous connection between the compacting of mud and individual destiny. However, on closer scrutiny we find the dream plainly centred on the theme of karma. The journey by car symbolizes the journey through life, which may leave deep grooves (of habit and compulsion) in its wake. Also, the grooves made by a previous vehicle (a past life) make the road bumpy, thereby making the present life a rough ride. The crops of rice and sugarcane are apt symbols of reincarnation and karma. Rice is planted twice, first the seed, which sprouts into a seedling, and then the seedling is replanted; it is thus a natural symbol for rebirth. In Hindu rituals and ceremonial oblation the importance of rice is also borne out by the fact that food is considered to be the basic medium for the transference of merit to the dead.[25] The ritual of *shradha*, performed for the dead, involves offering cooked rice shaped in a particular form (called a *pinda)* to transfer karma to the dead. The soul feeds not only on actual food (the *pinda*), but also on its own past experience – its karmic food. Sugarcane is a crop that yields multiple harvests, perhaps representing the idea that the harvest of karma is realized through multiple lives rather than in a single season. Unlike rice, which is planted as a seed, sugarcane is propagated from the cuttings of the parent plant. The tenors and tendencies borne from a life become the cuttings capable of producing another plant, another life. The fields on either side of the track are also a symbol of karma. The Bhagavad Gita calls the entire human body a 'field' (*ksetra*), and it informs us that this body ('field') is nothing but the instrument by which human beings are propelled towards their actions and corresponding results – good or bad karma. Fields in which crops are sown and harvested are mud fields, and 'mud' thus becomes a potent symbol for death and rebirth. Christians say: 'For dust you are and to dust you will return'[26], and the Koran has a similar equation between the body and earth when it states, 'Behold! thy lord said / To the angels: "I am about / To create man, from sounding clay / From mud moulded into shape."'[27]

Even though the body is destroyed at death, it is mysterious how a new body, given by a different set of parents, inherits the karma allotted to it from its previous lives. Puranic literature of ancient India establishes this karmic connection through a series of mediating elements. It states that 'at the time of the ejaculation of the semen, the *jiva* [incoming consciousness] united with the cause and enveloped and joined with its own karmas enters the womb. The semen and blood in their united form become an embryo in one day.'[28] Elsewhere it is said, 'At the moment of conception, the *jiva*, marked with all its acts and enslaved to passion and wrath, enters the womb by the following means: the sperm combines with the blood of the female and enters the womb to form the "field of good and bad actions".'[29] And it is also stated that semen, which gives birth to the body, is born from food.[30] And food is born from earth, thereby identifying the primary substance involved in the transfer of karma – 'mud'. In short, every image in the dream – the road, and the grooves in it, the crops, fields, and mud – all allude to and converge on karma and rebirth.

My mother-in-law symbolizes a wisdom born of a panoramic view of both states – life and death. The living do not know what happens after death, the dead at least do not suffer from any such confusion. She thus symbolizes knowledge about the after-death state and rebirth, which was otherwise unavailable to me.

Within this context, my dream's correlation between karma as compacted from one's past lives into this life and mud being briquetted into a block is really not such a bizarre statement. What the dream suggested was that the karmic residue is initially like an amorphous mass (of mud), without definite form or shape. This loose, formless sludge is then closely and firmly kneaded or compacted into a pattern imprinted on the life coming to birth. Similarly the first stirrings of life arise within the amorphousness of the fertilized ovum from which the human foetus is compacted, passing during its embryonic state through every form of organic evolution and finally to the crystallized consciousness of a human being. Death merely reverses this compacting, stripping away the physical body and its psychic raiment, and returning the person to the amorphousness of undifferentiated being. The ripple in the boundless ocean of existence whose waves are life and death has been quietened, and its momentary non-identification with phenomena is symbolized as amorphousness. All is quiescent, dormant, and calm. Then a yearning arises. The calm becomes a mist. Out of the myriad possibilities the yearning identifies with its past patterns, its past longings. And out of the mist a cloud of desire is precipitated. In the amorphousness a space has been delineated – a body of propensities has been generated. The paradigm for a new life, a new birth, has been chosen.[31] One step now remains – drinking the waters of forgetfulness. Then it re-emerges into life where it once again is compacted into a psychophysical organism within a womb. The strange portion of my dream could then indicate that we oscillate between an amorphous existence and a compacted material reality.

If we were to take the words spoken in the dream literally, then karma is not perceived as a retributive force but as the sum total of our strongest desires and inclinations. The doctrine of karma has been often associated with fatalism, the tightening noose of a blind law, under whose suffocating grip free will and opportunities wither. The iniquities, the injustices, the misfortunes one undergoes in this life are considered a direct consequence of some past misdeeds that are now catching up with us and demanding payment. My dream seemed to be outlining a different metaphysics of karma: there is no outward agency or entity that dispenses retribution. Instead, our choices, our needs, and deeds, our limitations and inadequacies, our unaccomplished tasks become their own 'retribution'. It suggested that in being reborn we ourselves choose our circumstances; they are not thrust upon us. What we deeply desire is what we become. The Brihad-Aranayaka Upanishad states: You are what your deep, driving desire is. As your desire is, so is your will. As your will is, so is your deed. As your deed is so is your destiny.

This dream perspective most certainly does not view the individual as a hapless victim of an implacable and unknown outward agency; what it proposes is that a person lives a particular life because it best reflects his or her strongest inclinations.

Karma is seen as a cyclic process through which personal proclivities of the current life – a person's *axis of inclination* – are preserved across the barrier of death and affect the choices exercised in the next life. The difficulty remains in apprehending how events from previous lives, of which we have no memory, can have a causal connection with the circumstances of one's current life. The psychological discovery that forgotten events of early childhood unknowingly continue to mould our behaviour later in life may provide an analogy of how forgotten experiences of past lives can continue to affect this life.[32]

Once again, it was Freud who discovered that all experience is recorded in memory below the threshold of waking consciousness, with only a small part of it normally available for recall in the waking state. But the record itself is virtually indestructible.[33] When it comes to our past lives, perhaps even death is not able to wipe this record clean, and adds its content to the karmic inscription of past experience. In the symbolism of Jung's dream imagery, the conclave imbibes the experience of the recently dead representative. And analogous to the Freudian discovery, out of this karmic storehouse only a small portion becomes available to bear upon the waking consciousness of the next life – a new representative is sent forth with another task.

This dream was probably providing a clue as to how karma is transferred from one life to another. Maybe at death, as Jung's vision evoked, the many individual desires pouring into various life concerns and interests are withdrawn – '*sloughed away*'. However, what remains with the person is the quintessence of that desire, which is now without its specific point of focus. To give a simplistic example: an individual may desire meaningful relationships and this urge is specifically directed towards the spouse, such that there is a unifocal preoccupation with marriage. Suppose the marriage proved unsatisfactory. Then at death the crystallized desire to find happiness through the spouse may fall away and sink back into its primal form, remaining as an inchoate urge to discover meaningfulness through the 'other'. Earlier sullied by its own potent need, it now exists merely as an amorphous longing, not necessarily involved with a specific person (spouse) or circumstance (marriage) through which it had once sought fulfilment. Thus the casting and crafting of desires, which, when expressed in life, may seem like intricate, ornate pieces of jewellery, at death melt down to their primary substance – formless gold.

It is not being suggested that at death the individual is resolved back into a single desire – there may certainly be more than one. What is being implied is that this desire (or desires) does not exist in a state of sharpened clarity, but in an amorphous manner. No wonder the discarnate Jung felt that though everything (personal) had been stripped, something (impersonal) remained. The sharply defined wants of personality had sunk back into a diffused state. What possibly gets stripped away at death is the whole preoccupation with one's earthly existence, as Jung's experience suggests. All the familial, social, and cultural skins we wore, the roles and relationships we identified with, our goals and aspirations, all disappear. What remains is the unqualified essence of the representative who had once set forth. The details of our earthly life – the suppressed rages, the unfulfilled longings, the ideals that allured, in short, all that held us in thraldom – are not present at that moment. What prevail are the strongest impressions and feelings left as the residue of that life. Only now they are bereft of specificity, or of any involvement with circumstances. What endures is an axis of inclination that the person takes to the rock-cut temple to confer with the conclave. Together they will redefine what needs to be addressed, perhaps not as a hard charter detailing the new representative's life, but again in a loosely defined agenda.

To illustrate, the scion of a business family may work throughout his life to put his personal stamp on the business he inherited from a successful father. He may want to streamline the various business divisions along new lines, an action that is resisted by the old guard. Let us say his goal was not fulfilled and he died consumed by this passion till the end. His life would be resolved along this axis of inclination.

When he takes birth again it is not necessary that he needs to be reborn into a business family to fulfil his earlier mission. He could be born into a poor farmer's family wherein he may have to argue and convince the elders of his family to plant new hybrid wheat on their meagre landholdings and adopt non-traditional farming techniques. The circumstances radically differ, but the challenge presented is quintessentially the same. In short, there is space within the broad agenda for the incarnating entity not only to succeed or fail in fulfilling his or her axis of inclination, but also to have the freedom to explore and discover unknown parameters.

My dream countered our speculation that the agenda of the Jungian representative is indelibly etched on him or her when he or she takes birth. Instead, it proposed that when the representative plunges into birth this task is but a dim and amorphous memory; the task has been more or less forgotten. However, despite its lacking definition, this task continues to exert a tenacious pull on the thoughts and circumstances of the individual, ostensibly from some hidden part of the psyche. When circumstances – events or emotions – concur with this 'inner' urge, the karmic intent of the person finds some sympathetic soil in which to develop and fructify – the amorphous mud of my dream becomes compacted.

This forgetting of the karmic task is not merely a convenient invention of mine. The Greeks visualized that the incoming soul had to cross the plains of forgetfulness and drink the waters of unmindfulness from the river (Lethe) as it journeyed towards birth, explaining why we have no memory of our former lives. Maybe the forgetting is important, for if that does not take place there would be an unbearable burden of memories that would prevent the current life from being lived as a new episode. The past, if not forgotten, would counterproductively intrude upon the present. The sacred Hindu text Brahma Purana (217.23-32) states that 'while in the womb, the embryo remembers his former lives and is thus subject to the twin tortures of chagrin for his past misdemeanours and *Angst* over the anticipated repetitions of his stupidity ... The embryo then resolves to make a better job of it this time; but like all New Year's resolutions, this one is short-lived, and at birth the *jiva* is deluded by the force of *maya* [illusion], so that he forgets his former lives.'[34] Other texts believe that 'the embryo remembers its many transmigrations, and it is distressed because of this one and that one, and therefore it becomes depressed'.[35]

The Greek conception of the soul's state as detailed by Plato in Book 10 of *The Republic,* the Vision of Er[36], supports other elements of my dream. It states that before taking birth the souls of the dead gather together to choose a *lot* (*kleros*), a portion of fate that somehow had represented or characterized that particular soul in the previous life. This lot is not allotted to them by a god or judge, but they are free to choose one from the lots available. My dream had suggested that this choice is guided by the residual desires from the last life. What a lot entails is clarified by going into the etymology of the Greek word *kleros*, which combines three closely intertwined meanings. It is (a) a piece of the earth (mud), which expands to mean (b), the 'space' that is your portion in the overall order of things, and (c) an inheritance, or what rightfully comes down to you as an heir.[37] The lot the soul will choose becomes its destiny compacted into a portion and a place in life that has been selected prior to birth. Plato calls it a *paradeigma* or pattern. My dream had made the bizarre statement that karma (life circumstances) is *compacted* like mud (earth).

Building on this Grecian conception of fate in his book *The Soul's Code,* James Hillman, currently a leading Jungian analyst, states that each of us is allotted a unique *daimon* before birth, and this daimon selects a pattern that is subsequently lived out in that individual life. Hillman understands this pattern to be an image that embraces the whole of a life all at once. This image, like Plato's lot, is chosen on the strength of an intuitive attraction: 'This is the one I want, and it is my rightful inheritance.'[38] This innate image carries with it an intention, akin to Jung's representative. The daimon guides us to birth, however, in the process of arrival we forget that image and believe we have come empty-handed into this world. But the daimon does not do so. It constantly directs you towards choices that are aligned to its innate intention.

Hillman convincingly demonstrates through the biographies of many eminent and famous people how their lives have been charted by invisible dictates; there is an unknown vision or ideal that 'calls'. Sooner or later this 'calling' unwittingly directs them to a particular path. For some this was a 'signal moment in childhood when an urge out of nowhere, a fascination, a peculiar turn of events struck like an annunciation: This is what I must do, this is what I've got to have. This is who I am.' For others, the call may not be this vivid or definite; it may have been more like gentle nudges in the stream in which the person drifted unknowingly to a particular spot on the bank. Looking back, he or she sensed that fate had a hand in it.[39]

The lives of extraordinary people display this calling most evidently. Perhaps they are extraordinary because their calling is simply more transparent than for us ordinary folks. Most ordinary people are less motivated and more easily distracted. Yet for both the ordinary and the extraordinary, the same underlying principles apply. Each person, including you and I, is born with a defining image, a personal uniqueness that asks to be lived, being already present in us before it can be lived – the design contained in the seed.

This only leads us to wonder whether Kavita Nayar, the painter we met earlier, was adhering to the wishes of her representative by answering its call to explore life through the medium of painting. We did witness that even though her conventional and unresponsive parents tried hard to stifle the impulsion of her destiny, she defiantly found ways to express its calling. One only wishes that her parents had not equated her doggedness with maladaptation; had they entered her imagination they may have realized that her non-conformance was a gift, the whisperings of her representative.

We are using the term *representative*, of course, because of our amplification of Jung's dream; other cultures have known it by other names. The Greeks knew the representative as *daimon;* the Romans as *genius;* the Christians as *guardian angel*; and the Egyptians alluded to it as the *ka*, or the *ba* with whom one could converse. The Romantics, like Keats, said the call came from the heart.[40]

This call is aptly exemplified in the life of Dr Sudhir Kakar, the well-known Indian psychoanalyst. Dr Kakar's great passion to explore the mind was compacted within him suddenly, at a signal moment, after what seemed like a long journey on a meandering path punctuated by vacillation and indecision. I rely on his 'Personal Introduction' in his book *The Indian Psyche* for the personal details of his life. We look to his life story as one biography that shows us how we carry within us a latent psychic idea, an urge, a specific purpose that gets compacted almost out of nowhere after what seems to have been an age and a half of confusion.

Sudhir Kakar graduated in 1959 with a degree in engineering. The choice of his career, like for other boys his age, was not decided by his talents and inclinations, but by the elders of the family. Since he himself could not express any preference for a particular profession, he acquiesced to their collective wisdom. Within this context the young man was sent to Germany for further training with the tacit expectation that he would return home to a job immediately after completing his training.

Kakar's calling obviously lay elsewhere, for he confides that his studies soon became a 'burdensome chore and though I did not know what I was going to do with myself, I was certain I was not going to be an engineer'.[41] He wrote to his father and told him about his dilemma; that he could not go on with engineering and instead wished to pursue philosophy. While his father appealed to his better reason and heavily enjoined on him his family duty, he was 'discovering the attractions of a West ... I learnt ... the slang German of docks and shipyards, full of interesting expletives. I learnt to dance the boogie-woogie and the cha-cha ... and took music lessons on the clarinet'.[42] Apparently he was not the 'driven' kind of student. After eight months of postal admonitions the family finally relented, but they felt studying philosophy was out of the question. The father and son eventually compromised on a degree in economics. However, this too was another impasse for Kakar. 'I studied economics as I did engineering, with half my mind and none of my soul. In my youthful affair with the world I needed passion and surprise; engineering and economics had neither.'[43] His disinterest notwithstanding, he completed his economics degree and after five years returned to India to the welcoming warmth of the family, and enrolled in the Indian Institute of Management at Ahmedabad as a research fellow in the faculty of Agricultural and Rural Development. Everyone, including the young man, seemed to have accepted his altered vocation, and the family now awaited his next logical step into marriage and family life.

Unknown to them, however, his daimon or representative was lying in wait for him. It would not let him settle down and kept him in a state of constant unrest. He travelled widely in rural India on work, interviewing people in villages, but his heart was in turmoil about what his direction should be. Mirroring the vacillation of his earlier student days, he lived in a swirl of contradictory pulls as he toyed with the idea of becoming a writer, of applying to film school, of packing his bags and going back to Europe. Once again ambivalence had entered the young Sudhir's mind, for we hear him musing: 'Should I marry one of the three girls my parents had so carefully selected for me ... or should I ... search for the great passion of my life?'[44]

But what was this 'great passion' and when and where had it taken birth? All that he had exhibited till now were amorphous urges and conflicting pulls. Conspicuously absent throughout was a compacted goal, a focus. Quite naturally his indecision left him and his family bewildered. 'They could not understand why, after I had had my way and done (or almost done) what I had so stubbornly wanted, I could not now settle down to a career and to the raising of a family; I did not understand it myself. I needed help to fathom the depths of confusion gripping my soul.'[45]

Such was his tortured confusion that Kakar confesses: 'I needed to understand the ambivalences of my desires, to unravel my tangled perceptions of the world and assess the realistic possibilities it afforded for the fulfillment of my wishes.'[46]

Destiny lying in abeyance stirred in the form of a chance encounter with Erik Erikson, a man who was well known in the field of psychoanalysis, even though at the time he was not the world-famous figure he would eventually become. Serendipitously, Erikson, researching his book on Gandhi, had rented Kakar's aunt's house. Kakar himself was living in an annexe of the compound. Unaware that his daimon was staring him in the face, Kakar writes: 'Caught up in my own youthful turbulences, I was unaware of Erikson's stature and in fact confused his name with that of Erich Fromm.'[47] In the evenings he would go over to visit Erikson at the main house and sitting companionably on the balcony, overlooking the Sabarmati river, they would talk about Gandhi and the people whose lives he had transformed, or just savour the silence. It is surprising that despite the fact that Kakar was suffering from an acute identity crisis and was desperate for direction, he did not ask the master therapist, who had invented the term identity crisis, to mentor him!

But then suddenly Kakar came to a realization: 'What I really wanted, I discovered, was a special kind of life of the mind which I believed psychoanalysis could give me. I wanted to be like him.'[48] This 'suddenly' did not mean a matter of months or weeks, but a few days, as the cryptic and significant webbing of circumstances that were to follow indicate.

Perhaps this is the signal moment of his annunciation. All of a sudden, out of nowhere, it seems, the young man, whose dalliance with life had bordered on fickleness, apprehended his call: what he wanted to do and become. His identity crisis suddenly vanished and his path stood clear before him. How and from where did this realization strike?

Could it have been that something forgotten had been recalled and given recognition?

By the time the realization dawned on Kakar, Erikson had already left Ahmedabad for Delhi, on his way back to the United States. Kakar was in a quandary. The train journey to Delhi would take twenty-three hours, by which time Erikson would have left India, and Kakar could not afford to fly. Out of the blue he had seen a ray of hope that could resolve his crisis, but equally suddenly it would now be swallowed by geographical distance. Then came a dramatic turn of events bordering on the miraculous. Once again destiny came to his rescue: the chief representative of the Ford Foundation was visiting Ahmedabad for a day and was returning to Delhi that same evening in his private aircraft. All Kakar did was to ask him for a lift. I am not going to dwell or elaborate upon the probability of a person travelling by private jet giving a ride to a research fellow just because the fellow has a sudden hunch about switching his profession. Kakar was granted the favour, and it was as simple as that.

It appears that the pieces of the jigsaw puzzle had begun to arrange themselves as though they were intent on creating an event. Landing in Delhi at ten that night, he went straight to the hotel and found himself asking Erikson if he would mentor him and allow him to work under him at Harvard. The impossibilities multiply. With degrees in engineering and economics, Kakar was asking to be trained as a psychoanalyst. Erikson pointed this anomaly to him. At this stage perhaps something significant occurred. Despite the odds, Erikson made him a promise: 'If you get your doctorate in the next two to three years, I'll try my best to get you an appointment at Harvard to work with me.'[49] May we consider this as an example of a calling, which despite many twists and turns finds its anointed destiny. I will let Kakar summarize it in his own words:

'In the years to come, I would finish my doctoral studies at Vienna, work as Erikson's assistant at Harvard, go through my psychoanalytic training at Frankfurt. I would teach, practise, write books, marry and have children. I would know loneliness and sadness; but never again would I know the panic and confusion of that year I travelled through the villages with no idea which direction I should turn, when I alternated between holding fast to a stubborn self-hood and surrendering to the family of which I was a part, when I spent many sleepless nights in the construction of private Utopias that crumbled in the morning.'[50]

In a strange kaleidoscopic movement, all fell into place in this biography. Kakar's despairing confusion lasted only till he realized that he wished to train under Erikson. After that he never looked back. Had Kakar's confusion been sparked by an identity crisis, he, presumably, would have felt a similar angst sometime later in life when confronted by other crises. Instead, as he himself so eloquently admits, he would encounter many anxieties, but he would never know the confusion of that year when he felt rudderless and adrift. Was this because his daimon had finally led him to encounter the central axis of inclination that the representative had been sent to explore? Once the representative had correctly aligned itself in the intended direction, the rest of Sudhir Kakar's life fell into step. As Jung observed towards the end of his life, 'What happens to a person is characteristic of him. He represents a pattern and all the pieces fit. One by one, as his life proceeds, they fall into place according to some predestined design.'[51]

We presume that random coincidences, the quirks of destiny, are devoid of a design, but in Kakar's case they had followed an invisible pattern that led him to discover the central 'plan' of his life. Each stitch was important in the emerging tapestry. What if Kakar had never met Erikson? What if the Ford Foundation plane had not been available? What if, after meeting Erikson, he had discouraged him to become his assistant? But none of this happened. It was as if, against all odds, events were being directed towards a single defining conclusion. It is not being suggested that he was ordained to become a psychoanalyst, but that his profession provided the platform from which he could explore life in the way his representative had been sent to investigate. Perhaps we can be bold enough to say that Sudhir Kakar was led to his *spot* in life!

Life had seemed like an amorphous experience until it was compacted into his calling. His identity crisis was not a symptom of some deep-rooted psychological problem, but, as Kakar discovered, 'another chance to re-align the shape of one's outer life with the core of one's being, with one's true self'.[52] And is not this 'true self' what we have come to birth to explore?

At this point I am going to venture a correlation between the traditional Hindu view of karma and the two dreams we discussed earlier – Jung's dream of the rock-cut temple and my dream about the compacting of mud. My dream is a comment on death and rebirth, while Jung's dream is about how the concerns of a particular life are shed at death and the manner in which an axis of inclination develops for the next life. The amorphous muddy sludge in my dream is compacted; the predispositions of the conclave in the rock-cut temple coalesce into the calling of the representative sent to earth. The underlying content of both these dreams is strongly reflective of the karma doctrine, even though it may not be apparent at first glance. Here I am going to digress into an explanation of what karma actually is (as opposed to some popular misconceptions about it) and whether there is any need for such a doctrine. This may then enable me to explore the connection between these two dreams and karma theory.

Karma is commonly understood as a retributive law, a predetermined course in which certain types of actions will always have the same karmic consequences – a doctrine that generally fills people with disquiet. However, the theory of karma is far ahead of this conception, and it remains the bedrock of life in the Hindu, Jaina, and Buddhist traditions.

One way that karma may be appreciated is to view it as an attempt to explain the perplexing questions of human existence – the haunting problems of inequality, human suffering, and the varying results produced by an equal amount of human effort within an identical environment. 'If two seeds planted in the same earth and given the same warmth and moisture develop differently, one has to postulate another cause.'[53] That cause is what karma attempts to outline. Contrary to popular conceptions, we are not assuming that karma theory alone can explain this. For example, some of the individual characteristics of a person can be causally traced to the parents (genes) or to developmental influences within the nurturing environment. However, none of this can explain the unequal and often unfair starting conditions of life. Why is one child born into a rich household and the other into the home of a poor landless labourer, ravaged by poverty, shackled by debt? Malnourished in its formative years, deprived of play in childhood with no education to school the mind, and with only the harshest conditions surrounding life, what meaning can profundities like will, talent, effort, perseverance, efficiency have for such a child? The disparity precludes opportunity and that forever determines the limitations of a life. This is the puzzle that demands an explanation, and in seeking such explanations, the doctrine of karma evolved by degrees from a primitive principle of retribution to the idea of an equalizing justice.[54]

Though the beginnings of the karma doctrine are shrouded in mystery, the rudiments of some of its features can possibly be traced to the oldest sacred texts of Hinduism, the Vedas: transmigration of the soul and accumulation of karma, which matures in a subsequent existence. But initially, in the Vedic literature of the Brahmanas, this was conceived only as ritual karma (*yajna* karma), tied to the performance or neglect of specified religious rites, sacrifices, or oblations. These ritual acts essentially celebrated the interrelationship between this world and the divine orderliness of the cosmos (*rta*). They were also a means of purification and expiation from evil or sin. Thus in the Taittiriya Samhita of the ancient Yajur Veda (V.7.7.2) the gods are called upon to recognize a man, who after death, goes to heaven and 'to disclose to him his *istapurta* (that is merit which he had accumulated through sacrifice) and liberality to the priests'.[55]

In the Upanishads and subsequent Sanskrit literature, karma acquired an entirely new significance. Perhaps in the attempt to explicate suffering and inequality, karma was transformed into an ethically retributive doctrine, which distinguished between ritual and moral action. The utility of ritual worship in the accumulation of karma was discounted. Instead, karma was associated with the nature of actions, good or evil, right or wrong. In the earlier texts (Samhitas and Brahmanas) the terms *punya* and *papa* – merit and sin – were not reflective of ethical acts, but alluded to ritual purity or pollution. It is the Upanishads that imparted an ethical colouring to these words. Upanishadic karma was no longer a rite but relied on deed and conduct. 'According as one acts, according as one conducts himself, so does he become. The doer of good becomes good. The doer of evil becomes evil.'[56]

Further evolution of the doctrine led to its classical formulation as a law of personal responsibility. It did not rely on an omnipotent, omniscient, and all-pervasive Creator to execute its edicts. Rebirth was treated as an aspect of worldly existence, which is perpetually fed and renewed by karmas, good and bad. Further, there is no escape from its law, its consequences manifesting as the conditions of life. Thus human inequality was traced to karmic residues accumulated in past lives. In contrast to *yajna* karma, where the sins of the father could be visited on the son and the son could transfer merit to his deceased father by ritual ceremonies (*shradha*), the individual was now personally responsible for bearing the consequences of his or her actions. Karma thus became self-operating, inescapable, and inexorable.

Buddhism developed this formulation one step further: it is not the act itself that is significant, but the motives that inspire actions that are supremely important. An unintentional harm or injury to another does not invoke retributive karma. On the other hand, someone could perform a good action yet reap unfortunate karmas. For example, if one donates money or works for charity in order to gain recognition or fame, then the outwardly good act will turn to unhappy karmas since the motive is wrong. It was a natural progression of the argument to identify desire or *trsna* as the originating source of all karma. This became the cause of the bondage of the soul to the cycle of birth, death, and rebirth.

What this bare bones of a historical perspective makes evident is that my dream was not carving out a new strategy for karma; it was merely restating what has been said since Buddhistic times. It is our strongest desires – our axes of inclinations – that frame the circumstances of our next life. As we desire, so shall we be. All the unsatisfied desires the deceased has left behind, all the longings left unfulfilled, come back to haunt in the world of death, as though these desires were things. When it is time for rebirth, a yearning to recover the lost opportunities of the last life may arise. Residual desires will define these longings along the restrictive grooves of old patterns (the ruts in the road). Past desires will become the parents of the new life, their limitations becoming its karma.

We thus see that the doctrine of karma gradually evolved from the Vedic transgression of rituals, to the Upanishadic focus on moral aberration, to the Buddha's injunction of the primacy of motive. The Upanishads had instituted an important shift in the doctrine, from being a meritorious sacrificial act to a causative force that leads to rebirth and suffering.

Good and evil karmas accumulate and bear fruit in subsequent lives, and these accumulated karmas are known as *sancita* karma. They represent the karmic residues of all previous lives, and are like seeds that retain all the plant energy till they sprout. However, only a portion of *sancita* karma will begin to bear fruit in the next life, as all of them cannot fructify in one life. Karmas that will fructify in the life to come are called *prarabdha* karma.

This second type of karma is what will determine a human being's destiny in the current life. It is, as the great Indian philosopher Sankaracharya (circa 780–822) says, like an arrow already in flight – it will continue until its energy is exhausted, unless something obstructs it.[57] Nevertheless, what remains a mystery is which karmic residues from the storehouse of *sancita* karmas will work themselves out in the current life. Sankaracharya seems to think that in general the more intense and proximate residues when one dies, be they sinful or meritorious, tend to mature first.[58]

We can, however, never wholly rid ourselves of all accumulated karma, because in each lifetime we are gathering fresh karmas. *Agami,* the third type of karma, pertains to actions that are being created in the present life. The *agami* karmas of this life will, after death, merge into the pool of *sancita* associated with the person.

Perhaps we are now in a position to appreciate the strong concordance of Jung's and my dreams with the traditional Hindu understanding of karma. The group soul, or the conclave in Jung's rock-cut temple, could be likened to the Hindu *sancita* karma, the storehouse of accumulated karmas of all previous lives, which Jung referred to as all *'that has been, and what has been accomplished'*. From the *sancita*, a representative is compacted and sent to birth with a particular task or agenda, which is its *prarabdha* karma – the destiny of that current life. If, as Sankaracharya said, the more intense and proximate karmic residues tend to mature first, this may be likened to the group soul deciding on the most immediate needs that the representative will need to address. The fresh experiences gathered by the representative in the new life (*agami* karma) will then be reabsorbed after death into the *sancita* or the conclave, further influencing the direction that another representative will take when it comes into a new birth.

It is possible that the compacting suggested by my dream does not take place only once in the mysterious zone of death and rebirth. In life *prarabdha* karma is also compacted in a mysterious way that seems to attract circumstances that fulfil a particular person's needs, like in the case of Sudhir Kakar. In Hindu terms it is called karma *vipaka*, or the maturation of karma. The consequences of actions done in the present or former births ripen and show effect or compact into a set of consequences and circumstances. It shows in an individual as a particular set of proclivities, aspirations, and drives that will translate into a choice of circumstances that will fulfil these inclinations. Out of the various options presented, the individual will be drawn only to those that best serve his or her innate tendencies. So though we may seem to have various options – an amorphous and large playfield of possibilities – they will be compacted only within a narrow band of circumstances because it is these that will attract us. *Prarabdha* karma, therefore, is not the irrevocable lines of destiny etched on the palms of our hands that we bring to birth, but the innate need of the representative that draws towards itself specific life circumstances. My dream seems to say this in shorthand: 'This is how an individual life is crystallized into a definite pattern. Like this amorphous soft mud, our strongest desires, our inclinations come together and are compacted to become a life, a destiny, the joys and sorrows of a particular human being ... When compacted and solidified it becomes a particular set of circumstances – karma.'

I would now like to return to the end of my dream. I watched a potter create a pot, and arrived at the notion that any individual with all his or her particularities, needs, and circumstances is finally but playing a role – signifying a transience to it. The imagery of the potter throwing a pot is reminiscent of the Hindu conception of the body being an earthen pot that houses the soul. In the cremation ceremony, the deceased's son circumambulates the pyre with an earthen pot filled with water placed on his shoulder, the water slowly draining out as he walks. The pot is then thrown on the ground and smashed, symbolizing the release of the soul and the disintegration of the body.

My dream could be hinting at the need to step back and witness the role assigned in this life as being merely a script. Possibly, this 'witnessing' might effect an important separation, a necessary disengagement from the role and the player of the role – the 'pot' and the 'potter'– and allow me to comprehend the web of desires that have sewn my circumstances together. This separation of the essential from the inessential, from who I thought 'I' was to who 'I' really am, leads back to the question my earlier dream had posed: Who are you?

Could it be that the question in my dream aimed at alerting me to *where* to seek, and not *what* to seek? Was it pointing towards what I am not? Simply stated, the dream's question has no answer in everyday consciousness; it therefore may be necessary to go beyond ordinary consciousness – much like normative dreaming has to be transcended by another dimension of dreaming if we are to experience the full range of the dreaming mind. The rest of the book is dedicated to exploring this gateway of the dreaming consciousness that can alert us to the imperishable 'I' in us.

I know full well that critical rationalism has eliminated the idea of life after death and of rebirth, believing these may only be projections of human desire. It is argued that rebirth and karma are a figment of a compensatory imagination expressive of a desire for immortality: the body perishes but 'I' live on. We cannot be certain who is right about rebirth and karma, the Hindus in their affirmation or the rationalists in their denial. The only certainty we do possess is that all of us will pass through the gates of death, and perhaps only then will we know for sure whether the entry into the rock-cut temple is a metaphorical rendering of a literal process of life, death, and karma or merely the fanciful imagination of C. G. Jung's sleeping psyche.

Meanwhile, as Jung said, we can do no more than imagine by listening to the strange myths the psyche weaves through dreams. Perhaps the power of going beyond the shores of the known world rests with the dreaming consciousness, as the waking mind baulks when it has to step over the restrictive boundary of reason. That is my only justification in attempting to vivify a conception of the afterlife with the aid of hints sent by dreams. I fully appreciate that it is merely a hypothesis that cannot be proved. The only verifiable argument able to address these rational doubts is that at least a part of the psyche is not subject to the laws of space and time. Proof of this began to trickle in with J. B. Rhine's experiments at Duke University, and the Maimonides research by Ullman and his associates, which have already been described earlier. Besides these formal research attempts, there are many people who have experienced a dream that has transcended the barriers of space and time. More importantly, we need a conception of what happens to us at death, a compass that guides us to meet this unknown realm. Whether that conception is true or false is not the issue. As Jung said, 'Truth is the wrong criterion here. One can only ask … whether man is better off and feels his life more complete, more meaningful and more satisfactory with or without them.'[59] Perhaps my aunt's fortitude in meeting her death when confronted with cancer stands as a testimony to Jung's statement. He who has a *why* to live, said Nietzsche, can bear almost any *how*.

My speculating about the after-death world is not mere cultural indulgence, but because it is an intermediate world – a reality between our everyday materiality and the incandescent life of the mystic. The dimension of dreaming that I wish to explore in the following chapters will take us not into the nether worlds of death and rebirth but beyond them, into the transcendental home of the mystic.

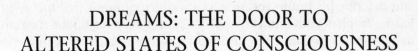

Chapter 21

DREAMS: THE DOOR TO
ALTERED STATES OF CONSCIOUSNESS

Leave nothing of myself in me;
Let me so read thy life that I
Unto all life of mine may die.

Saint Teresa

*I*n the previous chapter, the dreaming mind, for the first time, stepped away from the psychological and paranormal realms, and explored a still different reality, as it attempted to penetrate what the Tibetans call the *bardo* planes or the after-death world. However, this does not represent the upper limits of dreaming. The after-death realm is, after all, only an intermediary between the solidity of this tangible world of sticks and stones, and the mystery pervading the transcendental Beyond.

Perhaps, it is only the elasticity of the dreaming mind that can stretch far beyond the familiar dimensions of dreaming into this transcendental reality, whose outer form is glimpsed in traditional religions and its practices. History shows that dreams have served as an important vehicle for religious inspiration. In fact, we find that some form of dream imagery is embedded in the beginning of most if not all major religions of the world.

In Christianity many of the events surrounding the birth and early life of Christ were announced by dreams. Joseph was told the source of

Mary's pregnancy in a dream and was instructed to name the child Jesus. In later dreams Joseph was warned that he should flee to Egypt with Mary and the child to avoid Herod's dictat of killing all male infants. Judaism also places a lot of emphasis on dreams. In the 63 volumes of the Talmud there are 217 references to dreams attributed to many different sages and scholars.[1]

Even a cursory look at Buddhist literature reveals that the Buddha's mother, Queen Maya, dreamt in 544 BC of the future Buddha's birth. Also, 'five of the Buddha's dreams, along with dreams of his father, King [S]udhodana, and his wife, Gopa, appear in the Pali scriptures and describe his future vocation as a wandering monk'.[2] Similarly in Islam, Prophet Muhammad (AD 570–632) received his divine mission in a dream. In fact, much of the Koran was revealed in his dreams over a period of several years. Every morning he would share his dreams with his followers, as well as ask them for their dreams and offer interpretations.[3] It was during his lifetime that dream interpretation became a science called *Ilm al-tabir*.[4]

That dreams have played a very important role in the development of specific religions is undeniable. Lest it be assumed that these announcement dreams happened only in the past we will give two modern examples. The birth of Gauri Ma (in 1857),[5] religious renunciate, friend of Sri Sarada Devi (wife of the mystic Sri Ramakrishna Paramhansa), and founder of the Sri Sri Saradeshvari Ashram in Kolkata, was heralded by a dream. She was born to Giribala 'after a dream in which the Divine Mother had smilingly handed over to her a beautiful baby, accepted by the mother with reverent gratitude as a divine gift'.[6] In still more recent times, in 1953, a poor couple in a rural fishing village in the southern Indian state of Kerala had parallel dreams about an extraordinary child on the night before her birth. Damayanti, the mother, had a dream of giving birth to the god Krishna, while Sughunandan, the father and a devotee of Krishna, had a dream about Devi, the Universal Mother.[7] To them was born Mata Amritanandamayi (Ammachi), the founder of a religious movement that has an impressive network of educational, medical, and social service institutions, and arguably has the largest following among Indian gurus outside India.

At this point, an objection could be that if these religious dreams simply announce future circumstances like the paranormal dream, then why do we need to identify a different dimension of dreaming? There is a difference between them because ordinary dreams of prophecy are primarily concerned with mundane events and mostly affect the dreamer. Dreams of religious prophecy can sometimes affect an entire race, like the dreams announcing the birth of Gautama Buddha and Jesus Christ. Such visions act as the eyes of the race, transcending personal biographies to announce the intersection of the transpersonal with the mundane. Further, the religious dream or vision is not limited only to the announcements of the coming of world saviours. Its mystical component penetrates beyond material things to that immaterial Reality that some call the Absolute and most theologians call God.

For example, the Muslim philosopher Ibn Arabi (AD 1164–1240) argued that there exists a type of dream that is not sourced from our ordinary everyday experiences, but directly from the 'Universal Soul' or the 'Guarded Table'. 'In such a dream man's (rational) soul perceives the archetypal ideas contained in the Universal Soul ... Imagination does not enter into it, and the "inward eye" reproduces the exact reflection of the impression received ... They are the direct vision of Reality, of Universal Truth.'[8] This knowledge, it was argued, is possible only in a state of suspension from the outer senses, which normally occurs during sleep or in deep contemplation.

Differentiating between the two types of religious dreams, one of the great Christian theologians and contemplatives, Denis the Carthusian (1402–1471), succinctly clarified the distinction between them: 'The first kind are to be concealed, the second declared. The first are truly mystic, the second prophetic.'[9] The mystical dream has not been written about that openly or that frequently as the religious prophetic dream.

The distinction of a special kind of dream from normative dreaming was also made by early Christian thinkers. They called it a *vision*. We have already seen how St Augustine had gone to great lengths to isolate the true vision from ordinary dreaming by distinguishing a state of *ekstasis*. Not only were these visionary dreams considered legitimate, but they were also viewed as canonical.

In a vision the mind is in a state of deep absorption without conscious thought, and there is no intrusion from external reality. Even pain inflicted is not cognized or felt. This may indicate that the person is 'asleep' to the world and waking thought, even though the contemplative awareness is awake within a sleeping body. In short, the religious dream / vision is apart from normative dreaming.

We will, however, not concern ourselves primarily with the prophetic religious dream, nor should this dimension of dreaming be confused with the 'god-sent' dream of antiquity. A further consideration: we will not confine ourselves to those dreams that necessarily possess symbols grounded in Scripture. This will allow us not to be limited to orthodoxy, permitting us to investigate what remains of religious dreaming when it is shorn of its monastic robes and theological preconceptions. Instead, we will concern ourselves with dreams that alert the dreamer to a supramundane world, a suprasensible reality; those that are truly mystical. I would thus prefer to include within the ambit of religious dreaming the experience of mystics.

It might be more relevant to allude to these dreams as transcendental dreaming. They reflect on the pervasive and eternal human enigmas: who we are; the nature and meaning of life; the forces that shape it; and the reality that lies beyond it. From time immemorial people have pondered these perplexing questions. Seldom recognized is the fact that dreams have helped provide some answers. Possibly, long before the advent of sacred texts, it may have been through dreams that our ancestors got inklings of a realm beyond the physical, inspiring religious innovation and providing the basis of many beliefs including the concept of the soul.[10] The transcendental dream or the vision offers a link to a domain not otherwise accessible to mundane consciousness.

It may be important to appreciate from the outset that the mystic's search, the actual fount of all religion, is not confined merely to visions in a state of ecstasy, but also to the dream life of the seeker. The mystical dream goes beyond normative dreaming because it reflects the quest for the ultimate source of being. It transcends all the elements that are intrinsic to tradition: superstitious belief, unconscious symbolism, the misrepresentation of emotion, and the invasion of cravings from the lower nature, or the disguised fulfilments of an ungratified wish. Transcendental or mystical dreaming takes the person beyond personal motivations and extra-sensory perceptions to a realm that is at once perceived as foundational to the waking and sleeping state, and yet stands apart from both, for it affords a direct and penetrating insight into the whole of consciousness. The mystic seeks to engender an awareness that is unattached and independent of waking and sleeping consciousness – a state of calm incandescence that is untainted by desires or fears.

This is a very subtle dimension of dreaming that becomes a conduit for a line of communication between a seeker entangled in the sensory world and transcendental reality. The mystic seeks to reconnect the individual self with the Universal Self and loses him or herself in that union. Anything less than this merging is shunned. It is said that St Francis of Assisi, praying in the house of Bernard of Quintavalle, was heard saying again and again: 'My God! my god! What art Thou? And what am I?' This was the only question he thought worth asking; and it is a question that all mystics ask at the beginning and sometimes answer at the end of their quest.[11] This is characterized by the experience of Sri Ramakrishna, the great Indian mystic-saint who lived in the second half of the nineteenth century. Desirous of mystical union with the Supreme Reality personified by the Mother Goddess, he was unwilling to be satisfied by any substitutes. The intensity of his aspiration had reached such a state of yearning that he felt that if he could not have a personal vision or *darshana* of the Mother, there was no use in his staying alive. One day his eyes fell upon a sword in the temple and in acute anguish he decided to put an end to his life. Running towards the sword, he recounts, 'suddenly I had the wonderful vision of the Mother, and fell down unconscious. I did not know what happened then in the external world – how that day and the next slipped away. But in my heart of hearts, there was flowing a current of intense bliss, never experienced before ... It was as if the houses, doors, temples, and all other things vanished altogether; as if there was nothing anywhere! And what I saw was a boundless infinite conscious sea of light! However far and in whatever direction I looked, I found a continuous succession of effulgent waves coming forward, raging and storming from all sides with great speed. Very soon they fell on me and made me sink to the abysmal depths of infinity.'[12]

This is not an ordinary state of consciousness, as Sri Ramakrishna states that he was incognizant of what happened in the external world. Yet we cannot characterize his state as simply being unconscious. Clearly he was aware, but a different order of awareness pervaded his consciousness. In whatever manner we may want to define his experience – vision or dream, mystical union or divine bliss – here the boundaries between his self and the transcendental have become blurred. It consists of an elevation of awareness where the unifying experience with the transcendental eliminates perception of the concrete and abstract elements of the sensate world. The vision is not characterized by specific images, but is more descriptive of a state of consciousness conveyed by the 'effulgent waves' rapidly coming towards him. Soon even the metaphorical bridge of the waves is discarded as the individual sinks into and is immersed in the all-consuming folds of infinity. In this imageless silence, in the union with the greater life, nothing of the person remains.

This religious urge, sometimes finding its expression through dreams, is not singularly the realm of the spiritualist or mystic. As Evelyn Underhill observed: 'All men, at one time or another, have fallen in love with the veiled Isis whom they call Truth.' Most treat this love as a passing passion; their unrequited search makes them turn to more practical things. Others, despite their hopelessness, remain all their lives the devout lovers of Reality, though their vision of the beloved varies enormously. 'Some see Truth as Dante saw Beatrice: an adorable yet intangible figure, found in this world yet revealing the next ... Some have seen her in a test tube, and some in a poet's dream: some before the altar, others in the slime. The extreme pragmatists have even sought her in the kitchen; declaring that she may best be recognized by her utility.' The sceptic, after an unsuccessful courtship, has drawn philosophical comfort that his mistress does not really exist. Whatever their chosen path, none of these seekers have ever been able to assure us that they had lifted the veil and glimpsed Reality. However, if we are to trust the reports of the mystics – despite their strange descriptions – they appear to have succeeded where all these others failed in establishing communication between their essential self and the ultimate Reality.[13]

It therefore seems only fair that we explore the journey that mystics have undertaken – to discover what the dream state has yielded in their goal to reach the source of their being. These are dreams that explore an altered state of consciousness, by the sheer absence of the 'ordinary self'. Here a dream may be illustrative:

> *I saw that the entire universe, in the structure it presents, consists of light. Everything had become one colour, and all the atoms of all the beings proclaimed 'I am the Truth', each in the manner proper to its being and with the force particular to each. I was unable to interpret properly what manner of being had made them proclaim this. Having seen these things in my vision, an intoxication and an exaltation, a desire and an extraordinary delectation were born within me. I wanted to fly in the air, but I saw that there was something resembling a piece of wood at my feet which prevented my taking flight. With violent emotion, I kicked the ground in every possible manner until this piece of wood let go. Like an arrow shooting forth from the bow, but a hundred times stronger, I rose and moved into the distance. When I arrived at the first Heaven, I saw that the moon had split, and I passed through the moon. Then, returning from this state and absence, I found myself again present.[14]*

The landscape of the dream is grandiose. A purely psychological reading would lead us to understand that the dreamer has garbed in universal terms his childhood desire for omnipotence. Unable to fulfil this fantasy, he feels obstructed by a piece of wood at his feet. This method of interpretation may prompt some to believe that the dreamer, like a psychotic, has relinquished his hold on reality in favour of a narcissistically potent world. However, understood in metaphysical terms, this dream moves away from the darkness of psychotic regression. While it may submerge one dreamer into the depths of ungratified desires, it may lead another beyond the unconscious to a numinous experience full of 'light'. The individual circumstances of the dreamer may perhaps dictate this choice. There are essential differences between the psychotic and the transformed consciousness of the mystic. To the psychotic the dream becomes a symptom of his or her defence against the harsh demands of reality. For mystics, it is a vision that helps them see the underlying unity and interconnectedness of life and their place in it. It would integrate their personality in the deep abiding security of the experienced oneness of existence. Divine intoxication cannot be confused with psychological disintegration. A transcendental dream cannot be reduced to mere ego disorders.

The above dream is attributed to the Sufi mystic Shamsoddin Lahiji (d.1506). The description does not clarify where the dream ends and where the vision begins. We are not at all sure whether it is a dream or a purely mystical vision in which Shamsoddin is absorbed in ecstasy – and this is hardly the point. What is overpoweringly evident is that the experience bears little resemblance to the ordinary state of dreaming.

The dream or vision begins with an expansion of the dreamer's consciousness, which encompasses the whole universe bathed in light, with each individual atom proclaiming its truth by virtue of its divine origin. Those familiar with mystical literature will recognize a similarity in this account with traditions across many ages that report the ineffable experience of being flooded with light, often culminating in the feeling of the oneness of existence. Anyone who experiences this unitive vision cannot but be swept by its majesty and be transformed in some profound way. This is a very different state from that experienced in an ordinary dream. The personality of the dreamer seems to go into the background, submerged in the magnitude of the cosmic revelation. Despite the dreamer being immersed in the participation of the dream events, he is not unaware of himself. Instead he can view the events apart from himself.

Over a century ago, William James wrote in *The Principles of Psychology* that central to consciousness is the self-as-observer, what he called the 'knower'. The notion of self-as-observer implies dual levels of awareness – the participation in the experience itself and the awareness of one's own thoughts, feelings, or behaviour during participation. This concurrent splitting of awareness between participation and observation is the human quality of self-reflection. This self-reflectiveness is typically considered the prerogative of the waking mind only since it is often found absent in ordinary dreaming. Yet in the above dream, self-reflectiveness is its most distinctive feature. The dreamer is not only aware of the 'vision' as separate from himself, but also differentiates it from the sense of intoxication it generates in him. Though identified with the truth of every atom (participation) the dreamer observes his wonderment at how this truth got its certitude (witnesses his participation). The vision is the participation, while self-reflection observes the feelings *'born within me'*.

This sort of witnessing cannot be done in ordinary states of consciousness. The experience is such that the person is transported out of him or herself, away from the dictates of the mundane personality. Most mystical accounts describe this absence of the personality as its annihilation, similar to this dreamer's experience – as a flight away from the self, the personality. Some vestiges of his personality, however, remain and this is perceived as inhibitive to the attainment of the purity of this altered state of consciousness. In other words, even if the vision is soaked in a transpersonal awareness there may be some elements in it that are personal to the dreamer. The dreamer allegorically alludes to it as an obstacle, a piece of wood, impeding his flight. If he is to fully realize this transpersonal state, he must pierce through his mental structures (splitting the moon). In Sufi cosmology the moon symbolizes the intellect. Only then is his ascent (from banal reality) possible.

The dream describes a paradoxical state where there is an absence of selfhood and yet there is self-reflection. At one level the dreamer, Shamsoddin Lahiji, observes his own thoughts and feelings, and is therefore aware of himself. At another level we are led to believe that his normal personality is absent as evidenced by his *'returning from this state and absence'* and finding himself *'again present'*. Ostensibly, his vision/dream has taken him to another state of consciousness where the concerns of his mundane personality are not in operation and yet the capacity to self-reflect is intact.

This perhaps is the paradox underlying mystical states of consciousness. The mundane personality is transcended while at the same time the power to observe the experience is maintained. The very self that is transcended is retained in some way so that what is observed in the transpersonal state can be brought back to ordinary consciousness. If there were total self-annihilation, the rationalist argues, nothing would remain and there would be nothing to bring back. The mystic witnesses the dream events and is also capable of merging into a state that dissolves all personal distinction in the unitive oneness of existence. Since we have difficulty in conceiving this state, the rationalist denies this transcendental dimension of dreaming by equating it with the delusional state of the psychotic.

The above denial is perhaps reflective of a difference in the philosophical approach to life between the East and the West. In the East the whole of life is viewed as a dream from which we awake at death. When life is consistently viewed as such it becomes less real and loses its hold on us. Also one may realize that the activity of normal experience is composed largely of the mind's projections. This perspective may help us to withdraw from our total identification with the personality by releasing us from our ties to possessions and attitudes. When fully realized, that life is but an ephemeral dream, it may lead to liberation from the endless cycle of births and deaths. In stark contrast, the modern Westerner cannot bring him or herself to regard life in this manner. In fact, the ability to see life as a dream would induce the psychoanalyst to conclude that there is a schizoid loss of reality – a defensive symptom of escape and isolation from which the person needs to be alleviated. Harry Hunt summarizes this difference when he comments: 'Whereas it is schizoid to question reality and find it dreamlike in the modern West, in the Eastern tradition it is "deluded" not to question reality.'[15]

The incontestable hold of waking experience on reality was questioned in the West in 1985, when lucid dreaming was irrefutably demonstrated in the laboratory. Typically, in a lucid dream the dreamer knows that he or she is dreaming. Lucidity is often triggered when the dreamer finds something odd (bizarre) within the dream and wonders whether this is real, like when in the midst of a very frightening dream. This thought could lead to the realization that if this isn't real then I must be dreaming, and the dreamer becomes lucid. However, some episodes of lucidity can be spontaneously triggered.[16]

It has been established that in a lucid dream waking memory is available to the dreamer, thought can be directed, and the dreamer can reason while continuing to dream. When awake we voluntarily decide on our course of action – whether to turn left or right, or to talk to a stranger or not. This volitional control was also found to be present within some lucid dreams. All the while laboratory equipment certified that a dream was being experienced. More than that, it is even possible for a person who is fast asleep and dreaming to signal that he or she has turned lucid within the dream as also communicate the dream content. We will discuss this state of dreaming in more detail in chapter 23.

The reality of lucid dreams has important implications for transcendental dreaming. If dreaming shares with waking experience common capacities and abilities – like to reflect and make choices – then wouldn't the boundaries between waking and sleeping, conscious and unconscious, or real and imaginary break down? This questioning is necessitated by the capability of lucid dreamers to be simultaneously awake and asleep. The most important question that lucidity raises pertains actually to the waking state. In lucidity we realize that we are dreaming while dreaming. Do we ever notice or question whether we are awake while we are awake? Furthermore, do we enquire what in fact it means to be 'awake'? Lucid dreams force us to revise our understanding of the awake-asleep boundary.[17] Perhaps 'awakeness' is a form of consciousness that is not always chained to the waking state, just like being asleep is not the fundamental property of dreaming alone.

It is this uneasy relationship of what it means to be awake or asleep that mystics explore in one way or another. For example, G. I. Gurdjieff (1866?–1949), the Russian mystic, did not adhere to the normal definitions of being awake and being asleep. Instead, he taught that human beings usually live in two states of consciousness, of which the first is 'sleep, in other words a passive state in which man spends a third and very often a half of his life. And second, the state in which men spend the other part of their lives, in which they walk the streets, write books, talk on lofty subjects, take part in politics, kill one another, which they regard as active and call "clear consciousness" or the "waking state of consciousness".' He felt that although the waking state appears quite different from sleep at first glance, if we take a closer look we find that human beings live when awake in an equally subjective world, a bubble of loves, likes, and wants. Gurdjieff stated, '[Man] is a machine, everything with him *happens*. He cannot stop the flow of his thoughts, he cannot control his imagination, his emotions, his attention ... The real world is hidden from him by the wall of imagination.'[18] What is the difference between this and the subjective state of dream? Gurdjieff concludes that human beings are asleep; their waking state is another kind of sleep.[19] 'Only by beginning to *remember himself* [amidst everyday experience, like in a lucid dream] does a man really awaken.'[20] These perceptions are not particular to mystics only; most religious texts also exhort the novice to 'awake', 'watch', 'sleep not', and so on.

Also, the awakeness in a lucid dream is of a different order to our habitual waking experience. Though it shares some aspects, this awakeness is not derived purely from waking cognition, nor is it a refinement of it. May we then not presume that lucidity points to another state of consciousness that Gurdjieff calls '*self-remembering* or self-consciousness or consciousness of one's being'?[21] Gurdjieff was possibly recommending the inculcation of a lucidity-like awake-awareness during normal waking activities, 'which would cultivate a continuous sense of "self remembering" in the midst of everyday settings, where otherwise we lose ourselves and forget that we are alive'.[22] Perhaps the realization of this state is what transcendental dreaming also strives towards: 'awakeness', a form of consciousness not readily available during everyday waking experience.

Some mystical schools pay attention to the hypnagogic images we experience at sleep onset – the transition between waking and sleeping, when consciousness has not entirely relinquished control as in sleep, and nor has its freedom been overwhelmed by the harsh dictates of wakefulness. In fact, the modern-day researcher Fred Travis, on investigating the various states of consciousness, suggests that waking, sleeping, and REM dreaming emerge out of a pure consciousness, a silent void. He asserts that where one state meets another there is a little gap in which everybody very briefly experiences transcendental consciousness. When we go from sleeping to dreaming, or from dreaming to waking, these little gaps or junction points occur where pure consciousness is revealed.[23] And maybe this happens because consciousness is in transition and therefore less encumbered. It is this new-found awareness, its development, stabilization, and refinement, that has engaged the mystic through the millennia. Momentarily intoxicated with the liberation of its pristine awareness, consciousness may have the capacity to converse in a language that uses neither image nor thought.

This dimension of dreaming begins by distinguishing the essential nature of the self from the psychophysical involvements of the personality. The other two dimensions of dreaming were preoccupied with the content of the dream, identifying it as real or illusory, inner or outer, psychological or phenomenological. In its most refined form, the dreamer withdraws from the narrative flow of the dream, preferring to observe rather than participate in it. The dream is now no longer a set of images but, as we said, a state of consciousness, and the mystic, rather than strive to decipher the imagery, attempts to refine this state. In other words, one is not engaged by the reflections in the mirror of dream, but instead in investigating the mirror itself – one's essential self.

Transcendental dreaming concerns itself with what lies at the root of human consciousness. Negotiating the dream world without being enraptured by its content, the mystic aspires to penetrate other levels of awareness where he or she is truly 'awake'. The next few chapters are devoted to this paradigm of dreaming. In these we will explore lucid dreaming, the harnessing of consciousness, and the more evolved state of contentless awareness. We will also explore the numinous dream, which first alerts us to the possibility that there may be something beyond our sensory perceptions. This kind of dream traditionally confirmed the aspirant's readiness for initiation into the religious life. It was the dream of 'calling'. The numinous dream, however, need not clothe itself in religious robes; it often manifests in non-sectarian symbols, as we will see in the next chapter.

Chapter 22

THE NUMINOUS DREAM:
A SENSE OF THE SACRED

Though inland far we be,
Our souls have sight of that immortal sea
Which brought us hither

William Wordsworth

*I*n ancient times it was the primary function of religion to provide a purposeful structure and meaning to the universe, but religion has lost its persuasive power, leaving in its wake what Sartre called 'a god-shaped hole in human consciousness'. The loss of reverence for religious symbols coincided with the emergence of collective values that psychologically alienate us from our essential roots. Unfortunately, the rapid strides of modernization, the pace of technological change, the dominance of large impersonal institutions, and the demands of urban life have led to a spiritual dislocation leaving many people adrift, alienated, and lacking in any sense of purpose.[1] 'About a third of my cases,' wrote Jung, 'are not suffering from any clinically definable neurosis, but from the senselessness and aimlessness of their lives. I should not object if this were called the general neurosis of our age.'[2] The privilege of believing that our life has some ultimate meaning has been annihilated by scientific rationalism, while conventional religion has lost its inspiration, often leading to fundamentalism. Given this context, it makes absolute sense that dreams should step in and fill this vacuum in our lives, providing a direct experience of numinous energies within us.

Initially the dream life may spontaneously introduce the dreamer to 'something more'. This may happen to people who may or may not have any religious aspirations. The dream experience may vary from being singularly different from the ordinary dream in its unusual clarity and vividness, to being imbued with numinous imagery that creates a sense of awe in the dreamer.

The numinous and the mysterious have forever been a part of humankind's life. 'Every epoch has given this mystery its own appropriate guise; but our era has not yet found a suitable cloak for the numinous. It either lays bare the secret or veils it beyond recognition.'[3] This mystery cannot, perhaps, be apprehended through rational discourse; the most appropriate expression for it still remains the image, the symbol. The appearance of the numinous through dreams may provide the modern man or woman a bridge to the irrational, through symbols that are charged 'nuclei of meaning'.[4] The great value of *numinous* dreams is that they bring us in direct touch with the transpersonal, penetrating our being like a shaft of light, permitting truths that are otherwise inaccessible to the waking mind.

Jung, who was no stranger to the numinous dream, called it the *big* dream. For him big dreams are related to the primal substance from which all religions have their origin. Such dreams, he believed, could initiate human beings into the secret ways of the universe. The other dreams, the *small* dreams, were considered mere reflections of personal aspects of the dreamer. Anyone may receive the benediction of big dreams. Indeed, they are a benediction, for big dreams rarely come to us. But when they do appear they can radically alter our perceptions and help us penetrate deeper into the mystery and meaning of life. Clothed in the symbols we revere, these dreams represent our higher aspirations, bridging the gap between our outer, circumscribed, personal existence and a vaster transpersonal reality.

I call these dreams *numinous*, based on Rudolf Otto's description of the 'numinosum' in his book *Idea of the Holy*: that which is 'inexpressible, mysterious, terrifying, directly experienced and pertaining only to the divinity'.[5]

The dreams I am going to relate are the experiential truth of ordinary people. They do not constitute objective statements, the truth of which becomes apparent to anyone who hears them. Instead, their validity springs from the impact they had on the dreamers. Through these dreams they felt they had been touched by something greater than themselves. For some the dream was a mere fleeting brush with the numinous; for others they were an involuntary initiation, without the dreamer in any way having sought it; while for still others they seemed the direct result of an inner quest. Whichever way, for the dreamers these dreams interrupted the flow of the waking world, challenging their conceptions, and thereby soliciting inclusion of the dream insight into their lives. This mediation by the dream helped them comprehend their world in ways not previously available to them.

Most of us may sense that there is more to life than the sensible world we inhabit. Numinous dreams, in some strange way, provide the dreamer with a confirmation of the intangible, the 'other' reality. Megha Kashyap's dream of Shiva (chapter 12) on the night of her engagement was a comment on her personal life and not a voice of her transpersonal aspirations. However, a subsequent dream she had many years later seemed to be addressing a need beyond the web of personal conflicts.

Megha, caught in a loveless marriage in which unfaithfulness was the only constant, had felt adrift for many years. She found herself turning to spirituality, but was plagued with doubts about whether this was but another form of not facing up to the failure of her marriage. The result was that she neither put her heart into her new interest nor discarded it. Often the sheer intangibility of the spiritual path, which does not yield quick, discernible results, induces many of its followers to question the wisdom of putting faith in such a pursuit. Megha wondered if she was chasing yet another mirage. This rather common anxiety is voiced in the Bhagavad Gita (6:38), when Arjuna cries: What if, midway, not having arrived at the goal, torn from both ends, the pursuer of the spiritual path of Yoga just perishes like a stray cloud?

She believed that a dream had felicitously, and greatly, helped her:

> I am being chased and I am running in fright. I seem to have run for miles before I see these beautiful tall gates, which open up and permit me to enter. As soon as I enter the gates I feel protected and fearless. When I look around I see a beautiful sight. Just ahead are the most brilliant emerald green waters, above which are big stone arches with smaller arches attached to them like wings. Each of these wings has a small image of Ganesha on it, carved exquisitely. Far

*in the distance is the outline of a temple, where the bells are ringing
for the evening service, and the soft distant sound reaches me like
the call to prayer.*

At first glance the dream opens as a typical anxiety dream, where
the pursuer either never catches the dreamer, or the dreamer is never
able to escape the pursuer. What distinguishes this dream from other
anxiety dreams is that she is able to shake her pursuer off and enter,
through '*beautiful tall gates*', a place where she immediately feels safe.
The tone of the dream changes, perhaps alerting us to a different set
of parameters.

Her entry into the gates signifies a new way of living, as do the
images of Ganesha – the Hindu elephant god who sanctifies all new
beginnings. The arches are the entrance to a temple and thus allude to a
life of the spirit. The temple bells pealing in the distance are beckoning
her to a transpersonal aim. Perhaps such a life would afford her greater
dignity.

A dream like this provides a non-verbal assurance of non-cognitive
truths, the perception of which often serve as a far more effective form
of reassurance than the discursive power of our waking thoughts.
Megha's dream relied on motifs grounded in her specific upbringing:
the Hindu god Ganesha and the temple in the distance. However, in
'Pradeep Sanyal's' dream even religious symbols were surpassed to give
way to a universal symbol of transcendence.

Pradeep Sanyal has been a practising psychoanalyst for more than
twenty years. He believed that psychoanalysis had answers to the
human dilemma, besides providing an intellectually satisfying model
of the mind. If people accept and confront their unconscious conflicts
they would be drained of their potency and this would purge them
of emotional blocks, thereby paving the way for personal fulfilment.
However, over the years, his experience proved otherwise. He discovered
that conflicts that plagued his patients often did not cease; problems
went into temporary abeyance, but given a fresh crisis they reappeared,
proclaiming their entrenched existence. Initially, in true Freudian
tradition, he perceived his task as helping his patients recall early
repressed traumatic memories, allowing them to surface in the hope
that once faced they would free the person from current conflicts.
But when, despite this exercise, there was no discernible change in
the person's symptoms, he wondered whether the real trauma had, in
fact, been identified, and if it had been determined, why a cure did not
necessarily follow. Pradeep also found that outside the analytical space,

without the safety net of the analyst's skilled support, any curative gains that may have been achieved by the client did not always hold in the rough and tumble of the real world. Beleaguered identities resurfaced and the once-felt timidity or aggression, anxiety or fearfulness of his patient would reassert itself. Pradeep wondered whether this was an intrinsic limitation with psychoanalysis. But if psychoanalysis does not heal, he asked himself, what does?

A long period ensued in which Pradeep struggled with the limits of his discipline, and considered exploring other avenues. It was difficult for him to accept anything beyond the modern rational paradigm, yet in adhering to it he had reached a dead-end. He was bordering on intellectual despair, feeling robbed of what he had believed was the new-found truth – the curative powers of psychotherapy. He then had a dream:

> *I am in a rather small and confined room, where I find my movements restricted. There is a small window on the opposite wall, which is barred. I go to the window and look outside. I am struck by the dark, starless night sky. I hold onto the bars of the window and feel a sense of despair grip me as I see no way out between the confines of my room and this blanketing darkness surrounding me.*
>
> *Suddenly a long tapering finger, like Ramana Maharshi's forefinger, etches the sky with the figure of infinity – the horizontal eight eked out in silver against the dark background of the sky. I am awestruck by the figure as I attempt to identify its beginning or its end. It is inexhaustible and overwhelming in its vastness. I instinctively bow my head in reverence to the wonder of what I behold.*

The dream accurately portrayed Pradeep's dilemma, where his dwindling belief in psychoanalysis was symbolized by the suffocating darkness surrounding him. The small room represented the limitations of his discipline, the barred window expressive of the restrictions imposed by the rational paradigm. The dream depicted his incarceration in this darkness. Perhaps the sage (Ramana Maharshi) was pointing out to him that life and its problems are not a linear episode, lived between a beginning and an end. It is, in fact, connected to something greater – the Infinite.

'Infinity' is derived from the Latin *infinitus* or 'without limit' and it is often associated with God or the Absolute. The symbol of infinity can be read at various levels, each level interconnected to the other because of the inherent mystery contained in it. In mathematics, infinity is seen as that concept which is not numerically quantifiable, but goes into abstraction. On subtracting any number from infinity, the result is always infinity. If anything is added to infinity, it still remains infinity. What, then, is infinity? It is not a concrete number, but more an expression of the inherent limits of our ability to count, measure, or assess; ultimately an expression of something the mind cannot comprehend – unquantifiable, much like the transpersonal. Perhaps the finger of the maharishi is pointing to realities beyond representation. It is said that when the Buddha was questioned about the ultimate mystery of the universe he only answered with silence – and a finger pointing the way.

It is also significant that the dream does not show the face or form of Ramana Maharshi, save only his long tapering finger. Could this be because the emphasis is neither on a figure nor a particular human personality, but on something transcendental?

Even though Pradeep's dream was powerful, it did not immediately alter his life. Yet it perhaps began a significant process. Much time would elapse before its effect surfaced in his life.

Here I digress briefly to introduce a friend of Pradeep's who became instrumental in furthering his quest: Maurice Frydman, a Polish engineer. Maurice had made India his home many years earlier, and had given up his profession to devote himself to the study of Indian philosophy. In the early thirties Maurice had joined Mahatma Gandhi and had worked with him for a while, after which he lived briefly at Ramana Maharshi's ashram. Later in his life he frequently visited another mystic, Nisargadatta Maharaj, who lived in a rather humble tenement in the back-lanes of Khetwadi in Bombay. He visited him almost every day, with Pradeep often driving him there. Maurice would note down all conversations that took place between visitors who came from around the world and Nisargadatta Maharaj. This record of questions and answers became the modern spiritual classic *I Am That.*

Maharaj was a simple man, who had no formal education, but came to be loved and respected for his spiritual insights pertaining to the crux of human suffering and its transcendence, without recourse to conventional religious formulations. Pradeep, on the odd occasion, had wandered into the flat with Maurice, and was struck by Maharaj's presence: a short man dressed in dhoti-kurta sitting cross-legged in a tiny room, enveloped by the fragrance of incense sticks, answering with radiant energy people's age-old questions of origins and the awakening of their true nature. In those days Pradeep had viewed this only with the passing interest of the curious.

Maurice Frydman then passed away, and Nisargadatta Maharaj performed his last rites. This was the last occasion when Pradeep saw Maharaj. Years passed till Pradeep had his dream and an urge to meet Maharaj gained intensity within him. He knew Maharaj lived in Khetwadi, but Pradeep could not recall the address. Maurice was dead and he knew no one else through whom he could relocate Maharaj.

He set off for Khetwadi where he asked many people about Maharaj's residence. But he could not find it. Two nights later he dreamt:

I'm at Khetwadi and find myself turning left. There I meet a man in a white kurta pyjama who says, 'You have been looking for Nisargadatta Maharaj's place. I've been told to take you there.' The man takes me through by-lanes which were now becoming familiar to the ones that led to Maharaj's house. The man then stops, points to a cigarette-vendor's shop as a marker, then turns towards the opposite building and says, 'Go to the first floor. You are being awaited there.' I realize that it is Maharaj's house.

Pradeep awoke from the dream with absolute certainty of where Maharaj's house was located. However, due to work pressures he postponed his visit for several days. The directions given in the dream faded away. On his next attempt Pradeep tried to locate the by-lane with the cigarette vendor, but without success. He was back to square one: he still yearned to meet Maharaj but didn't know his address.

A month later the dream repeated itself:

I find myself again turning left at Khetwadi, and being taken by the same man through the back-lanes. Only this time, on reaching Maharaj's house, the man says 'This is the last time I'm bringing you here. Next time you will have to do it by yourself.'

These are amazing dreams because of their sheer repetition. And any residual ambiguity he may have had was dispelled. The dream was no longer an elusive hint, but a command. Its warning was compelling Pradeep to act upon his desire to meet Nisargadatta Maharaj. Forgetfulness was no longer a permissible excuse for inaction. The next day Pradeep reached Khetwadi, found the house, and climbed the steep steps leading to the mezzanine floor, where Maharaj sat as though awaiting him.

Most of the dreams we have discussed seem to either encourage, as in Megha's case, or introduce, as in Pradeep's dreams, the need to establish a connection with something transpersonal. Geeta Prasher's dream provides another dimension on this pilgrimage towards faith.

Every summer Geeta and her husband would head for the hills of Kulu-Manali in northern India. They would have to stop at the Kulu barrier to pay the necessary toll tax and would use the opportunity to stretch their legs, and then drive on. An ordinary activity like this became extraordinary when one night Geeta had a dream:

We are approaching the Kulu barrier. It is drizzling and the mist is making our progress slow. We reach the toll barrier and I get out of the car and walk a few steps ahead to stretch my legs. I continue to walk for, maybe, another hundred yards, when I hear a voice informing me that a little below where I'm standing is a Shivalinga [a symbol of worship for the Hindu god Shiva], *that I should go down the hill, into the ravine, and offer water there. I find myself walking down some stone steps when suddenly I see this rather huge Shivalinga in black stone. The Shivalinga is placed on a flat stone and seems to rise out of nowhere – powerful, immovable, full of some invisible energy.*

As I circle the Shivalinga, offering water, I feel part of some cosmic mystery, in which Shiva the creator and controller of the universe, a god who protects all and who, on the day of dissolution, withdraws all, is in essence embodied in that lingam, *whose altar seems not just that flat piece of stone slab, but the entire earth.*

This dream impacted Geeta on more than one level. The awe she had felt in the dream for the Shivalinga persisted with as much intensity even after she had awoken. There was something that was strangely compelling about it. Geeta had seen many Shivalingas in various temples in the course of her life, but she could not understand what gave this dream the sense of the sacred.

Geeta was a Shiva devotee, but her devotion was relegated to a few rituals, a silent prayer offered whenever she was in trouble, or the occasional fast. Shiva was a part of her cultural and family heritage. However, she felt this dream established a direct link with her deity. The waters of devotion that had once been poured blindly on the altar of her faith were now purified by a personal connection.

At another level, the dream's force arose not only because of its inner significance, but because Geeta nurtured the belief that there was an actual Shivalinga somewhere near the Kulu barrier. She was convinced that her dream was a clairvoyant vision meant to draw her attention to its existence. The passage of days only strengthened her belief. It need not be stressed that she had taken the dream literally.

Fifteen days later, Geeta, accompanied by her husband and son, left for Kulu on their annual vacation in the hills. They reached the Kulu toll barrier at about four o'clock in the afternoon. While her husband paid the toll tax she and her son walked ahead on the road. She stopped and looked down the mountain. Nothing but a sheer drop stared back at her. She walked further, her gaze searching. After some distance she saw some steps leading down. She grabbed her son's hand and ran the rest of the distance. They took the fifty-odd roughly hewn steps leading down, and there she was confronted with the reality of her dream. Resting on a stone slab was a huge Shivalinga made of black stone. Awestruck by this confirmation, she stood transfixed as the deep mountain silence enfolded her. The only way she could articulate her joy was by ringing the overhead bell again and again. A miracle had been enacted. Where dream began and reality took over was difficult to ascertain as she beheld the Shivalinga and poured water around it, as if simultaneously enacting the libation both in the waking world and the dream state.

The sense of awe experienced by a person when confronted with an extraordinary and meaningful coincidence was termed by Jung as *synchronicity*. This often has a mysterious numinosity about it, which comes into even sharper focus when the 'meaningful coincidence' is a dream that finds its confirmation in outer reality. The emotional impact of this experience sears itself into the person's consciousness so that the dream message is taken profoundly to heart.[6] Both inner and outer forces intersect to confirm for the dreamer that it was no random, chance encounter, but a directed and purposeful message transmitted to establish an experiential link between the personal life of the dreamer and that which transcends his or her individuality.

In the realm of the inexplicable lies 'Nirmala Pandey's' unusual experience. She believed she was initiated through a dream. She had never met Anandamayi Ma (a prominent guru, with a very large international following), but had only seen her photographs. One night she dreamt:

Anandamayi Ma gives me semal [cotton tree] *flowers. She says to me, 'Look after them.' There is an expression of love on her face which I find very moving.*

Her curiosity aroused, Nirmala accompanied a friend to Anandamayi Ma's ashram. She had just about sat down when Anandamayi Ma looked her straight in the eyes and asked, 'So, did you look after the *semal* flowers I sent you?'

Stunned, Nirmala could only stare at Ma. How did she know? Could it be that she had sent the message? But how did she know me, since we had never met? And how and why did she choose me? Had she sent this message so that I would come to her? Questions darted through Nirmala's mind, but she did not have an answer to even one of them.

We can circumvent these questions by assuming that an unknown person (Ma) had telepathically 'sent' Nirmala a dream. Then the surprising bit is that the unknown person also knew that Nirmala had received the dream. Or, when put the other way, it still does not diminish its mystery. If Ma had sent a general message without specifically directing it towards Nirmala, then how did Ma instantly recognize Nirmala as the receiver of her message? Both ways, the immediate recognition is mysterious. Further, if we call this dream a telepathic communication we run up against the problem that both Nirmala and Ma were unknown to each other so that the necessary link between the sender and the receiver was absent.

Though these questions remain unanswered, to Nirmala it did not matter. What struck her deeply was that she had been initiated through a dream, and that her guru had chosen her, even before she herself had set out in search of one. She was awed by the manner of the 'call'.

The Tibetans recognize that dreams are integral to religious life, more so before one's initiation into it. The aspirant is enjoined to observe his or her dreams in order to ascertain whether the desire for initiation is confirmed or denied by the deity. The Tibetan tradition hinges this on a karmic connection between guru and disciple. 'In other words, a sympathy must exist between the initiate and the realms that she or he is seeking initiation into, or between the initiate and the deity of the initiation, and this sympathy can be revealed or denied through dreams.'[7]

Fritjof Capra, the author of *The Tao of Physics*, dreamt that the dance of particles in the subatomic world was Lord Shiva's dance, and with this he fused his background in physics with his understanding of Eastern philosophy.[8]

Once again it may be felt that most of these dreams are prophetic, heralding what is to happen in the future. Pradeep's repeated dream instructions to Nisargadatta Maharaj's house proved accurate, as did

Geeta's directions to the Shivalinga. Nirmala was informed by her dream that she would find her teacher in Anandamayi Ma. Instead of prophecy, Jung's principle of synchronicity would better characterize these dreams. Seemingly obscure inner promptings became charged with meaning as they found a new direction in an outer event. Or, an inner direction that had been set in motion was first expressed through a dream and subsequently found its confirmation in an outer event. After all, Pradeep was already disillusioned and perhaps open to something else, while Geeta and Nirmala were both ready for a deeper commitment to something spiritual in their life. Their dreams helped them find a container for their aspirations. However, synchronicity is not the only yardstick for a numinous dream. Some dreams directly address the transpersonal concerns of the dreamer, without any outer confirmation. Perhaps we may say that the above dreams were those that helped the dreamers find their paths. The next few dreams are ones of guidance and instruction to help deepen an inner search. The former heir-apparent to the Maharaja of Jammu and Kashmir, Dr Karan Singh, dreamt:

We were in Kashmir and were driving down from our house towards the polo ground. Just before the bridge we turned off the main road, evidently in a visit to some well-known woman saint. It was apparently our first visit, as we were not quite sure where she lived.

On the way Asha [the dreamer's wife] *and I were in the leading car, followed by a long convoy of official cars. Suddenly it struck me as absurd that on such a visit we should be followed by a long convoy. I stopped the car and asked the sentry to hold back the cars following us so that we could proceed alone.*

We drove on for about ½ a mile and came to a square where some people had collected. We got out of the car and assembled in front of a building which evidently was the residence of the woman saint we had come to visit. We were under the impression that the only way to get into the building would be to have to be hauled up on some kind of a platform.

After some time the woman saint came out of the house. She was middle aged and had a tilak [a mark on the forehead worn by Hindus] *but otherwise I had not seen her before.*

Looking around the group of people gathered outside her house, she quickly recognised us and asked Asha and me to come into the house behind her. Contrary to our earlier expectation, the entry was quite normal through a door. As soon as we entered the house she

*closed the door and led us through the house. On the other side the
scene was dramatically different. There was a huge lake with fish
and clumps of bushes and behind a range of impressive mountains.
The house was very narrow, and we were surprised at the radical
change of scene.*

*I remarked, 'I never knew there was such a big lake here; what
is it called?' 'Anchar,' she replied.*[9]

In fact, Anchar is a marshy lake that the dreamer's father, the
erstwhile Maharaja of Jammu and Kashmir, had used for shooting
snipes. At the very outset of the dream we are informed that this dream
is not about the ordinary – the dreamer turns off the main road. What
is also clear is that the subject matter is something very private to the
dreamer – he finds the convoy of cars absurd and asks it to be held back
so that he and his wife can proceed alone. Their going to meet a religious
person indicates that his is a religious quest. His uncertainty about
where the woman-saint lives perhaps signifies that he is journeying
to an unknown region within himself. The importance of the dream
seems to reside in the dreamer's belief that he would *'have to be hauled
up on some kind of platform'*, when, in fact, *'the entry was quite normal
through a door'*.[10] Through this metaphor the dream is clearly instructing
the dreamer that no special set of rituals has to be carried out to gain
admittance to that part of himself which is spiritual. The entry is as
simple as entering through a door.

It would be evident that there is a difference between this dream
and those we have just discussed. In the earlier dreams the dreamer is
being introduced to the fact that there is something more to our lives
– a reality or dimension beyond that of our mundane perceptions. Here
the dreamer seems to be already apprised of this dimension – he has
consciously set out to meet the woman-saint. Had he inadvertently
stumbled upon her house then we would have understood the
encounter to be an unintentional one. Furthermore, her recognizing
him may not be due to his royal lineage alone; we have already been
told that he has divested himself of those privileges by distancing
himself from the convoy. Her singling him out from the waiting crowd
to allow him entry into the house could be a further indicator that he
is already familiar with the spiritual dimension and is perhaps actively
seeking it. Her leading him through the house to a lake, which he finds
dramatic and impressive, may be a symbolic depiction of the inner
quest. The lake in actual fact belongs to his father, and therefore to

him, which may signify that the journey is an interior one and not a 'journey of the feet'.

Another example: a woman who was experiencing grave doubts about her friendship with 'Sujata' had the following dream:

> *Sujata and I are walking in front of the director's house in AIIMS* [All India Institute of Medical Sciences] *and what I am holding on to is a red balloon on which is written, 'Hold a meditative awareness'. Sujata and I have to pass this balloon to each other as we walk. At times the balloon bursts but it is immediately replaced by another one. The mood is of a withdrawn state of consciousness where both Sujata's and my personality are in no way interfering with the quietness and contemplation of the activity.*

Both the dreamer and Sujata had taken initiation from the same guru and that had led to a friendship between them, even though they lived in different cities. The basis of their relationship and the inscription on the balloon alert us to the level of interpretation of the dream. The passing of the balloon to each other is a metaphor that binds the two friends together. Its red colour tells us that their exchange is laced with (unexpressed) anger. Their walking in a hospital complex – AIIMS – is indicative of a malaise between them. On a non-personal level it could also be alerting the dreamer about her AIM. Further, AIIMS may be seen as an anagram of I AM, or the essential self that the inner enquiry aims to discover. Not only is the dream enunciating her problem, but it also seems to be showing her how to resolve it. After all, they are walking in front of the director's house, which could be a reference to 'direct' one's attention to this aim. That aim could be to view her everyday interactions, specifically with Sujata (the balloon of anger), not merely as an investment of the personality, but something that must be overarched by a meditative awareness. In other words, her understanding should be reflective and imbued with self-awareness. The dream acknowledges that this is a difficult goal as the balloon periodically bursts. But its immediate replacement by another one urges her to continue unbroken her effort to foster a detached awareness. The dream appears to be instructing her not to polarize everyday actions as spiritual or mundane, but to use them to *direct* her attention to her *aim*. The balloon symbolizes daily actions and thoughts, and the inscription on the balloon suggests a way of dealing with them.

'Anjali Berry', who is now in her mid-forties, has been visiting the Ramakrishna Mission since she was twenty. She had been initiated into the order and thought of Sri Ramakrishna, one of India's most respected and influential spiritual teachers, as her guru, and tried to live by his precepts. Being an anxious person, worries crowded her day, and, by her own admission, she was a hypochondriac. During one of her anxiety-ridden phases she recorded a dream:

I am in a street in Kolkata, which is absolutely deserted. The street is lined on either side by old houses and the striking feature is that all the doors and windows of each of these homes are shut. Suddenly I see a rickshaw-puller come down the empty street with a passenger whom I cannot see at first. As he comes nearer I realize it is Sri Ramakrishna. He stands up in the rickshaw, flings his arms out vigorously, and proclaims energetically, 'Open all the doors and windows. Let the light in. Open them immediately. Don't keep them shut.' As the rickshaw-puller draws near Anjali, Sri Ramakrishna repeats, 'Open up ... open up,' and the empty street resounds with his words.

We could treat this as a psychological dream. All the doors and windows being shut allude to the closed personality of the dreamer. We presume that her anxieties are responsible for this. But this interpretation ignores two aspects of the dream that convinced Anjali that it was a *teaching* dream: the presence of her guru as the central protagonist of the dream and the exhortation to open her personality – to let the light in, which surely alludes to something beyond personal concerns.

Ramakrishna's life represented self-abandonment. He was prepared to disregard everything else for his central passion, his love for the divine. Even in Anjali's dream he was not a calm, passive figure. Instead, he was flailing his arms, passionately calling for the doors and windows to be thrown open for the light to enter. Many of us know what light meant to Ramakrishna – his vision had portrayed the divine as effulgent light in the previous chapter. To let the light in would then be an exhortation to Anjali to let the divine into her life. Also, Ramakrishna's abandon stood in direct contrast to Anjali's anxieties. And perhaps therein lay the lesson. He was gesticulating to Anjali to do the same.

This brings us to the question: If the guru appears in a dream, what does the image signify? Has the guru actually come to deliver a message of significance, as some are inclined to believe? My Teacher observed: 'In most cases, the living guru will seldom admit to having any knowledge of the dream. He himself has played no part in it. The figure in the dream is not him, but a representation of what the guru means to the disciple.'[11] Nirmala's dream seems to be an exception. Thus if in a dream you see your guru is unwell, in the majority of cases it is not a comment on your guru's health, but an indicator that your inner aspiration is presently lacking energy. At other times, the guru may be a symbol of your 'higher' self that is urging you in a particular direction, as in Anjali's dream and in the next example.

A woman and her husband, who live in America, had taken initiation from a guru in India, whom they visited every time they came to India. The woman had the following dream:

We are living in an old house overstuffed with furniture and other stuff. Our Guru has come to visit and is involved with our many 'running around' type activities – he follows us everywhere – weaving around the furniture. I keep thinking that we should find time to sit down with him at some time. We have to find him a place to sleep as well. I put some sheets on a sofa but wonder if it will be broad enough. I try it out myself by lying down on it. He says it is fine. He lies down on it and as he does that the sofa expands out to the size of a single bed, then retracts when he gets up.

The previous few months had been intensely hectic for the couple with various children- and work-related activities. Also, a spate of visitors and houseguests left them very little spare time during the day to pursue their inner work. This is aptly described in the dream: despite their guru being in America (in fact, a virtual impossibility) they are involved in their '*running around*' activities to the extent that instead of the couple making time to sit with him, he is following them around. I believe the dream is not so much a chastisement as it is a teaching dream. The strange part of the dream that immediately attracts attention is the expanding-retracting bed. And it is the guru's bed, alluding to the set of practices given to them by their guru: their inner work. The dream suggests: If there is no time during the day for spiritual practice then why not use the night for inner work? But the bed is too small for the guru to sleep on, indicating that she is doubtful whether it is at all possible to do inner work at that time. Her guru, however, does not concur. He lies down and shows her that the bed expands, symbolizing that the nocturnal space is broad enough for spiritual practice, or that sleep and dream are suitable vehicles for the disciple's effort. Needless to say that 'sleep' does not allude to the sleep of forgetfulness, but to the idea that it is possible to negotiate sleep with awareness. And to achieve this 'awareness' in sleep and dream some preparations would have to be made before going to bed. The relationship of sleep and dream to the meditational effort of the disciple will be discussed in later chapters.

Moreover, in the dream the sofa retracts when the guru gets up, suggesting that though this effort to remain 'aware' may recede and contract during the day with the pace of work and activities, it should subtly pervade the dreamer's consciousness, almost as a backdrop. This last thought is expressed in the image of the guru following them everywhere, the implication being that, in time, after having gained enough strength through practices of awareness, this backdrop may inform the dreamer's day world. In fact, the sofa expanding and retracting for day use and night use could represent that the holding of awareness (self-remembering) during the day and the nocturnal effort should continuously interact and strengthen each other.

Anamike Sharma is a Dutch woman married to an Indian and settled in New Delhi. She is a healer and has a steady stream of people coming to her. She recounted a dream experience during a phase when she was particularly troubled by the mental and physical sufferings of the people she was treating.

> There is a circular area enclosed by very high walls. On the ground people are crawling, grasping, fighting for space. Many of them are trying to climb the wall but fall back either because they are being pushed aside or cannot get a foothold on the wall. I try to climb it too, but find it impossible. I keep thinking that there must be another way to get out of this prison, for I now know that this is a realistic picture of life on earth – the clamouring frenzy of the human struggle and the hopelessness of there being no way out. As I'm thinking this I begin to rise and I fly over the high walls. As soon as I cross the walls I look back and see the fight on earth where people look much smaller but the blur of their frantic struggle is still palpable. As I rise higher everything changes. I feel a tremendous sense of freedom and am enveloped by a force so intense that it is love itself. Suddenly everything becomes pure light ... I'm enveloped in it, cradled by it, and yet feel one with it. There is a sense of joy and the wonder of oneness.

The dream opens by telling us the dreamer is feeling swamped by the 'clamouring frenzy' of everyday life and the 'hopelessness' of the human situation. She has also tried to climb the same walls of hope that have lured everyone else to fight for a foothold. Soon she realizes that rather than free people, these walls imprison them; that the solution does not lie in 'fulfilment' within ordinary coordinates, but elsewhere, in another dimension, as shown in the dream by her rising above. As she ascends, people become smaller, and their struggle, though still palpable, begins to blur. The dream further informs her that if she continues to rise higher everything changes – the blizzard raging below miraculously subsides and gives way to an effulgence (light) that can only be described as sheer '*joy*' and a vision of '*oneness*'. This change in perspective is possibly achieved only by a change in consciousness, towards which the mystic ceaselessly strives. It is a state of being, the dream informs her, where particulars of desire and attachment are erased, duality is transcended, and in the relinquishing of the personal, oneness is found.

This is perhaps not a teaching dream but a perspective of the human predicament, and it seems the only dimension from which it can be resolved is a transpersonal one – the vertical ascent. There seems to be a commonality of content in most of these dreams. In the dream about Sujata the balloon of anger obliquely alluded to the need for a meditative awareness as the backdrop of ongoing everyday involvements. Similar advice of being self-aware during both sleep and dream was also given to the woman in whose dream the sofa-bed expands and contracts. In both these dreams, this transpersonal state is something the dreamer has to strive towards, while Anamike was spontaneously given a glimpse of it.

What was shown more explicitly to Anamike was only given as a hint to Anjali – light. The experience of 'light' appears very often in dream and prayer when people describe their transpersonal experience; the Bhagavad Gita describes this luminescence as the light of a thousand suns blazing. Whether this is an expression of surrender to something beyond oneself or a metaphor for something much more subtle and far more powerful than any of our daily experiences can perhaps only be ascertained through personal experience. Its universal appearance is perhaps the only proof of its reality.

The numinosity experienced in the dreams we have just looked at has been the greatest mystery that man has struggled with. That there is something that empowers human life has been felt by many. What it is in itself has been the experience of very few. Yet those who have glimpsed it have found that it transforms their view on the purpose of human existence. It reveals to them the bedrock of the eternal in the transitory, the radiance of the universal in the particular.

This is what J. B. Priestley discovered in his dream, which he recalls in his book *Man and Time*:

> *I was standing at the top of a very high tower, alone, looking down upon myriads of birds all flying in one direction ... It was a noble sight, this vast aerial river of birds. But now in some mysterious fashion the gear was changed, and time speeded up, so that I saw generations of birds, watched them break their shells, flutter into life, weaken, falter, and die. Wings grew only to crumble; bodies were sleek and then, in a flash, bled and shrivelled; and death struck everywhere and at every second. What was the use of all this blind struggle towards life, this eager trying of wings, all this gigantic meaningless biological effort? As I stared down, seeming to see every creature's ignoble little history almost at a glance, I felt sick at heart. It would be better if not one of them, not one of us all, had been born ... But now the gear was changed again and time went faster still, and it was rushing by at such a rate, that the birds could not show any movement but were like an enormous plain sown with feathers. But along this plain, flickering through the bodies themselves, there now passed a sort of white flame, trembling, dancing, then hurrying on; and as soon as I saw it I knew that this flame was life itself, the very quintessence of being; and then it came to me, in a rocket-burst of ecstasy, that nothing mattered, nothing could ever matter, because nothing else was real, but this quivering and hurrying lambency of being. Birds, men, or creatures not yet shaped and coloured, all were of no account except so far as this flame of life travelled through them. It left nothing to mourn over behind it; what I had thought was tragedy was mere emptiness or a shadow show; for now all real feeling was caught and purified and danced on ecstatically with the white flame of life. I had never felt before such deep happiness as I knew at the end of my dream.* [12]

The dream needs no further elaboration. Any attempt at interpretation would only sully the dream with the analyst's beliefs.

Chapter 23

LUCID DREAMING:
WHO DREAMS THE DREAM?

From the power that binds all creatures none is free
Except the man who wins self-mastery

Johann Wolfgang von Goethe

The fourth seeker in the ancient Indian scripture Prasna Upanishad (IV.I) questions his teacher: Sir, what sleeps in a person? What is it that remains awake in him? Who sees the dream? Who is the enjoyer of sleep? In essence, who is he? With these simply framed straightforward questions we step into a different metaphysic altogether. We will have to address their philosophical substratum before we can find the answer to the conundrum: Who dreams the dream?

The obvious answer is: Me, of course! But then who is this 'me'? The daytime personality – this bundle of tissues and memories? Or something more? While asleep the body is inert, the personality dormant, yet the sensory perceptions and emotional tenor in a dream are sharply vivid. So who is it whose nocturnal space is equally fraught with fears and terror, suffering and despair, and at times shines with hope or is suffused with transcendence? Who is this 'I' who feels this whole spectrum of waking life without the instrument of the body or normal consciousness? Whoever it may be, it is not the 'I' that I habitually call myself. Is the participant in the dream the same as the viewer of the dream? Furthermore, the desires that find expression in dreams are those that were unacknowledged by the waking personality. They seem to belong to a being who is wider and deeper than what I know myself to be; one whose memory is greater than mine and whose perceptions are different from my own.[1] This applies especially to numinous dreams, like Pradeep Sanyal's or Anamike's. They certainly hinted about a state of being that was not their own. Where do such numinous dreams come from? In fact, where do all dreams come from?

We tacitly believe that the dream is the property of the sleeper, even though the sleeper has no control over the dream and feels no responsibility for the acts committed in it. Yet when the dream is vivid and meaning-rich in the context of his or her circumstances, it is very difficult for the dreamer to persuade him or herself that these images have no significance. Under such conditions, whether as protagonist or as witness, the dreamer believes that the dream comes from some superior power, and that he or she is the privileged recipient of something sacred. Hence the Upanishadic question: Who dreams the dream?

A variety of questions are intertwined with this one, and answers to them would have a deep influence on our understanding of dream formation and, consequently, who we consider to be the dreamer of the dream. These are not questions about the interpretation of dreams, but they relate to the source of the dream. Different schools have presented widely differing answers as we have seen.

The ancient Greeks saw dreams as an external entity, as visitations from the people residing in the Village of Dreams (*oneiros demiros*). The Islamic world, much like the Jews, postulated an intermediate world of *khayal* (imagination) that fathers the dream. The Hindus believed that the real dreamer is Lord Vishnu, who dreams the Universe. They asserted that although the individual, blinded by the heresy of separateness, imagines it is he or she (or the subtle body) who is the dreamer of the dream, the truth is that consciousness, whether allied to the waking, dreaming, or sleeping state, is actually trapped in the illusion of *maya*. If the essence of the question were sought, then all these identifications of consciousness would have to be transcended to find in the fourth state of *turiya* the real 'dreamer'. In other words, they believed the dreamer of the dream to be the greater life in which the 'I' is but a wave, a passing form that moves upon the sea of consciousness that gave it birth.[2]

In contrast, dream theorists in the earlier part of the twentieth century hypothesized that the genesis of the dream is in the unconscious – as mythical a conception as that of the ancient world. Later, dreaming was attributed to memory processes: they are largely plucked from the memory bank of the dreamer, and their substance is usually based on the manipulation or reorganization of these personal memories. However, as we noted earlier, not all dreams are personal testimonies; sometimes the concerns of others find their way into the dream – as in the shared or telepathic dream. They counter this objection by stating that dreams that deviate from the 'ordinary' constitute a mere 10 percent of the bulk of dreaming and can thus be safely ignored. In short, they advocate that the dream is essentially a memory structure.

This memory-based model believes that the subliminally perceived images from the waking world (the day residue and forgotten memories) are the building blocks of the dream and that the dream is an appendage to waking reality. This pejorative dependence of the dream on the day world is completed when we discover a bridge (the interpretation) that will lead the dream back across from the remote night world to the real life of the dreamer. After all, the aim of all interpretation is to rescue or reclaim (Freud's own metaphor) the dream from the delirium of sleep to the sanity of the day world. Even the function of dreams is limited to serving the needs of the day world: 'We read them for messages about living situations, choices, and relationships of our conscious life, its problems, feelings and thoughts. By means of the dream we may remember what was forgotten in the past, perceive what we missed in the present, or decide about the future, reading the dream prophetically, oracularly'[3] – so that we may be better able to cope with our waking lives.

We are thus confronted with a conflict about the dreaming process. On the one hand we firmly believe that the dream essentially belongs to the night world. On the other hand we insist on identifying in this child of the night the colours of our waking reality (memories), always forcing it to return to the day world by translating it into the language of waking life, 'either as a message to be decoded for the day-world (Freud) or as a compensation to it (Jung)'.[4]

The compromise between the demands of the romantic night world and the needs of the rational day world results in our inability to ascertain who dreams the dream, and to which realm the dream belongs.

We believe that dreams are private and therefore subjective, while when awake we are in a public domain and it is therefore objective. Being a personal one the dream world is lonely, while waking is a shared social reality. The former is irrational, the latter sensible. During the day we preserve continuity in one form or another; the dream world, on the other hand, is disconnected, thus making the dream wholly an internal phenomenon, inaccessible, perhaps, even to the dreamer after he or she has awoken. Above all, in the dream we participate without volition, while our waking hours are characterized by exercising choices that we are held responsible for.

This dichotomy between the irrationality of the dream world and the sanity of the waking world was rudely shattered with laboratory confirmations of the *lucid* dream in 1985. The studies conducted fundamentally dissolved the reality-illusion barrier between the day and the dream worlds. With the dissolution of this boundary between the objective world of waking life and the subjective world of dreams, all distinctions between lonely or shared, private or public, involuntary or conscious melted. And, the age-old questions surfaced once again: Whose property is the dream? The day world or the night world? Which state of human consciousness is at work?

Perhaps it would be best to introduce the lucid dream as a form of dreaming that is completely different from all types of dreams discussed thus far. A very simple definition of a lucid dream is one in which you know that you are dreaming. The term 'lucid dreaming' was coined by Frederik van Eeden, who used the word 'lucid' to indicate mental clarity while dreaming. This contrasts with 'normal' dreams, where we are not aware that we are dreaming and we believe that the waking state participates only indirectly in the dream as recalled imagery; that having no access to waking memories the dream progresses on its own momentum. However, in a lucid dream there is a continuity of consciously accessible memory that directly links the dream to waking experience, allowing the dreamer to contrast dream events with the everyday world. This 'awakening' within the dream in no way disturbs, or ends, the dream state. The great contradiction of lucid dreaming is that the private, unconscious world of dreaming inexplicably melts into a state where you are both awake (conscious) and asleep simultaneously. An actual dream may best exemplify this:

> I dreamed that I was walking by the water on the ... shore. It was morning; the sky a light blue; the foam-flecked waves were greenish in the sunshine. I forget just how it happened, but something told me that I was dreaming ... I decided to prolong the dream and continued my walk, the scenery now appearing extraordinarily vivid and clear. Very soon my body began to draw me back. I experienced dual

consciousness: I could feel myself lying in bed and walking by the
sea at one and the same time. Moreover, I could dimly see the objects
of my bedroom, as well as the dream scenery. I willed to continue
dreaming. A battle ensued; now my bedroom became clearly visible
and the shore-scene dim; then my bedroom would become indistinct
and the shore-scene brighter. My will triumphed. I lost the sense of
dual consciousness. My bedroom faded altogether from my vision,
and I was out on the shore feeling indescribably free and elated.[5]

This dream highlights some typical elements of lucid dreams: the
dreamer is not completely immersed in the dream, but is also aware
that he or she is dreaming. Secondly, normal memory is available
during the dream: '*my body began to draw me back*'; '*my bedroom became*
clearly visible'. After becoming lucid, the dream becomes very vivid;
not only is waking memory accessible, but the attainment of lucidity
helps the dreamer experience the dream more clearly. Lastly, after a
little vacillation, the dreamer takes control of the experience, exercising
the choice to continue the dream walk along the shore, rather than
wake up.

It is not necessary that all these elements must be present in a lucid
dream. The quality of lucidity can and does vary greatly. At its height,
the dreamer is aware of a dual consciousness – everything experienced
is within the dream, yet there is a continuity of waking awareness.
Furthermore, there is volitional control over the course of the dream. In
the earliest stage of lucidity the dreamer may experience it in a variety
of ways. Lucidity can occur when the dreamer is not able to clearly
ascertain whether he or she is awake or dreaming; or, when there is
a false awakening – the dreamer awakes only within the dream, but
is left with the feeling that he or she has awoken from sleep. Usually
when inexperienced lucid dreamers realize that they are dreaming, this
sudden perception of lucidity may jolt them into actually waking up
and the dream experience then ends.

A short historical perspective may show us that lucid dreaming has
been prevalent since antiquity, affirming humankind's awareness and
interest in states of consciousness beyond mundane daytime reality.
As far back as the fourth century BC, Aristotle wrote: 'For often, when
one is asleep, there is something in consciousness which declares that
what then presents itself is but a dream.'[6] The earliest report of a lucid
dream is preserved in a letter written in AD 415 by St Augustine. We
have already described the two dreams of Gennadius in chapter 19. In

the second dream Gennadius has clearly become lucid as he continues to dream and converse with the youth, all along aware of his body lying asleep in bed. By the eighth century the Tibetan Buddhists had already worked out a sophisticated experiential technique designed to maintain full waking consciousness while dreaming, which we will discuss in detail in the next chapter.

In the thirteenth century St Thomas Aquinas referred to lucid dreaming, citing Aristotle's supposition that the power of the senses remains undiminished during sleep. He said, 'Not only does the imagination retain its freedom, but also the common sense is partly freed; so that sometimes while asleep a man may judge that what he sees is a dream, discerning, as it were, between things and their images.'[7]

The advent of the nineteenth century heated up the debate on lucid dreaming. Pioneering work was done by many scholars who assiduously maintained a log of their dreams. Possibly, the most detailed study was done by the Marquis d'Hervey de Saint-Denys, a professor of the Chinese language, who documented about twenty years of dream research in his book, *Dreams and How to Guide Them* (published in 1867). F. W. H. Myers, a classical scholar at Cambridge University and one of the founders of the Society for Psychical Research, tried very hard to become lucid in his dreams, complaining that he succeeded on only three nights out of three thousand nights in realizing that he was dreaming.[8]

Freud was aware of such dreams, believing that lucidity was fundamental to the dreaming process: 'I am driven to conclude that *throughout our whole sleeping state we know just as certainly that we are dreaming as we know that we are sleeping.*'[9] According to him this presumably occurred at the level of the censor or the preconscious as a purely defensive function. Taken unawares by a dream that has already slipped past and gone too far, and being too late to suppress the threatening symbolism that may awaken the dreamer, the censor is thus forced to dismiss it as 'it's only a dream' and set at rest the anxiety caused by the dream. However, Freud did concede that 'there are some people who are quite clearly aware during the night that they are asleep and dreaming and who thus seem to possess the faculty of consciously directing their dreams. If, for instance, a dreamer of this kind is dissatisfied with the turn taken by a dream, he can break it off without waking up and start it again in another direction – just as a popular dramatist may under pressure give his play a happier ending.'[10]

The increasing debate on lucidity in dreams did not mean that scholars or the scientific community recognized such dreams. On the contrary, despite many individual accounts of lucid dreaming these claims were strongly discounted on philosophical grounds: How can a person be conscious that he or she is dreaming? The dreamer's feeling of being aware within a dream was explained away as a brief or partial arousal – a micro-awakening. Any arousal, whether partial or brief, implies a physiological change of state from dreaming to waking. In other words, the dreamer actually wakes up for a fraction of a second and the memory of that micro-awakening lingers through the dream, leaving an impression of being awake during the course of the dream. Seductive though this reasoning was, we now have concrete proof that this is not the mechanism of a lucid dream. Dreamers became lucid while their sleep patterns were being closely monitored in a laboratory. Since human physiology registers differently in the three states of waking, sleeping, and dreaming, researchers would immediately be able to detect the onset of a dream, and know whether the dreamer had momentarily awoken before wafting back into the dream. Laboratory research belied the arousal mechanism, but the truly impressive aspect of these studies was not simply the confirmation of lucid dreams, but that the researchers devised a way by which the dreamer could communicate with them while simultaneously continuing to experience a dream.

Since the muscular system is inert during the currency of a dream the only way to signal the onset of lucidity would be through eye movements. It was decided that a prearranged number of exaggerated eye movements would be used as a signal to indicate that the dreamer had experienced lucidity, for example, moving the eyes left to right three times. During ordinary dreaming the eye movements are usually involuntary. So it was reasoned that if, while dreaming, a person made specific, prearranged ocular movements it would convincingly demonstrate that the person was lucid, while the laboratory equipment would testify that he or she was asleep and experiencing a dream. The eye movements could be picked up by the EOG pen tracings, which would constitute an objective record of the onset of lucidity within the currency of the dream.

In 1975, Alan Worsley, a long-time lucid dreamer from Britain, had the usual REM monitoring equipment attached to him by Keith Hearne, a fellow graduate student at the sleep laboratory of Hull University in England. Worsley had been instructed to move his eyes from left to right a certain number of times if he became aware that he was experiencing a lucid dream. When Worsley experienced dream lucidity, he remembered the signal and did make the specific eye movements.

The EEG recordings indicated that Worsley was fully asleep in a REM period and the EOG bore witness that he had given the prearranged eye signal.[11] Over the course of a year, Worsley had spent forty-five nights in a sleep lab and had eight lucid dreams, in each of which the EOG showed that he made the specified eye movement signals whenever he became aware he was dreaming.[12]

Unaware of Keith Hearne's work, Stephen LaBerge, a young chemical physicist-turned-dream researcher in the U.S. and the author of *Lucid Dreaming*, conducted essentially the same experiment with himself as the dreaming subject. He also succeeded in making the required ocular signals. Once again, the lucid dream had been successfully isolated. Objective laboratory evidence had now been obtained from both sides of the Atlantic to confirm that lucid dreams do exist.[13]

The fact that lucid dreamers know that they are asleep and can communicate with the waking world through prearranged signals made possible a whole new approach to dream research. The dream world was no longer isolated from waking reality; subjects could be asked to perform any chosen action while dreaming, which could be recorded. Experiments conducted by LaBerge at the Stanford University Sleep Research laboratories addressed a range of issues that helped understand the dream state, as well as explore its connections with waking reality.

These experiments opened a whole new area of debate in philosophy, psychophysiology, and the neurosciences. These three disciplines have a longstanding interest in the relationship between mind and body. The misconception that dreams are pure mental activity and have no effect on the body was dispelled by lucid dreamers. Through carefully controlled experiments, it was demonstrated that if the breath was held (or the sleeper breathed rapidly) in the dream, then corresponding changes were initiated in the sleeper's actual pattern of breathing.[14]

It is known that the left hemisphere of the brain shows increased activity during the use of language and analytical thinking, while the right one shows increased activity during spatial tasks and holistic thinking. Both sides of the cerebral hemispheres show markedly different brainwave activity depending on precisely which type of mental activity the person is engaged in at that moment. Research on lucid dreamers showed that when they sang or counted in their dreams, their brain activity was similar to when they performed the same functions during the waking state.[15]

A very interesting experiment was done concerning the lapse of time during the dream state. The lucid dreamer would signal the commencement and end of a session of counting to researchers, who would measure the time taken with a stopwatch. It took the dreamer thirteen seconds (by the stopwatch) to count from one to ten. The intention of the counting was to measure the lapse of time (ten seconds) in the dream state. This would seem to indicate that the passage of time is slower in dreams than in the waking world. However, when the same dreamer was asked to count up to ten while awake, it still measured thirteen seconds by the stopwatch![16]

Sexual activity seems to form a prominent part of the lucid dreams of many individuals, especially women. Patricia Garfield reported that two-thirds of her lucid dreams have sexual content and about half of these dreams culminate in orgasm.[17] In a pilot study with two lucid dreamers, both reported experiencing sexual arousal and orgasm in lucid dreams, and revealed patterns of physiological activity during dream sex that closely resembled those accompanying corresponding experiences in the waking state, except the heart rate.[18]

What these experiments proved was that lucid dreams seem to break all rules that we have framed for reality. If dream sex is like the waking experience, if the lapse of time in dreams and waking is the same, if counting and singing in dreams are like 'real' singing and counting, then would this not suggest that lucid dreaming (and by extension dreaming in general) is more like actual *doing* than merely *imagining*? If dream reality produces the same physiological changes that a similar event in waking life would, then why should we assume that one set of experiences – the waking ones – is 'real' and the other – the dream experiences – is unreal? In fact, like the Hindus believe, all that we can actually state is that the dream experience is as 'real' or 'unreal' as a waking one. But how will we then answer the related question: Who dreams the dream?

The quality of vividness in a lucid dream is such that it seems to verge on full wakefulness. Yet the lucid dream is distinct from most of our waking experiences. However, it also appears to be different from our normal dream experience. Lucid dreams refuse to be billeted into the traditional definition of dreaming. The hallmark of 'normal' dreams is that the dreamer does not have the ability to reflect like we do when awake. However, when lucid, the dreamer does have this self-referential ability. Is lucidity then an aberration of the dreaming process, a dream gone bizarre? Is the dreaming process going against its own grain?[19] Because the dreaming brain exhibits very different characteristics from the sleeping brain, dreams have been called paradoxical sleep. Similarly, lucidity has been viewed as paradoxical dreaming because it is very different from ordinary dreaming – it involves dual consciousness. Perhaps this is why lucid dreams constitute a challenge to our worldview: they can effortlessly mix an attitude of active participation, which characterizes our waking life, with the passive flow associated with dreaming. Harry Hunt has pointed out that without the lucid dream we would have been left with a falsely simplified idea of what dreaming is and can be. However, he maintains, it would be a mistake to treat the lucid dream as a totally unique and unparalleled form of consciousness.

Hunt's research had led him to link lucid dreams with meditation. He believed that lucid dreaming can help clarify the obscure aspects about the nature and goals of meditation. Both states exhibit a detached receptivity in the midst of everyday involvements – the former while dreaming and the latter while awake. Prolonged meditation can gradually extend into states of 'lucidity' and lucid dreams can become more and more visionary and insightful. In other words, lucid dreaming may be viewed as a spontaneous invocation of the state sought through meditation – a quiet mindfulness. He thus thought of lucid dreaming as a kind of meditative state – perhaps as even a necessary first step towards insightful meditative consciousness. Hunt experienced a dream that dramatically informed him that meditative states can be reached without lucidity. The dream adhered to the descriptive criteria of lucidity – dual awareness of context and involvement – and yet was not actually lucid:

> I dreamt I had returned to a small house full of sleeping cots called the 'rest house'. I was about to lie down when a disembodied but familiar voice said, 'You're acting like you really think you're in the rest house, but you're not, you know. Try and figure out where you really are.' Fascinated, I looked about me with the sharpened sense of clarity and excitement that I associate with my own, all too few lucid dreams. I knew things weren't as they seemed and I stared at the walls waiting for them to collapse into my 'real' surroundings. But they just got more and more crystalline and radiating until I woke up.[20]

Clearly, this is not a lucid dream wherein the dreamer has control over the dream surroundings. We are not even sure whether he is aware that he is dreaming, as at no point in the dream is it actually suggested. Yet the clarity and the heightened state of excitement are reminiscent of lucidity, as is his attempt to exercise control over the dream by trying to change the walls to those of his familiar waking surroundings. However, the walls do not oblige; instead they get sharper and brighter, indicating that it is not a lucid control dream. On awakening, Hunt says, 'Slightly chastened, I realized that it had never occurred to me that I might be dreaming, although it was a spontaneous meditative-like state.' Ordinary dreaming, so to speak, had induced in him a state which he associated only with lucidity and dream control.

Are we then to treat this as merely a normal dream with different (bizarre) walls? Perhaps not. There is a quality of wakefulness in it that is alien to ordinary dreaming. Besides, whose is the *'disembodied but familiar voice'*? It would be too pat to dismiss it as the dreamer conversing with himself, like we sometimes do while awake. Also, it would be too convenient to attribute this voice to dream bizarreness and ignore it. This was neither an ordinary nor an irrelevant element of the dream because the dreamer, on awakening, felt chastened by the admonition. He felt he was being 'told' that he should not rest confident in his belief that he had understood this state, but should explore and discover its actual truth. Was the voice alluding to a state of awareness that lay beyond the cognitive boundaries of waking, sleeping, and lucidity? The appeal certainly appeared to emanate from an impersonal source that 'knew' the distinction between these states of consciousness.

Let us take a closer look at the dream. At first we presume that the *'small house full of sleeping cots'* and the *'rest house'* allude to lucidity. We assume that the rest house is just a repetition, a descriptive label for lucidity. However, we are alerted by a voice that it does not allude to this referent, and the voice warns the dreamer that he is only presuming that he knows what the true rest house is. The *'small house full of sleeping cots'* possibly does refer to lucid dreaming – that small house within the domain of sleep. But what does the rest house allude to? We are then told that the dreamer was about to lie down – re-emphasizing sleep, and perhaps drawing attention to the question: why confuse the rest house with the sleeping condition of the body? This makes one speculate whether the rest house is something apart from the lucid state and possibly not even tied to the supine condition of the body. This is once again highlighted when the fascinated dreamer strives in the only direction familiar to him – dream control. He stares at the walls, willing them to collapse into the walls of his 'real' surroundings – a repeated emphasis on the word 'real' – for he knows in the dream that things are not what they seem to be. The unresponsiveness of the walls may signify that he was 'looking' in a direction different from what the 'knower' or disembodied voice in the dream was alluding to.

In exploring the primary meanings of the word 'rest' – that which remains or is left over, a remainder – we may get a clue to the dream allusion. Could the rest house be referring to a foundational state of consciousness that remains (left over) after collapsing our definitional walls? A state apart from the state of lucidity or its derivative dream control? A state that exists beyond the boundaries of the sleeping (or waking) condition of the body? In short, a transcendental consciousness that is attained after the mind has been brought to 'rest' (quiescence). Walls are, of course, reflective of a definitional boundary – confining this state of consciousness to lucidity. The dream does not concur with his definition and the unexpected change in the walls suggests that this foundational state is something entirely different from what he expects. Perhaps cognitive definitions have to 'collapse' when approaching another state of consciousness whose 'walls' can only be described as 'crystalline' – transparent, revealing, and pure. In the dream they begin to radiate, dissolving all distinctions. Was the dreamer approaching a foundational consciousness from which emerge the three states of waking, sleeping, and dreaming? An unalloyed consciousness that is autonomous and beyond these distinctions – radiant and luminous. Was the disembodied voice in the dream actually urging the dreamer towards a 'real' encounter with that level of human consciousness that penetrates beyond the sleeping and waking state? For finally belief does limit perception and in the dream Hunt was being asked to question where his beliefs were limiting him, preventing him from collapsing the walls of the sleeping and waking state to enable him to step beyond to the source of the three states of consciousness, their origins. Perhaps this higher state of consciousness cannot be given a name or a form, for it is without any quality. It permeates consciousness, and yet is beyond consciousness – 'like a hole in the paper is both in the paper and yet not of paper'.[21] Could this state be the source of the dreaming mind – the real dreamer of the dream?

Chapter 24

DREAM YOGA:
HARNESSING THE DREAM

Great dreamers' dreams are never fulfilled, they are always transcended.

A. N. Whitehead

*L*ucidity is in itself an unusual if not exceptional state. Its laboratory confirmation revitalized a much older debate: can dreaming become a bridge to altered (higher) states of consciousness? We can certainly see that lucidity, with its sense of dual awareness, may act as a bridge to other states of consciousness, but can ordinary dreaming also act as a conduit to greater self-awareness? Hunt's dream suggests that it can. It forces us to review dreaming from a new perspective. Perhaps even our everyday dreams may be a continuum in which there are gradations of self-reference or self-reflection; a complete absence of it at one end and by incremental advances reaching a stage in which the dreamer has a sustained awareness of what is actually happening – specifically that he or she is asleep in bed and dreaming.[1]

At the lowest level of this continuum the dreamer is not present in the dream and the dream involves unknown people and unfamiliar objects. For example, *the police were chasing a man down an alley*.[2] The dreamer is not a part of the dream and hence there is no self-reference in the dream. Self-reference in dreams moves a step upwards when the dreamer is a part of the dream, and the dreamer's attention is completely soaked in the action within the dream – *the police were chasing me; I was cornered in an alley with no chance of escape*. These are our normal dreams. One level higher on the scale and the dreamer is able to think over an idea, and reflects upon the action in the dream or communicates with someone else. For example, *I watched the police chase a man down my alley and wondered if he was a terrorist. My neighbour tells me, 'This is a fake encounter, a set up.'* An even higher stage is attained when the dreamer has multiple levels of awareness, and notices oddities while dreaming. For example: *As I was running from the police I wondered whether they would believe me if I surrendered and told them I was innocent. I then noticed that there were no doors opening into the alley, only windows, and all of them were barred. My only chance of escape was to scale the wall.* Here, the dreamer, while participating in the dream action, also reflects about intentions, monitors progress, and ponders over behaviour modification. One more step and the dreamer from simultaneously participating and reflecting within the dream may consciously deliberate whether he or she is dreaming.[3] *The police were chasing me and I saw my father standing at each doorway in the alley looking disgustedly at me. I found this very odd – how could my father be in so many places at the same time? I then realized that I was dreaming and all the anxiety of the police chasing me disappeared. I turned and faced the police and they all smiled at me.* The dreamer has become lucid by noticing the oddity in the dream.

Is lucidity then at the upper end of the continuum of self-awareness, in a totally unique and unparalleled state? Some researchers believe it is only a midway point that can lead to more refined states of consciousness. If the waking state is at one end of the sleep or dream continuum, could the other end be pure consciousness, 'a state in which all ordinary activity of thinking, feeling and perceiving has come to a complete rest, yet awareness remains wide awake within itself', and lucidity lies midway within this continuum? Typical lucid dreams may then be viewed as a commingling of the waking state with the dream state, and what is awakened in lucid dreaming is nearer the ego, the bounded 'I' of experience. May there not be another state beyond ordinary lucidity that makes apparent an awareness that centres on pure consciousness and transcends the everyday self, and is identified with a silent inner unbounded Self?[4] According to Hunt, maximum development of lucidity leads not to greater cognitive alertness or wakefulness, but to subjectively powerful states involving forms of enhanced self-awareness, which are reminiscent of meditational states in Eastern traditions.[5]

This is where meditational schools step in: to use such dreams as an aid to harnessing consciousness. The Hindus have always maintained that dreaming is a plane of experience just as the waking state is one. They believe that to win freedom from the cycle of birth, death, and suffering, the aspirant has to achieve detachment from the participatory pull of not only the waking state but of the dream state as well. In short, by turning lucid while dreaming the first necessary step is taken by the aspirant in the practice to transcend the dream state itself. A tenth-century Tantric text enjoins neophytes to retain their consciousness while sleeping. This can be achieved by cultivating a profoundly contemplative state before placing themselves at the junction of waking and sleeping.[6] As Hunt maintains, perhaps lucidity transforms dreams in the same way as meditation transforms wakefulness.

Lucidity and meditation appear to be related, and psychological studies affirm this link. It is estimated that nearly six out of ten people have experienced a lucid dream once in their life. Maybe only two people out of them have a lucid dream once a month. However, if the sample interviewed comprises people who practise meditation, then the average goes up to once a week.[7] Other studies confirm that experienced meditators have significantly more lucid dreams than non-meditating dreamers. Also shown is that the longer a person has been engaged in meditative practice (an average of five years) the more frequent the reports of lucid and control dreams – to the point where some subjects could not tell whether they were having a lucid dream or whether they had awakened and were spontaneously meditating.[8] Still other studies have demonstrated that the physiological state during lucid dreaming may be closely related to changes in EEG and other measures associated with meditation.[9] These findings have raised issues of similarities and parallels between what lucid dreaming and meditational states can achieve, especially in the attempt to harness consciousness towards higher levels of awareness.

Perhaps the onset of lucid dreaming initiates a process in which an actual separation takes place between a part of the self that consciously reflects that it is dreaming and another part that participates or is involved in the dream itself. In other words, there is a focus of awareness separate from the activity in the dream – the dreamer shifts from being a mere participant in the dream to also becoming its observer. This can evolve to a point where the action in the dream no longer remains the dominant focus; it does not grip the dreamer such that he or she stays identified with it. With this further separation the person climbs to the upper reaches of lucidity – by staying in sheer observation. Unlike the typical lucid state in which the waking-state self can function from within the dream, an unbounded Self now silently observes from outside the dream state.[10]

The meditational schools remind the novice that lucidity is not the mere process of self-reflection that we sometimes indulge in during our waking hours – the process by which we become aware of our thoughts, feelings, or behaviour. No doubt this also involves a division between a part of us that is observing and another part that is participating. However, the self-as-observer is not the same as the witnessing awareness of the mystic or the *sakshi chaitanya* of the Hindus. In self-reflection the observer evaluates (judges) and desires to alter the participant. The observer is identified with the participant. Here the division that is usually effected is between what we like in ourselves or what we imagine is strong within us and that which we do not like or consider to be weak within us.[11] This is not the division that meditational schools value. What they call *witnessing awareness* is an entirely different state of consciousness that goes beyond self-reflection. It may observe the participating self, but it has no investment in it. Unlike self-reflection, it witnesses without involvement, without any trace of fear or desire – good or bad. Usually in life this witnessing awareness is passive and seldom brought to the forefront of consciousness; it is not the self which thinks, acts, and reflects.

This is the point of departure between the mundane and religious/mystical schools. The former believe the actual state of lucidity is the ultimate destination – the thraldom of clarity and freedom to direct their effort towards creating new and different forms of experience within the dream. I have never been on a luxury liner, so let me have the thrill of a cruise vacation. More often than not, all that this will aim to do is to fulfil ungratified desires.

The mystic's approach, on the other hand, is directed towards transcending the dream state rather than simply subjugating it or fulfilling desires through it. The aspirant on the mystical path is not interested merely in a balance between observation and involvement, but aims to attain a state of total withdrawal from participation in the dream such that it leads to a condition of mindfulness.

The mystical/religious schools take a fork in the road that traverses a totally different terrain. For the religious novice the emergence of the simplest form of lucidness may become a bridge to this witnessing awareness. Since this observational state is initially fragile and can easily be shattered, the first step then is to stabilize lucidity – make it mindful – so that it does not lapse back into the unawareness of ordinary dreaming. The lucid state, and especially the dual awareness of being the participant and the observer, can be further developed by withdrawing the attention from the participant and resting it completely within the calmness of the observer. And this is to be effected with no deliberate intervention in dream content. In this instance, absolutely no feelings and ideas whatsoever stand between the observer and the events of the dream. The action in the dream goes on 'out there' but the observer chooses not to pay attention to it, identifying instead completely with the awareness that observes the dream. No interaction exists between the experience and experiencer but only tranquil observation resting in itself. If there is any vested interest (attachments and preferences) in any aspect of the dream then the observational mode is abandoned and the attention is sucked back into participation in the dream.

We could think of the dream as a river flowing within the mind of the sleeper. In normal dreaming the attention wades into the water and wets itself completely by immersing itself in participation and knowing no other reality besides the dream. When a separation from the action in the dream is effected – as in lucid dreaming – then the attention, so to speak, has come out of the river and stands on its bank; separate from the dream yet simultaneously aware that it is observing the flow of the dream – its waves and ripples. Yet another step of withdrawal can be achieved if the attention continues to hold this observational awareness, but now withdraws from the banks of the river and stands atop a hillock, watching the progression of the river below. It is now unattached and possibly oblivious of any ripple or wave in the river, viewing the performance of the river as a whole. Previously, when on the riverbank, there was always the chance that now and again the attention would identify with a particular eddy in the water and immediately succumb to the participative pull of the dream. Now, atop the hill, no such danger threatens the observer. This observing awareness can even turn its gaze away from the river and meditate on a featureless horizon.

However, it may be asked: In what sense is the dream continuing if there is no one to observe it? Are we then to presume that the dream stops when the attention of the witnessing awareness is turned away, and that the progress of the dream restarts only when the attention is turned back onto it again? Surely this would mean that attention powers or props the dream, and is its causation. May we then say that the witnessing awareness dreams the dream?

The story is told of the courtesan who danced in front of the king. She danced as long as the king's attention was on her. If his attention wandered away from her she would stop dancing, only to resume the dance when his attention was focused back on her. The parable illustrates how the mind and thoughts stay in motion as long as we pay attention to them. Turn the attention away and the procession of thoughts will immediately stop. Similarly the flow of the dream ceases once the attention is turned away.

When the detachment from the dream experience is preserved, and one's consciousness is encouraged to direct its gaze back on itself, this state may then become the gateway to transcendence – the goal of the mystic. In its most refined form, consciousness becomes aware only of itself. Only an imageless quiescence remains, beyond thoughts, free of imagery of any kind; a state of *contentless awareness* that is only aware of being aware.

Lest it be believed that these are but rarefied states of consciousness, mere metaphysical speculations, let us look at scientific studies that confirm some of these transformations of consciousness. North American researchers like Harry Hunt, Jayne Gackenbach, and Charles Alexander (among many others) have begun to identify and detail in their experimental subjects this initial separation of awareness from the action in the dream. Gackenbach, for example, conducted a study with sixty-six advanced meditators (people who had been meditating for more than twenty years) and was able to identify a state of awareness that she calls *witnessing dreaming*. In contrast to lucid dreaming, she defines witnessing dreaming as an experience of quiet, peaceful inner awareness or wakefulness, completely separate from the dream. She had to use a specialized group for the study because these states under investigation are so subtle that college students would not have been able to recognize or identify them.[12] The study yielded fifty-five lucid dream descriptions and forty-one witnessing dreaming descriptions. 'Most revealing of these categories was the one on feelings of separateness. In lucid dreaming only 7 percent of the cases were those in which people reported feelings of separateness. In the witnessing dream experience, 73 percent of the cases spontaneously reported in their dream description that the dream went on, but they were separate from it.'[13]

Gackenbach aptly describes these states through the experiences of a mathematics professor who had practised transcendental meditation for twenty years. 'In the beginning, this person talked about lucid dreams he had in which the actor was dominant. Here the role of the observer is to recognize that the self is dreaming, but despite this recognition, the feeling still exists that the dream is out there and the self is in here. When you are in the dream, the dream still feels real.

'As you become more familiar with lucidity it may occur to you that you can manipulate, change, or control the dream. In a second stage it occurred to this dreamer that what is "out there" is actually in some sense "in here." The dreamer may actively engage [in] the dream events or control and manipulate them.

'In a third stage his dreams became short. He described them as being like thoughts that arose, which he took note of and then let go.'[14] '"The action of the dream," he says, "is not dominant. It does not grip you so that you are [not] identified with it as opposed to the first step in which the focus was more on the active [participation]. In this case it's just a state of inner awareness that's really dominant. Awareness is there very strongly. The dream is a little dust flying about so to speak."

[In a fourth stage he discovered that] an '"inner wakefulness" dominates. "You don't have dreams or in any case you don't remember having dreams." He was not absorbed in the dreams but in witnessing.'[15] Gackenbach goes on to conclude that in witnessing dreaming the person can manipulate the dream, but simply does not desire to do so. Whatever the content of the dream, the person feels an inner tranquillity that keeps him or her removed from the dream. At times the dreamer does get snared again in the events of the dream, but the background of a peaceful inner awareness remains. Some subjects were also able to retain this witnessing state during dreamless sleep. They reported a silent state of inner wakefulness with no object of thought or perception. Gackenbach calls this state *witnessing deep-sleep*, in which there is a feeling of infinite expansion and bliss, and nothing else.

This, then, seems to be a totally different role of the dream. It is no longer merely a source of prophecy, nor is it yoked under the material weight of the day world. Herein dreams are the vehicles of salvational practices, capable of insights that are not borrowed from the rational waking world, but insights that can alter forever the way mundane reality is perceived. The dream is no longer the metaphor for the waking self; instead it is viewed as the training ground for the transformation of consciousness.

What the above makes evident is that the fascination with lucid dreaming finds its strongest focus not in dream control per se, but in using it as an aid in the search for meaning. This quest for an underlying meaning is not limited to modern man, but has been sought by all people irrespective of temporal or cultural boundaries. Lucid dreaming and the control of dreams only highlight that which has been known in India and Tibet for a very long time.

Dreams in some Buddhist traditions are a means to accessing higher states of consciousness, and make up an integral part of their spiritual practice. In Tibetan Buddhism this became formalized as 'Dream Yoga', and involves many different practices. The simplest one requires someone to gently whisper in the ear of a sleeping person, without awakening him or her: 'This is only a dream. What you are experiencing is only a dream.' This is meant to encourage the dreamer to become lucid while dreaming.[16] Other practices, which are more intense and elaborate, aim to harness consciousness during both day and night, and direct it towards enlightenment. Naropa, the Tibetan master, has outlined six yogas for this, the third of which, *Milam (rmi lam)*, pertains to the control of dreams. In the Tibetan tradition, the ability to dream lucidly is not an end in itself, but, rather, it provides an additional context through which the illusoriness of all existence is highlighted and grasped by the initiate.

Dream Yoga is actually a high form of meditational practice performed while dreaming. The initial part of the practice requires the novice to become aware (lucid) while dreaming. After coming *awake* in the dream the disciple is cautioned not to lose the still fragile awareness of knowing that the dream is a dream by 'preventing the spreading-out of the dream-content'.[17] This 'spreading out', or the loss of awareness, can happen because lucidity involves a razor-edge balance: neither becoming too conscious and thereby waking up, nor falling back into the ordinary flow of the dream. Once the novice can hold the dream in this manner, he or she then has to master it – by attaining volitional control over the dream.

After stabilizing the sense of lucidity, the disciple may experience another impediment – fear. Perhaps such is the importance of fear that the yoga reserves a special section for it – the second – on 'transmuting the dream-content'.[18] The disciple has to trample upon the fear associated with any dream image. Once rid of this fear he or she is advised to 'tread under foot whatever be dreamt'.[19]

If, for example, the dream is about fire, the dreamer should think, 'Why should I fear fire in a dream?' This questioning would separate the emotion (fear) from the object (fire) and help the dreamer disidentify from the fear of fire. Thereafter the dreamer investigates those elements in the dream that snare his or her interest, realizing that the interest is due to a fear or fascination with that object. Once again, they are mastered by trampling (disidentifying) upon them. These are those very dream elements that suck the dreamer into participation in the dream and are therefore considered as obstacles in the path to mindfulness. Transmuting the dream content helps the dreamer go beyond him or herself – the persona – and reach a more authentic layer of being. This can only be achieved if there is no longer any identification with the images in the dream, and when that happens, it in itself indicates that there is no longer the need to fear or cling to objects, thoughts, and emotions. Consciousness, freed from fearful content, does not grasp at anything; it also collects nothing and nothing clings to it. It simply withdraws from the participatory pull of the dream and stands apart, only witnessing the dream from afar. The aim is to enable the disciple to realize that all phenomenal things are, like the dream state, illusion (*maya*).

Once this is realized the disciple is ready to advance further. However, despite this refined state of awareness – witnessing or observing – the aspirant still encounters difficulties that impede progress. The obstacles are no longer thoughts or emotions but beliefs – the strongest and most deeply ingrained beliefs: the solidness and absoluteness of the material world, the self as being separate from others and the world, the limitations of space, and the belief that time is the backdrop of everything. If the disciple has to defy the normal correlates and go beyond the dualistic ways of the mind, freedom from the illusions of both the waking and the sleeping state also has to be achieved. The disciple can achieve this freedom by learning to change the content of the dream, not in accordance with ungratified desires, but by converting an object or emotion in the dream into its opposite, its very antithesis.

> And, if the dream be of fire, transform the fire into water, the antidote of fire.
> And if the dream be of minute objects, transform them into large objects;

Or if the dream be of large objects, transform them into small
objects:
… And if the dream be of a single thing, transform it into many
things;
Or if the dream be of many things, transform them into a single
thing.[20]

In this way the disciple learns to change the character of any
dream by willing it so. Another step onwards and the disciple realizes
that form and all the multitudinous content of dreams are merely
playthings of the mind, and therefore as illusory as a mirage. A further
step leads to the knowledge that form and all things perceived by the
senses even in the waking state are just as unreal as their reflections in
the dream state.[21] If the dreamer is successful he or she enters a phase
where perception and cognition are fused, and the sense-mind has been
subdued and provides no functional distinctions. These practices have
helped the disciple see beyond form into the *thatness* of things, their
essential nature – beyond duality and cognitive boundaries, beyond
form and non-form. Consciousness has been freed and emptied of all
content except the awareness of itself. Perhaps this is akin to the state
of *dreamless sleep*, not the deep sleep of oblivion, but a sleep where
awareness is iridescent with its own glow. One cannot help but wonder
whether the disembodied voice in Hunt's dream was nudging him in
this direction.

But before all this can be achieved the practitioner must resolve
to enter the dream state consciously. This is accomplished only if an
unbroken continuity of consciousness is maintained throughout both
the waking and dream states. If the novice is not able to view life from a
distance, it would be difficult to become detached from the dream. It is
therefore recommended that throughout the day he or she practise the
recognition of the dream-like nature of life until the same detachment
begins to manifest in dreams. Upon awakening he or she should
think, 'I am awake in a dream', and during the day he or she must
continue to imagine that all things are of the substance of dreams.[22]
Every object of waking experience is used to provoke awareness, which
may consequently help in becoming awake in dreams. As a result the
disciple would enjoy as vivid a consciousness in the dream state as in
the waking one, and the contents of both states would be found to be
the same, and thus things in both states would appear equally illusory
(*maya*). This would release him or her from the bondage of materiality

and aid in making the first step in the practice of Dream Yoga – to comprehend the nature of the dream state.[23]

The Tibetans use sleep and dream to access higher states of consciousness, while the Hindus give them credence in a different way. The Upanishads debate which state of consciousness – waking, dreaming, or deep sleep – provides greater access to the Self, the foundational state that animates our consciousness. It is this Self, in the Upanishadic view, that is also the dreamer of the dream. The Hindu idealistic conception frequently rejects the world of waking consciousness as the means to grasp the reality of the Self. In the Chandogya Upanishad, when Prajapati, the Hindu creator deity, is pressed for an answer, he initially declares: He who moves about happy in dream – he is the Self.[24] However, a difficulty arises in such a formulation: If the Self is the unqualified, blissful unity – free of evil and sorrow, not dependent on the duality of subject and object – how could this unitary Self be reconciled to the dream state where there are pleasant and unpleasant dreams, and where the duality of subject and object exists? In response it is argued that the attainment of the Self cannot be attributed to everyday dreams. Admitting this inadequacy of the dream state, the Upanishad instructs: When a man has fallen so sound asleep, and has so completely and perfectly been lulled to rest that he knows no dream image, that is the Self.[25]

Thus the state most conducive for realizing the Self passes over from dreaming sleep to deep sleep, where there are no longer any contrasted objects, and there is no consciousness in any empirical sense. Such bliss is found in deep sleep, a union with the eternal knowing subject – the Self. However, passing into deep sleep and merging into the Self is done in relative unconsciousness. We as sleepers remain unaware that we have made contact with the source of consciousness every night. We may awaken refreshed each morning after resting in the pristine bliss of the Self, but we have no memory of it. The Upanishad says, 'So, just as those who do not know the spot might go over a hid treasure of gold again and again, but not find it, even so all creatures here go day by day to that Brahma-world (*brahma-loka*) [in deep sleep], but do not find it.'[26]

In the Mandukya Upanishad (I.7), then, there is a fourth and highest state that is put above waking, dreaming, and dreamless sleep – *turiya*. This state is said to be higher than dreamless sleep because in it awareness is held of one's merging with the *Brahman* (the ultimate source of everything), so that memory of this blissful union is present on

awakening. It was with the rise of the Yoga system that the yogi passed
beyond dreamless sleep, maintaining full individual consciousness in
union with the eternal knowing *Brahman*. Perhaps the best exposition is
given by Gaudapada, Sankaracharya's guru's guru, in Karika, his treatise
on the Mandukya Upanishad:

> The dreamer's knowledge is false,
> The sleeper knows nothing at all,
> Both go astray, where all this vanishes
> There the fourth state is reached.
> In the world's illusion that has no beginning
> The soul sleeps; when it awakes
> Then there awakes in it the eternal,
> Timeless and free from dreams and sleep.[27]

Our allusions to old texts should not lead the reader to believe
that the mystical use of the lucid dream is buried in history. It is not.
In modern times, lucid dreaming has been used as a gateway to make
contact with 'non-ordinary' states of consciousness. In recent times
Swami Satyananda Saraswati, founder of the famous Bihar School of
Yoga, drew on the Tantric practice of *nyasa* (ritual consecration of the
physical body with higher awareness), to devise a technique he called
yoga nidra. It aims to instil through guided visualizations a one-pointed
awareness during sleep.[28]

However, the most well-known account of lucid dreaming is found
in the Carlos Castaneda books, which describe his apprenticeship under
a Mexican Yaqui Indian sorcerer, whom he believed to be 'a man of
knowledge'. Castaneda, a student of anthropology at the University
of California, Los Angeles, had gone to Arizona in the 1960s to study
the uses of medicinal plants among the Yaqui Indians for his doctoral
thesis. There he met don Juan, under whose tutelage he experimented
with psychotropic drugs. Don Juan repeatedly emphasized that these
psychotropic plants, when taken under skilled supervision, would
endow the user with power and with the means for entering another
order of reality.

Don Juan taught that our ordinary everyday world, which we
consider unique and absolute, is only one in a cluster of consecutive
worlds arranged like the layers of an onion. Due to the 'serious and
fierce effort' of human society as a whole, we are led to assume that
the world of daily life is the one and only possible world. According
to him, the sorcerers of ancient times had developed a set of practices

designed to recondition our capabilities to perceive these other realities. They called this set of practices the 'art of dreaming'.[29] It is these unseen worlds, which he called the 'second attention', that he would make accessible to Carlos Castaneda. Through the world of conscious dreaming don Juan taught that one could enter the 'second attention' or a heightened level of awareness. He began by telling Castaneda, 'I am going to teach you how to *set up dreaming*.' He explained that to 'set up dreaming' means to have concise and pragmatic control over the general situation of a dream. As we make choices in waking life, be they to walk, eat, or read, in dreams we should be able to make similar conscious choices, without the dream carrying us along as a passive player. To be able to do this, don Juan advised, 'You must start by doing something very simple. Tonight in your dreams you must look at your hands.'[30] There was no special reason behind don Juan's choice of hands as a focal object; it was merely an example of something one is comfortable with and that is conveniently accessible as a focus. The only criterion was that he had to pick it in advance and then find it in his dreams. Concentrating on a particular part of the dream helps the dreamer not to awaken in case he or she is turning lucid. Besides, it aids in stabilizing the sense of lucidity. This is exactly what the Tibetans advocate in their dream practice.

However, in the process of stabilizing lucidity, don Juan warned that the dream hands might begin to change shape. (The Tibetans called this 'the Spreading-out of the Dream-content'.) When that happens he instructed that the dreamer move the gaze away from them and pick something else, after which the gaze must be returned to the hands again. He warned that it would take a long time to perfect this technique. By doing this, dream lucidity and its control are established as a gateway to something beyond.

Much controversy surrounds the authenticity of the Castaneda experience – whether he had actually met a Yaqui Indian sorcerer called don Juan Matus, or whether he was simply the figment of Castaneda's (and his editor's) imagination. The sceptics contradict the notion that these books are factual accounts of an apprenticeship, believing that Castaneda did not actually experience the events described in them. 'An ethnobotanist has argued that based on the flora and fauna Carlos claims to have encountered in the Sonoran [Arizona] desert, it would not be outrageous to conclude that Castaneda, the anthropologist, has never been there. In any case, the desert that Castaneda, the author, describes is apparently not the one he claims it is.'[31] Castaneda defenders counter that he was presumably trying to protect don Juan's privacy and may have purposely obfuscated places, dates, and other mundane details, while the novelist Joyce Carol Oates has praised their beautiful construction, faultless dialogue, and unforgettable characterization.[32]

It may be difficult to decide whether Castaneda created don Juan from imagination or whether he had actually met such a man. The fact is that the methods outlined by don Juan are informative accounts about lucid dreams and the ability to control them. His books have had a deep influence on people, helping them to define some of their own experiences. One of Castaneda's interviewers admits: 'It would be dishonest for me to pretend that his works have had other than a strong effect on me. They helped me organize my own responses to altered states of consciousness.'[33]

Rather than debate the Castaneda experience, I prefer to discuss another modern teacher – my guru, Sri Madhava Ashish – who made use of dreams in the development of the inner life of the aspirant. The spiritual training of the individual was his only frame of reference for dreams; the other roles of dreams became subservient to this aim. He had, perhaps uniquely, reformulated the mystical training of the disciple in terms of the analytical tools of modern psychology, without partaking of its assumptions and goals.

Ashish asserted that dreaming is essentially a realm whose stability lies only within the observer, never in the images observed. And it is the duty of the disciple to discover who this observer is. For it is this same observer who during the day looks outwards and observes this mysterious universe, and at night observes the dream. If this observer can be made to observe only itself, as in meditative absorption or by becoming 'awake' in a dream, then the disciple can reach a realm where the distinction between the knower and the known dissolves. It is in this realm, perhaps, that we can find out who we truly are and ultimately discover who dreams the dream.

Chapter 25

DREAMING AND THE
MYSTICAL ENQUIRY

He who does not flow,
Does not grow;
He who flows,
Drowns.

Sri Madhava Ashish

Any allusion to mysticism tends to pose difficulties, conjuring variegated associations when invoked. Orthodox believers are apt to label it as heresy, while the rationalist relegates the mystical to a state of downright confusion. Still others tend to associate it with visions of some sort. However, in its root sense a mystic is concerned with a mystery. More specifically with the mystery of being: Who am I? Perhaps the essence of the mystery lies at the root of our being, somewhere within our awareness. The mystic attempts to trace this awareness back to its source by enquiring: In itself what is this awareness that allows me to participate in life, but through which I can also observe myself? When the mind is not full of thoughts and the senses not filled with stimuli, what remains?[1] In this enquiry nothing depends on the acceptance of dogma or belief. Any person, anywhere, at any time, can take the plunge into the source of his or her awareness to discover what is there. The less people believe about what they ought to find, the more likely are they to see with undistorted vision. The mystical journey then becomes a process of trying to 'awaken' to that awareness; its discipline and practice an attempt to identify and weed out all that stands in the way. And dreams may be used as a vehicle for this effort.

For Sri Madhava Ashish the dream was important initially as a tool for self-discovery on the mystical journey, and later as a vehicle to access meditational states of consciousness. He ascribed a dual role to dreams, viewing them both as a mirror and as an aperture. He was apt to compare them to a window: after dark, windowpanes reflect the light from objects within the room; they can also allow light from the outside into the room. Similarly, dreams can mirror many of our psychological propensities, yet by changing the focus of our perception, dreams can become the aperture through which we may glimpse the transpersonal. Let me illustrate with a twenty-four-year-old's dream:

> An ochre-robed numinous figure asks – 'If everything belongs to the Lady, what would you choose: Control or the Crown?'

This dream can be interpreted in many different ways. The Lady alludes to the Madonna, about whom he had seen a film, set in the Reformation, the previous evening. The day's residue could have triggered repressed infantile urges. His dream would then be understood as symptomatic of his Oedipal strivings which, in a disguised form, are *crowning* his waking thoughts about women. His mother-image subtly governs his perceptions and thus insidiously controls his choices. This is the standard Freudian template. Other theorists may perceive that the dream is an obvious allusion to superior-inferior feelings that are *crowning* his interactions with the mother/women and about his need to *control* these feelings. Still others may believe that an imbalance in his feminine function needs redressal as he has neglected this side of himself. The dream compensates by emphasising that everything belongs to the Lady. Furthermore, if he is able to subdue (*control*) his over-dominant masculine tendencies and make space for his feminine function, then this compensation may *crown* his efforts to individuate.

Perhaps all these interpretations may be relevant to our dreamer. The dream, then, is a mirror reflecting the ambivalences of youth and a choice that he has to exercise about his relationships – is he really in love? Should he marry? His life situation certainly fortifies such a rendering of the dream. He had successfully completed the transition from his university days to working life, and had by then grown a little more comfortable in his work environment. He had established a home space away from his parents and had fostered new relationships, but was unsure whether it was premature to commit more firmly and deeply to the girl he was dating. Could the dream be highlighting his amorous dilemma, urging him to make up his mind?

The content analysis school would read the dream as an indication that his self-conception needs further elucidation and that this is the quandary assailing him. Confirming its continuity hypothesis its proponents would say that the lack of emotional clarity in his waking hours has continued into and invaded his dream space. This assessment of the dream is also correct. In fact, none of the above appraisals can be denied, yet our psychological interpretations are not sensitive to another dimension of the youth's life that is begging the question in his dream.

We have totally ignored in our interpretations the figure who asks him the question – a *sadhu* (a Hindu ascetic or yogi). Surely, what the ochre of his robe represents should occupy some space in our interpretation. In short, we have neglected the religious aspirations of the young man in our comprehension of the dream. For the past four years he had been making week-long annual visits to Ashish's ashram, and seeking his advice on fundamental life issues. Also, the Lady (Virgin Mary) is primarily a religious symbol. Most importantly, an anomaly in the metaphorical question alerts us to a totally different rendering of the dream. Ostensibly, both *crown* and *control* are symbols of power. The crown usually stands for temporal authority and control is its natural corollary. Then what is the choice being offered in the dream? Ashish perceived that the dream was asking the youth to exercise an actual choice: between material significance (crown) and dominion over his whole nature (control), which would help him discover what belongs to the Lady (Godhead). The young man, as we know, was keen to pursue this mystical self-enquiry, but was unsure if he was ready to embrace the mystical life. Viewed thus, the dream becomes an aperture revealing something beyond the sensible world. It becomes an initiatory dream, asking for the dreamer's commitment to the greater life of the spirit.

All mystical teaching has described some sort of fundamental division of experience into two realms – the sensory world of our everyday perception and the unseen 'other' reality. In their attempt to explain the 'other' world mystics have largely explored two broad avenues. One is to talk about a magical world of elemental powers, of divination – the description of the shaman, the tantric, or the healer. The other avenue has been to describe the 'other' world in abstract concepts of theology, or in religious phraseology. Even though the 'other' reality suffuses our everyday world, it remains obscured from us because this sensory world is analogous to an opaque covering enclosing a flame.[2] The Hindus epitomize this in their belief that only *Brahman* is real, the rest is *maya*. They believe that the essential awareness in human beings gets identified with the physical (body) and psychical (personality) layers, and the world is then perceived as something external, and standing against and separate from them. Understood in personal terms, the sensible world and our psychophysical structure – including thoughts and emotions – are the opaque covering shielding our view of the Real. The task of the mystic is to recapture that pristine awareness in which the Self and the Universe are one.

To fulfil this task Ashish was not prone to reject the psychological dimension of dreams in favour of a purely mystical one. He felt that the personality, or the nature of the disciple, is the starting ground of the search. The above mentioned young dreamer, by understanding his motives, inhibitions, and compulsions would gain dominion over his nature and this would prevent it from becoming an impediment in his mystical aspirations. According to Ashish, the dream at one level is the mirror of our anxieties, fears, and sexual dilemmas. But if the disciple is prepared to work on the psychic web of the personality, then the mirror of dream can become an aperture to a higher reality. Ashish's work with dreams, therefore, included wading into the waters of the personal nature, not merely to help the individual remain afloat in work and relationships, but to create a pathway through the tangle of personality to reach the source of being.

If the disciple eschews this probing into him or herself, if the ground is not cleared, then there is the risk of allowing unaccepted psychological material to emerge and sometimes stymie the inner effort. An example may make this more explicit:

'Nirmala' came from a large orthodox family where her male siblings enjoyed considerable freedom, while it was expected that she and her sisters would restrict themselves to the home. It was but natural that Nirmala wished she were a boy. All through her youth she fantasized that she would one day become an artist. This desire had been sparked when she had heard of a woman artist who was able to live an independent life. Thus emboldened, she started to learn to paint. In due course she was married and her marital circumstances afforded her the leisure to pursue her interest in painting.

The passage of years saw both husband and wife take initiation from Ashish. The dreams she had were indicative of unaccepted material seeking expression. However, despite Ashish's emphasis on paying attention to these aspects, Nirmala preferred, instead, to enthusiastically pursue meditation. One day while meditating, behind closed eyelids she saw a ghost in the room. Needless to say, she was terrified of this apparition. It was the ghost of a female artist.

It was months before Nirmala dared to meditate again.[3]

Ashish believed that the tools of modern psychology are useful and often necessary to prepare for the mystic's journey towards the root of his or her being. In her attempt to see beyond the windowpane, Nirmala found that her own unaccepted desires stood between her and what lies beyond – just like psychological projections stand between the outside world and us. It often happens that when the neophyte attempts to transcend everyday consciousness the effort is met with a barrier. A 'guardian of the threshold',[4] so to speak, bars entry to the 'other' world.[5] Modern psychology is familiar with a similar 'guardian' who stands on the threshold of the conscious-unconscious divide – the Freudian censor, which prevents the entry of repressed material into one's consciousness. Possibly, we encounter a similar guardian at the threshold of our ordinary consciousness when we attempt to transcend it. This may dredge up repressed images when the aspirant attempts to meditate, or these images may surface in dreams. Ashish was not alone in perceiving this difficulty. Mystics believe that often the 'way' is through the murky waters of the unconscious and the foot of the ladder by which the candidate ascends rests in its slush.[6] My personal experience attests to this. Soon after I had begun to meditate I experienced a bewildering dream, which I have already discussed in chapter 2. I found the dream about Annie Besant and the dead child so frightening that I did not meditate or attempt to recall my dreams for months afterwards, till my guru helped me resurrect that child. The 'guardian' had barred my entry, though it had simultaneously indicated the cause of the block.

It is certainly not being suggested that this is inevitable and that anyone who starts to meditate will experience frightening dreams. The threshold is guarded not only by repressed images rising to the surface, but also by a much more common barrier encountered when the neophyte attempts to go inwards in meditation: the incessant chattering of the mind. One of the means by which the disciple can learn to identify the essential self and to differentiate it from the ego-personality is meditation, dreams being the other. This is the reason why most mystical schools believe that the trans-egotistic observer – the Self – cannot be discovered or isolated until these distracting influences have been put to rest.[7] Expressed differently, when the mind has been brought to a state of rest, only then can the Self stand in its true nature. So long as waves and ripples cover the surface of a lake, neither can we look down through the clear waters to see what lies beneath the surface, nor can the undistorted image of the heavens be reflected on the surface of the lake.[8] Similarly, if the ripples of thought constantly disturb the mind, the disciple will not be able to penetrate to its deeper recesses; nor will the mind be transcended. Therefore, the first and most important task on this path of inner enquiry becomes the stilling of the mind. Most schools recommend but one medicine for all such problems: Meditation. Stop the mind. Drop the worries. Calm the desires. That is standard teaching. The problem, however, remains in the doing. As the disciple attempts to weed out these distracting influences during meditation, he or she realizes that thoughts have a compulsive power. Independent of the will, they tend to drag him or her along as a captive.

Ashish suggested that these thoughts have to be traced to their roots, understood, and then checked with a combination of intelligent analysis and disciplined control. If the disciple analyses these uncontrollable thoughts over a period of time, he or she may find that one or two themes endlessly repeat themselves in the chatter of the mind. These may be clothed in different thoughts everyday, but an essential commonality in their content may be determined. These thoughts remain unappeased, persistently replaying their theme over and over again no matter what method the disciple employs to silence them. Possibly, their insatiable presence stems from a deep-seated compulsion, and the disciple's intent is not able to address the source of the conflict. In such situations dreams can be particularly helpful to locate and identify the main source of the trouble, as 'James' learnt. His efforts to meditate were met by a mind conversing without respite. His thoughts constantly flitted around typical work worries – his fear of not being able to meet deadlines and challenges; of being left behind; of being ineffective and unable to cope. How could he build his self-worth so that the chattering of the mind would quieten? He did not know where to begin. He then had a series of very vivid dreams in which he returned to his childhood days. I relate one of them:

I am in my parental home, as it was when I was twelve years old. Adjacent to the kitchen, I see the dining room. It was the room of the house where everything happened. It had a coal-fired fireplace with the chimneybreast jutting out. On the left was a large cupboard standing from floor to ceiling. Its wooden doors hid everything the cupboard may have contained. The white paint appeared a bit dull.

Ashish probed his associations to this cupboard, which seemed to hide the message of the dream. James could not recollect anything. Ashish asked him to mentally open the cupboard door and ascertain what it contained. James, after considerable effort, remembered that it contained the crockery and the top shelf the household linen. On top of the linen, inaccessible to the child, lay a whippy cane with which his father, a teacher in a London Catholic primary school, beat the young James if he broke any rule of the house. The other dreams also had symbols that when decoded pointed towards an authoritarian father. These dreams helped him excavate from memory a crucial incident when he was eleven years old. He had done exceedingly well in the 'eleven plus' exam and was offered a full scholarship to a reputable public school. The Catholic headmaster and James's father decided to refuse the scholarship because the public school was Protestant. From the next term onwards, attending the Catholic grammar school his father had been to, James's grades fell to the lowest in the class and never recovered. He lost confidence in his mental abilities and became slow and uncertain at expressing himself both in speech and writing. Not until he was forty and with the help of these dreams did he see the connection between his lack of self-confidence and the devastating shock and disappointment deriving from his father's decision.[9] Small wonder then that the above dream had described the room as one where '*everything happened*'. The cupboard held hidden the secret to his sense of personal worth. The dream had taken him back to the time when he had changed schools – a move which would eventually rob him entirely of his self-worth. This cathected experience was invisibly obstructing his efforts to quieten his mind in meditation.

The disciple has, with the help of dreams, dug deep into his or her emotional past and excavated something significant. However, Ashish cautioned that this glimpse into the past would not miraculously release the chattering mind from its bondage, but it was susceptible to yet another pitfall – that of recrimination and self-indulgent emotions. Since the material excavated is often painful, the tendency to blame others and one's circumstances may surface in an overwhelming manner and swamp the disciple's focus. At this juncture it would do well to remind oneself that the aim of reclaiming the trauma is to break the identification with compulsive thought patterns. Recriminations would only lead to identification with other trains of thought and feelings of 'poor me', and the whole exercise would be vitiated.

Instead, Ashish advised that the disciple must practise what the Buddhists call 'bare attention'[10] to the events that foster his or her compulsive thoughts. This requires only a clear appreciation of 'bare' facts without nursing or strengthening them by adding judgements or reflections that lead to excessive sensitivity, self-pity, or resentment. And if mental comments do arise they are neither to be repudiated nor pursued, but to be dismissed with mindfulness. The intent is to penetrate and be free of the root cause that holds meditation hostage to rampaging thoughts. This can only be done if the disciple views everything, even his or her painful past, with dispassion, learning not to identify with the child to whom the events once happened. The attempt is to encourage that vulnerable and intimidated child to grow up and so see that these fears are not relevant to the adult state. Once the mechanism of compulsion has been grasped, then simply by the act of detached observation of such thoughts – bare attention – the bondage may relax its grip. It may then be taken in a quite different way: what had been hurt is not my essential being. 'I' – the true I – am only a witness to the hurt.

Unfortunately, life is not so uncomplicated, and Ashish fully recognized that we are captive not to one compulsion alone. Even though one fear or compulsion has been acknowledged, that does not mean it will lead to a quiet mind. Instead, as when unravelling a tangled ball of string we start by finding a loose end and proceed from there, similarly the dreaming power provides a starting point to lead one through a labyrinth of compulsions. There is no easy way out and the disciple 'has to make the effort to clear away the mind's activities which seem like a shining screen of images lying across the inner gateway'. He or she has to pass beyond that screen. Ashish formulated these steps as an effective method to combat the waywardness of the mind. He had utilized the dream not merely as a psychological tool but as an important vehicle to help still the chattering mind.

It thus becomes apparent that the neophyte's entry to the 'other' reality is blocked, perhaps, not so much by the thoughts themselves but by his or her compulsions – the inarticulate powers of fear and desire, and that possibly is the real 'guardian of the threshold'. Dreams can become the vehicle to alert the aspirant to unresolved conflict areas in the personality that give our thoughts their seemingly uncontrollable drive; and frequently dreams provide the necessary connections between the disturbing factors and their roots. Simultaneously, meditation helps the disciple to perceive the 'light' beyond the glass – light that at first seems to be darkness. At a later stage, dreams may also help penetrate this darkness to realize a state of meditative consciousness. Then dreams can become the interface wherein it is possible for both the realities – this and the 'other' – to countenance each other.

Accordingly, Ashish expected the disciple to make a two-pronged effort – to work on the personal nature, and to directly reach the source of being. This may express itself in different types of dreams – the *purificatory* dream and those dreams that lead to meditative states of consciousness.

Initially every disciple must presume that most dreams, if not all, are purificatory. Dreams, regardless of their vivid images and the familiar cast of characters in them, are not about other people. The dreaming power is primarily concerned with the dreamer and will aim to keep the dream discourse limited to him or her.[11] On recalling a dream, the novice must first ask: What is it in myself that is being represented by the content of the dream? It is another way of stating the famous injunction of the Delphic oracle: Know thyself.[12]

Purificatory dreams tend to be critical of attitudes in the aspirant that need looking into and changing. To illustrate from my dream journal:

I'm telling the gardener that simply watering the lawn is not enough. There are weeds that have to be pulled out too. I plead to him not to take care of only a part of the garden, but the whole of it.

The dream is obviously not about gardening. The garden represents the whole of me, including those aspects that I am unaware of. Thus I am being directed to pay attention to every part of myself. The weeds represent negative thoughts, laziness, vague depressions, which have to be uprooted through meditation or otherwise.[13] Ashish had earlier spoken to me about this difficulty. The dream highlighted that I was unwittingly diluting the focus of my aspirations because of the small indiscretions in my thoughts and emotions – the weeds. My energies were being wasted in these indulgences. Individually viewed they could not be considered hindrances that had to be 'weeded' out of my personality, but if left unchecked they could choke the garden of my being.

To address the criticism of dreams the novice must be prepared to descend into the 'lowest' and 'dirtiest' region of him or herself. The mystic's urge to wholeness demands that nothing remains outside its totality. The disciple must therefore be free to move at will through the psychic house in which he or she dwells, through the cellars and toilets, to the living rooms and bedrooms. The house cannot be called one's own until there is nothing hidden, nothing in it to fear or be ashamed to admit as one's own. 'The Spirit encompasses everything, from its own numinous calm to tumultuous action, from high seriousness to dirty jokes, from celibate asceticism to passionate expressions of sexuality.'[14] Only if the disciple consciously accepts this premise will he or she be free to interpret dreams, which open up unacceptable areas of the self. Drains cannot be cleaned if you refuse to admit their existence. 'We cannot understand the need to clean our vessels if we refuse to admit that our vessels are dirty.'[15]

Often enough the aspirant will be faced with dreams that must be interpreted in relation to the lowest levels. This is so because all efforts must be grounded on a firm understanding of one's personal nature and because the full implications of the higher levels of interpretation cannot be grasped without accepting the relationship to the 'lower' nature. An example:

> *I am worshipping the deities with* aarti (lighted wicks in a metal container) *in one hand and a hand bell in the other. Suddenly, the hand bell stops ringing because the central gong has got stuck to the side. Several women devotees start running in panic and the act of worship comes to a stop. Then I find myself telling Kamla that my mother is sick, no doubt, but she has not died.*[16]

The central gong is an obvious male sexual symbol and it has stopped functioning. We can only conclude from this that sexual inhibitions are marring the dreamer's emotional life. The dreamer tells Kamla (his wife) that his mother is sick, giving the vital clue that his mother complex is the cause of his inhibition. In actual fact, his mother had died long ago, but the dream informs him that she continues to live in his mind (unconscious) and thus is not dead. The women devotees represent the dreamer's 'feeling-life', which has panicked and disrupted his worship. The traditional *aarti* is a ritual offering of the elements to the deity, aiming to centre the disciple in the act of worship. The sexual inhibition it seems has stopped this centring process, and his dream has quite directly informed him about his block.[17]

Ashish believed that when confronted with sexual dreams, we need not recoil from them. He felt that they show that in some specific manner the novice is degrading the divine creative power of Eros either by exploiting it for selfish ends or by thinking of it in negative terms.[18] The above dreamer had darkened it with his mother fixation. The dreaming mind was advising him that his next step on the 'path' would require him to attend to this block. The need to do this is not merely to release the energy from repressed psychic material for the sense of well-being and better adaptation that follows its release. The main purpose in attending to these blocks, these clogged drains of compulsive thought patterns, is that they may hinder progress inwards.

Those who are introspective would be quick to apprehend that the criticism of dreams is essentially challenging the basic assumptions that they have formed and lived by in life. The purificatory dream aims to make them aware of the areas they need to disentangle themselves from. When the energy locked in these issues is released, the disciple may increasingly find that his or her response to dreams may begin to change. Consequently, like Ashish, the disciple may also come to feel that 'a night without a dream was a wasted opportunity, a forgotten dream was a breach of trust'.[19] This kind of receptivity towards the dream will come about only if the neophyte accepts that the full gamut of human frailties lies potentially dormant within. Then, it may be possible to face the criticism inherent in the dream without any resistance.

If dreams tell us what we do not know, then how can we be sure of their veracity? This is where the mystical work comes in: the windowpane needs to be cleaned. At first those windows appear only as reflecting surfaces on which images of the darker qualities, of repressed or unacceptable psychic material, are seen. As the aspirant assiduously cleans them, they gradually become transparent membranes. Soon he or she will find that the content of dreams, instead of remaining confined to reflected images, reveals other aspects of objective being. In this way the disciple may pass beyond the surface of the waking and dreaming mind, and glimpse what lies beyond.

This cleaning of the windows involves the stilling of the mind (meditation), introspection, identifying the essential self (self-remembering), and squarely facing the criticisms made by dreams.

Psychological work and meditation gradually free the mind from the limitations imposed by psychological propensities, releasing the energy imprisoned in the turbulence of desire and fear, thereby making it available to the neophyte to plunge into the inner worlds. Then, instead of perceiving the two worlds – the mystical and the sensible – as being at variance with each other, they are seen as two aspects of the one ultimate reality. When this happens the individual begins to lose him or herself in the universal, the mundane world revealing itself as the mirror of cosmic ideation. And the guru hopes that the dimly glowing potential of self-awareness in the disciple will come to the incandescence of full 'witnessing'. The mirror of dreams may slowly transform into the window of vision.

To achieve this, the disciple has to follow certain practices. It is recommended that sleeping conditions should not be too comfortable. The mattress should not be soft, the pillow should be hard, and there should be no more covering than is absolutely necessary. The intention is that the sleep be light, so that sleeping and dreaming may be negotiated with some measure of awareness. Similarly, sleeping soon after the last meal is to be avoided, and if that is not possible then the meal should be kept light. It would be ideal if sleep were preceded by a period of meditation. For those who cannot sleep without reading, it is advisable for them to read a book related to the inner enquiry. The reading list could include mythology and mysticism – apart from introducing the disciple to great spiritual traditions, they abound with symbols. This may afford the architect of dreams a larger spectrum of colours to paint the disciple's nightlife with by allowing it access to meaning-rich symbols. All this would help in shepherding the dream content towards the aim of the disciple.[20] Modern-day studies also confirm that presleep conditions do influence dream images.[21] It is also said that the disciple should not engage in negative emotions, and avoid any indulgence in fantasy as this burns psychic energy, on which the inner effort is built. If the mind is idle, one should ponder over the dream of the previous night. In fact, there is always time during the day to think about a dream, as there is always time to quieten the mind in meditation. The intention is not to enunciate dictums, but to help the aspirant in distinguishing between actions and habits that are consonant with the 'work' and weed out those contrary to it.

The disciple is also advised to discuss his or her dreams with the guru,[22] it being a very effective method through which the preceptor stays attuned to the disciple, alerting the guru when the novice's inner effort needs a push.[23] The dream becomes for the guru a window into the inner world of the disciple. These dream sessions with the guru also help the disciple to become familiar with the language of the dream so that, in time, an ability to interpret them can be acquired.

The purificatory dream, as enunciated by Ashish, incorporates much of the work done by Freud, Jung, and Hall. We have seen how Ashish, like Freud, utilized the dream to dig out from the unconscious sexual inhibitions blocking the disciple's effort to withdraw inwards. Like Jung, he believed that the dreaming power knows more about the dreamer's needs than what the dreamer consciously knows. He therefore subjectively characterized the dream content and was apt to enquire, 'What is the dream telling me about myself that I am unaware of?' The purificatory dream's criticism highlights those aspects of the personality that are neglected or underdeveloped, like my dream of the gardener. These neglected aspects often became the barriers that restrain the disciple from going within. And, like Hall, Ashish believed that dream content reflects the conscious attitudes of dreamers, indicating their current conflicts. Rather than deal with these as personifications of angry or wrathful powers (the traditional religious approach), Ashish preferred to deal with them as projections of psychological factors – subconscious fears, uncertainties, doubts, ungratified desires, angers, or anxieties. However, unlike the psychological schools, his comprehension of a dream was not limited to psychological insight only, but found a connection of the individual with the Universal.

Interpretation along these lines does not imply that the source of dreams is under the egotistic control of the dreamer. Like the mystics, it was Ashish's firm conviction that the dreamer of the dream is the *Atman*,[24] the Self, that 'strange autonomous being who both is and is not the person of our waking personalities'.[25]

The disciple initially relies on the analytical tools of psychology, but the 'mystical work' itself is something quite different. Although control may help to quieten thoughts, the still mind is only a step towards transcending the mind itself. Analysis and control may be the first leg of the journey, however, the disciple's enquiry will lead to nowhere unless certain preliminary qualifications are present in the enquirer.[26] A different order of yearning is demanded from the aspirant.[27]

To begin with, the inner enquiry has to become the central focus, and the requirements of total self-dedication cannot be sustained merely by an hour or two's practice. Disciples cannot be totally 'given' for a few hours of the day and then follow their own selfish interests at other times. They have to bring the totality of their nature – waking, sleeping, and dreaming – into harmony with their perception of the nature of the source of being.[28] What is required is a radical change in outlook, a process perhaps best described by the Greek term *metanoia*, or a transformation of mind.[29]

An example here, and one taken from someone not connected with Ashish, may be both illustrative and interesting. Sivananda Radha, a German woman who had once been under the tutelage of the respected spiritual teacher and yoga proponent Swami Sivananda, had started to teach a group of men and women in Canada. She advocated the use of dreams to her disciples as a guide on the inner journey, believing that if they are prepared to grapple with their psychological problems and are willing to learn, then they can be given some more 'spiritual food' through dreams. This she knew from personal experience. She recounts in her book *Realities of the Dreaming Mind* a telling dream that she calls 'Solitary Confinement'. In the dream she finds herself in a strange prison where the inmates do not realize that they have been incarcerated and, astonishingly, are quite happy with what they are doing there. In fact, they are captivated by it – prison activity is their sole focus. The warden then takes her to the upper levels of the prison where the more dangerous inmates are kept in solitary confinement. She notices a particular prisoner, a man in a small cage-like cell that has a simple blanket spread on a very straight bed. He is sitting in a perfect lotus posture and meditating. He looks peaceful. After a little while he opens his eyes and when she enquires if he knows he is in prison, he confidently says, 'Yes'. When further questioned he states that he does a little work in the prison, but to her great surprise informs her, 'I leave the prison. I go somewhere else.'

She asks him, 'Where do you go?'

'To places of great knowledge. And because of this freedom I do not mind being here, as there is always time to do what is important after I have done what is requested of me.'

'But how do you get out?'

'Oh, I just sit here quietly and "think" my way out.' Puzzlingly, he adds, 'I leave my body and come back without anyone knowing. Only in solitary confinement are we free.'

The dream ends with Radha asking herself – Where is this prison? The world? The body? The mind?

The dream outlines the process of *metanoia*. It is advising the dreamer to study the prison we inadvertently build around ourselves.

Any psychological appreciation makes us realize very quickly that our actions and thoughts are governed and bound by habit and compulsion, so that we are held hostage within their prison walls. Can a life obsessed by desires and fears be called free? To be constantly torn by feelings and tortured by thoughts – is that freedom? Perhaps the dream has accurately portrayed what can be said for most of us – we are unaware that we are imprisoned and like the prisoners in the dream are content merely to pursue our mundane activities. Furthermore, the 'upper levels' of the prison where the dangerous prisoners are kept are reflective of the conventional norm to consider dangerous the penetration to the 'upper' or 'higher' reaches of consciousness. It is dangerous because it is unknown. And yet these 'dangerous' men and women – the mystics – are the ones who give us the clue to where real freedom lies.

Ironically, one of the prisoners says, 'Only in solitary confinement are we free.' In the dream the allusion is to a 'space' that is inwards and unfettered, reached by meditative silence and therefore peaceful. It is not bound by the emotional and mental dictates of concepts, beliefs, and thoughts that normally confine us. The man in solitary confinement is thus referring to a state of mind that can be reached where the normal notions of space and matter are transcended, and he is able to approach 'places of great knowledge'. Radha's puzzlement of how this *metanoia* can be achieved is, however, only answered in a sequel to this dream.

The setting is identical to her first dream – the same prison, the same prisoner in solitary confinement – perhaps underscoring its deep significance. However, this time the dreamer asks the prisoner:

> 'Would I have to commit something in order to be sentenced to solitary confinement?'
> 'Exactly,' he responded.
> 'Why did you get solitary confinement?'
> 'I killed.'
> 'Oh my God!'
> And he said, 'One day you will have to kill.'
> 'No, I can't do this. Do I have to kill?'
> 'Yes.'
> 'There is no other way?'
> 'No.'
> Then he looked at me and asked, 'Do you know what you have to kill?'[30]

Even within the dream she realizes that she has 'to kill the part of the mind that constantly creates and produces desires'.[31] She has to eschew all thoughts and, like the prisoner in solitary confinement, seek in meditative silence that which goes beyond thought. The killing alludes to the removal of the mental and emotional 'dust' that blinds us, obscuring and isolating us from the 'places of great knowledge'. *Metanoia* removes the 'dust' by shifting the attention away from the demands of the personality to something beyond it. Like the prisoner in the dream observes – though he does what is demanded of him, his attention is not held hostage to it. For only when we move our gaze away from the traffic in the street below, can we become aware that the room we are standing in is actually a silent one.

Clearly this phase of the disciple's journey requires a radical change in outlook. This transformation may coincide with changes in the disciple's dream life, with an occasional precognitive dream bursting through the haze of personality dreams. Sometimes, an insight may be afforded into the problems that beset the disciple. A hint of guidance may also come through a dream. In ordinary dreaming the dream mirror shows little more than the reflection of the dreamer's personality. As the disciple cleans the windowpanes, it may reflect the light from the minds of other people – telepathic and other paranormal dreaming may happen spontaneously. These can serve to inspire and encourage as they tend to introduce the disciple to a more mysterious and subtler level of energy, hitherto hidden from him or her. The disciple may feel the wonder of a magical universe through the spontaneous expression of these powers. However, one must not cling to such dreams. As Ashish said, 'If these paranormal dreams come, observe them, get used to them, read any message they may seem to give ... and [move] on.' For these are not the mystic's goals.

This entire practice must not be looked at as a linear process – first the disciple makes the effort, then the dream comes, and then understanding dawns. Sometimes visions are granted to the aspirant struggling to control the mind or battling with negative emotions, as if to inspire and provide a glimmer of hope in the engulfing darkness. Soon he or she may recognize that these dreams have a different feel to them. They are not to be construed as untapped powers of the individual, but are a comment on the disciple's universe and its numinous origins. They call for an examination and, consequently, a reformulation of the terms of the disciple's search. Perhaps what had guided him or her thus far was only the warming-up exercise. The climb is yet to come.

Another example may further clarify this:

Last night I had a series of strange and powerful dreams. First I dreamt that I was in a Hindu temple but not in India (Indonesia?). The main image was indistinct; after looking at it for a while I thought it perhaps was an ancient stone Ganesha, and so I recited a Sanskrit hymn to him. Then I realize that it was a mixed Shiva/Shakti. On coming out of the temple I found myself on a narrow, precarious scaffolding from which I fell to the ground (or, rather, jumped/fell) but without hurting myself.[32]

The dreamer is apparently on the threshold of an attitudinal change. Transition points are often accompanied by uncertainty, a blurring of boundaries or definitions, perhaps because a new orientation may be required to challenge or change one's habitual view. This uncertainty is amply represented in the dream – he isn't sure where the temple is located, and neither is the main image well defined. Initially perceived as Ganesha it soon metamorphoses into a mixed Shiva/Shakti. He, then, is not certain whether he *'fell to the ground'* or *'jumped/fell'*. Everything abounds with possibilities, each image is nebulous. Nothing is what it seems when first perceived and changes on further cognition. Had the dreamer been a young boy his uncertainty may have been reflective of his lack of self-definition, but this is the dream of a forty-three-year-old man. The dream portrays him on a narrow, precarious scaffolding (transition) outside a temple. This sets the context of the dream and his ambivalence. Are his religious beliefs, imbibed through his upbringing, consonant with the needs of his inner enquiry? He is, after all, inappropriately reciting a hymn to Ganesha in front of the androgynous Shiva/Shakti. It seems his beliefs are poised on the threshold of reformulation, possibly where the 'familiar have to make way for the unfamiliar'.

Ashish interpreted this reformulation to mean that Ganesha, the god of beginnings, transforms into the mixed (united) Shiva/Shakti, the symbol of the primal 'union of opposites' from which all things arise. Shiva and Shakti also represent that 'union' through which a human being transcends opposites to find unity. The temple is set outside India, which could mean that it is not to be understood as typically Hindu, even though the dreamer's reaction to the image is typically that of a Hindu in that he recites a Sanskrit hymn. In effect, the dreamer needs to separate the essential perception of the spirit in human beings from his Hindu religious predilections. The falling off the scaffolding is significant. Ashish pointed out that scaffolds are structures erected in order to build something else, and are demolished once the building is ready. He therefore advised the dreamer: 'Any religion is thus like the scaffolding of outer and temporary structures within which the real temple is built. Factually it is better to leave (jump / fall) the supporting scaffold of religion as soon as one has gained the beginnings of perception that no religious system as such can lead one to the ultimate truth.'[33] This is so because often the belief in particular religious symbols (gods and goddesses) makes one take them as facts in themselves, when they are only representations of the Truth, not the Truth itself. In the mystical enquiry, Ashish emphasized that 'one must never stop content with a particular form. Form and change are almost synonymous. What is eternal and unchanging may be sought through form, but it is not in itself form.'[34] This transition in perception, where the dreamer falls off the scaffolding without getting hurt, suggests that even though many of us need the tangible foothold of an image or symbol, be it Ganesha or Shiva and Shakti, to travel from the concrete to the abstract, the familiar to the unfamiliar, the outer to the inner, the scaffolding has to be discarded at some point, and it seems this is done without any ill effects on the dreamer.

This sacrificing of familiar symbols of religious belief to enable oneself to see beyond them was something that Ashish was acquainted with. He was an aspirant schooled in orthodox Vaishnavism, the dominant Hindu tradition distinguished by the primary worship of Vishnu (or Krishna). While he was young in his search he had an overwhelming vision of Radha-Krishna, shining in all their glory. Within a few days another dream chastised him by implying that if he thought his vision to be the end of the journey it was an immature view. His traditional schooling had conjoined his way of life to the routine of the temple. Under those circumstances, he had seen the Deity as he saw 'Them' in the temple, but appearing much younger. What he had 'seen' reflected his own beliefs. Perhaps, his 'vision' was asking for a *metanoia* in his conceptions. Ashish concluded that his vision was asking him, Who is Krishna?[35] thereby urging him to transcend a specific religious symbol and see the non-sectarian Truth behind it.[36]

The Kashmiri Saivite mystic-saint Lalla describes this state poetically:

There in that state is, neither speech or thought,
Neither '*kul*' [family, lineage] nor '*akul*' [without or beyond lineage]

Neither meditation nor ritual has entry there.
Shiva and *Shakti* [Radha & Krishna] have no dwelling there.
That Something which remains – that is what the teaching sets forth.[37]

From merely reflecting the distorting projections of our nature, slowly dreams begin to comment on our search, providing inspiration and clarification on perceptions that need further thought. By helping us expand our definitions of what we are searching for they urge us to come closer to what it is in itself that is being sought and not what we believe it to be.

If we cast a backward glance at the early practices of the disciple, it becomes apparent that a *metanoia* was being attempted even in the simplest of exercises. The disciple had been advised not to lay blame on others in the outer life, but to always search for motives within him or herself. The benefits of this practice, which were not always apparent to the novice earlier, are subtle and go beyond the conquest of compulsion. If the cause for outer actions is habitually internalized, then one is forced to accept two modes of identification: The ubiquitous 'I' immediately polarizes into a self that observes and another self that indulges in action – the 'observer' and the 'participant'. The normal identification is with the participating 'I', but introspection will focus the disciple's consciousness on the observing 'I'. And he or she may then be forced to enquire: Who is this 'I'? Similarly, if in the realm of dreams the effort is always to identify the dream content with oneself, then soon the question that will arise will be: Who is this 'I' that surfaces in the dream – the 'I' that is me and yet not me, and who perennially comments on the waking 'I'? The common substrate of both these practices is to help the disciple identify an observing self capable of standing apart from the participative self of both the waking and dream states.

We can perhaps now restate that the real intention of the mystical journey is to forge a new awareness, by bringing the disciple to a stage where the essential awareness is distinguished from the empirical self. Textually, this is considered the preparatory part of the work – the purification of the disciple.

This brings us to a watershed in the mystical journey, and the next step would entail a quantum jump in perception. The disciple has now to take a further step inwards by isolating within him or herself 'something' that observes the observing self; to use J. Krishnamurti's words, the 'observer' becomes the 'observed'. This state is not easily reached, and once attained it takes much practice to stabilize.

The disciple knows that the purpose of meditation is to still the mind, but the exercises employed till now to control thoughts can only quieten them temporarily. Even in his or her most rewarding moments the disciple remains in the midst of stilled mental thought, which could and does start again at any moment. However, as Ashish advised, 'If one holds quiet, the next thing to look for is a slight dissociation from the thinking process, which makes it relatively easy to stay in this quiet state. It is peaceful but eventually unsatisfying. This can deepen into the state ... where the body passes into sleep and one is awake within it. Deliberately invoking sleep, while keeping in a position which discourages sleep, is an aid in this process. It also points to the fact that this movement is not, initially, anything that you can achieve by intention. In practice, you have to hold yourself in the quiet state and let yourself get tired.'[38] In short, the disciple attempts to dissociate from his or her usual mode of cognition (*metanoia*), from thoughts in meditation, from dreams by attaining lucidity, and by attempts to stay 'awake' even while in dreamless sleep. As we noted earlier, current laboratory research has begun to confirm that sleeping subjects, particularly long-time meditators, are able to make prearranged ocular signals while asleep,[39] suggestive of a state of 'witnessing' during sleep.

Perhaps there is a parting of ways here, depending on the reason why the sleeper aims to become lucid in the dream state. If it is to manipulate and control the dream as a compensation for waking experience, or 'if one thinks of this sort of "waking dream" merely as one of many psychic powers, it is not very important. But if one sees it as an index of the capacity to stand with controlled mind, with vision undistorted by hopes and fears, without the ballast of a body to recall one from one's fantasies',[40] then it has immense significance. The attempt after becoming lucid is to withdraw from the pull of the dream, to shift from being the 'participant' in the dream to the 'observer' of it.[41] As in the waking state, where one has to restrict the rush of desire, in the dream state too the disciple has to learn to withdraw the identification from the dream narrative and limit his or her focus on being only the 'observer' of the dream. Previously we had noted that this involves a tenuous balance: if the dreamer withdraws completely from the dream there is the risk of lapsing into sleep. On the other hand, if the dreamer is unable to adopt a detached receptivity he or she will be sucked into the flow of dream events. It requires arduous practice to stabilize this fragile sense of 'witnessing', but once established, it will help master the dream state like meditation helps order wakefulness.

If the central aim is to distance the essential self from the content of the dream, then the practices to remain 'awake' in sleep will become different from the earlier nocturnal discipline. 'One of the recommended exercises is to attempt to carry waking consciousness into the sleep state. There are various ways and the first is to hold the intention throughout the day and while falling asleep ... Do a lot of physical work during the course of a day. Then, being exhausted, instead of lying down to go to sleep, quietly remain sitting up [in meditation]. This may allow the body to actually go to sleep while you are in the sitting position, whereas the conscious mind, functioning through the brain, remains awake.'[42] In other words, to learn how to be fully 'awake' in the state where most of us dream, the disciple must allow him or herself to fall asleep in meditation.[43] The disciple must not chastise him or herself if he or she does fall asleep; he or she should wake up and again try to hold his or her awareness through the barrier of sleep. Ashish does not see falling asleep pejoratively as he expects the aspirant to go to sleep again after waking up. 'Let yourself fall asleep in meditation, wake up and continue. Fall asleep, wake up and continue. Fall asleep ... and [one night] wake up inside.'[44] The confusion is, perhaps, in the two kinds of waking up: one is what we are familiar with (ordinary wakefulness) and to which, at this stage, Ashish accords no great importance and merely advises the disciple to persist in the effort; while the second kind of waking up seems a different state of consciousness altogether, one that is the object of the meditational effort.

Ashish himself had serendipitously learnt of the possibility of being asleep yet awake. After a day of hard manual work on the farm Ashish would sit for hours every night massaging his guru's aching feet, and fall asleep while doing so. His hands would stop moving and his guru would awaken due to the pain. Not only that, if his attention wavered his hands would inadvertently touch certain extremely sensitive spots on his guru's feet and the pain would again jolt his guru awake. His desire to be of service to his guru made him struggle night after night with his fatigued body's need to sleep. One night he found that something within him was awake even though his body was asleep. He soon discovered that if he could get past a certain point, where that 'something' happened, he could go on all night if necessary, without fear of his consciousness being overwhelmed by sleep – no matter how tired he was after the day's work. It was only years afterwards that he realized he could make use of the same 'technique' to remain 'awake' beyond the sleepiness of the body while meditating. Then, of course, he discovered that staying awake was itself a 'method' for passing into a state of real meditation. It was again many years before he learnt that others had experienced the same thing. Ashish called this process natural – it was something that happens naturally if one can hold against the tug of sleep.[45] Needless to say, this staying 'awake' is not lucidity, but a state of contentless witnessing awareness.

By now it seems fairly clear that the attempts in meditation and the exercises during sleep merge together. The effort made in meditation infuses a change in sleep; more 'awakeness' in sleep allows greater access to deeper states in meditation. The endeavour in meditation to invoke higher states of consciousness becomes parallel to the stages traversed in sleeping and dreaming. The earliest stage of meditation begins with the observation and understanding of thoughts in an effort to still them. This corresponds to the purificatory dreams that indicate the specific knots of desire. The stilling of the mind in meditation, where the attention has been shifted away from thoughts to a state of quiescence, perhaps is akin to becoming lucid in dream and then learning to dissociate (withdraw) from the dream content, to finally rest in the purely 'witnessing' mode of consciousness.

The acolyte's effort to reach these higher states of consciousness, by withdrawing both in meditation and in sleep, may result in dreams where the sleeper dissociates and feels exteriorized from the body, akin to an out-of-body experience (OBE). The sleeping awareness, when seen as dissociated from the body, provides the novice with a personally convincing demonstration that 'I am not the body'. It must be appreciated that there can never be any hard proof to convince others whether the sleeper is spatially separate from the physical body or not. It becomes authentic for the sleeper to the extent he or she is 'awake' during the experience.[46]

The above aim is very similar to the first practices advised in the Tibetan Dream Yoga – comprehending the nature of the dream state.[47] The Tibetans advocated 'holding the dream' through a fine balance between active and non-active energy;[48] remaining lucid while dreaming, neither waking up nor falling back to sleep into the ordinary flow of dreams. In an OBE, dissociation is possible if there is expectancy without anxiety.[49] And when the disciple 'lets go' in meditation, the resulting effect is a metaphorical exteriorization – a standing-apart by withdrawing from thoughts and witnessing them from afar.

This withdrawal, however, often faces difficulty; the 'guardian' raises its head once again. Now fear and projection may impede the disciple from progressing further. We have seen that throughout this journey the disciple has had to cope with one kind of fear or another. Initially, an acceptance and understanding of it helped the disciple disentangle him or herself from compulsions. Later, fearlessness in challenging assumptions aided the disciple's withdrawal to become the 'observer'. Now another face is being shown – a much more subtle face of this beast. Buddhist anecdotal literature abounds with accounts of the demon Mara plaguing the inward-turning efforts of the Buddha, even on the eve of his enlightenment.[50] The allusion is, perhaps, to a deeper and more fundamental fear.[51] For example, the fear of relinquishing personal beliefs, the comfort of habits, the subtle identifications that support the intrinsic sense of self; in short, the fear of self-annihilation[52] – the *fana* (extinction) of the Sufis.[53] A simple example of fear as an impediment to increasing the length of meditation may be the sheer habit of sleeping a fixed number of hours, with the accompanying belief that this is absolutely imperative for good health. This is not so much a biological issue, but one of fixed mental belief operating subliminally. It would need to be tackled if the disciple is not to be blocked from prolonged periods of meditation.[54]

The fear experienced by the disciple is understandable: 'The process of withdrawal behind the sense organs is so similar to the withdrawal from the body at death that it is *like* dying.'[55] All along, the discipline has forced the disciple along a continuum of ever-subtler streams of refusals: refusal to abandon him or herself to fantasy; refusal to be swept along by the stream of thoughts in meditation; refusal to participate in the flow of the dream. The silencing of the mind will slow his or her respiration; any attempt to annihilate thought would appear akin to a refusal to breathe.[56]

Ashish, presumably through personal experience, had observed: 'In sleep and in deep meditation, breathing is also affected ... In the waking state, breathing is partly volitional and partly under the control of the autonomic nervous system ... But when we fall asleep, the control of breathing is taken over by the autonomic nervous system entirely, ... the transition of control from one part of the brain to the other is usually smooth. In passing from a meditative state of the waking mind into deep meditation, a similar transition occurs: volitional breathing is handed over to the sympathetic system ... In both sleep and [deep] meditation, this change is associated with a dissociation of mind from body which is not necessarily spatial. But whereas in sleep the awareness of the person passes into relative unconsciousness, in [deep states of] meditation the waking awareness of the mind remains while the body falls asleep. In this case, the transitional stage is often marked by a momentary blurring of the focus of awareness.'[57] This process can be very frightening, especially when it happens for the first time and one does not know what to expect. A pause is apt to occur. 'If his breathing appears to have stopped, he thinks he is dying, and if he cannot move his body, he thinks he has had a paralytic stroke. Few people can contemplate such unexpected symptoms with equanimity. Many people, therefore, panic and return to waking consciousness only to realize that they are as normal as before and then consider what happened as a frightening dream.'[58] 'But if he [the meditator] remains calm, the autonomic system takes over, as in sleep, while his awareness "stands in its own nature".'[59]

Fear is, perhaps, not the only obstacle that confronts the disciple as he or she plunges deeper into the inner worlds. Projection may become a bigger hindrance. While awake, we normally imbue an object (or situation) with a particular colouration based on our desires and hopes, distorting it with psychological projections. In much the same way the disciple emits or projects his or her psychic state in the dream world,[60] which can make the unreal appear as real. And therein lies the danger of projection: visionary accounts are prone to be coloured by the projected content of the dreamer. In Shamsoddin's vision (chapter 21) the subjective element was symbolized as a piece of wood that was dragging him down, preventing him from taking flight. This does not mean the entire experience is merely subjective, but that some projective content has unwittingly crept into the vision. If the aspirant has to negotiate the subtle inner worlds, then he or she would have to know how much is objectively real and what has been projected as real. Nirmala's ghost was a subjective projection of a denial. Presumably, the disciple by now has cleared some or much of the ground by the work of psychological purification. However, another kind of projection may hinder the disciple at this stage. This has to do with beliefs that have been assimilated without questioning. For example, our concept of the divine. In a study, a transpersonal psychologist asked thirty-five lucid dreamers about their experience of the divine. 'These concepts were categorized as either personalized, such as encountering a figure like Christ or Buddha, or impersonalized, when the divine was considered to be all-encompassing, energy, formless, and so on. She found that

83 percent of the subjects who believed in the divine as a person encountered a personalized divine presence in their lucid dreams, while 87 percent of the subjects who believed in an impersonal divine experienced the divine in forms other than a person in their lucid dreams.'[61] Perhaps we could say that they saw what they expected to see, a personification of a personal belief. Lucid dream content had been overlaid by personal projections.

Another example is the near-death experience (NDE). When we compare cases collected from Americans and Hindi-speaking North Indians we find that they resemble each other in some respects but differ in others. Most of these accounts report of 'being met' by a discarnate person, although they differ about who meets the dying person. For Americans this usually is a deceased relative or friend. Prominent in the Indian accounts are the 'messengers' sent by Yamaraj (Hindu lord of the dead) to bring the subject before him, who then discovers that a mistaken person has been brought, whereupon the dying person revives. In contrast, American subjects usually give no reason for their recovery; if they do give one it is because thoughts of their living loved ones pulled them back. Also, 'Indian NDEs do not report seeing their own physical body during the NDE, although American subjects usually do.'[62]

Perhaps the variations are expressions of the prevailing conceptions about what happens at death. Once again, our beliefs are projected on to what is experienced, and colours it. This tendency to project manifests even when the disciple is 'awake' in the 'exteriorized'[63] dream state. Ashish advised that one always has to be vigilant when traversing the inner realms, irrespective of the level of advancement of the disciple. Some of the objects encountered in vision or dream will appear different – distorted due to personal psychic emissions; very rarely will he or she find everything like its waking counterpart. Tibetan dream-yogis are expected to trample underfoot all dream images. They believe that not only are the emotionally charged images projections, but that all images have projective content. In fact, the extent of projection rests largely on the degree of the person's 'awakeness'. A lesser degree of 'awakeness' leads to a greater degree of projected content intruding into the vision of the observer. Mostly, projected content is superimposed on objective reality. A more 'awake' disciple may, perhaps, see only one or two objects changed. For instance, in a dream about a familiar room everything may appear normal except the wooden floor that has been changed to one of patterned stone. A further decrease in 'awakeness' leads to a situation where many other objects in the scene appear changed. In that case, continuing with the above example, besides the floor, the fireplace may appear as an altar, an existing wardrobe becomes a door, the glass windowpanes have been replaced by carved panels, and a flowering tree has replaced a standing lamp – the dream scene ceases to have any recognizable connection with the dreamer's material surroundings. So strange is the setting that only on reflection can the dreamer recognize that the scene had been imposed on waking reality. Ashish always cautioned that anyone learning to negotiate the inner worlds should be more concerned with preventing the intrusion of projected content than with analysing it.[64] If the disciple is not to identify with what is encountered, and aims to withdraw into a detached observational awareness, he or she has to distinguish between the counterfeit currency of personal expectations and what is objectively stable (dream content that is not propped by projections). Perhaps it is obvious that distortions can be recognized only if the dreamer finds him or herself in familiar dream surroundings. 'In strange surroundings, or in surroundings familiar only to the exteriorized state, he cannot know whether they are purely visionary or whether they have material counterparts ...'[65] To be able to withdraw all projections, the dreamer has to learn to assert the power of 'awakeness' over the projected content by forcing these apparently changed objects to return to their normal form.[66] Was this not exactly what Hunt was attempting to do with the crystalline walls in his dream of the 'rest house' (chapter 23)?

The earlier purificatory practices will greatly help in this effort. If from the beginning the disciple has been unafraid about identifying his or her projections, then at this stage the separation between the warring tendencies of 'sleep' (tendency to project due to unawareness) and staying 'awake' (ability to distil the real from the projected) can be made. If discrimination has not been practised up to this juncture, once the waking focus relaxes, the unregenerate aspects will leap out – projections alluring the person into participation in the dream content.

Mystics are not concerned with the techniques that enable the conscious manipulation of the dream state by the 'awakened' dreamer. Their aim is to see clearly, whether 'awake' in this world, 'awake' in dreams, or 'awake' in sleep. For, finally, all contents of the dream have to be turned away from, in the same manner that thoughts are to be eschewed in meditation. The focus of awareness has to shift away from the 'seen' to the 'seer'.

We have already witnessed how dreams have consistently beckoned the dreamer to question his or her projections. Perhaps that was what my dream had demanded when it had questioned, 'Who are you?' I had found the dream perplexing because I had attempted to define myself in the usual manner by 'I am this' or 'I am that'. I had never separated the 'I am' from the 'this' or 'that'. In the final analysis every form of 'this' or 'that' is a projection. Never had I tried to feel what it means to *be*, just *be*, without being 'this' or 'that'.[67]

Even Ashish's overwhelming vision of the Deity required him to withdraw his projections on to the object of his search. His attempts to withdraw projections were finally rewarded. Over time his dream/vision had repeated itself, the Deity kept appearing as images whose shapes shifted and kept changing forms. Each time he questioned whether this was truly what the mystics have experienced through millennia. Each time he resolved to see beyond the image. On each questioning the form changed.[68] As his awareness became more discriminatory it did not continue to wander from form to form. Instead, his awareness collapsed inwards and turned in on itself – a state where images subside into an imageless quiescence, and vision dissolves into pure 'seeing'; where, the 'seer' and the 'seen' fuse into an indivisible unity.

The following is an exercise that encapsulates the journey of the disciple and gives us a flavour of the goal.[69]

Step 1: Choose an object, like a candle, set on a table.
Step 2: Observe the candle. (If your attention is not wandering, then all that you will see is the candle.)
Step 3: Become aware[70] that you are observing the candle.
Step 4: Become aware that you are aware that you are observing the candle. Remove the candle from view.
Now, you are only aware of being aware.

This practice demonstrates the attempt of the mystic to directly reach the stage of witnessing awareness.[71] It also symbolically expresses the early aims of meditational practice: See only the candle; the outer life must be made consonant with the aim.[72] The candle can also represent normal dreams that are usually overwhelmed by the identifications of the everyday self. The psychological work introduces the novice to the 'observer'. This stepping back or disidentification is further strengthened when the dreaming self comments on the actions of the waking self or becomes aware that he or she is observing the candle. Then, as the mind begins to be silenced in meditation, the disciple perceives both the thoughts and their thinker. The disciple therefore concludes: I am not the thinker or the 'observer', and proceeds towards what is called the 'house without support'.[73] This distinction is brought into sharp focus when the disciple comes 'awake' while dreaming. The disciple has become 'aware that one is aware of observing the candle'. One more step inwards and there is a dissociation from any involvement with the dream, perceiving it to be totally separate from oneself. If the disciple can turn back completely on the dream, he or she would be in a state of contentless awareness – 'aware of being aware'.[74]

The contemporary mystic Nisargadatta Maharaj has elegantly summarized the attempt to pierce into the higher states of consciousness and finally to go beyond: 'It is like washing printed cloth. First the design fades, then the background and in the end the cloth is plain white. The personality gives place to the witness, then the witness goes and pure awareness remains. The cloth was white in the beginning and is white in the end.'[75]

To pass beyond the witnessing awareness, requires prolonged effort, aspiration, and, hopefully, grace – or what appears as grace because one has no control over it.[76] Only then does the witnessing awareness dissolve into a state where no differentiation exists between subject and object, since there is no focus of awareness to which anything can appear as an object. Then, there is no 'I' and there is no 'it'. No 'here' and no 'there', no 'now' and no 'then'. Mystics describe this both as nothingness, and as being-consciousness-bliss (*sat-chit-ananda*).[77] Perhaps this is the state of *turiya* – the fourth state of consciousness – in which, paradoxically, the plenum is also the void.

NOTES

(The surname of the author followed by the year in brackets refer to the corresponding bibliographical entry for the publishing details. The relevant page numbers are given after the comma. Page numbers of articles in periodicals downloaded from the internet are not mentioned. All allusions to 'Freud' refer to Sigmund Freud, while Anna Freud is mentioned such whenever she is referred to. The 'CW' in Jung references allude to Jung's Collected Works (19 volumes). The numerals before the colon refer to the volume number and the relevant paragraph numbers are given after the colon. The numerical references to Plato allude to the marginal sigla derived from the pagination and page subdivision of the 1578 edition of Plato by Henri Estienne (Stephanus), the most commonly used one.)

PART 1

Chapter 1 – The Multiplicity of Dreams

1. States (1992).
2. Hunt (1989), 4.

Chapter 2 – My Dialogue with Dreams: A Personal Introduction

1. Tandan (1997), 67.
2. Nisargadatta Maharaj (1973), 270.
3. I am not using this term in the specialized sense employed by the German philosopher Edmund Husserl (1859–1938) with whom it is usually associated, but as a more general term descriptive of experience and alluding to something that is visible or directly observable.

Chapter 3 – The Interplay between Belief and Bizarreness

1. Bulkeley (1997), 109–10.
2. I am indebted to Kelly Bulkeley for these questions formulated in Bulkeley (1997), 4–5 and 109–10.
3. Shakespeare, *Julius Caesar*, Act II, Scene 2.
4. Ibid.
5. Artemidorus, *Oneirocritica* (I.45). Quoted in Miller (1994), 85.
6. Hunt (1989), 85.
7. Castle (1994), 54.
8. Hobson (1988), 204.

Chapter 4 – Dream Paradigms

1. Franz (1966). Quoted in Ullman, Krippner, and Vaughan (1973), 27.
2. Presumably, Shakespeare had sourced the story of Julius Caesar from Plutarch's *Lives*, which chronicles Calpurnia's premonition. But then Plutarch tended to look more at the personality than at absolute historical accuracy.
3. Ullman, Krippner, and Vaughan (1973), 65.
4. Ibid., 66.
5. 'They are merely an anticipatory combination of probabilities which may coincide with the actual behaviour of things ...' – Jung CW 8: para. 493.
6. Cayce (1962). Quoted in Ullman, Krippner, and Vaughan (1973), 6.
7. Quoted in Ullman, Krippner, and Vaughan (1973), 6–7.
8. Hunt (1989), 9.
9. Young (1999), 119.
10. Foulkes (1993), 11–12.
11. Jung distinguished between the process of active imagination and what we commonly regard as imagination. Active imagination consists of setting aside the critical faculty and allowing emotions, fantasies, and images to surface into awareness. The images and emotions that emerge are encouraged to be identified with; to be treated as if they were objectively present. 'This imaginative process is one of involvement; not merely a spectacle. The idea is to regard these interior events exactly as if one were in a similar exterior situation. Emotions are felt, not just noted ... A real lion elicits fear; an active imagination lion should do no less.' – Price-Williams (1987), 247.

PART 2

Chapter 5 – An Insignificant Dream and the Biology of Dreaming

1. Some people, to protect their privacy, have requested their names to be changed. Whenever this has been done, the first allusion to the name is enclosed in quotation marks.
2. Dement, (1972), 28.
3. My description relies on that given by Castle (1994), 228–35 and Dement (1972), 24–29.
4. Woods and Greenhouse (1974), 34.
5. Rechtschaffen and Siegel (2000).
6. Hobson (2003), 80.
7. Shakespeare, *Macbeth* Act II, Scene 2.
8. Freud (1932), 9.
9. Hobson (1988), 150.
10. 'In one respect the term "quiet sleep" is a misnomer: it is during NREM sleep that snoring occurs.' – Dement (1972), 26.
11. Hobson (1988), 146.
12. Jouvet (1967).
13. Fontana (1994), 15.
14. *Newsweek*, 9 August 2004, 47.
15. Stevens (1995), 85.
16. Crick and Mitchison (1983), 111–14.
17. Freud (1900), 50.
18. Jouvet (1967).
19. Hobson (1988), 207.
20. Hunt (1989), 10.
21. Hobson and McCarley (1977), 1347.

22. Ibid.
23. Hobson (1988), 272.
24. Ibid., 15.
25. Bulkeley (1997), 61.
26. Freud (1900), 47.
27. Hobson (1988), 296.
28. Ibid., 299.

Chapter 6 – The Legacy of Dreams: A Backward Glance

1. Castle (1994), 49.
2. Oppenheim (1956), 179–373.
3. Ibid., 186–91.
4. *Encyclopaedia of Religion and Ethics*, 34.
5. For example: The Chronicle of the Abbey of Waltham, in southeast England, begins with an account of a wondrous dream dreamt by a blacksmith at the beginning of the eleventh century. 'For three successive nights, the venerable figure of Christ appeared to him in his sleep and ordered him, in an increasingly pressing fashion, to go find the parish priest and guide him to the summit of a mountain where they would discover, buried in the earth, a marvellous cross. The abbey itself was founded as a result of this holy "invention."' – Schmitt (1999), 281–82.
6. Feuerstein (2002), 353.
7. Chandogya Upanishad (5.2.4–9) in Hume (1931), 229–30.
8. Fraser points out an interesting element of Greek dreams: 'An analysis of Homeric dreams shows them to be predominantly auditory with the visual elements obscure and shadowy, whereas in contrast, dreams of early Greek drama are predominantly visual ... [V]isual descriptions of events tend to stress the spatial, whereas auditory descriptions stress the temporal ...' – Fraser (1975), 12.
9. The Parisistas of the Atharvaveda (68.1.52). Quoted in O'Flaherty (1984), 19.
10. Brelich (1966), 297–98.
11. 'Unlike the Greek Cosmos the Hindu World lay seventh, or the lowest of the upper worlds, in a vertical arrangement. The Visnu-Purana places *Bhuvarloka*, extending up to the Sun, above the terrestrial sphere (*Bhu*). From the Sun to the pole star is *Svarloka* or the heavenly sphere. Below the Earth and above the seven Nether worlds are the Hells (*Narak*) starting with *Avichi*. The Devi Purana states that there are 34 Hells. The lowest Nether world is *Patal* and yet below is Lord Vishnu bearing the entire world as a diadem and dreaming his dream.' – Woodroffe (2001), 26.
12. Brelich (1966), 299.
13. *Encyclopaedia of Religion and Ethics*, 30.
14. Euripedes, *Iphigenia in Tauris*. Quoted in Miller (1994), 21.
15. *Encyclopaedia of Religion and Ethics*, 31.
16. Freud (1900), 433n1.
17. Ibid.
18. Hemacrandra. Quoted in Sharma, and Siegel (1980), 15–16.
19. Oppenheim (1966), 346.
20. Rig Veda (2.28.10, 10.37.4, 5.82.4–5). Quoted in Young (1999), 135.
21. Atharva Veda (IV.17.5, VI.45 and 46, X.3.6). Quoted in Gupta (1971), 52.
22. The Parisistas of the Atharvaveda (33.1.3). Quoted in Gupta (1971), 53.
23. Homer, *The Iliad*, bk. II, 15.
24. Homer, *The Odyssey*, bk. XIX, 302.
25. Miller (1994), 81.
26. Cancik (1999), 172.
27. Ibid.
28. Gupta (1971), 47. Woods and Greenhouse (1974), 41. Freud also quotes this dream:

'Alexander dreamt he saw a satyr dancing on his shield.' – Freud (1900), 131n2. Also see Freud (1916), 274–75.

29. Brahmavaivarta-Mahapuranam, vol. II (77.17), 502.
30. Ullman and Zimmerman (1979), 34–35 and Castle (1994), 56.
31. Castle (1994), 57.
32. Brahmavaivarta-Mahapuranam, vol. II (Shri Krishna Janam Khanda, 77 Adhyay), 501.
33. Ullman and Zimmerman (1979), 35.
34. Young (1999), 33.
35. Oppenheim (1956), 209.
36. Castle (1994), 57.
37. Gupta (1971), 78–79.
38. Freud (1900), 129.
39. Ibid., 130–31.
40. The Matsya Puranam (242.35), 266.
41. The Parisistas of the Atharva Veda (68.1.13–19, 29–37, 44–47). Quoted in O'Flaherty (1984), 18.
42. Brahmavaivarta-Mahapuranam, vol. II (77.10–13), 502.
43. 'Patients dream in the dialect of whatever physician happens to be treating them. The dreams are "made to order" and produced in the form that will best please the analyst.' – Stekel (1962), 13–14. Quoted in Castle (1994), 181.
    Freud also conceded that dream content is influenced by the analyst, and that patients dream of things which the analyst has discussed, or aroused expectations in them. – Freud (1923a), 113–14. Also see Freud (1916), 276–77.
44. Kakar (1997), 14.
45. Stroumsa (1999), 191.
46. 'I had the following vision ...' wrote Perpetua, the African Christian martyr. She only clarifies later that it was a dream. – Stroumsa (1999), 189.
47. Ibid., 194.
48. Ibid., 193.
49. Schmitt (1999), 278.
50. Ibid., 278.
51. Stroumsa (1999), 203.
52. Schmitt (1999), 279.
53. Ibid., 279.
54. Artemidorus, Oneirocritica. Quoted in Bulkeley (1997), 10.
55. Ullman and Zimmerman (1979), 43–44.
56. Tedlock (1987), 2.

Chapter 7 – Freud Fashions a New Pathway: The Unconscious

1. Taylor (1997), 13–15.
2. 'On several occasions Freud compared the injury which he inflicted upon man with his findings with the effect of the unwelcome realization (by Darwin) that man descended from the apes and the no less unwelcome discovery (by Copernicus) that the earth is not the centre of the universe.' – Anna Freud (1986), 131–32.
3. Ratcliff (1996), 111–12.
4. Foulkes (1978), 94.
5. Walde (1999), 129.
6. Freud (1916), 153.
7. Freud (1923), 442n2.
8. Freud (1916), 249.
9. Anna Freud (1986), 132.
10. Bulkeley (1997), 21.

11. Freud (1932), 14–15.
12. 'By the early 1920s, Freud's topographical model had become a "structural" model. This ... was now divided into the Id / Ego / Super-Ego. The Id (the It) is the realm of drive representations and repressed materials; the Ego (the I) is the part of the psyche that mediates between inside and outside; and the Super-Ego (the Over I) is the source of values and ideals and by implication enables the making of moral judgements.' – King (2002), 104.
13. This example and much of my description closely follows Castle (1994), 117.
14. McDougall (1997), 62.
15. 'Faulty acts' or 'faulty functions'. The term is special to Freudian terminology. Freud has devoted a whole book *The Psychopathology of Everyday Life* to discuss the impact of these in our lives, including mispronouncing of words in a foreign language.
16. Freud (1900), 163.
17. Ibid.
18. Ibid., 449.
19. Freud (1910), 35.
20. Freud (1900), 180–82.
21. Ibid.
22. Freud (1901), 89.
23. Ibid., 89–90.
24. Barry (1995), 99.
25. Freud (1916), 207.
26. Freud (1932), 21.
27. Ibid., 12.
28. Palombo (1978), 4.
29. Freud (1900), 133–36.
30. McDougall (1997), 64.
31. Hunt (1989), 7.
32. Freud (1932), 12.
33. Stafford-Clark (1967), 63–64.
34. Freud (1900), 557.
35. Stevens (1995), 36.
36. Freud (1916), 183–84.
37. Hall (1953a).
38. Freud (1900), 389–90.
39. Freud (1932), 23.
    Calvin Hall points out that 'the Greek word for ladder or staircase is *klimax* which is the source for the English word *climax*, a term that is used to denote the sexual orgasm'. – Hall (1953c), 238.
40. Freud is quoting from Robert Eisler. Freud (1932), 24.
41. Freud (1916), 203.
42. Breger (1967), 5.
43. McDougall (1997), 54.
44. Auden, *The Collected Poetry of W. H. Auden*. Quoted in Young (1999), 18.

Chapter 8 – Are Dreams 'Dumb' Biology or 'Smart' Psychology?

1. States (1992).
2. Breger (1967), 8.
3. Hobson (1988), 217.
4. Ibid., 213–14.
5. 'In this model the substrate of emotion is considered to be a part of the forebrain; it will not be further distinguished here because we have no specific physiological

evidence as to how this part of the system might work in any brain state.' – Hobson and McCarley (1977), 1336–37.

6. Ibid., 1336.
7. Hobson (2003), 112.
8. A few of the many species whose sleep has been carefully studied are elephant, chimpanzee, whale, shrew, pig, sheep, monkey, rat, mouse, cat, bat, dog, donkey, guinea pig, frog, alligator, lizard, fish, pigeon, chicken, eagle and snake. – Dement (1972), 30.
9. My description of sleep and dreaming in the animal world faithfully relies on Rechtschaffen and Siegel (2000) and Dement (1972), 29–30.
10. Ullman, Krippner, and Vaughan (1973), 63.
11. Stevens (1995), 91.
12. Winson (1990), 94.
13. Hobson (2003), 72, 76.
14. Dement (1972), 30–31.
15. Ullman, Krippner, and Vaughan (1973), 63.
16. Winson (1990), 86, 88.
17. There are strong indications that sleep is also concerned with maintenance of body or brain temperature. This thermoregulation is what characterizes any species as cold- or hot-blooded. Reptiles have to rely on the surrounding environment to regulate their internal body temperature. It has been observed that body and brain temperatures are usually reduced during sleep, and heating the hypothalamus induces sleep in animals. Rats that are chronically deprived of sleep show a marked preference for warmer locations, indicating that sleep tends to regulate their body temperature. Prior body heating also induces sleep in humans; perhaps that is why we prefer a covering when we sleep. Contrarily, in the REM state, adult mammals – including human beings – are not able to regulate their body temperature on their own. This means that they are unable to shiver while in the REM state. The foetus is also unable to regulate its body temperature, presumably because the mother maintains body temperature. These facts suggest that sleep has thermoregulatory functions, however the exact mechanism is still unclear. – Hunt (1989), 26, and Rechtschaffen and Siegel (2000).
18. Dement (1972), 40–41.
19. Rechtschaffen, Vogeh, and Shaikun (1963). Quoted in Dement (1972), 44.
20. Foulkes (1978), 89–90.
21. Ibid., 90–91.
22. Ibid., 11.
23. Hunt (1989), ix–x.
24. Hobson (2003), 105.
25. This letter was written on 12 June 1900 to Wilhelm Fleiss, who had considerable influence on the final shape of Freud's manuscript on dreams, having critically commented on it on a regular basis. – Freud (1900), 154 and xx.

PART 3

Chapter 9 – Jung Liberates the Unconscious

1. Rechtschaffen (1978), 97.
2. Jung CW 17: para. 187.
3. Dostoevsky (1866). Quoted in Foulkes (1978), 4.
4. Foulkes (1978), 5.
5. Ashish, citing A. N. Whitehead, emphasizes that the perception of observable frequencies of light is a physical phenomenon—a 'neurosis', or a state of the nerves—while the experience of colour is a state of consciousness – a 'psychosis', or a state of the psyche. – Ashish (2007), 10.

6. Foulkes (1978), 5.
7. Jung CW 8: para. 288.
8. Jung (1963), 182–83.
9. Hunt (1989), 143.
10. Jung CW 8: para. 149.
11. I am thankful to Sri Madhava Ashish for introducing me to this debate.
   It is said that Jung questioned the Freudian belief that a church steeple stood for a penis and nothing more: 'If a church steeple stands for a penis, how does one interpret [the image of] a penis?' – Mattoon (1978), 97.
12. Jung (1963), 26–27.
13. Hunt (1989), 143.
14. Jung CW 16: para. 322.
15. My description of Jungian psychology relies heavily, if not exclusively, on Calvin Hall and Vernon Nordby's excellent exposition in their *A Primer of Jungian Psychology* from which I have quoted many passages.
16. Jung CW 9(i): para. 63.
17. Jung CW 9(i): para. 490.
18. Jung (1964), 57.
19. Hyde (1993), 41.
20. Quoted in Hall and Nordby (1973), 41.
21. Hyde (1993), 59.
22. Ibid.
23. Jung (1964), 13–14.
24. Quoted in Hall and Nordby (1973), 116.
25. Hall and Nordby (1973), 116.
26. Ibid., 117.
27. Jung CW 10: paras 304–05.
28. Jung CW 10: para. 305.
29. Jung CW 18: para. 509.
30. Fordham (1953), 103.
31. Jung CW 18: para. 469.
32. Jung CW 18: para. 473.
33. Jung CW 8: para. 493.
34. Ibid.
35. Ibid.
36. Jung CW 16: para. 335.
37. Jung CW 18: para. 519.
38. Mattoon (1978), 114.
39. Ibid., 117.
40. This example of the bull has been taken from Castle (1994), 166–67.
41. Kutz (1993), 3.
42. Jung CW 5: para. 5.
43. Castle (1994), 175.
44. Hunt (1989), 143–45.
45. Ibid., 146.
46. Mattoon (1978), 110n 12.
47. Ullman (1987), 5. Quoted in Castle (1994), 200.
48. Ullman (1987), 4. Quoted in Castle (1994), 199.

Chapter 10 – The Metaphorical Language of Dreams

1. Hunt (1989), 14.
2. Hazarika (1997), 94.
3. Quoted in Arendt (1981), 106.

4. Quoted in Rycroft (1981), 75.
5. Ullman and Zimmerman (1979), 29.
6. I read this example a long time ago, and I have forgotten from where.
7. Delaney (1991).
8. Ullman and Zimmerman (1979), 101.
9. Ullman (1999), 222.
10. While interpreting a long dream, Jung observed: 'It is very difficult to grasp it as a whole; it is so long and there is so much detail that one can hardly take it all in. Therefore the ordinary technique in such a case is to divide the dream into scenes or parts, and to look at each part separately. Only in the end shall we try to bring it all together.' – Jung (1928), 662.
11. '… [I]t does sometimes really happen that nothing occurs to a person under analysis in response to particular elements of his dreams … [I]n a great many cases, with perseverance, an idea is extracted from him. But nevertheless there remain cases in which an association fails to emerge … [W]e are tempted to interpret these "mute" dream elements ourselves, to set about translating them with our own resources. We are then forced to recognize that whenever we venture on making a replacement of this sort we arrive at a satisfactory sense for the dream …' – Freud (1916), 182–83.
12. I am grateful to Sri Madhava Ashish for having introduced me to this phonetic metaphor.
13. Hunt concurs: 'Sometimes assonance constitutes the only possible interpretive key to an otherwise semantically unrelated aggregate of dream objects and actions.' He exemplifies this by citing a study by Berger on the influence on dream content of names spoken while the subject is asleep. It was found that assonance was by far the most significant determinant of incorporation into the dream, accounting for 65 percent of all rated incorporations. Typically the spoken word 'robber' entered a dream as 'a rabbit'; the name 'Naomi' entered as a friend who said 'oh show me' – to quote two examples of linguistic metaphors. – Hunt (1989), 106.
14. Anna Freud (1946), 152.
15. 'There is no other period in life when the growing child is more in need of help and guidance than in this transitional stage with its almost overwhelming inner and outer struggles. Yet, there is no other time when parents and teachers find themselves equally powerless to help.' – Anna Freud (1949), 168.
16. Campbell (1949), 90–91.
17. Ibid., 19.
18. Ibid., 92.
19. This categorization is given by Parsons and Bales (1955). Quoted in Stevens (1982), 106–07.
20. Kakar (1981), 80.
21. Jung (1974), 97. Also see Jung CW 16: para. 319.
22. Frazer (1922), 694.
23. Kakar (1981), 206–07.
24. Pandey R. (1969), 128–32.
25. We want him (the child) to have control over his sexual desires, for if they are constantly breaking through, there is a danger that his development will be retarded or interrupted; that he will rest content with gratification instead of sublimating, with masturbation instead of learning; that he will confine his desires for knowledge to sexual matters instead of extending it to the whole wide world. – Anna Freud (1935).
26. Erikson (1965), 255.
27. Bhagavata Purana (10.8.21–45). Quoted in O'Flaherty (1984), 109–10.
28. Quoted in O'Flaherty (1984), 111.
29. Gaston (1996), 26.

30. Campbell (1949), 12.
31. As a matter of fact they were the Indian School Certificate examination, equivalent to Class XI. The scoring was not as percent, or percentile, but a point system – 1 being the highest and 9 was failure.

Chapter 11 – Typical Dreams and the Nightmare

1. Stevens (1995), 36.
2. Freud (1900), 274.
3. Ibid., 274–75.
4. Stevens (1995), 248.
5. Ibid., 73.
6. Castle, (1994), 335.
7. Ibid.
8. Ullman and Zimmerman (1979), 110.
9. Garfield (1995), 104–09.
10. Moss (1996), 53.
11. Domhoff (1985). Also see Young (1999), 167–69.
12. Schacter and Crovitz (1977). Quoted in Castle (1994), 338.
13. Freud (1900), 305–06.
14. Fontana (1994), 104.
15. Hazarika (1997), 133.
16. Castle (1994), 338.
17. Freud (1900), 308.
18. Ibid., 308–09.
19. Gutheil (1951), 226–28.
20. Ullman and Zimmerman (1979), 102.
21. These are the findings of T. Benedek and B. B. Rubenstein, which are reported in the *Psychosomatic Medicine Monographs* nos. 1 and 2 for 1942. Quoted in Hall (1953c), 241.
22. Hall (1953c), 48.
23. Karacan, et al. (1976). Quoted in Castle (1994), 236.
24. Rogers, et al. (1985). Quoted in Castle (1994), 238–39.
25. Ten young married men were asked to abstain from sexual activity on three occasions during a period of ten days. Their nocturnal erections were monitored on the last night of abstinence as well as on the following night after each subject engaged in sexual activity. Fewer and longer periods of time between erections were found on the nights following periods of abstinence in comparison to those following intercourse. – Karacan, Williams, and Salis (1970b). Quoted in Castle (1994), 236.
26. Karacan (1970a). Quoted in Castle (1994) 236–37.
27. 'Often enough a symbol has to be interpreted in its proper meaning and not symbolically; while on other occasions a dreamer may derive from his private memories the power to employ as sexual symbols all kinds of things which are not ordinarily employed as such.' – Freud (1900), 387–88.
28. Hall (1953c), 49.
29. Ibid., 60–61.
30. Fontana (1994), 75.
31. Gutheil (1951), 144.
32. Sudhir Kakar in an interview with Michelle Caswell of AsiaSource on 8 July 2002. Accessible on http://www.asiasource.org/arts/kakar.cfm
33. O'Flaherty (1984), 59.
34. Hazarika (1997), 135.
35. Freud (1900), 277–79.
36. Young (1999), 48–49.

37. Brahmavaivarta-Mahapuranam, vol. II, 522.
38. Lorand (1957). Quoted in Delaney (1991), 360.
39. Delaney (1991), 361.
40. Castle (1994), 339.
41. Freud (1900), 422n1.
42. Ibid., 423.
43. Castle (1994), 340–41.
44. Bettelheim (1975), 18.
45. Ibid., 6.
46. Castle (1994), 341.
47. Jung (1964), 40.
48. Castle (1994), 347.
49. Hartmann (1996), 107.
50. Galvin and Hartmann (1999), 236.
51. Hartmann (1996), 111–13.
52. Galvin and Hartmann (1999), 239.
53. Delaney (1991), 358.
54. Castle (1994), 347.
55. Hartmann (1996), 100.
56. Ibid., 109.

Chapter 12 – Archetypal Dreams at a Crossroads

1. Kakar (1981), 62.
2. Ibid., 58.
3. Ibid., 73.
4. Young (1999), 9.
5. Quoted from an exhibition handout titled, 'Kavita Nayar: A Journey Out of Despair.'
6. Suneet Chopra, *The Economic Times*, New Delhi: 14 September 1993.
7. Campbell (1949), 11.
8. Jung CW 6: para. 401.

Chapter 13 – Calvin Hall and the Content Analysis of Dreams

1. Hall and Nordby (1972), 104.
2. Hall (1953c), 72.
3. Reis (1951).
4. Hall (1947).
5. Ibid.
6. Hall (1953c), 23.
7. Ibid., 25–26.
8. Hall and Nordby (1972), 39.
9. Domhoff (1996). Quoted in Bulkeley (1997), 71.
10. Bulkeley (1997), 71.
11. Castle (1994), 305–06.
12. Hall and Nordby (1972), 36.
13. Ibid., 104.
14. Hall (1953b).
15. Hall (1953c), 95.
16. Hall (1953b).
17. Hall and Nordby (1972), 51.
18. Hall (1953c), 2.
19. This enumeration relies on the accounts given by Castle (1994), 302–03, and Hall and Nordby (1972), 107–08.

20. Hall and Nordby (1972), 41.
21. Castle (1994), 303–04.
22. Hall (1953b).
23. Ibid.
24. Hall (1953c), 84–85.
25. Domhoff (1999).

Chapter 14 – A Dream Series: A Chapter in a Life

1. Hillman (1979), 228n50.
2. Hall (1947).
3. Hall (1953b).
4. Jung CW 18: para. 1095.
5. Hall (1953b).
6. Erikson (1965), 260.
7. Okri (1997), 21.

PART 4

Chapter 15 – The Unsolved Mystery of Dreams and the Hindu View

1. Jung CW 17: paras. 117–22.
2. Jung CW 18: para. 471.
3. Jung CW 16: para. 323.
4. Jung CW 18: para. 471.
5. Ibid.
6. Jung CW 17: paras. 121–22.
7. Fodor (1967). Quoted in Ullman, Krippner, and Vaughan (1973), 25.
8. Hall (1953c), 239.
9. Ibid., 239–40.
10. Freud (1901), 89.
11. Hall (1953a).
12. Calvin Hall noted every slang expression in Partridge's *A Dictionary of Slang and Unconventional English* to find 200 expressions for penis, 330 for vagina, and 212 for coitus. Many of the dream symbols are identical with those enumerated in Partridge. – Ibid.
13. Ibid.
14. Freud (1922), 77.
15. Jung CW 18: para. 473.
16. Jung CW 8: para. 493.
17. Ibid.
18. Ibid.
19. Mattoon (1978), 144.
20. Antrobus (1978). Quoted in Hunt (1989), 20.
21. Rupprecht (1999).
22. Kilroe (2000).
23. Tedlock (1991).
24. Yeats (1974), 130.
25. States (1992).
26. Ibid.
27. Caillois (1966), 27.
28. Brihad-Aranyaka Upanishad (4.3.14–16) in Hume (1931), 135.
29. O'Flaherty (1999), 74.

30. Kurma Purana (I.9.6–13). Also see Mahabharata III.194, 8–14. Much in this paragraph has been quoted from Young (1999), 132.

31. This is an archetypal dream that I heard from Sri Madhava Ashish and other people later on.
Please also see Nisargadatta Maharaj (1973), 230, where he continues the story by answering the riddle posed.
It is also prevalent in other cultures. For example, Chuang-tzu relates: 'Once upon a time I, Chuang-tzu, dreamed I was a butterfly, fluttering hither and thither, to all intents and purposes a butterfly. I was conscious only of following my fancies as a butterfly and was unconscious of my individuality ... Suddenly I was awakened, and there I lay, myself again. Now I do not know whether I was a man dreaming I was a butterfly, or whether I am a butterfly now dreaming I am a man.' – Quoted in Ullman and Zimmerman (1979), 40–41.

32. *The New Encyclopaedia Britannica*, 308.
Socrates also asks: 'What evidence could be appealed to, supposing we were asked at this very moment whether we are asleep or awake, dreaming all that passes through our minds or talking to one another in the waking state?' – Plato, *Theatetus* (158c), (tr.) F. M. Cornford, 863.

33. O'Flaherty (1984), 12.
Admittedly this is only the position of the Advaita Vedanta school of Hindu philosophy, but then this is not intended to be either a comprehensive or exhaustive exposition of the philosophy. It is the common, if not the dominant, view held by most Hindus.

34. Jaimini's Mimasa Sutra (circa AD 200) states, 'When a shell is perceived as silver, the sense-perception is wrong; and if sense-perception may be wrong, it follows that inference and other means of cognition, based on sense-perception, may also be wrong.' – Kuppuswamy (1993), 168.

35. Lankavatara Sutra (10.498). Quoted in O'Flaherty (1984), 262.

36. O'Flaherty (1984), 17.
A classic ancient reply to the question of what is real comes from Taoist Chuang-tzu around 350 BC: 'And one day there will come a great awakening, when we shall realize that life itself was a great dream.' – Creel (1953). Quoted in Ullman and Zimmerman (1979), 40.
The nineteenth century American poet Edgar Allan Poe feared, as did Hamlet, that the 'sleep of death' was not dreamless, and pushed the dilemma of reality one step further. 'Is all that we see or seem but a dream within a dream?' – Quoted in Ullman and Zimmerman (1979), 45.

37. O'Flaherty (1984), 14.

38. 'Let us consider them together – waking and dreaming. The difference is merely in continuity. Were your dreams consistently continuous, bringing back night after night the same surroundings and the same people, you would be at a loss to know which is the waking and which is the dream.' – Nisargadatta Maharaj (1973), 58.

39. Freud (1900), 658–59.

40. Miller (1994), 4.

41. O'Flaherty (1984), 14.

42. Jung said that the subconscious is usually regarded with the pejorative connotation of an inferior consciousness. – Jung CW 9(i): para. 40.

43. Brihad-Aranyaka Upanishad (4.3.21) in Hume (1931), 136.

44. Brihad-Aranyaka Upanishad (2.1.16) in Hume (1931), 95.

45. Sri Ramakrishna (1947). Quoted in O'Flaherty (1984), 45.
To clarify, Sri Ramakrishna was not commenting on the reality / unreality of dreams but stating that the mystic needs to transcend fear even in the dream state. Similarly,

Freud, citing Stricker, acknowledges that 'dreams do not consist solely of illusions. If, for instance, one is afraid of robbers in a dream, the robbers, it is true, are imaginary – but the fear is real.' – Freud (1900), 106.

46. Caillois (1966), 33.
47. Expressing a similar sentiment, the Yogavasistha (3.3.17) states: 'The universe is like a dream of sexual intercourse with a woman; for by the imagination of something unreal we experience real emotion.' Quoted in O'Flaherty (1984), 45.
Such examples are not limited to Hindus immersed in their theory of *maya*; the Western tradition has similar accounts, e.g., Perpetua, who was martyred in the third century AD for professing to be a Christian, 'awoke from her dream of eating paridisial cheese with the taste of something sweet in her mouth'. – Miller (1994), 4.
48. O'Flaherty (1984), 46.
49. This quote is from Marianne Moore's poem 'Poetry'. In *A College Book of Modern Verse.* (eds.) J. K. Robinson and W. B. Rideout (New York: Harper and Row, 1958), 325. Quoted in Miller (1994), 4.
50. Similarly, Heraclitus describes sleep as 'death in life' in Gupta (1971), 18, and Tertullian as the 'mirror of death' in Stroumsa (1999), 191.
51. Brihad-Aranyaka Upanishad (4.3.9) in Hume (1931), 134.
52. Deussen (1919), 303.
53. *Padartha-dharma-sangraha of Prasastapada*, 387.
54. The Parisistas of the Atharvaveda (68.1.51). I am grateful to Dr Trinath Mishra for translating from Sanskrit many of the verses of this text.
55. *Padartha-dharma-sangraha of Prasastapada*, 387.
Also see *Vaiseshika Aphorisms of Kanada*, 293–95.
56. Kuppuswamy (1993), 289.
57. Brihad-Aranyaka Upanishad (4.3.10) in Hume (1931), 134.
58. *Susruta Samhita* (Sa, 4, 33–36), 18.
59. O'Flaherty (1984), 59.
60. 'Susruta advances a theory that dreams are warnings about future happenings, specially about diseases or death. It has been said that the eternal soul (*jivatma*) may convey glimpses of things, not cognizable to the conscious mind, to the semi-conscious *rajasika* part of the mind in sleep. These dreams are glimpses of things unknowable in the normal state, but known to the *purusa*.' – *Susruta Samhita* (Sa, 4, 35), 19.
61. Hunt (1989), 86.
62. 'It would be truer to say instead that they give us knowledge of the past. For dreams are derived from the past in every sense ... By picturing our wishes as fulfilled, dreams are after all leading us into the future. But this future, which the dreamer pictures as the present, has been moulded by his indestructible wish into a perfect likeness of the past.' – Freud (1900), 660.
63. Freud, while reviewing the earlier dream theories, glosses over Fechner's suspicion (even though he italicizes his paraphrase) that 'the scene of action of dreams is different from that of waking ideational life' by wondering: 'It is not clear what Fechner had in mind in speaking of this change of location of mental activity; nor, so far as I know, has anyone else pursued the path indicated by his words.' – Ibid., 81.
Also, while discussing Indian mystics, Freud admits: 'But it isn't easy to pass beyond the limits of one's nature.' – Letter to R. Rolland, 19 January 1930. In Freud (1960), 392. Quoted in Kakar (1991), 7
64. Green (1968a), 17.
65. Freud (1900), 143n2 and 564. I am grateful to Bulkeley (1999), 214, for highlighting this connection.

Chapter 16 – Dreams That Have Changed the World

 1. Gandhi (1927), 348.
 2. Ibid.
 3. Stevens (1995), 283.
 4. Koestler (1964), 118.
 5. Ullman, Krippner, and Vaughan (1973), 178.
 6. Stevens (1995), 283.
 7. Bryson (2003), 184–87.
 8. Becker (1968), 96–97.
 9. Castle (1994), 34.
10. Koestler (1964), 146.
11. Kaempffert (1924). Quoted in LaBerge (1986), 187–88.
12. Castle (1994), 36.
13. Loewi (1960). As quoted in Edwin Diamond, *The Science of Dreams* (New York: MacFadden Books, 1963). Quoted in Garfield (1995), 68–69.
14. Stevens (1995), 285.
15. Koestler (1964), 116–17.
16. Kedrov (1957). Quoted in LaBerge (1986), 187.
17. Coleridge (1912), 296.
18. Stevenson (1925), 'A Chapter on Dreams'. Quoted in Garfield (1995), 71, and in Woods and Greenhouse (1974), 55–56.
19. Stevenson (1925), 'A Chapter on Dreams'. Quoted in Garfield (1995), 70.
20. Ibid., 71.
21. Gaskell, *The Life of Charlotte Bronte*. Quoted in Ratcliff, 88–89.
22. Garfield (1995), 64.
23. Raine (1971). Quoted in Garfield (1995), 65, and Garfield (1996), 201.
24. Castle (1994), 11.
25. Breton (1969). Quoted in Castle (1994), 11.
26. Kinder (1988). Quoted in Castle (1994), 12.
27. Manaceine (1897). Quoted in Castle (1994), 39.
28. Koestler (1964), 151.
29. Dement (1972), 101.
30. Whyte (1962). Quoted in Koestler (1964), 153.
31. Freud (1905), 95–96. Quoted in Hunt (1989), 12.
32. Caillois (1966), 31.

Chapter 17 – Paranormal Dreams: The Echo before the Sound

 1. Plato, *Timaeus* (71e), tr. B. Jowett, 1194.
 2. *Caraka Samhita* (5.5.42), 564. Quoted in O'Flaherty (1984), 24.
 3. *Caraka Samhita* (5.5.43), 564.
 4. Bulkeley (1999), 212–13.
 5. Young (1999), 87.
 6. Ibid., 21.
 7. Ibid., 88.
 8. Ibid., 90.
 9. Eisenbud (1947), 26.
10. Ibid., 263.
11. Ibid., 263–69.
12. Caillois (1966), 34.
13. The story of Vikramaditya and Malayavati is given in *Kathasaritasagara* (18.3.24–110). Quoted in O'Flaherty (1984), 63.
14. Jung (1963), 178–79.

15. Castle, (1994), 412.
16. Freud (1901a), 263–64.
17. Freud (1932a), 37–38.
18. Freud (1932a), 38.
19. Eisenbud (1949), 9.
20. Freud (1932a), 39.
21. Freud (1922), 69.
22. Freud (1925), 88.
23. Ibid., 89–90.
24. In his technical 'Recommendations' Freud says: 'All conscious exertion is to be withheld from the capacity for attention, and one's "unconscious memory" is to be given full play.' [The analyst] 'must bend his own unconscious like a receptive organ toward the emerging unconscious of the patient ...' Freud (1912). Quoted in Deutsch (1926), 136.
25. Freud (1925), 89.
26. Deutsch (1926), 139.
27. Ehrenwald (1954), 39.
28. Freud (1921), 56.
29. *Mysteries of The Unknown*, 8.
30. Freud (1932a), 55.
31. The Parisistas of the Atharvaveda (68.2.57–59); Agni Puranam (229.16–19); The Matsya Puranam (242.16–20); Brahmavaivarta-Mahapuranam (Krsna-Janma Khanda) (77.4–8). The period in which the outcome fructifies varies slightly between texts.
32. *Mysteries of The Unknown*, 29.
33. Ibid.
34. Barker (1967). Quoted in Castle (1994), 408.
35. Dunne (1927), 42–43.
36. Ibid., 44.
37. Ibid., 53.
38. Ibid., 67.
39. Ibid., 82.
40. Hill (1967). Quoted in Ullman, Krippner, and Vaughan (1973), 6.
41. *Mysteries of The Unknown* , 50–53, 69.
42. Ullman, Krippner, and Vaughan (1973), 114.
43. The English translation of Hall's study was titled 'Experiments with Telepathically Influenced Dreams' and published in Freiburg University Institute for Border Areas of Psychology's journal *Zeitschrift fur Parapsychologie and Grenzgebiete der Psychologie*, 10 (1967): 18–47. Quoted in Ullman, Krippner, and Vaughan (1973), 115.
44. Ullman, Krippner, and Vaughan (1973).
45. Krippner, Ullman, and Honorton (1971). Reproduced as Appendix D in Ullman, Krippner, and Vaughan (1973), 235–46.
46. Ullman, Krippner, and Vaughan (1973), 148–49.
47. Krippner, Honorton, and Ullman (1972). Reproduced as Appendix E in Ullman, Krippner, and Vaughan (1973), 247–57.
48. Tabori (1951). Quoted in Ullman, Krippner, and Vaughan (1973), 25.

Chapter 18 – Prodromal Dreams of Illness and Healing

1. Freud (1900), 57.
2. Ibid., 70.
3. Ibid., 271.
4. ASD *Newsletter* 6 no. 2 (1989): 9. Quoted in Castle (1994), 369.
5. Dement (1972), 102.
6. Kasatkin (1967). Quoted in Castle (1994), 362.

7. Castle (1994), 363–64.
8. Garfield (1991), 35.
9. Quoted in Castle (1994), 364.
10. Garfield (1991), 101.
11. Quoted in Castle (1994), 367.
12. Mitchell (1923). Quoted in Castle (1994), 368.
13. Lockhart (1977). Quoted in Castle (1994), 36.
14. Siegel (1989). Quoted in Castle (1994), 366.
15. W. Dick and H. Gris, *National Enquirer*, 18 March 1975, 8. Quoted in Castle (1994), 364.
16. Quoted in Castle (1994), 364.
17. Garfield (1991), 95.
18. Gupta (1971), 7n2.
19. Garfield (1991), 77.
20. Hunt (1989), 87.
21. Castle (1994), 364.
22. Garfield (1991), 82.
23. Ibid., 98.
24. Ibid.
25. Castle (1994), 364.
26. Ibid., 364–65
27. O'Flaherty (1984), 18.
28. The Parisistas of the Atharvaveda (68.1.51). Quoted in O'Flaherty (1984), 19.
29. *Susruta Samhita* (I.29.68). Quoted in O'Flaherty (1984), 23.
30. Potter (1977). Quoted in O'Flaherty (1984), 25.
31. Master (1999).
32. Jung CW 5: para. 78.
33. Garfield (1991), 69.
34. Ibid.
35. Ibid., 94.
36. Ibid., 82–83.

Chapter 19 – Dreams of Mortality: Is Death Our Only Destiny?

1. Boa (1994), 213.
2. Garfield (1996), 187.
3. Ibid.
4. Garfield (1996).
5. Ibid., 198.
6. Ibid., 201.
7. Homer, *The Iliad*, bk. XXIII, 315–16.
8. Gennadius's dream has been amalgamated from the accounts given by LaBerge (1986), 21–23 and Castle (1994), 440–41.
9. Miller (1994), 10.
10. Fourtier (1972). Quoted in Bulkeley (1994), 163.

PART 5

Chapter 20 – Dreams and Karma: Do We Live but Once?

1. Green (1968a), 13.
2. Tart (1977), 8.
3. Brahma Purana (217.1–16). Quoted in O'Flaherty (1983), 16.
4. Garuda Purana (Uttara Khanda, 2.22–25). Quoted in O'Flaherty (1983), 16.

5. Brahmavaivarta-Mahapuranam (2.32.27–32). Quoted in O'Flaherty (1983), 16.
6. Jung (1963), 320–23.
7. Ibid., 320.
8. Sri Varahapuranam (98.24); Markandeya Purana (43:11, 15–17, 28); Agni Puranam (229.1–14); Brahmavaivarta-Mahapuranam (82.4); Vayu Purana,548.
9. At the time of this dream / vision, Jung's attitude to India and things Indian can only be described as alien. He admits: 'The question of karma is obscure to me, as is also the problem of personal rebirth or of the transmigration of souls.' He could not discover in his own world or experience anything that would convince him of the authenticity of this belief. It was only towards the end of his life that he observed in himself a series of dreams which would seem to describe the process of reincarnation in a deceased person. – Jung (1963), 351.
10. 'In one country whose intellectual culture is highly complex and much older than ours – I am, of course, referring to India – the idea of reincarnation is as much taken for granted as, among us, the idea that God created the world ...' – Ibid., 348.
11. Ibid., 349.
12. Ibid., 321.
13. I am grateful to Sri Madhava Ashish for this rendering of the dream imagery. See Ashish (2007), 86.
14. Jung (1963), 322.
15. Ibid., 338.
16. Ibid.
17. Ibid., 338–39.
18. Ibid., 336.
19. Ibid., 349–50.
20. Ibid., 349, 354.
21. I am grateful to Sri Madhava Ashish for this illustration.
22. Coward (2001), 121–22.
23. Jung asks, 'Is the karma I live the outcome of my past lives, or is it the achievement of my ancestors whose heritage comes together in me?' – Jung (1963), 349.
24. Ibid., 350.
25. In Tibet there is the holy cake, while Christians place emphasis on the Eucharist as a symbol of the essence or nutriment.
26. Genesis 3:19.
27. Sura Al-Hijr-Meccan Verses (xv.28) The Holy Qur-an: English translation of "the meanings and commentary". Rev. and ed. by The Presidency of Islamic Researches, IFTA, Al-Madinah Al-Munawarah,Saudi Arabia. Also see Suras xviii.37; xxii.5; xxx.20; xxv.11.
28. Bhavishya Purana (4.4.9–11). Quoted in O'Flaherty (1983), 20.
29. Mahabharata (Asvamedhaparvan 18.1–13). Quoted in Long (1983), 55.
30. Bhavishya Purana (4.4.9–11). Quoted in O'Flaherty (1983), 20.
31. The Upanishads offer several accounts of what happens. Potter's reconstruction, which follows Sankara, briefly says, 'Thus at the "moment of death" the *jiva* is caused by its karma to develop a *vasana* which determines the direction in which the subtle body will go as it leaves the "heart" – by which veins and points of egress, by what path, and to what kind of birth it will eventually proceed.' – Potter (1983), 250–51.
32. Ashish (2007), 81.
33. Ibid., 83.
34. O'Flaherty (1983), 20.
35. Markandeya Purana (10.88–92). Quoted in O'Flaherty (1983), 19.
36. Plato, *Republic*, bk. X (617–24), (tr.) P. Shorey, 838–44.
37. Hillman (1997), 45.
38. Ibid.

39. Ibid., 3.
40. Ibid., 9.
41. Kakar (1996).
42. Ibid., 10.
43. Ibid., 11.
44. Ibid., 14.
45. Ibid.
46. Ibid.
47. Ibid., 15.
48. Ibid., 17.
49. Ibid., 18.
50. Ibid.
51. Jung, 'Men, Women, and God.' In the *Daily Mail* (London) on 29 April 1955. Quoted in Jung (1953), 322.
52. Kakar (1996), 17.
53. Quoted in Krishan (1997), 566–67.
54. My description of the evolution of the Karma doctrine closely follows Krishan (1997), x–xiii and 559–65.
55. Ibid., 5.
56. Brihad-Aranyaka Upanishad (4.4.5) in Hume (1931), 140.
57. Quoted in Potter (1983), 256.
58. Ibid, 258.
59. Jung (1960), 147. Quoted in Jung (1953), 326.

Chapter 21 – Dreams: The Door to Altered States of Consciousness

1. Castle (1994), 52.
2. Ibid., 39.
3. Ibid., 39–41.
4. Sviri (1999), 257.
5. Her biographies do not provide a specific date. One of them says 'around 1857', while another claims she was born in 1858. – Anderson (2004), 79n2.
6. Ibid., 66.
7. Raj (2004), 205–06.
8. Bulkeley (1999), 211.
9. Underhill (1911), 279.
10. Young (1999), 117.
11. Underhill (1910), 9.
12. Sardananda (1983), vol.1, 162–63. Quoted in Kakar (1991), 14.
13. Underhill (1911), 3–4.
14. Bakhtiar (1979). Quoted in Wilde (1995), 148.
15. Hunt (1989), 217.
16. Moffitt, et al. (1986).
17. Ibid.
18. Ouspensky (1950), 141–43.
19. 'Plato implies (*contra* Heraclitus) that everyone in the world is actually asleep, with the exception of a few philosophers, who are awake ... Finally, Plato points out that the beginning of true wakefulness comes only when we realize that we are in fact dreaming ...' O'Flaherty (1984), 39, alluding to Plato's *Republic* bk. 5 (476c–d) and bk. 7 (534c–d).
    Also the Aitreya Upanishad (1.3.12) alludes to the first three states of consciousness (waking, dreaming, and profound sleep) as sleep. As explained by Sankara and other commentators on this passage that it is in contrast with the desired metaphysically awakened self that the ordinary condition of waking is regarded as 'sleep'. – Hume (1931), 297n4.

20. Ouspensky (1950), 143.
21. Ibid., 141.
22. Hunt (1986).
23. Gackenbach (1997), 109.

Chapter 22 – Numinous Dreams: A Sense of the Sacred

1. Doniger and Bulkley (1993).
2. Jung CW 16: para. 83.
3. Jacobi (1959), 117.
4. Ibid., 117–19.
5. Jung (1963), 416.
6. Ullman, Krippner, and Vaughan (1973), 35.
7. Young (1999), 55.
8. Radha (1996), 100.
9. Singh (2004), 151–52.
10. Ibid., 153.
11. Ashish (2007), 121.
12. Priestley (1964), 306–07.

Chapter 23 – Lucid Dreaming: Who Dreams the Dream?

1. Prem (1976), 83.
2. Ibid.
3. Hillman (1979), 11.
4. Ibid., 13.
5. Green (1968b). Quoted in Hunt (1989), 119.
6. LaBerge (1986), 21.
7. Ibid., 25.
8. Ibid., 26–28.
9. Freud (1900), 610.
10. Ibid., 611.
11. Castle (1994), 444.
12. LaBerge (1986), 76.
13. Castle (1994), 445.
14. LaBerge (1986), 85–86.
15. Ibid., 87–88.
16. Ibid., 82.
17. Ibid., 89.
18. Ibid., 95.
19. Hunt (1989), 120.
20. Hunt (1986).
21. Nisargadatta Maharaj (1973), 34.

Chapter 24 – Dream Yoga: Harnessing the Dream

1. I have abbreviated the scale of dream self-reflectiveness given by Purcell, Moffitt, and Hoffmann (1993), 211–13.
2. The example dreams for each level of dream reflectiveness have been modified from the examples given for dream control in Purcell, Moffitt, and Hoffmann(1993), 219.
3. Moffitt, et al. (1986).
4. Alexander, Boyer, and Orme-Johnson (1985).
5. Hunt (1989), 119.
6. LaBerge (1986), 25.

Also see *Vijnanabhairava* (v. 75): 'When sleep has not yet fully appeared i.e. when one is about to fall asleep, and all the external objects (though present) have faded out of sight then the state (between sleep and waking) is one on which one should concentrate. In that state the Supreme Goddess will reveal Herself.' Similarly verse 55 prescribes breathing and meditational techniques while going to sleep that will help the aspirant acquire the freedom to control dreams.

7. Gackenbach (1997), 103–04.
8. Hunt (1989), 121–22.
9. Gackenbach, et al. (1987). Quoted in Hunt (1989), 121.
10. Alexander, Boyer, and Orme-Johnson (1985).
11. Ouspensky (1950), 147.
12. Gackenbach (1997), 109.
13. Alexander, Boyer, and Orme-Johnson (1985).
14. Gackenbach (1997), 108.
15. Quoted in Gackenbach (1988).
16. Young (1999), 120.
17. Wentz (1958), 218.
18. Ibid., 220.
19. Ibid.
20. Ibid., 221.
21. Ibid., 221n1.
22. Tulku (1989).
23. Wentz (1958), 215.
24. Chandogya Upanishad (8.10.1) in Hume (1931), 270.
25. Ibid., 271.
26. Ibid., 265.
27. Deussen (1919), 311.
28. Saraswati (1976), 1–7 and 69–74.
29. Castaneda (1993), viii.
30. Castaneda (1972), 113–14.
31. LaBerge (1986), 59.
32. Cravens (1973), 92.
33. Ibid.

Chapter 25 – Dreaming and the Mystical Enquiry

1. Ginsburg (2001), 229, 264.
2. Woodroffe (2001), 27.
3. Ashish (2007), 4–5.
4. In the Greek Myths, the entrance to Hades was guarded by Cerberus, the monstrous hydra-headed watchdog. The actual Underworld was preceded by a vestibule called the Grove of Persephone, which had to be crossed before reaching the gate of the Kingdom of Hades. At the gate was posted Cerberus. – Larousse, 188.
5. Ashish (2007), 4.
6. 'The ladder by which the candidate ascends is formed of rungs of suffering and pain; … its foot rests in the deep mire of thy sins and failings…' – Blavatsky (1975) frag. 1, v. 69, 30–31.
    This, however, does not mean that anyone who has disturbing dreams is on the verge of entering the mystical enquiry.
7. The *Abhedopaya* states that for the complete identification of 'I' with Shiva (the Godhead), the I, which is a psycho-physical complex (*nama-rupa*) must disappear before the real I, as the real Self is experienced. '…for this experience occurs when there is complete cessation of all thought constructs.' – Siva Sutras, xxxiii.
8. Ashish (2007), 12–13.

9. Ashish (2007), 59–60.
10. Thera (1996), 30–35.
11. Freud, in his later writings on dreams, explicitly endorses this view of dreams: 'Thus, we know that dreams are completely egoistic and that the person who plays the chief part in their scenes is always to be recognized as the dreamer.' – Freud (1915), 230.
12. The Kashmir Saivite school calls this effort *anusandhana* – close (mental) examination with a view to union with the Godhead. – Siva Sutras (I.22), xl.
13. I am grateful to Sri Madhava Ashish for this interpretation of my dream.
14. Ashish (2007), 20.
15. Ibid., 21.
16. S. D. Pandey (2003), 158.
17. Ibid., 159.
18. Ginsburg (2001), 224–25.
    'In the Upanishads sexual relationship is described as one of the means of apprehending the divine nature, and throughout oriental literature it is constantly used metaphorically to express the true relationship between the human soul and God.' Havell (1964), 158.
    See also Eliade (1958), 254–73.
19. Ashish (2007), xviii.
20. This tradition goes all the way back to Pythagoras who recommended that his disciples listen to music before going to bed in order to prepare the mind for sleep. – *Encyclopaedia of Religion*, 31.
21. Castle (1994), 241–250.
22. Sri Varahapuranam (98.19), 287.
23. Akin to Calvin Hall's continuity hypothesis whereby dreams are the reflection of the dreamer's current waking thoughts and concerns. – Hall and Nordby (1972), 104.
24. Prasna Upanishad (IV.5) in Hume (1931), 386.
25. Ashish (2007), 7.
    In this regard also see Katha Upanishad (2.5.8) where it is explicitly stated: 'He who is awake in us shaping objects of desire while we are asleep … that is Brahman.' – Brahma Sutras (3.2.2), 284.
26. Bhagavad Gita (XV.3) 'These qualifications are usually given as four: *viveka*, discrimination between the constant and the transitory; *vairagya*, a turning-away from what is transitory; *shat-sampatti*, a group of six attainments comprising control of mind, control of sense, endurance, a turning-away from the outer (whether in experience or in religion), faith (in the Gita's sense) and mental balance; *mumukshutva*, desire for liberation from the bondage of ignorance.' – Prem (1938), 147.
27. Siva Sutras (II.8–9) state that after a certain stage the neophyte's formal rituals have to change (*metanoia*) into spiritual practices, meaning thereby: he or she must learn to pour the self into the fires of *cit* (universal consciousness), thoughts of the essential self should become the food that nourishes him or her. The quest for the Divine, which is not an object of thought, becomes the neophyte's yoga. The limited 'I' dies to live in the universal 'I'. – Siva Sutras, xlvii–xlviii.
28. 'According to the *Lankavatara-Sutra* the arbitrarily discriminating intellect can only be overcome if a complete "turning-about" has taken place in the deepest seat of consciousness. The habit of looking outwards, i.e., towards external objects, must be given up and a new spiritual attitude established of realizing truth or ultimate reality within the intuitive consciousness …' – Govinda (1977), 79.
29. G. I. Gurdjieff, the Russian mystic, used it to describe what must be done to change perspective from the relatively real to the objectively real. – Ginsburg (2001), 241.
30. Radha (1996), 206–10.
31. Ibid., 209–10.

32. Singh (2004), 145–46.
33. Ibid., 147.
34. Ibid., 138.
35. Ashish (2007), xviii–xix. I am grateful to Kersy Katrak for fleshing out Ashish's dream/vision.
36. O'Flaherty's comment on this subject is interesting: 'There are several ways in which the Tantric image of God resembles and does not resemble the child's "transitional object", described by Winnicott. Where the child, in playing, uses the transitional object to move from internal reality to external reality – to redefine his dreams – the Indian Tantrics use the image of God to move in the other direction, to move from material objects to the greater reality of *brahman*. In both cases, the transitional object – the teddy bear, or the image of God – is ultimately discarded; it is the ladder that one kicks away when one has climbed to the right place. But the child has climbed to a place where the teddy is replaced by a *real* bear, while the yogin has climbed to one where there are no bears at all.' – O'Flaherty (1984), 59.
37. Singh (2004), 77.
38. Ginsburg (2001), 228.
39. 'We have begun to conduct research to determine if pure consciousness can be maintained outside of meditation – especially during sleep. In a pilot study of an advanced TM meditator ... we found when compared to the sleep of two lucid dreamers and a non-lucid dreamer, that this particular subject seemed to physiologically maintain a deeper state of rest. He had lower respiration rate, lower heart rate, and less REM density, but he also appeared to be alert and could signal from REM sleep, Stage I, and Stage II sleep with strong lateral eye movements.' – Alexander, Boyer, and Orme-Johnson (1985).
40. Ashish (1998), 9.
41. 'Our work supports the notion that these three states of consciousness in sleep are qualitatively as well as quantitatively distinct but none-the-less probably exist along a developmental continuum with lucid dreaming emerging prior to witnessing dreaming or [witnessing] deep sleep.' – Gackenbach (1988).
42. Ginsburg (2001), 41–42.
43. 'The novice in *pranayama* almost always falls asleep as soon as he has succeeded in reducing his respiratory rhythm to that characteristic of the state of sleep.' Eliade (1958), 56n23.
    Also, the Buddha's advice (Vinaya Pitaka, I.129) is to fall asleep in the state of mindfulness. – Young (1999), 129.
    The contemporary mystic Ramana Maharshi was once told by a disciple: 'But when I have stilled everything, I almost fall asleep!' He replied, 'That does not matter. Put yourself into the condition as deep as sleep, and then watch: be asleep consciously; then there is only the one Consciousness.' – Ramana Maharshi (1998), 64.
44. Ashish (1998), 24.
45. Ibid., 30–31.
46. Ashish (2007), 73–74.
47. Wentz (1958), 215.
48. Tulku (1989).
49. According to one account: 'A certain balance of attitude seems necessary – expectancy without anxiety, intense concentration of imagination, but no effort of will.' – Green (1968a), 110.
50. One of the most common attitudes displayed in Buddhist iconography is to show the right hand of the seated Buddha to be hanging downwards, the middle finger gently touching the earth, in what has come to be known as the *bhumi sparsh mudra* (touching the earth). This *mudra* (gesture), along with other *anguli mudras*, symbolizes mental activity. Legend has it that on the eve of his enlightenment the arch-tempter Mara, in a last bid to avert Prince Siddhartha from crossing the boundaries of

Manifestation, assails him with his great army. The most potent weapon at their disposal is the power of projection: 'The warriors could alter their faces in many ways and change into a thousand forms.' The only way the prince could resist this onslaught of Mara was by *grounding* himself to earth, thereby diffusing the *charge* of the witnessed projection. 'And the Bodhisattva touched the earth', calling upon it to stand witness. In other words, no sooner do we refer our projected fantasies to the test of reality they immediately evaporate, their mesmerizing power broken. 'And at this testimony of the earth, Mara and his hosts fled in all directions...' – Zimmer (1955), vol. 1, 175–77. (I am grateful to Dr Trinath Mishra for pointing out this connection.)

51. Bhagavad Gita (XVIII.66) explicitly alludes to this kind of fear, which is experienced when the normal conceptions that support the sense of self are surrendered. Krishna, prefacing his words to Arjuna by informing him that what he is about to tell him is the ultimate Mystery – the supreme teaching – says:

> Abandoning all supports, take refuge in Me alone.
> Fear not; I will liberate thee from all sins.

The fear that Krishna alludes to is not the ordinary state of fear because this verse comes near the end of the discourse, when much of the teaching has already been enunciated. – Prem (1938), 186.

52. Sankara commenting on Gaudapada's Karika (III.39) talks about the same fear of non-being:
'In other words, the *Yogis*, being devoid of discrimination, who, through fear, apprehend the destruction of their self, are afraid of it which is, in reality, fearlessness.' – Mandukya Upanishad, 200.

53. Lings (1975), 25.
54. Ginsburg (2001), 229.
55. Ashish (1998), 50.
56. Patanjali (Yoga-Sutras, II.49) defines this refusal as: '*Pranayama* is the arrest [*viccheda*] of the movements of inhalation and exhalation...' – Eliade (1958), 55.
57. Ashish (2007), 77.
58. Ibid., 76–77.
59. Ibid., 78.
60. Many years after his seminal work on dreams, Freud categorically stated: 'A dream is, therefore, among other things, a *projection*: an externalisation of an internal process.' (emphasis Freud's). – Freud (1915), 231.
61. Bogzaran (1991). Quoted in Castle (1994), 457.
62. Pasricha and Stevenson (1986).
63. Harry Hunt, while eschewing the twin explanations of 'illusion' and 'astral travel', finds the OBE (an 'awakened' dreamer's images coinciding with their material counterparts) and lucid dreams (an 'awakened' dreamer's images ceasing to have any connection with their material counterpart) have 'a close logical and definitional similarity, involving the unusual development of a detached observational attitude and its tenuous balance with participatory involvement. In addition, if the out-of-body experience ends in "dream travel" to a setting that no longer includes the imagistic construction of one's own body percept, it is indistinguishable from lucid dreaming; and if the lucid dreamer attempts to become fully aware of his / her sleeping body, the situation may be indistinguishable from classic out-of-body accounts.' – Hunt (1989), 121.
64. Ashish (2007), 74–75.
65. Ibid., 74.
66. Tibetan dream yoga requires the disciple to transform dream content into its opposite – like fire into water – so that its essential nature is realized to be *maya*. – Wentz (1958), 221.
67. Nisargadatta Maharaj (1973), 59–60.

68. I am grateful to S. D.Pandey for this elucidation of Ashish's continuing vision.
69. Personal conversation with Sri Madhava Ashish.
70. 'It is common to confuse awareness with attention, or even concentrated consciousness. The vocabulary for this subject has not been fully worked out ... and one tends to get bogged down in clashing jargons of different schools. I find it useful to use "consciousness" to refer to all the processes concerned with sensing (seeing, hearing etc.) ... I prefer to restrict awareness to the faculty/power which *observes* the images/thoughts/feelings. Awareness does not think: it observes the thinking process. It does not concentrate: it observes the concentration of attention. This is why it usually has to be found/identified in a meditation practice which aims at *stopping* all perception of sensation, thought etc. When the operations of the mind are stopped, then what is left is awareness.' – Ashish (1998), 33–34.
71. The *Pratyabhijnahrdayam* (sutra 13) states that the individual consciousness (*chita*) by eschewing extroversion becomes introverted and rises to the level of the knowing subject (*cetana*). By the dissolution of limitation it becomes the universal consciousness (*chiti*). – Siva Sutras, xxxix.
72. In the Mahabharata (I.123.45) the Pandavas, during their final examination in archery, were asked by their teacher: What do you see? All save Arjuna answered by describing the bird and its surroundings. Only Arjuna, whose skill in archery was based on his absolute power of concentration upon his target, restricted his gaze to the eye of the bird. – Katz (1989), 44.
73. Ashish (1990).
74. This exercise need not begin with an external object (the candle), but the body can be used as the initial focus of attention: 'recognise first that there is the body. Experience the body. Then experience what experiences the body. Then forget the body.' You are now experiencing that which experiences. – Ginsburg (2001), 224.
75. Nisargadatta Maharaj (1973), 401.
76. Ginsburg (2001), 228.
77. Ashish (1990).

SELECT BIBLIOGRAPHY

(Titles of books and periodicals are in italics; titles of papers and essays in anthologies are in inverted commas. Numerals in thick type refer to volumes; ordinary numerals refer to page numbers. Std. Edition in Freud entries refers to the 24 volumes of The Standard Edition of *The Complete Psychological Works of Sigmund Freud* published by Hogarth Press and the Institute of Psycho-Analysis.)

Agni Puranam. 2 vols. (trans.) Manmatha Nath Dutt Shastri. Varanasi: Chowkhamba Sanskrit Series, 1967.

Alexander, C. N., R. Boyer, and D. Orme-Johnson (1985). 'Distinguishing between transcendental consciousness and lucidity'. *Lucidity Letter*, **4**(2): 68–85.

Anderson, Carol S. (2004). 'The Life of Gauri Ma'. In Pechilis, *The Graceful Guru*, 65–84.

Antrobus, J. S. (1978). 'Dreaming for cognition'. In *The Mind in Sleep: Psychology and Psychophysiology*. (eds.) A. M. Arkin, J. S. Antrobus, and S. J. Ellman, 569–81. Hillsdale, New Jersey: Lawrence Erlbaum.

Ashish, Sri Madhava (1990). 'A Return to Intelligent Inquiry'. Address, Conference of the Indo-European Neurosurgeons. New Delhi, November 1990.

—— (1998). Untitled collection of extracts of letters. Compiled by John Donovan. Unpublished manuscript.

—— (2007). *An Open Window: Dream as Everyman's Guide to the Spirit*. New Delhi: Penguin Books.

Arendt, Hannah (1981). *The Life of the Mind. Volume 1: Thinking*. New York: Harvest Books (HBJ).

Bakhtiar, Laleh (1979). *Sufi Expressions of the Mystic Quest*. London: Thames and Hudson.

Barker, J. (1967). 'Premonitions of the Aberfan Disaster'. *Journal of the Society for Psychical Research*, **44**: 169–81.

Barrett, Deirdre (ed.) (1996). *Trauma and Dreams*. Cambridge, Massachusetts: Harvard University Press.

Barry, Peter (1995). *Beginning Theory: An Introduction to Literary and Cultural Theory*. Manchester: Manchester University Press, 2002.

Becker, R. de (1968). *The Understanding of Dreams, or The Machinations of the Night*. (trans.) M. Heron. London: George Allen and Unwin.

Bettelheim, Bruno (1975). *The Uses of Enchantment: The Meaning and Importance of Fairy Tales*. London: Penguin Books, 1991.

Blavatsky, H. P. (1889). *The Voice of Silence*. Adyar: The Theosophical Publishing House, 1975.

Boa, Fraser (1994). *The Way of the Dream: Conversations on Jungian Dream Interpretation with Marie-Louise von Franz*. Boston: Shambala.

Bogzaran, F. (1991). 'Experiencing the Divine in the Lucid Dream State'. *Lucidity Letter*, **10**(1–2): 169–76.

Brahma-Sutras. (trans.) Swami Vireswarananda. Calcutta: Advaita Ashrama, 1993.

Brahamavaivarta-Mahapuranam. 2 vols. (trans.) Shanti Lal Nagar. Delhi: Parimal Publications, 2001.

Brelich, Angelo (1966). 'The Place of Dreams in the Religious World Concept of the Greeks'. In Grunebaum and Caillois, *The Dream and Human Societies*, 293–302.

Breger, Louis (1967). 'Function of Dreams'. *Journal of Abnormal Psychology*, Monograph no. 641, vol. 72, no. 5, part 2, 1–28.

Breton, A. (1969). *Manifestation of Surrealism*. Ann Arbor: University of Michigan Press.

Bryson, Bill (2003). *A Short History of Nearly Everything*. London: Black Swan, 2004.

Bulkeley, Kelly (1994). *The Wilderness of Dreams: Exploring the Religious Meanings of Dreams in Modern Western Culture*. Albany: State University of New York Press.

——— (1997). *An Introduction to the Psychology of Dreaming*. Westport, Connecticut: Praeger.

——— (1999). 'The Interpretation of Spiritual Dreams throughout History'. In Krippner and Waldman, *Dreamscaping*, 198–220.

Caillois, Roger (1966). 'Logical and Philosophical Problems of the Dream'. In Grunebaum and Caillois, *The Dream and Human Societies*, 23–52.

Campbell, Joseph (1949). *The Hero with a Thousand Faces*. London: Paladin Books, 1988.

Cancik, Hubert (1999). 'Idolum and Imago: Roman Dreams and Dream Theories'. In Shulman and Stroumsa, *Dream Cultures*, 168–88.

Caraka Samhita. 5 vols. (trans.) A. Chandra Kaviratna and P. Sharma. Delhi: Sri Satguru Publications, 1996.

Castaneda, Carlos (1972). *Journey to Ixtlan: The Lessons of Don Juan*. Harmondsworth, Middlesex: Penguin Books, 1974.

-------- (1993). *The Art of Dreaming*. London: Aquarian, 1994.

Castle, Robert L. Van de (1994). *Our Dreaming Mind*. New York: Aquarian.

Cayce, H. L. (1962). *Dreams: The Language of the Unconscious*. Virginia Beach, Virginia: Association for Research and Enlightenment Press.

Coleridge, E. H. (ed.) (1912). *The Poems of Samuel Taylor Coleridge*. London: Oxford University Press, 1957.

Coward, Harold (2001). 'Karma, Jung, and Transpersonal Psychology'. In *Karma: Rhythmic Return to Harmony*. (eds.) V. Hanson, R. Stewart, and S. Nicholson, 115–33. New Delhi: Motilal Banarsidass Publishers.

Cravens, Gwyneth (1973). 'Talking to Power and Spinning with the Ally: The Glossed Carlos Castaneda'. *Harper's Magazine* February 1973.

Creel, H. G. (1953). *Chinese Thought from Confucius to Mao Tse-tung*. Chicago: University of Chicago Press.

Crick, Francis and Graeme Mithchison (1983). 'The Function of Dream Sleep'. *Nature* (July) **14**: 111–14.

Delaney, Gayle (1991). *Breakthrough Dreaming*. New York: Bantam.

Dement, William C. (1972). *Some Must Watch While Some Must Sleep*. Stanford, California: Stanford Alumni Association.

Deussen, Paul (1919). *The Philosophy of the Upanishads*. (trans.) Rev. A. S. Geden. New York: Dover, 1966.

Deutsch, Helene (1926). 'Occult Processes Occurring during Psychoanalysis'. In Devereux, *Psychoanalysis and the Occult*, 133–46.

Devereux, George (ed.) (1953). *Psychoanalysis and the Occult*. New York: International Universities Press, 1973.

Domhoff, G. W. (1985). *The Mystique of Dreams: A Search for Utopia through Senoi Dream Theory*. Berkeley, California: University of California Press.

——— (1996). *Finding Meaning in Dreams: A Quantitative Approach*. New York: Plenum.

——— (1999). 'The "Purpose" of Dreams'. Accessible on http://dreamresearch.net/Library/purpose.html

Doniger, Wendy and Kelly Bulkley (1993). 'Why Study Dreams? A Religious Studies Perspective'. *Dreaming*, **3**(1): 69–73.

Dostoevsky, F. (1886). *Crime and Punishment*. New York: Random House, 1956.

Dunne, J. W. (1927). *An Experiment with Time*. London: Faber and Faber, 1964.

Ehrenwald, J. (1954). *New Dimensions of Deep Analysis: A Study of Telepathy in Interpersonal Relationships*. New York: Grune and Stratton.

Eisenbud, Jule (1947). 'The Dreams of Two Patients in Analysis Interpreted as a Telepathic *Reve a deux*'. In Devereux, *Psychoanalysis and the Occult*, 262–76.

——— (1949). 'Psychiatric Contributions to Parapsychology: A Review'. In Devereux, *Psychoanalysis and the Occult*, 3–15.

Eliade, Mircea (1958). *Yoga: Immortality and Freedom*. (trans.) Willard R. Trask. Princeton, New Jersey: Princeton University Press.

Erikson, Erik H. (1965). *Childhood and Society*. Harmondsworth, Middlesex: Penguin Books.

The New Encyclopaedia Britannica, vol. 27 Macropaedia (Fifteenth Edition). London: Encyclopaedia Britannica, 1997.

Encyclopaedia of Religion and Ethics, vol. 5. (ed.) James Hastings. Edinburgh: T. and T. Clark, 1960.

Feurerstein, Georg (2002). *The Yoga Tradition*. New Delhi: Bhavana Books.

Fodor, N. (1967). *Between Two Worlds*. New York: Paperback Library.

Fontana, David (1994). *The Secret Language of Dreams*. London: Piatkus, 1997.

Fordham, Frieda (1953). *An Introduction to Jung's Psychology*. Harmondsworth, Middlesex: Penguin Books, 1975.

Foulkes, David (1978). *A Grammar of Dreams*. Hassocks, Sussex: Harvester Press.

———(1993). 'Data Constraints on Theorizing about Dream Function'. In Moffitt, Kramer, and Hoffman, *Functions of Dreaming*, 11–20.

Fourtier, Millie Kelly (1972). *Dreams and Preparation for Death*. Ann Arbor, Michigan: University Microfilms.

Franz, M. L. von (1966). 'Time and Synchronicity in Analytical Psychology'. In *The Voices of Time*. (ed.) J. T. Fraser. New York: Brazillier.

Fraser, J. T. (1975). *Of Time, Passion, and Knowledge: Reflections on the Strategy of Existence*. Princeton, New Jersey: Princeton University Press.

Frazer, Sir James (1922). *The Golden Bough: A Study in Magic and Religion*. Ware, Hertfordshire: Wordsworth Editions, 1993.

Freud, Anna (1935). 'Psychoanalysis and the Training of the Young Child'. *The Psychoanalytic Quarterly*, **4**: 15–24.

——— (1946). *The Ego and the Mechanisms of Defence*. (trans.) Cecil Baines. New York: International Universities Press, 1964.

——— (1949). 'On Certain Difficulties in the Preadolescent's Relation to His Parents'. In *Selected Writings – Anna Freud*. (ed.) Richard Ekins and Ruth Freeman, 165–74. London: Penguin Books, 1998.

——— (1986). 'Introduction to the Concept of the Unconscious'. In Freud, S., *Essentials of Psycho-Analysis*, 129–33.

Freud, Sigmund (1900). *The Interpretation of Dreams*. (trans.) James Strachey. New York: Avon Books, 1965.

——— (1901). 'On Dreams'. In Freud, S., *Essentials of Psychoanalysis*, 81–125.

——— (1901a). *The Psychopathology of Everyday Life*. (trans.) Alan Tyson. London: Ernest Benn Ltd., 1966.

——— (1905). *Jokes and Their Relation to the Unconscious*. (trans.) James Strachey. New York: W. W. Norton, 1963.

——— (1910). 'Five Lectures on Psychoanalysis'. Std. Edition vol. 11. (trans.) James Strachey. 9–56. London: Vintage, 2001.

——— (1912). 'Recommendations for Physicians on the Psycho-Analytic Method of Treatment'. Collected Papers, **2**: 323–33. London: Hogarth Press, 1924.

——— (1915). 'A Metapsychological Supplement to the Theory of Dreams'. In *On Metapsychology: The Theory of Psychoanalysis*. (trans.) J. Strachey, (ed.) A. Richards, 229–43. London: Penguin Freud Library vol. 11, 1991.

——— (1916). 'Dreams'. In *Introductory Lectures on Psychoanalysis*. (trans.) James Strachey, 111–278. London: Penguin Freud Library vol. 1, 1991.

——— (1921). 'Psychoanalysis and Telepathy'. In Devereux, *Psychoanalysis and the Occult,* 56–68.

——— (1922). 'Dreams and Telepathy'. In Devereux, *Psychoanalysis and the Occult,* 69–86.

——— (1923). 'The Ego and the Id'. In Freud, S., *Essentials of Psychoanalysis,* 439–83.

——— (1923a). 'Remarks upon the Theory and Practice of Dream Interpretation'. Std. Edition vol. 19. (trans.) James Strachey, 109–21. London: Vintage, 2001.

——— (1925). 'The Occult Significance of Dreams'. In Devereux, *Psychoanalysis and the Occult,* 87–90.

——— (1932). 'Revision of the Theory of Dreams'. Std. Edition vol. 22. (trans.) James Strachey, 7–30. London: Vintage, 2001.

——— (1932a). 'Dreams and Occultism'. Std. Edition vol. 22. (trans.) James Strachey, 31–56. London: Vintage, 2001.

——— (1960). *The Letters of Sigmund Freud.* (ed.) E. Freud. New York: Basic Books, 1960.

——— (1986). *The Essentials of Psychoanalysis.* Selected, with an introduction and commentaries by Anna Freud, (trans.) James Strachey. London: Penguin Books, 1991.

Gackenbach, J. (1988). 'From Sleep Consciousness to Pure Consciousness'. Presidential address to the annual meeting of the Association for the Study of Dreams, London. Accessible on http://spiritwatch.ca/from.htm

——— (1997). 'Lucid Dreaming'. In Varela, *Sleeping, Dreaming and Dying,* 101–10.

———, W. Moorecroft, C. Alexander, and S. LaBerge (1987). 'Physiological correlates of "consciousness" during sleep in a single TM practitioner'. *Sleep Research,* **16**: 230.

Galvin, Franklin and Ernest Hartmann (1999). 'Nightmares: Terrors of the Dreaming World'. In Krippner and Waldman, *Dreamscaping,* 236–44.

Gandhi, M. K. (1927). *The Story of My Experiments with Truth.* Ahmedabad: Navajivan Publishing House, 1972.

Garfield, Patricia (1991). *The Healing Power of Dreams.* New York: Simon and Schuster.

——— (1995). *Creative Dreaming.* New York: Fireside Book.

——— (1996). 'Dreams in Bereavement'. In Barrett, *Trauma and Dreams,* 186–211.

Gaston, Anne-Marie (1996). *Bharata Natyam: From Temple to Theatre.* New Delhi: Manohar.

Govinda, Lama Anagarika (1960). *Foundations of Tibetan Mysticism.* New Delhi: B. I. Publications, 1992.

Ginsburg, Seymour (2001). *In Search of the Unitive Vision: Letters of Sri Madhava Ashish to an American Businessman 1978–1997.* Boca Raton, Florida: New Paradigm Books.

Green, Celia (1968a). *Out-of-the-Body Experiences.* Oxford: Institute of Psychophysical Research.

——— (1968b). *Lucid Dreams.* New York: Hamish Hamilton.

Grunebaum, G. E. von and R. Caillois (eds.) (1966). *The Dream and Human Societies.* Berkeley, California: University of California Press.

Gupta, K. Das (1971). *The Shadow World.* New Delhi: Atma Ram.

Gutheil, E. A. (1951). *The Handbook of Dream Analysis.* New York: Washington Square Press, 1966.

Hall, C. S. (1947). 'Diagnosing Personality by the Analysis of Dreams'. *The Journal of Abnormal and Social Psychology,* **42**: 68–79.

——— (1953a). 'A Cognitive Theory of Dream Symbols'. *The Journal of General Psychology,* **48**: 169–86.

——— (1953b). 'A Cognitive Theory of Dreams'. *The Journal of General Psychology,* **49**: 273–82.

——— (1953c). *The Meaning of Dreams.* New York: Harper and Brothers Publishers.

—— and V. J. Nordby (1972). *The Individual and His Dreams*. New York: Mentor.

—— (1973). *A Primer of Jungian Psychology*. New York: Meridian, 1999.

Hartmann, Ernest (1996). 'Who Develops PTSD Nightmares and Who Doesn't'. In Barrett, *Trauma and Dreams*, 100–113.

Havell, E. B. (1964). *The Art Heritage of India. Comprising 'Indian Sculpture and Painting' and 'Ideals of Indian Art'*. Revised edition with notes by Pramod Chandra. Bombay: D. B. Taraporevala Sons and Co. Private.

Hazarika, Anjali (1997). *Daring to Dream: Cultivating Corporate Creativity Through Dreamwork*. New Delhi: Response Books.

Hemacandra, *Trisastisalakapurusacarita*. 6 vols. (trans.) Helen M. Johnson. Baroda: Gaekwad's Oriental Series, 1931–52.

Hill, R. (ed.) (1967). *Such Stuff as Dreams*. London: R. Hart-Davis.

Hillman, James (1979). *The Dream and the Underworld*. New York: Perennial Library.

—— (1997). *The Soul's Code: In Search of Character and Calling*. London: Bantam Books.

Hobson, J. A. (1988). *The Dreaming Brain*. New York: Basic Books.

—— (2003). *Dreaming*. New York: Oxford University Press.

—— and R. W. McCarley (1977). 'The Brain as a Dream State Generator: An Activation-Synthesis Hypothesis of the Dream Process'. *The American Journal of Psychiatry*, **134(12)**: 1335–48.

Homer. *The Iliad*. Ware, Hertfordshire: Wordsworth Classics, 1995.

——. *The Odyssey*. (trans.) E. V. Rieu, London: Penguin Books, 1946.

Hume, R. E. (trans.) (1931). *The Thirteen Principal Upanishads*. Delhi: Oxford University Press, 1995.

Hunt, Harry T. (1986). 'Lucid Dreams and Meditation'. *Lucidity Letter*, **5(1)**: 31–37.

—— (1989). *The Multiplicity of Dreams: Memory, Imagination and Consciousness*. New Haven, Connecticut: Yale University Press.

Hyde, M. and M. McGuinness (1993). *Introducing Jung*. Cambridge, England: Totem Books.

Jacobi, Jolande (1959). *Complex / Archetype / Symbol in the Psychology of C. G. Jung*. (trans.) R. Manheim. Princeton, New Jersey: Princeton University Press, 1974.

Jouvet, Michel (1967). 'The states of sleep'. *Scientific American*, **216(2)**: 62–68.

Jung, C. G. (1928). *Dream Analysis: Notes of the Seminar given in 1928–30 by C. G. Jung*. (ed.) William Mcguire. Princeton, New Jersey: Princeton University Press, 1984.

—— (1953). *Psychological Reflections: A New Anthology of His Writings 1905–1961*. (ed.) J. Jacobi. London: Routledge and Kegan Paul, 1979.

—— (1960). 'The Art of Living'. In *Doctors Without Drugs*. Gordon Young, Epilogue 133–53 London: 1962.

—— (1963). *Memories, Dreams, Reflections*. (trans.) Richard and Clara Winston. London: Fontana Press, 1995.

—— (1964). 'Approaching the Unconscious'. In *Man and His Symbols*. (ed.) Carl Jung. London: Picador, 1978.

—— (CW). *The Collected Works of C. G. Jung*. 19 vols. (trans.) R. F. C. Hull. (Second Edition) London: Routledge, 1969.

—— (1974). *Dreams*. (trans.) R. F. C. Hull. Princeton, New Jersey: Princeton University Press, 1974.

Kaempffert, W. (1924). *A Popular History of American Invention*, vol. II. New York: Charles Scribner's Sons.

Kakar, Sudhir (1981). *The Inner World*. In *The Indian Psyche*. New Delhi: Oxford University Press, 2002.

—— (1991). *The Analyst and the Mystic: Psychoanalytic Reflections on Religion and Mysticism*. New Delhi: Viking.

—— (1996). 'A Personal Introduction'. In *The Indian Psyche*. 1–18. New Delhi: Oxford University Press, 2002.

—— (1997). *Culture and Psyche: Selected Essays*. New Delhi: Oxford University Press.
Karacan, I. (1970a). 'Clinical Value of Nocturnal Erection in the Prognosis and Diagnosis of Impotence'. *Medical Aspects of Human Sexuality*, 4: 27–34.
——, R. L. Williams, and P. J. Salis (1970b). 'The Effect of Sexual Intercourse on Sleep Patterns and Nocturnal Penile Erections'. *Psychophysiology*, 7: 338 (abstract).
——, P. J. Salis, J. I. Thornby, and R. L. Williams (1976). 'The Ontogeny of Nocturnal Penile Tumescence'. *Waking and Sleeping*, 1: 27–44.
Kasatkin, V. N. (1967). *Teoria Snovidenni* [Theory of Dreams]. Leningrad: Meditsina.
Katz, Ruth Cecily (1989). *Arjuna in the Mahabharata: Where Krishna Is, There Is Victory*. Columbia, S. Carolina: University of South Carolina Press.
Kedrov, B. M. (1957). 'On the question of scientific creativity'. *Voprosy Psikologii*, 3: 91–113.
Kilroe, Patricia (2000). 'The Dream as Text, The Dream as Narrative'. *Dreaming*, 10(3): 125–37.
Kinder, M. (1988). 'The Dialectic of Dreams and Theater in the Films of Ingmar Bergman'. *Dreamworks*, 5(3/4): 179–92.
King, Richard H. (2002). 'Sigmund Freud'. In *From Kant to Levi-Strauss: The Background to Contemporary Critical Theory*. (ed.) John Simons, 97–112. Edinburgh: Edinburgh University Press.
Koestler, Arthur (1964). *The Act of Creation*. London: Arkana, 1989.
Krippner, Stanley and M. R. Waldman (eds.) (1999). *Dreamscaping: New and Creative ways to Work with Your Dreams*. Los Angeles: Roxbury Park.
——, Montague Ullman, and Charles Honorton (1971). 'A Precognitive Dream Study with a Single Subject'. *Journal of American Society for Psychical Research*, 65: 192–203.
——, Charles Honorton, and Montague Ullman (1972). 'A Second Precognitive Dream Study with Malcolm Bessent'. *Journal of American Society for Psychical Research*, 66: 269–79.
Krishan, Yuvraj (1997). *The Doctrine of Karma*. Delhi: Motilal Banarsidass Publishers.
Kuppuswamy, B. (1993). *Source Book of Ancient Indian Psychology*. Delhi: Konark Publishers.
Kutz, Ilan (1993). *The Dreamland Companion*. New York: Hyperion.
LaBerge, Stephen (1986). *Lucid Dreaming*. New York: Ballantine Books.
Larousse Encyclopedia of Mythology. New York: Prometheus Press, 1960.
Lings, Martin (1975). *What is Sufism?* London: George Allen and Unwin.
Lockhart, R. A. (1977). 'Cancer in Myth and Dream: An Exploration into the Archetypal Relation Between Dreams and Disease'. *Spring*, 1: 1–26.
Loewi, Otto (1960). 'An Autobiographic Sketch'. *Perspectives in Biology and Medicine*. Autumn, 1960.
Long, J. Bruce (1983). 'The Concepts of Human Action and Rebirth in the *Mahabharata*'. In O'Flaherty, *Karma and Rebirth*, 38–60.
Lorand, S. (1957). 'Dream Interpretation in the Talmud'. *The International Journal of Psycho-Analysis*, 38: 95.
Manaceine, M. de (1897). *Sleep: Its Physiology, Pathology, Hygiene and Psychology*. New York: Charles Scribner's.
The Mandukya Upanisad. (trans.) Swami Nikhilananda. Calcutta: Advaita Ashrama, 2000.
Markandeya Purana. (trans.) F. Eden Pargiter. Delhi: Indological Book House, 1969.
Master, F. J. (1999). *Dictionary of the Dreams in Homoeopathy*. New Delhi: B. Jain Publishers.
The Matsya Puranam. The Sacred Books of the Aryans, vol. 1. (ed.) J. D. Akhtar. Delhi: Oriental Publishers, 1972.
Mattoon, Mary Ann (1978). *Applied Dream Analysis: A Jungian Approach*. Washington, D. C.: V. H. Winston and Sons.
McDougall, J. (1997). 'Dreams and the Unconscious'. In Varela, *Sleeping, Dreaming and Dying*, 54–78.

Miller, Patricia Cox (1994). *Dreams in Late Antiquity: Studies in the Imagination of a Culture.* Princeton, New Jersey: Princeton University Press.

Mitchell, E. (1923). 'The Physiological Diagnostic Dream'. *New York Medical Journal,* **118**: 417.

Moffitt, Alan, Milton Kramer, and Robert Hoffman (eds.) (1993). *The Functions of Dreaming.* Albany, New York: State University of New York Press.

———, S. Purcell, R. Hoffman, R. Pigeau, and R. Wells (1986). 'Dream Psychology: Operating in the Dark'. *Lucidity Letter,* **5(1)**: 180–96.

Moss, Robert (1996). *Conscious Dreaming.* London: Rider.

Mysteries of the Unknown: Psychic Powers. Alexandria, Virginia: Time-Life Books, 1995.

Nisargadatta Maharaj, Sri (1973). *I Am That.* (trans.) Maurice Frydman. Bombay: Chetana, 1997.

O'Flaherty, Wendy Doniger (ed.) (1983). *Karma and Rebirth in Classical Indian Traditions.* Delhi: Motilal Banarsidass Publishers.

——— (1984). *Dreams, Illusions, and Other Realities.* Chicago: University of Chicago Press.

——— (1999). 'The Dreams and Dramas of a Jealous Hindu Queen'. In Shulman and Stroumsa, *Dream Cultures,* 74–84.

Okri, Ben (1997). *A Way of Being Free.* London: Phoenix Books.

Oppenheim, A. Leo (1956). 'The Interpretation of Dreams in the Ancient Near East with a Translation of an Assyrian Dream-Book'. *Transactions of the American Philosophical Society,* **46**, **Part 3**: 179–373.

-------- (1966). 'Mantic Dreams in the Ancient Near East'. In Grunebaum and Caillois, *The Dream and Human Societies,* 341–50.

Ouspensky, P. D. (1950). *In Search of the Miraculous.* London: Routledge and Kegan Paul.

Padartha-dharma-sangraha of Prasastapada. (trans.) Ganganatha Jha. Varanasi: Chaukhambha Orientalia, 1982.

Palombo, Stanley R. (1978). *Dreaming and Memory.* New York: Basic Books.

Pandey, Rajbali (1969). *Hindu Samskaras.* Delhi: Motilal Banarsidass Publishers.

Pandey, S. D. (2003). *Guru by Your Bedside.* New Delhi: Penguin Books.

The Parisistas of the Atharvaveda. (1909) (eds.) G. M. Bolling and J. von Negelein. Hindi notes by R. K. Rai. Varanasi: Chaukhambha Orientalia, 1976.

Parsons, T. and R. F. Bales (1955). *Family, Socialization and Interaction Process.* Chicago: Free Press.

Pasricha, S. and I. Stevenson (1986). 'Near-Death Experiences in India'. *Journal of Nervous and Mental Disease,* **174(3)**: 165–70.

Pechilis, Karen (ed.) (2004). *The Graceful Guru: Hindu Female Gurus in India and the United States.* New York: Oxford University Press.

Plato, *The Collected Dialogues of Plato.* (eds.) Edith Hamilton and Huntington Cairns. Princeton, New Jersey: Princeton University Press, 1973. (Bollingen Series 71).

Potter, Karl H. (1977). *Indian Metaphysics and Epistemology: The Tradition of Nyaya-Vaisesika up to Gangesa.* Princeton, New Jersey: Princeton University Press.

——— (1983). 'The Karma Theory and Its Interpretation in Some Indian Philosophical Systems'. In O'Flaherty, *Karma and Rebirth,* 241–67.

Prem, Sri Krishna (1938). *The Yoga of the Bhagavat Gita.* London: Stuart and Watkins, 1969.

——— (1976). *Introduction to Yoga.* Delhi: B. I. Publications.

Price-Williams, Douglas (1987). 'The waking dream in ethnographic perspective'. In Tedlock, *Dreaming,* 246–62.

Priestley, J. B. (1964). *Man and Time.* London: Aldus Books.

Purcell, S., Alan Moffitt, and Robert Hoffmann (1993). 'Waking, Dreaming, and Self-Regulation'. In Moffitt, Kramer, and Hoffman, *Functions of Dreaming,* 197–260.

Radha, Swami Sivananda (1996). *Realities of the Dreaming Mind.* London: Shambala.

Raine, Kathleen (1971). *William Blake*. New York: Praeger.

Raj, Selva J. (2004). 'Ammachi, the Mother of Compassion'. In Pechilis, *The Graceful Guru*, 203–18.

Ramakrishna, Sri (1947). *Tales and Parables of Sri Ramakrishna*. Mylapore: Advaita Ashram.

Ramana Maharshi, Sri (1998). *Conscious Immortality: Conversations with Sri Ramana Maharshi*. Recorded by Paul Brunton and Mungala Venkataramiah. Tiruvannamalai, Tamil Nadu: Sri Ramanasramam.

Ratcliff, A. J. J. (1996). *A History of Dreams*. London: Senate.

Rechtschaffen, A. (1978). 'The Single-Mindedness and Isolation of Dreams'. *Sleep* **1**: 97–109.

———, G. Vogel, and G. Shaikun. (1963). 'Interrelatedness of Mental Activity during Sleep'. *Archives of General Psychiatry*, **9**: 536–37.

——— and J. M. Siegel. (2000). 'Sleep and Dreaming'. In *Principles of Neuroscience*. (eds.) E. R. Kandel, J. H. Schwartz, and T.M. Jessel, 936–47. New York: McGraw-Hill.

Reis, W. (1951). 'A Comparison of the Interpretation of Dream Series with and without Free Associations'. Doctoral dissertation, Case Western Reserve University. Abridged version in *Dreams and Personality Dynamics*. (ed.) M. F. DeMartino, 211–25. Springfield, Illinois: Charles C. Thomas, 1959.

Rogers, G., R. L. Van de Castle, W. S. Evans, and J. W. Critelli (1985). 'Vaginal Pulse Amplitude Response Patterns during Erotic Conditions and Sleep'. *Archives of Sexual Behavior* **14**: 339.

Rupprecht, Carol Schreier (1999). 'Dreaming and the Impossible Art of Translation'. *Dreaming*, **9(1)**: 71–99.

Rycroft, Charles (1981). *The Innocence of Dreams*. Oxford: Oxford University Press.

Saraswati, Swami Satyananda (1976). *Yoga Nidra*. Munger (Bihar), India: Yoga Publications Trust, 1998.

Sardananda, Swami (1983). *Sri Ramakrishna, The Great Master*. 2 vols. Mylapore: Sri Ramakrishna Math.

Schacter, D. and H. Crovitz (1977). 'Falling while falling asleep: Sex differences'. *Perceptual and Motor Skills*, **44**: 656.

Schmitt, Jean-Claude (1999). 'The Liminality and Centrality of Dreams in the Medieval West'. In Shulman and Stroumsa, *Dream Cultures*, 274–87.

Shakespeare, William. *Julius Caesar*. (ed.) G. B. Harrison. Harmondsworth, Middlesex: Penguin Books, 1937.

———. *Macbeth*. (ed.) Kenneth Muir. London: Methuen and Co., 1961.

Sharma, J. P. and Lee Siegel (1980). *Dream Symbolism in the Sramanic Tradition*. Calcutta: Firma KLM.

Shulman, David and Guy G. Stroumsa (eds.) (1999). *Dream Cultures: Explorations in the Comparative History of Dreaming*. New York: Oxford University Press.

Siegel, B. (1989). *Peace, Love and Healing*. New York: Harper and Row.

Singh, Jyotsna (ed.) (2004). *Letters From Mirtola: Written by Sri Krishnaprem and Sri Madhava Ashish to Karan Singh*. Mumbai: Bhartiya Vidya Bhavan.

Siva Sutras: The Yoga of Supreme Identity. (trans.) Jaideva Singh. Delhi: Motilal Banarsidass Publishers, 1979.

Stafford-Clark, David (1967). *What Freud Really Said*. London: Penguin Books.

States, Bert O. (1992). 'The Meaning of Dreams'. *Dreaming*, **2(4)**: 249–62.

Stekel, Wilhelm (1962). *The Interpretation of Dreams*. New York: Grosset and Dunlap.

Stevens, Anthony (1982). *Archetype: A Natural History of the Self*. London: Routledge and Kegan Paul.

——— (1995). *Private Myths: Dreams and Dreaming*. London: Penguin Books, 1996.

Stevenson, R. L. (1925). *Memories and Portraits, Random Memories, Memories of Himself*. New York: Scribner.

Stroumsa, Guy G. (1999). 'Dreams and Visions in Early Christian Discourse'. In Shulman and Stroumsa, *Dream Cultures,* 189–212.

Susruta Samhita. (trans.) P. Ray, H. Gupta, and Mira Roy. New Delhi: Indian National Science Academy, 1980.

Sviri, Sara (1999). 'Dreaming Analyzed and Recorded: Dreams in the World of Medieval Islam'. In Shulman and Stroumsa, *Dream Cultures,* 252–73.

Tabori, C. (1951). *My Occult Diary.* Quoted in *They Knew the Unknown.* M. Ebon. New York: World, 1971.

Tandan, Madhu (1997). *Faith and Fire: A Way Within.* New Delhi: HarperCollins Publishers India.

Tart, Charles (1977). 'Introduction'. In *Journeys Out of the Body,* Robert Monroe, 5–18. New York: Anchor Press, 1977.

Taylor, Charles (1997). 'What's in a Self?' In Varela, *Sleeping, Dreaming and Dying,* 11–21.

Tedlock, Barbara (1987). *Dreaming: Anthropological and Psychological Interpretations.* Cambridge, England: Cambridge University Press.

―――― (1991). 'The New Anthropology of Dreaming'. *Dreaming,* 1(2): 161–78.

Thera, Nyanaponika (1996). *The Heart of Buddhist Meditation.* Kandy: Buddhist Publication Society.

Tulku XI, Tarab (1989). 'A Buddhist Perspective on Lucid Dreaming'. *Lucidity Letter,* 8(2): 47–57.

Ullman, M. (1987). 'The Experimental Dream Group'. In *The Varieties of Dream Experience.* (eds.) M. Ullman and C. Limmer. New York: Continuum.

―――― (1999) 'Context and Metaphor: The Message of the Dream'. In Krippner and Waldman, *Dreamscaping,* 221–25.

――――, Stanley Krippner, and Alan Vaughan (1973). *Dream Telepathy: Experiments in Nocturnal Extrasensory Perception.* Charlottesville, Virginia: Hampton Roads Publishing Co., 2002.

―――― and N. Zimmerman (1979). *Working with Dreams.* New York: Tarcher / Putnam.

Underhill, Evelyn (1910). *The Essentials of Mysticism and Other Essays.* Oxford: Oneworld, 1995.

―――― (1911). *Mysticism: The Nature and Development of Spiritual Consciousness.* Oxford: Oneworld, 1999.

The Vaiseshika Aphorisms of Kanada (1873). (trans.) Archibald E. Gough. Delhi: Oriental Books, 1975.

Sri Varahapuranam. (trans.) Ch. Shrinarayan Singh. Varanasi: Sarvbhartiya Kashirajanyas, 1983.

Varela, F. J. (ed. and narrator) (1997). *Sleeping, Dreaming and Dying: An Exploration of Consciousness with The Dalai Lama.* Boston: Wisdom Publications.

The Vayu Purana. In The Puranas, vol. 3. (trans.) Bibek and Dipavali Roy. Delhi: B. R. Publishing, 1994.

Vijnanabhairava or Divine Consciousness. (trans.) Jaideva Singh. Delhi: Motilal Banarsidass Publishers, 1979.

Walde, Christine (1999). 'Dream Interpretation in a Prosperous Age?' In Shulman and Stroumsa, *Dream Cultures,* 121–42.

Wentz, W. Y. Evans (1958). *Tibetan Yoga and Secret Doctrines.* London: Oxford University Press, 1973.

Whyte, L. L. (1962). *The Unconscious Before Freud.* New York: Anchor Books.

Wilde, Lynne W. (1995). *Working with Your Dreams: Linking the Conscious and Unconscious Mind in Self-Discovery.* London: Blandford.

Winson, J. (1990). 'The Meaning of Dreams'. *Scientific American,* November 1990, 86–96.

Woodroffe, Sir John (2001). *Introduction to Tantra Sastra.* Madras: Ganesh and Company.

Woods, R. L. and H. B. Greenhouse (eds.) (1974). *The New World of Dreams*. New York: Macmillan Publishing Co.

Yeats, W. B. (1974). 'Among School Children'. In *Yeats – Selected Poetry*. London: Pan Books.

Young, Serinity (1999). *Dreaming in the Lotus: Buddhist Dream Narrative, Imagery, and Practice*. Boston: Wisdom Publications.

Zimmer, Heinrich (1955). *The Art of Indian Asia: Its Mythology and Transformations*. 2 vols. Compiled and edited by Joseph Campbell. New York: Pantheon Books. (Bollingen Series 39).

INDEX OF DREAMS
AND SELECT SYMBOLS

INDEX